PRAISE FOR

The Selected Letters of Thornton Wilder

"Wilder's writing is sharply etched and generous of spirit. [In *Selected Letters*] he consistently discharges the obligation he imposed on his correspondents: that their letters 'intimate the alterations of climate in their hearts and minds.' "

—*The Times Literary Supplement* (London)

"A staggering range of acquaintance. . . . Wilder was a charmer. . . . His letters are chatty, intimate, appealingly self-deprecating."

—*The New Republic*

"Wilder and Bryer provide considerable insight into a protean American novelist and playwright. . . . [An] essential gathering of letters, carefully edited and abundantly annotated. . . . Like the best collections of correspondence in the hands of sensitive editors, this one peels away the quotidian to reveal the underlying personality of its subject."

—*Publishers Weekly*

"A useful companion to [Wilder's] literary work." —*Library Journal*

"If you'd like to know how it feels to be a distinguished and popular author of both plays and novels for a good part of the twentieth century, and to correspond with famous friends and a talented family, and to be a central figure in the events of one's time, then this is a good book to roll around in."

—A. R. Gurney, author of *Love Letters*

"A remarkable collection. . . . What emerges from these pages is a new and sometimes surprising self-portrait of a great American artist."

—Marian Seldes

About the Authors

THORNTON WILDER (1897–1975) was an accomplished novelist and playwright. His many honors include three Pulitzer Prizes, the National Book Award, the Gold Medal for Fiction of the American Academy of Arts and Letters, the Presidential Medal of Freedom, and the National Book Committee's Medal for Literature.

ROBIN G. WILDER is an independent scholar with a Ph.D. in history who specializes in archival research. She is the niece by marriage of Thornton Wilder and knew him well.

JACKSON R. BRYER is Professor Emeritus of English at the University of Maryland. He is the coeditor of *Selected Letters of Eugene O'Neill* and of *Dear Scott, Dearest Zelda: The Love Letters of F. Scott and Zelda Fitzgerald.*

The Selected Letters of THORNTON WILDER

EDITED BY ROBIN G. WILDER
AND JACKSON R. BRYER

Foreword by Scott Donaldson

HARPER PERENNIAL

NEW YORK • LONDON • TORONTO • SYDNEY • NEW DELHI • AUCKLAND

HARPER PERENNIAL

A hardcover edition of this book was published in 2008 by HarperCollins Publishers.

FIRST HARPER PERENNIAL EDITION PUBLISHED 2009.

Designed by Kris Tobiassen

Library of Congress Cataloging-in-Publication Data is available upon request.

ISBN 978-0-06-076508-8

09 10 11 12 13 DIX/RRD 10 9 8 7 6 5 4 3 2 1

Letters are the only form in all literature, in all the arts, which reposes on the communication of one to one. It is this condition which renders [them] the pre-eminent vehicle for that aspect of life which is generally excluded from all literature except the novel: those innumerable trifles of the daily life, that rain of trifling details, pleasing and vexatious, which falls upon the just and the unjust and which is also an inescapable concomitant of all human life.

—THORNTON WILDER,
JOURNALS, AUGUST 20, 1951

CONTENTS

ILLUSTRATIONS

EDITORS' NOTE

AS WE CONTEMPLATED HOW BEST TO PRESENT THORNTON Wilder's correspondence, we were guided, as it were, by two seemingly contradictory statements. One was Wilder's own remark, in a February 12, 1964, letter to his close friends Gilbert and Janet Troxell: "Did I ever tell you I once heard my mother saying to a friend (my mother who never made wise cracks) 'It's hard enough to write novels anyway, but it's especially hard for Thornton because he's illiterate?' " The second was playwright and director Garson Kanin's oft-quoted response when he was asked where he went to college: "I never did; I went to Thornton Wilder."

Wilder's correspondence certainly gives more evidence of the extensive range of his vast store of knowledge and learning than it does of his "illiteracy." Nonetheless, we believe that the paradox implied in these two statements is one of many puzzling and challenging aspects of Wilder, and we have sought to preserve it in this collection. We have corrected only the most obvious slips of his pen—the same word repeated twice in succession, uncrossed *t*'s, letters transposed within a word—and, for the most part, retained his misspellings, poor punctuation, misquotations (corrected in footnotes), and inadvertent omissions. Only in cases where meaning is unclear have we supplied, in angle brackets (used here because Wilder occasionally used square brackets), missing punctuation, missing words, or corrected spellings. Where we supply a correction to Wilder's text, we do not leave a space between Wilder's word and the angle-bracketed correction; in instances where we supply a missing word, we leave a space.

While some of Wilder's epistolary infelicities can probably be attributed either to the fact that he surely wrote many letters rapidly and almost exclusively in holograph form or to the fact that his mind often moved more quickly than his pen, we feel that his carelessness about such details also testifies to something quite important about him. He was much more concerned with communicating concepts and dealing with large issues than he was with such mundane matters as spelling and punctuation. We believe that retaining these errors preserves an important aspect of the flavor of Wilder's correspondence and that doing so in no way interferes with the reader's appreciation of his skills as a letter writer.

From the very beginning, Wilder's wide-ranging acquaintance, even as a teenager, with literature, music, and the visual arts was apparent in his correspondence. He was fluent in four foreign languages—French, German, Spanish, and Italian—and his letters are frequently peppered with quotations in those languages, as well as with the occasional Latin phrase. We have translated all of these foreign-language passages, no matter how brief, unless they appear in a standard English dictionary. Similarly, we have tried to identify lesser-known public figures, writers, composers, artists, and their works to which Wilder alluded in his correspondence. He had a large worldwide circle of friends and acquaintances, and we have attempted to explain references to them as well. Readers should assume that any person we do not footnote could not be identified. We feel that, in aggregate, these references suggest the extraordinary scope of Wilder's social and cultural landscape and are a testimony to his seemingly insatiable desire to learn more and to meet new people from all walks of life. Although this means that our edition is heavily footnoted, we have tried to keep our notes brief and succinct, and to provide more detailed background information in the introductions to each of the book's six parts.

Of necessity, we have had to make compromises in the interests of clarity and consistency. We have standardized all of Wilder's dashes to one em in length, although he sometimes used a hyphen instead of a dash (especially in his very few typewritten letters), or, in other instances, used dashes longer than one em in holograph letters. Especially in his later years, Wilder frequently used an equals sign instead of a colon. In most instances, we have rendered these as colons. For items of correspondence on which a return address is printed as letterhead, we have transcribed that information and placed it within parentheses at the head of the item. In cases where Wilder wrote a return address, we have placed that at the top of the letter. Sometimes Wilder wrote a return address above the letterhead of the stationery, but we have always placed it below the letterhead, regardless of where he put it. We have, however, tried to place his holograph return addresses accurately with respect to whether they appeared on the left or right side of the page or were centered.

When Wilder provided a date, he almost always did so at the head of the letter; when he placed the date at the end of the letter, we have moved it to the head and noted the change. When Wilder did not provide a date or gave a partial or inaccurate date, we have added an approximate or conjectured date (usually with a question mark) in angle brackets; or we have supplied one in angle brackets based on internal evidence or a postmark (indicated by the abbreviation P.M.); or, in a few instances, we have used a date supplied by the recipient (as indicated in a footnote). We have also used a question mark in angle brackets or an angle-bracketed word or words to denote a conjectured reading of Wilder's handwriting. Wilder occasionally added text in the margins or above the salutation of his letters. We have noted the location of this added text in angle brackets. When Wilder indicated that this marginal material should be inserted in the text of a letter, we have placed it in the text in boldface type and have given, in angle brackets, the reason for the placement. Often, probably in an effort to keep his letters to one or two pages, Wilder wrote text or a postscript perpendicularly in the margin of the last page. We have not noted these additions and have treated such material as part of the text of the letter.

We have used the following abbreviations in the headings to describe physical form: ACS (autograph card signed); AL (autograph letter unsigned); AL (Draft) (unsigned autograph letter found only in draft form); ALS (autograph letter signed); APCS (autograph postcard signed); TL (Copy) (letter found only in transcribed typewritten unsigned form); TLS (typewritten letter signed); and WIRE (telegram). The number of pages cited at the head of the letter refers to the number of sides of paper on which the original is written, regardless of whether or how Wilder numbered the pages. We have listed the repository of each letter in the heading. In cases where we located photocopies and/or transcriptions as well as the original copy of an item, we have noted only the location of the original. For items owned by private individuals, we have provided no identification of those individuals. We have used the following abbreviations for repositories:

Academy of Motion Picture Arts and Sciences	Academy of Motion Picture Arts and Sciences Library, Beverly Hills, CA
Albers Foundation	Joseph and Anni Albers Foundation, Bethany, CT
Berea	Berea College, Berea, KY
Berg	Berg Collection, New York Public Library
Billy Rose	Billy Rose Theatre Collection, New York Public Library Performing Arts Research Center
British Library	British Library, London
BU	Boston University
CalTech	California Institute of Technology, Pasadena
Chicago	University of Chicago
Columbia	Columbia University, New York, NY
Cornell	Cornell University, Ithaca, NY
Harvard	Harvard University, Cambridge, MA
Hobart/William Smith	Hobart & William Smith Colleges, Geneva, NY

Houston	University of Houston
Huntington	Huntington Library, San Marino, CA
JFK	John F. Kennedy Library, Boston, MA
Lawrenceville	Lawrenceville School, Lawrenceville, NJ
LofC	Library of Congress, Washington, DC
Morgan	Morgan Library, New York, NY
National Archives of Canada	National Archives of Canada, Ottawa
Newberry	Newberry Library, Chicago, IL
New Dramatists	New Dramatists, New York, NY
NYU	New York University
Oberlin	Oberlin College, Oberlin, OH
Penn State	Pennsylvania State University, University Park
Pennsylvania	University of Pennsylvania, Philadelphia
Princeton	Princeton University, Princeton, NJ
Private	Privately owned
Redwood	Redwood Library & Athenaeum, Newport, RI
Rice	Rice University, Houston, TX
Schlesinger	Schlesinger Library, Radcliffe College/Harvard University, Cambridge, MA

Smith	Smith College, Northampton, MA
SUNY-Buffalo	State University of New York at Buffalo
Syracuse	Syracuse University, Syracuse, NY
Tennessee	University of Tennessee, Knoxville
Texas	University of Texas, Austin
Theatermuseum	Österreichisches Theatermuseum, Vienna
UCLA	University of California, Los Angeles
Vassar	Vassar College, Poughkeepsie, NY
Virginia	University of Virginia, Charlottesville
Wisconsin	University of Wisconsin, Madison
WisHist	Wisconsin Historical Society, Madison
Wooster	College of Wooster, Wooster, OH
Yale	Beinecke Library, Yale University, New Haven, CT

Literally hundreds of people have assisted in the decade that we have spent gathering, selecting, and editing the correspondence in this volume, and we can acknowledge only a few of them here. Our debts of gratitude must begin with Tappan Wilder, the literary executor of the Wilder estate. It was his idea that we undertake this project. Thereafter, he did the seemingly impossible by continually giving us the benefit of his knowledge, contacts, and expertise without in any way interfering in our selection process. Among the many tasks he performed generously and cheerfully was being one of our readers, going through the first draft of our edition, correcting errors and supplying missing information. Our four other readers were Penelope Niven, who took time from researching her biography of Wilder to be of great assistance; Hugh Van Dusen, our editor at HarperCollins; Barbara Hogenson, our agent; and Mary C. Hartig. We also acknowledge with gratitude the support of the late Catharine Kerlin Wilder. The vast majority of Wilder's correspondence is to be found at the Beinecke Library of Yale University; we are deeply indebted to Patricia Willis, the curator of the Beinecke's American Literature Collection, and the staff, especially Diane Ducharme and Stephen C. Jones, for a great deal of assistance over many years.

It is impossible here to list the names and affiliations of the numerous librarians throughout the world who provided us with photocopies of the Wilder correspondence in their collections. Others who assisted us in locating or annotating frequently elusive items were: Andrew Arnold, John Auchard, the late Jonas Barish, John Barnett, Roland Baumann, Sally Higginson Begley, Eric Bentley, Alice L. Birney, Charles Boewe, Roger Bourland, Jaime H. Bradley, Clarissa Hutchins Bronson, Andreas Brown, Dalma Hunyadi Brunauer, Elizabeth J. Bryer, Edward Burns, David and Denise Carlson, Claus Clüver, Robert Cowley, Jonathan Croll, J. S. Cummins, Barry Day, Suzanne del Gizzo, Russell DiNapoli, Frederick DuPuy, Elizabeth Edminster, Barbara Eggleston, Lewis W. Falb, Ruth Farwell and the late Byron Farwell, William Ferris, James Fisher, Neil Fraistat, Robert Freedman, Nola Frink, Greg Gallagher, the late Donald Gallup, Julia Gardner, Thierry Gillyboeuf, Charles Glenn, the late Richard Goldstone, Linda Gordon, Catharine Wilder Guiles, Jennifer Gully, the late Mel Gussow, Christopher G. Hale, Naomi Hample, G. Laurence Harbottle, Ralph Hardee-Rives, the late Gilbert Harrison, Maurene Y. Hart, Elisabeth Hartjens, Jacqueline Haun, Gary Heyde, Bobbie Hopper, Mrs. Edward Hopper, Israel Horovitz, Kathryn Johnson, Merrie

Martin Jones, Michael Kahn, Jerome Kilty, Lotte Klemperer, Mario Laserna, Hugh Lee, Julian Le Grand and the late Eileen Le Grand, Theodore Leinwand, Mary Lincer, Annemarie Link, Michael A. Lofaro, Robert Longsworth, Nita Walter McAdams, J. D. McClatchy, the late Mary McGrory, John McIntyre, S.J., Vera M. McIntyre, Marilyn McMillan, Richard Mangan, Theodore Mann, Caroline Maun, Anne Marie Menta, E. Ethelbert Miller, Tom Miller, James Morton, Geoffrey Movius, Tommaso Munari, Joseph A. Mussulman, F. J. O'Neil, Sharon Peirce, Barbara Perlmutter, Yves Peyre, Howard Pierson, Charles A. Porter, Margaret Powell, Diana Prince, Pamela Rankin-Smith, Chad S. Reingold, Diane Rielinger, Harriet Robinson, Ned Rorem, Lois Rudnick, Jessica Ryan, Jeffrey L. Sammons, Judith Schiff, Paul Schlueter, Marian Seldes, Ed Smith, Joseph Thomas Snow, Edita Spinosi, Peter Stansky, Jan Stieverman, Irvin Stock, Cecilia and Peter Sturm, Sue Swartzlander, G. Thomas Tanselle, Liffey Thorpe, Harry J. Traugott, June Trolley and the late Leonard Trolley, Serge Troubetzkoy and the late Dorothy Ulrich Troubetzkoy, Nick Tsacrios, Jay Tunney, Fred Walker, Julia Walworth, Barbara Whitepine, Catharine Williamson, Martha Wilson, Autumn Winslow, Peter Wiseman, Douglas Wixson, Luke Yankee, Matthew Young, and Waldemar Zacharasiewicz.

The arduous task of transcribing the correspondence fell entirely to helen DeVinney, who not only solved the difficulties of reading Wilder's handwriting but also made certain that our editorial procedures were consistent. Robert Bowman was of great assistance in tracking down often obscure information for our footnotes. The staff of the Department of English at the University of Maryland and its successive chairs, Charles Caramello, Gary Hamilton, and Kent Cartwright, provided photocopying and mailing facilities.

FOREWORD

I

These letters of Thornton Wilder are a pleasure to read: as entertaining and enlightening, almost, as a conversation with the man himself. They also introduce us to the mind and heart of one of the great American writers of the twentieth century. Wilder belonged to a literary generation that included Ernest Hemingway, William Faulkner, F. Scott Fitzgerald, and John Dos Passos—all of them born between 1896 and 1899—and was proud of it. "[N]othing interests me more than thinking of our generation as a league and as a protest to the whole cardboard generation that precedes us," he wrote Fitzgerald. Wilder had a long and sparkling career, highlighted by three Pulitzer Prizes: for his novel *The Bridge of San Luis Rey* (1927), and for the plays *Our Town* (1938) and *The Skin of Our Teeth* (1942). Altogether he wrote seven novels and three major plays. *The Bridge of San Luis Rey* became a best-seller. *Our Town* became part of the American experience. The third play, *The Matchmaker* (1954), was adapted into *Hello, Dolly!*, a tremendously successful musical comedy. Almost everything Wilder produced found its audience, including his last novel *Theophilus North* (1973). Yet he remains, in Malcolm Cowley's phrase, "the most neglected author of a brilliant generation."

Why should this be so? Amos N. Wilder, Thornton's older brother, devoted much of his short book on *Thornton Wilder and His Public* to puzzling out the answers. Most commentators on his work, he concluded, did not know what to do with him. Wilder's works did not fit into the critical imperative of making it new. True, he demanded of himself the same compression of language that Ezra Pound was lobbying for in poetry and Hemingway was practicing in prose. And his plays were highly experimental in stagecraft and technique. But then there was the subject matter, where Wilder was reaching beyond his grasp toward a fusion of the modern and the traditional, the present and the past, with an emphasis on ordinary people. On the surface, as among George and Emily and the Stage Manager in *Our Town,* this seemed to smack of the sentimental, than which in critical opinion nothing could be worse. But this conclusion ignores the play's purgatorial third act, and Emily's disastrous return to her twelfth birthday.

Wilder's popularity worked against his reputation among those who regarded starving as a precondition of artistic excellence. Nor was he political enough to please the doctrinaire. "Yes, Wilder writes perfect English but he has nothing to say in that perfect English," Mike Gold, editor of the communist *New Masses,* commented in a review of the 1930 novel *The Woman of Andros.* Where were the streets of New York in his "little novels"? Where the idealists in union halls? Their oppressors at country clubs? Wilder did revisit the Midwest of his boyhood in *Heaven's My Destination* (1935) and *The Eighth Day* (1967), but these novels were not saddled with proletarian propaganda. Universal questions spanning the centuries interested him, and to those there could be no fast answers. In his books and plays, he followed Chekhov's dictum that the "business of literature is not to answer questions, but to state them fairly."

II

Thornton Wilder has been somewhat unlucky in his biographers, a situation that promises to change with the arrival of Penelope Niven's book. Meanwhile, this selection of his correspondence, judiciously edited and annotated by Robin G. Wilder and Jackson R. Bryer, serves nicely as a Life in Letters. The editors' headnotes to each of the six chronological sections provide an excellent summary of significant events in the lives of Wilder and his family. The letters themselves show how he reacted to these circumstances. Fact: We learn from the editors' Introduction that during an eleven-year period between

Thornton's ninth and twentieth birthdays, the boy himself, his four siblings, and his father and mother lived together under the same roof for only twelve months altogether. What that felt like: Thornton at fourteen, alone at prep school in China, writes, "Oh, but Father, I wish I could see Mother. It seems many years since I saw her last. I want to see her very very much. When you make your plans try and let me be near her and [his brother] Amos. And of course father dear, I want you too; my dear Papa—all together."

Amos P. Wilder, journalist and lecturer and internationalist, commanded the household—often from a distance—with an iron hand, directing where his sons went to school and college and on what farms they were to spend their summers at hard democratic labor. With daughters Isabel and Charlotte and Janet, he was marginally less domineering, but all the children were expected to issue regular bulletins on their activities and accomplishments. Thornton's were notably aesthetic in nature. From Thacher School in Ojai, California, on January 13, 1913, he reported that he was making progress on the piano and the violin, and noted that he'd received his "Chefoo [China] music prize and thank you for your part." Nine months later, he announced that a "little one-act farce" he'd written had been chosen for a benefit performance at the Berkeley, California, high school he was then attending. In his sixteenth year Thornton was on his way toward becoming a playwright—a prospect that did not entirely satisfy his father, who had more lofty pursuits in mind. He likened his son's writing to "carving cherry-stones." When it came time for college, he enrolled the lad at Oberlin.

With its compulsory chapel and mandatory scripture study, high-minded Oberlin had connections to the Wilder family in generations past, and his older brother Amos had just completed two years there before going on to Yale. But Thornton objected that "a boy—if possible—should have some say about the college he's going to." He would have chosen Yale or Harvard himself. Or have elected to travel and write, subsisting in European attics or in steerage on boats. Father decided otherwise, and dutifully Thornton spent two years at Oberlin, and three more at Yale, where he graduated in the class of 1920.

College brought Wilder new friends, but he hardly needed classrooms to educate himself. All his life he was a perambulating autodidact, a perpetual graduate student in love with learning. His letters are full of fragments from the languages he mastered: French, German, Spanish, Italian, Latin. He read widely, driven by a "seemingly insatiable desire" to know more. Often he raided the masters for techniques and approaches—Dante for *Our Town,* Molière and Bacon for *The Matchmaker,* Joyce for *The Skin of Our Teeth,* the Marquise de Sévigné for *The Bridge of San Luis Rey.* He was like the woman caught for shoplifting in Los Angeles. "I only steal from the best department stores," she said in defense, "and they don't miss it,"

Like any fervent researcher, Wilder sometimes got caught up in scholarly investigations that distracted him from his own work. He spent countless hours obsessively attempting to decipher Joyce's *Finnegans Wake.* He threw himself into the magnificently inconsequential project of dating the plays of Lope de Vega between 1595 and 1610, becoming the leading authority on a subject that, he knew, no more than twenty people in the world might conceivably be interested in. In other ways, too, Wilder sloughed off the discipline of the professional writer to pursue peripheral interests. "I'm Jekyll and Hyde," he admitted in 1934. "With the side of me that's not Poet, and there's lots of it, I like to do things, meet people, restlessly experiment in untouched tracts of my Self, be involved in things, make decisions, pretend that I'm a man of action." He was forever on the move, spending two hundred days a year away from the Hamden, Connecticut, home he'd built in 1930 on the proceeds from *The Bridge,* where sister Isabel kept house for him. He wrote aboard ships, and at "spas in off-season." Late in life he escaped to the desert, yet even in Douglas, Arizona, found fresh distractions and new people to talk the night away with. Always there were too many things to do. In addition to novelist and playwright, Wilder functioned, the editors point out, as "translator, adapter, essayist, screenwriter, opera librettist, scholar, cultural emissary, lecturer, teacher, actor."

III

A prolific correspondent, he turned out as many as 25 letters a day to friends, family, and professional associates. He also read a great many letters, including the correspondence of major writers of the past. He was interested in what distinguished the accomplished letter writer from run-of-the-mill correspondents. Only in letters, he thought, could people communicate one to one the "innumerable trifles" of everyday life, "that rain of trifling details, pleasing and vexatious, which falls upon the just and the unjust." Successful letter writers, such as his friend Alexander Woollcott, could make such unpromising material engaging through "high vivacity"—a quality Wilder shared with Woollcott. But there was more to writing good letters than merely entertaining the recipient. For over a period of time, reading two or three hundred letters, one could conjure up a "profile of a personality" above and beyond the wit and the anecdotes. The personality that emerges from Wilder's letters is that of the enthusiast, a man who "fizzed like champagne," whose effervescence was like a force of nature.

This gift made him an excellent teacher. Fresh out of Yale, Wilder earned his keep as an instructor in French and assistant housemaster at Lawrenceville School in New Jersey. "People said to me <u>Never</u> <u>teach</u> <u>school</u>. <u>You</u> <u>will</u> <u>be</u> <u>so</u> <u>unhappy</u>. <u>It</u> <u>will</u> <u>deaden</u> <u>you</u>," he wrote from his post at Davis House in November 1921. "But what happy surprises you find here; how delightful the relations of the teacher and an interested class; casual encounters with retiring boys on the campus, and at lights-out the strange big protective feeling, locking the doors against dark principalities and powers and thrones, and the great lamp-eyed whales that walk ashore in New Jersey."

To amuse his mother and poke fun at himself, Wilder composed a wonderful letter to her supposedly written by one of his students. "We get on very well with [Mr. Wilder] in the house. . . . He doesn't come out and watch our football much, but perhaps if he were the kind that did he wouldn't be able to help us in Latin etcetera. In class he talks so fast and jumps on you so sudden for recitations that often you don't know a thing. Please write him for his own good to speak slowlier, as it would be for his own good. . . . Can you explain why he hasn't any pictures of girls in his room, nor even of you, everybody has pictures of women in their room, can you explain this?"

Humor pervades these letters. Wilder declared a classroom triumph fifteen years later, when he was teaching at the University of Chicago under the aegis of President Robert Maynard Hutchins. "I was sublime on the two Oedipuses the other day—sublime," he wrote

Woollcott. As Hutchins himself reported at Wilder's memorial service, Thornton had once described to him the humiliations of receiving a bad review: "My barber lost his tongue and cut my hair in silence. The waitress at my *stammtisch* at Howard Johnson's murmured, 'Never mind, dear. Maybe you'll do better next time. You'll be wanting the eighty-five cent blue-plate lunch. It's hash today.' My dog hid behind the woodpile when I called him, and when I spoke to the little girl next door, her mother called through the window, 'Come inside, Marguerite. I think it is going to rain.' "

Then there was the American Academy of Arts and Letters awards ceremony when Arthur Miller and Dorothy Parker were honored, with Mrs. Miller (Marilyn Monroe) in the audience applauding. "So who did they place me between at lunch?" Not between Dottie and Marilyn, but between novelists Carson McCullers and Djuna Barnes. McCullers neglected her roast beef until Wilder, "synchronizing with the television cameras," cut it for her "very nicely." He attempted to engage Barnes in conversation. "I just saw that exhibit of your work in the Paris show about American-Expatriates-in-the-Twenties, Miss Barnes." "Must've been horrible." "No—very attractive. I went with Miss Toklas." "Never liked her!" "Really—and Miss Stein." "*Loathed her.*" "I was especially interested also in the Joyce exhibit." "Detestable man."

Another dimension comes to light when Wilder is moved to high dudgeon. In a 1955 letter, he scolded the poet Marcia Nardi for too readily succumbing to sorrow. She'd told him about "shattering emotional experiences" that left her "ill in both body and soul." Well, Wilder knew about such experiences, but he was afraid that Nardi cultivated and actually enjoyed them. She sounded like a willing victim in a bad French novel, he told her. She sounded "Greenwich-village-y, 1912." He doubted she'd write any poetry worth reading until she shook out of it. And then, to take the curse off, he finished with "I think you know that I write you this way because I believe that you will outgrow all these stages and write beautiful things. . . . You know that, don't you?" And enclosed a check.

Unsympathetic to ostentatious self-pity in others, Wilder allowed no trace of it in himself. In 1968, Richard Goldstone commiserated with him after he'd undergone a hernia operation. Each year he understood Wilder better, Goldstone maintained: "I understand that your life has been difficult, filled with profound disappointments, with strivings and struggles, that the rewards have not been many." "Where the hell do you get that?" an outraged Wilder asked, and immediately answered, "You get that out of your own damp self-dramatizing nature." He was damned if he would feel sorry for himself: "Struggles? Disappointments? Just out of college I got a good job at Lawrenceville and enjoyed it. I made a resounding success with my second book. The years at Chicago were among the happiest in my life. I got a Pulitzer Prize with my first play. What friendships—Bob Hutchins, Sibyl Colefax, . . . Gertrude Stein, Ruth Gordon. . . ." Obviously angry, he advised Goldstone to leave him alone. Goldstone, undeterred, went on to commit the first biography of Wilder.

Outbursts like these take us beyond Wilder's bubbling personality into the territory he called "News from Within," inner views only to be glimpsed in the finest letter writers. His intolerance of any display of unhappiness and unwillingness to court the sympathy of others bespeaks a withholding of the self more characteristic of his Maine ancestors than his midwestern roots. Yet, between the lines of his letters, we begin distantly to know him. Wilder was a bachelor all his life, with a series of young male protégés. Did he love this one, or that? There are only hints here, as when he signs off a 1927 letter to William I. Nichols. "Letter-writing bridges next to nothing. Goodbye my dear Bill. Is my affection some help to you when you are depressed and restless?" In his understated way Wilder was forever reaching out to others. He thought of himself as an observer and onlooker, with "an interest in human beings so intense and unremitting that it approaches and resembles love." He stood at the opposite pole from Nick Carraway, the unwilling confidant who in the opening pages of *The Great Gatsby* deplores having to listen to the confessions of "veteran bores." People did not bore Wilder.

Little as we know of Wilder's emotional life, his letters reveal ample evidence of his genius for making and maintaining friendships. Good letters, he believed, resulted from friendship plus absence, with absence supplying the tension that "raise[d] them above even good talk." His correspondence with the elegant and charming Sybil Colefax, the English interior designer, may serve as a case in point. Wilder was only rarely in London, and Colefax rarely left the continent, so they kept in touch through letters—four hundred of them, he estimated. Here, encapsulated, are the contents of but one of them: his May 15, 1949, letter from Washington, D.C. He began mundanely with an account of recent activities. He was getting some work done, his only distractions "being visits to great poets—Ezra Pound, Alexis Léger, and Czeslaw Milosz." Upcoming was a trip to the Goethe Bicentennial Celebration in Aspen, where he was to deliver the opening talk to a gathering that included Albert Schweitzer and José Ortega y Gasset. The moving force behind the Goethe festival was his friend Robert Hutchins, the controversial educator. Colefax had heard charges that Hutchins was "an enemy of humanism," and Wilder defended him vigorously.

His letters were all about people—usually celebrated people—and in this case one dog. Wilder asked Colefax to grieve with him over the illness of Basket III, Gertrude Stein and Alice B. Toklas's French poodle, and reminded her that Basket I had been a gift to Stein from Picasso. Next he did a characteristically thoughtful thing: he told Colefax about a talented young artist—Robert Shaw, "the wunderkind of choral directing"—whom he was sending to see her. He was afraid that Shaw might shrink from presenting the letter of introduction, for the lad was shy. He often thought, Wilder added, that the people "we would most wish to see walk three times around the block and then decide not to call on us, fearing that they have nothing which could interest." In a closing burst of rhetoric, Wilder addressed the issue of when he and Colefax might next meet. Could she come to Arizona in the fall? If not, he would cross to see her. He had "100,000 irremoveable marks in Germany," so they could go to Bad Homburg or Bad Nauheim or Baden-Baden and she "could lie in the mud-filled copper baths where [her] sovreign, Edward VII, renewed his youth like an eagle."

IV

Some of Wilder's most interesting letters, unsurprisingly, were addressed to or commented on prominent figures in the literary and theatrical worlds. He met Gertrude Stein—"a great, sensible, gallant gal and a great treat"—when she came to Chicago in 1934 and he was pressed into service as her "secretary, errand boy-companion." The next year he stayed with Stein and Toklas for eight days in Bilignin, coming away feeling rather daunted by Stein's "difficult magnificent and occasionally too abstract and faintly disillusioned alpine wisdom." He never doubted her genius, though, and other happy meetings ensued. When she died in 1946, he wrote Toklas offering to serve as literary executor of her works. "[L]ong after you and I are dead," he said, "she will be becoming clearer and clearer as the great thinker and the great soul of our time."

If he admired Stein, Wilder was quite swept away by Hemingway. The two men met in Paris in the autumn of 1926, each at the beginning of their careers. Hemingway was living alone at the time, separated from his first wife, Hadley. On November 9, Wilder wrote him from Munich, waxing enthusiastic about the city and deploring the dullness of the youth he was accompanying as chaperone-companion. He hadn't read *The Sun Also Rises* yet, Wilder said, but would have by the time they saw each other. He suggested that Hemingway write a play for Richard Boleslavsky and his Laboratory Theatre in New York, and in closing asked Hemingway to give his regards to Sylvia Beach.

This letter constitutes at least a minor discovery in Hemingway studies. It has not been cited in the several biographies of Hemingway, nor has any mention appeared of a meeting of the two writers. That there was such a meeting, quite possibly at Beach's Shakespeare & Company bookstore, and subsequent encounters as well, marking at least the beginning of a friendship, is borne out by Wilder's November 28 letter to his three sisters, written in Paris. He was considering "going over to live with Ernest Hemingway" in his studio apartment, he reported, but "[Ernest's] wife is about to divorce him, and his new wife is about to arrive from America, so I think I'd better not try." Hemingway himself, he thought "wonderful" in his devotion to his work. He was the only writer of his generation he had met who inspired his respect as an artist.

Ten days later Wilder wrote his mother that Hemingway "remains the hot sketch of all time, bursting with self-confidence and a sort of little-boy impudence." Hemingway was at work on a play about Mussolini, he wrote—again, a revelation, if true. Its accuracy seems doubtful, though, for Wilder goes on to report that Hemingway in yarning mode claimed to have dabbled in secret service and to have certain knowledge that most of the attempts on Mussolini's life were orchestrated by Il Duce himself in order to create a martyr-legend. His mother could judge, Wilder dryly observed, "how full of astonishments" Ernest's conversation was.

Stagestruck since boyhood, Thornton Wilder took immense pleasure in his contacts with prominent men and women of the theatre. "Mary Pickford wants me to write a play with her!" And on Saturday, "Aleck, Kit, Gert (Alexander Woollcott, Katharine Cornell, Gertrude Macy) and [he]" were going to the summer home of Alfred Lunt and Lynn Fontanne "to sleep on army cots." So he announced excitedly in a letter of June 1933 to actress Ruth Gordon—"best of all Ruthies"—who with her husband, the writer and director Garson Kanin, became his lifelong friends. Two months later he alerted Woollcott to look out for an eighteen-year-old actor coming to New York and armed with letters of recommendation from Wilder. He was "a rather pudgy-faced youngster with a wing of brown hair . . . and a vague Oxford epigrammatic manner." The name, he added, was "Orson Welles," and he was going far.

Wilder's profound understanding of the stage is demonstrated in letters of advice to aspiring actors and playwrights. An actress, he warned Rosemary Ames, must expect to be regarded socially as a freak. She would be too busy to pay calls, and people would cast "their curious and fascinated gaze" upon her. Ames should beware of the temptation "for praise and lively suppers" that followed a performance. It was not easy "to go soberly to bed at eleven after a superb climax." Best friends were likely to seem dull; the actress required bright new admirers instead. Eventually, though, if she were good enough, she would become "something more than a lady: an artist."

The best thing a young playwright could do was to immerse himself in the theater, Wilder believed. Climb walls, get thrown out by guards, hide behind back rows—do everything possible to see hundreds of hours or rehearsals, he wrote in 1954. Fifty hours backstage were worth a thousand in the audience. The beginner might have to work at some other occupation to earn a living, but that would not hurt him. It was important, however, not to earn that living by writing rubbish. Writing down could do real damage.

More than forty years later, he dispensed savvy advice about the writing process itself. Select a subject "close to you—not autobiographically but inwardly." Think about it. Take walks. Block out the main crises. Begin not at the beginning but at some scene that has already started to "express itself in dialogue." Take your time. Don't write too much in a day. Keep a regular steady pace, and the next day's writing will take shape while you are sleeping.

In other communications Wilder addressed specific issues of stagecraft. He liked opening a play in silence, as Shakespeare did in *Hamlet*. He heartily disliked ending with a message, as T. S. Eliot had in *The Cocktail Party*. He was "grateful and absorbed" by the play until the last fifteen minutes, Wilder wrote Laurence Olivier and Vivien Leigh, but "angry as a boil" when the "answers" began to descend. To another famous actor, Cary Grant, he offered his thoughts about how a film might be made of *Gulliver's Travels*. Play it straight, he counseled. Treat it not as a fantasy but as "dead-pan sober-serious travel-experience." And don't be afraid of taking liberties, for it would be difficult to keep audiences interested in the giant-pygmy situation for two hours.

In 1957, Wilder proposed a book of letters about the theater, written by and to himself, to his editor Cass Canfield. These would include his correspondence with Ruth Gordon about *The Matchmaker*, with Sybil Colefax about the London and New York theater, with Max Reinhardt about *The Merchant of Yonkers*, with Jed Harris about *Our Town*, and with Laurence Olivier about *The Skin of Our Teeth*. It would make for a lively book, and his sister Isabel could edit it. Unfortunately, this volume was not published, but these *Selected Letters* present most of Wilder's side of that conversation.

Wilder suggested the theater-letters book as a way of benefiting a friend and fellow artist. He was collaborating with composer Louise Talma on an opera based on *The Alcestiad*, he explained to Canfield, and Talma "was living on very narrow means." The question was how "to get money to her—across the barrier of her pride and independence." Wilder thought that she might accept royalties from such a book, inasmuch as it would contain some of their letters back and forth about *The Alcestiad* and the funds could be considered as subsidizing their common project, the opera. Perhaps his idea wasn't practical—he even wondered if it was in good taste—but surely it originated in a wise and largehearted sensibility. Thornton Wilder wanted to do more with his life than to give pleasure to those who read his novels or saw his plays. The trouble with T. S. Eliot, he decided after seeing *The Cocktail Party,* was that he didn't like people. Wilder did, went out of his way to make them happy, and profited from doing so.

Armed with that outlook, he bucketed along well into his seventies. He was thankful, as he wrote John O'Hara in 1965 (the year O'Hara reached sixty), not to be "tormented by that panic over the passing of youth that beset Scott Fitzgerald and Hemingway." He hoped that O'Hara enjoyed each new decade as much as he had. If you welcomed each decade, Wilder said, you could keep the past ones green inside you. And you could continue to do your work as well, for, as he observed in a 1972 letter, there was no age limit for creativity. There *were,* however, "two required conditions: EROS at your right hand, Praise of life at your left."

Scott Donaldson
Scottsdale, Arizona
May 2008

INTRODUCTION

> The rewards of reading letters come to us in extent, not in bright single moments.
>
> —THORNTON WILDER
> "THREE ENGLISH LETTERWRITERS" (unpublished lecture, May 13, 1930)

Thornton Wilder (1897–1975) had a sixty-year career as a successful author—from his first play, *The Russian Princess,* produced in 1913, when he was sixteen (to reported raves from schoolmates), to his seventh and last novel, *Theophilus North* (1973), published two years before his death and a best-seller for twenty-six weeks. In the intervening decades, he had far more success than failure, playing such varied roles as translator, adapter, essayist, screenwriter, opera librettist, scholar, cultural emissary, lecturer, teacher, actor, and, of course, novelist and playwright. He remains the only writer ever to receive the Pulitzer Prize in both drama and fiction.

Throughout his life, Wilder played yet another role, one until now neither adequately acknowledged nor sufficiently documented: He was an avid connoisseur and practitioner of letter writing. In retrospect, it is no surprise that, in the spring of 1928, in the midst of international acclaim for his second novel, *The Bridge of San Luis Rey,* he accepted an invitation from Yale University to deliver the Daniel S. Lamont Memorial Lecture on the topic of "English Letters and Letter Writers," the first of some two hundred public lectures he would give during his career. He devoted a section of his talk to the virtues of the letters written by Mme. de Sévigné, whom he had memorialized in *The Bridge of San Luis Rey* through the figure of the Marquesa de Montemayor. Letters were to continue to play an important role in his fiction and drama—from an entire novel, *The Ides of March* (1948), written in epistolary form, to the amazement Rebecca Gibbs expresses in *Our Town* (1938) that "the postman brought . . . just the same" a letter addressed to "Jane Crofut; The Crofut Farm; Grover's Corners; Sutton County; New Hampshire; . . . . United States of America; Continent of North America; Western Hemisphere; the Earth; the Solar System; the Universe; the Mind of God."

There is ample evidence as well that Wilder was himself a prolific practitioner of the art of letter writing. In a typical aside in a March 1935 letter to his mother and his sister Isabel, he reported, "Last night I sat up til two and added 18 new letters to the 8 I had got off earlier in the day." On March 20, 1948, he wrote William Layton, "This evening I mailed 24 [letters], all written today." It is estimated that the total number of letters Wilder wrote exceeds ten thousand. Thanks to the Wilder family's habit of preserving correspondence as well as to the passage of enough time since his death for letters to migrate into places where they can be found, we have been able to read some six thousand in the process of compiling this volume, which is the first to present examples of Wilder's correspondence across the entire span of his writing life. Our choices from scores of fine letters represent the range of his friendships, public achievements, and private interests. We have included letters that do indeed encompass almost his full life: The earliest letter we found was written, we believe, when Wilder was about nine years old. The first we have selected finds him at age twelve in 1909, while the last is dated December 3, 1975, four days before he died.

Until recently, of course, letters were a primary means of personal and business communication and letter writing was a routine part of a person's life. Wilder became a letter writer at a young age because of his personal circumstances. When he was growing up, his family was together as a unit very infrequently. During the eleven-year period between 1906, when nine-year-old Thornton left Madison, Wisconsin, for China, and 1917, when he enrolled as a sophomore at Yale College in New Haven, Connecticut, where his parents had recently moved, all the Wilders were under one roof for a total of only twelve months. Distances between one or more absent family members were more often than not measured by oceans. Even Thornton's summers from 1913 to 1917 were spent away from home, working on farms in California, Kentucky, Vermont, and Massachusetts. Given these circumstances, letters became the only way he could communicate with his friends and, especially, with his family. Letters to his father were particularly important during Wilder's youth. From his consular posts in China, with his wife and children rarely present, "Papa"—described by his elder son, Amos, in *Imagining the Real* (1978), as a "very intensive parental planner"—sought through a flood of letters to guide his children's activities. He expected and received frequent status reports from them. This early letter writing may have played a part in turning the younger Wilders into authors; each of the four children born between September 1895 and January 1900 became a published writer. Thornton Wilder grew up in a family where reaching for a pen and a blank piece of paper (all his life, he handwrote almost all of his letters and creative work) was first, second, and third nature—and had to be.

Wilder's peripatetic lifestyle persisted for the rest of his life. After 1928, from the earnings of *The Bridge of San Luis Rey,* he built a house for himself and his family in Hamden, Connecticut. He maintained the house and, for the rest of their lives, supported the members of his family who lived there. But Wilder himself, despite a handsome study on the second floor, treated the family home as a base to which he returned periodically, rather than as a primary place to live and work. He was an artist who had to go away in order to write—to hotels or occasional short-term rentals in North America, the Caribbean, Mexico, and abroad; to the MacDowell Colony, an artists' retreat in New Hampshire; or to cabins on transatlantic steamships, the slower the better. Given this lifestyle, letters were crucial for keeping in touch; they knit his world together, just as they had when he was growing up. He reportedly disliked talking on the telephone, employing it chiefly for the exchange of necessary details, while using letters for more expansive conversations.

By the late 1920s, Thornton Wilder's world had, of course, grown far larger, literally and figuratively, than when he was a boy. His travels had accelerated and widened in scope, his experiences had become more varied, and he had accumulated an extremely large group of friends and acquaintances, a small circle of whom he corresponded with over many years. Among those represented in this volume, his friendships with Gilbert Troxell, C. Leslie Glenn, Amy Wertheimer, Sibyl Colefax, Alexander Woollcott, Gertrude Stein and Alice B. Toklas, and Ruth Gordon and Garson Kanin were of especially long duration. He met Troxell when they were both Yale undergraduates, and they remained friends until Troxell's death in 1967. Wilder and Glenn met in 1922, when they were both assistant housemasters at the Lawrenceville School, and the last letter we have included from Wilder to Glenn is dated 1973, although they continued to correspond until Wilder's death two years later. Wertheimer met Wilder in the summer of 1925 and they corresponded until her death in 1971. And Wilder exchanged lengthy letters with Colefax between 1928 and 1950, the year of her death. Wilder also had a large coterie of "honorary nieces and nephews" (in addition to his actual niece and nephew), young people who became his protégés. Among those whose careers he encouraged and to whom he regularly dispensed advice were June and Leonard Trolley, Byron and Ruth Farwell, Sally Higginson Begley, Mia Farrow, and Marcia Nardi.

Until poor health intervened toward the end of his life, Wilder personally answered a staggering number of the cards and letters he received, whether from producers or directors wanting to stage his plays, strangers seeking advice or praising one of his works, or students acting in one of his plays or writing papers about him. He explained this generosity by famously referring to himself in a January 12, 1953, *Time* cover story as an "obliging man." Although he meant this phrase somewhat ironically, he also intended that it be taken at face value, for Wilder saw his far-flung audience as a worthy and important part of his life.

While we have attempted in this volume to present the variety of Thornton Wilder's correspondence, we have had to omit a number of valuable letters, especially those relating in detail to Wilder novels or plays or to specific works by other writers, because they would have required the reader to possess extensive knowledge of the material discussed. Furthermore, because all of Wilder's letters to Joyce scholar Adaline Glasheen have been published (*A Tour of the Darkling Plain: The* Finnegans Wake *Letters of Thornton Wilder and Adaline Glasheen,* edited by Edward W. Burns with Joshua A. Gaylord [2001]), we have included only one from their extensive correspondence. Wilder's many letters to Gertrude Stein and Alice B. Toklas appear in *The Letters of Gertrude Stein & Thornton Wilder,* edited by Edward W. Burns and Ulla E. Dydo, with William Rice (1996); therefore, we have cut back our selection of these to permit other inclusions. Numerous Wilder letters either have not survived or remain unlocated in libraries (this is especially true of repositories outside the United States) and in the possession of their recipients (or the latter's descendants). As a result, gaps do occur; this is most noticeable during the first twenty-five years of Wilder's life. For that period, the great majority of the letters we found were those to his family; so while such letters undoubtedly did represent a high percentage of those he wrote during this time, our selection probably increases that ratio somewhat. We also elected not to include any of the several letters he wrote entirely in a foreign language, because we felt that to present these in translation would not satisfactorily convey their tone and flavor. As to our criteria for selecting among the items we did locate, they simply echo those standards Wilder believed a letter should reflect: a sense of the "historical—data relative to social implications of a period"—and "a natural gift for letter-writing," as he indicated in an August 1951 letter to scholar and critic Robert W. Stallman, his former student at the University of Chicago. Basically, we have included letters that either shed light on Wilder's many activities and interests and those of his friends or display his skill with words. Often, we were able to find letters that we believe do both.

Today, Thornton Wilder is best known as the author of *Our Town,* a play that is performed every night of each year; and of *The Bridge of San Luis Rey,* a novel widely taught in secondary schools. Altogether, he published seven novels, five full-length plays, and a score of one-act plays, translations, adaptations, and essays. Thornton Wilder's literary record is not complete without his correspondence. Letters and letter writing played a major role in Wilder's personal and creative life. He wrote letters prolifically, took the task seriously, and was keenly aware of the epistolary tradition of which he was a part. If this volume helps to familiarize readers with a vivacious, erudite, and multitalented man with a myriad of interests—a man of letters both literally and figuratively—and, above all, if it leads some of them to a broader reading of his work, it will have accomplished its intentions.

Part One

BEGINNINGS: 1909–1920

THORNTON NIVEN WILDER WAS BORN IN MADISON, WISCONSIN, on April 17, 1897. His twin brother died at birth, and, according to family lore, Wilder himself was so frail that he was carried around on a pillow for the first months of his life. At the time of Wilder's birth, his father, Amos Parker Wilder, was editor and part owner of the *Wisconsin State Journal.* By 1901, when Thornton was four years old, his father had acquired a controlling interest in the paper and was well-known in Wisconsin political circles.

Because his parents exerted an unusually strong influence on their children, a brief account of their backgrounds is necessary here. Amos Parker Wilder was born in Maine in 1862, grew up in the state capital of Augusta, and graduated from Yale College, where he was a scholar, singer, orator, editor of one of Yale's literary magazines, the *Courant,* and a member of a senior secret society. After graduating in 1884, he taught for two years and then became a journalist, working first as a reporter in Philadelphia. He returned to New Haven to edit the *New Haven Palladium,* while also working on a doctorate at Yale. He wrote his dissertation on the difficulties and possible solutions of governing American cities, and received his Ph.D. in 1892. When he lost his editorship at the *Palladium* for attacking political figures who had a financial interest in that newspaper, he left New Haven for a position as an editorial writer on a New York City paper. In 1894, he traveled to the Midwest, intent on finding a newspaper to invest in and work on. He realized his ambition in the university town of Madison, Wisconsin, where, with his savings augmented by loans from friends, he bought a one-quarter interest in the *Wisconsin State Journal*.

Before the year was out, another important change occurred in his life: twenty-one-year-old Isabella Thornton Niven of Dobbs Ferry, New York, accepted his proposal of marriage, and on December 3, 1894, they married and returned to Madison to live. Isabella was the daughter of the minister of the Presbyterian church in Dobbs Ferry. Her maternal grandfather was Arthur Tappan, cofounder of the American Anti-Slavery Society, who, with his brother Lewis, did much to support the antislavery movement. Both men were also prominent in backing the Oberlin Collegiate Institution and probably ensured its survival as Oberlin College. Isabella was a graduate of the Misses Masters School in Dobbs Ferry, where she published poems in the school paper and studied languages, piano, art, and literature. Before her marriage, she attended concerts, the theater, and lectures in New York City and was attuned to the cultural offerings of the day.

The literary interests of Amos Parker Wilder and Isabella Niven Wilder were reflected in their habit of regularly reading aloud classics and Scripture during the childhood of the four children who were born during the next five years: Amos Niven (September 18, 1895), Thornton Niven (April 17, 1897), Charlotte Elizabeth (August 28, 1898), and Isabel (January 13, 1900). Amos Parker Wilder, an active Congregational layman, was also very concerned with his family's religious life and with the cause of temperance.

During the first years of their marriage, because of the loans on the newspaper that Amos Wilder had to repay, money was scarce. Nonetheless, in 1901, they managed to build a cottage on the shores of Lake Mendota in Maple Bluff, just outside the city of Madison, where the family lived each year from early spring until late fall, and Isabella Wilder was able to take a European trip with Madison friends. Amos Parker Wilder almost certainly supplemented his income with lectures on municipal government at the University of Wisconsin, and, as he was becoming a well-known speaker, with engagements on similar subjects around the state. His eloquence was often grounded in his moral certainties, which sometimes strained relationships with political allies. In 1903, this occurred when he changed his paper's editorial policy from support for the "progressive" wing of the Wisconsin Republican party to the more conservative "stalwarts." Around this time, he began to explore professional opportunities outside the newspaper business.

In 1906, he sought a position in the consular service, and with the support of Yale friends within the Republican party, he received an appointment as U.S. consul general in Hong Kong. After twelve years of residence in Madison, the Wilder family sailed for Hong Kong from San Francisco only days before the earthquake there. They arrived in Hong Kong on May 7, 1906, shortly after Thornton's ninth birthday. Life in Hong Kong offered a complete change from the neighborliness of Madison and the activities associated with its homes, shops, and public schools.

Just five months after their arrival in China, the new consul general and his wife decided that Hong Kong was not a good place to rear and educate their children. On October 30, 1906, Isabella Niven Wilder and the four children left Hong Kong, returned to San Francisco, and settled in Berkeley, California, another university town, where the children were enrolled in the local public schools. Their father sent money to support them, supervised their upbringing long-distance through detailed instructions in letters, and saw them on home leaves. Their mother supervised their daily lives and kept Papa informed of their progress; his children wrote to him regularly about their activities and thoughts.

In early spring 1909, Consul General Wilder was promoted and transferred from Hong Kong to Shanghai. Before taking up his new post on June 1, 1909, he paid a short visit to his family in Berkeley. In the fall, he made another trip from Shanghai to California, with a plan for reuniting his family in Shanghai, because he believed it would be a better situation for them than Hong Kong had been. The family reunion did not take place until more than a year later, for Janet Frances, the fifth and final Wilder sibling, was born on June 3, 1910.

In December 1910, Mrs. Wilder embarked on the S.S. *Mongolia* for Shanghai with her four youngest children. The eldest child, fifteen-year-old Amos, was sent to the Thacher School, a boarding school in Ojai, California, established in 1889 by a Yale acquaintance of the senior Wilder. This was one of the country's first "ranch schools," where each boy had a horse to care for, took camping trips, and learned wilderness skills, along with partaking in the usual sports and college-preparatory course work.

Mrs. Wilder was physically unwell in Shanghai and distressed by the unsettled political situation in China. Her doctor suggested a change in climate, and in mid-August 1911, she sailed for Europe through the Suez Canal with her two youngest daughters, Isabel, now eleven, and Janet, just over a year old. They landed in Genoa and proceeded to Florence, Italy, where they joined Mrs. Wilder's younger sister, Charlotte Tappan Niven, and their widowed mother, Elizabeth Lewis Niven. Mrs. Wilder's sister was running a hostel for the international arm of the Young Women's Christian Association.

After some time at a German school in Shanghai, Thornton and Charlotte were sent to the China Inland Mission Schools in Chefoo, approximately 450 miles from Shanghai. They enrolled in the spring term of 1911 and remained there until August 1912. Charlotte attended the Girls' School and Thornton the Boys'; they were permitted to visit with each other for an hour each week. Wilder's friends at Chefoo included Theodore Wilder (no relation) and Henry Luce.

Amos Parker Wilder took home leave after his wife sailed for Europe. He visited his elder son at Thacher, conducted business, and saw friends in Madison. He consulted with doctors, because he had developed Asian sprue, a digestive disease that had left him in a weakened state. While still in the United States, he made arrangements for Thornton and Charlotte to leave Chefoo before the fall term and to take passage on the S.S. *Nile* for San Francisco. They arrived in San Francisco in early September 1912. While Charlotte boarded with family friends in Claremont, California, and attended the local public school there, Thornton joined his brother, Amos, at the Thacher School. During Christmas vacation, Thornton and Amos visited Charlotte and stayed with her and the family with whom she boarded. For the three older Wilder children, the important news was that their mother and two youngest sisters, whom they had not seen in over a year, were planning to return to Berkeley in the spring of 1913. A few months later, the family was reunited, although again without their father.

Amos graduated from Thacher in June 1913 and was sent to work in an orchard in northern California before leaving in the fall for Oberlin College. Thornton attended an arts program at the local public school in Berkeley and helped his mother get settled. He did not return to Thacher. He and Charlotte (although she was a year younger than Thornton) began their junior year together at Berkeley High School, while thirteen-year-old Isabel attended the local McKinley Elementary School, and three-year-old Janet remained at home with her mother.

In the spring of 1914, Amos Parker Wilder, whose Asian sprue disease had worsened in the Shanghai climate, resigned from the consular service and returned to Berkeley, where it was decided that Isabella would stay until Thornton and Charlotte had graduated from high school in June 1915. Charlotte's father took her on a trip to Yosemite Park, but the trip was cut short when he became so ill that it became necessary for him to travel to New York City earlier than anticipated to receive medical care. He remained in the East, returning to his old college town of New Haven, where he accepted the position of secretary and treasurer of the Yale-in-China program and prepared for the arrival of his family after Charlotte's and Thornton's high school graduations.

Although separated from his children in California, the elder Wilder carefully planned their summer activities. He believed that his sons should use their school vacations to exert themselves physically in healthy outdoor labor, to expand their experience to include practical, homely tasks, and to associate with people in a setting that contrasted with the more familiar urbanity of Berkeley. Between his junior and senior years in high school, Thornton was sent to work on a farm in San Luis Obispo. After his graduation from high school in 1915, Thornton came east and learned from his father that he was to work on a farm in Vermont before following his brother to Oberlin. The Wilder brothers, however, did not overlap at Oberlin; Amos, under his father's guidance, had transferred to Yale College for his last two years.

Oberlin College was founded in 1833 by members of the Congregational denomination, which played a significant role in the abolitionist movement. It was the first college in the nineteenth century to have a racially integrated and coed student body. Oberlin also had a music conservatory attached to it. The Oberlin College that Thornton Wilder attended for two years, beginning in 1915, represented the continuing tradition of evangelical Congregationalism, which combined a concern for social causes, personal religion, and missionary work; in a more secular but related mode, the college emphasized teaching and public service. It was a high-minded, serious institution, and while supporting athletic teams and literary and drama clubs, it was much given to religious pursuits such as class prayer meetings.

At Oberlin, Thornton continued to develop his musical interests—he sang in choral groups and took instruction in violin, piano, and organ—which was traceable to and encouraged throughout his boyhood. He also published fiction and plays in the college literary magazine. His Oberlin experiences helped him to shed some of his social awkwardness among contemporaries, an endeavor encouraged, perhaps, by this public acknowledgment of his literary talent. At Oberlin, he renewed his Chefoo friendship with Theodore Wilder and forged close new relationships with undergraduates Robert M. Hutchins, Ruth Keller, and Nina Trego, and with Professor Charles H. A. Wager, the chairman of the English Department. During the summers after Thornton's freshman and sophomore years at Oberlin, his father continued to arrange for him to work on farms attached to institutions the senior Wilder admired: the Mount Hermon School farm in Massachusetts in 1916, and the farm at Berea College (often referred to as the "Oberlin of Kentucky" because it had been founded on the same ideals as its sister school in Ohio) in 1917.

In the fall of 1917, at his father's behest, Thornton Wilder entered Yale College. He had to repeat his sophomore year, possibly because some of his Oberlin credits were not transferable. The family was housed in nearby Mount Carmel, approximately eight miles by trolley from the center of New Haven. Now they were living together, or at least near one another, with the exception of the eldest child, Amos. He was driving an ambulance in Paris, then later on the western front and in Macedonia, before he joined the American Field Artillery after the United States entered World War I. Charlotte, a junior at Mount Holyoke College in South Hadley, Massachusetts, was not far away, and Thornton lived on the Yale campus in downtown New Haven. With the exception of a job in Washington, D.C., during the summer of 1918, and a little more than three months' military service in the Coast Artillery on Narragansett Bay in Rhode Island, Thornton spent the next three years at Yale, in proximity to his family. In fact, after his brother's discharge from the army, the two roomed together at Yale before both graduated in 1920.

As at Oberlin, Thornton Wilder's literary output at Yale was prodigious and his talent noted and appreciated. His pieces were published in the *Yale Literary Magazine* almost upon his arrival on campus. At Yale, however, he gained recognition in a literary milieu that tested his worth against other gifted writers and expanded his acquaintance with others interested and influential in the arts. During those three years, he was elected to esteemed Yale literary societies, among them the Elizabethan ("Lizzie") Club; Chi Delta Theta, a senior literary society; and the Pundits, a group of undergraduates known for their wit and high spirits. He was elected secretary of the Pundits, and he also won writing prizes for two genres: short story and drama. At Yale, he reunited with Henry Luce and Robert M. Hutchins; began lifelong close friendships with musician Bruce T. Simonds and librarian Gilbert Troxell; and met poet Stephen Vincent Benét, playwright Philip Barry, and publisher John Farrar. He found mentors in Yale English professors Chauncey B. Tinker and William Lyon Phelps. In June 1920, as Thornton Wilder completed his undergraduate education, he knew he wanted to be a writer, but he had very little notion of how he could afford to become one.

1. TO ELIZABETH LEWIS NIVEN.[1] ALS 4 pp. Yale

<Berkeley, California>
April 24. <1909>

Dear Grandma,

I had no trouble in cashing the check, for which I thank you very much. My income is not large and I am always thankful for a gift.

I am to join the church very soon. Also Amos.[2]

Mr. Miles our new minister has had preparatory class for several weeks. He is a Yale man a friend of Mr. Parsons and Father.

I would <be> very happy if—I could live in Europe but Mother is not at all sure we can go.

You know I am in the Episcopal choir. Tomorrow the Bishop comes and is to give two gold pins, one for deportment and one for attendence. I am to recieve the one for good deportment.

We feel glad that uncle Thornton[3] likes to go to Washington.

We had a Bach Festival Thursday in which the Mass in B miner was given with great succes.

The Chicago Symphony orchestra is coming. The Ben Greet players[4] are also to be here in the Greek Theatre, where the Mass was held,[5]

your loving grandson
Thornton Niven Wilder

---

1 TNW's maternal grandmother (1847–1923).

2 The First Congregational Church. Amos (1895–1993) was TNW's older brother.

3 Thornton MacNess Niven III (1876–1943), younger of TNW's mother's two brothers.

4 Sir Philip "Ben" Greet (1857–1936), English actor and impresario, who toured North America with spare productions of Shakespeare's plays.

5 The Greek Theatre was given to the University of California by newspaper tycoon William Randolph Hearst in 1903; TNW saw many rehearsals and performances there. The Mass in B Minor was performed there on April 22, 1909; the Chicago Symphony Orchestra appeared there on April 26; and the Ben Greet Players performed *A Midsummer Night's Dream* there on May 1 and *The Tempest* on May 8.

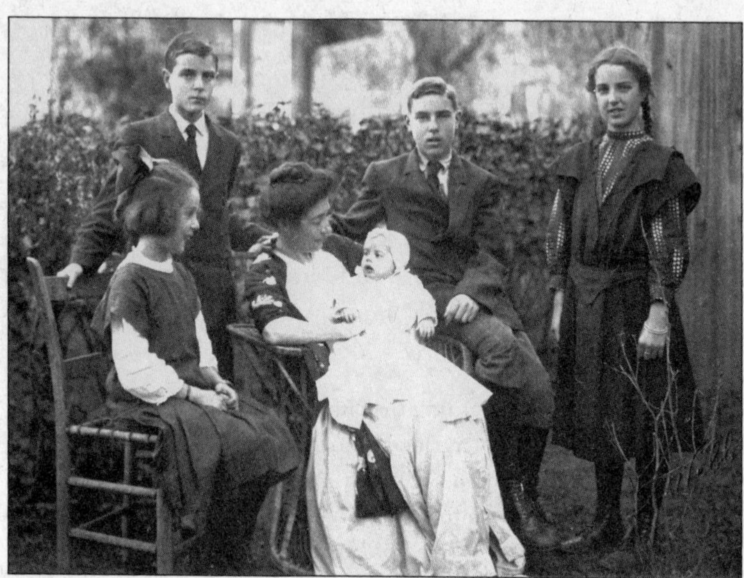

Wilder family in Berkeley, 1910. Left to right: *Isabel, TNW, Isabella, Janet (*in her lap*), Amos N., and Charlotte.*

2. TO AMOS P. WILDER.[6] ALS 2 pp. Yale

<Berkeley, California>
<mid-December 1910>

Dear Papa,

Tonight I am going to Rev. Browns Church to hear Handel's great Oratorio "The Messiah," sung. Do they ever have anything like that in China?

Our Piano has been taken away now, and the sitting rooms little cold without it.

We are going to Miss. O'Connor's for tea this afternoon.

Janet Frances Wilder[7] now weighs 12½ lbs at 6 months.

---

6 TNW's father (1862–1936) was consul general in Shanghai at this time. TNW's mother, Isabella Niven Wilder (1873–1946), and her five children lived in Berkeley.

7 TNW's youngest sister (1910–1994).

Yesterday afternoon I left the letter unfinished, as we left for the O'connors. I came home early and started for "The Messiah" first I went & met Margeret Miles, who invited me, and then we went way over to North Berkeley and got her friend a Mrs. Nipper (I think). She was once a missionary in Turkey. She is very, very sweet. When we got to Dr. Brown's Church it was 7.15. We went in and found that it was not the "Messiah" this year, but Saint-Sean's Christmas Oratoria "Noel".[8] I was not at all disappointed as Margeret expected. The music was beatifully discriptive; angel and shepard Chorus and recitatives of the first Xmas.

Lovingly
Thornton Wilder

3. TO AMOS P., ISABELLA N., AND ISABEL WILDER.[9]
ALS 4 pp. Yale

<C.I.M. Schools, Chefoo, N. China>
<Spring(?) 1911>

Dear Family,

This is a letter we write instead of a composition, I suppose. It is a specimen of grammar, spelling and writing and it passes through other hands than your own.

I have been (relabled) relabeled and rechristened. No. 10 cell 19; Commonly known as Wilder Minor, because of a Major a roommate of mine.[10] He is about my age and about my size; I know a few others too. I am put in a class much higher than I ever expected and there is some doubt of how long I will stay. Im allready tackling the six major declentions in a Latin grammar and the rudiments of Algebra.

8 Christmas Oratorio (Oratorio de Noël), by French composer Charles-Camille Saint-Saëns.

9 The second of TNW's younger sisters (1900–1995).

10 Theodore Wilder (1897–1985), the elder of two sons of Dr. and Mrs. George D. Wilder; Dr. Wilder was an American medical missionary in Tehsien and his wife was a teacher. They were not related to TNW's family.

The Officials in the streets here wear the sensational looking Cholera noseguard.[11]

The journey up wasn't so very calm, and I was seasick once, but it wasn't at all bad. There was a Baron on board with a son and daughter. The son read a french edition of "Anna Karénina"[12] and the daughter slept. On board there was also a french officer who could not talk any english; But he stuck on me thinking I was a french scholar somehow and talked french to me for quite a while. I went away as soon as an excuse came up and played with two black cats. Later for the dare of it I returned and asked him (I dont know how to spell it right)

"Parlez vous Allegmanne, Monsier?"[13]

The man admiring the suberb accent and unapproachable grammar pour<ed> out his soul in french to me with much gesticulation. I went away.

The boys here talk a kind of slang of there own which is very funny at first. They spoke a while ago of a ship going "horribly" slow, and of one another being "abject" clowns. The boys on the ship gave me the scare but I'm over it now; the thing of it is "that they always are calling one another silly idiots" and "abject fools" and any other thing of the sort. Last night as I was lieing in bed I heard from all the other rooms the goodnights and parting thrusts. They were very funny. I wish I could have taken them down. Most of the boys have nicknames; "Ape", "Parsee", derived from Percy, "Spadger<">, "Iago", "Pollywog" and many others.

We just had singing a few minutes ago. The boys all learn by the Sol-Fa System and the music-books looks like Hiroglyphics (tell it to the cook, mater).

You can send this to Amos?

Lovingly
Thornton Wilder.

---

11 In late 1910, a pneumonic plague epidemic broke out in north China and the port near the Chefoo schools was quarantined. Anyone who had to leave the school wore a mask soaked in disinfectant.

12 TNW sometimes added accents in titles or names that did not have such.

13 French: "Do you speak German, sir?"

4. TO AMOS P. WILDER. ALS 4 pp. Yale

<C.I.M. Schools, Chefoo, N. China>
<Early May(?) 1911>

Dear Papa,

I have just received your letters. I see you saw that I could not find your picture. I did not know how you would take it, I see you have or else some one else has, and as for mama's idea of my looking for it, that is impossible, the trunks being kept in inner sanctuaries, and I would not ask the matrons to let me go and search after it after they vowed it wasn't there. And about Mother's picture it has been blown around the room by the Chefoo monsoons (Janet's too) untill the "fall of the house of Wilder" is complete. Now a roomate has lent me a frame of his and she swings on the wall.

For Mothers and Auntie's[14] <u>bene</u>fit (From the latin bene—good) (ahem!)

I will recount our meal today.

<in the margin appeared a diagram of three tables, labeled with names> <left-hand table: at head> music teacher <at foot> Helper <middle table: at head> Mr. McCarthy <at foot> Chief Housekeeper <right-hand table: at head> Mr. Murry, Lea or Mr. Alty <at foot> Wardrobe mistress <below the drawing> <u>Females</u> all helpers! A whole army each with a nickname.

At the end of the tables sit the teachers who deal out the soup and meat. The plate with the meat on is passed to the centre of the table where the prefects sit. The prefects pour on vegetables and gravy. (If the decks-out<prefects?> are mad at you they either pour on Mts. of food or just a little.) Today we had

soop
Entrée a crust to be eaten with (soup)
Vegetable soop (commonly known as Dishwater.)
Meat (lamb) Rice, potatoes and greens (weeds).
Dessert Yellow Tapioca in flowing liquidity

14 The Wilder children's nurse, Margaret ("Aunt") Donoghue.

This last is call<ed> tuck-shop pudding because it is given on candy-shop days. I do not buy candy any more, but buy photos of the cricket teams etc that have the portraits of my friends in. I have begun violin with (Mr) Murray commonly known as Shinter).

I am learning a few trios to play with him-self (he play cello also) and the piano-teacher. I am also in a dozen, stands for the glee-club—I suppose. Tonight again is bath night. I suppos you saw in my next to the last letters that I found that which I thought was lost. I'm glad I found it.

My german has also begun, we have a sharp, irratable lady-teacher who gives us (that Walter Hearn and I are the only German pupils) awfull hard prep. (from the word preparation meaning Home-work). I went to the beach today after Sweet-cupboard and found a cats-eye. Wilder I found nine! He has much better eyes that<than> mine (Cats-eyes)<.> Both of us are called "Wildcat"<.> About the Boracic Acid, she told me to come every saturday morning and made me wash my eye in one of those new-fangled eye-buckets, she calls it a (gentle) Eye-bath. I guess thats all right. I am sorry to say that I was not a good enough rower to get in the boat-club, but I am in the tennis-club.

Lovingly,

Thornton Wilder

(P.S.) Last Cricket day I made 3 runs.

(P.S.) We drill with Indian-clubs. I am just beginning to learn how.

5. TO ISABELLA N., ISABEL, AND JANET F. WILDER. ALS 4 pp. (Stationery embossed C.I.M. Schools, / Chefoo, / N. China) Yale

Friday, <August> 11th 1911

Dear Family

I am in doubt as to wether I did, or did not, send my sunday-letter. I remember the post-boxes were not there when I went to bed, but I could not find it in my pocket next morning so I thought maybe I had mailed it early-morning or not. I think there was nothing more important in <it> than a mountain of love, and that is free. My sweet-cupboard in the form of Aunties box gave out a while ago but Fathers is open now. But Auntie is not forgotten even if the symbol of herself has given out. Today is bath night, I think it is my fifth bath. You told me to describe more minutely a few things. Now comes the bath. The First night I was here I had a great deal of Su<r>prise given to me. Mr. Taylor one of the masters called out:

"All those who have not had a bath lately come up here."

I went forward to my great imbarrasement, there were a few others too. "Allright" he said, I was to have a bath. The Bathroom is a great hall made in to stalls in which is a tub of boiling hot water, one honest inch high, I went down and tried it. From all parts of the room come shrieks of Pain. "Ow! Ow!" I was told that these were from unfortunates who had projected their toes into the brimestone. Later, after fifteen minutes for dressing undressing and bathing a prefect calls out

"One minute more!" Wild shrieks of protest greet this proposal.

"Aw, Wobbles (one of the prefects) give me so<me> more time."

Wobbles with a watch in his hand hollars out:

"Half a minute."

Screams.

"All Out"

Silence. Wobbles never knows which people are in which bath and the doors are shut. By and by boys rush out their doors and run past the prefect who gives a resounding spank as the fugitive's pass. This is the bath.

Violin begun today. Mr. Murray gives me two half-hours a week, and I am to practice as much as I like. (He's very kind, I'm sure) He's evidently been selftaught but he teaches alright. Thank you very much for that San Juan Fernandez stamp it is a fine one; the school is subjugated at my feet for they all wish the stamp. Had cricket again the other day; the worst game out (sorry)

Thornton Wilder

Mother—I tried my white suits today. Good fit. Mother? How about those flannel ones you made? There are more in my trunk, she says: There must be some mistake.

6. TO AMOS P. WILDER. ALS 4 pp. Yale

<C.I.M. Schools, Chefoo, N. China>
<September 1911>

Just a few snatchy mid-week (on Friday night) words with two important things to say.

1st. About Amos's birthday present sadly delayed as it is.[15]

In birthdays I saved up (from a interesting assortment of occupations) 2 gold dollars (pumping organs and vending programs are hard work in a dignified guise). One went to the plague that time in Shanghai, and the other I wish to send Amos. If you think that he would take it as a insult and send me Mr. Thatcher's[16] grandfathers embroidered glove with the finger holes, if I say, he would take it as a affront on his pecuniary wealth, then we might steep it in—may I say—permit me—steep it in a volume like "The Scarlet Pimpernel" (Dickens)[17]

I myself not being embarrased by affairs of the wallet, or being bowed down by the weight of a empty pouch, do submit and approve the present of the sum in question without as the poet says "without the garb of secret Charity." And impress him with the overwhelming regret which floods me from the neglect and tardiness with which I seek to accomplish this duty. I have bequeathed (?) it to you to despath the bounty, but I will write him my emotions. (Samual Johnson very weak)

"It is enough."

---

15 TNW's brother's birthday was September 18.

16 Sherman D. Thacher (1861–1931), founder and headmaster of the Thacher School.

17 *The Scarlet Pimpernel* was written by Baroness Emma Orczy (1865–1947).

—·—

2nd. The subject for the Taylor Prize History exam is out.

"The Life and times of Alcibiades"[18]

Please try and gather something about him from some learned friends etc. I have the Plutarch's lives (arr. for Children)[19] at Hand (Charlotte[20] has it in the Girl's School). Try and get some quotations about him from Heroditus, Xenophon, Thucydides and some other old chapies![21] You live in a very mixed society maybe you have some unbusy scholars for friends.

I thank you very much for the offer you have sent me. I have chosen two. The first of Kipling, is short stories of which I have read one.[22] Very eager for the rest. "The more you eat the more you Want!" (Egg-o-see?) I will give that to Charlotte when I have finished.

The next is by a favorite of Mr. Phelps of Yale.[23] Mother and we read all of his other books in Berkeley. It is much heavier reading. I am glad to see the Ymca approves them. Remember Alcibiades and Amos's birthday gift. Lovingly

Very Lovingly, my dear Papa
Thornton Wilder.

---

18 Athenian general and politician who, because he switched allegiances during the Peloponnesian War, was finally marginalized in Greek affairs.

19 In *Parallel Lives,* by Plutarch, the careers of prominent Greek and Roman statesmen and generals are presented mainly in contrasting pairs. Two editions for children were F. J. Gould's *Tales of the Romans: The Children's Plutarch* (1910) and F. J. Gould's *Tales of the Greeks: The Children's Plutarch* (1910).

20 TNW's oldest sister (1898–1980).

21 Herodotus wrote a history of the Persian Wars; Xenophon was the author of *Anabasis* and *Hellenica,* which continued the history of the Peloponnesian War; Thucydides wrote the most famous history of the Peloponnesian War.

22 The volume of Kipling's short stories to which TNW is referring may be *Rewards and Fairies* (1910).

23 William Lyon "Billy" Phelps was a professor of English at Yale University. A close family friend of the Wilders, he had been TNW's mother's Sunday school teacher at her father's church in Dobbs Ferry, New York.

China Inland Mission Boys' School.

7. TO AMOS P. WILDER. ALS 4 pp. Yale

<C.I.M. Schools, Chefoo, N. China>
<September 1911?>

<appeared vertically above and along the margin of page one>
Dear Father,

I have taken care in Part I of this letter to express what I mean. Mothers letter held no words that I would not have you see. There was that part of my self that Mother shares with me: the expression of Sentimentality. If you had seen it I would feel your pooh-pooh recieval would have been sure. I have tried hard to explain, as I know it lies heavy on your mind-heart. There is the milky, sensarous, even slovenly side of affection in which I cannot imagine you partaking, the face-gazing, and silly part of it, which is to weak and light for big, powerful people.

Dear Father,

I see you were rather worried about Mother's Private Letter. It has become a delicate subject, and it was a tactless thing of mine. But if I could explain and glaze it as it should be glazed and smooth there would still be a rankling in you, I suppose. The only thing to do is to tell of its drift. First, it was very lush and sentimental, the mood that Mother can accept, if she is ready in her mood of a letter from the son. Again I sought to make a letter show how I had grown very different in my opinion of her while I was away from her and explain that I did see a difference her being near or in far-away Europe. To make it more solemn—or more special—I also named it "Private." You had been begging private letters for long. Mother expected none, I did not think that she would not feel a little pleased. Is this enough?

I received "Molly—make-believe."[24] I read it before, on the "Mongolia,"[25] but I was very glad to get it, I have nothing but praise for the way it is written. It is so very original. Did you not think so?

The only thing that seem<ed> to cast a shadow was the falling away from Cornelia of Staunton. It was the same with "David Copperfield." Davids ardour for both Dora and Agnes seemed to lessen his loves for one or the other, and here Cornelia enlists my sympathies to a great extant. The characters are but the types of many a story, nothing new there; but the idea of a Serial-letter Company is so finely original that it would rescue anything. I consider a book fine according to its originality. That is why I dislike Scott[26] and the costume Romantists. As for the Parody and the swear word, they I suppose are the acrobatic gymnastics necessary to the atmosphere of the "best-sellers." Just like a pistol shot in a Melodrama, or a trill in a popular song, all un<nec>essary necessities.

The last of the boys are expected soon. Yesterday another of my intimate circle arrived.

Yesterday also we were invited to the Malpas's for tea. After tea we took a walk. I went ahead with Mrs. Malpas and talked advanced Music. She played one of those difficult, flashy pieces in a concert not long

---

24 *Molly Make-Believe* (1910), best-selling novel by American novelist Eleanor Hallowell Abbott (1872–1958).

25 S.S. *Mongolia* was the ship that TNW, his mother, and his sisters took from San Francisco to Shanghai in December 1910.

26 Sir Walter Scott.

ago, but I liked Dr Smiths singing of Shuberts "Erlkönig"[27] more. He sang beautifuly, dramaticaly. Mrs. Malpas played "Alice where art thou"[28] with variations, I would rather have heard a classic

Lovingly,
Todger Wilder.

8. TO ISABELLA N. WILDER. ALS 3 pp. (Stationery embossed C.I.M. Schools, / Chefoo, / N. China) Yale

Feb. 10.—<19>12

Ma Caro Donna,[29]

It has been said somewhere (you may know where) that "a house divided among itself can not stand;"[30] I dare not say that that aphorism may have an exception but still this house has managed with help of some of the boys to keep a-going in spite of a strike of the servants!

The Revolutionary headquarters here have offered $18 a month for all men who will join the army as recruits,[31]
Result = All of are<our> "boys" who work on $8 a month leave for higher wages
Result = No servants have got,
Result = Boys work.
Result = Wilder II washes dishes and cleans carrots, serv<e>s table, and carries water for other people (boys) to wash in (not himself! Oh No!).

---

27 Song for solo voice and piano, based on a poem by Goethe.

28 "Alice Where Art Thou?": a song for solo voice and piano by Dutch composer Joseph Ascher (1829–1869).

29 Italian: My Dear Lady.

30 "A house divided against itself cannot stand" is the most famous line from Abraham Lincoln's June 16, 1858, speech at the Republican State Convention in Springfield, Illinois, where he accepted the nomination to run against Democrat Stephen A. Douglas for the U.S. Senate. The line paraphrases Matthew 12:25 and/or Mark 3:25.

31 In October 1911, a mutiny broke out among army troops against the ruling Manchu dynasty. By the end of the year, the Manchu regent had been deposed and his representative had begun negotiations in Nanking, where the provisional revolutionary republican government had been established.

But, my dear Mother, that is not the reason that that “cherub” Thornton does not write to his martyr Mother and Grandmother. If he is as you might say a “cherub” surely he would not neglect his folks without a very believable excuse, but again if the “little darling” has no excuse then by Euclid and common sense he is not a “cherub” but a very thoughtless youngster.

All this juvenile raillery is the desired thing for a school letter like this one, which will, “si possible” be followed by another with something above “ennui” in it (and with out any <“>bad french quotations”<)>

Directions pour la Musique

Lento á la valse — And now “Believe me” as the lady said to the cocatrice

Largamente — I am yours as the toad stool said to the Ostrich

Appasionate — Lovingly

Humilisimo — Thornton Niven Wilder

Grazioso — Best Remembrances to my Grandmother and her other daughter, “My Lady of Patience.”[32]

(Later) Evidently, Mr. Lea our Master does not think this to be the “desired thing,” maybe he would like me to tell you how “Evan’s Bunny died” and how I lost my book and such trash.

9. TO AMOS P. WILDER. ALS 3 pp. Yale

<C.I.M. Schools, Chefoo, N. China>
Sunday Night
March 3—<19>12

My dear Father,

This is my first letter since you have been ill. I suppose you look to it with interest, to see how I have taken your leave. Oh, my father,

32 TNW’s maternal aunt Charlotte Tappan Niven (1882–1979).

of course I am very sorry that you have gone but if you needed it, may there be no complaint from here.

I am afraid you will not get this letter until you get to Madison which will probably be a <u>long</u> time; yet if you have stayed with Amos very long (which I hope you will have done.)[33]

I have no cause to complain of being left here because Amos has been left alone in the continent with no other members of the Family.

Oh, but Father, I wish I could see Mother. It seems many years since I saw her last. I want to see her very very much. When you make your plans try and let me be near her and Amos. And of course father dear, I want you too; my dear Papa—all together.

I have a little duty here now. A Doctor Jones came up here a little while ago and left his son here. When he went away I saw he was much moved by going (and remembering another farewell that was hard not long ago) away from his laddie. I came up as he was going and spoke to him a little in a friendly tone. Immediatly the man opened up and left the boy in my charge. I have just written the Father a little note about the boy.

A boy that was here in the boys school when I first came, who graduated and left last graduation Day, has come back for a little stay here. He and I have always been very familiar. We are having a fine time together now.

A very perplexing thing has happened. In your departure you forgot to pay Miss Richard's violin Music lesson bill. It amts. to about $43. She says she has been "advised" to send it to me<.> I of course will send it to my "men-gardians" Mr. Dorsey or Lobenstein. It is a difficult thing to settle, but I guess it will be all right.

Rowley Turbeville Evans wishes to be remembered to you. He is not yet a prefect but we all expect he will be soon. He is a fine boy.

33 TNW's father was on home leave in the United States and visited his son Amos in California before going to Madison, Wisconsin.

It is communion tonight but I have firmly decided on once in two months. Mr. Lea gave a talk at Communion lately against people setting a time for communion like that. But I think unless I feel that definitly I must go, I will keep to <a> fixed time.

Was that hint at sending me home only a false alarum. May it be so!

Remember <me> with all affection to the Madison Friends. To Mrs. Sheldon Johnson, Stevenson, Kellog (and Miss Kellog) Whitney and above all Miss Donoghue to whom I yet will write.

Remember me to my friend Mr. Taft. Ask him when he's going to give me my papa for good and all,[34]

And now good night

May love and peace attend you always

Lovingly

Thornton Wilder.

I am sorry I can have no more definite address.

10. TO ISABELLA N. WILDER. ALS 6 pp. Yale

<C.I.M. Schools, Chefoo, N. China>
July 14—<19>12
Sunday Evening

My Dear Mother,

You will easily forgive my writing with pencil on this school Exercise Paper? The intimate aire of these will appeal to you I'm sure?

Mr. Alty who is on duty today exhorted us boys to get our letters written before we go to bed. Not that these are the class letters to be

---

34 William Howard Taft was a great admirer of TNW's father, an admiration partly traceable to their ties to Yale. As secretary of war (1904–1908) and then president (1909–1913), he was instrumental in getting TNW's father appointed consul general, first in Hong Kong and then in Shanghai.

perused by the master, but that because yesterday was a holiday (& so we were unable to write our class letter)—for that reason is firm about our writing private letters to you now.

I am going when I finish to ask him to lend me his "Elijah" or "Messiah."[35] But if I went to him now he would ask me if I had written my letter and I would very modestly (eyes on the floor) lisp "No, thir." "Well go along and write your letter first." That's the way things are done!

The boys of the upper school were, this morning—in the rain, invited to a funeral. The daughter of Mr. Roe the Head of the Sanitarium, Partner in the Business Department (the store here) and teacher of Bookkeeping to the Upper Fifth Form had died of unexpected fever evening before last.

Mr. Roe came to the grave supported by strong men & deadly white. They say that he may die. Poor Mrs. Roe who walked beside—far frailer than Mr. Roe was visibly trying to comfort her husband.

There were visible effects on Mr. Murray who has lost more than five children & has only one—& the other extreme Mrs. McCarthy who has 5. Mr. Murray had his only Duncan beside him & Mrs. McCarthy was beside her Brian.

I am glad you approve of my Latin poetry researches. Charlotte hates Latin and spurned Horace Odes Book III and Aeniados I which I offered to her. I have now added to my other collection: Aeniados Books II & VIII & all of Horace Odes, Epodes, Satires (fine!) Epistles & fragments, & a book of Selections from Ovid. I have done nothing more in French or German other than learning occasional lists of words.

To continue my self-educating theory in other realms, I have been doing a good deal of Piano lately Both for Practicing in reading & general playing<.> I go thro' the set of Beethoven Sonatas that have separate names to them viz: Moonlight<,> Pathetique, Waldstein (L'Aurore Dawn), Pastorale & a little of Charatristique & then of course I do my Mother's, which I am preparing for Exhibition Day (although I will probably not be here.) I have also Chopin's Preludes, one flashy

35 TNW is referring to the oratorios *Elijah* (Felix Mendelssohn) and *Messiah* (George Frideric Handel).

one of which I am learning by heart for those people who ask & papa will not allow me to refuse. Now Dear Mother good night and Isabel & my little sister Janet (oh lovely photo!) do you feel lonely without Auntie & Grandmother? I am there, I am—Before long you will see me—no—I will see you till then.

Very, very Lovingly
Thornton Wilder.

Lots of love for Isabel & Janet—can Janet understand Goodnight does she know she has a little Brother?

Just another little note to put these stamps in with the letter. These are just some of those sent me by Father not long <ago>. The others are really too good—ancient kind. But there are three real nice ones here.

I can imagine the lady as a little elderly german with bright and red cheeks. She has a shawl on and she spends most of her time in hotel corridors.

I am getting along pretty well with both piano and violin. I (by myself) am learning by heart a Grieg "Ballade" to play you.

All my examinations were above 80 out of a hundred.

Spelling 100, Cicero 93 English 87 Algebra 80 Lat. Comp. 82

In a few moments I am going to my Music teacher's Mrs Lord's house with my violin. She has called an assemb<l>y of most of the violin pupils with Mr. Cook (a teacher who plays viola) that we—with her husband who plays cello may have a practice on Schumanns Quintet for Piano and String. Won't it be fine.

I am reading "Joseph Vance" over again.[36] I can remember just the parts you liked.

Do you remember good old Janey and Lossie? And the Shipwreck and Beppino. It half kills me trying to say whether "Joseph" or "Clayer" is better.

Lots of Love
Thornton N.

---

36 *Joseph Vance: An Ill-Written Autobiography* (1906), a novel by English ceramic artist and author William Frend De Morgan (1839–1917).

11. TO AMOS P. WILDER. ALS 4 pp. Yale

Thacher School[37]

Dec. 13?<January 13, 1913?> Sunday P.M.[38]

<appeared perpendicularly beside first paragraph>
I can ride a horse pretty well now. Isn't this a long letter? Dear Papa

Dear Papa—

I'll try to give you a topical, typical letter for once—after your own heart. We'll begin with

Music.

Out of my two lessons a week I think I am making progress. On the Piano I take up that musical staple—Czerny.[39]—velocity exercises to corrospond to the examples on velocity which we are taking in Algebra (of course they're really physics ($S = \frac{1}{2}gt^2$).). Besides that they are parts of Beethoven Sonatas and Chopin Preludes. (What's in a name! Those aren't so imposing as they might be judged.) Then besides there are scales, finger-movements...

On the violin I am taking another set of exercises also for velocity. And some pieces. When in Claremont, as there was no orgonist in town, I took violin of a Prof. Staples.—Prof in the college of Music. He tried to graft a new method on me but I can not keep it up with my other teacher. On the violin I have already had six teachers to only two on the piano. In Claremont I played in the Sunday-School Orchestra twice. I recieved my Chefoo music prize and thank you for your part. Beethoven's Sonatas have been called the musician's Shakespeare and if ever you live in the same house as I do you'll get to know them.

Let us now take up the study of school-mates.

Boys

None of the Thacher boys are original. They are all of the same cast whereas at Chefoo each boy was to any other as blue to red. Some

---

37 TNW was now attending the Thacher School in Ojai, California, with his brother.

38 TNW probably misdated this letter, as he refers in it to having spent Christmas in Claremont with the Maynard family. His sister Charlotte was living with the Maynards while attending public school in Claremont.

39 Karl Czerny (1791–1857), Austrian pianist and composer.

people might like the Thacher plan. Do you? Some of the boys are nice and polite and very proficient in small talk and white lies, but so are waiters! N'est ce pas? One of the boys—my especial—altho' by no means kindred—spirit, is named Harrington Shortall.[40] He hails from the fashionable side of Chicago and is ever-so aristocratic. Altho' he looks at me as a common little street-gamin nevertheless he plays duets both 4 hands at Piano and Piano & violin (I being the violinist). He <His> views on music and musicians, book<s> and authors are delightfully conteradictable and afford many pleasant arguments. He will cling to Mozart as a staff of life whereas to me Mozart is merely tune & barber-shop chords except in a sonata for two pianos that I heard in Claremont. But as sometime in the far future you will hear somethings more I will pass on to the subject of

Claremont

We had a lovely Xmas time at Claremont. The Maynards are ever so nice and Charlotte couldn't help but have a continual picnic.

The astronomy lessons we had were wonderful.[41] They were the most interesting things too. We saw the craters on the moon and learnt a few of them by name. We saw Venus one of the morning-stars that sang together the "Sanctus" of Bach's Mass in B Minor. We saw Saturn and the 2 rings. We saw the Nebula in Orion. Billions <appeared below "Billions"> **"2 x 4"** of miles square and yet you can't see it with <the> naked eye. And we got talked to—the man like the ever-juvenile Mme. Bottu would stay over time and be late to his meals.

We went to two or three parties, one of them a surprise party which was lots of fun. An awful lot of High-school girls and boys were waiting when we got there. I hope you'll get something yellow out of your house there. The house itself is Rheumatic but the lot is worth while. Maybe the college'll offer you a castle in Spain and a genii bottle for it. You never can tell (G. Bernard Shaw.)[42] We were waiting eagerly for our Lady of Florence to dawn<?> upon us, but we are yet to wait.

---

40 Shortall (1895–1984) became a composer and teacher and remained friends with TNW and, especially, Amos N. Wilder for the rest of their lives.

41 TNW's father arranged special instruction during the holidays for TNW, Amos, and Charlotte at the Frank P. Brackett Observatory on the Pomona College campus in Claremont, California.

42 *You Never Can Tell* (1899), a four-act comedy by George Bernard Shaw.

Thank you ever so much for your two dollars, I'll probably get some soulful music with <it> or some instrument of { the muses
Torture

From Mother I got this writing Paper and some cuff buttons.
" Amos a dollar—thereby hangs a tale
" Charlotte all Shakespear in one volume!
" Isabel a part of Mothers.
" Janet " " " "
" Miss O'connor a lovely Japanese Print Hokusai's The Wave![43]
" Mr. O'connor Arnold Bennetts "Milestones".[44] Etc.

Now Father this has been a long letter to make up for the Seven Egyptian Years of drought. But Father look at my correspondence list.

Father
Mrs. Malpas & Mr.[45]
Mr. McCarthy }
Mr. Murray } Chefoo
Mr. & Mrs. Lea }
Miss Shepherd }
Mother Isabel
Grandma
Aunt. Charlotte
1 About 5 chefoo boys
2
3
4
5
Mr. O'connor
Miss O'connor
Vincents
Hannas
Robertsons

---

43 *The Great Wave at Kanagwa,* a famous print by Japanese painter and wood engraver Katsushika Hokusai (1760–1849); it hung in the Wilder home in Hamden, Connecticut.

44 Play (1912) by Bennett, in collaboration with Edward Knoblock.

45 Members of a circle of Wilder family friends in Shanghai; Mrs. Malpas put TNW and Charlotte on the boat from China to San Francisco in the summer of 1912.

Mrs Moore (neé Maxwell)[46]

A young lady I met at my orgon lessons who demands letters.

The length of the list scares me. Where shall I begin<?> Mr. Murray'd be mad if I wrote to Mr. Lea only. Vice versa etc. Telegraph solution

Now adieu my dear Poppy—well, strong, and happy, glad, good and gumptious.

With lots of love from
Thornton Wilder or Nifty Niven
the petrified Sleuth.

12. TO ISABELLA N. WILDER. ALS 4 pp. Yale

Thacher School
Jan. <19(?), 1913> Sometime ad 20
Sunday.

Dear Mother,

Whenever anything happens during the week of any real interest I put it down on my mind for my corrospondence but today there is only one thing to tell so we must dig up some past treasures. That one thing is told soon but long remembered. "Namely", as Cicero would say; that after much waiting the play for the Dramatic club here was at last decided upon. It was to be given at the time of the Tennis Tournament when all the Parents come from far and near to various feats of their children. Their is the Tennis Tournament, a big dance in the evening and the next evening the play. All the days are planned out—with a feature of every morning and afternoon such as shooting-matches, gymkhana's etc. Well the play decided on was Oscar Wilde's "The Importance of being Earnest," a very funny frivolous farce. We had the tryouts and I was cast for one of the leading characters: Lady Bracknell, a very sharp, lorgnette-carrying old Lady. I began learning my part

46 The O'Connors, the Vincents, the Hannas, the Robertsons, and Mrs. Moore were close Wilder family friends in Berkeley.

right off and fell to work trying not to laugh at the clever epigrams I had to say. I was never so happy in my life (never mind that phrase) until that evening I was in the parlour looking at some Magazines and Mr. Sherman T. came in.[47] He stood against the mantel and put his back to the fire. Then he coughed and called me up to him.

"Oh Thornton" he said, "your Father said in a letter that he would rather not having you in the plays taking female parts, so, altho' he didn't absolutely order you, I think we had better do as he says." I was terribly disappointed. Now another boy has the part. It'll be very un-funny to watch the part I might be taking. The worst part of all comes in the explaining to other boys all about how my puritanical pater disapproves etc

---

Now to rake up a page and a half of other news.

You remember that there is a prize of books to the boy who reads the most during the year? Here is my list so-far

William DE Morgan

Joseph Vance
Somehow Good[48] } fine, both of them.

Arnold Bennett

Milestones Mr. O'C. Xmas Present fine.
How to live on 24 hrs. a day[49] fine too
The Truth about an Author[50] " "

Charlotte Brontë

Villette Very fine.

Jerome K. Jerome

Passing of the Third floor back.[51]

Yeats.

---

47 Sherman D. Thacher.

48 Morgan's novel *Somehow Good* was published in 1908.

49 *How to Live on 24 Hours a Day* (1910) offers practical advice on how one might live (as opposed to simply existing) within the confines of a twenty-four-hour day.

50 Bennett's humorous memoir, *The Truth About an Author* (1903), emphasizes the commercial aspects of authorship.

51 *Passing of the Third Floor Back* (1908), a modern morality play set in a boardinghouse.

The Land of Hearts Desire[52]
Kathleen Na Houlihan[53] } Very lovely

and quite a few more.

In prospect I have

Mrs. Gaskells

Life of Charlotte Brontë[54]

Cranford[55] (for a second reading)

Charlotte Brontë

Shirley

Jane Eyre.

Margerite Audoux

Marie-Claire That novel by Parisianne Sempstre[56]

Robert Browning & Mrs B

Letters.[57]

Fitzgerald, Edward

Letters.[58]

They say these last are very fine but Father won't let me read the Rubaiyat of Omar![59] I'm sorry I've left it till now but I want to thank <you> very heartily for this papier and the cuffbuttons, one think <thing> I have on and the other I'm writing on.

Lots of love to Isabelle Janet and yourself

from

T. N. Wil.

---

52 *The Land of Heart's Desire* (1894), a play by William Butler Yeats.

53 The play *Cathleen ni Houlihan* (1907).

54 A biography (1857) by Elizabeth Cleghorn Gaskell (1810–1865).

55 A novel (1853).

56 *Marie Claire* (1910; Eng. tr., 1911), novel by French author Marguerite Audoux (1863–1937), who was in fact a seamstress by trade.

57 The correspondence of Elizabeth Barrett Browning and Robert Browning was published by their son, Penini: *The Letters of Robert Browning and Elizabeth Barrett Browning,* 2 vols. (1899).

58 The correspondence of Edward FitzGerald: *Letters and Literary Remains,* edited by W. A. Wright (1899).

59 *The Rubáiyát of Omar Khayyám,* Edward FitzGerald's translation (1859) of the Persian poem, which concentrates on the pleasures of the senses as the primary reason to live.

13. TO AMOS P. WILDER. ALS 7 pp. Yale

<Thacher School>
March <1913>

Dear Papa

(Having received your letter of admonition, I resume the letter-writing. I find it conveniant to mention the matter very little.)

Dear Papa

I have one piece of news which will perhaps please you. Altogether now I have ridden to Norhoff[60] and back (10 miles) 5 times. Your clipping of Admiral Dewey would do as an advertisement for Wilkinson's Horseshoes but hardly as a lure.

I like riding all right but the only thing is its hurts. It made some huge blisters on me. I'll probably get used to it some day.

My horse is the nicest old thing ever bridled. He is old—well on in his teens—and white—really white, not white like a white man—but not slow or dull or lifeless. He was called Blanco before I got him but as he doesn't seem to recognize it, I offer you to cho<o>se one of these for him

Harlequin
Cathay or
Pax.

Until then I will probably call him pax after my twin.[61] If you think its a crime to call him pax why then—cable. He really is awfully nice tho' of course after all the only thing he does is to keep his eyes open for hay or keep them shut in sleep, which polite society does not consider the best Formula for living. Now to talk about some other things you have asked me about. Books I have been reading. Not long ago I read Mrs. Gaskell's Life of C. Bronte. Most people think that next to Boswell[62] it is the greatest Biography ever written tho hardly the most cheerful. To make a glorious comparison pretend that our Charlotte (that adorable

---

60 Nordhoff, a town near Ojai.

61 TNW's twin, who died at birth, was frequently referred to as Pax by the Wilder family.

62 TNW is referring to James Boswell's *The Life of Samuel Johnson, L.L.D.*

minx) was that Charlotte; grant Mother to have died some six years ago leaving on her the whole burden of a Mother then suppose that you have two more daughters both of whom die of consumption; In the meantime (There is no room for Amos in the illustration) I go very directly to the bad and cause much worry. In the mean time you get blind and cross (incredible!) and Isabel (Emily Bronte) writes a great book (Wuthering Heights) and dies of consumption before it is ever published or accepted as immortal. Also Janet writes a nearly great book (Anne Bronte and her <">Tenant of Wildfell Hall"[63] all about me and my fall) and then she dies of consumption. <appeared at top of page next to page number and before text> **(What page five? Infandum![64] incredible)** If you feel like <it> by all means read it. I have also been reading Charlotte Brontë's "Villette" and am now on "Jane Eyre" Now about some of the other things in which you are interested—classmates. I think I have already told you about the boy who has a room next to me Spencer Hancock Logan, son of the Chicago Millionaire wheat broker (I suppose thats what they're called.) The other day he got a telegram running something like this—no economy in sight—

"Dear Spencer We are feeling lonely now and unless you want to take your trip into the mountains very badly we would like to have you come home for the Easter Vacation."

Of course it's very plain that Mrs Logan (scilicet $1000 paris gowns) is unwell because Spencer will only be able to have 4 days in Chicago at the most. He went this morning after a affecting farewell with me. When I get an invitation to spend my holidays in Chicago your not to stand in the way even if it is The Theatre or a dance every night—excepting Sunday of course. Please don't write him a separate letter because he doesn't think very much of your not letting me act in the play. On the other side of my room is Frank Bromwell<?> whose Father and Mother have just come down from Seattle in their $5,000 Packard Automobile. Beyond him is Russel Tracy whose parents have two automobiles. Mr. Tracy has just been at Shanghai I hope you met him; he

63 *The Tenant of Wildfell Hall* (1848).

64 Latin: unutterable or unspeakable.

went out with Mr. Goss, your new vice-consul. I may learn a little more about your private matters—from other people. Here are a few jokes <remainder of letter missing>

14. TO AMOS P. WILDER. TLS 1 p. Yale

<Berkeley, California>[65]
<September 1913>

Dear Father,

Art School over and High School on, what can I do but take time seriously and wright (rather good, eh) you. I am again prepaired to perhaps fall in with another school (did you get the split infinitive, a sign of superior litery apprenticeship). I have just finished my first week at the Berkeley High, and notwithstanding my dislike for the national Philistinism, I rather like the school from my third-personal impersonal view. The beauty of the school is that so far it has left me entirely alone. I confess that I never expected that. I got a little of that at Chefoo, but never a drop at Thacher. I like it on that account very much. I am taking Vergil Aneidos Book Four. English and Geometry, the same as Sharlie, and also beginning Greek. I hope that it will be many years before that study of Greek stops. It will start something like this: First week—study. Second week—Xenophen. Third week—Testament. Fou<r>th week—Plato. Fifth week—Homer. Sixth—Venerable Tragedians. Seventh—Slangy Comedians<.> Eighth—Sappho. But I think I will reverse the order. The only other study I take is German. I think I will make a new paragraph, if you dont mind.

About those postal-cards, or better, panaramas, I assure you that I did not intend to send them to you for circulation, as you said. That would be the expression of mere ridiculous childish enthusiasm, the kind that rises suddenly from nowhere demanding cooperation, hurraying and eagerness from every hand. (How foolish and didactic that

65 TNW and Charlotte ("Sharlie") were now enrolled as juniors at Berkeley High School.

last sounds, meant to be a mood-or-point-of-view-picture, also a kind of fierce at my own youth, buttered-over with that very thing. And what an inane kind of thing it is, but maybe you havnt recognize<d> it, I dont know whats arroused me, but here I am with my hair up.) What an awful dirth of periods ive left behind me. Moral: Keep your hair on.

Kwong Ling[66] goes to church with us every Sunday, but we let him out, after childrens sermon. The poor boy doesnt understand a word, I myself taught him for a while. I cant imagine what he does when the teacher asks him to read the Heading to the Paragraph or the Title of this Poem (registered in K. Lings vocabulary as song). I suppose he just gollops for a while and then says to himself in Chinese that four times three are twelve and three times—Oh well you know what hes like. Ugh. We cant change, but we can drop him. A new paragraph by all means.

(Later in the evening) School begins again to-morrow, but I do not dread it as at Th-etc, which after all as an institution was not equal to itself as a—supply the word yourself—I refuse to preach even in the good cause of disillusionment. After all a letter cant be like a verbal communication—in fact I dont believe that I would ever slush to you like this personally—so I guess I might as well end here as at the end of the fourtieth page, for ther would still be left the things one never writes and seldom says, and for one like me, never says; meaning, not that I do not feel gushy but that I am swathed in my Anglican Calm. (tommy-rot; how I have unwapped it this evening<)>.

Lots o Love
Cleaned of gush;
Come early and
Avoid the THE ANTIDOTE FOR
SENTIMENTALISM IS
LUNACY even the types
going crazy. Hurray

(Thornton)

---

66 Chinese orphan "adopted" by TNW's father in Shanghai; he was sent in 1913 to live in Berkeley with the family and attend school there. He later became a minister, the Reverend John K. L. Yong.

15. TO AMOS P. WILDER. ALS 2 pp. Yale

Berkeley Calif
Sept 21—<19>13.

Dear Papa,

I guess it's been a good-sized "spatium"[67] since last I wrote but this time it was not idleness or distraction that caused it but real preoccupation. You may have heard that I have a dramatic venture on the Market and have on me the heavy habiliments of an Impresario. After a contest or try-out my little one-act farce "The Advertisement League"[68] was chosen as a "vehical" for a few of us in a vaudeville given by the Berkeley High School for the benefit of the New School Gymnasium which is the Reno Skating Rink made over! Of course the play is a magnificent treatment of all the problems that ever ruined the worrying-powers of man. Its dynamic force in the way of social uplift is almost as tremendous as it is negligible. My "cast," 3 boys and 4 girls, all secured at a tremendous expenditure of debate and exhortion, are some zealous for it some pulling the other way; and our rehearsals, when there are no teachers present, are perfect nightmares for me. I get corrected to the left and uncomfortably pushed at the right. The performance will come off next friday night before an audience of 1200+. Of course I have adhered to your demand that I remain in masculine clothes. When you have changed your mind as to it please notify.

———·———

I am expecting a good report card tomorrow for my first semester.—. I went to the station with Amos the other evening<.> I think that if you had been there you would have wondered how such a thing ever came into your head. Let us hope that Amos's "surrounding circumstances" in a strange land are favorable to a youngling and such as an average parent would wish for his son. Many fathers would consider themselves fortunate in having <u>their</u> son with at least one parent already in a University town knowing that home-life is quite as good

---

67 Latin: a period of time.

68 This one-act play has not survived.

as a higher education, but we've heard that Oberlin is well spoken of in that portion of Ohio.[69]

What a lot of your best friends are away from Shanghai just now. Mrs. DeGray, Mr. Hinckley, (from Kwong Ling I hear bad reports of him), Malpus, Stedmans, Kwong Ling, and Ravens.

Mr. Darrach (Shakespearian corrector.)[70] has sent us $6 (gold!) worth of tickets. $2 per. for us to attend a super-quasi-hyper-post-fashionable recital at which "carriages are requested to call at 12.30 AM."
Kwong Ling, the gem, left the house-door key on the outside last night.

Lovingly—
Thornton Wilder

16. TO AMOS P., ISABELLA N., ISABEL, AND JANET F. WILDER.[71] APCS 1 p. Yale

<San Luis Obispo, California>[72]
<P.M. June 15, 1914>

Dear Familie,

I have had two lessons in milking now. About two hours in all. Am still getting up to a four-o'clock alarm altho' I don't have to. Tell Violet <Vincent> and Miss O'C that I'm sorry I didn't see them for an au-revoir. Typewriter is consideration. Watch still going nicely, tho' I sometimes wish it wouldn't say 4 A.M. Illuminating sidelights on the

---

69 TNW's brother was now attending Oberlin College.

70 Marshall Darrach, a noted English solo performer of Shakespeare, was in San Francisco for six weeks in the fall of 1913 and gave a Shakespeare recital on September 27.

71 TNW's father was now in Berkeley with his family.

72 TNW was spending the summer working on the farm of Ellwood Varney, Jr., as arranged by TNW's father.

comparative values of pigs, cows, calves and horses, and human nature continue to reveal themselves. Went to Presbyterean Church last night. Sleep well as can be expected. Remember to Janet in reference to moo-cows and grunts. Wanted—Amos' address. Tell Mother that I bought overalls and will probably not need my suits except for Sunday evenings! The great crises of life resolve themselves into milking-times and pig-feeding hours

Lovingly T.W.

17. TO AMOS N. WILDER. ALS 2 pp. Yale

<Berkeley, California>
Nov. 18—<19>14—

Dear Amos,

I sure hope we can keep a room at Yale, but it<I'll> probably never get there.[73] Some small college Wooster und so weiter[74] is probably waiting for me and before I see the shaky New York-New Haven R.R's Depot[75] you'll be leaving it for a missionary post on the Koko-Kola Is—east of the moon. Whether next Thanksgiving Dinner be held—a tutti—in New Haven or with "remembrance for our loved ones scattered over the earth" is a matter that rests entirely on the strength of the adjectives in the Little Colleges' Pamphlets on father's desk.—N.B. Note for Essay = The Parcel-Post Xmas, or the House divided.

Mother here is working very hard for the Red Cross Society of Berkeley. She has been writing letters to all the ministers in town ask-

73 There appears to be no question that TNW's father wanted both his sons to graduate from Yale; it was his plan that, after two years at Oberlin, his son Amos would transfer to Yale for the last two years of his college education.

74 German: and so forth.

75 The present New Haven railroad station was not built until 1918.

ing them to announce to their flocks that contributions will be received in Room 420 1st Nat. Bank Bldg.[76]

Charlotte is a red cheeked, so-so plump girl in glasses; everything she says would be described as "stoutly" or "emphatically" put. She has a habit of talking protestingly which is the lighter side of her infallibility. You may not realize it but its positively serious, the way Charlotte can't be corrected. <appeared perpendicularly in left margin> **Critique Sevère sur une famille.**[77] Reprove her; point out that she is in the wrong, and she says "All right" then if Mother continues to reprove, comes a "Oh, you'll talk forever," and then Isabel and I sit on her by roaring. It's all based on great underlying consciousness of being perfect that often shows up curiously. You mention such a slight and plain fact as that she "cant sing—any more, that is, than any other person who can follow the choir in church" and immediately she raises her back with: "I can sing better than Isabel," or a direct, "I can too." Perhaps that isn't a good illustration, but it may show where the wind blows.

Isabel is <a> very self-conscious, fluffy headed person, getting a little slangy, a little loungy-about, and a little vain, but all smiles when the sun shines. When she is told that her hair-ribbon (this is me this time) is crinkly or that she only two-steps to her waltz, she tries to whistle—like Uncle Toby in "Tristram Shandy."

I will flay Janet and myself hereafter. I've left out the unconscious charm of Charlotte—a kind of tantalizing childishness, or the companionable good heartedness of Isabel, (when she gets there)—but again:

Love

Thornton Wilder

76 After the assassination of Archduke Franz Ferdinand on June 28, 1914, the world was preparing for war.

77 French: severe criticism of the family.

Wilder family in Berkeley, 1914 or 1915. Left to right: *Isabel, TNW, Isabella, Charlotte, and Janet* (in front).

18. TO AMOS P. WILDER. ALS 2 pp. Yale

<Berkeley, California>
"Happy New Year" Jan 1. <1915>

Dear Papa,

San Francisco and Oakland and in its mild way Berkeley, howled in today last night; which was an appropriate beginning of the year, if you like that kind of thing.

I'll be very glad to get out of school—any kind of school—and into something that doesn't feel quite as much as if it were made—and run—with extensive equipment for educating forcibly—you-know-whats. No doubt Oberlin contains a greater amt. of it than Yale—Oberlin with its compulsory chapels and prescribed Scripture-class-work and its suggested Christian Endeavors, Bible-class, YMCAs and Temperance Society.[78] It does seem awful to hear me talking so; I who am the ridiculous ever-present of my own sunday-school boy's division. The only one of my class of 12 to be present often; the official organist; the performer of official odd-jobs; moving tables and passing messages. <appeared perpendicularly in left margin> **Excuse the Messes we're crowded about this table.** And while I play beaten-out hymns, I know how much more expressive and "religious" even simpler music can be, and how much more impressive and awesome pictures may be than Hoffman's[79] saccharine representations; to say nothing of a better way of presenting the lesson to the others. Blagh!

I don't know whether Oberlin will introduce me to another Mrs. Varney or Cecil-Smith with Elwoods and Lagerquist Minor thrown in.

I hope the $400 plus—that I will save by going to Oberlin will be really used; the rejuvenating of Mother, and the spanking of Janet are two humble suggestions. I feel a donor in the matter and will watch with great eagerness a blossoming out of freedom and breath from the chrysalis of care and pinch. As you know I am very fond of Theodore Wilder—I am often angry at myself for liking merely the niceness of people, but we did a great deal of laughing at each other, and I am fearful of mutual rasping—where I would like to be alone at Harvard or Yale with the Amy[80] and The Family—Love from

Thornton W.

Thanks ever so much for the dollar: Shall I put it with the static $10 in the bank or into cubist Music <illegible; letter torn> Valses Nobles et Sentimentales.

78 TNW was scheduled to enter Oberlin in the fall of 1915.

79 German painter Heinrich Hofmann (1824–1911), famous for his religious works depicting the life of Jesus.

80 Amos N. Wilder's nickname.

19. TO ELIZABETH LEWIS NIVEN. ALS 4 pp. Yale

<Berkeley, California>
Jan. 7—<19>15

Dear Grandmother

I am still thinking of some very nice way of using your dollar: there is my bank-account; and there is my growing collection of modern (therefore "discord-y" music,) then I could put it into typewriter rent and try and arrest and find nests for some of my wild ducks; or could go to every one of Forbes-Robertson's four plays on his farewell tour when he comes to Oakland;[81] or I could take Mother or Charlotte to better 50c seats to, say, "Passing of the 3rd Floor Back <">—as for myself I don't mind the highest gallery. Then I could buy some really beautiful picture to hang over my bed. In the art store downtown is Whistler's Battersea Bridge,[82] and whenever your eyes go on it, you are there on the bridge in the evening with the lights of London above and "below" the Thames. Then there is one more day at the Panama-Pacific Exposition when it opens.[83] I have never in my life seen a well-known or great painting in the original, but there will be some there, and that is fine.

I guess when the fog has lifted over the "wortwechsel"[84] which is now on—it will be decided that I go to Oberlin next year. There is a family there, the boys of which were my room mates at the Chefoo boarding-school, and by coincidence called "Wilder"—that will probably take me in as a boarder. Their oldest boy Theodore Wilder—which Mama says might have been my name—will be at college, too.

---

81 English actor Johnston Forbes-Robertson (1853–1937) performed *Hamlet,* Jerome K. Jerome's *The Passing of the Third Floor Back,* George Fleming's *The Light That Failed,* and G. B. Shaw's *Caesar and Cleopatra* at Oakland's Cort Theatre in December 1914 and early January 1915.

82 *Nocturne: Blue and Gold—Old Battersea Bridge,* painting by James Abbott McNeill Whistler.

83 The Panama-Pacific International Exposition opened in February 1915 and ran until December 1915.

84 German: dispute.

I don't much—very much—like going to Oberlin, and I think that a boy—if possible—should at least have some say about the college he's going to. I want Harvard because it is more serious-minded and academic than Yale, and broad than Oberlin. It may sound awful, but I don't like to fall into the folding-of-the-hands attitude about doing what father says all the time. Amos has got into that, and helped to make his college career weaker. When they ask him what his college is he must say: "I had two years at Oberlin and two at Yale." He will not feel himself to be a real Yale man either, who has had at least three years to form a close friendship with his class. It looks at present as tho' my college life will be thusly:

1 year at Oberlin

3 years " Yale

2 years " Harvard (Prof Baker's postgraduate playwright course.)[85]

I'd like to just not do it at all, tho. Just travel and write, and live in ordinary, city boarding-houses and in the second class and steerage of boats, and in European attics and among the people of China. And "accidentally" brush myself up against writers etc whom I admire, and get out of feeling that I'm always being hurt by father and always hurting him.

But my page is almost filled and it's 10:10 P.M. so I will close thanking you again for your very kind and useful remembrance and sending much love to you and Aunt Charlotte. Maybe when I see you I will have finished this tiresome education—tho' it will probably have taught me how to appreciate you and everything even better than now—

Your Loving Grandson,
Thornton Niven Wilder

85 George Pierce Baker conducted the famous 47 Workshop, begun in 1905 in the English Department at Harvard University. It was an undergraduate course on playwriting techniques and a laboratory for experimental productions.

20. TO AMOS N. WILDER. ALS 3 pp. Private

2350 Prospect St. <Berkeley, California>
April 7—<19>15

Dear Amos,

It's about time I began finding out about Oberlin from you and working out what I'd better do there. I submit this—:

English—anything—

Latin—Horace—

Botany—2nd year—

German—"Willhelm Tell"!!![86]

(Greek?) I want to take College very mildly and be able to keep all my irons and waffle-pans in the fire. I'd like to take choral work and harmony of music, but I dread piano or violin lessons. I've such a rough-and-tumble preparation.

I'm a perfect Firebrand in the Berkeley Oratorio Society here. I approach Herr Paul Steindorff on the choir's singing Bach or something à capella. I open the windows when the contraltos find the air close and close them when the sopranos feel a draught. I show late comers the place, and vote for incumbent officers. We and lots of other local choral Societys gave the Stabat Mater[87] in the Greek Theatre on Good Friday and Repeated it in Festival Hall at the Exposition and each recieved two free gratis passes (50¢ value) into the grounds!

We've been having a two week vacation at Berkeley High and I'm picking up fine. I was beginning to feel like a saleslady on Xmas Eve. Along of my two complimentary tickets I've been to the Exposition three times. Its most wonderful. I almost feel I'd rather wander about among its courts and Lagoons and the waterfront (Marina) than in thru the miles of little streets insides the huge buildings. I wish you could come out. You might not be able to pick up with California again at

---

86 *Wilhelm Tell* (1804), a play by Friedrich von Schiller.

87 "Stabat Mater Dolorosa," a thirteenth-century Roman Catholic hymn attributed to Jacopone da Todi. The Berkeley Oratorio Society performed Italian composer Giocchino Antonio Rossini's version in the Greek Theatre on April 2 and repeated it on April 4 and 25 at Festival Hall in San Francisco.

first ie. in the morning<.> Sat. I sobbed and swung incense-burners in the Stabat Mater; in the afternoon I onestep-ped with Isabel and a friend of hers in the Thé Dansant in the California Building, I don't mean that to be shocking—hommes angeles—schockire non passant—just illustrative—(Is there a verb for not able as theres one for not-wishing volo nolo—[nollo?]?)

Theres a lady here who knows the young Australian composer Percy Grainger[88] whos arrangements of old English etcs "Shepherd's Hey" "Molly on the Shore" etc you heard the New York Symphony play. She says he's got a perfect aureole of yellow hair—and he invited her to take tea with him and his mama. Send me the Aureole's program if he comes your way. We get programs here, too. Our Berkeley Musical Society corresponds to your Artist Recital Course, only its probably not so cheap: We've had this season Arrigo Serato Italian Violinst; Efrem Zimbilist; Alma Gluck (alone); next Tues Julia Culp.[89] and then another. Student, single ticket $2.00.—and so on 11:20 P.M.

Affectionately, fraternally, insidiously yours
Thornton—eee—E-E-E- O!

21. TO AMOS P. WILDER. ALS 2 pp. Yale

<Berkeley, California>
<May(?) 1915>

Dear Papa,

Rowley Evans, of Shanghai, is a commissioned officer—according to Theodore Wilder and will soon be at the front. I wrote as evasive a nice letter as I could. Maybe I told you all this before.

---

88 Grainger (1882–1961) settled permanently in the United States in 1914.

89 Italian violinist Serato (1877–1948); Russian-American violinist Zimbalist (1889–1985); Rumanian-born American classical soprano Gluck (1884–1938), Zimbalist's wife; and Dutch mezzo-soprano Culp (1880–1970).

¶ Charlotte and I took a long walk over Dwight Way hill for new flower specimans for Botany Class. Charlotte's always threatening to go to all the lonesomest and most distant mountain-tops alone, and because of her perverseness she probably will some day, but until then I have to act as guardian and "take" her everywhere. We had a fine view of Mt. Diabolo from where we were today. ¶ I now play violin in a little orchestra conducted by a self important little Johnny, who knows all about conducting and taking tempos. This orchestra plays at the social evenings etc of our church. He keeps us sawing catgut on cheap waltzes, Spanish Dances etc from 7:30 to 9: + every Monday Evening. ¶ Then Tuesday eve. is Oratorio Society. I met a Thacher Alumnus, the Kerr Boy—he says he hasn't paid any attention to the School for a long time—he's in business now—; and that's another side of the coin. ¶ Civics at school is a little more hopeful. We've been having "lectures", lately à la College & Government Appropriations, Election information, etc. ¶ Mother got a letter from Amos lately in which he grows real sob-by about leaving Oberlin. He hasn't known anything better yet; he'll know what he's missed soon. I feel that I know before hand. I feel I don't want to go to College at all. College is just a broader, more roaring brighter world for a bounded High School Boy anyway. It seems that there Religion-Family-Obligations can be given up for a life with boys and glimpses into the Book-Experiance. There will be a change of happiness for the coming year, won't there? Amos will be at Yale. I at Oberlin<.> Mother and Janet at<and> Isabel at the Plantation and Charlotte on the Hill.[90] And you with your sheaf of plans won; ¶ Janet has one eye almost closed with mosquito bite; Charlotte has a poison oak cheek—this has been "finely" written so I may now make my bow & withdraw. I remain, sir,

lovingly Yours

Thornton Niven Wilder.

90 TNW's sister Charlotte would be attending Mount Holyoke College in the fall of 1915.

22. TO AMOS P. WILDER. ALS 4 pp. Yale

<Berkeley, California>
Tues. May 25—<1915>

Dear Papa,

The other letter has been sealed, so I will send this under separate cover.

Dr. Henderson, after several careful search found some very valuable archaeological deposits in my mouth which turned out to be the debris piles such as mark the site of Troy. He careful<ly> removed the valuables to a less secluded spot and filled up the caves so that no rival explorer could find any careless leftovers to parade. What minor blasting and drilling and excavating there was called<caused> a good <deal> of trouble to the surrounding country. He foresees further work in the neighborhood—however he found the environs pleasant and well-kept.

I am going to get two more $.50 (cent) admission entrances to the fair free. On saturday we rehearse and on sunday we repeat Brahms—German (Protestant) Requiem. I wanted to send you a program but couldn't get an extra before—this time I hope to. ¶ The fair-ground grows better and better on seeing. Mr. Torrey[91] took us <to> two Boston Symphony Concerts lately and I went to one last night (yesterday afternoon) as Mother's birthday present. (Your birthday is yet to be spent unless it has already gone into my collection of Modern Dissonental Music.) It was Russian night and very fiery and sad—and stormy and—hopeless.

Thank you ever so much for the Granville Barker Iphegenia in Tauris program. I hope you went—if so were you able to overlook the primitive-futuristic manner? I swear by Granville Barker and his wife, whose pictures hang at intervals upon my wall. I'd rather know G. than anyone in America or across. I can't see how it could help being impressive even with the striped toward<?> and feather-headed soldiers. Lillah McCarthy must have been wonderfully dignified and

91 Art and antiques dealer Frederic C. Torrey was a Berkeley neighbor.

expressive—I guess you got the best thing in the theatre way in the whole world except for their Trojan Women which is more vital. Very little choice tho'.[92]

We graduate next Friday night. I do not feel it as a solemn occasion<.> I don't think even mother can go and here it, because that will leave Isabel alone with the baby and possibly Kwong Ling—and we never leave the baby alone, and Charlotte graduates, too so "what to do?"

Graduating's the strongest turn-of-the-thumb-screw anyway.

I've been doing worse and worse in School but better and better out. The last four weeks have brought more friends of<than> the previous twelve. All this rich concerting and the following of the latest things in my line all over the world.

Mrs. Williams burst out crying when she mentioned the assassination of Lincoln today!

—Lovingly

Thornton Wilder

23. TO AMOS P. WILDER. ALS 4 pp. Yale

<Berkeley, California>
June 20—<19>15

Dear Papa,

The last week is about to begin since mother says I am to leave a week from tomorrow on Santa Fé.[93] Wed, Thurs & Fri. I take Yale entrance Exams

---

92 English actor, producer, director, dramatist, and scholar Harley Granville-Barker (1877–1946), whose innovative productions of new translations of such classical works as *Iphigenia in Taurus* and *The Trojan Women* by Euripides, starring his wife, English actress Lillah McCarthy (1875–1960), played in outdoor venues at American colleges and universities.

93 Amos P. Wilder arranged for his son's train fare east so TNW could visit him in New Haven; he would then provide TNW with a plan for his summer activity.

English I & II (a & b)
German a
U.S. History and Civil Gov^{nt}.
Virgil-Ovid.

And if you say I have to do full entrance requirements I must refurbish this summer & take in October

Caesar-Nepos[94] (failed when taken at Thacher; never had him in class work because of jumping him at Chefoo!)

German b
Plane Geometry
and?

I have already passed in

Cicero-Sallust[95]
Algebra (a & b)

If I don't pass some of the exes next week (and its at a six day notice) I'll have to try again in September.

Prof. Nutting tells me that without these I would have to go from 1st year Oberlin into 1st year Yale and make a 5 year College course, or else stay two years at Oberlin and enter 3rd Yale as allowed and it's lucky you found it out in time. You've promised me one year at Oberlin to put off the time when the bloom is smudged and I have it in writing. Pleadings and resentful deportment when Jeptha is forced to keep his promise would not be the thing, either.[96]

I have just got back from hearing Prof. Walter Rauschenbush[97] speak at the Baptist Church. Hes the man who wrote the prayers I

---

94 Roman general, statesman, and writer Gaius Julius Caesar; Roman historian Cornelius Nepos, whose major work is a collection of biographies of Roman and non-Roman leaders.

95 Roman orator, statesman, political theorist, and philosopher Marcus Tullius Cicero; Roman historian Gaius Sallustius Crispus, known as Sallust.

96 TNW ultimately spent two years at Oberlin, then repeated his sophomore year at Yale, from which he graduated in 1920. Jeptha (Judges 11) impetuously promises God that if he is victorious in battle, he will sacrifice the first person he meets on his return: That person is his daughter Iphis.

97 Rauschenbusch was a noted Baptist preacher and a leading spokesman for the Social Gospel movement.

wanted to introduce in family prayers, but I never think of when I'm at the library.

He was highly coarse "of the earth earthy" at the beginning of his talk and quite a few ladies around me left in loud indignation; but he was very good.

I'm looking forward to my train ride. I can't be sure yet whether you'll be able to meet me at New York. I can see myself jumping at you from the train-steps now and your <">Well, well, well, well" that we've <had> at so many restorations. Of course I'm looking forward terribly to Amos too; I feel very much ashamed of myself, he is so much the real thing with the testimonial from every one. I dont seem to know anyone or to hold anyone long, but after Berkeley—again. Sometimes I wish I were a Japanese or a Chinese in America; it almost seems like being physically disembodied and holds humiliations of a kind I wouldn't mind so much.

Rev. Brooks[98] has asked me to come up and see him some evening before I go. He doesn't know me however and can't give me what you wish he would in the soul-gouging way. Today I and Bower (the Soph in College) walked down to the Bay and out onto the long pier. I wish I had known of that pier before.

Will you try and arrange it so that Amos will be at the Summer Camp too? or has he tennis engagements?[99] Will you be there? I wish he'd be at Oberlin, Wilder Major (Theodore) used always to become very impatient in his amiable way of impracticable me, and would allow me to even ask him the date or such parasitic questions.

I will remember the Santa Fé as Your and My Route. With lots of love to you at the other end I remain your expectant

Thornton W.

98 Raymond C. Brooks served as minister of the First Congregational Church of Berkeley from 1913 to 1921.

99 TNW's brother was a nationally ranked amateur tennis player.

24. TO AMOS P. WILDER. ALS 4 pp. (Stationery embossed The Bisonte / Hutchinson, Kansas) Yale

Dummerston Station
c/o Myron Dutton[100]
Wed—13?<14> July <1915>

Dear Papa,

I'm almost too tired to write, but I'll try some. I have a little gallery of blisters on the "cushions" beneath my fingers. Today there were three separate thunderstorms and between them ordinary summer weather. We had to work like fits yesterday aft. and this morning to get some hay in from the rain; since cut hay thats been wetted turns black "and the caows doant eat it with the relish they deoa other hay." During thunderstorms farmers fold their hands so it wasn't a too strenuous afternoon, but this morning I almost walked into my grave. First I cleaned the horses stalls, and washed the milk pails, then I helped wash the breakfast dishes since the eldest daughter was brought up sharp with appendicitis last night; <letter shifts from pen to pencil> then I swept and mopped the floor of the "inner room<">—separated etc.; then I fed chickens and emptied swill pails; picked currants for a pie; raked hay and tossed it onto a wagon under a swiftly approaching storm; then it was about eleven o'clock; after the storm more haying until dinner; dried the dinner dishes and then, thank goodness was taken for a ride, until the short routine of the evening. <appeared perpendicularly in left margin> **Forgot to say that I hoed beans for a while**

The change from pen to pencil meant that at about half-past nine last evening Amos's pen went dry and I had to put off the letter til the afternoon of the next day; this morning I had to be entirely domestic, and in addition to servant-maid work, I pared potatoes for two

---

100 TNW and his brother spent a portion of the summer working on the Dutton farm in the southeastern corner of Vermont.

meals for seven; ! I can't say anything and neither can you if it gets worse. Mrs. Dutton is approaching 0 thru worry over the appendicitis daughter and I have to help the one remaining. After dinner tho' I did some more haying and I go back in a minute. At present while their putting hay in the barn there's literally no room. Three big men are at it.

I tried my hardest to milk the first night but they haven't thought <it> wise to call on the little stream I draw again

Lovingly
Thornton W

I like it all right.
Amos gets sick-spells and semi-faintings; I felt sick the first few days myself. What to do about him?

25. TO AMOS P. WILDER. ALS 4 pp. Yale

221 N. Prof. St. Oberlin
<Fall(?) 1915>

Dear Papa,

I have spoken to my class English teacher, Mr. Beattie and to Prof. Wager,[101] head of the department of English, about my choosing Psychology as a major: They see very much why I don't want to take their English major highroad. It's not made for me. Its made for people who have to be talked to for two whole years before they know what to look for in Elizabethan poetry or Ruskin etc. Even majoring in Psych. I would probably take all the "disciplinary" courses in composition etc that I could get in.

101 Charles H. A. Wager, professor of English and head of the Oberlin English Department for thirty-five years, became one of TNW's most important mentors.

Prof. Wells says that of course there are hardly any opening<s> for teaching Psych. in secondary schools, but that its very good in small colleges.

As for Psych. being suited to me of course I don't know. I know that I'm interested as I can be in all the points of it that come my way, and that I'm speculating on sides of it in my own mind all the time. The laboratory courses in experimental Psych. would be most interesting of all. The d<r>udgery part of it would be the physiology of the brain, which they lay great stress on here. Zoology is required for such a major.

All I know is: that I can not major in English as its taught in Oberlin College, and that I believe myself suited to the study of Psych.

Besides, Mr. Wilder, my friends here don't consider it very problematic whether or not I'll be able to earn a living. When the Prof's advise me not to give my work into the College magazine because I ought to be able to sell it someday, it must be an advanced case.

Here's my money bill as near as I can make it. In the meantime my account has sunk to $4:40.

Board 9.70

Room 15.00

Train (16.00) (I called up the station and asked fare Oberlin to New York and they said $13.95. In the meantime I've forgotten what the N.Y. New Haven Hartford costs, and what a berth or so forth costs. So you add this item in yourself.)

Extra 10.00

Unpaid (50.70)

I seem to be writing you a letter every day. I'm not good-humored in this letter, tho',

---

I ran the 220 in 32 seconds. I was about fifth from worst in a class of 35+.
They consider Psych. so impt here that they require every Junior student to take the year course.

Lovingly
Thornton

26. TO AMOS P. WILDER. ALS 4 pp. Yale

<Oberlin, Ohio>
Dec 20—<1915>

Dearest Papa—

You say you especially like letters to yourself PRIVET so I'll pretend this is one. ¶ I really think that the older I get the more homesickness threatens and it doesn't really work at me in the right way—that is, of course, I ought to be feeling especially for you and Mama, but the person upper most in my mind is little Isabel. I'd love to walk her around here and show her to my friends and have her at table & Funny!—I've got a real lot to say so I'll enclose a general letter, too. I find there is room-subject for a PRIVET after all.

What are you going to do about my Xmas vacation after all. I dread every mail that blows. I didn't realize at first what it would be to have my Xmas three days after I enter an absolutely strange and unpleasing family. Amos used to give me "dramatic readings" of that household the only impersonation I can remember tho' is the father & his accent. Oh, let me stay where I am. I'll take my walks just as regularly as in term time! and longer. Quite a few other boys are staying here for me to get to know; and Mrs. Duncan has offered to me to earn my room-rent if I attend to the furnace. I hate to say to questioners that I'm going on a strange farm to do a little work during the Xmas vacation. And how can I go and do a little work? It was a little work that I was going to do at San Luis Obispo—(how did I ever get up at 4:15?), it was a little that I was given permission to do in Vermont, and it was a lot whatever Amos may say. I don't want to go away; I'll be good; I'll be good. But I'm afraid this letter's too late.[102]

Lovingly
Thornton.

27. TO CHARLOTTE E. WILDER. ALS 6 pp. Yale

221 N. Professor St
Oberlin Ohio
<March(?) 1916>

Dear Old Girl

Its been some weeks since I wrote you so I'll take up my pen now. I didn't see much of you during the Xmas vacation so I'll take the opportunity now to write to you now and thank you for the pocket diary. I'll tell you about how it works.

Into it I only put memorandums of original work I do. And occasionally if I hear some especially beautiful piece of music, or read something very fine, I put that in too; but chiefly what I write. I'll copy out a little just to show you.

Jan 5 Wrote sketch for Act II of "Graves Family". Copied out Act I mostly.

Jan 6 Took four mile walk and thought out scenes of Act II—wrote them out in the evening

Jan 8 First Rehearsal of "The Last Word about Burglars." Completed "A Fable for Those Who Plague."

Jan 11 Wrote Finale Act I Graves Family.

Jan 12 Wrote Dorcas-Ella scene in Act I

Jan 28 Wrote opening of Act II with song.

Feb 12 Wrote sketch for Act II of "Ventures Joyous"

102 TNW spent his Christmas vacation in 1915 at Oberlin.

Feb 18 Sat up till 1:00 AM on Shakespeare Essay

Feb 20 Handed in "Sealing-Wax" to Magazine

Feb 21 Wrote "Brother Fire" <">Three Minute Playlets for Three Persons" No 6, and projected "Archangel's Fires."[103]

Feb 26 The New Belinda (Ventures Joyous) growing in mind.

Feb 27 Informed of winning of Shakespeare Essay Prize, $10.

March 8 Verse Libre: 1. Gaby Deslys[104]
2. Mirandolina[105]

Sometimes whole weeks go by when I don't do a thing, then two or three days running! I think that Feb 21 is the most important day there. Did you foresee this?

Now don't you wish you were here. Oh, I know lots of girls you could room mate with, and not irritate each other, either way. They say you've almost improved to perfection now. Think of that!

Uncle Harry Peabody[106] spent the whole day here yesterday. I re-

---

103 Many of the items TNW mentions in this letter were completed; some were published, while others can be found in parts or fragments in the Beinecke Library at Yale University. An undated manuscript notebook contains act 1 of "The Graves Family," as well as undated holograph manuscript fragments. There is a holograph manuscript of "The Last Word About Burglars" and a program for the production of this play with "A Fable for Those Who Plague," for May 9, 1916. Nothing remains of any work titled "Ventures Joyous," or "The New Belinda." TNW's Shakespeare essay was published as "The Language of Emotion in Shakespeare" in the *Oberlin Literary Magazine* for March 1916. The following month, his short story "Sealing Wax" was published in the *Oberlin Literary Magazine*, as was "Brother Fire: A Comedy for Saints," in the May 1916 *Oberlin Literary Magazine*. Another of his "Three Minute Playlets for Three Persons," No. 6, may have been "Solus Inter Deos Protens: No. 6," which was never published but exists in an undated manuscript notebook at Yale. There is no record of the projected "Archangel's Fires," although there is the possibility it could have been reworked and retitled.

104 French actress and singer (1881–1920), notorious in France, England, and the United States for her daring on and off the stage; reference may be to a poem TNW wrote about her that has not survived.

105 Comedy (1751) by Italian dramatist Carlo Goldoni (1707–1793) about how a woman treats four suitors, each of whom personifies a different attitude toward her sex. Again, the reference may be to a poem by TNW that has not survived.

106 Harry Ernest Peabody (1865–1940) was a Congregational clergyman who was related through marriage to TNW's father.

membered him when I saw him. He preached in my church and I sat behind him in the choir. Then I took him to dinner at Dascomb.

Miss Marion Knight[107] said she saw you on the train going or coming from Holyoke.

Do you see anything of boys up there? You must get them to call on you, too, remember. I can't have a sister who scares the boys away. I'd be pleased to death if I heard you'd become engaged—even if it was only a butcher-boy. Of course, I wouldn't allow the match to procede; but still, I'd be feeling that you weren't quite dead. I don't want to come and hear your organist play a sentimental concert in the half dusk with a lot of sickening schoolgirls saying "Isn't this just too lovely!" And I don't want to sit up in the gallery and watch a pedal couplers—I'll go to an organ recital where an organist attempts a huge Bach fugue, and tears your scalp off amid screams from the sensitive. No silver collection tip toe affair, but a carry-out-the-corpses, women-and-children-first function.

I'd like to give your Dr. Wooly[108] a try, but I wouldnt be impressed by the fact that she <with> the colored hoods down her back would turn my fren' Gaby Deslys pea-green with envy. Gee, but I'd hate to be the president of the girls' college and be aware of that waves of foolish admiration and unstemmed enthusiasms that rock of the "sea of upturned faces."—Wouldnt it be fierce!—

I'm very seriously worried. My dear Charlotte if I sent you a picture of myself would you promise not to tell that it was your brother.

I'd sign it Yours Herbert or

Would you? It would give you a "new dignity" and "added prestige" and, Lord, it<'s> what you need. You

107 Marion E. Knight (1891–1941) was at this time a graduate student at Oberlin after attending Mount Holyoke College.

108 Mary Emma Woolley, president of Mount Holyoke College from 1901 to 1937.

could put it all over your room mate. Get Amos to send his in tennis flannels, with the inscription

Don't Forget
Percy

You send me yours: But none of your I'm-content-to-just-be-good-and-let-who-will-be-pretty. If you cant put any smartness into the picture any other way, stick out your tongue.

I'd be ashamed to write such a silly letter to anybody else, but in writing it to you I show my remarkable instinct of adapting my letter to the letteree—even father ought to write you silly letters

So long
Thornybush.

P.S. Its great to be able to draw!

28. TO AMOS P. WILDER. ALS 8 pp. Yale

221 N. Prof St, Oberlin Ohio
April 4 <1916>

<appeared above salutation>
Make this as PRIVET as you think best.

Dearest Papa

Still vacation. I'm feeling very fine this morning after a bath and a hair-cut—I need it I tell you:

Our weather is very changeable; we haven't had snow for some time but we have days snow-cold and then sunny ones.

I tell you I like vacations. I get up at 7:00 o'clock tho, and go to bed at 9:30, spend a few hours in the library; hang around and talk to people after meals; take my walks and come home and write down what I thought out during the walk. The difference between Vacation and term-time in that respect is that during term-time I only write when I've got a red-hot idea, while now I have to make use of my time and sit down and write anyway. You won't be mad if I tell you about it. The worst thing about Oberlin here is that I have no one to talk it over with. Just out of a kind of necessity I read the thing aloud to Mrs. Orpha Grey, the "elecutionist" down the Hall and to Mrs. Gammon[109] and Theodore Wilder and even Hotchkiss[110]; but all they do is to laugh at the broadly humorous parts and say "it's very good," and make encourageing prophecies! But partly because it's not a professional printed book, and partly because I'm a freshman they wont take it as more than something I amuse myself with. Ugh.

Miss Grace George a prominent and distinguished New York actress-manager says she's "looking high and low for an American play" and has offered a large prize for the best play by an undergraduate in an American College. Now I'm such an undergraduate and I write plays as I eat so I feel that without much audacity I ought to be allowed to enter that contrast<contest>. The things against me are that I'm not Harvard, and that I'm not an upperclassmen. I don't really see why I

109 Mrs. Charles Gammon (Mary Stanley Gammon), Theodore Wilder's maternal aunt, whom he called "Aunt Mame."

110 Edwin DeWitt Hotchkiss was at this time a student in Oberlin's Conservatory of Music.

ought to expect myself to be able to picture "American life" with any big eye, but I'm swimming through the second act, and I want to read it to somebody who can tell me whether its ridiculously immature or not. I'm not worrying about the special details of its construction, I'm probably over-confident that the dialogue's a paragon of natural vivacity and vividness, and the characters real, and so forth

I often wish that I could plant you impersonally at the foot of my bed and read the thing to you.

I read as much as I had finished a week and a half ago to Prof. Wager, head of the English Department. He thought very highly of it, and confessed to a weakness of being interested in the story and wanted to know how things were going to turn out, wanted me to read it to him as it grew. But: he was sorry that he didn't see many modern plays—familiar as he was by teaching with the Greek and Elizabethan—and couldn't quite judge as to the modern atmosphere. I was glad to hear that a "classicist" could enjoy it at all, but wanted someone who knew New York and the Middle West very closely to sit in judgement on the very atmosphere.

The story briefly concerns a young lady of a quiet, old wealthy family in Chicago who suddenly disturbs her family with a violent attack of ideals she has had:

Anabel (in exalted strain, impressively) I'm beautiful; I'm brilliant; I'm rich; what can't I do?—I will surround myself with famous men and women; I'll form a new school of literature; a new circle of Art and Music.

Why do I have to stay in a little ugly dark house in Chicago? I will live in a temple in New York. (challengingly) Now, Phil.

Phil (her brother, deeply moved and disturbed, getting up and pacing the floor.) You may be able to do a little along that line, but you mustn't hope to go very far.

Anabel (to the World!) Why not?

Phil You may not have the personality—the magnetism. I don't like the idea of your voting yourself into the place.

Anabel But it's <u>small</u> to be afraid to be conceited. Let me call out again:—I'm beautiful, clever, rich—the new Madame Récamier;

Lady Wortley Montague;[111] with something of Cleopatra, Sappho—

Mother (shocked) Cleopatra!

Anabel How little I've been until this came! I'll wear striking gowns in a marvellous house. I'll be all graciousness, all distinction, all charm. My very ambition will give me dignity. I will appear in the public eye; I will learn to speak in public—

Phil (almost trembling) Stop, Anabel—maybe you can't do any of these things; and there will be nothing left, but the collossal foolishness—a sentimental schoolgirl—you've begun too high.

Anabel I won't plan any lower

Phil (burning) If you could! I<f?> you can!

Anabel You'll be along with me. You will write it down—the new Boswell—but not my glory—but what my own idealism lends me!

Mother Well, the hairdresser's waiting for you upstairs.

End of Act I

In a way its a big idea for a kind of High Comedy. And in Acts II and III we see her in <her> new N.Y. Home "Room of Honor" and her brother—a young fellow who until this came was a Chicago society man, and amateur patron of the arts; we see her, (now named Helena!) receiving her first call from a famous novelist, and trying pathetically to be brilliant and a super-woman, and doing very well. There is an equally important sub-plot woven in, showing her abounding good intentions equally miss-directed.

In the end <the> way<?> of "The Joyous Ventures" fail, where she seems to be most successful, and she retires to a small farmhouse in Illonois. The public misunderstood her principally; she had acted in a

111 Jeanne Françoise Récamier (1777–1849), French socialite well-known for her beauty, whose salon was a gathering place for the leading political and literary figures of her day; Lady Mary Wortley Montagu (1689–1762), English writer known primarily for her letters, which were first published in 1763 and which revealed her to be a highly intelligent woman in a male-dominated society.

tuberculosis-propaganda moving-picture play for them, and the benefit of the Red Cross Society (!), and she had made sincere and good little speeches to working girl leagues and to school-children in Central Park; she had discovered some new philanthropic veins; she had found some artists and poets in Indiana etc, but the dear public thinks she is trying to be notorious instead of lofty, and she becomes a kind of public "hit," a preacher holds her up as a warning to American girlhood, as the personification of American crudity—and her strength gives out.

But the play is not cynical in holding up the folly of youthful idealism and enthusiasm. The whole answer to the play is in the spirit (not the words) of the conversation on which the final curtain falls. This is between the girl and her brother, in which he coaxes her out <of> her heart's soreness and brooding and before long they are laughing and playing together in a kind of warm affection, like two young animals,—youth again.[112]

I don't know whether I have entirely misrepresented the thing to you or not. I wish I had you here to give it word for word. I got to go now to lunch!

Lovingly

Thornton

How are you? You're dear old photograph accidentally got a smudge on it. I must take it and have a photografer remove it. Hein?[113]

---

112 The play variously called "Ventures Joyous" and "The New Belinda" (see letter number 27) became "The Rocket: An American Comedy in Four Acts," which can be found as an undated corrected typescript in the Beinecke Library at Yale University. It is not known whether or not TNW sent "The Rocket" to American actress, producer, and director Grace George (see letter number 36).

113 French: Eh?

29. TO AMOS P., ISABELLA N., ISABEL, AND JANET F. WILDER. ALS 4 pp. Yale

221 N. Prof
<Oberlin, Ohio>
Sunday night May '6 <1916>[114]

Dear Family,

Nothing especial has happened. I'm being dragged through the trigonometry book. Tues. night comes the very first performance of any serious dramatic work by T.N.W. when "The Last Word about Burglars" and "A Fable for Those who Plague" will be produced before Dascomb Family and friends at a quarter-before-seven. We've been rehearsing our heads off. The next week comes the May Festival. We've been rehearsing our heads off again.—Such is Life

---

Tomorrow morning I have to get up before six and take breakfast out at the Arboretum with the New England Club. I couldnt refuse. I had waived going to their dinner about a month ago because I could <not> afford to go alone—to say nothing of asking a New Englander—in. But this is only twenty-cents.

I have grown very fond of Grandmothers present—The Giorgone "Concert"[115] and now I have temporarily traded it with another boy for a Corot landscape. This is not a permanent swap. We just want to live with a new picture for a change.

The green fern is doing very well. We're thinking of getting it a bigger dish. I never was so happy as when I got the photos. Now that I think of it, I'm struck by the fact that I've never mentioned receiving these—to say nothing of enjoying them. Isabel's pastel shows great advance. Try and afford to take her to good exhibitions. We've just finished one her<e> with a splendid canvas by Mother's favorite George Bellow's.[116]

---

114 In 1916, May 6 was a Saturday; TNW probably misdated this letter.

115 Giorgione's painting *Pastoral Concert*.

116 Painter George Bellows.

Papa's money I am still carrying around in my mind as open to profitable investment. I think it is just as well if I put it into the daily round of New England Breakfasts, Latin Plays (25c), Church Collections, and Class dues.

I probably told you that I had sworn off sending anything more to the Magazine this <year?>. It is atrociously bad taste to have so many things in succession—a Freshman, too—but Miss Martin came all the way to my boarding-house to beg me for "that little thing about St. Francis of Assisi, that I read to her and her guests once." I fought fearfully but at last gave in—"Brother Fire: A Comedy for Saints. Three Minute Playlets for Three Persons, No V." One of the few short things I've written while in Oberlin.

The Big One is almost done.[117] One conversation at the end of the Fourth and last Act is left and then I'll be glad. I have no regrets at parting with these people's company. The typiste has begun already. I've suddenly discovered that she's too expensive and I'm going to shake her off at the end of the Second Act.

Lots of love to Everybody
Thorntony

30. TO AMOS P. WILDER. ALS 4 pp. Yale

You know where
<Oberlin, Ohio>
May 14—<19>'16.

Dear Papa,

The majestic contract for my valuable labor I return signed.[118] I suppose its what's called an efficiency document. I really am very glad

---

117 TNW is probably referring to "The Rocket: An American Comedy in Four Acts."

118 Apparently a formal contract for the farm labor TNW was scheduled to do during the summer of 1916 at the Mount Hermon School in Gill, Massachusetts.

to have my work organized. With the Dutton housework it was—"You can do this next if you want to." and all my work was an extravagant favor to the family. But this admirable paper says I'm to get up at this dot and report to work at this dot, and submit myself to Mr. Dot this; and refrain from profanity on this dot. I hope my Mr. Dot isn't the pretentious, upright reformer that got up the sheet.

Did you know that you were doing what the psychologists call "infringing on my personality" when you ask me to sign a blank agreement in which you fill in the details. You have impaired my self:consciousness when I am told that you bound me over to 9 hours a day; made inroads on my "mental acceptance of conditions of living" when I see that my term of labor is ten weeks.

So Watch Your Step

I really think you've solved the problem very well for yourself but as for the men who want me to milk Mt. Hermon cows, or stack Northfield Hay, or "carry on the work which Mr. Moody began"[119]—well, I suppose your attitude is They Should Worry.

I don't like the idea of getting money. And I don't believe in your speaking of it "as a work I have had some experience in". If you don't be very careful—and you know I'm going to major in Psychology at Oberlin—you'll find that the Spirit of Wishing on <has> been painting pictures on the unstained Walls of Truth, in your mind.

So Watch Your Step

I've got a room mate for next year. Mr. Walter Smith of Dascomb. I've always liked him for a quiet concientious and clever-minded boy. He's no Alexander like Mr. Spore, but he's very good solidity for daily wear. He just beat our religiously-sentimental, chaplain all to nothing in a gloriously funny argument on whether God underwent change at

119 Dwight Lyman Moody (1837–1899) was an evangelist who founded the Mount Hermon School for Boys (1881) and its sister institution, the Northfield Seminary for Young Ladies (1879), both designed to serve students with limited means.

all. The chaplain had a vague idea that God underwent everything, so he would relinquish his right to a change (not-withstanding the old text.) But Walter Smith proved something like Time is fluid change, embodied in the super-intellect—of course I can't carry it any further, and I haven't even got the subject of the debate right, but you're impressed anyway. Walter Smith is the one I exchange pictures with so you can see he has taste. He both teaches Geometry at the Academy and urges me to borrow his beloved copy of Theocritus.

Lots of love
Thorny Bush.

The date I signed that thing was the 14th. I didn't know whether to leave it to the next signer or not

31. TO ISABEL WILDER. ALS 4 pp. Yale

221 N. Prof St Oberlin <Ohio>
May 18—<19>'16

Dear Old Isabel,

This is to thank you in person for the pastel of Lac Leman[120]—and its really all kinds of improvement—and to enclose t<w>o more Oberlin poster stamps. You might be interested in the program, too; I know the boy quite well, he can't compose worth a bean but he can argue and argue as long as I want.

I'm glad you're going to Chataqua.[121] I'm getting afraid that your being kept at the same age as you look, and that would never do. I ad-

120 Lac Léman, the French name for Lake Geneva.

121 TWN is referring to the Chautauqua Institution. Founded in western New York State in 1874 to provide religious and secular instruction to Methodist Episcopal Sunday school teachers during the summer, Chautauqua later offered summer courses in the arts, sciences, and humanities, as well as lectures and performances by musicians, artists, and well-known political figures.

vise you to do two things to make yourself feel more grown up: ① open your mouth wide when you talk, and let the words be long and full of real grown-up bluff-talk without wrinkling your forehead, or lisping or smiling—just stare mother in the face, and say "Did they guarantee the poppy seeds?" or "I've just discovered that my stationary has a translucent water-mark."

② Always know more than you're saying. When you tell Janet to put on a shall<shawl> over her head you must be thinking to yourself "Now I'm using the imitative instinct; and when I make her walk in step, I've got her attention just that much more because I'm using her sense of rhythm." It's really time you felt terribly conscious of your towering height over Janet. I say again I'm getting terribly afraid that your getting into the kind of girl, who is so behind hand that when she's with people she's so busy just wondering and being bewildered that she's no time to slap other people's faces and generally make herself felt.

③ I like your letters very much. Next time tho, don't even stop to form the letters. A young lady just runs across the polished floor to her shining desk, throws it open and dashes off a note, as tho she were drawing a cartoon; then she licks it, pounds it to make it stick and calmly places it in the mail-box and the thing—the little chance trifling thing is over.

I'll be home soon; and then I'll have to act wilder than I feel like doing, so I can scare you, and push you and worry <you> into a real modern storming young woman.

Maybe you are after all, tho'.

What?

Thorny Bush.

32. TO ISABELLA N. WILDER. ALS 8 pp. Yale

May 20—<19>16
221 N. Prof St.
<Oberlin, Ohio>

Dear Mother only—[122]

There are lots of things to tell—stark stiff things—but I have a mood to communicate first and the things need not be too sure of an appearance;—for when one has disclosed a mood, a feeling one is so proud that one goes to bed and snores with an undercurrent of brazen triumph.

There is a senior at Dascomb named Ruth Keller. She is majoring in Latin, and knows the latin poets very well. She is taking Italian and reads Dante. But she does not mix with the other girls very well, partly because she has a reserve of her own and partly because she spends so much time studying hard,—a grind. But I have come to know her very well, and I am the only one that really knows what a delightful, colored personality she has. I try to explain it to Mr. Spore—who is too nice to demand of me why I "sit out" with that large old grind—but he can't see it. And I ask Miss Tritschler whether she sees ever—just a glimpse of it.

But they'd see it alright if Miss Keller were pretty. But she is not. I must be remorseless in describing her. She is "large"—I used to think that her face looked a vulgar italian—the kind with little curls greasily fringeing the forehead. But now I know she is like a handsome Roman matron. Part of her air of reserve comes from the height at which she holds her head, and the classic severity of her mouth. But to give the public's opinion of her I must return to the remorseless details. When she has an evening dress on, in charity one must refuse to notice the large arms, and the unbalanced neck. She maintains an upright retirement at table—she will not laugh at the foolish teasing that is the greater

---

122 TNW originally wrote "Dear Family" but crossed out "Family" and substituted "Mother only."

part of table conversation here,—she busies her self conscientiously in seeing that the waiters bring enough for the boys to eat, but apart from that she refuses to enter into the hilarity. Except when I am there—and Miss Parker places me at her table very often, since I am the only person she is at home with. Then we two exclude the whole table and talk about anything we darn please.

But when we are together she is like a little girl; we're both willing to laugh at the humblest and most ridiculous joke in the world. Or else we're as sober as reformers. The other day we had a long walk in which we discussed what she was going to do next year and then on. She's going to teach Latin in the High School of her hometown, New Kensington, Penn. She'll do it alright, of course, but she needs a lot more than that to keep her living. She gets great fits of perfect despair with herself—her not being able to be one girl among many, and her not being at least on ordinary friendly terms with the boys;—its all the tragedy of not being pleasing and beautiful. I told her that she had to find something to do hard out of school times. She can't just live at home in her flat with her mother talking and sewing and gossiping. And I was thinking so hard of the awful folly of Miss Hanna and Miss Day[123] that I must have been little short of eloquent. I told her she must always be forcing herself to read good things she didn't want to read and join Women's Clubs she didn't want to join and spending money on concerts and plays she didn't want to spend just to keep herself from thinking that she was living a full life, as a teacher. I took as an example the concert of the May Festival the night before, where we had sung the "Nuova Vita" of Dante. She had gone—altho she hardly ever goes to "anything" and had thot it very beautiful. She saw that if she kept seeing and reading things like that she would feel different than if she just stayed in a rut.

The next morning she said with a little laugh that she'd hardly been able to sleep at all.

---

123 Miss Hanna and Miss Day were Berkeley friends of the Wilder family.

Wouldn't it have been a wonderful thing if I had really at least put a disturbing influence into a potential Miss Hanna?

Another thing is that there is a young man, a Mr. Howard, who writes to her very often. He came down to see her the other day and I happened to see them. He was a spruce young man, very attentive to her. I don't pretend to understand it, but I know for one thing that he's not attentive to her because he sees her charm too. She says he doesn't do anything—he just drifts—he's quite wealthy. I asked her why she didn't make him get down to something like work. Oh—she was vague about it—"it couldn't be done, he was just born that way."

"Oh well," I told her, "you're just the kind that would work and slave yourself to death, just so such a man wouldn't have to lift a finger."

She repudiated the idea with indignant laughter.—But today she told me that she had changed her mind<.> She wasn't going to send him an invitation to her graduation after all. Now imagine what it means to a neglected girl like her to hold off a nice young <man>. ¶ I won't say the whole affair is a case for Strindberg—poor girl.[124]

This afternoon almost all the rest of Dascomb was down to the lake. I talked it over with her, and said I was afraid I couldn't afford to go. If I didn't go it meant that she didn't go for there's no one else in the house who couples off with her. "She was glad she wasn't going—she had to study."

We went to the library to study for an hour and a half and then we were to go out <remainder of letter missing>

---

124 After graduating from Oberlin in June 1916, Ruth Keller (1894–1973) taught school for two years in her hometown, worked for the U.S. government in Washington, D.C., married, and had six children (one son's middle name was Thornton).

Wilder men in New Haven, 1915 or 1916. Left to right: *Amos N., Amos P. (sitting), and TNW.*

33. TO ISABELLA N. WILDER. ALS 4 pp. Yale

c/o The Mt. Hermon
School, Mass
July 2—<19>'16.

Dear Mother,

By tomorrow evening I will have completed two weeks of work. I am becoming used to the deeficulty of the work—used that is not so much to doing it physically as to accepting it with resignation mentally; my fatalism increases with my blisters.

I suppose father has told you that I earn 15 cents an hour and work ten hours a day, and sixty a week. I was a little pleased at the thought of nine dollars a week (although that is very low wages), when suddenly a Portia[125] stretched out her hand and announ<c>ed with or without blood four dollars was to be deducted from my living wage to cover board, room, light and laundry. I now see that the earning of money is degrading to the spirit of man; such avarice and greed is growing in me that I can plainly see that before long I will be getting up early with some of the other "workers" in order to grind out a few more fifteen cent's before the sun rises. I hope to come home Saturday, July the twenty-ninth, or else go up to the Duttons for that weekend.

I get in about an hour and a half of reading every evening. By that time I am so tired that everything that I read which is beautiful or impressive finds tears in my eyes! This phenomenon in turn reacts to even deeper emotion; farm life would make the weeping philosopher of Syracuse out of me.[126] So far I have endamped the pages of "Hedda Gabler" "The Master Builder" "Boswell's etc" and the "Religio Medici."[127]

---

125 TNW is referring to Portia in Shakespeare's *The Merchant of Venice*; disguised as a lawyer, Portia cleverly and fairly wins the case in which Shylock has demanded a pound of flesh owed to him by her husband's friend Antonio.

126 The Greek philosopher Heraclitus was often referred to as "the weeping philosopher."

127 *Hedda Gabler* and *The Master Builder*, plays by Henrik Ibsen; Boswell's *The Life of Samuel Johnson L.L.D.*; and *Religio Medici*, a prose work by English author and philosopher Sir Thomas Browne (1605–1682).

There is a very interesting paper on "My Street" by that Earnest Poole in the July Century.[128]

You will be surprised to hear that the boy I often hay beside is a cousin of Miss Eleanor Hague. He is a freshman from Washington and Jefferson College, Penn. quondam Mt. Hermon.

Amos telephoned my boss from Northfield this noon with orders for me to stay in my room since he is bring<ing> over a "cousin" of mine. I suspect its Mr. Peabody. It can't be Max! can it?[129]¶ You ought to be glad that I can only write to you on these slow resty Sundays. Father gets the frantic mid-week ones; tho' I must say they don't seem to disturb at all—he's positively pleased by them, the complacent one!—Tell Isabel to assume this duty on her heart: Find somewhere to hand in my room the packet of my bookplates. Enclose one to me. The waiter at my table is going to start putting himself thru Harvard next year with a printing press, and I want to show him something in his line that he never heard of—something Harvardiensian, too.

Affty Thornton.

34. TO AMOS N. WILDER. ALS 4 pp. Yale

July 11 <1916> c/o Mt. Hermon School,
Mass.

Dear Amos,

I am very sorry to find you in so low a mind and I don't know what to do. I agree with you that the prospect of the time involved, the weeks and days, is more discourageing than the separate duties. I myself however can see how I came to my present attitude of philosophical stoicism from positive frenzy and I hope that you will come, too. The

128 American journalist and novelist Ernest Poole (1880–1950), whose essay appeared in *The Century Magazine.*

129 Max Wilder (1894–1962), TNW's cousin, the son of TNW's father's older brother Julian Wilder (1860–1938).

principal alleviations of my life have been the evenings, my reading and my thoughts. I am sure that you have as beautiful a place as this, altho' you may not have the last hours of the day free to enjoy it as I have. But steal an hour from sleep if necessary and walk along the sides of some pond or brook. And try to get a little reading in.

I will send you the "Religio Medici" which is a "devotional" book but written in the most exquisite style. The marks are father's and refer to the sentiments not the style. The discussions of the supernatural especially are written in the most stunning eloquence I ever read. My chief interest here however has been Boswell's Life of Johnson which I read every hour I can. I'd send it to you—only it weighs a ton. I am often able to be by myself "hoeing a row" or "turning the hay" and look forward to such jobs as chances to think over everything and anything.

Please do not think me any the less sincere because of the frightful wording of this letter. All this stiffness is the sign that Boswell has me all over. I see myself writing down a archaism, or latin construction and I have to howl at myself, but I cannot help it. My style will either come out from this ordeal saved or ruined. Wash out your eyes, remember that life's a kind of illusion and this pain and dis-ease is merely funny—and that you are tenderly loved by

Thornton N. Wilder

35. TO AMOS P. WILDER. ALS 4 pp. Yale

Sunday Morning July 16 <1916>
Mt. Hermon School.

Dear Papa,

I have begun to take an unusual pleasure in writing letters. I suppose that in spite of my fatigue I have found time to write as many letters in my short time here as in months of Oberlin time. You must confess that you have received many, besides which I have written several and divided them among Mother, Amos, Mr. Spore, Prof Wager and Ruth Keller, my classical friend. But it might grow to a danger to talk about letters as such, so I will stop.

The grounds today are covered by a thousand plus of old Hermonites. Last night they held a faculty reception on the lawn and afterwards until late into the night they tramped around like a herd of cattle, giving yells and spelling words to the tramp of their feet: H-E-R-M-O-N, D-L-M-O-O-D-Y. They all show that the prep school can leave a tremendous impression but they are a dissappointing crowd. Their faces are heavy and they stand and walk hideously. A great many are oily, repressed and apologetic, some are stout and have pockets showing a battery of sausage-like cigars, and give the picture of a Senator from Kansas. Their wives are unusually secondary because they are visiting a men's school and a men's reunion. The whole crowd has cheapened itself by wearing huge blue circular tags with their names on. I cannot but remember the more enlightened masquerade on the New Haven campus, altho' I suspected there that the cheer and life of the occasion owed something to translucent bottles and a barrel swishing as it was lifted onto the table. At the dining-hall during supper last night I discovered these alumni to be of the kind who strike their plates with their knives when supper is delayed; and signify applause by beating on the table cloth with the handles of their forks. Nevertheless I have seen much better stuff in the present graduating class and conjecture that the religious pressure in this school finds out the best students & sends them to the foreign field while the rest—who are considered as corn that did not pop, a necessary surplus—return to their farms unlighted.

My friend Sibley from Chefoo, a fine boy, hopes to go to China soon, is in this graduating class of eighty boys. I forgot to mention altho you probably guessed it that this is a reunion of Ford cars as well. The banquet—workers invited too—is Monday evening—do but picture the enthusiasm!—I see the toastmaster is a Wilfred Fry of Philadelphia. Isn't there a famous Chinese art-connaiseur of Philad. named Fry, too?—I hope not Wilfred, tho!

All these Captains & Kings depart Tues. night and leave the wearied worker to take up his regular meal hours and routine.

Now that I've vented my spleen I'll sign my name. This crew has turned my stomach more than the food and the dirty room and the cheap attempts at disgustingness of my would-be sophisticated fellow workers.

Ugh!

Thornton.

P.S. I honestly thot I was going to write a nice letter but the cat got out of the bag.

36. TO RUDOLF KOMMER.[130] ALS 4 pp. (Stationery embossed Monhegan Maine![131]). Princeton

Men's Building
Oberlin, Ohio.
Sept. 15—<19>16

Dear Mr. Kommer,

I am back at College and about to start in work again. Two of the courses that all Sophomores are required to take I will find very hard. These are Economics and Chemistry. I am not afraid of the rest, though: Exposition and Essay-Writing, "Classics in Translation", and a short history course in English Institutions and the Reformation. My father is having me add to this a little work with the organ in the Conservatory of Music. In all I have tried to see to it that I have plenty of time to myself outside. During the service in which the new Senior class was inaugurated yesterday afternoon the Parsifal music was played. I was reminded of the last time I heard the Motif of the Holy Graal, at the close of that great evening.[132]

---

130 TNW met Kommer, a Viennese drama critic (1885–1943) and assistant to Austrian theatrical producer and director Max Reinhardt, during his summer vacation in 1916 at Monhegan Island, Maine, after he finished his work at the Mount Hermon School. The island had long been the site of an artists' colony.

131 TNW added this exclamation point after "Maine" on the letterhead of the stationery.

132 Richard Wagner's opera *Parsifal* tells the story of a Knight Templar and his search for the Holy Grail. The Wilder family possesses a completed undated typescript of a three-minute playlet, "The Lost Miracle of the Graal," which may have been written at this time.

I thought for a while that the picture you drew of living in a city and mixing in with the "newest thought" would make little old Oberlin look mild for me. But I think I am too much of an American, and a middle-westerner—to ever really go in for the Continental Method in earnest. Perhaps you can explain my mind in the matter to me?

I had two days in Boston on my way back. My mother always told me how great an actress Mary Shaw was in "Ghosts" and so I thought a play in which she appeared could not be altogether lost. Such awful stuff as "The Melody of Youth" I never saw, and as for Miss Shaw, all she did was to lift her hand and make her points, and then stare at the audience.[133] How much better it would have been to have gone to "Hit-the-Trail-Holliday" which was my only other choice.[134]

I couldn't find Eulenberg's "Schattenphantasie"[135] in the great Boston Public Library itself. I'll have our local library send to Washington for it.

I am overhauling the Dr. Johnson-Boswell affair.[136] When I re-read the thing it struck me hard how excellent your suggestions were. I hope I can follow them appropriately.

As for the assault on Grace George—"The Rocket; an American Comedy in Four Acts"—my father says he'll send it to me in a week. He's been making marginal comments on it that it'll take me a week to erase. His point-of-view is "antipodal" to yours.

I am very interested in Mr. Strunsky's play.[137] Please let me know if it reaches anywhere. Could you let me know the name and mold of it?

---

133 American actress Mary Shaw (1854–1929) portrayed Mrs. Alving in Henrik Ibsen's play *Ghosts* in numerous productions, most notably in New York in 1916–1917. *The Melody of Youth,* a play by Irish-born American dramatist, actor, and director Brandon Tynan (1875–1967), also played in New York in 1916, although Mary Shaw was not in the cast.

134 *Hit-the-Trail Holiday*, a play by George M. Cohan.

135 German poet, dramatist, and prose writer Herbert Eulenberg (1876–1949) does not seem to have a published work called *Schattenphantasie,* but his *Schattenbilder: Eine Fibel für Kulturbedürtige in Deutschland* was published in 1910. TNW mentions this book in his foreword to *The Angel That Troubled the Waters and Other Plays* (1928).

136 In a July 12, 1916, letter to his mother, TNW mentions that he has written a three-minute playlet for three persons, "Mr. Bozzy," which is about Johnson, Mrs. Thrale, and Boswell. It survives as an undated typescript in the Beinecke Library at Yale University.

137 Possibly, TNW is referring to Russian-born American humorist and journalist Simeon Strunsky (1879–1948).

"Young writers live with most enthusiasm on books they have not read; pictures they have not seen; scores they have not heard."

Wish me well with my Chemistry, as I do for your piece. I am bound to you for much encouragement and many new ideas—difficult to assimilate!—

Sincerely yours
Thornton N. Wilder

P.S. Do you want to see my book-plate?
Funny, Hien<Hein>?

37. TO CHARLOTTE E. WILDER. ALS 2 pp. Yale

<appeared above salutation>
Use Spacing and Deep Margin's Elegantly.

October 16—<19>16
Men's Bldg Oberlin.

Great Scott, Charlotte

I never saw such impudence in my whole life. Just because a person pretends to show you a little deference, you feel you have to write your own obituary, and open shop as a patron of belles-lettres. When I read your gentle strictures my eyes popped out of my sockets, and when I came to your favorable comments I felt as tho I were being stabbed from behind. As I read my manuscript I began to miss some of my cherished phrases; every now and then I saw that someone had inserted perfunctory bridges over which the timid mind might step—with petticoat lifted = when the art of writing is a matter of alpine climbing—peak to peak, and let the chasms snatch the fearful.

However the mistake was mine to attempt expository prose in which I wasn't over-interested. Now, Madam, I am sending something, if you touch a curl of which you shall surely die. The very rhythm of the sentence is important and if you supply a polite "over which" or "wherefore" the web will fall. I trust that you are in a better position to enter into the confusion of mythologies in the Revival of Learning, than improvisation.

Send me your magazine; and I will send you mine. My contribution is not an article and so your search for signs of illiteracy are entirely beside the point. A sweet pale girl on the magazine staff came to me and said: "After we read your story for the magazine we sat there perfectly silent, it was so beautiful."[138] I won't expect any such effect upon you until you are "educated in reverence" but you shall eat your words someday!

Lovingly Thornton.

P.S.I Why don't you go to France as a nurse or a hay-maker or streetcar conductor?

P.S.II My hair is still white and curled from reading your letter. Why the idea! I hope you have removed all the poison from your system. Oh, most incredible venom, Judicatrix incredibilis, quouseque tandem abutere nostra patientia![139]

38. TO ISABELLA N. WILDER. ALS 4 pp. Yale

Men's Buildg. Oberlin, Ohio.
Oct. 22—<19>16.

PRIVATE

Dear Mother,

I suppose I have to be very tactful in my letters these days. Amos' going away has intoxicated you and Papa so with swelling emotions that letters from oberlin will surprise you by their thinness. Soon letters

---

138 TNW may be referring to his story "Two Miracles of Doma Y Venuzias," which appeared in the November 1916 issue of the *Oberlin Literary Magazine.* Charlotte Wilder's article "Of the Class of '52" was a humorous comparison of her era and the Mount Holyoke class of 1852; it appeared in the October 1916 issue of *The Mount Holyoke.*

139 Latin: Unbelievable judge, how long will you abuse our patience. This line is TNW's play on Cicero's line "Quo usque tandem abutere, Catilina, patientia nostra?" from the *Orations Against Catiline.*

will be coming to you from Red Cross hospitals with censor-stamps on the back and Papa will feel that at last he has a son in the foreign field; how relentlessly I am shown up by it all—a minor who doesn't study hard and who needs money from time to time.[140]

So read my letters with charity. Few other mothers have sons where your's is but many have sons where your other is!

I told you that while I was at Hermon Mr. Wager wrote me that he had a subject to treat if I could. Well, its il gran tradimente ([The Great Betrayel" (?)] of the Baglioni family of Perugia.[141] <)> It's a superb affair but would be too ambitious for me. Did you know anything of it?

I went to see Elsie Ferguson.[142] It was a most lovely performance. The play is light but not negligable. Her peculiar voice and walk brought back the Outcast continually but throughout this play she is for the most part happy. And such acting in the graceful or tender moments.

With all my new clothes I feel like a new person and I can hardly go back to wearing my old overcoat. I've had it ever since Chefoo days in and out. Its a perfect give-away in texture and shape. However I could recall St. Francis' vow of Poverty and wear it another year if necessary. You write me privately your own secret and inner opinion of father's money state and tell me whether it would be adding the last straw to an impossible load if I presented the question to him. He himself recognized the fact that it was a "wierd" garment when he was last here but has probably forgotten it. Don't feel any hesitation will crush

140 On September 26, 1916, eight days after his twenty-first birthday, TNW's brother enlisted as a volunteer ambulance driver. He sailed for France on October 21 to begin a three-month assignment with the American Field Service (AFS) in Paris.

141 The Baglioni family dominated political life in the Italian city of Perugia from the fifteenth century through the early sixteenth century. In 1520, Gian Paolo Baglioni was lured to Rome and beheaded by Leo X.

142 American stage and film actress Ferguson (1883–1961) appeared in the stage production of *The Outcast* (1914), by English dramatist Hubert Henry Davies, and repeated her role in the film version (1922).

me. I am quite often surprised by evidences that I have a little pleasant "prestige"; it can help me "live down" lots.

This afternoon I saw Leonard Peabody[143] and called on Latin Professor Lord. Mrs. Lord is a wealthy and very beautiful lady. They have a handsome home. Mr. Lord has been to Europe about twelve times and their rooms are full of old furniture and beautiful painting reproductions.

Often I'm dissatisfied and unhappy; I want to leave college and live on a Desert Island. Would it cost much?—Everything beautiful I read or hear reminds me that I ought to be finished with all this and be at it. But I have finished a beautiful new 3-minute that Charlotte's typewriting for me.[144]

Lots of love to Isabel; I have more fellow-feeling for her with her Algebra than with Father and his Gratified Wish

Love Thornton—.

39. TO ISABELLA N. WILDER. ALS 4 pp. Yale

Men's Bldg, Oberlin Ohio
Nov 13—<19>16
On this day the exquisite Nell Gwyn died
and R.L.S. was born—or vice versa.[145]

Dear Mama,

There is considerable to tell you (and all interested) today. I recognize with a rueful smile that it is some time since I last wrote. I shall

143 Leonard Clough Peabody, a member of the Oberlin class of 1920 and son of "Uncle Harry" Peabody (see letter number 27).

144 Probably "Prosperina and the Devil: A Play for Marionettes," which appeared in the December 1916 issue of the *Oberlin Literary Magazine.*

145 English actress and mistress of King Charles II, Eleanor Gwyn (known as "Nell") died on November 14, 1687; Robert Louis Stevenson was born on November 13, 1850.

bind up my thoughts into sheaves as usual in order to conceal the lack of unity. This letter will be a little more cheerful than usual because it is Monday morning and during the weekends I have time to take long walks and forget how far behind in Laboratory work and in the Major Prophets I am. Besides I am met on every hand with congratulation on—

Saturday night the Latin Department presented a metrical translation of Plautus' "Menaechmi."[146] I had the role of Peniculus, the Sponge, the Parasite. I had a light beard the color of fried apples and a red nose. We acted in front of a picturesque Roman street and the play was happily over-flowing with the customs and manners of Ancient Roman Bourgouisie.

The Oberlin Magazine has at last appeared with my Saint's Story. I hope Papa will like it. The whole issue is I think better than any last year. The George Ade affair is by Robert Watson my little tenor boy. It has three acute moments, but is swamped in the banal[147]

My new overcoat is thick and warm and only seventeen dollars. Both Mrs. Gammon and Agnes[148] felt obliged to come down and see the launching. The only real joys and fears are those I experience in Whitney and Hill's.

Mr. Rudolf Kommer, to whom I sent "the Rocket" put himself out to write me a long letter. Most of the letter was analysis of the play for my own good but he said many nice things too. My letter had followed him to c/o The German Consulate, Los Angeles. Altho "I was very excited over the proclamation of the new Kingdom of Poland, which would not mean much to you, I sat right down and read your

---

146 The comedy *Menaechmi,* by Roman dramatist Titus Maccius Plautus; it was the inspiration for Shakespeare's *The Comedy of Errors.*

147 TNW's story is "Two Miracles of Doma Y Venuzias"; Watson's story is "A Pessimist's Perspective of Life." Both appeared in the November 1916 issue of the *Oberlin Literary Magazine.* TNW befriended Watson and introduced him to a wider musical repertoire for voice. Ade (1866–1944) was an American humorist and dramatist.

148 Agnes Gammon, Theodore Wilder's first cousin and Mrs. Gammon's daughter.

play." So I am tangled among the intrigues of german diplomatists. He thinks that Oberlin is on his way back and wants to get a glimpse, "a real glimpse," of such a college. I welcomed him to Oberlin with reserved gladness—I don't know what on earth would attract so perfect a flower of Vienna—but he can come if he likes. I added tactfully enough, to give me good warning so that I could put my cell in to unwonted Monastery neatness, and arrange with the Dean to throw off the unvarnished harness, and to meet him at the cross-roads.

It will be curious. I shall insist on his going to Church and Chapel to hear the choirs.

Prof. Wager couldn't meet his classes on Sat. because of hoarseness and he didn't come down to the doorbell on Sunday. I hope he isn't worse. I am a correspondent of Mrs. Wager's—who is away at the bedside of her father who is failing of Bright's Disease in New Jersey—and I feel responsible! Oh, he's the most wonderful man.

Do start reading the last series of your Edith Sidgwick.[149] Begin with A Lady of Leisure. Then there are Duke Jones and the Accolyte. Most brilliant dialogue, charming characters! all in memoriam H. J.

Lots of Love Thornton.

40. TO AMOS P. WILDER. ALS 4 pp. Yale

M.B. Oberlin, Ohio.
Nov. 14—<19>16

Dear Papa,

There is no reason why I should feel so comfortable and happy this evening. Heaven knows I was all at sea during Chemistry class this morning and that I handed in a paper more remarkable for substance

---

149 English novelist Ethel Sidgwick (1877–1970), author of *A Lady of Leisure* (1914), *Duke Jones* (1914), and *The Accolade* (1915).

than form to Exposition-and-Essay-Writing class this afternoon. But after that I practiced sturdily and with surprising absorption at the organ for fifty minutes, then paid a call on the lonely wretched Mr. Carr my ex-Trigrometry teacher. In a veiled way he exposes his distraught shy life and his dissatisfactions. I'm the only person he knows in the town, for all his many classes and his talkitive blind-headed aunt; and again Heaven knows that of a necessity he must be a post script in my life. This may sound very sketchy and imaginative on paper but when you come I can amass evidence—the tragi-comedy details of the poor young man's sensitiveness. The strange thing is that with him I am clear almost curt, with a cross-examination manner, but I in turn "lean" and am drawn out—sometimes on the very same evening by the Man in the Old Brick House.

After the heartrending interview with Mr. Carr I went to supper. I'll make no bones of saying that I am developing into a kind of Breakfast-table Kaiser. I insist on dominating! I become educative. I call them up short when they utter bromides. I demand that one of them read a certain magazine story that throws light on herself and report to me. (And they do.) I ask them what they thought of the Chapel service and then disagree with them noisily. I insist on giving them informations I have extracted from the Encyclopoedias so that they can go to the Concert and listen intelligently. To put it short—I see you in myself and laugh, and then go on exagerating what I saw.

So I enjoyed a fictitious importance at the supper table and then returned to the Men's Bldg. I spend some time in visits in boys' rooms. ¶ Not long ago I had a long talk with Mr. Wager. Usually our talks are ornamental both e- and al- lusive. But in this one he directed his fine subtlety on me and before long I had spread myself shivering all over the place. Drawing richly from his own experience he put me together again with just enough appreciative pats to start me off. The effect may seem remote from the cause but now it is observed that I can stand in the door of any boy's room and be greeted normally and be asked to come again and be "cussed" at and joked with. And not only this but the Dissector laid it on me that I should be able to get all this but more—that by my inherited personality (that's one for you!) and by the associations I carry in College I ought to bring out the idealler strains—

As he put it it was transendentally beautiful and winning and I have started life over again as it were. I always thot that I was constitutionally disgusting to all men. But now I know I have four friends among the Philistines where before I had one. And I do like them more and more. There are two men on the football team itself that pass the campus gossip with me in the gentlest amiability. I will always say that Prof. Wager did half but my new coat did the other half.

After these calls among a strange but charming nation, I drew up my rocking-chair before my murmuring radiator and read into Jeremiah for class tomorrow. At 9:30 I took up a brisk walk out in the cold (our first snow-fall today!) When I came home I drew up my chair again in my own blessed happy room, and a feeling of such contentment stole up my shoes from the steel-purring-stand that I was determined that I would write an untroubled letter to the Atlas of my sphere

So Lots of Love
Thornton.

Can you forgive the ego? I'm a sophomore—but well-born.

41. TO ISABELLA N. WILDER. ALS 2 pp. Yale

<Oberlin, Ohio>
Nov. 23—<19>16.

Dear Mother I may have complained of lack of time last year but it was mere illusion compared to this year. I have almost literally no afternoons. On Monday I have Economics lecture at 3: to 4:00, Tues. a class until three and organ practice from four to five, Wednesday, laboratory from 3 to 4:30 cutting into my organ time which ends at five; Thursday like Tues. Friday, lab. from 1:30–4:30. Sat. I have to come back early from my walk to take up the organ at four. Today I was lying down when the two o'clock class bell rang and immediately through my head ran a string of excuses I might offer the Dean for absence, but I went.

I take every measure however to fence off the week-end from the routine. Sat. afternoon I walk as many miles to the east or west as I dare. I don't go to the football games. Sunday I walk again; I don't go to Church very often<;> if I do I go in the evening or Vespers in the afternoon. Monday morning I take my walk again.

I am getting to dread the week. I put off a serious consideration of my studies until Wednesday morning; and I take liberties with study requirements on Friday.

But I have really done a good deal of original writing this year. The best has been the Saint Story in the Magazine and a 3-minute playlet called "Proserpina and the Devil" for Marionettes. And a "Masque of the Bright Haired" for the Red Headed Club = "Order of the Golden Fleece" they call themselves.[150] I shall send this Masque to Percy MacKaye since it is his line—reminding him of the ridiculous urchin during the rehearsals of Antigone.[151]

I have collaborated with Miss Marion Tyler the brightest and most charming girl in College (slim and great dark eyes with quaint embroidered things on her dark dresses; shy but vivid.) in writing two essays and a one-act play for the market. I supply some purple patches and general ideas, she adds some more ideas and reduces the whole to structure. One of these is a curious mystico-religious fantasy, the other, called "Stones at Nell Gwyn" is a defense of Nell and Catullus and Earnest Dowson and Villon etc—that kind of person! The Play is for the Washington Square Players and is unique. It is about the China coast![152]

Lots of Love
Thornton.

---

150 An undated manuscript of "The Masque of the Bright Haired" is in the Beinecke Library at Yale University.

151 American dramatist and poet Percy MacKaye (1875–1956) assisted on the production of Sophocles' *Antigone* that ran at the Greek Theatre in Berkeley during the summer of 1910; TNW also attended a performance of MacKaye's *Anti-Matrimony* (1910) that same summer.

152 "Stones at Nell Gwynn" has not survived. Gaius Valerius Catullus was a Roman lyric poet. Ernest Dowson (1867–1900) was an English poet. François Villon is considered the greatest French poet of the late Middle Ages. The Washington Square Players was founded in 1914 as an alternative to the commercial Broadway theater; when the group disbanded in 1918, its leading members went on to form the Theatre Guild in 1919.

Mention me regularly to Janet; speak cheer of me to Father; let Isabel think me not unromantic; bless me when the westerly wind blows.

42. TO AMOS P. WILDER. ALS 4 pp. Yale

Men's Bldg, Oberlin, O.
<Fall(?) 1916>

Dear Papa,

I received your money. $16 of it will have to go out immediately in Room-rent. With the $4 which I have now I imagine I can last 'til the new year. You have a way of not being open about money matters that is perfectly harrowing for us. With great solemnity you hope that we can do the college year under $550 and then express delight that we were able to; of course you didn't expect we could. You ask me to get a coat between sixteen and eighteen dollars, but in your heart of hearts you expect it will be twenty-two. Just because Amos and I have been so minutely brought up we comply to the letter when our whole life and thought would be happier if we could feel proud of working out our own economies on our own money. Money and money-matters will be the last end of our family anyway. Poor mother has almost been robbed of her mind by worry over money; she can get so wrought up over the price of a pair of shoes that she is intellectually nil for a week. You are secretive and furtive about it; you may sometime become suspicious and injured. I hate to ask for money or talk about it, and so I drag on for weeks without soap or equally absurd details just because I feel that money is such an oppressive difficult thing.

The first thing St. Francis of Assisi thought about was poverty. When he changed from his old life to the new he ran naked out of his father's house. A lovely girl at about the time of the reformation had mystical visions and was in terror of the integrity of her soul because her parents were forcing a distasteful marriage upon her. So she planned to run away. She took up a penny saying "This will buy me bread at noonday." But she felt hindered as she ran. At last she threw it away and was happy. When money grips you at the throat the only thing to do is to read these old stories. We cannot give up everything for the comforts of poverty in our home We have been so settled in respectability. You must retain "position", mother must retain "appearance" and at college we must "appear well." The position of a farmer is only happy in this way. But not today. He must send his daughter to school; his sense of emulation pushes him to vie with the passersby. Besides no farmer ever recognized himself that he had at hand opportunities for a perfect spiritual life; they long to take on the cares we trudge about with. A missionary in chinese clothes in remotest Szechuen province is the free-est state I can imagine. But very likely his religious beliefs there are anything, but spiritual. They are full of the ten commandments, and the Christian austerities.

When you say with your sober manner "I hope that no Wilder will fail in class" you are saying more than you feel again. You were surprised that I did not fail last year. You honestly expected it. How much happier and free-er it would be for me if I only had to live up to what you really expected, instead of what you professed. I suppose I should be thankful that you're not as demanding and exacting as you sometimes sound. You like to make little German drives against chance evidences of impracticality that I leave around, but you know that if I weren't that way I wouldn't love you with the kind of love I love you with. I don't love you with a patriarchal bond like Amos, or like a rebel, secretly in eternal debt to your patience, like Charlotte or Isabel's shy acknowledgement of your felicity in talking to her best nature. I don't know how I do love you, but I know the edges of the ocean, the impatience with your solicitousness, your overemphasis of the rigid necessity of being moral and "good"; when there's really such licence allowed to personality to do honorably such unspeakably un-moral things. Now do confess that to be glad and aspiring and intimate makes "being a Christian" and doing one's iron duty and "weeping over the unsaved" negligable. So don't ask me to pass all my classes; cultivate oneself like a rose-tree and poverty—the end—will burn you in the end with the greater trees—But you were a rose-tree. Well its probably not clear, but never mind. Its well meant

Thornton

43. TO AMOS P. WILDER. ALS 4 pp. Yale

Oberlin O—
Jan 11, <19>'17.

Dear Papa,

You are often urging me to devote myself to my studies, but you do not say how far. Beyond a certain point I could gain nothing by close study. What I won in discipline would be balanced by what I lost in "integrity of temperament." There are higher goods in pursuits consistent to oneself than in reaping iron flowers in a foreign field. Should I by a (hypothetical) self-control force myself after hours of work into a student I should be like those whom Pascal describes as going to Mass, and going to Mass, until they at last find themselves Christians, "making animals of themselves."[153] ¶ I do not pretend yet to have reached the point where the equilibrium of gain through discipline and loss through integrity balances itself, but I have at times overleaped it, and been wretched.

Why we should go to College at this time of our life it is hard to see. Our minds are in a ferment; we cannot realize an idea; or imagine a conviction. Art, sex and religion are driving us mad, and time or mood for reflection we have none. There are long periods, sometimes a whole week when I am so miserable because I cannot think of a beautiful thing to write that I seem to <be> beating my head in despair again<st> a stone wall. Sometimes when the din and voices of these years of my life become too insistent, I say:

"Come, I'll stop all this. I'll not try to answer anything, or right anything or aspire <to> anything. I will be an ordinary boy; I will eat and study and wash and be full of polite attentions to other people. Then after a few months I will come back to this inner room, and perhaps I being older can put it in order."

But within a few hours something has happened: someone has spoken, or glanced or snow has fallen and I am up in the air again.

---

153 In his *Pensées* (1670), Blaise Pascal contended that reason was insufficient to solve man's dilemmas and satisfy his longings.

I cannot tell whether I suffer from this restlessness more than other boys or not. We all conceal it, and from our parents first of all. But College is not an answer to it—not Oberlin with its fat Christian optimism.

I want either to go to Harvard next year where life is handled in the idiom of art instead of YMCA. I am sick of Affirmations.

Or else I want to go and live on Monhegan. Even during the winter. Perhaps a year until all this fever is over, and I have grown up, or grown stiff or whatever it is that allows one to accept the world, and be content with a life of Houses and dinners lived on a life of Dreams and Cries. Why should there be such a tremendous and pressing apparatus of Bricks and Vegetables and Clothes and Calling-Cards on what they insist is a life only for the Spirit?

Lovingly
Thornton

44. TO ISABEL WILDER. ALS 4 pp. Yale

Men's Building Oberlin O
Jan 11 <19>17

Dear Isabel,

I hear that you are becoming reconciled to N.H.H.S.[154] and see that your letters are improving. There is a very nice man here who taught in a summer-camp where some boys from your school were staying. He said that some were all right, but that there were others he couldn't say much for. So look sharp, petite, and carry your own books. The girl who insists on carrying her own books will surprise the boys who like a girl to be surprising. You avoid too that akward moment when he piles them back into your arms. Even if he is nice about it.

There is a greater difference between High School and Grammar

154 Isabel attended New Haven High School in 1916–1917, after having applied too late to be admitted to Northfield Seminary in Massachusetts.

School than between High School and College. You would enjoy being in one of these girls' Dormitories like Dascomb, but you would hate some of the rules such as all Freshman girls must be in their rooms by 7:30.

So Mother is going to New York. So father casually noted tho why the lady or yourself did not mention the Why and When I cannot imagine. Whenever any of the family want to go to New York and there are any slight chances of their going to the theatre I want them to ask my advice. I know altogether too much about what is going on at the New York Theatres as it is, but since I have the knowledge I want to put it to some use if I can and prevent such awful mistakes as Amos going to see "Hush" when there were such stunning thing<s> as "Pierrot the Prodigal" and "The Yellow Jacket" in town. Tell Mother to go to either "A Kiss for Cinderella" or "Shirley Kaye" with Elsie Ferguson or Nazimona <appeared in the left margin> **or Getting Married of Shaw** and to send the Bill to me; and I'll abstain from shoestrings and clean linen in order to pay it.[155] Tell her too that she must for this send me an exact account of the whole performance. But if she goes to "Turn to the Right" or "Cheating Cheaters" or "Nothing But the Truth" let her never see a footlight again.[156]

And you, Isabel, might even ask my advice about the movies because for Wilders to spend a dime and be disappointed is a crime, when there is a censor of censors born right in the family

Lovingly,
Thornton.

155 *Hush!*, by Violet Pearn, ran in October and November 1916; *Pierrot the Prodigal*, with music by André Wormser and book by Michel Carré, ran between September 1916 and January 1917; *The Yellow Jacket*, by George C. Hazelton and J. Harry Benrimo, ran in 1916–1917; *A Kiss for Cinderella*, by J. M. Barrie, ran between December 1916 and May 1917; *Shirley Kaye*, by Hurlbert Footner, ran between December 1916 and March 1917; *Getting Married*, by George Bernard Shaw, ran between November 1916 and February 1917. Russian actress Alla Nazimova (1879–1945) appeared in *'Ception Shoals*, by H. Austin Adams; the play ran in early 1917.

156 *Turn to the Right*, by John E. Hazzard and Winchell Smith, ran between August 1916 and September 1917; *Cheating Cheaters*, by Max Marcin, ran between August 1916 and April 1917; *Nothing But the Truth*, by James Montgomery, ran between September 1916 and July 1917.

45. TO AMOS P. WILDER. ALS 4 pp Yale

Feb. 14—<19>17
Men's Bldg. Oberlin.

Dear Papa,

I want to go away to Italy but not to relieve suffering—tho' while I am there by all means let me do it.

—not to see pictures and Classical landscapes

—not to get away from the uninspired complacency of Oberlin.

Let me go to have some time to myself. Not just a day, or a week-end, or a week—but half a year.

There always seems to be a thot waiting for me to find it out, just around the corner of my mind.

And I know that when I have dropped the net I both hold and am held by, that I can dig out a most lovely play or story. Everything I have done so far has had to be turned out during other things. Let me have liesure to examine the thing fully, (as I had in part during the "Tragedy" in my one week! at Monhegan) and I will give you something which <will> not only cheer you by it's achievement but not vex you by its imperfections.

Barrie brings forth a major work every three years! A student could not hammer at a thing for three years; he is too feverish about getting his thing before his teachers, father's or judge's eye. He lets it go by unbrushed. He'd rather receive acknowledgement for its promise that <than> lurk without appreciation in the hope of finally submitting an unquestionable achievement.

A person like me has got to keep writing things or it irks us to pain; when we think we have written a good thing we feel as tho' it had justified our existance and we don't know what "plain people" satisfy that self-demand with.

Make a business arrangement with me. Give me three or four months on Monhegan, or a year alone somewhere, and I will give you something final and convincing.

And yet I do not need your faith in me. I know by what Catholics call their "vocation" that I can now, with time, "trespass among superlatives." This elation and confidence follows the completion of "The Little Turtle a play in five scenes"[157] brooded upon for years, but written in a month of chemistry lessons; imperfect and skimpy to the point of tears; but authentic in parts and in birds-eye view as an axe

T.N.W. Letter to follow.

46. TO ISABELLA N. WILDER. ALS 5 pp. Yale

Men's Bldg.
March 14 <1917>

Dear Mother,

I can write you a letter (now that the appraising eyes are in Chicago),[158] as full of everyday small-talk as ordinary common speech is.

Besides you are home alone and the empty mail-box has a hollower ring.

I have at last read "Ghosts." This does not mean that your influence over me has at last totally dissapeared. It only means that I imagine you as giving me your consent, since our Classics in Translation class is about to read Oedipus Rex. Oedipus makes Oswald sweet and sane in comparison! Besides I'm reading "Evelyn Innes"[159] and after that there is no pathology. I confess to being a little disgusted with "Evelyn," but I must go on. George Moore and I are twin-knit. We are what—before they found a better term—were called Affinities by the Movie-makers.

George Moore spends half of his time—the better half—dropping aphorisms, reflections and phrases; and they so suit me that I cannot

---

157 This play has not survived.

158 TNW is probably referring to his father here.

159 Novel (1898) by Irish writer George Moore.

miss any one in the most obscure of his books. Besides his tone! his mood!

When I told Granville Barker that our mutual friend Rudolph <Rudolf> Kommer (of Monhegan) was collaborating with George Moore on a play, Mr. Barker smiled wryly—"I'm about the only person he hasn't collaborated with," he said. And the quaint impudent personality of George M. was reflected in his eyes and smile.

You remember that the only other author who has engrossed me this way is Barrie. And always will. But the side issue with George Moore, his interest in the forms and spirit of the Catholic Church and his Cadence—his great contribution to the English sentence borrowed by him from the Anglo-irish, intrigue me as greatly as do the stage-direction of the Scotsman.

You will be appalled to hear that I am preparing two of the "Affairs of Anatol"[160] for local benefit performance. Fear not, I will brush away the highest flashes of sophistication and no one need ever know more than that a charming man happened for a quarter-of-an-hour to share the umbrella of Mrs. Gabrielle Somebody on Christmas in Vienna. There they stood, witty and whimsically tender, and then she goes off saying that she might have been happy with him and sending her greetings to her sucessor. The things would seem ridiculously inconsequential and rubbishy if we did not have four sensitive actors who could at least approach the wit and irony of the perfect things.

I got into a little difficulty yesterday. I take a nice interest in two High school boys who are literarily inclined and yesterday one of them came to me and asked me whether I could go up to Cleveland to see Leo Dietrichstein[161] or not. I said that I had better not; I had been up so often (four times) and I always felt as tho' I were taking the clothes off my family's back . . . etc. Oh, he said, he would provide the tickets. I had never heard of such a thing. I laughed and said that if we went at

160 In his play *Anatol* (1893), Austrian dramatist Arthur Schnitzler depicted the amorous escapades of a Casanova-like adventurer who goes from one woman to another.

161 Hungarian-born American actor and dramatist Leo James Dietrichstein (1864–1928).

all we had better be democratic with it. I walked down the hall with my arm around his shoulder, and pleasantly repeated the democracy of it. When I spoke to Mr. Carr he said it was perfectly proper and accepted for one boy to go as the guest of another, and that I'd probably hurt Baird's feelings. Mr. Wager said of course it was perfectly natural and that I should have thanked him and gone. "But" I said ruefully "I never heard of it before." "Oh" said Mr. Wager disappearing behind a door, "There are lots of things you've never heard of."

So I'm in a fix.

And mind you, lady, I lay it at your door. You with your money-obsession brought us up to feel continually self-conscious about the transfer of coin... you have made us desperately afraid of putting ourselves under obligations to anyone.... we seem no longer able to tell when a person is trying to be kind to us... we suspect them of endeavoring to put us at a disadvantage.

And the moral is: Never think about the dirty shining pieces. Fret not yourselves with bills and loans

Etc. Etc.

Love
Thornton.

47. TO AMOS P. WILDER. ALS 4 pp. Yale

The Square Tower
The First Day of Spring
The Third Year of the War.
<March 21(?), 1917>

Dear Papa,

and I am tired again tonight. A long day, full of a hundred distressing interruptions: today I have wished to contemplate peace and religious repose, as the sun with constancy contemplates the tender earth.

Two dull classes: Miss Fitch on Evidences of Gnosticism in the Letters to Collossae; Harold King on Wages.

An organ lesson wherein I play my first hymn "Holy Holy Holy" and am introduced to rules governing the repitition of notes.

I write some rhymed jokes for the College annual.

I go to Laboratory and fail to get results from some dismal experiments with Antimony and Bismuth. But the errant gases from sixty students' experiments pass through my dried and coated lungs.

Then to rehearsal of the French Play. I remember myself as merry there, but there was no reason for it that I remember, so we must have been fools together.

Through all of this I was waiting for the dark. When people are tired in the day the thought of dusk is present in the back of their mind, not only because it brings sleep, but because it hides one face in the shadow. A tired person is a wounded person, and his eyes are his wounds;—to them night brings a balsam.

Tonight I had to deliver bills for the College annual—to the Assistant Business Managership of which my class in compliment elected me. So I took a long, wandering walk, as I went dropping envelopes onto the mail-tables of the boarding-houses. I have enjoyed the walk. In the streets is the smell of leaves burning, whence I know not. It is one of the things Rupert Brooke mentioned as loving:

"These I have loved:
    White plates and cup, clean-gleaming
..... Wet roofs<,> beneath the lamplight; the strong crust
Of friendly bread; and many-tasting food;
Rainbows; and the blue bitter smoke of wood.<...>"[162]

And as I went along I thought of your beautiful letter to me, as good as any letter I ever received. I do not think it a less spirit in me to say that perhaps I liked it partly because you spoke well of my letters, in turn. There are two insidious ghosts in our family and this exorcised one of them away; we in our way are not abundantly generous to one another—think us all over in turn—we are a grudging family. And

162 The lines are from "The Great Lover" (1914) by Rupert Brooke, who was killed during World War I.

now let me take another shoo at the other ghost—the fear of poverty, abject.

But we all seven of us are so splendid individually (we are more like a case of blue weapons than a flower-bed) that it would be presumptious to as<k> for a sweetest<sweeter?> ensemble. If we were a sober, New England, around-the-lamp, co-praying family I insist, we should be less. Amos would be more docile; I less modern, Charlotte less promising, Isabel less vivid, Janet more sophisticated, Mother less concentrated<.> You more demand-ative. We should be cut into pieces.

Love Thornton.

48. TO AMOS P., ISABELLA N., ISABEL, AND JANET F. WILDER. ALS 2 pp. Yale

Men's Bldg
April 10—<19>17

Dear Family—

We begin drilling tomorrow.[163] All the honorary trustees of the College have been using their influence to try and secure us an Army officer for instruction, but they cannot obtain one, so we begin under some Seminary men who took four years of such training in the U. of Missouri. We are to combine Theory and Practice in three hours a week, and add to it extra marches and field-excursions. We have begun study in the little Government handbook. Only four boys in the whole College have enlisted, (one my friend Hankinson for the Navy)—and Those Who Know advise us to begin this work. Those who enlist now will be put in Concentration camps with the hoi poloi, whereas College boys, (with this advance we will make by June) will be recommended for non-commissioned officerships. It doesn't seem to me

163 Oberlin, like many American colleges and universities, had begun military instruction on their campus when it became increasingly clear that the United States would enter the war in Europe.

to much matter whether one learns with their hoi-poloi now—I suspect its a survival of Eligance. ¶ This is to say that I have to buy a pair of shoes tomorrow. Trust me! I buy nothing without counting a hundred.

This drilling does not mean that I have committed myself to enlistment. I have committed myself to something severe in the physical way—I should smile. It seems to me now that I must go. Putting aside that odd insistant self-ridicule that I am not meant for this: not made of remotely heroic grain, a mere wisp whom the first shock will shrivle to a cinder; putting aside to<o> the feeling of responsibility and bewildered solicitation for my Little Gift; putting aside, as I can most of the time, the feeling that the issues for an American are not great enough to risk everything for. The only way I see going is for what it can do to me in sudden maturing, completing; and what it can do to put greatness into my Little Gift. From such sights and sounds; and from the conviction that I am suffering for great ends I will come or live long enough—deo certe volente[164]—to leave a great little thing somewhere. Other<s> fight for their country or for their sheer love of great action, but the artist is the great egoist, and counts the world well lost for one created perfect thing

Love-in-a-hurry- Thornton

49. TO ELIZABETH LEWIS NIVEN. ALS 4 pp. Yale

The Men's Building,
Oberlin, Ohio
April 29, 1917.

Dear Grandmother,

This month—stirring, exciting month, tho' it is!—shall not go by without my thanking you warmly for your remembrance. At this

164 Latin: God willing certainly.

time when we young men are being commissioned to represent the whole country, we begin individually to feel the joy in relatives and family, the solid background to our perplexities. So now in addition to my personal love for you, you may feel my veneration for you as my Tradition.

What is being planned for me? I do not know. Perhaps in two or three weeks the machinery of conscription will be set in order and I will be tested and examined. It is likely that they will not consider my eyesight good enough to "fix" a spikéd helmet at twenty yards. But if I am passed I think by that time I will be reconciled to the soldier's life. In my funny, sensitive way of being distressed and despairing over my life and my fitness, I am always at odds with life; I am a personality perculiarly isolated. And to me in my dark (and true) mood the simplification of a soldier's life—the reducing of the jangling wires to an orderly routine—offers sweet compensations. But let no one mistake my acquiesence with the positive fire of patriotism.

Perhaps Father will soon put me on a farm. Seventy boys have left College already (with credit for College work given them) to "serve the agricultural need of their country and their countries' allies." Another thirty has enlisted in the Mosquito Fleet, a subdivision of the U.S.N.[165] Gradually the Male Student Body is breaking up—or rather petering out. A dozen boys leave every day. I had better try a farm until the Gov[nt] ferrets me out.

In reality I am not as upset and excited over all this as I should be. I suppose I am built along the lines of The Artistic Temperament (Oh, perilous sea!) and for such the stress and tossings of wars, domestic and national, can be shut out as secondary to the process you so charmingly referred to as "my catching of wild ducks." To slay or be slain in battle will always be of less consequence than the turning of an expressive phrase; and one story achieved is more satisfying than the taking of a strong city.

So I go doggedly about my peculiar life, at variance with other

---

165 On April 2, 1917, the U.S. government had signed contracts to begin construction of over three hundred torpedo boats to be used in detecting and chasing enemy submarines. Their tonnage restricted the size of the crew and necessitated the use of as much automatic equipment as possible.

peoples ideas as to how I should live and yet not conforming to my own—but thankful and grateful for tokens and kind wishes from you

Your loving grandson
Thornton.

50. TO RUTH KELLER. ALS 3 pp. Private

Mens Building Oberlin,
May—about the 8th or 9th <1917>

Dear Ruth,

I can't understand your card. It sounds snappish. As though perhaps you were doubting my sincerity in wishing you back to see me. "Ah, Seraphina, you do me wrong."

I suppose you want a frank statement of what you (so distressingly) call the-person-who-would-not-demand-too-much-attention who succeeded you, I will furnish it. Miss Nina Trego[166] and I—(I began the sentence wrong.)

I am often found plaguing and worrying the life out of Miss Nina Trego. Our conversations consist of that same sharp commentary on passing events that I enjoyed so with you; and our friendship takes place on the same high, independent, Platonic plane. But I am often reminded by contrast that compared to you she is merely clever and sharp-tongued; whereas you were more human, and something of a philosopher too.

Now, Ruth, treat me straight. Perhaps soon you will write me a letter offering me up to my country, closing characteristically enough—for I first came to know you thru Latin poetry.

"Dulce et decorum est pro patria mori."[167] I irresistably think of you on Sunday morning, but no other Senior girl ever dares to take

166 Trego (1893–1932) graduated from Oberlin in 1917 and was a close friend and literary confidante of TNW.

167 Latin: It is sweet and fitting to die for one's country.

Nina Trego.

TNW at Oberlin.

walks with me then. You and I were unique in a delightful way—we were like characters of a mock-heroic novel, touched with fantasy. I will besides always remember the tea-room in connection with you

Afftly
Thornton.

51. TO AMOS P. WILDER. ALS 4 pp. Yale

<Oberlin, Ohio>
May 10 <1917>

Dear Papa—

This receiving of two letters a day is very brightening and encouraging. It gives me the thrilling impression that you are doing nothing all day but stoke the furnace of my interests. But there are two kinds of coal that are impractical as fuel:

① I could never take the Yale entrance exams in the subjects I have covered in the last three years. Tutors and thumbscrews could not effect. You and I have a tacit agreement, a common law, that I am not in College to learn any subject per se except English and Languages; that Chemistry, Economics, Civics, Botany have been only the pegs on which to hang the COATS of spiritual qualities: Persistance, fidelity etc. The pegs have lost all individuality—they are cold steel to me.

If I must be examined in the virtues—let my literary work be scanned.

Imagine giving me an examination in Botany or even special textbooks in German. Assiduous study avails nothing then or now.

---

② I do not want to go to Yale. My aims in life lie clearer before me everyday; they reach me every day as the complaints of the Engineer float up to the Captains deck from the hidden energies.

One is that there is no conviction stronger in me that<than> when I sit under Prof. Wager "it is good for me to be there." I might say of him what he says in his only revealed poem—from Atlantic Monthly—"the thought that runs along thy brain is mine." The situation (paradoxical enough) is simplified by the fact that he is not particularly fond of me. He likes the great, boyish, naive, accepting boys, and I am odd, over-learnèd, distressed and adrift, but ruddered by my own conceit. So I remain no less fond of him than ever but with a subdued deference that is not satisfying, but is best for what I really want. I have been attending two of his classes regularly now; one just finishing Cardinal Newman,[168] and now the other on Dante. When I consider what I know of Phelps and Tinker, Copeland and Baker[169] I admit they may be brilliant and literary but they have not got that spiritual almost ascetic magnetism of Mr. Wager. His great background of St. Francis Literature and the Newman, Erasmus and St. Augustine periods are always making themself felt. If you can find me another mystic

168 English churchman and author John Henry Newman (1801–1890) resigned his position in the Church of England, converted to Catholicism, and was made a cardinal in 1879.

169 William Lyon Phelps and Chauncey Brewster Tinker were leading faculty members at Yale University at this time, while Charles Townsend Copeland and George Pierce Baker held similar positions at Harvard University.

for my Gameliel[170] I will come but better I live in an ordinary routine College and Mr. Wager than in a World-famous University without him. Albeit if you hear well of some Catholic college I will discuss that seriously. I think that after all I am an acutely religious temperament and that beside it nothing else matters.

I have reconciled myself to staying here and going to Berea.[171] If my age is drafted I shall acclaim its compensations since nihil humanum me alienum puto—[172]

Love Thorny.

52. TO AMOS P. WILDER. ALS 4 pp. Yale

<Oberlin, Ohio>
May 15 <1917> Wednesday

Dear Papa,

I have received the beautiful the supreme letter, and the check for twenty. You have referred to me as noisily expressing my love to you; it is what I have so often intended to do and never felt that it was reaching you with sufficient intensity; there is that ignoble restraint that civilization and middle youth brings that ties me tongue before it has spoken the heart's pourings. If I loved you less I could find it in my conscience to express it more showily; but you must gather my depth from the short declarations and stray hints that I leave lying about. If you are soon in New York you will see the case put on the Empire Theatre stage in a one-act by my Sir James Barrie.[173] A boy before leav-

170 Highly respected rabbi with whom the apostle Paul studied.

171 TNW's father had arranged for his son to spend part of the summer of 1917 working and taking a class in typing at Berea College in Kentucky.

172 Latin: I consider nothing human foreign to me.

173 *The New Word* (1915) ran in New York between May and June 1917; it appeared on a bill with two other Barrie one-acts, *Old Friends* (1910) and *The Old Lady Shows Her Medals* (1917), the latter of which also dealt with the war.

ing for the trenches comes in his khakis to say goodbye to his father. They have been tongue-tied all their lives but in this last moment they arrive at a new understanding. It is a wonderful, touching, dialogue, and an example of the greater Barrie; the same performance contains another little warplay even greater, of a wonderful pathos and tenderness, but not concerned with the subject of this paragraph.

You ask me where I got a quotation in my letter, and quote: "until he reached a place of considerable comfort." I do not remember seeking aid elsewhere, in that letter, altho I remember dimly taking down from the shelf for a previous letter. If not too much trouble please copy out the passage in full and send back. Be gorry perhaps I said something and unconscious too. Please be frank and send it me. The only context I imagine it in is where Dr. Donne began to recieve livings and deaneries, like plums falling into his lap.[174]

I try to assure that since I saw myself in one illumined and flaring hour as a soldier, I have taken pains to read the most elevated literature. The sermons of Newman, three dialogues of Plato, "Macbeth<,>" St. Augustine (unsuccesful). Ike Marvel[175] long ago proved too mellow and unarroused for me; there is no mood more distasteful to me than the regrets and pipe-dreams of a reminiscent bachelor. Perhaps when I am older. At present I am ordering a golden trumpet from the forge, built on designs of those in the lower circles of Paradise; not shrill however but persuasive of those sempiternal lawns and the pulsating radiance that bathes them. ie legands of the saints in bliss shall be my theme, and the manner in which they gloriously won that desired rest.

Thornton

---

174 Among the honors John Donne received toward the end of his life was being named dean of St. Paul's Cathedral in 1621.

175 Ik Marvel was the pen name of American essayist and novelist Donald Grant Mitchell (1822–1908); he was best known for his books of sentimental essays, *Reveries of a Bachelor* (1850) and *Dream Life: A Fable of the Seasons* (1851).

53. TO AMOS N. WILDER. ALS 4 pp. Yale

Men's Bldg—
Oberlin, O.
May 26—<19>17

<appeared perpendicularly above salutation>
I drilled for 2 hours this afternoon. Corporal again. Send me a photo of you in kahki. Some very nice Oberlin boys coming out to you. I am associate Editor of Hi-O-Hi; want to resign.[176] Monday night I appear in Dramatic Assoc. play. The Poet in Lord Dunsany's one act The Lost Silk Hat.[177] Chem class visited grand Lorain steel plant yesterday. Am I going to get thru Chemistry? Lots of love

T.

Dear Amos,

I got your beautiful letter ten minutes ago and hurry to go over it with you.

All the fever about my going into the army has passed—there were moments perhaps hours when it seemed to me the perfect thing for me to do—but with the news that the Registration age is from 21–30, the fever has passed with the necessity. For the present Fathers plans carry. For seven weeks beginning about June 7 I go to work on <a> farm at Berea College, Ky, among the Mountain Whites. It will be hard but I face it this year with a new motive, and with some anxiety about Father. Our domestic life approaches the piteous. But I would not allow blame to be thrown on Mother—her undemonstrative temperament wreaks greater havoc than she knows; but what eats at the happiness of them both is their preoccupation with money and economy. They admire the generous mind that refuses to harbor prying

176 *Hi-O-Hi* was the student yearbook at Oberlin.

177 Play (1914) by Irish dramatist and poet Edward John Moreton Drax Plunkett (1878–1957), the eighteenth baron of Dunsany.

obsessions, but about their own souls stalk wolves and lynxes! Neither of them will age prematurely for all their cares, but when they do it will be unwillingly—no acquiescence.

Oh, to be with you in the Lake country, or to have you with me on Monhegan.[178] But most I would like to have you here now—tho, more to myself than your return to Oberlin would really allow—among the little waves of this cove. Perhaps it is with the thought I may not come back next year that I look upon Oberlin now as a forest of paths I have not ventured: the friendships I have omitted to seek out, the experiences I have failed to fling myself into, the habits I have avoided forming. Noble boys like John Allen, the runner Fall, Farquhar, men like Prof. C. B. Martin and Ian Hannah.

Will I find a compensating variety at Harvard or Yale for these few unworked mines?

Your religious self-examination I cannot duplicate. I am a less conscientious nature and do not examine my faith. I fling myself upon my knees as though at a divine compulsion, mostly when I am happy, tho also in extremis. I am happiest in loving and being loved by human people and next to that in writing words and being commended for them, and next to that in mysteries of the spirit, into which I penetrate I believe more every year, until perhaps God will be my whole life. I suppose that everyone feels that his nature cries out hourly for it knows not what, but I like to believe that mine raises an exceeding great voice because I am a twin, and because by his death an outlet for my affection was closed. It is not affection alone but energy and in it I live and because of it I believe I seem to see life as more vivid, electric and marvelous than others so placidly do. I am continually surprised at people's lukewarmness; I am perpetually enthusiastic over some composition or book, some person or some friend.

I thank you for the photos. I thank you for your assurance of "backing me up" in my ideas on fighting; the issue may yet rise to face me. It will never confront you, will it, who have your duty marked? In war one says that the lives of young men are on the knees of God and

---

178 After serving for three months as an ambulance driver in the Argonne region, TNW's brother began a seven-day leave on May 16, 1917, visiting London and England's Lake District.

that only such bullets as he permits ever strike the human heart. [Alas, those times when one thinks one is on the verge of a new thought and then sees that it <is> nothing but an old platitude!]

I am glad you received my letter, and more glad to receive yours—always in love

Your loving brother
Thornton.

54. TO AMOS P., ISABELLA N., ISABEL, AND JANET F. WILDER. ALS 4 pp. Yale

Men's Bldg Oberlin O
June 3—<19>17

Dear Family,

This is my last Sunday in Oberlin, perhaps for a long time? A mixture of leaves overburdened with sunlight and of blue, benignantly threatening clouds. As I leave Oberlin I do not find myself regretting my commissions so much as my ommissions. I hear father telling me that I should groan for the evasions I have learnt, the sidestepping of duties through which others have had to plow, but I don't—I justify them completely to myself. But I regret intensely acquaintanceships I have not made, and friendships I have not improved. There are three names that seem to call me back to Oberlin as much as imagined openings beckon me elsewhere. The brown study, Prof Martin darkened but not embittered, whose wife is my Tante. We not only have much in common—which is not necessary anyway—but we appeal imaginatively to one-another, for I have been told <a> remark he has let drop about me. And he likes nothing better than to read aloud with some one which is dearer to me than solitude itself. Then there is Farquhar, the great runner, a kind of gaunt intense boy, all silence and awareness.

Then there is Katharine Hubbard, Fra Elbertus'[179] daughter, by an early alliance, an excellent performer on the piano and a wonderfully vivid girl, and pretty as a mermaid and as fresh and strange. I know all three of these a little, but I have neither laid siege to their confidence as I have with so many—for in friendships it seems I have always to take the initiative, seldom being myself pursued—. On the other hand I have known intimately Mr. Wager, Walter Smith and Nina Trego and last year Harold Spore, Theordore Wilder and Ruth Kellar.

How many times, after making a new acquaintance I have said: now I know all that are in this village, between whom and myself an acquaintance would prove valuable. And before evening new personalities suddenly strike me as necessary to my human education and I go out to find.

All this curiosity has taught me a hundred tricks of getting to know people, of fastening on them, accidental-like, and of making them say things illuminative of themselves. I have developed a kind of conversation method of insisting on saying sudden significant things in order to bring others to contributing sudden significant things, and becoming restless unless the conversation darkens with revelation. It is like drama, in which the dialogue must for always be throwing light before or behind and at the same time be searching itself.

This is not to give the idea that what I want is earnestness and starting tears; anything will do for me—the atmosphere of the other person's homelife, his interest in electricity, her opinion of X,—no I can't explain what I want but I recognize it when it comes and quiet myself like a child at a fairy story. Enclosed find picture of Nina. I received suitcase. Leave for Berea next Friday morning

Thornton

179 American editor, publisher, and writer Elbert Hubbard (1856–1915) was known as "Fra Albertus." He is best known for founding the Roycroft Community in East Aurora, New York. Roycroft, established in 1895, was an important part of the American Arts and Crafts movement. Katherine Hubbard, born in 1895, was one of the children born to Hubbard and his first wife, Bertha.

55. TO WILLIAM GOODELL FROST.[180] ALS 1 p. Berea

Men's Building, Oberlin, O.
June 10, 1917.

Rev. Wm. Goodell Frost
Berea College, Ky.

Dear Dr. Frost,

My father writes that he has arranged for me to work at Berea College during the summer. I am looking forward to the experience and have been much interested in the catalog. I hope that my comparative lack of experience will give the minimum of trouble.

Unless I hear that it is inconvenient to you I intend to arrive at Berea on Friday afternoon, June 15. Thanking you for the opportunity your kindness has extended, I remain

Sincerely yours,
Thornton N. Wilder

56. TO AMOS P. WILDER. ALS 4 pp. Yale

c/o Berea College
Berea Ky.
July 1 1917

Dear Papa,

Thank you for the ten dollars. Five of it are gone for tuition. I hoped less but one can't be surprised at that for seven weeks @ $2\frac{1}{2}$ hours a day. The teacher is really very good and walks around under the name of Livengood. Then one and eighteen cents when<went> to pay for two little textbooks of business letters etc. I will probably not want more for a great while now that I've bought me a straw brimmy hat and have raked out some more old trousers.

---

180 Frost, who had been a professor of Greek at Oberlin College from 1876 to 1892, was now president of Berea College.

I was sick for four days, but except for one of them went on with my work. They had put us into the room next to the washroom and we found that the hot pipes went the whole length of one wall and acted in the nature of steam heat day and night. The room was hot just as an oven is hot. I carried the thing to Mr. Trosper, our dormitory monitor, who promised to see about it, but he kept delaying. He's one of these persons who believe that the most forgivable excuse in the world is to say "Now frankly I tell you: it clean went out of my mind." I kept pegging at him and extracting nothing but hearty promises; and all the times my headaches and perspiration baths continued. At last I jumped to the official beyond him one step and now we have a new room, cool as a cellar.

The custom with farmers around here is to work until eleven and then lay off until two-thirty, but we poor drudges leave the farmhouse after twelve and are back and started before one. The heat in the fields is often intense and I am almost broken up by it, until the later clouds sail before the sun.

The stupidity and primitiveness of my roommate drives me to tears of vexation. He brought here no change of clothes for himself, and he so wide-eyed envies me everything I have that I have been driven to lend him some pieces of my delicate finery that will be hard to ask back from him. He never saw light union suit underwear before and gasps at the price of it. He is as vain in the suit I lent him as a girl with a feather. He takes a bath just so the boys can see the slim whiteness of it as he comes and goes in the hall.

Thanks for the Ole Virginia days.[181] I will get to them soon. I am now on Froude's Life and Letters of Erasmus, that Mr. Wager brought to my attention.

I have given some of my new and lighter MSS to Mrs. Embree[182] to read for fun. What can she find to keep her aware in Berea. You will be interested in the Pres. Frostiana I have collected. As one remarked in Berea: Its the first time I was ever in a real Oligarchy.

I'm learning more Ira Sankey Hymns than I ever learnt even in

---

181 TNW may be referring to *In Ole Virginia* (1887), a book of short stories by Thomas Nelson Page (1853–1922).

182 Etta Parsons Embree (1882–1962), the wife of a Berea trustee.

Mount Hermon.[183] The Mountain Peop<l>e are a vague element and I don't know whether I have laid hold of it or not. There is certainly nothing of Lincoln around here. Perhaps they are all asleep with hookworm—Like my roommate. Explanations are so easy

Lots of love
Thornton

57. TO AMOS N. WILDER. ALS 4 pp. Yale

Mt. Carmel <Connecticut>
Sept. 7 <1917>

Dear Amos

The hateful red-tape of entering College is being unwound around here in order to transfer me to Yale. All the rattling skeletons of the past are being un-graved ie the application blank is being filled out by Thacher, B.H.S. and Oberlin. I have lost all interest in entering Yale or any other College, but Father prophesies that the war will end before next September—which isn't committing himself very much—and then says that all three of us will be seniors at the same time.[184] I don't want to go to College any more and I don't need it. It has come to the place where it positively harms me. And a lot of Papa's money that hes grown to be almost tearful about, is spent in just keeping me mediocrely respectable and all the fidgety apparatus that goes up to make "Mr. Wilder's son—a junior at Yale." I could take half of this gentlemanly money into my own victorious developement if he only let me take a year in strenuous quill-driving about Washington Square, talking til fifty o'clock in the morning with the young blood of American

---

183 Sankey (1840–1908), a gospel singer and composer, was one of the compilers of and contributors to *Gospel Hymns and Sacred Songs* (1875). He composed the music for many hymns. Sankey was closely associated with fellow evangelist Dwight Moody, the founder of Mount Hermon School.

184 Had TNW not repeated his sophomore year when he transferred to Yale and had his brother returned earlier from Europe, the three eldest Wilder children might have graduated from college in 1919.

literature, instead of the corrected and sandpapered etc etc from the prep. schools. But you must have heard invective like this before. With me its à propos because I have an offer from the Cincinnati Little Theatre to join their Repertory Company. Its just that practical experience I need to almost finish me off as dramatist, but the familie won't hear of it.

I am sending you the last copy of your class Oberlin Magazine, with myself representing you.—(with a study in abnormal psychology more suitable to a Pathology museum than a sweet college magazine.) Note the poem by Nina, Trego.[185] I send you also a playlet illustrating the history of religion—(oh no! nothing's too pretentious for me!) in which the whole idea is in the title and the last lines. This playet illustrates the Roman Catholic tendency in me that pains dear Papa so, and Mama too, who has become so full of Theology and metaphysics that I'm afraid of her. Charlotte is typeing some others that illustrate better my dramatic method. This one is only a baby oratorio.[186]

In these war days and with you so intimately engaged, we are ashamed to mention that we went to such-and-such-a movie, or spent a fortnite at such-and-such a seaside place. I wonder how you picture America in wartime anyway?

There are a good many khaki men on the street cars; all the women knit all the time; flags droop to the right and left; everything costs more; and all the nicest young men are wearing silver on their shoulders.

But still loungers smoke on the corners, still young men play tennis on the University courts; and Yale boys with their hair scrupulously parted in the middle drive up in huge cars to the street corner and ride off with wonderful girls in astonishing clothes. And still the Waterbury street car is overcrowded between 2 and 4 P.M.

lovingly for your 22nd Birthday
Thornton aged 20 $\frac{6}{12}$

---

185 TNW's contribution to the June 1917 issue of the *Oberlin Literary Magazine* was a short fictional fable, "The Marriage of Zabett," which dealt with a young woman's struggle to choose between marriage and the call of the church. Nina Trego's poem was titled "Confession."

186 It is unclear to which work TNW is referring here; no work matching this description appears to have survived.

58. TO CHARLES H. A. WAGER. ALS 4 pp. Smith

414 Berkeley Hall
New Haven
Sept. 25 <1917>

Dear Mr. Wager,

This is my first night in my room. I have just come back from seeing Sara<h> Bernhardt. The white stones I lay upon important days are my envelopes to you.

Just before I moved here I read the first part of Sinister Street.[187] It is a wonderful picture of the amenities and atmosphere of Oxford life—(The second part is of course an entirely different matter as The British Censorship said.) And it is with that illustration that I cannot help hunting for resemblances. College does not open until day after tomorrow, but already the boys are coming in. Quite a number of windows are brightly alight in the walls that overhang Berkeley Oval.

I am happy and expectant, but my family is troubled. The entrance-board has sat upon my application and decided that I am a Sophomore. But Dean Jones is a classmate of father's and promises a successful subterfuge.[188]

I saw Bernhardt in the Fourth Act of "Merchant of Venice" and the Last of "Camille." In the former she had that nervous technical proficiency of Mrs. Fiske. That flecking of a point with the hand and the turn of the shoulder; and she smiled and laughed far too much. But Camille was very wonderful. What a great tragic face she has to begin with. And the voice.

I am awaiting minute by minute by<my> roommate that the Authorities will assign to me. Bob Hutchins wrote a splendid letter from the Oberlin Ambulance Unit, regretting that he couldn't be with me.[189]

---

187 *Sinister Street* (1913), a controversial novel by English author Compton MacKenzie.

188 TNW did repeat his sophomore year. Frederick Scheetz Jones was the dean at this time.

189 Robert Maynard Hutchins (1899–1977), whom TNW first met at Oberlin, eventually transferred to Yale, graduated with the class of 1921, attended Yale Law School, of which he became dean in 1927, and then went to the University of Chicago, where he served as president and then chancellor.

Did I tell you that my Mother and I were reading the Fioretti[190] that you gave me, all summer. And that at our Cape Cod hotel I sat next to the Colgate Geology Professor who spoke very highly of you & wanted to be remembered? (I forget his name; what the ladies called "the nicest man!"<)>

Like Henry James' hero we burn our candles Thursday for your Bricharis birthday altho the office really fell on Aug. 22—lagging not far behind Samma in our protestations.[191]

Excuse this ink and paper. Amos writes that he is near Jimmy Todd in Saloniki.[192]

I am learning shorthand and typing at a Business College from 9–1:00 every day so that when my hour strikes I may be as useful as the 7th clerk of a sub-quarter master.

Afftly

Thornton

59. TO THEODORE WILDER. ALS 4 pp. Yale

Box 414 Yale Station, N. Haven
Feb. <19>'18

Dear Ted,

I received your humorous letter and the trunk, and all's well. I was a ninny to leave such a tiresome job to anyone else anyway and I hope you will forgive me for inconveniencing you. ¶ The social notes at the end of your letter were intense reading: I was absorbed in finding out

---

190 TNW is referring to *Fioretti del Glorioso Poverello di Christo S. Francesco di Assisi,* a collection of stories about the life and teachings of Saint Francis of Assisi.

191 TNW is probably referring to George Stransom in James's story "The Altar of the Dead." Stransom lights candles as a rite for his dead friends; he begins this ritual on his birthday. Bricharis and Samma may refer to pets belonging to the Wagers.

192 TNW's brother was now an AFS ambulance driver in Macedonia.

that Theodore Wilder will resume sharing an elegant apartment with Mr. Durand Wilder,[193] the idol of the Freshman class, during the Spring. Agnes' engagement came to me as a greater shock than my gentlemanly reserve can express: but it was a model of womanly delicacy and fine feeling that she did not send me the embittering news herself. I never could quite make out whether I was on the point of being engaged to Agnes or Nina Trego. An alliance with the former would have been exhilirating, and the quarrels would have been fine, vigorous and as tonic as <a> sneeze. With Nina life would be close-centred, nervous, with only oases of serenity and the quarrels would have been silent, repressed, dark and intense. In considering a possible wife—this is a real ipse dixit,[194] Ted—choose her in the light of her quarrels. Ascertain her style in argument, her method in animosity. ¶ But I hear you laughing at me.

You didn't tell me enough about your Grandmother, Aunt and Sister. These deficiencies are not to be excused. If I stepped (without knocking) into the good old house on N. Professor St (imagine me as returning from my solitary four-mile walk!) would I find everything very much as it used to <be>? Grandmother at her desk? Agnes the sudden-smiling busy at the telephone, endlessly farewelling? You and Durand on the point of leaving on the other's wheel?—(there is only one wheel but it always seemed to belong to the one who wasn't using it, and had to be petitioned for.) And our much enduring Aunt Mame sewing upstairs in the frontroom or in the kitchen, finishing some fragrant bread and generous of it? Or have I imagined it wrong, and does Margaret, instead of holding her head upstairs over her Algebra, now usurp Agnes' place at the telephone chair?[195] Keep me in touch with these alterations; they are of more moment to me than the hopping crowns of the Balkans.

---

193 George Durand Wilder, Jr. (1908–1984), Theodore Wilder's younger brother.

194 Latin: he himself said it (meaning an unproven assertion).

195 When TNW arrived at Oberlin, he already knew both Theodore Wilder and his younger brother Durand from Chefoo. While at Oberlin, he became acquainted with their sisters, Margaret (1898–1987) and Ursula (1902–1997), as well as with their maternal grandmother (Mrs. Charles A. Stanley), their cousin Agnes, and their Aunt Mame, who kept house for them all.

There are no changes in my life to report, except that now I reside in the oldest dormitory in Yale, the celebrated Connecticut Hall, once roomed in by Nathan Hale, Horace Bushnell and Edward Rowland Sill.[196] The floors tip like the ocean through a porthole, and the ceilings sink to meet them, but Yale traditions and Yale history leaks from every crack and wormhole. It is the best we can come to in America that bears the flavour of old Oxford and Cambridge. I am still taking eighteen heavy hours, Business College three hours a week. I am still "writing" much, both for the waste-basket and for posterity which is only a temporary postponement of the waste-basket. I received a fine letter from Harold Spore, a charming one from Marian Tyler that I intend to answer momently—and Oh Ted! a wonderful one from Mr. Wager. A marvel, boy.

Amos is in the artillery,[197] I suppose you know. Bergström, Oberlin ex '19 is here in the Yale R.O.T.C. Tell me what news you can of the Oberlin bunch at Allentown.[198] Will they move to France en masse? ¶ Tell me if Hotchy[199] is in town; if he is remember me warmly to him and tell him to send me his address. I owe a letter to Mr. Jeliffe that I am ashamed to have delayed so long to answer. Remember me affectionately again to your whole household, with great wishes for yourself

Thornton

---

196 Bushnell was a nineteenth-century Congregational minister, and Sill was a nineteenth-century poet.

197 TNW's brother had enlisted in the U.S. Army in Paris in November 1917 and was assigned to field artillery in the Second Division.

198 The military training camp in Allentown, Pennsylvania.

199 Edwin DeWitt Hotchkiss (see letter number 28), who, in May 1918, entered the army.

60. TO BRUCE T. SIMONDS.[200] TLS 2 pp. (Stationery embossed: War Industries Board / Washington)[201] Yale

July 19, 1918

Dear Bruce, my bonny,

From now on address me: c/o Chevy Chase School, Washington, D.C. where all your letters will find me happy, tired and temporarily excited. I have moved from the gloomier (that's my little joke!) atmosphere of the Perpetual Carousal, finding that four boys in a small apartment whether it belonged to a literary Marquise or not, was both warm and excitable, especially when the noise is created by that perpetual competition in cleverness which constitutes the relation of Steve and John.[202] My home is now almost three quarters of an hours ride away from Washington and them. It is in a fashionable old-colonial-fronted Girls' School which for the summer is turned into a suburban mens' club. There are lawns and verandahs and great halls, and although I arrive there every evening at about seven very wan and staggering a little I am usually able to pick up a little spirit before I go to bed. In other words I have written two whole new scenes into Vecy,[203] and the two that I like the best in the whole play. But here in this whole town I have no one to whom I would care to read them, except William Rose Benet,[204] whom I have got to know very well, and he me. I

---

200 Simonds (1896–1989) was a concert pianist and a Yale classmate and close friend of TNW; he taught at the Yale School of Music, where he also served as the dean.

201 With his father's help, TNW got a thirty-five-dollar-a-month job as a clerk typist at the War Industries Board during the summer of 1918.

202 When he first went to Washington, TNW shared an apartment with Yale friends John F. Carter, Jr., and Stephen Vincent Benét. Benét, who was in Washington as a clerk in the State Department and was a class ahead of TNW at Yale, was already recognized as a major literary talent. He served on the *Yale Literary Review*'s editorial board and published three volumes of poetry while still an undergraduate.

203 A typescript of the unfinished comedy "Vecy-Segal" is in the Beinecke Library at Yale University. A fragment, "Sea Chanty: 'Vecy-Segal,' Scene IV," was published in *S_4N* in December 1919.

204 William Rose Benét, Stephen Vincent Benét's older brother, was a leading American poet and anthologist.

havent read them to him yet, but he is coming out to hear them some near Sunday afternoon under the wide elms of the Chevy Chase Tea-rooms. And dear Brucekins, you cant imagine how starved I am for music. To a large extent it was my hungar for music that took me to see Hearts of the World[205] three times, for there was a large orchestra that played from time to time the more conspicuous of the melodies (though which of his melodies are there that are not conspicuous?). After a while even the commoner tunes in it had a strong appeal for me and I induce a grand melancholy in myself at any time just by singing over a few, and remembering the great marvelous face of Lillian Gish who has succeeded in my opinion to Mae Marsh[206] as the greatest screen actress. I realize however that that is an argument in which you have not yet achieved a full locus critici.[207] One of the greatest omissions of my faltering life lies there: I did not introduce Bruce to the celuloid.

Drop me now and then a card of some cool shore you come to on your trip, for the weather here shows signs of breaking its matronly temperateness and becoming in Falstaff's figure, characteristically misquoted be<by> me, "a wench in flame colored taffeta." I wish it would occur to you to give a red cross trip to open the hearts of the arrogant worldly stiffnecked art-supercilious Washingtonians. There is scarcely none of the lovable middle-class in this city Bruce dear, just a lot of marble-faced limousiners and a lot of wretched women clerks living on a farthing a day, forty thousand of them, desperately driven.

I told you I guess that I sent my ten playlets to the yale press but except for a cordial note from mrs day (i am too tired to strike the capitals—) saying that the press was forwarding THEM to her—(i am never to<o> tired to capitalize that kind of thing.)[208]

My mother and three sisters are all up at Mount Holyoke together where Charlotee is doing War Farm Work. Arthur Hopkins will be in Washington the last week in august putting on a play. Shall I try to

205 *Hearts of the World* (1918), a silent film directed by D. W. Griffith.

206 The career of American film actress Marsh (1895–1968) spanned fifty years.

207 Latin: critical vantage point.

208 The volume TNW submitted probably contained some of the five short plays he had published in the *Oberlin Literary Magazine* in 1915 and 1916 and the six playlets he had published in the *Yale Literary Magazine* in 1917 and 1918.

make an appointment to read to him do you suppose, or just send it in to his bored readers? Did you know that he had secured the new great matured John Barrymore as his star for the coming season and was to produce him in a series of plays, and was going to do the same with Alla Nazimova, probably putting on the greatest play since Hamlet, namely the Master Builder?[209] I weep at these beautiful things. I want to write a play for J.B. about a young Lord Sands a fated gifted tragic boy of the Yellow Ninties period, with a highly colored background of Whistler, not Wilde, a little Beardesly, Dowson etc. A boy that took a rococo period too seriously and died like L'aiglon.[210]

As you love me, do not laugh at my silly plans.

Conceit and ambition are the first luxurious of a tired frustrated man.

I long to hear you and Arthur doing the D'Indy Symphony[211]—I cannot even remember that great rhthmic figure; I cant even remember the Motto.

Wouldn't it be beautiful if my little book were published—eventually why not now? as they say of razors.

Forgive me if I stop now. I am leaving this hot <office?> for my nightly vacation in my place of carpets and shrubs.—and great dignitary officers, very kindly and a little communicative.

love
admiration
curiosity
everything else good
Thornton

<handwritten> My best to Caroline

---

209 Producer, director, theater owner, and writer Arthur Hopkins (1878–1950) produced *A Very Good Young Man*, by Martin Brown, in Washington in August. In the spring of 1919 and then again in September 1919–February 1920, he produced *The Jest*, starring John Barrymore. Although Nazimova appeared in three Ibsen plays produced by Hopkins, she did not appear in a production by him of Ibsen's *The Master Builder*.

210 *L'Aiglon* (1900), a play by dramatist and poet Edmond Rostand about the tragic life of Napoléon's son.

211 Symphony on a French Mountain Air (1886), by French composer Vincent D'Indy (1851–1931).

61. TO AMOS P. WILDER. TLS 2 pp. (Stationery embossed War Industries Board / Washington) Yale

August 14, 1918

Dear Pops,

Dings are going shplendidly. I took my Advisory Board Exam. and probably passed it. But this is not certain. However I think so. So I went today to the office of the Coast Artillery and put in my application for an induction into that service. IT ONLY TAKES MEN WHO ARE IN GENERAL MILITARY SERVICE OF THE DRAFT (and of course general enlistments.) and Men who have had at least one year of College. So that if they find out from my Branford office—the only people who are allowed to tell me the result of last night's exam—that I am fit for general milit. service they will immediately call me to go to Fort Adams on Narragansett bay, Long Island or somewhere near Connecticut. But if the Branford board says "limited service" they will refuse to have anything to do with me and I will be left where I am. So you see either alternative is desirable; and the grand Mt. Carmel send-off with hot coffee and hymns is off the horizon. Besides this process does not introduce the ambiguities and uncertainties resting on the disposition of further medical exams, whose inter-se disagreements and conflicts has until now been my trouble. They take you as you come from the draft board and ask no questions.

First thing we are sent to train until September—near the end of Sept.—when the bonny promising ones of us are selected <u>by our own application</u> to go into a training camp, the graduation of which, a one or two-month's course—confers a Second Lieutendantcy on us. Then we go to France and deal with the very heaviest artillery, the Big Berthas etc. If this goes through as indicated and there are no hitches any where—the snow this winter should fall on me in France, and that before Xmas. This no doubt sounds incredible to you, but remember that it is only men with at least one year of College that are called, or others who pass bravely an exam in Plane Trignometry and Logarithms, both of which I had Freshman year in Oberlin, and can polish up.

To make this letter really impressive I should stop here, but I am going on.

I sent the enclosed too hastily written critique of a play to the Boston Evening Transcript which keeps a whole page open to Drama three or four times a week, after a scholarly analytical type. The reason this copy is so dirty is because it is the carbon copy and the erasures on the original turn up as smudges on the copy.[212]

I wrote the producer Arthur Hopkins who is in town with this play, saying that I had a play of the China Coast and the effect of the war on the social and political exiles there, that might be of interest for the use of John Barrymore, and since he, Mr H. was in town perhaps he might have liesure to read it or have it read to him. I finished up saying that if I did not hear from him I would infer that he prefered the manuscript to be handed in to his New York office in the usual manner. But I did hear from his secretary in a very nice note saying that Mr.—but I will enclose the note.[213]

I am being drawn into a Bohemian crowd here. The ladies dye textiles and write, the men serve in the Fuel or Food administration or the War Industries Board by day and write by night. And they meet at a tea-tavern called THE SILVER SEA-HORSE which you must confess is a happy stroke. They put on plays from time to time, want me to appear in a Chinese pantomime and insist that I hand in some of my playlets immediately to the play-reading committee. So you see the low company to which I must relapse if I am not called to Fort Adams in two weeks.

All possible luck, my dear family, to <t>he Maine trip. I am half mad to be going on with you. This hot weather makes every primitive pore of your body sing for the sea of one's origin, which, by felicity, will be always near me, in the Coast Artillery.

---

212 TNW's review of *A Very Good Young Man* appeared in the *Boston Transcript* on August 17, 1918.

213 TNW submitted the play "The Breaking of Exile" to Hopkins, but it was never produced; a copy survives as a holograph and undated incomplete typescript and undated typescript carbon manuscript in the Beinecke Library at Yale University. The note from Hopkins's secretary has not survived.

How soon can we tell Amos that little brother is in the Artillery—the unskilled emergency-rush section of it, to be sure? Tell little lady mother to keep her shears poised in air and her needle threaded for the sewing of the star.[214] One knows not the day or the hour, except that it will come within a week and a half. It was something artful of me to avoid the terrible drilling camp-days during the worst days of heat. When I played at Camp Meigs they said that that afternoon about twenty soldiers had fainted during afternoon drill. Perhaps I would have fainted during morning drill.

Give my love to every sloping wave, especially to the long low urgent ones that come in towards evening with a sense of distress, as though the whole long-sighing night tide were pressing even then upon them. Of<If> it <is> Gran manan[215] you are going to, give your afternoons and mornings to the search for porpoises under the sky-line for the child-races felt that busy rolling of school<s> of them in the distance was a religious thing, noting with simple quickness of the primitive mind that of all the animals of the world, these seem most to be moving in an inspired trance, with their heads always under the water and the solitary, self-sufficient, world-alone air. But do not interrupt them, for wh<e>ther it be minnows they are pondering over, or whether it be The Divine Nature, it is best that we respect the folk-lore of the ruminative south sea-Islanders.

Can you realize that Washington can see me perhaps no more in two or three weeks? We never know our fate; we never know our fate.

Lots of love
Thornton

---

214 TNW is referring to the small flags (a blue star in the center of a red-bordered white rectangle) that families during World War I hung in their windows. Each star represented a son serving in the military.

215 Grand Manan Island at the mouth of the Bay of Fundy, New Brunswick, Canada.

TNW as a corporal in the army's First Coast Artillery Corps, 1918.

62. TO AMOS P. WILDER. ALS 3 pp. Yale

<Fort Adams, Rhode Island>[216]
<November–December 1918>

Dear Papa,

I have been so busy transferring fatheads preparatory to their discharge, and writing letters to your old friends, that I'ven't been able to drop a stitch home.

I have received and written two letters to Mrs. Weed, who is now an old fast friend of mine. And I have just mailed my regrets to Mr Chapman. These letters have been simple, my dear parent, but under

---

216 On September 14, 1918, TNW was inducted as an office orderly into the army's First Coast Artillery Corps stationed at Fort Adams, Newport, Rhode Island. He was discharged as a corporal on December 31, 1918, and returned to Yale.

their simplicity the very virtuosity of letter-writing. The gem-like salutations and valedictions will very likely die of faint admiration. In both cases the body of the letter contained a fanciful picture of the officials in Washington issuing the Bulla forbidding any personnel Officer or clerk, in any post, Camp, fort or Headquarters to be given any 24-hour pass, furlough or discharge until further notice. Then followed "to slow music" a depressing of we clerks after the last man has been discharged, "limp, overworked, disillusioned soldiers, dragging ourselves under the snows of February, joylessly home."

I have spoken to the Adj. about Yale's Jan. 30 opening. He says no force as yet known can break through Mimeo 91, quoted above. The Gov. of R.I.<,> Beekman, sent a special telegram for the discharge of one of my fellow-workers, and was disregarded. However I think we may be out by New Year anyway. The Coast Defenses are supposed to be on a Peace Basis by next Sunday. This is laughably impossible. The slow sleepy Officers downstairs were suddenly shaken last Sunday by an irate phone-call from the Department Hdqrs. in Boston: "The U.S.A. has discharged 200,000 men: why have you not done your share?"

We've been working like mad ever since. The red-tape and forms of the Government must be seen to be believed. Seventeen separate little paper forms for each discharge, where three years ago, there were only four operations. Now you have a little poster to account for the disposition of your very shoe strings.

The spectacle of the great heavy-moving opaque gov't guarding itself against remote and inconsiderable frauds in its divine stupidity is so depressing that it affects one physically. The lucid, deft, swift French mind would make a wonderful facile channel of the process, and a million men would be discharged with <a> bow and a smile

love

Thornton

Part Two

BRIDGES: 1920–1929

WHEN THORNTON WILDER GRADUATED FROM YALE IN JUNE 1920, he was the only one of the five Wilder children who had never been to Europe. His youngest sisters, Isabel and Janet, lived in Italy and Switzerland with their mother from 1911 to 1913 while Thornton and his sister Charlotte were in school in China and then California. After her college graduation in 1919, Charlotte worked in a YWCA hostel in Milan, Italy. In June 1920, Thornton's brother, Amos, who had served overseas during World War I, returned to Europe after receiving his Yale degree and began a fellowship at the University of Brussels. Thornton's immediate future was decided when he was accepted as a paying visiting student and boarder in the School of Classical Studies at the American Academy in Rome for the term beginning in October 1920.

Worried about his second son's employment after college, Wilder's father encouraged him to enter the teaching profession as a prep school Latin instructor. The elder Wilder believed that his son's enrollment in the School of Classical Studies would enhance his credentials on job applications. Despite the family's limited resources, the foreign exchange rate was so favorable that nine hundred dollars—which the senior Wilder doled out in installments—fully covered his son's year abroad. Before Wilder sailed for Italy on September 1, he completed six weeks of work in the last of five farm jobs he had held over the past seven summers.

Wilder arrived in Rome on October 14, 1920, and remained at the American Academy for seven months, taking graduate courses and participating in student social life. His social circle widened due to informal introductions to young American embassy personnel and more formal introductions from family and friends that provided him entrée to the large English and American community in Rome. He especially enjoyed his visits to the home of the Italian poet Adolfo de Bosis and his family, where on one occasion he met Ezra Pound. Wilder continued his writing, focusing on playwriting. He hoped to complete "Villa Rhabini," a play with strong Jamesian overtones, and to read it to some of the literary ladies whose tea parties he frequented. He made short trips to other parts of Italy, such as his "Umbrian week" in Perugia and Assisi. After leaving the American Academy in Rome on May 18, 1921, he explored Florence and nearby Siena and stopped off in Milan to see his sister Charlotte.

From the time Wilder learned he was to go to Rome, he longed to spend time in Paris. He wanted to see a close friend who was studying music there, and to attend performances at the Vieux-Columbier, a theater established in 1913, whose founder, Jacques Copeau, employed novel stage techniques Wilder had read about and wished to experience firsthand. In early June, Wilder arrived in Paris, where he spent two and a half months. Although he had initially planned to stay there a shorter time, his father cabled him to say that the Lawrenceville School in New Jersey had offered Thornton a position as a French teacher. Once Wilder accepted the offer, he felt it necessary to study and immerse himself in French grammar and conversation.

While Wilder was in Paris, his mother and two youngest sisters sailed for Southampton, England. They spent time in London with Wilder's maternal aunt, Charlotte Tappan Niven, and visited Amos, who had completed his fellowship year and was living and working at Toynbee Hall, the oldest settlement house in London. When Amos matriculated that fall at Mansfield College, Oxford, to study for a degree in theology, Mrs. Wilder and her daughters took up residence in that academic community. While the foursome settled down in

Oxford, both Thornton and Charlotte left the Continent at the end of the summer. Charlotte gave up her job in Milan to work in Boston, and Thornton left Paris on August 31, 1921, on board the French liner *Roussillon*, to begin his teaching job at Lawrenceville, a private boarding school for boys. Their father had remained in New Haven, where he was now associate editor of the *New Haven Journal-Courier.* Once again, the Wilder family was separated by an ocean.

From September 1921 to June 1925, Wilder taught French and served as the assistant housemaster of Davis House, a dormitory at Lawrenceville. The school and the surrounding community provided a congenial place for Wilder to earn his living and continue his writing projects. He became especially close to Edwin Clyde Foresman, the housemaster at Davis, his wife, Grace, and their young daughter Emily, and to C. Leslie Glenn, a young math teacher who later became a distinguished Episcopal clergyman. Glenn remained a close friend for the rest of Wilder's life. Nearby Princeton University had a wonderful library and kindred groups of musicians and literary figures. Lawrenceville was also only a short train ride from Trenton, Philadelphia, and New York City, where the off-duty schoolmaster could easily enjoy the current theatrical fare. As a result, during this time, Wilder broadened his ties to literary and dramatic circles in New York. These associations fostered his writing life, provided informal but professional criticism of his work, introduced him to Off-Broadway theatrical groups, and opened doors to residential programs for aspiring writers.

In the fall of 1925, Wilder, the successful teacher and housemaster, took a two-year leave of absence from Lawrenceville to enter the graduate program in French at Princeton University. The three siblings closest to him in age had either completed degrees or were about to enter graduate programs. Charlotte, who had received her M.A. in English from Radcliffe in June 1925, began teaching at Wheaton College in Norton, Massachusetts. Amos returned from England in 1923 (as did Mrs. Wilder and her two youngest daughters) and completed his B.D. degree at the Yale Divinity School in 1924. After a year of tutoring and travel in the Middle East, Amos was ordained in 1925 and became the minister of the First Congregational Church in North Conway, New Hampshire. When Isabel returned from England in 1923, she worked for two years in New York before entering the three-year certificate program at the Yale School of Drama. The youngest sister, Janet, now fifteen, attended high school and lived with her parents, who had moved from Mount Carmel, Connecticut, to Mansfield Street in New Haven. In the fall of 1925, the members of the Wilder family were not only all together on the same continent but living near one another in the Northeast.

Thornton Wilder's commitment to graduate studies did not affect his determination to pursue a writing life, nor did it stifle the ideas, characters, and plots that filled his imagination. During July 1924, when he was awarded his first residency at the MacDowell Colony, an artist's retreat in Peterborough, New Hampshire, he concentrated on a group of "Roman Portraits" he had begun in 1921, probably in Paris. He had worked on these pieces intermittently, but there was a new impetus to complete them. In March 1925, he had received welcome news from a Yale classmate who was working at a publishing house. He had requested a copy of Wilder's manuscript months before and had shown it to the directors of his firm. Now they were interested in publishing it. Wilder expanded and revised the manuscript, and in November 1925, a month after he began his graduate studies, he signed a contract for his first novel. *The Cabala* was published in the United States by Albert & Charles Boni in April 1926 and in England by Longmans, Green in October of that year. Most reviews were positive and sales were strong, although not sufficient for Wilder to live by his pen alone.

After Wilder received his M.A. degree from Princeton in June 1926, he returned to the summer routine he had followed since his second year of teaching, dividing his vacation into two parts. He reserved one month to write and another to earn money tutoring at a boys' camp. In July 1926, he was accepted for a second residency at MacDowell, where he began a new book. In August, he returned to Sunapee, the tutoring camp where he had been employed for the past two summers. From late September until the beginning of December, Wilder toured Europe as the paid companion of a boy he had tutored the previous spring. By December, he was in Paris, where he remained when his duties as companion had ended. There he met another young American author, Ernest Hemingway, whose second novel, *The Sun*

Also Rises, had been published that year to excellent reviews, and whose writing Wilder admired.

Wilder enjoyed a banner year in 1926: In addition to the publication in April of his first book, on December 10, 1926, *The Trumpet Shall Sound,* a slightly revised version of a play that had won a Yale writing prize in 1920, was directed by Richard Boleslavsky at the Off-Broadway American Laboratory Theatre. Although it did not receive favorable reviews, the play remained in repertory for several months. Wilder was not overly concerned about its reception, because he was then deeply engaged in a new work, a novel set in Peru. He worked on it over the Christmas holidays, which he spent at a pension on the French Riviera with some Yale friends who were now studying at Oxford. There he met Glenway Wescott, another contemporary author he admired.

On January 31, 1927, Wilder sailed for New York on the *Asconia.* He rented rooms in New Haven, where, away from the hubbub of family life, he would have a quiet place to work on his second novel. Shortly thereafter, to supplement his small income, he accepted a six-week residential tutoring job in Briarcliff, New York, from February to early April, and also agreed that spring to translate a French novel for his English publisher. In July, at the urging of his father and the headmaster of Lawrenceville, he accepted the position of housemaster of his old dormitory, following the untimely death of Edwin Clyde Foresman. Throughout this period, Wilder worked on his Peruvian novel. In July 1927, a year after he began it at the MacDowell Colony, Wilder delivered the final manuscript of *The Bridge of San Luis Rey* to his publisher. In August, he resumed his tutoring position at the camp in New Hampshire.

The academic year 1927–1928 at Lawrenceville began inauspiciously. The new housemaster, with his three-thousand-dollar-a-year salary, settled into his six-room quarters and prepared for the customary trials and tribulations that punctuated residential life at a boys' school. The first trial, however, had nothing to do with his charges. A few weeks into the fall term, Wilder had a mild attack of appendicitis but was able to return to his duties. Another flare-up later in the fall required surgery and an absence from teaching.

The Bridge of San Luis Rey was published in the United States on November 3, 1927 (the English edition had appeared the previous month), to rave reviews and stunning sales on both sides of the Atlantic. By the time Wilder traveled to Miami, Florida, over the Christmas holidays to recuperate from his surgery, it had become clear that his second novel was already a huge success. The implications of this became apparent when he returned to Lawrenceville for the spring term: His dormitory home was deluged with telegrams and letters requesting interviews and speaking engagements, and packages of books to be signed were delivered daily. Most gratifying, perhaps, were invitations to meet notable authors whom Wilder, hitherto, had admired only from afar. In May, his novel won the Pulitzer Prize. Wilder had suddenly become an acclaimed author with a popular following and a great deal of money in his pocket.

In June 1928, Wilder resigned his position at Lawrenceville, but his association with the school was not entirely severed. At the beginning of July, he sailed for Europe with three Lawrenceville boys he had agreed to chaperone for a few weeks in England. After some travel, they joined Wilder's mother and two younger sisters in a large house in Surrey he had rented for his family. Wilder stayed on in Europe for the rest of the year. During his recuperation in Miami the previous December he had made a new friend, someone just his age, and had planned a walking trip in the Alps with him for September. His companion was the book-loving heavyweight boxing champion of the world, Gene Tunney, an acclaimed athlete and international celebrity. Because Wilder's recent success had turned him into a literary lion, it was not surprising that this seemingly disparate pair attracted widespread press attention, which continually interrupted their trip. The press surveillance ended only when the two men were able to slip down to Rome for Tunney's private wedding.

With that furor behind him, Wilder retreated to the south of France, where he spent a month writing, exercising, and socializing before meeting his sister Isabel for a round of theatergoing, concerts, and visits to museums in Munich and Vienna. After spending Christmas with their aunt Charlotte in Switzerland, Wilder and Isabel returned home at the end of January 1929. No longer could he pursue his vocation as a writer in relative anonymity. From this point until the end of his life, forty-six years later, Thornton Wilder was to live the life of an internationally renowned and acclaimed literary figure. In this climate, the privacy and seclusion he needed to pursue his vocation became increasingly difficult to find.

63. TO AMOS P., ISABELLA N., ISABEL, AND JANET F. WILDER. ALS 4 pp. Yale

Oct. 14 <1920>
Roma

Dear Family:

I have this minute arrived in Rome, and am waiting up in my room at half-past ten for some supper. The train was two-and-a-half hours late, and I know no more of Rome than can be gained on rainy evenings crossing the street that separates the station from the Hotel Continentale (the last room left for 22 lire). I had resolved not to write you until I had received your letters forwarded, but they failed day by day to come so I have hurried up to Rome to get them. French Lemon[1] may have decided not to forward to Cocumella on the Wagers' casual advice, or they may be found at the Boston. Tomorrow will straighten out.

In the meantime (while my hunger resounds in my stomach like a great bell) I must tell you some of the news of the last week and a half in Sorrento. One day for instance when I had been walking enraptured for hours among the bronzes and marbles of the Museo Nazionale I returned at 3:30 to the Immaculata to take the Sorrento boat. I bought my ticket, went aboard; it was expected<inspected> by three guards. We started and I settled down to read my Paris Temps and Berliner Tageblatt.[2] I fell into conversation with an Italian sailor who had had a fruit store on upper Broadway. Suddenly I found I was on the wrong boat: I was bound for Procida and Ischia, and there was no return that

1 French, Lemon & Co. was a place where foreigners picked up their mail.

2 Daily newspapers.

night. Seaman Esposito embarrassedly offered to take me into his home at Procida but I laughed it off, saying that I would go on to the Ischia that had been good enough for Vittoria Collonna and Lamartine.[3] Then I fell into conversation with a handsome middle-aged Anglo Italian who is employed between London and Rome in the wheat business. There are half a dozen exceedingly beautiful villas on Ischia because the bathing is so perfect for children, there being no cliffs as at Sorrento. This gentleman tried to be as helpful to me as possible, but with a touch of caution. I was hatless, in an eccentric-looking baggy grey-suit, and with a strange air of being at my ease that suggested arriére-pensée.[4] We drove up towards his villa, whereupon he extricated himself, telling the coachman to carry me on to the Floridiana Hotel ("the best one" on the Island, but not very good.) In the glass of my Italian, darkly, I found the Floridiana closed for the season, and was waved on to the second best which was full. Then I was sent to the Albergo del' belli guiardini<giardini> which turned out to be a rather ambitious kitchen-in-the-wall, peopled by several suspicious old women in black dresses who discussed things in whispers among themselves. I feared I was going to sleep in Vittoria Collonna's castle, now a house of correction, but one of the women emerged and beckoned to me ungraciously to follow her. We passed to an outdoor court (the beautiful gardens perhaps of the title) and on the second story through four spacious dark funereal bedrooms, there being no hall, and no light, and no privacy. The last was offered to me, to my simulated delight, and I gazed at the great shapeless shabby bed where so soon (I foresaw) my throat would be cut. I wanted to keep my relations with my hosts as sweet as possible and so refrained from bargaining until the morning. I slept very well; I was awakened only once by a dog under my bed eating the Paris Temps, the Berliner Tageblatt having been used in a more humble and not inappropriate way elsewhere. The return boat for Naples left at six the next morning and I had told them to call me at five, so I lazily replied to a knocking in the dark. It seemed to me, as always on waking, that I was happily

---

3 Italian poet Vittoria Colonna (1492–1547) lived on the island of Ischia for many years. French poet Alphonse-Marie-Louis de Lamartine (1790–1869) visited Ischia and wrote a poem by that name.

4 French: ulterior motive.

back at 72 Conn. or on Whitney Avenue.[5] Soon the truth came to me that I was in a dubious situation on the island of Ischia. I threw some cold water at my face from a washstand in the corner, dressed and descended. There was a yellow streak in a dark sky visible above the narrow blanching street. By lamplight my padrona made me a cup of coffee and presented her conto.[6] Twenty-two lire for that wretched room, a supper and a breakfast! It was too late to argue. I paid it and threw myself on circumstance. Except for my Express checks which were uncashable until late in the morning I had only three lire left, and the fare to Naples was five lire. I asked the woman if she'd give me two more, and I'd mail her five, but she concealed her obduracy under a flow of rapid Neapolitan dialetta.[7] I left quickly without mancia[8] and reaching the ticket-kiosk explained myself to the official. Suddenly it occurred to me that 3 lire would at least buy me a 3rd Class passage, and so it did with a lire to spare. So at ten o'clock I reached Naples and going to beloved piazza dei Martiri cashed another Express at 25 lire to the dollar! Suddenly I passed an American soldier (as I thought) in the street. I ran back and spoke to him, inviting him to have an ice-cream with me. He turned out to be a Princeton boy of <an> imposing New York family who ran away from bank servitude to join the Near Eastern Relief. He was actually in the Wall Street Explosion.[9] The J. P. Morgan skylight fell on him, and he's got the scars! He came over and spent two days with me at the Cocumella, and we went to Pompeii and climbed Vesuvius together. (I keep going to the window. Outside in wonderful Rome, it is drizzling. Carriages and trams pass. Not far away the Pope and forty cardinals are sleeping, the coliseum and the forum are lying dampish, and silent and locked up but with one burning light at least, the Sistine chapel is glimmering, and somewhere further off, in the struggling starlight, your graves, John Keats and Percy Shelley, lie, suc-

---

5 72 Conn. was TNW's room in Connecticut Hall at Yale; Whitney Avenue was the road that ran past the Wilder family home in Mount Carmel, approximately eight miles from the Yale campus.

6 Italian: bill.

7 Italian: dialect.

8 Italian: a tip.

9 On September 16, 1920, an explosion rocked the heart of New York's Financial District, killing over thirty people; those responsible for the bombing were never apprehended.

ceeding to establish, if anyone can, that it is better to be in a moist hell with glory, than live in an elegant hotel with stupidity.) When we got quarter way up Vesuvius, at a hotel where are<our> horses were supposed to be waiting saddled for us, there were suddenly no horses. So we cut the price of our agents in half and agreed to walk. It's a wicked mountain, half of every step you take is lost in the sliding blue-black dust, yet so steep that every step for two hours and a half is palpably lift. I suddenly got anxious about Charley White; he has been shut up in a bank for a year and a half and was unprepared for this. He insisted on going on, though he was on the verge of palpit<at>ions and heaves and blood-coughing the whole way. Yet Father and I had wisely let pass the call of the Near Eastern Relief because of my constitution: I who talked Italian all the way up with our guide, Nicola!

(Now it is morning and Stupidity is impatiently waiting for café-au-lait. A busy modern city with only a hint of romance is riding the tide under my window. In a few moments I am going to dash over to French-Lemons; then to the Londres-Cargill, an almost unheard of hotel with a room at about eight lire! Then this afternoon to the Academia.)

Love to you all. I'm dying to know about you.

Will write again tonight

Thornton

Looking in the cheval-glass I see a young man of about twenty-one who implicitly, or by his reason of his large shell glasses, presents an expectant eager face to the view. His shoes and clothes are in travel-state, but he is carefully shaved and brushed. On his pink cheeks and almost infantile mouth lies a young innocence that is not native to Italy and has to be imported in hollow ships, and about the eyes there is the same strong naiveté, mercifully mitigated by a sort of frightened humor. He is very likely more intelligent than he looks, and less charming. Alone in Italy? To study archaeology! Why each single tooth in that engaging upper row is an appeal in the name of Froebel and in the name of Wordsworth to let childhood enjoy its rainbow skies and imagined gardens while it may.[10] A delicious little breakfast has come,

10 German educator Friedrich Wilhelm August Fröbel (1782–1852) was the founder of the kindergarten system.

TNW's Yale graduation photograph, 1920.

with a marmalade of orange and pineapple, and though I want you all here all the time, for this particular meal I choose Isabel.

64. TO AMOS P. WILDER. ALS 2 pp. Yale

Am. Acad. At Rome
Dec. 4, 1920

Dear Papa:

I have received the remittance and acknowledge statim.[11] I was told it was coming the latter half of November and had planned things

11 Latin: immediately.

down to a science. Its delay by so much as a week (to say the least) compelled me to ask the Secretary here to forward one hundred and fifty lire, as you will see on the bill enclosed. I was also told that you were sending me eighty dollars, which on the day of your mailing would have been at l<e>ast Lire 2160 and more likely £2300. I presume of course that you got full exchange (otherwise you would have left the exchanging to me as the advantage lies here) and that your remittance was $55. about.

If this means that your method of conducting my arrangement has changed it deserved explanation before it was put in practice. I gratefully accept anything, but like to know the worst. If I am to <be> paid with you getting the benefit of the exchange, I shan't be able to go with the Classical School for three weeks to Pompeii; I shan't be able even to buy the pocket microscope we must have for the numismatics study in the course on Roman Private Life. I shan't be able to go to the Opera, which definitely narrows my visit to Europe as being purely Classical Study.

Out of the 1500 I have already paid:

The bill for November	Lire 709.45
10 Italian lessons	70.00
A pair of gloves	45.00

I've immediately stopped Italian lessons.

Is the idea for me to stay in Italy as long as I can for $900, or is it to stay for one year under as pinched conditions as possible?

We parted on the first agreement.

① On a generous amount of money I could make quite a little agitation on this Roman scene that recognizes extraordinary eccentric sharp young men, as it did when Emperors adopted them! Enclose yesterday's cards received.

② On a discreet amount I could still do the name Wilder modest credit and gain entrance to regions incomputably valuable to a younger writer who misses nothing, as far as observation goes.

③ On an adequate student allowance I can walk about and see things and meet rather complacent Americans at the hotels, and do a little work without worries, and with an extraordinary amount of pleasure.

④ At present, as a shabby repressed soul, I can breathe and go into museums (not too often) and get a great deal of pleasure in a denied, envious sort of way with all my capabilities still in the cocoon.

love
Thornton

<appeared perpendicularly in left margin>
On my margin I couldn't b<u>y any Xmas presents on time. Photos later,—

65. TO AMOS N. WILDER. ALS 4 pp. Yale

Porta San Pancrazio
Roma Italia
Dec 13, 1920

Dear Amos:

I'm so ashamed at not writing before, especially in view of your closely-written and -observed letters, that I don't know what to say. I have certainly be<en> idler than you, too, full though my days have been with sightseeing and lectures. I think I must unconsciously have postponed writing you from pique at your intimation that I was probably on the point of borrowing money from you, a terror which Charlotte also experiences, and gratuitously reminds me from time to time that she hasn't enough to live on herself. Hug your avarice as closely as you please; it never occurred to me to borrow from either of you! Though, since both of you got the idea simultaneously I suppose penury and dependance are as conspicuous as two red flags in my temperament, or else father, whose idée fixe about borrowing is perfectly Freudian, has been warning you about what he calls the Leech of Rome. I have every intention of being parasitic all my life, but always on those who can easily afford so expensive an encumbrance and who take a special delight in subsidizing those talents to which I make so modest a claim. I have at last found in Italy a mecca for just such patrons, and am myself presenting myself as a sort of objet-d'art of a most singular and quaint charm, rentable for teas, dinner-parties and dances;

will read MSS plays to adoring ladies; will sit in their palaces and talk to them about their own uniqueness; will — and so on, in a catalogue that you blue-nosed Flemings can only envy and disapprove of.

A vacation from dalliance comes to me with the visit of Harry Luce and Bill Whitney over Xmas.[12] I have just trod the <u>via dolorosa</u> of Roman pensions (unprecedentedly overcrowded) and finally found them a room-and-pension for 25 lire a day—less than a dollar in present exchange: Within stones-throw of the house where Keats died (little as that will mean to <u>them</u>!) and the College of the Propeganda of the Faith[13] (little distinguished in your mind, you Calvin, from the Inquisition and other practices of the Whore of Rome,[14] about which you have only the vaguest and most superstitious of ideas). This last thought of mine is so important that I am going to drag it out of brackets and continue it, by belaboring you for your ignorance and prejudice before the most beautiful religious system that ever eased the heart of man; centering about a liturgy built like Thebes, by poets, four-square, on the desert of man's need. You and I will never be Roman Catholics, but I tell you now, you will never be saved until you lower your impious superiority toward this magnificent and eternal institution, and humbly sit down to learn from her the secret by which she held great men, a thing the modern church cannot do; and a church without its contemporary great men is merely pathetic.

¶ Charlotte is spending Xmas with the Blakes[15] in Florence, I hear, then coming on to me. I receive this indirectly. ¶ Don't acquire a barbarous lowland accent to your French. ¶ I'll try and pick you up something for Xmas, though I must borrow to buy it. ¶ Tell me any intimate dope you may get from America on our parents; Mother's letters are delightful quiet dining-room table affairs, and Father's are trenchant homiletic. It's foolish to expect other people to write as revelatory let-

---

12 Henry R. Luce, later the founder of *Time, Fortune*, and *Life* magazines, was TNW's classmate at both Chefoo and Yale; William Dwight Whitney was TNW's classmate at Yale. Luce and Whitney were Rhodes scholars at this time.

13 Probably TNW's wordplay for the Sacred Congregation for the Propagation of the Faith.

14 TNW no doubt meant the Whore of Babylon, a derogatory term for the Roman Catholic Church.

15 The Blakes were aunt Charlotte Tappan Niven's closest friends; he was an Anglican priest.

ters as I do, but I wish that they'd at least intimate the alternations of climate in their minds and hearts. ¶ I'm not at all sympathetic with your shockedness over fellow-students conduct: you haven't learned Morals, you've learned the Code of Morals. Politeness and Celibacy are a matter of indifference to God. Go deeper. If possible, sin yourself and discover the innocence of it.

love
Thornton

66. TO AMOS P. WILDER. ALS 4 pp. Yale

Accademia Americana
Porta San Pancrazio, Roma
Feb 1, 1921

Dear Papa:

I have been shamefacedly conscious all these last few weeks that you were just about to receive, or had received, an ugly-toned letter from me. I would give the world to recall it, especially now that your beautiful grave reply has come. Now I am conscious that you are receiving two more "financial" letters, not bad-spirited I hope, but violent and despairing. You see the date on my letter and will be glad to hear that I have payed my January bill with a little help from a discreet unexpected source, and can now live weeks and weeks without raising my voice. The whole original trouble lay in the fact that I did not realize my monthly Academy bill was £500 (now £600) and that my original Express checks gave out soon after I arrived in Rome and could no longer eke out the transoceanic remittances. I think I have now learnt how not to spend lire; and am out of the danger of ever exhibiting myself in such a disgusting uncontrolled state as you've had to look at lately.

Just the same I'd like to go away from this crowd about Easter time. My two courses in Epigraphy and Roman Private Life will be finished by then, and I think the new one, Numismatics. They are full

Post-Graduate School courses, and although I have groped, and scrambled and lagged behind the PhD fellow-students I think I can get the professors to sign a little document to the effect that I passed the courses. Teas and dinners increase, and I hope it can be said I have improved those opportunities too, but I would be glad to leave that. There is only one friend I shall greatly miss. The dim churches, the pines, the yellow sunlight you will see in my eyes for years—it doesn't matter when I leave them. I should like to leave for a week or two in Florence and the hill towns about the middle of April—then up to Paris until sailing home in late June,—either by the Fabre Line again from Marseilles or if I can find one cheaper from northern France.

In imagination I hear you quite clearly wondering reproachfully why Thornton—in the middle of great natural beauties, amid masterpieces, with a great deal of free time, well-housed and fed, among friends—shouldn't at least be docile and simply grateful. My only answer is that the very complexity of things flays one's peace of mind to the point of torment. You are haunted by the great vistas of learning to which you are unequal; continuous gazing at masterpieces leaves you torn by ineffectual conflicting aspirations; the social pleasures and cheap successes bring (against this antique and Rennaisance background) more immediate revulsions and satiety. A snowy walk in Mt. Carmel, Mother's sewing and you with your pipe hold for me now all I hold of order and peace. Your queer "aesthetic" over-cerebral son may yet turn out to be your most fundamental New Englander and most appreciative of the sentiment of group; when Amos and Charlotte have set up independent self-centred institutions, I shall turn out to be a sort of male Cordelia![16]

Your enclosures give me the keenest pleasure. I miss only one sort; the "Alumni" and newspaper reports of your recent speeches. I am very pleased and proud of all these menu-cards and the letters that come in to you. I can't have too many of these, and am jealous of every one you sort out into Amos' or Charlotte's mail: if I can't claim a great part of the inheritance of your patience and sublime endurance (virtues you

16 TNW is referring to King Lear's daughter, who is disinherited by her father because of her refusal to flatter and fawn over him but who eventually proves to be the only daughter who truly cares about him.

have consigned to my light-haired fellows) I can at least rush forward and stake out reflections of your animation and vitality and (hear, ye Heavens!) your eloquence.[17] You will always turn to find my eyes bright with delight and admiration at your wit and charm, even if I am occasionally (Oh, for the last time!) thoughtless of your sacrifices. And I can already see Amos and I, whiteheaded at the age of eighty, disputing amicably as to which of us knew you best, Amos who could not take his eyes off of your labors, so beautifully and quietly sustained, or I who was always after cajoling you into those moods of quickness and inspiration that you were allowing to grow less frequent. Either aspect alone could make the reputation of a great father, but with both we have a right to feel a little bewildered and hide ourselves from the responsibility of standing up to so much privilege and love. Here I am, a sort of Arthur Pendennis,[18] breaking down in front of you, and wishing old words unsaid and old silences forgotten, and remembering you so intensely as you were when you came to Litchfield, or to Mt. Hermon, or to the Duttons'. I hope this letter will get to you at about your birthday and if you sit down on that day to think us all over, I hope it may lift from my record some of the discredit left there by my last three letters.

Much love
Thornton

67. TO ISABELLA N. WILDER. ALS 4 pp. Yale

Accad. Americana
Roma: Aprile 13 • 1921

Dear Mother:

I have just sent off letters to Father and Amos, and feel so virtuous that I must write you two<too>. I left you after my last, hung up in

17 TNW's father was a nationally known orator and often spoke at private schools and before such groups as the National Municipal League.

18 Hero of Thackeray's *The History of Pendennis,* who has a sheltered and spoiled childhood.

suspense over my luncheon at the De Bosis.[19] It fell out almost as I anticipated, only twice as delightful. The reddish-yellow villa, hung with flowering wistaria at the end of a long avenue of trees; choked garden plots with various statues of Ezekiel glimpsed through foliage; the rooms of the house furnished in rather ugly Victorian manner—all modern Italian taste in music and art being deplorable, perhaps because they are so discriminating in literature. Some guests, a young Englishman named James; a Miss Steinman; the young Marchese di Viti whose sisters I had met, a beautifully bred discreet medical student. Signor de Bosis himself has a sort of abstracted gently humorous air, silent, that sits agreeably upon one who having so many over-intelligent children doesn't have to descend into the arena of conversation very often, and then only to kill. These days—perhaps I told you—he is revising his verse translation of Shelley's The Cenci for immediate performance by Italy's foremost company now in Rome. He is one of the best Italian poets (conservative) and as such made an address in the Protestant Cemetary on the anniversary of Keats' death last month. [Upstairs he showed me his recent discovery of the meaning of the first two lines of the Epipsychidion, and if you turn to the lines you will be glad two <to> find that the Emilia Viviani's sister spirit is not (as she herself thought and Ed. Garnett) Mary Wollstoncraft, but Shelley who puns here on his name Percy—in Italian "lost"—as Signor De B. found in a few casual lines where Shelley began translating his poem into Italian.][20] At table things went merrily in and out of both languages. Lauro—my friend—and the Arabic-Arimaic sister I admire, so began throwing at each other in latin and from memory the ridiculous list of beautiful books which Rabelais says Pantagruel found at the library of Saint-Victor.[21]

---

19 Adolfo de Bosis was an Italian poet and translator. His son Lauro de Bosis (1901–1931) translated TNW's 1927 novel, *The Bridge of San Luis Rey,* into Italian. Lauro de Bosis was one of the two people to whom TNW dedicated his 1948 novel, *The Ides of March.*

20 Shelley's epic poem *Epipsychidion* was dedicated to Emilia Viviani. Richard Garnett was an editor of Shelley's poetry.

21 Pantagruel is the principal character in Rabelais's *Gargantua and Pantagruel.*

April 14 • 1921

I went with some of them last night to the last Symphony Concert conducted by Arthur Nikisch; the program was "popularissimmo" Beethoven's Egmont and 5th; Lohengrin and Tristan and Tannhauser Overtures and the Liebstod, but I have never heard such conducting in my life. ¶ Signór de Bosis has sent me a book of his verses inscribed. ¶ I have found an Italian playwright whose plays I adore, the Sicilian Luigi Pirandello. Philosophical farces, actually,—strange contorted domestic situations illustrating some metaphysical proposition, with one eccentric raissoneur in the cast to point out the strangely suggestive implications of the action. The very titles evoke an idea of his method: "Se Non Cosí" "Cosí è (se vi pare)" "Il Piacere dell' Onestà" "Ma non è una cosa seria."

¶ One of our boys here is developing such serious hallucinations that he may have to be treated for madness. He is insanely in love with a lady more clever than considerate, and altho' she is away fancies her arrival momently, prepares imaginary teas under the delusion that she is arriving, rushes out as each streetcar climbs the hill. He fancies also that she is just around the corner but refuses to come in, that she stands evening-long under the arc light opposite gazing at his window, or prowling about the iron fence of the Villino Bellacci. By an impossible chain of logic he fancies me in league with her, dictating letters for her to have mailed from Siena (where she is in fact) while she obscurely fixes her gaze upon him in Rome. I no longer try to reason with him; (as Freud will tell you) the idee fixe is only agravated by contradiction. The woman is a pure adventuress,—like the woman in my play strangely enough, a Bohemian countess.[22] ¶ I had myself a strange little sentimental experience that made concrete the warnings that Continental women however impersonal, comradely and full of good sense they seem, cannot understand friendship that is without romantic concommittants, cannot, cannot. Queer!

love Thornton

---

22 TNW is referring to "Villa Rhabini," which survives in holograph and in a typescript carbon in the Beinecke Library at Yale University.

68. TO AMOS P. WILDER. ALS 2 pp. Yale

American Express Co. 11 Rue Scribe Paris
June 27, 1920<1921> • Sunday

Dear Papa:

A letter came from Mother dated June 1, Mt. Carmel, giving me directions to write her at the boat's landing Southampton. But it only reached me on the 16th and I could never meet her then, so I await further addresses. People about here are full of the delays and losses of mail in the American Express Co; I hope I am missing no one's letters altogether.

Well, I have begun conducting a column in the Telegram called The Boulevards and the Latin Quarter. It takes no time to do it and I am already following up openings that lead to jobs to combine with it. But there is so much "call Thursday, if you can. Mr. Y will be here," calling over and over. If I get enough of these, I hope you will approve of my staying until Xmas. I am making as little inroad as possible into the money that is understood to be my passage money. I have still over 1500 francs there, and if the readers and advisers of the new Telegram write in that the chatty theatrical column is an ornament I shall be taken on regularly and perhaps given more—interviewing and so on. In the meantime I am provided with addresses of American movie people who want someone to write cinema "titles" etc.[23]

Don't worry or think about me. I wear clean linen, brush my teeth, "hear Mass" and drink much certified water. Without sticking to Americans I meet many people you would like to feel near me in ambiguous Paris—Mrs. Sergeant Kendall, for instance. Polly Comstock (of Trumbull St.) asked me to lunch at her pension the other day, and there was a Mr. Winslow of Madison who remember<s> me as a baby. I couldn't tell him that Mr. Cushing and himself were the two people always held up as object-lessons to avoid. Bill Douglas is here, too.[24]

---

23 The *Telegram* was the only English-language evening newspaper in Paris. TNW submitted several articles on the theater to them, but none were published.

24 Mrs. Kendall and Polly Comstock were New Haven acquaintances; William Douglas was a friend of TNW's from Yale who published poetry in the *Yale Literary Magazine*.

Steve Benét returned to America, but will be back in October. I have met his fiancée here, a journalist on the Tribune.[25] She has made him give up drinking so, or almost. Mrs. Wells is here, though I haven't seen her yet. It seems quite true that Danford Barney[26] is incredibly mean and brutal to his wife. I ran into Frank Brownell of Thacher and his mother the other day; and a young Mr. and Mrs. Holcomb York of New Haven. I don't know what's become of Amos and Charlotte since last I wrote you. Charlotte hasn't even acknowledged the receipt of the twenty-eight dollars which vexes me: I have all the receipts however.

I buy little penny paper copies of the great French classics and read indefatigably, but I am increasingly at a loss how to find opportunities to speak French at <a> stretch. I go often to the clubrooms of the American University Union and there are some notices hung up there of students wishing to exchange hours with an American but inquiry at the desk reveals that the notices are months old and the requests long filled. This is something to worry about for me—since you must—and also about the difficulty of keeping one's stomach working regularly. And the distastefulness of having to go to public baths for one's shower; a vulgar practice that I resent, universal and respectable though they are over here. I am often homesick for America or Italy. The Frenchmen are not so immediately "sympathetic" as the Italians, and I am eager for letters from you and mother. I should like to know if the Mt Carmel house is given up, and if you are left to the depressing emptiness of Taylor Hall.[27] I hope you have made a homely room in the Graduate Club,[28] with your photographs, Thoreau, and the neckties (from which Amos and I long since rifled the best) about you—I remember against the wall, too, long envelopes bursting with matter that I have always supposed to be your notes on the years in China. They will be in your

---

25 Rosemary Carr.

26 Barney (1892–1952), Yale class of 1916, was a poet and photographer.

27 A residence hall at Yale, also known as West Divinity Hall, it was torn down in 1931 to make way for Calhoun College.

28 Located on the edge of the Yale campus, it was a private club that contained rooms for boarders.

new room. A cup or two of Amos's.[29] You may feel quite free to smoke, too, for even if it's example should penetrate to me, it would do little harm for I don't finish a cigarette a week. An arrangement so that you can read in bed, read Walpole and Burke and Mrs. Montague and Swift—all the inexhaustible standards that wait for me someday when I have lost both legs in a streetcar accident, and need stout trenchant reading. Copies of The Literary Digest and other sources to transmute into public reflection.

You see I wish you happy. When you have counted your troubles with a certain Puritan satisfaction in the reflection that the Inexplicable Disposer of Things has thought you worthy of trials beyond the endurance or even sympathy of most men—leave me out. Consider me as some other man's son, strange and remote, loving you at that distance prodigiously and unaccountably.

Thornton

69. TO ISABELLA N. WILDER. ALS 4 pp. Yale

269 Rue St. Jacques.
<Paris>
Thurs. <August 1921>

Dear Mother:

I'm so amazed I don't know what to do! All the millions of French books I've read this last year haven't helped me the slightest in speaking or in grammar? However I am bold to bluff. I rushed right out to take a lesson every day with a certain lady who has been taking my fellow-pensionairres; she will supplement my forced marches through grammars at home.

I shall come over and see you very soon but not until the day

29 Tennis trophies TNW's brother won in amateur tournaments.

before my <u>mois</u>[30] is up here—money must be saved at every corner, and although its worth a hundred dollars that I should see you again before going back, it is hardly worth ten that I should see you seven days instead of six. So I shall probably come over—following your directions—the night of the 26th of August. More later.

Let Isabel be very cautious about her movie course. The magazines are flooded with inducements to take courses. Let us talk over.[31]

I shall try and see Aunt Charlotte tomorrow morning, although I have heard no word of her.[32]

I have not cashed the money yet but am sure it will go through as quietly as the other did. ¶ A letter from father Aug. 1. in which from what he says he seems not to have received my cable YES nor my S.O.S!

Lawrenceville you know is the smart prep. school for Princeton and entertains only big husky team material. Oh, how well dressed I must be! I'd better grow a moustache for maturity.

Well, well, I'm as excited as a decapitated goose. Will see you soon. I might perhaps get a later sailing but I'd rather not and I dont think Father'd mind, since my stay has been a month prolonged as it is.

None of you say how you like London. It has finally broken into Rain here and the whole world seems better. You must polish up your French and find a neighbor or two, a French maid perhaps who will sit on the area steps with me gently exchanging subjunctives.

Isn't it perfectly mad of Father; but it'll be awfully good for me in the long run.

Love to the whole caboodle.

Thorny—soon

---

30 French: month

31 During this period, Isabel Wilder was writing one-act plays, two of which TNW copyrighted for her in 1922; apparently, she saw in a magazine an advertisement for a course in writing for the movies, which interested her.

32 TNW's aunt was probably in Paris in connection with her work for the YWCA.

70. TO AMOS P. WILDER. ALS 4 pp. Yale

Oct. 3 • 1921
Lawrenceville

Dear Father:

I didn't realize until I got your letter, on returning from Trenton that the suit and the other obligations were to be separate. I didn't send you enough, of course. So I am enclosing the first of my checks. Will send on more whenever you say.

I hope they can cash this for you without delay; otherwise let me know by card and I will send you the same thing by postal money-order.

The work goes on by strange ups-and-downs. The heart of the matter is that no amount of good intentions or mental coërcion can really bring my interests into our table conversation, our discussions of verbs, of athletics. I am still in Europe. I especially cannot forget Italy. The boys see instinctively that I am not the collegiate live-wire.

But then again—especially mornings before I am tired by the awful excitement of dragging a class through the iron teeth of an assignment—I seem to be irresponsible and "good fellow" and we exchange the expected breakfast remarks with all the spontaneity in the world. There are a number of boys in the house for whom Mr. Wilder is quite an adequate Assistant House Master. I get on well with Mr. Foresman too, but I suspect he regrets not have<having> the vigorous snorter assigned to him.

There are times of great pleasure in the class-room when I know I'm not merely adequate, but really good. It only took me a day to reach perfect composure; I usually stroll about if a class is reciting well directing olympianally now from the side now from the back. With my older class—we are reading a French classic—quite unconsciously I get drawn into some exposition of idea or technical expression—and I suddenly think that that art of holding twenty intelligences in hushed attention is going to justify my coming down here in the capacity of unprepared teacher and unsuitable companion

—afftly
Thorny

Davis House, Lawrenceville School.

71. TO CHARLES H. A. WAGER. ALS 1 p. Oberlin

<Lawrenceville>
Nov. 4 • 1921

Dear Dr. Wager:

Four evenings a week I sit up in my study from seven until ten while my thirty-two boys do their preparation for the morrow. They begin to drop in, a difficult phrase in Caesar, a little Trig, "Please, sir, what does mendacity mean?" some French, a little chat, "would you like some fudge my sister made, sir?" Every now and then there is a sound of scuffling on one of the three floors. I rise, and descend the stairs with majestic and perfectly audible advance, dispensing awe and order like fragrance. Finally fifteen minutes freedom before lights-out; sudden activity, four Victrolas play, rushings to the bathroom, four-part harmony. Then the last bell and I lower the lights. An expensive benevolent peace invests us; my heavy reconnoitring footsteps flower into symbolic significance as I lock the backdoors and try the windows. Follows about ten minutes of furtive whisperings from bed to bed, and they fall off to sleep—most of them having sustained the incessant impacts of football practice throughout three hours of the afternoon. People said to me Never teach school, You will be so unhappy, It will deaden you. But what happy surprises you find here; how delightful the relations of the teacher and an interested class; casual encounters with retiring boys on the campus, and at lights-out the strange big protective feeling, locking the doors against dark principalities and powers and thrones, and the great lamp-eyed whales that walk ashore in New Jersey—

Thornton

72. TO AMOS P. WILDER. ALS 4 pp. Yale

Davis House
March 4 <19>'22
night

Dear Father:

I wish I wrote you often. My natural inertia is now fortified by my professional lack of quiet time, and I write even less often than before. ¶ It is agreed that I am to stay on here another year. I had no way of knowing whether I "suited" or not,—at times it seemed to me that the Headmaster loathed me, my housemaster longed for a change of assistant, and the boys on the point of petitioning my removal. But these must have been phantoms of an (at times) overworked nervous system, for the day, March 1, when you must announce your decision about next year, and when—so says the contract—the H'dmaster must announce his objection to you, if such there be, has gone by. Mr. Foresman was amazed when I told him that I had expected to be called into the Foundation House, told that I was an entertaining guest but that they required a more athletic type. He told me that I was considered a pearl of great price, that he for the first time felt secure about the house when he was absent, and that if the vote of the boys counted for anything I had reason to feel signally pleased. There is a considerable amount of double-reading in all this that mitigates its flattery, but on the whole I feel like one who has come out of a perplexed bad dream into a more confident waking.

My little English Club is coming along in the most delightful manner. The boys read very earnest bad original poems to oneanother. We take, eight of us, walks through the bare tree trunks of a hesitant Spring; its really too easy for me—imaginative boys from homes and schools that never fed an imagination—my flattest remarks on books or style or even people are manna to them. I'd like to give you all their innocent names if I thought they would evoke for you as they do for me, the awkwardness and charm and rush of their opening minds. ¶ We have almost found, you and I, that, with food and shelter, I can be happy almost anywhere. If the Amherst offer comes after all, and now I can no longer accept it, without doubt it indicates a scene where I might too have been happy; but not happier than my second year promises to be. Now I have learned some of the principles of teaching, now that I have mastered all but the obstinate core of the problem of classroom discipl<in>e (the core—those one or two fundamentally bad boys who are bored and restless and vindictive anywhere except in a pond of mud); and that I have made many friends and got over my worried distressed eager-to-please attitude,—I look forward to reaping a harvest after my real labors of this year.

Will you send an occasional letter of mine to Oxford. I write to the mad air-fed ladies every now and then myself. To you I can write hurriedly, between bells, but to them I compose like an artificer, and the result <is> I write them with despicable infrequency. Keep urging the wild witch Charlotte to tell me how it goes.[33] ¶ If I save hard, am I justified in looking forward to months on it at Monhegan this summer?

love from

Thornton

---

33 Charlotte Wilder had moved to Boston, where she worked as a companion/secretary to a family, then as a governess, and then as a proofreader at *The Atlantic Monthly.*

73. TO THE EDITORS OF *THE DIAL*. TLS 1 p. Yale

Box 282, Newport, R.I.
August 3, 1922

The Editors of The Dial
152 West 13th Street
New York City.

Dear Sirs:—

I am submitting under separate cover the MSS of a series of imaginary memoirs of a year spent in Rome, entitiled The Trasteverine. These give the appearance of being faithful portraits of living persons, but the work is a purely fanciful effort in the manner of Marcel Proust, or at times, of Paul Morand.[34]

Attached hereto find return postage.

Very truly yours,
Thornton N. Wilder

74. TO ISABELLA N. WILDER. TLS 2 pp. Yale

Box 282, Newport, R.I.
August 22, 1922

Dear Mom:

I have told the family where I tutor that I must go away Friday; so now I give a lesson every day and am a solid fellow. In the afternoons I take the ferry to Jamestown, walk out to a remote point of land, so far from the World (that father cannot get over his fear I am in town to cultivate!) that I need only wear the trunk of my bathing-suit. Here I

---

34 During the summer of 1922, in a rented room at the YMCA in Newport, Rhode Island, TNW, stimulated by his reading of French authors Proust and Morand, continued writing what later evolved into *The Cabala*.

read and read, exposing myself to the ultra-violet rays of the sun that give me a thorough sunburn. Every now and then I plunge in and swim a big arc, then come back to read some more. The other day as I was just about to enter the ferry on my return a boy came running out of breath to shake hands; a Laurentian whom I didn't remember from Adam, but an auspicious beginning of the new year.

There is a new, very radical magazine, called the Double Dealer, published in New Orleans, that has accepted two "Sentences" of mine, drawn from the Roman memoirs. I've never even seen a copy of the paper; but will forward all to you when it comes out.[35] "The Dial" a very high class, though ultramodern, review is flirting with the publication of the whole Memoir. I only sent them the first book, ten or twelve thousand words. They write back that it is hard to estimate a fragment, that some pages are interesting, and those that aren't may be so because of their relation to the unfinished whole. They enco<u>rage me to send them the rest. Well, I can hardly send them books seven and eight when I have not begun Book Two. And I am unwilling to kill myself with the composition of an interminable Book Two without still greater assurance of their using it.[36]

You remember that I told you how when I met Mrs Augustus St Gaudens in Rome? She confided to me that her son, Homer, the stage designer, was engaged in dramatizing General Ople and Lady Camper, a long short story of George Meredith, for Maude Adams, their very good friend.[37] I suddenly became curious to see it and send<sent> to Trixie Troxell,[38] my friend in the Yale Library, to send it to me. It is quite amusing, but utterly unsuited to stage arrangement; and the idea of Maude Adams as the sophisticated dictatorial Lady Camper is the crowning absurdity. Since then I am mulling a play about the riotous

---

35 The short sections appeared in the September 1922 issue of *The Double Dealer,* a little magazine that in that same year published early work by William Faulkner and Ernest Hemingway.

36 *The Dial* did not publish any of TNW's fictional memoir.

37 Augusta Homer Saint-Gaudens was the widow of the noted American sculptor; their son, Homer Saint-Gaudens, was an author, art critic, and museum director. At one time, he worked as a stage director for American actress Maude Adams.

38 Gilbert McCoy Troxell (1893–1967), a friend of TNW's while they were both Yale undergraduates, was at the time working at the Yale library, where he later became the curator of the Yale Collection of American Literature. They remained good friends until Troxell's death.

character of the Countess of Saldar in *Evan Harrington*.[39] I tell you all these tentatives because it may set you reading the old books to distract your mind, and because even as unfinished impulses they might interest you.

The fleet has been in the harbor and the community is after giving them a block dance. A stretch of well-paved Washington Square, as wide as the Yale campus and twice as long was roped off and sprinkled with corn meal. The moon was shamed by strings of colored electric bulbs and by batteries of searchlights with petticoats of amber gelatine in front of them. Up until eight oclock a twenty-foot hem of craning citizens was held back by the police, while in the center of the naked acre on a few precarious chairs sat the patronesses, Mrs Admiral Sims, the mayoress, and some ladies from the Summer Colony whose closest connexion with the navy resided in the fact that they were great-granddaughters-in-law of Cornelys van der Bildt,[40] the ferry-boy of Staten Island and pseudo-commodore. The grand march was so long that it reminded me of the armies of David Belasco[41] where, as soon as a soldier passes out of sight of the audience, he rushes around behind the scenes and re-enters on the other sight<side> as some one else; it was headed by a great deal of gold braid and brought up by a million gobs and their girls. There were two alternating bands composed of musicians off all the cruisers and very good they were too. I went and stood near them to subject my deliciously suffering spine to the rages and hurricane of the great brasses; just as in Rome (when the *lira* was at twenty-eight) I would get a seat for Verdi's *Otello* fairly on the percussion, so that during the Taking of the Oath at the end of the Second Act my nervous system might happily be reduced to rags. Someday I shall take a camp stool and sit inside the bass drum during a performance of *Elektra*.

You will have a great headache from seeing all these misprints. I will close by saying that I shall not be able to see Charlotte after all; she

---

39 Novel (1861) by George Meredith.

40 Cornelius Vanderbilt began his career by ferrying passengers from Staten Island to Manhattan.

41 Belasco (1853–1931), American director, dramatist, and manager.

is gone on a few vacation trips until the thirtieth. I take the night boat for New York Friday night and will be with Father Monday morning to help him on the Journal Courier for two weeks while he goes to Maine. I don't know what he thinks I can do, but I am willing to try. Love to you all, named Wilder and to Aunt Charlotte. I am eager to hear anything you can snatch time to say.

love
Thornt

75. TO ISABELLA N. WILDER. ALS 4 pp. Yale

Davis House Lawrenceville NJ.
Sept 19 • 1922

Dear Mother:

I must write you something at this psychological moment. This is the first night that the boys are back in the house. Mr Foresman is away at committee meeting and I have just turned out the last lights. A most well-omened silence wraps the house. Thirty-three heads have fallen back on their pillows as though they had been chopped off. The excitement of arriving and shaking several hundred hands has fatigued them, just as football practice and Latin will next week. There are a dozen new boys in the house and of course we are all looking each other over furtively. There are almost a dozen new masters in the School, too, all young but three. They come from all sorts of backgrounds and are much shyer than even the new boys. Mr. and Mrs. Foresman, with whom I live are looking well; he is a little stout man, an old football celebrity, with blunt ideas and a jovial reticent manner; she is much superior intellectually, a Cornell graduate, but domesticating rapidly—her not inconsiderable good-looks gradually approaching the benignant maternal. Her French and Latin are in astonishingly good repair, and we play piano four-hands after a fashion. The baby Emily, age three, is a squirming little girl with a piquant French face. Contrasting though we are, Mr. Foresman and I get on finely. I often think that the reason I have got on in the House so well, is because his personal affection for me is always forseeing and averting things that might embarrass me. The result is that I am being extremely well paid for being happy. In return fortunately I am able tacitly to help him; today, for example: Mr. Foresman has a horror of meeting the fathers and mothers and making conversation. Consequently in the face of express orders from Foundation House to stay at home, he drives off to Trenton, and leaves to me to a dozen fascinating encounters with mamas depositing their sons in our spiritual Pawn-shop* Human nature is often as simplified as the comic supplements represent it: I have had exactly twelve proud, deprecating, anxious accounts of some priceless sons. The same apology for their inability to study, the same confidence that the fundamental gray-matter is all right, the same anxiety about blankets.

I have written now into profoundest night. The last mattress has creaked, the last slipper flopped back from the bathroom, the last yawn-blurred words between room-mates, exchanged.

lots of love
Thornt.

* (asterisk) The elaboration of this metaphor is as follows: Cornelia deposits her jewels with us and we give her the coin of relief from responsibility for her sons' character, of the terrors of disciplining them, and from their noise crudity and moods. In due time we render them back to her, and she wears them, the jewels, in the most public places, pretending that they<their> care had been her's all the time.

Dear Mom:—

I forget whether I sent you a copy of The Plain<Double> Dealer, so if I send you another put it down to utter indifference to the honor of print, rather than to pride. I shall send you Lefty's novel[42] too, when I can get into Trenton. You should see my room. I got an introduction to a department store and started shopping on account. Two deep blue

42 Wilmarth Sheldon "Lefty" Lewis (1895–1979) was TNW's schoolmate at both Thacher and Yale; his 1922 novel was *Tutors' Lane.*

rep curtains as a portere between my study and my bedroom (there was a dusty red thing there last year) two deep blue strip rugs crossed the empty bit of floor by my desk, a really beautiful blue, without design except for two inches of still darker blue around the edge; and white curtains for both windows. Vous m'en direz des nouvelles![43] I just controlled myself from buying one big deep blue rug a foot thick, that would pervade the room and (being a little too big) would turn up to climb the walls for about an inch all around, like the toe of a Turkish slipper. I have a big rectangle of blue cloth that says YALE on it, but it seems to have been lost over the Summer; it was to be, of course, the keystone of the decorative plan!

I am to teach 24 hours this year, if there is still pressure on me to take an hour of Bible. Naturally with such a load I don't have to take any Study hour supervision in the Big Study (that I am very glad to be out of). I have no 1st Formers to teach, though I was supposed to have shown some aptitude for the wrigglers last year: instead I teach a 2nd 3rd 4th and 5th—these last two mature ones are, of course, my dulce decus.[44]

I am fashioning a new 3-minute playlet, very strange called And The Sea shall give up its Dead,[45] which I shall send you, if it comes to anything.

Excuse now if your grown-up and busy son rushes away to help boys arrange their schedules to direct tramping negroes on the stairs as to the destination of trunks, and to brush the teeth of his thirty three stoopids. Love to Isabel, who may find an outlet for herself and a chance of helping Charlotte enormously on that page of the Youth's Companion.[46] I've just about broken my neck looking around for something else odd to send Janet, but I swear there's no originality in our shops. To Amos a salute, as we may be on the brink of new wars, wars in Palestine too for a generation that can see no irony. love

Thornts

43 French: You tell me what you think!

44 Latin: sweet glory.

45 This playlet was published in the January–February 1923 issue of the little magazine *S_4N*, where TNW's writing appeared with some regularity.

46 Charlotte was a junior editor of *The Youth's Companion*.

76. TO ISABELLA N. WILDER. ALS 2 pp. Yale

Davis House, Lawrenceville, N.J.
Oct 9, 1922

My Dear Mrs. Wilder,

Your son has asked me to write to you in his stead for two reasons. The first is that he is so ashamed of not having written you for so long that he has no idea of how he should begin. The second is that since you have never received a letter from Lawrenceville written by anyone except himself, you might enjoy someone else's view of the life there. I am not only in his house, but in two of his classes and can give you some idea of how he appears to us.

If you are going to excuse his silence, it will be a shear act of grace. It is only fair however to tell you the few arguments he might put forward. He teaches twenty-four hours; most of the masters have between eighteen and twenty-three. The correction of papers for so many is enormous, to say nothing of the tiredness that follows it at night. Besides just as he was about to write you last week something urgent arose. One night while we were at supper I was bidden to answer the telephone. It was for him—a long distance call from New Haven. When I told him they were waiting for him, he changed colour, dropped his spoon into the soup, and ran. It turned out to be Mr. De Lacy of the Brick Row Book Shop. Mr. Hackett had been struck by an editorial in the Journal-Courier during the Summer on the Shelley Century, and had called up your husband, thinking he had written it. Dr. Wilder redirected him to your son. They wanted a longer article in the same vein, to be printed in the Yale Alumni Weekly as an introduction to the collection of Shelleyana they were offering for sale shortly. The collection was to include a locket containing some of the poet's ashes, set in fourteen aquamarines and listed at three hundred and fifty dollars, a beautiful portrait of Mary Wallstonecraft Shelley, for the first time drawn out from the obscurity of a private collection, and many first editions. The Book Shop assumed that the article would be a labor of love, but would instruct its treasurer to mail him ten dollars. This was Thursday night and the material must be in New Haven Monday. The school pressure was hard enough without this, but he undertook it. He has intimated that if the article is printed in the Weekly and meets the favor of such Tinkers, Phelps, Berdans,[47] as have hitherto watched him but doubted his adequacy to conventional tasks, like that, it might lead to offers of college teaching. Again, it is probably a delicate sounder from the Book Shop that has now three branches and is looking for cultivated young men to station at their outposts. At present he feels disinclined to join either connexion, but he would like to have them offered to him. The finished essay was amusing, although it had serious weaknesses of structure. To me it has a tremendous air of learning, though Mr. Wilder says that is merely the result of a hasty pillage of some source books that can be found in any good library. It is not unlikely however that the article will not suit the requirements of the Book Shop; it does not go into ecstacies over the brooch filled with ashes, and a repulsive portrait of Shelley (companion piece to that of his wife) is given a cold notice. Everybody knows that the Brick Row Shop has grown more and more bloodlessly financial, and the economic interpretation of your son's piece is temperate; he refused to boot-lick. However, it is at least suave; they may have to use it for lack at that eleventh hour of other material. If it goes in, he is almost certain of its attracting notice. In parts it is green, but in others it is trenchant and witty with his characteristic precision of words tempered of late by his much French reading.[48]

We get on very well with him in the house. He almost never interferes with us, and we do not play dirty tricks on him like they do in other Houses. He doesn't come out and watch our football much, but perhaps if he were the kind that did he wouldn't be able so well to help us in Latin etcetera. In class he talks so fast and jumps on you so sudden for recitations that often you don't know a thing. Please write him for his own good to speak slowlier, as it would be for his own good. Of course this year he is an old master now, and has the hang of keeping a classroom down and never has to give marks, any more, or even fire us out of the room, like new masters do. He must have learnt

47 Like Tinker and Phelps, John M. Berdan was also a celebrated member of the Department of English at Yale.

48 The article was published as "The Shelley Centenary—A Notable Exhibition of Shelleyana at the Brick Row Book Shop" in the October 13, 1922, issue of the *Yale Alumni Weekly.*

summers somewhere. Can you explain why he hasn't any pictures of girls in his room, nor even of you, everybody has pictures of women in their room, can you explain this? Why did you give him a name like Thornton for, didn't you know it would be a thing we would hold against him, you might have made it Theodore through<though> even Theodore is bad, and Bill or Fred is best. Don't think I'm crabbing, because after all he's all right for the present and you don't expect a master to be everything. He says he has some sisters, are they good-looking, or are they like him, and nothing can be done about it. Thanking you for your patients, I am

faithfully yours
George Sawyer Naylor.

77. TO ISABELLA N. WILDER. ALS 2 pp. Yale

Davis House Lawrenceville N.J.
Feb 10 • 1923

Dear Mama:

Your wandering boy tonight is very contrite. If Father however forwarded to you my playlet, as I bade him, let me count that as a letter, and the case is a little less damaging.[49] My letter before that described to you my Xmas vacation. Since then I have lain very low in Lawrenceville, teaching without respite. Last Tuesday however a fellow-Master, Mr. Rich, two faculty ladies and I acted Barrie's The New Word[50] before the Woman's Club. This choice one-act play was in the volume Isabel sent me a year ago with the inscription "bought in a shop in Tottenham Court Road." We are to repeat our performance Thursday night in front of the boys, our most exacting public. I am including

49 TNW is probably referring to "And the Sea Shall Give Up Its Dead."

50 TNW had recommended this play to his father during its 1917 New York run (see letter number 52).

a review I wrote of our student Dramatic Club's latest effort.[51] So much for "events."

Isabel's letters from Paris to yourself, to Father, and to me—I receive them all ultimately, are absorbing reading. My stomach faints with emotion at the very address: 269 Rue St. Jacques. I expect I shall have saved enough for a trip by this Summer, but I am afraid to use it. Any sums I may be able to put by (and even such will be less than a thousand) will be too valuable as a resource for us Wilders and I do not want to touch it until the year following. No doubt you are astounded to notice this touch of avarice; but believe me, I am a very naughty boy and the reverse of avaricious. I am just about agreed to join one of two Summer Camps that are angling for me—to do a little French tutoring, spend the days in a bathing-suit under breezes smelling of the pines, with almost no fixed or disciplinary duties. There will be a considerable interim at the beginning and end of the Summer, and generous leaves of absence during it, so if you are back here I shall <be> transported with joy and at your side. Father says the Adams are urging you to take their house for the Summer months, and in combination with the reduced fare to Mamauguin[52] it seems a good start. Turn it over for yourself however, carina[53]; I'm behint you.

Great long stretches of my Roman Memoirs are now done, and I've a good mind to group together the Society sections and try and send them out into the world first, under the title: Elizabeth Grier and her Circle. To many readers they will seem (this show of the low-life and ecclesiastical material with which in the ultimate version they are relieved) too gossipy and feminine. Many passages however are of a valuable mordant satire, and others drenched with restrained pity; I am not ashamed of it. You would be a great help, but I cannot send my forlorn unique text across the ocean.

---

51 TNW's review of English dramatist, poet, and novelist Oliver Goldsmith's *She Stoops to Conquer* ran on the front page of the student newspaper *The Lawrence* on February 8, 1923.

52 Momauguin was a beach community and resort in East Haven, on Long Island Sound; TNW's family probably spent some of the summer there.

53 Italian: dear.

Charlotte's essay in the Atlantic[54] has made a pretty stir in Lawrenceville. She has been sending me some sonnets of her writing that will make you hold your breath. If she keeps on right she may discover herself as something of a very high order that will scatter our magazine poetesses, as a hawk does the hens. Don't say I didn't tell you. What is the secret, madam, of having astonishing children? thousands of pretty, intelligent mothers growing old among their dull prosperous and unappreciative sons and daughters ask you that question. Their life threatens to be a decrescendo; have you any advice as to how young mothers can guarantie themselves a crescendo?

Albert Parker Fitch[55] of Amherst spoke at our School service today admirably. I met him here last year and twice this year; Stark Young[56] had told him about me too,—we had fine talks. He spent the Summer at Fiesole in perfect quiet at a nuns' nursing home. I have a letter from Gwynne Abbott[57] full of how charming you and Isabel are. She has gone on to Merano in the Tyrol.

Anybody care to know what I've been reading. I'm now in the XIII' th tome of Saint-Simon,[58] more adoring than ever. This influence, believe me, arrived most à propos—henceforward whenever I am endangered of falling into silken felicities and jewelled or flute-like cadences I have only to remember this memoirist whose three greatest virtues are energy and energy and energy. I have just read also "Siegfried et le limousin"[59] by Giraudoux which I like for the rather weak reason that it is interested in the same things that interest me. The second instalment of your Xmas present has come and I have just derived a vast amount of pleasure from Doormats and Outcast. Who is Janet

---

54 Charlotte Wilder's brief essay "Hail and Farewell," an impressionistic piece about places visited and remembered, appeared in the January 1923 issue of *The Atlantic Monthly.*

55 Fitch was professor of the history of religion at Amherst College and author of *Preaching and Paganism* (1920).

56 At this time, Young was the chief drama critic of *The New Republic* and an associate editor of *Theatre Arts Magazine.* TNW met him on shipboard when returning from Europe in August 1921.

57 Daughter of Mather A. Abbott, headmaster of Lawrenceville.

58 Saint-Simon's *Memoirs* offers a vivid account of life in the court of Louis XIV.

59 *Siegfried et le Limousin* (1922), a novel by French dramatist and novelist Jean Giraudoux (1882–1944), which the author later adapted into a play, *Siegfried* (1928).

that you mention in your letters? some Y.W. worker doubtless; you say she enjoyed The Mollusc—send me a photograph.[60] I can't abide women who aren't pretty; must I advance money for milk baths and electric exhilirators to make her more presentable? Is she by any chance interested in horses? When my book's published, and I'm very rich, I'm going to live in the Connecticut hills and own a large stable of horses that can tell time and play bridge etc. I shall need a capable women <woman>, sympathetic (and pretty) to put over them. If you know anybody who might suit, have her write me at once and enclose a photograph. You can see how my ink is turning quite red with eagerness, and quite illegible with fear that such a valuable woman can't be found.

—Quite a time has gone by since I began this letter and I want to add that my Eliz. Grier and her Circle is almost finished—watch and pray

love from a drying aging schoolmaster
Thornton

78. TO EDITH J. R. ISAACS. AL (Draft)[61] 3 pp. Yale

<Lawrenceville, New Jersey>
May 3 • 1923

Dear Mrs. Isaacs:

Please take your time over the four acts I sent you.[62] When reckoning comes do not spare me: I learn meekly. Besides they are from a closed chapter; after them came Dada.

---

60 *Doormats, Outcast,* and *The Mollusc* were plays by Hubert Henry Davies; all three were published in vol. 2 of *The Plays of Hubert Henry Davies* (1921), which may be the Christmas present to which TNW refers.

61 Between May 1, 1923, and December 31, 1923, TNW hand-copied many of the letters he sent into a "Letter Book." This unsigned transcription is from that copy; the original letter has not been located.

62 TNW sent his play "The Trumpet Shall Sound" to Edith Isaacs, the editor of *Theatre Arts Magazine.* The play had been published in four successive issues of the *Yale Literary Magazine* (October, November, December 1919; January 1920) and won Yale's Bradford Brinton Award. While Isaacs did not accept the play for publication, she was instrumental in arranging its first production in 1926 (for which TNW made some revisions to his text).

Last night I shook hands with Max Reinhardt.

In the summer of Sixteen I spent a week on the lonely island of Monhegan, off the coast of Maine. In the colony of surf-painters and solitaries, human sea-gulls, that such an island would attract I frequented a group of Germans that gathered every evening in the draughty pine-board studio of I no longer know what musician, There was Herr Doktor Kuhnemann, University of Breslau, author of a standard life of Schiller; a Fraülein Schmidt or Müller, head of the German department at Bryn Mawr or Smith (one could verify these in an hour); and a Viennese dramatic critic named Rudolph<Rudolf> Kommer, who answered with unfailing good humor and wit my thousands of questions. Even while I was on the island I heard that the group was suspected of espionage, but, after I left, my Aunt says they were convicted of midnight signalling to a submarine base nearby, and interned. All these years go by and I see in the Sunday Times of two weeks ago that the article therein on Reinhardt is by Rudolph<Rudolf> Kommer now travelling with him as interpreter and agent. Just after I had made my plans to go to *The Cherry Orchard* in Philadelphia last night I saw, again in The Times, that Reinhardt was running down from New York to see the same performance. Sure enough, at the close of the first act, there he was in a stage box (with a gloriously beautiful actress setting off her face with the waftings of a huge feather fan in Paris green), and there behind him sat Rudolph<Rudolf> Kommer. They did not leave the box until the next intermission, when I pushed down the alley. Kommer was very cordial; declared that he had been wondering how he could find me, etc. He introduced me to Reinhardt, with a rapid, "*nur als knabe er kannte mehr vom deutschen Literatur als die meisten Deutschen*."[63] You know that the producer is astonishingly young and homely, but with bright eyes, and with a pretty, deferential manner. After a few polite changes, he said in good English that he was with a lady and must go; and went.

Kommer then said that it was all settled that he would return for production in the Fall; that he would begin with a big pantomime

63 German: even as a boy he knew more of German literature than most Germans.

spectacle (though he is no longer fond of them); and that he ultimately hoped to do Strindberg's The Dream Play and Shakespeare. He is excited about America, stunned and bewitched by the Ziegfeld Follies, and by the negro entertainers (he mentioned The Plantations). Kommer said that they had been to many plays and that Reinhardt was always pointing out actors in roles of fourth and fifth importance who were full of possibilities; he added that some of the actors for his Fall season were selected already.

Perhaps you have met them yourself these days and know a great deal more than this.

In the afternoon I saw Henry Miller, Blanche Bates, Laura Hope Crews and Ruth Chatterton in The Changelings a jumbled comedy by a New Haven friend, Lee Wilson Dodd; a quilt of contrasted intentions—ten minutes of drama about misguided ladies stealing to bachelors' apartments; sudden rush for chairs and a poor Shavian badinage about morality; Blanche Bates suddenly turns farcical and does Hermione[64] (just before the curtain she will return to her Noble Mother tune); stretches of preachment about pretty wives who shirk light-housekeeping and on studious young husbands who do not admit their wives into their enthusiasms and Ph.D. theses. Oh, how bad it was; even Laura Hope Crews was bad. And in the intermission Blanche Bates made a speech about how they all loved Henry Miller, how they knew they were out of the beaten track of the theatre, but that they were glad and proud to be with him, who had always led out in the direction of the Best Things in the Theatre........and Stanislawsky[65] and Reinhardt both in town!

I should love to write you for seven days and nights, but I shall see you soon—unless you leave for Europe before the third week of June. You will have a glorious trip, but you will not regret too much arriving back in New York for the finest season in our history.

Give my very best to your husband and children. I hope I can see

---

64 Presumably, TNW is referring to the tragic Queen Hermione in Shakespeare's *The Winter's Tale*.

65 Russian director and actor Konstantin Stanislavski (1865–1938), cofounder of the Moscow Art Theatre.

you when I come up from graduation, but I shall not force you to choose between me and Italy.

Affectionately,

P.S. I forgot to say that Kommer mentioned by name Bel-Geddes[66] as one of the younger artists Reinhardt hoped to work with.

79. TO ISABELLA N. WILDER. ALS 2 pp. Yale

Davis House,
June 5 • 1923

Dear Mother;

Just a page to supplement the letters Father and Uncle Thornton wrote you about Grandmother's last days.[67] Father asked me if I could come up Sunday. I arrived at about two and turning into 44th St. from Broadway came upon Father leaning against the area-railings. He had waited in and around the hotel for three days, it seems, and was to be relieved that night when Uncle Thornton arrived on the midnight from St. Louis. He took me right up to Grandmother's room, nodding to the various people in the lobby all of whom were very concerned. She had been moved into a larger and lighter room, with a big bed and was attended by a homely middle-aged nurse whom Father claimed to find "superior," but who gained my confidence only by her stolidness. Father leaned down to Grandmother's ear and said that 'little Thornton from New Jersey had come up to see her'. She opened her eyes wide and I am sure she recognized me, for she framed with her lips the elongated O, and uttered the tremulous cooing noise with which she always greeted me when I knocked at her door for a visit. Father continued to

---

66 Norman Bel Geddes (1893–1958), American industrial and theatrical designer who pioneered the use of lenses in stage lighting. In 1957, TNW collaborated with Bel Geddes on the script for a film about the American experience, "The Melting Pot." Bel Geddes's death ended the venture, though TNW copyrighted the script, which survives as an undated holograph manuscript and as an undated corrected typescript in the Beinecke Library at Yale University.

67 Elizabeth Lewis Niven died in early June 1923.

repeat that it was grandson and not son Thornton, whereupon she broke into a musical but incoherent flow of words in which I read a reproach at his presuming her capable of such a mistake. Her words in themselves were clear and even beautiful; the difficulty lay not in speaking but in thinking. When after a few moments we made a motion to go, it distressed her, for she raised her hand and wrinkled her forehead in a characteristic expression of humorous reproach; so we sat down, until from fatigue or content she had closed her eyes and forgotten us. Somehow the interview was anything but painful; it seemed to breathe Grandmother at her best, sweetness and a touch of humor. Father has probably told you the many beautiful and characteristic incidents of the days he watched by her.

After that Father and I walked for a few hours in Central Park, and I left for School. I went up again for the Service on Thursday. There seemed to be quite a number of people in the Bible Study room behind the Church Auditorium (she and I had once sat there waiting for Church to begin). Father led me up to sit beside Charlotte; it had never occurred to me that she would be there and dressed in complete black. Dr. Kelman,[68] whom Grandmother admired so and had taken me to hear during my Christmas vacation, the great Dr. Kelman, opened with a wonderful prayer; it wasn't just good, for it was perfect. Then the Dobbs Ferry minister who conducted with him read some lines of your father's that Grandmother had once found for him. Then just the six of us drove out to the cemetery, to the knoll amid countless columns marked Lewis and Nitchie.

I shall miss her a lot, especially when I am in New York and suddenly realize that we cannot take up again our modest little lunches and expeditions (she so fearful lest I be ruined with the price of street fares) and our little accumulation of jokes and comments we had in common. To you who only received news of it by the cruelty of cablegrams it will seem more tragic than it has been for us who saw an end as gently disposed as is possible among us.

Lots of love
Thornton

68 John Kelman, the minister of New York's Fifth Avenue Presbyterian Church.

80. TO ISABELLA N. WILDER. ALS 4 pp. Yale

Sagawatha Lodge[69]
Lakeside, Litchfield Co.
Conn.

July 2. 1923

Dear Mother:

I suppose I've made a mistake in coming here; it's not terrible, but its hard in the queer duties laid on you and in the monotony. The whole problem of these camps is to keep the urchins amused on five acres for fourteen hours a day: nothing more difficult. They are pursued by boredom and fretfulness and homesickness. They practically desert their own baseball-games in the middle of an inning; no game (however passionately and stridently acclaimed at first) can hold them long; they adore singing, but their minds wander after twelve minutes of it; only story-telling can enthrall them long, and I hold that monopoly here, sitting on a piano-stool and narrating with my wiry hands and the changing horrors of my face. Two months of this and I see where I'll get thinner yet.

Passing through New Haven I picked up two second hand books, two by Couperus. Where was it that you and I used to read Small Souls and Dr. Adriaan? One of these Old People and Things that Pass promises—one of his complicated semi-aristocratic families of the Hague with at least five generations gradually revealing their not quite plausible secrets. The other The Inevitable I got because it was about foreigners in Rome, and its one of the poorest stories I ever read; I cant say a thing for it. Besides it has an erotic notion to proclaim that is untrue and revolting. It is surprising that there is not a single brilliant portrait among all the minor characters—one can hardly believe it's Couperus.[70] I have also just finished another amorous novel about

69 TNW spent part of the summer working at this summer camp for boys.

70 Dutch novelist Louis Marie Anne Couperus (1863–1923).

TNW at Sagawatha Lodge, July 1923.

modern Rome, Robert Hichens' The Fruitful Vine,[71] written with tremendous superficial cleverness (under that Paul Bourget-Edith Wharton bedazzlement in the presence of hotels and coronets)[72] but the love-love itterations are silly; nothing convinces; the humblest page of Dostoevsky would burn it up in a trice; I wonder why I read them. "Il y a trois choses" said La Bruyère "òu la mediocrité est insupportable: la musique, la poesie et. . . . ." I forget his third, but propose le roman.[73]

71 English novelist Hichens (1864–1950).

72 French novelist and critic Bourget (1852–1935).

73 TNW misquotes French writer Jean de La Bruyère (1645–1696). The actual quote is from *Les Caractères* (1688): "Il y a de certaines choses dont la médiocrité est insupportable: la poésie, la musique, la peinture, le discours public." ("There are certain things where mediocrity is insupportable: poetry, music, painting, and public discourse.") *Le roman* is French for the "novel."

Guess whom I at last met in New Haven? Sherman D. Thacher. I never pass through without calling on the Whitney sisters and this time (as one of their million cousins) he was staying with them. I had a long talk with him. He had the idea that I hated his school, and he was even a little ready to apologize for its inflexibility in regard to me & I hurried to reply that the school had been perfectly right and that (especially with my sharpened professional eye) I looked back upon it with increasing admiration and affection. While we were talking Pres. Hadley[74] came in with some books "for Marian"[75] (Father hints they were almost a match and what a match it would have been); he recognized me and said he was sorry not to have seen me the week before (when he was giving us our Commencement address at Lawrenceville), and left us gobbling adorably in the throes of fifty adieux. In parting S•D• said distinctly that he hoped someday I could give him a year in the Ojai. You can't estimate all that's implied there—though he hardly meant it and I wouldn't considerate it—the very fact that he could commit himself so far must mean that I've thrown off and fought off and outgrown so much. He used to despise me and shudder at the very sound of my high voice.

Tuesday.

Endless games of Flags, Authors, Birds, Flinch, Jack Straw, Dominoes, Checkers, Parchesi. Teaching stupid boys the simplest rules. Soothing the contempt bright boys feel for duller competitors. Moving Olympianly amid the shrill whirlpools of running games. Rebuking little Turks with a passionless firmness that must have come instinctively to "an experienced worker with boys." Sleeping in a log cabin with six youngsters and hearing their perpetual nagging of one another: "You dumbell". "It'd take a ton of dynamite to get through your head, you nut." "Aw, his head's ivory." "You come from a hick-Town, you hayseed—Hemstead is only a hick-town<.>" "It is not." "It is. Only one train goes to Hemstead everyday and that's a day late." "Gee, if I had a face like you got, I'd try an' get smallpox." In swimming

74 Arthur Twining Hadley was president of Yale University from 1899 to 1921.

75 Marian Whitney.

three times a day, warmish water, like swimming in tea; supporting boys' stomachs while they try their first strokes; taking out wide-eyed ten year-olds in canoes, in rowboats, drifting through lily-pads with the mysterious noise of stems and leaves brushing against the bottom of the canoe. You tell them its drowned men's fingers. They laugh and hold their breath.—Getting ready beds for Inspection; perfect neat corners. Shoes all in a row. Our little cabin Kwasind has twice won the prize. Everybody's thoughts are on prizes, medals, banners, honorable mentions.—Good food at table prepared by a cook who used to be at Lawrenceville, Winters, and now is at Miss Masters'. Endless announcements between courses—the self-importance of adults giving orders to ten-year-olds. "I don't want to see any boy without a sweater at meal times.... keep away from the Office unless you have special business..." Nobody impressed.

Thank you for The Adelphi; full of good things—poor hysterical D. H. Lawrence, soupy one minute and fine the next.[76] Did Isabel ever get the Molnàr plays[77]—I gave the money to a Philadelphian bookseller who hadn't them in stock, but promised to forward them in a week—was he honest?—A nice note from Lola Fisher.[78] If I were away from this Camp I could write her a perfect a little play.—Added some handsome brocades lengths to my Roman memoirs, vital, rich, crowded. Conscious of that inexhaustible invention that is so lacking these days where they can give you a thousand details without giving you a thousand lights; my portraits rise from my own pages to surprise me, solid, three-dimensional, speaking. All of them a little eccentric and all frustrated, wretched, but forceful, combative.

Lots of love, more soon
Thornt.

---

76 Lawrence's "Trees and Babies and Papas and Mamas" appeared in the June 1923 issue of the English magazine *The Adelphi*.

77 Ferenc Molnár (1878–1952).

78 American actress whose Broadway career extended from 1913 to 1924.

81. TO ISABELLA N. WILDER. ALS 4 pp. Yale

Davis
Mon. night
Oct 29, 1923

Dear dear

But don't I know just what you mean!

One has a low opinion of one's family and yet one is angry at oneself for appearing at a disadvantage before them at some public function.

Of course in the end you passed through the Williams' dinner like a charm, but I know what you felt.

Its the malady of the Wilders; each is better when the others aren't around. Father is ponderous when Amos and I are near; but I enter houses that he has just left and I hear wonders of his wit and nonsense. Hasn't Charlotte insisted a hundred times, almost with tears, that when we are not around she is Madame Recamier? I have even a suspicion that Isabel is more buoyant at those parties where there is no chance of meeting my depreciating eye over the shoulders of the dancers.

When you go out with me you may be as talkative or silent as you choose—you may stare at the carpet, or trip over the rug—it is too late to erase from my mind the conviction that you have the purest natural and cultivated talent for living that I have ever seen. Your technique ranges from diplomatic dinners to village book clubs; do not suppose that a Mrs. Williams cannot sense the presence of a lady and feel troubled. (The malice of her tea-table has become a scandal in New Haven; I heard indignation against her from all sides. Besides she hasn't the remotest idea that she should reach out to an unassimilated guest, or respect a newcomer's ignorance of her circle, and so on. However I do not need to expose her to make your gift the brighter; you are what you are.)

I read and read the endless tide of Madame de Sévigné's letters, and enjoy more and more the happy resemblance of your natures. If I could only give you a <u>Les Rochers</u>[79] where you could retire for a few

---

79 Château des Rochers, Madame de Sévigné's country home near Vitré, Brittany.

months every year, with a Breton climate, a son to read to you, your walks in the allées,—some books fallen on the gravel-path, as you sit thinking in the sunshine of Madison and Berkeley days. Don't be worried that you cannot fling Isabel into Hillhouse Avenue[80] by the sheer impetus of your welcome there; let you take your deserved rest. Presently you will encounter by nature some congenial friends—more delightful even than Mrs. Day and the old corps de venues.[81] Do not even read; compose your mind with an occasional unostentatious concert. You have something to talk with that hundreds of restless women have not,—the excellence of your own mind, with its monologue of temperate wise humorous comment. Only think of the poverty of their thoughts!—They have read nothing; they have been nowhere; they have not been favored by God with the slightest innate distinction to turn these things to mental magic if they had them.

Get ready to come down here, for interruptions arise until it seems that it will be impossible for me to see you for a long while unless you accept my invitation to come. But more soon from Him who Laughs at your Fears

Thorn.

82. TO MATHER A. ABBOTT. ALS 1 p. (Stationery embossed Lawrenceville School / Lawrenceville, N.J.) Lawrenceville

Jan 26 • 1925

Dear Doctor:

I have been hunting for an opportunity to tell you that I am planning to go to the Princeton Graduate School next year and roll up a

80 A fashionable and prestigious address in New Haven.

81 French: local group.

magister artium.[82] If all goes well my hope is to come around about this time next year and ask if I can be useful to you Fall after next. My father is especially insistant on the degree and has at last persuaded me to try for one. And I am glad I shall be still your neighbor,

Sincerely,
Thornton Wilder

83. TO AMOS P. WILDER. ALS 4 pp. (Stationery embossed Lawrenceville School / Lawrenceville, N.J.) Yale

Feb 4 • 1925

Dear Da:

I was intending to write as soon as the Princeton Graduate College had announced to me that my application was accepted. It will be here any day; in the meantime know that my bridges are burned at Lawrenceville. Now that the four years are drawing to a close I can feel regret at missing the class-room routine (and at not having done it better), but I can see more clearly the vulgarity, the superficiality of the present régime—above all the devestating lack of sympathy for boys (one side of which is exactly too great a sympathy for their complaints and requests and their wheedling). Nor can tongue tell the childishness of the chief: his cruel generalizations on absent masters (all the worse because he does not believe them himself and will instantly change his tone if the subject is suddenly cast in a more favorable light); his hard turning away of masters of twenty years service by a letter as late as May; his gorging on flattery; and so on. I will be right sorry to leave Mr. and Mrs. Foresman. He must have had a sinking of the heart when three and a half years ago he saw a slight and anxious (and ill-dressed) stranger coming up the path with an enormous suitcase, and personifying all that boys find most ridiculous. Oh là-là, I've gone through the machine.

---

82 Latin: master of arts.

Enclosed find insurance remittance. I shall enquire among my fellow veterans about my bonus. I am getting awfully alive to money. My article[83] is all proof-read and now all I have to do is to wait for the cheque that will reimburse me for all the expenditure of the holidays.

¶ I now do my running out-of-doors on a new board track, my bare knees among the snowdrifts. ¶ It's all settled that I get 300 bucks for tutoring at a camp on Lake Sunapee, Middle New Hampshire. ¶ When we were small in Berkeley you used on Sabbath to force us to read a book which now I dip into voluntarily (I won't pretend that I am dematerialising utterly): Law's A Serious Call.[84] It's pretty good but God had better hurry and raise up a new devotional literature for an age of Bessemer[85] and Radiotelegraphy—the impress of machines is more than skin-deep. My generation can no longer exclaim in the purple light of an eclipse that the heavens declare the glory of God; eclipses aren't at all strange; we have found that space is finite and we have chased the unknowable down into the kernals of an atom. If that explodes tomorrow I shall have nothing to pin my faith to except the music of Schubert, the prose style of George Santayana and the disinterested affection of two people in New Haven—(and even one of them is the most grudging Isaac sighed over Jacob.) ¶ Give my love to the other, whom it will not embarrass; tell her she's mostly right about Jennifer Lorn[86] but must trust in its successor. Be good and send me more clippings.

thine

Thornt—

83 At the invitation of Edith Isaacs, TNW wrote a review of sixteen new Broadway plays; titled "The Turn of the Year," it appeared in the March 1924 issue of *Theatre Arts Magazine.*

84 *A Serious Call to a Devout and Holy Life* (1729), by English spiritual writer and mystic William Law (1686–1761).

85 English engineer and inventor Sir Henry Bessemer (1813–1898).

86 First novel (1923) by American novelist and poet Elinor Wylie (1885–1928), wife of William Rose Benét.

84. TO ROSEMARY AMES.[87] ALS 4 pp. Yale

96 Bishop St. New Haven
Conn
July 4 • 1925

Dear Rosemary Ames:

If any of your friends would frown on our clandestine correspondence per se, how much more would they frown on it if they knew what I have to tell you. Remembering that you are the only living girl who never shocked Dr. Abbott I'm almost afraid to answer one of your questions. But.

People aren't far from the truth in assuming that the ladies of the stage are of entirely different stuff from our mothers and sisters and aunts. But the change in the actress has not come about from the kind of people she has had to associate with. If I believe what my sisters tell me a lady is not free from persecution in any walk of life?

The actress pays no formal calls; she is too busy to receive any; if she kept up social relations with her mother's friends she must suffer their curious and fascinated gaze; as a freak would. If she becomes famous she becomes loneliest of all, for then even her closest friends (I know Maude Adams' best friend[88]) must handle her with a certain insincerity. In other words she lives a life in which the What-Will-People-think becomes unimportant.

Worst of all the excitement and fatigue of acting (especially of good acting) make her hungry for praise and lively suppers. One can't go soberly to bed at eleven after a superb climax; one is so self-dazzled that one's best friends seem dull: one wants new bright admirers. Last of all, the actress feels herself becoming something more than a lady: an artist. The old things are no longer important and a new set of needs comes in sight.

I think there's only one school better than the Theatre Guild's and

---

87 Ames (1906–1988), whom TNW met at Lawrenceville, probably in the fall of 1924, when she was a guest of the headmaster, became a stage and film actress.

88 TNW probably meant Homer Saint-Gaudens (see letter number 74).

that is Boleslawsky's Laboratory Theatre[89]; but he long since picked his class and has been working with them for two years. I almost joined it. I have attached a clipping to show what good people you can learn from and what a close connection the Guild School has with the real stage. I distrust the Sargent School[90] and the Academy because they turn out good slick competent Broadway actors, not actors that work from within from a long painstaking experimented technique

Through<Throw> even the ghost of discretion to the winds and ask me everything you like. Pls let me know what happens next. All best wishes in your war with the Familly. Grim persistance is better than dramatic flare-ups. Promise them you'll live at one of those Y.W.C.A clubs. And so on.

Most sincerely—
Thornton Wilder

85. TO ISABELLA N. WILDER. ALS 4 pp. Yale

c/o Roger Coleman, Esq
Newbury. Lake Sunapee
New Hampshire
<Summer 1925>

Dear Mother

I had a postcard all written to you when your full crowded letter came to which only a piker could return such a jot.

To make a long letter out of jots let me begin by saying that although Part three of The Caballa is refractory (I don't <know> what the matter is for I see the whole thing quite clearly: Mlle d'Homodarme's veneration for the Cardinal gradually turning into hatred until in full Caballa dinner she fires an ineffectual revolver at him) altho that re-

89 Richard Boleslavsky (1889–1937), Russian-trained actor and director, began his career as an actor with the Moscow Art Theatre before coming to the United States and founding the American Laboratory Theatre, with Russian actress Maria Ouspenskaya in 1923.

90 Franklin H. Sargent was an acting coach at New York's Madison Square Theatre in the late nineteenth century.

fuses to be begun, I suddenly finished the Second Act of Geraldine de Gray[91] the other day, the obstinate, the insoluble Second Act. It finished with unexpected simplicity and I begin to see the mists rising from the Third.

Let me describe some diversions of wistful bachelors. We have been three times to dance at the Grauliden; the manager is only too glad to have us and introduces us at once to various damsels all forlorn. Meet Miss Corday, who en plein fox trot announces that she is a Beautician. Young though she is (some twenty-three) she has her own shop in New York, her own manicurist; the business pays well, she saves a good purse to squander on three weeks at a smart hotel, playing the lady, and looking for rich widowers. She had also been an exhibition diver at Long Branch, and a Five-mile International Swimmer. I know lots more about her..... Meet Miss Henry, pretty, rouged, and thirty-eight, who is an illustrator, yes, she illustrates medical journals and can be found sketching in the operating room of Johns Hopkins any time these winters. She saves a good purse to squander on three weeks at a smart hotel, playing the lady, and..... Meet Miss Pursley. She looks exactly like Katharine Cornell. Black evening gowns; enormous earpendants in seed-pearls. She is a designer for Lord and Taylor, or rather a disposer of fabrics and apportioner of materials among the different shops making clothes for that firm. She hopes next year to go to Paris and study with Paul Poiret. I spent the evening asking every partner whether they could present me to her and at last I found a Galeoto:[92] I still half believe it was Katharine Cornell on vacation.

The scene shifts to a dinner party at Mrs. Wertheimers. Left to right Mrs. Wertheimer,[93] a proud sad Jewess with literary yearnings, thirty-five on her own confession; Mr Dresser, headmaster of Woodmere, a preparatory school for Jewish boys on Long Island; Mrs. Rosenthal, a vivacious young matron who would be an actress if her husband

91 "Geraldine de Gray" was apparently never completed; incomplete holograph and typescript versions survive in the Beinecke Library at Yale University.

92 TNW is referring to Spanish dramatist José Echegray's best-known work, his play *El Gran Galeoto* (1881).

93 Amy Wertheimer (1890–1971) became a binder of rare books for the University of Connecticut; she remained TNW's friend and correspondent to the end of her life.

allowed her; Roger Coleman, Yale football, very tall and a little noisy with highballs; Mrs. Dresser, very sweet middle-age, a little shocked; Mrs. Giers, già Giersburger, comic falsetto manner, very funny, more stage yearnings, warm (nay, moist) sympathies; Mr. Taylor, fellowmaster; Mrs. Coleman, the prettiest woman in the world, the very face that magazine covers fall short of fixing, but with a difficult carping disposition; then me. Though it is little more than a camp and there is a shortage of table silver the food is wonderful. After dinner, movies, for the hostess owns her own motionpicture camera, charades, horseplay, scotch. Where you ask are Mr. Wertheimer, Mr. Rosenthal and Mr. Giers. Down in the law offices of N.Y., madam, far from the merry wives of Blodgett[94] who hold their parties in the middle of the week so that the broken glass can be swept up before the Friday night invasion of husbands.

But you don't like my letter. Try this.

I canoed over to church this morning, St. James of Birkhaven, a fine sermon, and Dean Wilbur Cross[95] passing the plate. I told him I was coming to see him soon, tho' how I shall explain my residence next year I cannot see.

Or this:

Dear Ellie Jones Campbell[96] and consort called on me and took me home to dinner. Good chops and things, a slightly confused rolly-poly husband, a nice house with canoes and motorboat. The Doctor inspires confidence, a research chemist with a taste for the Church Fathers. We swam and then they brought me home late across the black lake weaving in and out among the coloured signal lights, and buoys and poles.

Today I went with Mrs. Coleman (to whom in the absence of the husband I am playing a little perilously, the cavalière servante[97]) to a benefit bridge party and tea dance given at one of the great estates about the lake. Miles of cars parked en queue; a sprawling shingled house with fern gardens snapped from Town and Country; hundreds of

94 TNW's phrase "the merry wives of Blodgett" refers to Blodgett's Landing, one of the eleven original steamboat landings on Lake Sunapee, and the site of the summer camp.

95 Wilbur L. Cross (1862–1948) was dean of the Graduate School at Yale at this time.

96 Ellie Jones Campbell was the daughter of Dean Frederick Scheetz Jones of Yale.

97 Italian: gentleman-in-waiting.

people bowing, staring; a picture raffled; Turkish girl selling cigarettes; crowded dance floor; the hostess very condescending to the vulgar strangers who were peering at her rooms. Great satisfaction of dancing with Mrs. Coleman. The prettiest lady on the floor, being stared at, being pointed at—"there, the one in blue! She's coming now!"

I'm reading The Golden Bough, the one volume edition abridged from twelve. Tons of folklore, witch doctors, how to make it rain, May day myths, Spring ceremonies, resurrection legends.... the evidence accumulating like a great Juggernaut trying to flatten out any particular importance that might be reserved for Christian doctrine. But the theoretical interludes are a little pompous and repetitive and there remains a chance that the notions I learned at your knee may survive.

Give my love to the whole house. I think its splendid of you to have gone to Storrs and to New York. I feel as though I'd see you very soon. Love to Father and tell him I take great pleasure in all his enclosures. Your adoring son. Thornton.

86. TO AMOS N. WILDER. ALS 3 pp. (Stationery embossed Graduate College / Princeton University) Yale

Oct 2 • 1925

Dear Amos

You must not let the deliberations of these committees worry you. I'm now sure that you're not meant to be a preacher at all; I've been rereading your poems. Now I think that some passages in them are so fine that writing more should be your only business. I was just stupid never to see before that such passages as the "Muse on this epitaph...." And the "life's sufficient lures" ought to cut you off from being a clergyman.[98] The clergyman will kill the poet. It's the passages in which you talk least about "He" and "Himself" that are best.

98 TNW's brother had been writing poetry from boyhood. The first line TNW quotes is from his brother's poem "Ode in a German Cemetery Where Many Victims of the Great War Were Interred," and the second line is from "Lines by Arno." Both poems were published in Amos N. Wilder's *Battle Retrospect* (1923), a volume that was selected for the Yale Series of Younger Poets.

You must not allow yourself to believe that the verdicts of vestrymen have anything to do with your qualities; your pretensions are far above anything they can estimate. Father either. At heart Father is about sixty times more worldly than you or I. He is devoured by the College President Complex. There are times when I feel his perpetual and repetitive monologue is trying to swamp my personality, and I get an awful rage. He has wonderful and beautiful qualities, but he has one monstrous sin. Mother, Charlotte, you and I (and lately Isabel) have lived in a kind of torment trying to shake off his octupus-personality.

Don't you hesitate to suddenly turn down all the committees. Tell him you are not looking for a job. Settle down for at least six months in Mansfield Street.[99] Perhaps more. Perhaps forever. You have justification enough in your lines. I will defend you; Charlotte and Mother will.

Come down here for a week-end if you like. I have an extra cot in our study all ready for you.

Anyway don't you be afraid of anything on earth. You have the goods. I was a fool not to have been so sure of it before.

love

Thornt.

87. TO AMOS N. WILDER. ALS 4 pp. Private

Grad College Princeton N.J.
April 25 • 1926

Dear Amy:

Your remembering a birthday by more than a letter gave me that same Wilder mortification that Mother always experiences when one so much as pays her carfare for her. But I thank you very much and will try to do something with it that will allude to your good wishes.

99 The Wilder family now lived in a house at 75 Mansfield Street in New Haven.

You were very restrained in your glancing at the misprints and at the graver limitations of my book. Most of the misp– are not my fault. The final proofs were perfect, I feel sure. But at that stage the firm suddenly decided that the book was too short and began expanding it by all the devices known to the trade. In the respacing of lines therefore many must have been broken and crazily repatched by the typesetter: But a few of the errors remain my maxima culpa!—

heure de champagne

exampla gratia

The chronological tangles at the close of Book II and the middle of V. The misprint that lacerates me most is p. 196 the conversion of France!![100]

Almost no one likes the last book. I should have "prepared" it more consistantly thru the earlier. Well—all in all, I have learned lots of lessons—to be scrupulously attentive; to be more flowing; to extract all the possible resonance from repetition and echo etc. etc.

No big reviews in yet. Bonis not seriously advertising until some blurbs begin. The thought visits me every now and then that Bonis may give it a brief and decent interrment. They are very rich and keep their eyes mostly on their enormous successes. Even a thousand copies is chicken feed for them. Apparently both Princeton and New Haven villages are having a moment's tea-table excitement over it. After all I earn my living elsewhere and have elsewhere my real pleasures. Many delightful & reassuring letters have come. (they were as specifically phrased or as full of helpful aperçus as yours). You are right about IHS.[101] I am too young and too undedicated a person to achieve a restrained Grand Style (which I pretend after)—notes of burlesque, smartalecisms and purple-rhetoric creep in and are only discovered when it is too late. Let me promise you tho that tons of bunk were deported in the successive readings of the proof. Hope for the best.

The acct of your circle and your routine sounds beautiful to me.

---

100 The errors in the first edition of *The Cabala*, alluded to by TNW, were corrected in the second edition: "heure de champagne" to "heure du champagne"; "exampla gratia" to "exempli gratia"; and "the conversation of France" to "the conversion of France." In all, the first edition of *The Cabala* contained twenty-eight errors.

101 A Monogram for Jesus Christ.

Do be awfully wise about your health. I do my long run or my fierce handball every day and what began as an act of will has become a pleasure & a necessity. I hope you'll get married soon. As for your poems please be patient and self sufficient; in these matters early or late isn't so important<;> excuse me saying that I waited six years beyond the time when the Gossip Fair assigned me a début, and even now the real pleasure is in the insight of the few who could have read the stuff in MS anyway.

I wish you could have come in here for a weekend or so. I am almost an ardent son of old Nassau. Next year I will probably be tutoring a boy in Rochester. This Summer a month in Peterboro,[102] I hope<,> and some time by Mother<?>. Perhaps here in this very building—living cheap, proximity of a great library, terrible weather but on a slight hill.

Don't hesitate to write me your troubles, if I can act for you. Hope you have few. See you in Summer somehow, I hope. Thanks for the memento and comments.

Affectionately
Thornton

88. TO CHARLES H. A. WAGER. ALS 2 pp. (Stationery embossed Graduate College / Princeton University) Yale

May 25 • 1926

Dear Dr. Wager,

If I deserved to be happy no letter could have made me happier than yours. But every time I am commended by persons I greatly value a real shame goes through me. I become aware of all the negligences and greennesses that I let by. I shall try again and keep in mind such readers as yourself. Try and remember that I kept adding bits to the

102 TNW is referring to the MacDowell Colony, located in Peterborough, New Hampshire.

book during all those years at Lawrenceville, but always with the sinking feeling that nowhere a publisher or friend would read it.

What emotion went through you as you discovered your influence turning up on every page? It is fairly speckled with your favorite quotations, and it is always aspiring after effects that you taught me to admire in others. How many hours I sat under your rostrum, burning with awe and emotion, while you unfolded the masterpieces. Dear Dr. Wager, like Alix[103] you have "a form of genius that is seldom praised to its face" but which it is so satisfying to praise. I am an old-fashioned believer and when I assert that I believe that lives are planned out for us I am always thinking of the fact that my father, by the most unexplainable accident, sent his two sons to Oberlin where the younger could get the nourishment without which he would have remained a bright blundering trivial hysteric.

The book has been doing well; a second printing is ready (with all the twenty-eight errata corrected) and I hope to go in the Fall to the hills around Salzburg to write some plays.

Give my love to Mrs. Wager. I hope Italy does you both all the good in the world. Always remember me as your devoted and affectionate

Thornton

89. TO AMY WERTHEIMER. ALS 4 pp. Yale

June 21 • 1926
Princeton Grad College
until Thursday
Then 75 Mansfield
St. N.H. until July 1.

Dear Amy:

I must say I like your letters more and more, even though you don't like my new reason for liking them: their serenity. Now I walk

103 Alix d'Espoli is a character in *The Cabala*.

Wilder family at Mansfield Street. Left to right: *Amos N., Isabel, Janet, TNW, Amos P.*

into the Commons Room, read them by the window overlooking a vast perspective of lawn and woodland; I smile here and there; your likeness floats up from the pages; I am reminded that I have a good friend and that in my queer unsound and almost secret life I have a sturdy last resource against the occasional conviction that "I don't belong", that there's no room for me.

That is one of the things then that should be making me very happy. This very minute Andy is in taking one of his College Boards and my tutoring is practically over; the first flurry over the book is at an end, but I continue to get letters assuring me that friends and strangers are surprised and pleased by it; I am to be in Peterborough all July and am alive with wonderful little touches for the Peruvian novel.[104] But I'm not very happy, and that's all there is to be said. Perhaps it's because through distraction and laziness I haven't written a word for so long, i.e. denied my raison d'être.—however I mustn't try and shadow you with my depressions. I shall be all right when I'm home; there is one place in the world I am really at peace and that is on the little cot up in the hall in Mansfield Street, with my Father and Mother and Isabel tiptoeing about their affairs.

Now let me talk about a thousand stray things so that you can see that I'm at least alive enough to be interested. ¶ Been reading Spengler's Decline of the West with the greatest enthusiasm. I'm told a lot of it is wrong, I know that a lot of it is beyond my reach, but at least it's absorbed me beyond the call of dinner bells and movie-going. ¶ Boni's made me the following proposition: if I would turn back to them my royalties on the not-yet-sold first five thousand copies, twelve hundred and fifty dollars, they would add to it from their coffers the same amount, the whole sum to be used to plaster the country with adv'ts, to try and ram it down the public<'s> neck as one of the six best sellers of the Spring and perhaps recoup all that was invested. I replied no, thank you. In the first place I must eat. In the second, it would be absurd to make a little goldfish go through the antics of a whale. They're loony, and every now and then a little . . . . . a little . . . As they get much more than I per copy, shouldn't they have offered to contribute more than 50% of the advertising drive?—anyway, don't mention this bit of publishing gossip to a soul. ¶ You notice I'm writing this to you on a Monday—that's because Sunday is getting to be a little farcical—the telephones rings for dinners and teas. Now I've

104 TNW tutored Andrew Townson in English and French from mid-April to mid-June, while he was completing his M.A. He began work on what would become his second novel, *The Bridge of San Luis Rey* (1927), during his stay in the summer of 1926 at the MacDowell Colony.

moved into another entry and phonecalls can't reach me at all, and that's how blasé I am. So I telepathed you for half-a-day's delay on this letter and you made a moue and accorded me it. ¶ There's no denying that music is the first of all the arts, that literature even cannot hold a candle to it. Well, did I tell you about my Thursday nights at Prof. Menzies (pendants to my Sunday nights at Mrs. Franz's)? about our long sessions for two pianos eight-hands, hours with the Brandenberg concerti and the Brahms symphonies? with me being inept and requiring the other three proficients to go back to six bars before M, and to be reminded of the changes of key-signature.[105] There are two maiden-ladies from the Princeton Conservatory of Music, super-sight-readers taking the passage work with a great rattle of bracelets & heaving of shoulders and, Mrs. Menzies of Edinburgh, a still pretty young woman with an accurate if a little pedestrian accomplishment. The Cabala lies guiltily on the center table and the author is humored along when he falls out of time and key; others hurry to take the blame and declare stoutly that the<y> skipped three bars etc. ¶ This little M.A. has been drinking a little too much lately having fallen into a crowd after his own heart—tough-guys, chemists and physicists and other non-introspectives. Their major ordeals are just over and they are all for stealing the distilled alcohols reserved for experimental work in the biological laboratories and infusing it with whole groves of lemons and shaking violently at the level of the shoulders. Then I am almost happy, accepted as a mere fella among fellas, closing one eye and pronouncing upon the recipe of the concoction, strolling about Nassau Street and taking great pride in "not showing it." I long to be ordinary as Elinor Wylie longs to be respectable. ¶ You mention a review in the Post that says my book is too clever.[106] That makes the 3rd unfavorable review; they delight me most; but what Post is it—I have a review from a New York Evening Post Book Review Section (Stuart Sherman's) but there is no problem as to who it's by for it is signed (I

---

105 Alan Wilfred Cranbrook Menzies was a professor of chemistry at Princeton at this time. Sarah Morton Frantz was a resident of Princeton.

106 There was a review of *The Cabala* in the *Chicago Evening Post Literary Review* on May 14, 1926, signed by Louise George.

haven't the handsome leather scrapbook by me now) and moreover I hear that (I remember now her name is Eva Goldbeck) she is Lina Abarbanell's daughter.[107] The line she takes is that she "has heard" that it is a roman à clef and that her pleasure is practically spoiled because she does not know enough about Roman big-leef (as they call it) to identify my victims. If you have a different review from that, do copy out the two most significant sentences. Don't copy out the retelling of the plot or the opening salutations. ¶ The thought suddenly struck me last night that I owed Jean[108] a letter. I am mortified at having been so long. I will send that therefore during the week. ¶ I am finishing this up in the Octagonal Room of the University Library. Through the windows float the sounds of heavy green trees brushed by a breeze, the sound (I insist) of sunlight on ivy and that of applause for the class day exercises are being held before a vast crowd a stone's throw away. This may be my last letter to you from Princeton (I am still thinking of coming back here to work in August) and I should close with a majestic summary of what the whole chapter has meant, but you have known all the agitations and all the satisfactions and its not impossible that in the back of your mind lies a better evaluation of my year here than will ever lie in the back of mine. So, Madam, you draw the conclusions and add the column, mentioning always that changes of place and the completion of time-units have no power to alter my admiration for yourself.

So
Thornton.

---

107 Abarbanell was an opera singer. Goldbeck's review of *The Cabala,* "Real People Masquerade Behind Mask of Fiction in Story Laid in Rome," appeared in the *New York Evening Post Literary Review* on May 15, 1926.

108 Jean was one of Amy Wertheimer's two daughters.

90. TO LEWIS S. BAER.[109] ALS 4 pp. Morgan

The Lake Sunapee Summer School
Blodgett's Landing, N.H.
Aug 7 • 1926

Dear Lewie or Louie:

(Anyone who commits a shy message to a postal-card, as I did, deserves to be misunderstood.)

First, I haven't submitted my plays to any publisher, except you.[110]

My thought was that they were so frail that even if you did bring them out during the next two years, it would probably be bad for my "booksellers" and even perhaps for most of "my readers."

And yet I should love to get these little things out somewhere, quietly and even unprofitably.

The Bridge of San Luis Rey grows lengthier (in design) and can hardly be finished before Spring. Though it might be serializing from Jan. (The nice note in The Century encourages me to hope for them:[111] they like costume pieces: Messer Marco Polo and The Venetian Glass Nephew[112] (later Doran))

My thought then was that if they appeared for a few years in some obscure publisher's lists (if they would even take them) just enough to make presents for a few special friends and to give me the feeling that those Juvenilia were once <and> for all "off my chest"—it would be

---

109 A Yale classmate of TNW, Baer worked for Albert & Charles Boni and was responsible for soliciting *The Cabala* for the firm.

110 TNW is referring to his "three-minute playlets for three persons," most written at Oberlin and Yale and published in those schools' literary magazines. Sixteen of these "playlets" were published by another New York publisher, Coward-McCann, in 1928 in *The Angel That Troubled the Waters and Other Plays.*

111 *The Century Magazine* published a favorable brief review of *The Cabala* in its August 1926 issue.

112 The first book mentioned is a novel (1921) by American writer Brian Oswald Donn-Byrne; the second is a novel (1925) by Elinor Wylie.

nice. Then they could revert to you in say, 8 years and go through the 'Boom (if you chose) then.

However, as I say, its not anything I'm very het up about and if you think best, we'll say no more about it. Anyway you are my one and only House, of course & I tried to get Robinson for you—we even had a long confab. of which I shall someday tell you the details, but he's for MacMillan to his death.[113]

Ever Thine
Thornton

<appeared perpendicularly in the left margin of the first page>
Next Day: Gee I'd love to send you some hunks of The Bridge of San Luis Rey—but I haven't any copies and I couldn't be sure you'd be able to "foresee" all the treatment a first draft can rec've later.

91. TO ISABELLA N. WILDER. APCS 1 p. Yale

<Aix-les-Bains, France>
<P.M. October 22, 1926>

What the h— am I doing at Aix-les-bains, sleeping in royal chamber for ninety cents a night. Well, we're going from Paris to Rome (French Lemons Co. Piazza di Spagna) by relays, so as to avoid the 3,360 francs for the Rome Express. Tomorrow night we sleep in Genoa, and then in Rome.[114] Things are much brighter & cheerier than when I wrote you-alls last. ¶ Tell Isabel that stopping in at Shakespeare & Co, Miss Beach introduced me to Ernest Hemingway (one of the two other good novelists of my generation, the 3rd being Glenway

113 TNW met American poet Edwin Arlington Robinson at the MacDowell Colony in the summer of 1924 and tried to get him to switch publishers, although TNW was unsuccessful in this endeavor.

114 TNW was accompanying Andrew Townson on a European tour and acting as his chaperone during the fall of 1926.

Wistcott<Wescott>) and we had a grand long talk. Brentano's can't keep enough C-l-as in Paris, but I got one for Ernest at Gaglia's on the Rue de Rivoli. Mama, the franc is 3 cents today and prices not yet proportional. More tomorrow—love

Thornt.

92. TO ERNEST HEMINGWAY. ALS 4 pp. (Stationery embossed Hotel Bayerischer Hof / München) JFK

9th November 1926[115]

Dear Ernest:

This crazy journey is drawing to a close and I may show up in Paris one of these days and drag you out to help me find a room. I still think it would be best for me to go South and keep in the sunlight; but I need to hear a lot of good talk and be near some big libraries. This Munich is pretty wonderful; I keep imagining myself here. The theatres and the music put any other country in a green shade (quotation ended.)

Crazy journey is right. Andy hates all Europe. If he could he'd like to park all day in his hotel rooming (reading the Paris Herald and smoking Chesterfields) and never put foot in Paris, or Rome or Naples or Florence. He's not even got ordinary vitality for he hates to walk more than two block<s> and yet among those dozens <of> prep. schools that he honored for a couple of weeks each he was discovered by the examiners to be the strongest boy in school, etc. He doesn't even learn the names of the towns we're in and Naples and Florence remain for him as: <">what was that city we were in last?" He's quite taken with Germany because there are so many trick devices in street management and elevator service, and because he has heard their airplane routes are in such a good state. Even his interest in mechanics though

115 This date is written in handwriting that may not be TNW's.

is not a saving grace. Its only the passing observation that a boy of ten would give. The terrible epitaph for Andy is this: He's not even interested in the things he's interested in.

So you can imagine sitting through long blank meals with him. Naturally he thinks I'm as much of a mess as I think he is. But I know that any other kind of tutor would have been as poor a companion. Even if he had had a snappy nightclub collegiate tutor, he would have been left at home more and more, for Andy looks irresistably like a lonesome but conceited little boy when he's on a party. His whisky goes straight to his egotism and he will boast for three hours on end of what he regards as his achievements in polo, heavy drinking, cards and love. An ordinary common-sense tutor would have given him up because of his curious dependence, his inability to say where, what, why, how. He can complain afterwards, but he can never propose before.

However you see I can almost work myself up into a pathological state over my companion. Most <of> the time I can be found enjoying myself immensely in the cities. I'm a hound for museums and I don't care who knows it. Where the Baedekers are thickest, there am I in the midst of them. There aint no ruin that escapes me. So between the aesthetic excitements of the Sistine roof and the exasperations of the pie-face back at the hotel I get worked up into a curious state that may not be so bad for me after all. I get crazy to write. And ideas, and anecdotes and developements in my next book keep hitting me at all hours, even though I have only time to put them into a notebook. And notions for plays!—which reminds that I've been writing to Richard Boleslavsky back at the Laboratory Theatre and, Ernest, you must begin to think of a play for him. His group can't do the bold usual good Broadway play, but they can do quiet genre studies, and realistic character comedy, as no one in New York can. Besides they have repertory and though they only pay 10% of gate receipts (a very tiny theatre) they at least don't run the play until the audiences thin out and then cast it aside for ten years, they keep it alive in a shifting program for a long time. They're now considering a very poor Jim Tully-Robert Graves play about tramp life, that you could beat with one finger.[116]

---

116 There is no evidence that American writer Jim Tully (1886–1947) collaborated on a play with Graves, but Tully did collaborate with Robert Nichols on *Twenty Below* (1927).

I'm awfully eager to read The Sun Also. I shall have by the time you see me. Don't be harsh to me about mine: I'm rapidly deculturing. Be patient with me and there'll be less fooling with inessentials etc. Give my best to Miss Beach.

Ever

Thornton Wilder

93. TO ISABELLA N., ISABEL, AND JANET F. WILDER. ALS 6 pp. (Stationery embossed Hotel Édouard VII / 39 Avenue de L'Opéra / Paris) Yale

November 28 • 1926
Sunday

Dear girls:

Andy sails Wednesday and the farce is over.

Three more nights in this vulgar hotel (one hundred francs a night. 'magine! I protested all I could. But as he remarks so often: It's his money; and it's less than the Plaza!)

Then I'm either going over to live with Ernest Hemingway or else going to the pension de la Schola Cantorum for a month, or going straight South.

I'd love to go into the studio with Ernest, but there are no meals with it. He eats around with the enormous and flamboyant Rotonde crowd. And his wife is about to divorce him and his new wife is about to arrive from America, so I think I'd better not try. But he's wonderful. Its the first time I've met someone of my own generation whom I respected as an artist. Neither Steve nor Edna Millay inspired one tenth the confidence that he does, as a writer.

The pension Schola costs 800 francs a month for everything and I'll have Wednesday morning (I'll explain why I'm putting it Wedn. morning.) about 3,500 francs. You love money matters so I'll explain all. I have still one hundred dollars of mine. And (this will give you the staggers) I have still one hundred dollars of my expense account. Nine hundred dollars seems a horrible amount to have spent from Sept 25 to December 1, but even that was kept down with great adroitness. Andy must easily have spent two thousand, not counting a lot of tailoring in London and gifts everywhere. When Wednesday morning I pay my bill for this week's hotel (that will be 7 nights: 700 francs, a couple of breakfasts and baths and mineral waters & tips = 1000) I will have 1500 francs expense money left.

As Doug.[117] said that of course he would pay me the value of a return ticket, instead of returning the Expense Money left over after the hotel is paid, I shall keep it and tell him to deduct it from the Return Ship money.

The exchange today was 27 fr. to a dollar which brings my capital up still further: even 4,400 francs.

If that's all true I really should go right South, but these telegrams and anxious letters make me think I ought to stay for a while.

But I love your letters!! I just have a glorious time collecting them at Morgan Harjes[118] and strolling off to a café and reading them 12 times. Between you and me I don't like Paris. I never did. If I had somewhere to go in America I'd come straight home, but I don't want New York and I couldn't park on you adorable people in New Haven and that's that.

The important thing is that The Bridge is getting along fast and is just filling up with beautiful passages that take your breath away. The whole last week Andy has been sleeping all day and prowling around all night with his brother in dress-suits. (Brother Chick, not Douglas who couldn't come after all.) and I've stayed up in the old room and worked. I'm awful lonesome. I know a good many people in town, but none (except Ernest) that I really want to park around with. I go and sit and have good long talks with Sylvia Beach when I'm extra blue. Jack Kirkpatrick of Lawrenceville and Princeton I see everynow and then; and a certain Atkinson a phd grind at the Biblioteque nationale, and some girls; but for the most part, I write: all morning, take a late lunch somewhere (a dollar in American money, but dazzling to the French)

---

117 Douglas C. Townson, Andrew's father.

118 Morgan, Harjes was a Paris bank where one could receive mail.

drift forlornly into churches or louvres or buy a Berlin paper and read it through. (Oh, how I love Berlin compared to this dump.)

Andy and I are at last on pretty strained terms, but I have nothing to reproach myself with and don't think twice about it.

I feel awfully remote from the news about The Trumpet, though of course its exciting. I was horrified at a telegram from Boly saying that Dabney was going to read the Lord's prayer. I sent back one of the frankest telegrams ever committed to the wires: Please no prayer<.> I think he'll find he's made a mistake in telescoping the 3 & 4th acts, but I don't care. Its all sort of remote to me. If its well-done or ill done, or successful or unsuccessful, it's all one to me: its there on paper and someday when I'm older I'll revise it and get the ideas sound. It's scenario is too pretentious. If Dante had gone into the theatre he couldn't have carved himself a more ambitious subject. On the eve of performance I shall telegraph the company my thanks and go to bed.[119]

The English weeklies I see havent shown the C-b-la on the Longman's lists yet; but I haven't seen any for quite a while. Aunt Charlotte's keeping an eye out for me.[120]

Are you all well? Isabel's a saint for doing all these chores for me in addition to all her work. Your all saints, and like all saints—far away. Now I'm all in a stew about how to get some little Xmas trifles over to you. Andy's being sunk on me is pretty nice because it leaves me so much free time, but it prevents my asking him to carry home some items in his trunk. Mrs. Hemingway (she's a brick and we all secretly hope he'll go back to her: there's the most beautiful little 3-year old baby you've ever seen:[121] Ernest is just a Middle Western kid whose genius and health and good looks and success have gone to his head a little and I think the new wife is a mess) well, Mrs. Hemingway says

---

119 Richard Boleslavsky agreed to produce TNW's play *The Trumpet Shall Sound* in repertory at his American Laboratory Theatre in December 1926. Horace Dabney, a character in the play, is a former ship captain; he is a marked man because he deserted his sinking ship, leaving scores to drown.

120 English publisher Longmans, Green & Co. had published *The Cabala* in October; TNW's aunt Charlotte was living in London, working for the International YWCA.

121 John Hadley Nicanor "Bumby" Hemingway was born on October 10, 1923.

that your bundles arrived<arrive> in U.S. torn to ribbons and your friends are made to pay fantastic duties. However I'll get Sylvia Beach's advice and Rosemary Carr Benét's advice and a couple of others.

Every now and then I go to a concert. Tell Bruce[122] when you see him that I went to a concert at the Schola and it was terrible. And every concert I've been to in Paris is terrible. Everywhere they try and make charm take the place of rehearsals, and I don't get their charm.

The only thing that could take away the curse from Paris for me would be to live in it with my dear Mama.

Otherwise the only nice things about Paris are:

① Morgan Harjes on mail days
② The silly little franc and its troubles.
③ Ernest Hemingway.
④ Russians and their restaurants with Borsch.
⑤ The tombs of Racine and Pascal. St. Etienne du Mont[123]
⑥ The El Grecos in the louvre
⑦ The memories of the XVII and XVIII centuries (first decade), especially Mme de Sevigné's salon.
⑧ Memories of Stendhal
⑨ Sylvia Beach and Adrienne Monnier.[124]
⑩ I really can't think of a tenth

love in dejection
Thornton

<appeared perpendicularly in the left margin of the first page>
P.S. If I stay a month in Paris I shall rent a typewriter and do the glowing Bridge myself. Otherwise very soon I shall get hold of a good per-

---

122 Bruce T. Simonds.

123 Both French dramatist Jean Racine and Blaise Pascal are entombed in Paris's Église Saint-Etienne-du-Mont.

124 French poet, bookseller, and publisher (1892–1955) who founded the bookstore La Maison des Amis des Livres in Paris in 1915, across the street from where Sylvia Beach later opened her bookstore, Shakespeare and Company. She and Beach became lifelong companions.

son going to America and entrust the two unique cahiers to him or her to give to Bonis and Bonis or Mrs. Wertheimer can have them typed. P.S. I haven't mentioned Father in this letter. Give him my love. And he's to read all letters if he wants to, though most of them are just trivial gabble like this one.

94. TO ISABELLA N. WILDER. ALS 4 pp. Yale

Closerie des Lilas[125]
Blds Montparnasse et de l'
observatoire.
To be found there every morning
from 9:30 to 10:30.
<P.M.? December 9, 1926>

Dear Mom:

If I wrote you every day for hours I wouldn't get out of my system all the things I want to tell you. That means that we ought to <be> meeting daily. When last I wrote you that seemed imminent. Since then a little flurry of things have happened and I have decided to try and stay over here until my March allowance comes and then go home on that from Italy. The events that have made me change my mind are: one, just when I thought I was frozen over and the Bridge would never be finished, for lack of notions, suddenly I went to a performance of the Ninth Symphony (one thousandth as good as the Berlin one, but good enough) and was all broke up. I came home and wrote the pages you will someday know as the death of Manuel; and the next morning I wrote Doña Maria's visit to Cluxambuqua and I've been writing evenly ever since. Then came event no. two—letters from England. First Richard Blaker,[126] the novelist, whom I have never met but who writes me often invited me to his home from<for> Xmas. Roy Bower, vice-

125 Paris café that was a popular gathering place for writers.

126 English novelist (1893–1940), whose *Medal Without Bar* (1930) was considered one of the best novels about World War I.

consul at Southhampton, through whom I knew him, has just passed through Paris and told me a lot about him. For instance he is married to his uncle's wife, a bond not permitted in the prayerbook but offering no difficulties to commonsense. They had to travel about the world hunting for a country that would absolve them of their sin and presently both Holland and the U.S. Roy says they are both perfectly delightful. Well, I was on the point of spending Xmas with Dick and his aunt, or rather with Mayme and her nephew, when another letter came from Coleman Walker (football star, U. of V. and ex. Lawrenceville master, and Rhodes scholar) announcing that since I was on the Riviera I should at once engage him a room near me, for he was going to spend Xmas with me, willy-nilly, and right thereafter a whole horde of Oxonians would descend on us. Thirdly, I began to know the motley crowd in my house, the Polish pianists whose money doesn't come and another Polish pianist who is rich and famous and charming and trying to hide from the Princesse de Polignac, and other menaces. There's suddenly developed in our dreadful pension a thickness of local color that would stagger Balzac. The successful pianist is taking me to a tough dance tomorrow; and Sunday I am to go to a farewell party among the impecunious Russian composers and painters. And a French law student urges me to come and try the company of his cafe circle.

Ernest Hemingway remains the hot sketch of all time. He bursts with self confidence and a sort of little-boy impudence. The other day Mrs. Vanderbilt (she who is going through procedures to get her divorce that make my Mrs. Roy episode sound tame) asked him to dinner and he accepted addressing her in his note as Mrs. Vanderbuilt, "just to keep her in her place."[127] He's now at work on a play about Mussolini. Ernest claims to have dabbled in secret service and plots, and to have access to highly secret dossiers. He swears that of the attempts against Mussolini's life all except that of the mad Irish woman, were intentionally planted by Mussolini to create a martyr-legend. This last shot was not fired by the boy who was stamped to death by the

---

127 Through intricate political and social maneuverings, Mrs. Roy, a character in *The Cabala,* attempts to obtain a divorce at the Vatican under the Pauline Privilege, an arcane procedure. Consuelo Vanderbilt obtained an annulment decree from the Catholic Church despite having been married to the duke of Marlborough for twenty-five years and bearing him two sons.

crowd, but by someone else who escaped as planned.[128] The little boy was a sturdy Fascist Junior and made the mistake of turning to run when the shot was fired. You can judge by that how full of astonishments Ernest's conversation is.

I haven't the slightest idea whether the play has been produced yet or not. Isabel said about the 5th. I tried to read it the other night but I couldn't 'see' it, it was unreadable. But if I knew when the performance was I c'ld send a telegram of good wishes to the Lab. Perhaps there will be letters from somebody tonight.[129] Mail arrives here at 8:30 AM and PM and at those times I am like a lion at feeding hour. The more I think about all you treasure the more I pine to come home perhaps I shall go to Nice for Xmas with Coleman then hop a boat back after that.

Tonight I'm taking the almost-ex Mrs. Hemingway to a concert. She is a nice brave little soul, looks very like Mae Marsh and therefore a little like Mrs. Lincoln and no one knows how she feels about Ernest's cut-ups. I think she has ceased to be particularly in love with Ernest, but dreads being alone and divorced and back in America. Fortunately she has the most beautiful little boy in the world and all the royalties of The Sun also rises. ¶ I have sent Amos a book; now I must find Charlotte something. Mansfield St. must be content with the Century. Oh, honey, I forget to tell you that I filed an application for the Guggenheim—only I was as usual a little too high hat. I asked for residence in Munich & Salzburg (though I meant Vienna) in order to learn the theatre from the inside out etc through friends on Reinhardt's staff—(Rudolf Kommer). They want you to claim a definite piece of work even if you are one of the "Creative" fellowships (Steve pretended something in Old French History) and they must learn better. I'll probably not get it, so don't worry.[130] Do you realize that the Bridge

---

128 On April 7, 1926, Italian dictator Benito Mussolini was wounded in the face when he was shot by Violet Gibson; three other assassination attempts occurred between April and October 1926.

129 The American Laboratory Theatre production of *The Trumpet Shall Sound* opened to negative reviews on December 10, 1926, but remained in their repertory for several months.

130 TNW's application for a John Simon Guggenheim Memorial Foundation Fellowship to study drama in Germany was unsuccessful, unlike that of Stephen Vincent Benét, who received one in 1926.

is going to be a riot. Every twenty pages there's a tremendous emotional situation and between times it's as lyrical and beautifully written as....... It will help you build the most adorable little Engl. house and put a maid in it too. And then I'll never travel to Europe again but will sit reading aloud to you while you punch rugs. Sweetest lady in the world, au revoir

Thornt.

95. TO WILLIAM I. NICHOLS.[131] ALS 4 pp. (Stationery embossed Alpha Delta Phi Club / 136 West 44th Street / New York) LofC

Feb 4 • 1927

Dear Bill:

Excuse me for not having sent a letter for you the minute I got off the boat (Tuesday noon.) The nearest I came to it was this idiocy which I enclose and which was put through by the determination of the young lady. I like her only pretty well; and the last-day of the trip I surprised her in a not-very-nice action. However she's not so bad, and if it turns out that you liked her especially well, I can be brought around to a kind of acquiescence.

The trip was very long and pretty rough. The ship's company was below the average except for two astonishing friends I made—two beautiful examples of a high-class Hungarian and a high-class Swede. I projected a letter to you in which I would paint their full-length portraits <u>à la Cabala</u>, but I see now that they would take up four closely written pages and wld be out of proportion with the things I want to say to you.

---

131 TNW met Nichols (1902–1987) in 1921 or 1922 in New York, when he spotted him reading Keats in a restaurant, then met him again at Balliol College, Oxford, in October 1926, when TNW was touring England with Andrew Townson; he was also one of the Oxonians with whom TNW spent Christmas in December 1926. He and TNW remained friends and corresponded intermittently to the end of TNW's life.

The impetus you gave me to whip myself into publicity survived the voyage. I have paid amiable calls right and left. I wrote a letter to Eva Le Gallienne asking for an appointment. I called on Aswell,[132] whom I like very much (though fancy your trying to give me the impression that he was a sort of Nichols!) and who assured me that serial opportunities must be sought six months ahead of the first instalment. Bonis were full of deferense and good news. The C^{x}b^{x}la continues to sell with quiet obstinacy. The review in Punch had just reached them and so on.[133] Then I went to see a performance of my play. There are lots of beautiful things in the production and the great technical virtuosity of Boleslavsky discovers lots of good things but there are some pretty distressing moments. The last ten minutes aren't mine at all—they are sentimental and preachy beyond words. I am permitted, nay begged, to rewrite all the last part and it will go into rehearsal at once. I don't like the play. It's remote from me. If I came upon it as the work of someone else I doubt whether I would see a grain of talent in it. But the actors love it, are fairly revérent about it, especially the heavenly sweet face that plays Flora. She's an emotional little angel, doesn't know her lines yet even. I gave her a copy of The C^{x}b^{x}la, inscribed with all my admiration and gratitude "as a Valentine" and she cried and cried.[134] I took Ray Bridgman[135] out to dinner last night, and he haranged me for four hours about the stars, and the fourth dimension, and idealism and universalism. It's quite true: he almost lives in a trance;—his extraordinary mad eyes do not see any human being. I think there are no brains there: just yearning and escape from life. He is as thin as a pole, thin arms and hands, and a desolate face that won't give in. I think he regards himself as having been trapped into marriage (by nature) and all he wants for the rest of his life is to take an endlessly long walk about Staten Island reciting Adonaïs to himself.

I saw a splendid rich meaty performance of The Brothers Karama-

---

132 Edward C. Aswell was assistant editor of *The Forum* magazine.

133 The review appeared in the column "Our Booking-Office" in the January 19, 1927, issue.

134 The role of Flora in *The Trumpet Shall Sound* was played in repertory by two actresses, Helen Coburn and Florence House.

135 Ray Bridgman may be the husband or son of the Mrs. Bridgman whom TNW met during his Christmas on the Riviera in 1926.

zoff and another of Tchekov's The Three Sisters.[136] There are dozens of glorious new skyscrapers. The faces on Fifth Avenue this morning—eleven o'clock and sharp wintry sunshine—were 3 times as interesting as any European parade outside Germany.

Your letter doesn't say anything about your rooming problem and I assume that you have had to resign yourself to staying where you are. I keep thinking about crossing the ocean again just to see you. Nothing has given me so much quiet pleasure as being liked by you. Life is short, and has so little congeniality at best that I keep wanting to throw everything else aside and rejoice in the share that has been given me. I have been feared for my sharp tongue; I have been admired with a sort of distaste; only lately have I simplified out enough to be worthy of being liked (by men that is.) I don't dare say that my silly egotism is entirely buried yet, but it is with you.

Hurry on, hurry over, Letter. I was shy of writing you at once for fear I would give the impression of presenting you with mail (so unready am I to believe that I am welcome). I do not like the thought that a whole month will have elapsed before you will have heard from me again.

When various sides of me come forward that you do not like—the introspective side, perhaps, as on the bottom of the previous page; or the sentimento-demonstrative side (I have not known you very long after all and cannot be sure what strains make you impatient); or the I-did-this-and-that side, as on page 2—when such things come up, be patient and realize that after a long ill-adjusted awkward age I am only just beginning to be simple. Perhaps that remark makes you mad with the others.

I am going down to New Haven in a few minutes, to live for two months in great retirement. I shall finish The Bridge in 3 weeks. I shall be very thoughtful to my good father and mother, a sort of unexpected autumnal comfort. I shall write you often. And I shall prepare myself

---

136 The Theatre Guild production of *The Brothers Karamazov* ran on Broadway in January and February 1927. Eva Le Gallienne's Civic Repertory Theatre presented the first English-language production in the United States of Chekhov's *The Three Sisters* in repertory between October 1926 and April 1927.

for writing (ten years from now) such beautiful books that all kinds of things will be forgiven me.

Letter-writing bridges next to nothing. Goodbye my dear Bill. Is my affection some help to you when you are depressed and restless?

Ever
Thornt.

96. TO WILLIAM I. NICHOLS. ALS 4 pp. (Stationery embossed Alpha Delta Phi Club / 136 West 44th Street / New York) LofC

Feb. 16 • 1927

Dear Bill:

Here I am in New York again for 2 days prowling around after Advertisement. <appeared in left margin underneath the drawing of W.I.N.> **I hate to resign myself to the fact that certain of the fine arts are closed to me.** A tiger can't change his spots, and I've found out that I'm not much good at exploitation but I'm doing my best. For instance, there are signs that the University of Michigan and the University of Southern California want to put on my play.[137] At first glance that doesn't seem much. But if you can get to be a Little-theatre-author you can make thousands. The Middle West and West are lousy with little theatres; they copy one another's shows and they pay about twenty-five dollars a performance. So I'm trying to get the

137 According to a June 16, 1927, letter TNW sent to Roy Curtis at the University of Michigan, *The Trumpet Shall Sound* was presented for the first time outside New York by the Comedy Club at that university on March 30, 1927, revised and with a new fourth act not present in the New York production.

theatrical publisher French to bring it out (first wringing the permission from Bonis). Between I and you the play is almost no good, but that has Nothing to do with the Case.

The Lab. theatre has struck a great financial and prestige success with Clemence Dane's Granite.[138] Crowded houses. This brings refreshed audiences to all the alternating plays in the repertory, too, so even mine is getting new life.

New Haven is fun. A whole crowd in the Elizabethan Club bought a row for Abie's Irish Rose last night and I was in before I knew it.[139] We all put on wigs and dress suits with ambassadorial ribbons and medals and beards and some dreadful gin. We put our make-ups in our pocket long enough to get by the doorman, but the police put us out in the middle of the second act. You can imagine the P-rade of fourteen flagrant Jews and Irishmen filing drunkenly out during that solemn oratorio. And again you can imagine how I enjoyed it—being mistaken for a young man, or even for a lighthearted one.

I've been reading Spengler and Keyserling, and Santayana's Character and Opinion in the United States—the devil's own intelligence playing around the Puritans and other institutions. And the meanest deliberate effort to puncture William James and Royce,[140] and a long look at HARVARD and all American education. All sorts of beautiful things wilt at the breath of that damned Spaniard.

It seems more and more likely that I'm going off to New Mexico in the middle of March to concentrate. Get letters to Mrs Mabel Dodge and her primitivo-sumptuous colony at Taos,[141] and take long walks, look at color, listen to Brahms and concentrate.

---

138 This play (1926) by English dramatist and director Dane (1888–1965) played in repertory between February and April 1927 at the American Laboratory Theatre.

139 The Elizabethan Club is a private but Yale-affiliated organization for faculty and students interested in literature. *Abie's Irish Rose* (1922), a comedy by American dramatist Anne Nichols, ran on Broadway from May 1922 to October 1927.

140 Josiah Royce (1855–1916), American philosopher. Both James and Royce taught at Harvard.

141 Mabel Dodge Luhan (1879–1962) was an American patroness of the arts and was well known for her salons in Italy and New York. She settled in Taos, New Mexico, where she was the center of the art colony there, hosting such visitors as D. H. Lawrence, Carl Jung, Georgia O'Keeffe, Martha Graham, and, on several occasions, TNW.

Later.

Bonis are thrilled with the first instalment of The Bridge. Friday I'll give them the Twin-Brothers passage and if that doesn't knock them cold, I'll be.

Just got a letter from Jerry Hart's Marjorie, inviting me to the Chateau des Enfants.[142] Also a letter from Jerry two days ago. Also a letter from Coleman saying that he had had a long walk with you. To all these people I write better letters than to you because I don't know them as well. All I say is: Be patient, be patient with me, Benny.

There's a big hot article in the February American Mercury by a returned Rhodes scholar.[143] I'll send it to you as soon as I get back to New Haven. ¶ Ernest Hemingway writes from the Austrian mountains that at 2 bucks a day he's warm and well-fed and hard at work. Also that ski-ing is a sensation like something between tearing silk and........ ....Fill in the blanks from what you have heard of Ernest. ¶ I had tea with Muriel McCormick day before yesterday, the daughter of Harold and step of Ganna.[144] She was on her way to Palm Beach and suggested that it was an ideal place for a young author to do his best work. Remind me to tell you someday all the drama behind that there tea. I've been butting into turgid complicated lives all this year—never again shall I dismiss a play as "mere melodrama." Books are timid. God, how good for me to be always tangential to someone else's whirlwind. Even though every now & then they suck you in for twenty minutes.

Ever

Thornt.

142 Jerry Hart was another of the Oxonians on the Riviera during Christmas 1926.

143 TNW is referring to "Rhodes Scholars," by O. B. Andrews, Jr., in the February 1927 issue of *The American Mercury.*

144 Muriel McCormick, the granddaughter of both Standard Oil tycoon John D. Rockefeller and Cyrus McCormick, inventor of the mechanical reaper, was a prominent socialite. After Muriel's parents divorced, her father, Harold, married Ganna Waska, an aspiring opera singer.

97. TO CHARLOTTE E. WILDER. ALS 4 pp. Yale

75 Mansfield
New Haven
May 2, 1927[145]

Dearest and sweetest of Charlottes:

I forgot when you were here to thank you for this elegant stationery and to be very meek about the overtone of reproach involved. So an hour after putting you on the train I shall write you a letter though sheer astonishment may endanger your health. Many thanks; naturally I had that minute of terror with which any Wilder views any other Wilder buying anything. But if you always buy to such advantage, buy on and tell me when it's all gone.

Did you see the two sailors playing checkers on the train in the seat in front of yours and how they gasped for envy when I kissed you so loudly. Always kiss on trains; it gives the whole car something to meditate upon for the rest of the ride. A kiss in a railway station always reminds people that for all its appearance Life among the Anglo-Saxons is more than mere Amiability.

Try more and more to carry about with you a little secret deposit of contempt. Do not fill your late twenties and early thirties with the flutter of little friendships however comforting. Read, read the classics and the great critics on the classics. My motto is Prepare for the forties and fifties. Your friends are mostly gentle and sweet. They do not require enough of you. They lean on you (I'm sure) but after this Wheaton interval you will find, and I shall bring you, friends of a bigger mold. Not bigger by brains (at l<e>ast not Economics brains, or Social Message brains).

Be awfully wise about your health. Cut your classes in cold-blood and tear up exams if you are indisposed. Don't give a goddam for the Sour Spinsters. No pastry. No whipped cream. You are very good looking and you do nothing about it. That is criminal. Set aside money for cold creams, massages and nice things for your hair. Good looks

145 In the original letter, the date appears at the end of the letter.

are a tremendous blessing and every now and then you insult yours. Be a vain woman; use your glasses sparingly; stand well and walk without constraint. In your new evening dress you put yourself at an advantage that thousands of women cry all night after in vain. Good looks and good clothes are courage. Don't you think you'd better take up tennis—will you let me give you a raquet? have you one? don't be reticent about gifts with me, idiot.

love

Thornt.

98. TO EDWARD WEEKS.[146] TL (Copy) Yale

75 Mansfield St.
New Haven, Conn.
June 3, 1927

Dear Mr. Weeks:

I am sending you under separate covers two very untidy portions of The Bridge of San Luis Rey. Of course I should be prouder than I say if the Atlantic could use some of it. As you see there are two separate novelettes there, but the process in surgery would be beyond me. When I was in London Mr. Squire[147] wanted to run the chapter on the Marquesa de Montemayor (a treatment of the life of Mme de Sévigné) but at that time I didn't see how the piece could be extracted from its "theological" frame. If you saw possibilities in the story of the twin brothers; then to retain some of the poignancy I think the portrait of Madre María del Pilar whould<should?> be somehow lifted from the preceding chapter and inserted at the beginning.

The whole book will be very short (you have two thirds of it

146 Weeks was the associate editor of *The Atlantic Monthly.* This letter appears in a typescript of an essay on TNW that Weeks wrote; the original letter has not been located.

147 J. C. Squire was editor of the monthly *London Mercury,* an important outlet for new writers, from 1919 to 1934.

there; the Uncle Pio section excerpted would be a little strong for the Atlantic) and I should be dazzled at your liking the whole. But Boni's and Longmans, Green want to bring it out simultaneously (there is a copyright law about that) in the early fall, and I suppose your tables of contents are pretty well packed for many months to come. I don't mean it to look pretentious when I ask you to let me have the script back as soon as possible.... I haven't quite finished Parts Four and Five and am all flustered.

Whether you feel it suitable for your magazine or not, please write me an editorial-advice letter; I am eager for suggestion and if you found certain parts too sentimental or too didactic or others too summary etc., I should be very indebted to you for saying so. I am not haughty about alterations in matters of "taste" either!

I hear that you are doing Ernest Hemingway's Five Thousand Grand.[148] That's fine.

Well, whether anything comes of my ambitions for the Bridge and yourselves, thanks very much for writing to me, and excuse all this careless typewriting.

Very sincerely yours,
Thornton Wilder

99. TO C. LESLIE GLENN.[149] ALS 4 pp. (Stationery embossed The Elizabethan Club / of Yale University) Yale

Wed June 14 • 1927

Dear Les:

There is a piece of news here that I scarcely dare to tell you. Dr. Abbott has been after me to come back and teach at Laurenceville and

148 Hemingway's short story "Fifty Grand" appeared in the July 1927 issue of *The Atlantic Monthly.*

149 TNW met Glenn (1900–1976) when both were teaching at Lawrenceville School. Glenn left teaching to attend Virginia Theological Seminary and then became an ordained minister in the Episcopal Church. Glenn and TNW remained lifelong close friends.

today I telegraphed him that I would. That's an awful come-down after the pretentious outlines I laid down for myself in front of you. It was partly the result of my rereading The Bridge. The Bridge is far better than the other, but it is so sad, not to say: harrowing, that I doubt whether it finds as many readers as the other. There is a faint chance that its very earnestness may strike right into the need of a large number, in which case I might spend the Fall taking long walks in the Austrian uplands. But with a dear vague impractical family group like mine I don't dare stake on the margin of risk. If something happened to Father.....etc. Besides ① I love the Laurenceville atmosphere, my "running", the proximity of the Princeton library and the flights to New York and New Haven, and ② I shall ask for a very moderate wage in return for a modified teaching schedule. If you are very disappointed in me, just remember that it is for one year. In one more year I should be able to find a real niche somewhere.

We took our sick man from the hospital to the Pennsylvania station Monday. He still has no idea that he is as ill as he is. The doctors keep up the most amazing hopeful soft-soap as a matter of policy. He will not live through the Summer. I go down Friday for a week and a half.[150]

Someone told me by accident the other day that the Worcester Art Museum contain<s> three El Greco's. El Greco is a religious painter compared to whom Raphael was merely the inventor of the Christmas card. He is the perfect illustration of some of Rudolph Otto's finest pages.[151] Steal an hour away from Martha and invite Mary for a trip thither.[152] You will probably see pictures that look as though they were seen through the elongating mirror of an amusement park and painted in a bilious green. If you can accustom your eye to it you will be catching one of the most extraordinary transcripts of the numinous in all art.

---

150 Edwin Clyde Foresman, housemaster of Davis House at Lawrenceville, died on July 14, 1927.

151 German theologian and philosopher Otto (1869–1937) was the author of *Das Heilige,* or *The Idea of the Holy* (1917), one of the most important German theological books of the twentieth century.

152 TNW is referring to the biblical Martha and Mary, thereby suggesting to Glenn that he should refresh himself and leave his work.

C. Leslie Glenn.

(I shouldn't have said that about "stealing an hour from Martha"; you are never with one to the prejudice of the other.)

¶ The more I think about the girl at Smith and your way of thinking about her and her way of thinking about you, the more I think she is the real best find. ¶ Now that you see that I can write a sober simple letter will you do me the favor of tearing up the other two or three? The only part that you are to retain in them (mentally) is the notion that I was greatly helped by my stay and have gone about some amateurish attempts at trying it on other people. An awful hope is stirring in me. Perhaps..... well, it's too soon to tell. ¶. The proofs for the first 3 parts of <u>The Bridge</u> came this morning. I'm going to have Boni send you some duplicates and you tear them up when you have shuffled them. ¶. Isabel sails for England Friday just in time to avert a nervous breakdown. I threw a little party for my women downtown tonight. You wouldn't have known they had a care in the world. The wonderful resiliency of the human spirit when it is fed by affection from no matter where. ¶. Every now and then I would love to think of you at Worcester one more year, partly because I don't like to think of you climbing in and out of trains and meeting every day new faces and partly because the good people at Worcester are so fond of you and will probably have to discover in your place a 'busy' young curate, or an effortful one, or a smug one or something. ¶. My little millionaire tutoree Gibbs Sherrill is about to spend his second summer with Dr. Grenfell, and sends me from Groton a composition he wrote about the great doctor.[153] I wrote to Gibbs about the ministry and so on (he would not be so bad in Worcester ten years from now); he writes back with a tentative wonder and wants to know who, how and why you are! ¶ I enclose one of the English reviews of my book. If I were a bigger person I probably would not send it, but now that I am retreating, "declining" to an assistant-mastership again, in a last faint spurt of pride I want to show that I have a little corroboration for the claims I made for myself. My weaknesses are no secret to you and I suppose you can oversmile this as you have the others. ¶ The English language (as I'm always saying) does not comfortably permit of the expression of great regard between gentlemen; but let me indulge in a paroxysm of understatement and announce that I am pretty attached to you, pretty attached, as it were.

ever

Thornton

153 Glenn was serving as an assistant in a church in Worcester, Massachusetts. Gibbs Sherrill was a Groton student TNW tutored for six weeks in Briarcliff, New York, in March and April 1927. Sir Wilfred Grenfell (1865–1940), an English physician and missionary, was famous for his work among the fishermen of Labrador.

100. TO GRACE CHRISTY FORESMAN.[154] ALS 6 pp. Yale

75 Mansfield Street
New Haven
July 25 • 1927

Dear Mrs. Foresman:

As you may be in Pittsburgh I am sending this letter to Lawrenceville and hoping that it will not take too long in getting to you.

You may have suspected that even during the last weeks of Clyde's life Dr. Abbott had offered me the Davis House for the following year. I turned it down without even hesitating, partly because the very idea of taking his place (especially if he were still alive in retirement) seemed unfriendly, partly because the responsibilities and the details were distasteful to me and would even find me plain incompetent. But I did tell the Doctor for a while that I was really tempted by the idea of going in again as Assistant, if he could find a congenial Head. He was very pleased because he was eager to retain a continuity in the Davis Line and thought that a certain middle-aged master now in the Lower School, I forget his name, would do. But the next time I went back even that much house routine seemed to be not what I was looking for and so I declared for Mrs. Brearly's.[155]

But less than a week ago he telegraphed to me offering the House again. The message had to be forwarded to me in the North through my father's hands who begged me not to refuse, adding that it would do a great deal to ease some of the problems in the family also. So I accepted.

Oh, I shall be so bad when it comes to all those details of demotion and credits and signing the boy's allowance checks and a hundred and one other things. But at least I can hope to aim toward the simple wonderful thing that Clyde maintained. I should love to think that you wish me well and that you still feel that you are an active Davis House "master" and a part of us.

---

154 Widow of Edwin Clyde Foresman.

155 TNW probably means Brearley, a private school for girls in New York City, where he apparently was offered a teaching position.

If I knew when you were going to be in Lawrenceville I should come down and see you there and talk over with you buying the furnishings or some of them, or whatever suited you. I don't even know whether the School supplies some of the Housemaster's furnishings or not. Anyway do be sure that all the plans are yours. Yours to live there as long as you like, and I hope, to return often.

I am still at work on the last pages of The Bridge and trying to weave into it all the thoughts and the meanings of our last few months. I think of Clyde so often and now it seems to me that he knew, after all. I wish I had many months yet to assimilate it so that in the book it would come out beautifully and persuasively; but I must close it up soon and drop literature for a whole year.

Give my love to your Mother and keep me fresh in Emily's mind.[156] I wish she and I could steal away to another Secret meal. Perhaps you will be in the East soon and I shall see you again before long. I wish I could be useful to you in finding you something "to do". But for a while I hope, you are resting, best of all in Our House, by your garden.

Affectionately ever
Thornton

101. TO LEWIS S. BAER. ALS 3 pp. Berg

75 Mansfield St.
New Haven Conn.
July 25 • 1927

Dear Louie:

If your firm were in serious difficulties at the edge of bancruptcy I should be patient, but I cannot believe it is.[157]

---

156 The only child of Edwin Clyde and Grace Christy Foresman, Emily Foresman was two years old when TNW went to Davis House in September 1921.

157 The Boni firm told TNW that they felt that *The Bridge of San Luis Rey* was too short to justify a price of $2.50 and suggested that they add several illustrations to the text. There was also a dispute over the handling of foreign rights.

I have always been very grateful and loyal to you for having discovered me. This loyalty is a very real thing to me and I should never dream of leaving your Firm merely for bigger Terms elsewhere, though I have had them. But my loyalty is being thrown away, if you cannot be normally considerate of me these early difficult years. You have not yet caught up to the January statement; you promised me some of the Spring royalties; and surely some of the Advance on a book of which four-fifths is set up. In a few weeks the translation of Paulina 1880 will be ready which I am willing to sell en bloc for three hundred dollars down, but which will certainly be too expensive for your Firm.[158] I shall stay with Bonis', not only <for> the three stipulated books, but for a whole shelf-ful, if Bonis' shows some interest in me above and beyond the mere literary machine.

My new job at Lawrenceville requires my furnishing a house and sends me on a number of trips this Summer, so please send me my five-hundred, Louie, and let us keep the association cordial.

Ever

Thornton

102. TO ISABEL WILDER. ALS 4 pp. Yale

Blodgetts Landing
Aug. 22 1927

Dearest Isabel:

Look what befell me. I was on the way from a weekend at Cape Cod with the T-s to a week with Les Glenn at Champlain with perhaps a Sunday night supper at Mrs MacDowells.[159] Then I was going back to

---

158 TNW was asked by his English publisher, Longmans, Green, to translate the notorious avant-garde French novel *Paulina 1880* (1925) by Pierre-Jean Jouve (1887–1976). It is not known whether he completed the translation, and the manuscript has not survived.

159 TNW spent a weekend on Cape Cod with Douglas and Marie Townson, Andy Townson's parents, and planned to stop in Peterborough, New Hampshire, for supper with Marian MacDowell,

New Haven to finish Paulina and to sit with Mama. But I decided to stop in here a day or two and say howdy to my old camp. Presto, they wanted me to stay and teach. You know how I love an Even Tenour. So here I stay set. They offered me wages, but my pupils are so few that I allowed that board and lodge was enough. (Now I have a new pupil to tutor after hours and that's money.) The usual crazy thing has happened: I love it. I take twelve mile walks almost every day; I swim over a mile; I'm brown-black and roaring with health. And two of the nicest boys on the lot are to be among my 33 at the Davis House next year.

Of course Amy Wertheimer is in the vicinity. I only show up once a week. She's resigned and wistful. She always has house guests so that there isn't much occasion etc.[160]

The Bridge was finished etc. Longman writes about a nice format. Boni is revolted that it isn't long enough to keep up the fraud of a 2.50 book. He wants six to eight illustrations, and the Canadian and Esquimaux rights. I begin to see a lit. agent to keep Bonis quiet.

I've bought over all the Foresmans' furniture for five hundred bucks. There will be much additional outlay for linen. So I guess I'm a weighty schoolmaster for some years. With anyone else it would be wrecking one's talent for money and all that slop: but for very special reasons I think it is a subtly remarkable solution for me. I don't write in leisure. I don't write from any aspect of my life that daily life can exhibit. I am Dr Jeykel and Mr. Hyde. And the more ordinary and uneventful Mr. Hyde's life is, the better Dr. Jeykll pursues alchemical research.

The rumour reaches me that Dr. Abbott has grown so impatient with certain of the big housemasters' wives that he has decided to keep certain of the big houses as Bachelor Establishments. Men's Clubs; Camps, almost. He is wrong. Davis makes the third of these. But you and Mama can come and stay as long as you choose to the delight of the proprietor and of the boys, I wot.

---

widow of the American composer Edward Alexander MacDowell, before going on to visit Glenn. The MacDowells established the MacDowell Colony in 1907, and TNW had been there in July 1926, working on *The Bridge of San Luis Rey.*

160 Amy Wertheimer, five years older than TNW, wanted their relationship to be a more romantic one; TNW worked hard to maintain a platonic but close friendship.

Well, how are you? Do you love London? and Oxford? Are you tranquillizing out? Ach, honey, I should have joined you over there. I could have perfectly well. Boni just slipped me five hundred dollars on the Bridge.

How about the sentimental ghosts of New College (was it New?). All that assimilated long ago? I am going to write herr. Childers, I've decided, and ask him to come to Davis. He's the kind that haunts New York pretty often, pullman or no pullman. Next week I'm going down to Peterborough where Rosemary Ames is star pupil at the Mariarden Theatre Camp. Such letters—quite turn my head—also from Gwynne Williams. Eco[161] writes frequently elaborate introspective fantasias. I trot humbly along behind. I'd rather put my head in a lyon's mouth than spend a weekend at Chappaqua. But, God, what brains. She's getting raises and rolling up influence: if only she doesn't get fired on a touch of temper.

Our adorable mother misses you girls no end. They had some mean hot days, but on the whole the Summer has been very cool and the farmers crops are a month late and lack flavor (dope acquired from Doug Townson, the canner).

What shall I write next, by slow stages at the Davis? Plays, I suppose. Another letter from Charles Wagner wanting to see some and all that. But I have no burning ideas.

Go to St. Mary's, for me.

Reread the first part of Strachey's Eminent Victorians.

Take a scoot over to Cambridge and write a charming little essay for The Literary Review.

I hope your homeward trip is better than your outward, and that there are some nice gents.

Lots of love and ever thine

Thornton

I own a paino and a victrola. And a handsome dining room table and six chairs and a big sideboard. Wouldn't it freeze y'?

---

161 TNW may be using a name that he and Isabel used to refer to their sister Charlotte.

103. TO CHAUNCEY B. TINKER. ALS 3 pp. (Stationery embossed Thornton Wilder / Davis House / Lawrenceville, New Jersey) Yale

Dec 6 • 1927

Dear Mr. Tinker:

You may imagine how exciting your letter was for me and how happy and fit-for-nothing it left me the rest of the day.[162] It has decided me to fix on you as the judge in a new problem I have: more and more people are muttering to me that I must leave the little chicken-feed duties of the housemaster and teacher and go to Bermuda, for example, and write books as a cow gives milk. I do not know how to answer them, but I do feel (though with intervals of misgiving) that this life is valuable to me and, I dare presume, my very pleasure in my routine can make me useful to others. Anyway no one, except you and I, seems to believe any longer in the dignity of teaching. (Though to us even 'dignity' is an understatement.) Ach, you should see the Davis House and all the sincerity and contentment and application that keeps coming out of 32 potential roughnecks and Red Indians.

Well, you must think over this for me, though I don't know when I can pin you down for it, for, Xmas I am going South. I'm not all well of Dr. Verdi's adroit appendectomy and am finding some minor Florida beach to lie on for a few weeks.[163] But that will only make a short postponement for New Haven rather than New York is still my week-end privilege.

As for your questions, oh, isn't there a lot of New England in me; all that ignoble passion to be didactic that I have to fight with. All that bewilderment as to where Moral Attitude begins and where it shades off into mere Puritan Bossiness. My father is still pure Maine-1880 and I carry all that load of notions to examine and discard or assimilate.

No, I have never been to Peru. Why I chose to graft my thoughts

---

162 Tinker apparently wrote TNW a letter praising *The Bridge of San Luis Rey*, which had been published the previous month.

163 TNW had his appendix removed in New Haven in the fall of 1927 by Dr. William Francis Verdi, his father's physician.

about Luke 13[4] upon a delightful one-act play by Mérimée, Le Carosse du Saint-Sacrement, I do not know. The Marquesa is my beloved Mme de Sévigné in a distorting mirror. The bridge is invented, the name borrowed from one of Junipero Serra's missions in California.

It is right and fitting that you cried for a page of mine. How many a time I have cried with love or awe or pity while you talked of the Doctor, or Cowper, or Goldsmith.

Between the lines then you will find here all my thanks and joy at your letter

Ever
Thornton

104. TO F. SCOTT FITZGERALD. ALS 2 pp. (Stationery embossed Thornton Wilder / Davis House / Lawrenceville, New Jersey) Princeton

Jan 12 • 1928[164]

Dear Scott Fitzgerald:

I have been an admirer, not to say a student, of The Great Gatsby too long not to have got a great kick out of your letter.[165] It gives me the grounds to hope that we may sometime have some long talks on what writing's all about. As you see I am a provincial schoolmaster and have always worked alone. And yet nothing interests me more than thinking of our generation as a league and as a protest to the whole cardboard generation that precedes us from Wharton through Cabell and Anderson and Sinclair Lewis. I know Ernest Hemingway. Glenway Westcott, I think, is coming down here for a few days soon. I'd like to think that you'd be around Princeton before long and ready for some long talks. I like teaching a lot and shall probably remain here for ages; a daily routine is necessary to me: I have no writing habits, am

164 In the original letter, the date appears at the end of the letter, as well as here.

165 Fitzgerald, whose third novel, *The Great Gatsby,* had been published in 1925, apparently had written TNW a letter praising *The Cabala.*

terribly lazy and write seldom. I'd be awfully proud if you arrived in my guestroom some time.

I spent last Xmas with a pack of Rhodes scholars (I'm not one) at Juan-les-Pins. The dentist-doctor-ex-sailor-adventurer on the plage told me you were working on a novel based upon a pathological situation seen in the hotel crowd.[166] You'd do it wonderfully and to hell with Scribners. The new firm of Coward-McCann would do their share wonderfully well. I'm sending you my Second.

We're looking for some more tremendous pages from you. Thanks a lot for writing me

Sincerely yours
Thornton Wilder

Later: God, I write a bad letter. I hoped this was going to carry more conviction. Fill in with the energy I'd have had if I hadn't just taught four classes in French. T.W.

105. TO CASS CANFIELD.[167] TL (Copy)[168] 1 p. Yale

COPY
THORNTON WILDER
DAVIS HOUSE
LAWRENCEVILLE, NEW JERSEY.

Jan. 16, 1928[169]

Dear Mr. Canfield:

I wish to commit myself to the house of Harpers by putting on paper the following conditions:

---

166 In 1925, when Fitzgerald began planning the novel that would become *Tender is the Night,* his protagonist was Francis Melarky, a twenty-one-year-old southerner. In this early version, Fitzgerald intended for Melarky to join the fashionable young crowd on the Riviera and, after an alcoholic breakdown, murder his overly protective mother. The Melarky version was later abandoned.

167 Editor and publisher Cass Canfield (1897–1986) joined the publishing firm of Harper & Brothers (later Harper & Row) in 1924. He served in a variety of positions there and became the president of the firm in 1931. He remained an editor at Harper until his death.

168 This is a secretarial transcription of TNW's letter; the original letter has not been located.

169 In the copy of the letter, the date appears at the end of the letter.

That if the House of Harpers will consent to subsidize me to the extent of five thousand a year for three years beginning June 1929 (even though it covers some of the time when I must be completing the two remaining books that I am required to give to Albert and Charles Boni) I shall agree to consider all further books thereafter as belonging to the House of Harpers.

This shall except the book of short plays published by Coward-McCann;[170] and the money to be reimbursed if the time is consumed in writing plays or material of a specially limited type of interest.

The fifteen thousand dollars shall be considered as applying against the royalties of at least two novels of 50,000 words or more.

In the event that this guarantee arrangement is not necessary to me, I shall be willing to enter into a contract along the ordinary lines on terms satisfactory to both of us.[171]

Sincerely yours,
(Signed) THORNTON WILDER.

106. TO ISABELLA N. WILDER. ALS 4 pp. (Stationery embossed Thornton Wilder / Davis House / Lawrenceville, New Jersey) Yale

<February 23, 1928>[172]

Dearest of mamas:

I'm the worst of goofs. I write sixteen letters every two days but I never write the important ones! I haven't answered E A Robinson

---

170 *The Angel That Troubled the Waters and Other Plays* was published by Coward-McCann on October 29, 1928.

171 Unhappy with the Boni firm's treatment, TNW signed a secret agreement committing to Harper upon the completion of his contractual obligations to Boni. In return, Harper agreed to give him a five-thousand-dollar annual subvention for three years, even while he worked on books still owed to Boni. Because of the financial success of *The Bridge of San Luis Rey,* TNW never called on these moneys. His contract with Boni covered his three books after *The Cabala*; the firm published *The Bridge of San Luis Rey* (1927), *The Woman of Andros* (1930), waived its right to *The Angel That Troubled the Waters,* and ultimately sold the third, *Heaven's My Destination* (1935), to Harper.

172 This date is written on the letter in another hand, probably TNW's mother's.

yet, nor Robert Longman[173] nor sent Amos the book I promised him. Instead I write the queerest little letters. Well: here are the items for today:

You and I and Isabel and Janet or everybody are taking a house near London (Oxford or the Thames-side) all Summer. And we, all or some or more, are staying there until March. Then I am coming back to lecture for two months under Lee Keedick (the best: Margot Asquith and G. K. Chesterton and Hugh Walpole).[174] You stay on if you like.

2. I am sailing on the Adriatic July 7 with 3 boys[175] vaguely under my care. Their mamas would not let them have the Summer abroad without me being there. They are going to golf in Scotland and spend a week in Dea<u>ville with a friend, and are going to return to America as early as Aug. 20. (for college boards)

3. You are going over to England quite early in the Spring, probably alone to prepare the way. Find a house with a garden, please. Like Duff House in London; or somewhere very nice near it. And a big house.[176]

4. The book is going to go well above 100,000. Friday I was in N.Y. and the Bonis (who by the way have forgiven me) mentioned that on that day alone I had earned over 600 dollars (5,000 copies by telegraphic order). <appeared perpendicularly in left margin> **Just got $6000 from Boni. More monthly.**

5. You are to get the rental of a real house, big

These boys are going to drop in and out during the Summer and Gene Tunney in the Fall etc. If you don't go over and choose it for me I shall have to ask Richard Blaker or Robert Longman to find it and they will overdo. And it must be started before June 20.

---

173 Head of Longmans, Green, TNW's English publisher.

174 TNW signed a multi-year public lecturing contract with the well-known Lee Keedick Lecture Bureau to go on a lecture tour. Keedick also represented English writers Asquith, Chesterton, and Walpole. TNW lectured under the terms of this agreement until the spring of 1937.

175 The three boys, Henry Noy, Clark Anderson, and Duff McCullough, were Lawrenceville students.

176 TNW's mother and youngest sister eventually rented Axeland House, near Horley, Sussex, for the summer.

6. So be a honey: think this over and come to a decision soon.

7. I don't dare come home Easter. Three days in N.Y? or New Orleans: or Charleston; or Atlantic City. I'm tired, and good cause too. ¶ I am forwarding Father's accident. left behinds when I can find paper and cord.[177] ¶ love to all.

love

Thornton

107. TO F. SCOTT AND ZELDA FITZGERALD. ALS 2 pp. (Stationery embossed Thornton Wilder / Davis House / Lawrenceville, New Jersey) Princeton

<early March 1928>

Dear Scott, Dear, Zelda, dear Scott, Dear Zelda,

Why should I tear up three letters in an attempt at writing you. One was a long and over-literary catalogue of the things I enjoyed at your house,[178] with delighted characterizations of all the guests and of yourselves (hurry, come and get it; it's in my wastepaper basket here, Davis House), and one was a letter to little Scotty, the new planet. All I can say is that I filled my eyes with more than they can digest for a long while, and my affections with more than they can ever consent to lose. For instance I met the beautiful and wonderful Zelda and feel as though I'd been no-end awkward and inadequate beside her. Anyway I know that she understands that in my fashion I was happy and excitingly interested in everything. And now I'm more than ever eager to live near you someday on some European beach with long lazy days for talking and just mooning about. Since I got back the routine has been

177 TNW is referring to some items his father accidentally left behind during a visit to Lawrenceville.

178 TNW spent the weekend of February 25 and 26, 1928, at the Fitzgeralds' rented house, Ellerslie, outside Wilmington, Delaware, where he met for the first time Fitzgerald, his wife, Zelda, and their only child, Frances Scott, who was called "Scottie."

more complicated than usual, but I have been collecting a little bundle of things to say to you, which I shall not take the trouble to link together or even to interspace. ¶ If you are staying long at Ellerslie you should get a piano for Scotty. She's alive with some gift or other and that may be the one. Besides I can come down and give her piano-talks. (I went into Trenton on the streetcar yesterday with a little girl 8 yrs old and she wasn't anywhere near Scotty, and yet Barbara Baker's no slouch for brightness.) ¶ You, Scott, seemed to have the impression that I was restless under Miss Murphey,[179] under "the banyan-tree of her tragedienne's voice." No, I was delighted; we discovered the same enthusiasms in French memoir literature and I could have got on as happily as that for years<?>. ¶ I started my phonograph agency searching for copies of the Rosenkavalier and Pavillon d'Armide waltzes for Zelda, so please don't get them in the meantime. They'd make a deaconess's<?> eyes droop, if you get what<?> I mean. ¶ Rex Lardner was here to lunch nailing an option on the serializ. of my next for Hearst-Cosmop.[180] He says he knew you at Great Neck. I told him the opening of Scott's next was stunning. I hope that's all right, isn't it? ¶ Next Sunday night (we are allowed a half-hour's reading-recreation after House Prayers then) I am reading the boys: Rags and the Prince of Wales.[181] Is it all right with you. Seven-twenty, Eastern Standard Time. ¶ Can you-alls ever come up here? Can't I ever be hospitable to anybody? ¶ The ballet teacher at the American Laboratory Theatre 222 East 64th St. is Mme Irantzoff-Anderson and La Sylphe is retained for corrective gymnastics and something else; something new in sylphs.[182] (10:15 p.m. Just turned off the house-lights. 3rd Floor kinda restless. Organized

179 Among the guests at Ellerslie was Esther Murphy, sister of Gerald Murphy, the Fitzgeralds' friend from their time in Paris and the Riviera.

180 Reginald "Rex" Lardner, brother of American writer and journalist Ringgold "Ring" Lardner, was, like his brother, a neighbor of the Fitzgeralds when the latter lived in Great Neck, New York, and was an editor for *Hearst's International-Cosmopolitan* magazine.

181 Fitzgerald's story "Rags Martin-Jones and the Pr-nce of W-les" (1924) was reprinted in his collection *All The Sad Young Men* (1926).

182 TNW no doubt mentioned this because of Zelda's interest in ballet. She began to take ballet lessons in Paris in the summer of 1925 and, while they were at Ellerslie, took classes with the director of the Philadelphia Opera ballet.

rough-house brewing? Heaven help us thru the Winter Term. Spring Term is Housemaster's paradise.)

ever thine
Thornt.

108. TO JOHN A. TOWNLEY.[183] ALS 2 pp. (Stationery embossed Thornton Wilder / Davis House / Lawrenceville, New Jersey) Lawrenceville

March 6 • 1928[184]

Dear John:

The book is not supposed to solve. A vague comfort is supposed to hover above the unanswered questions, but it is not a theorem with its Q.E.D. The book is supposed to be as puzzling and distressing as the news that five of your friends died in an automobile accident. I dare not claim that all sudden deaths are, in the last counting, triumphant. As you say, a little over half the situations seem to prove something and the rest escape, or even contradict. Chekhov said: <“>The business of literature is not to answer questions, but to state them fairly.” I claim that human affection contains a strange unanalizable consolation and that is all. People who are full of faith claim that the book is a vindication of their optimism; disillusioned people claim that it is a barely concealed “anatomy of despair.” I am nearer the second group than the first; though some days I discover myself shouting confidentally in the first group. Where will I be thirty years from now?—with Hardy or Cardinal Newman?

Thank you for your fine thoughtful letter. I am carrying your messages to Mrs. Abbott. May we see you before June?

---

183 Townley graduated from Lawrenceville in 1923 and from Princeton in 1927.

184 In the original letter, the date appeared at the end of the letter.

A letter like yours does me lots of good. If you were here I would outline my Next[185] to you.

Ever

Thornton W.

109. TO ERNEST HEMINGWAY. ALS 1 p. (Stationery embossed Thornton Wilder / Davis House / Lawrenceville, New Jersey) JFK

June 20 • 1928[186]

Dear Ernest:

Wonderful to hear from you.

Talk about you all the time. I had <a> weekend with Scott and Zelda this Spring. Scott read the opening chapter of his new book to us, perfectly fine. Your ghost crosses the stage everynow and then, but so it does in all of our books willy-nilly, mostly willy. You haven't published anything, big or little, for ages. All agog about a novel plus a play.

I <am> writing from bed, laid up with four-day-grippe. Nothing compared to your pretentious ills—anthrax and finger-in-the-eye. Sailing for 2 months in Eng. (Adriatic July 7); then walking tour with Gene Tunney (vide press passim).[187] As fine a person as you'd want to meet; not much humour, but I've always had a taste for the doggedly earnest ones. Then another tutoring job from Oct 20th on with Xmas in Egypt, then some readings & lectures in America (March and April.). Hawaii to write two plays. But I dread and lose my enthusiasm before all this leisure. I need routines.

185 *The Woman of Andros.*

186 In the original letter, the date appeared at the end of the letter.

187 Latin: see the press here and there.

You see I haven't much to say, but I'm strong for you and wish we could sit down to some long talks. Honest. I'm more flexible than I was. And you modified me lots. If I can do any errands for you note the Ship's Date.

Ever thine
Thornt

TNW and Gene Tunney hiking at the Mer de Glace in the French Alps, October 1928.

Part Three

RÔLES: 1929–1939

BECAUSE OF THE LITERARY SUCCESS AND FINANCIAL REWARDS of *The Bridge of San Luis Rey,* Thornton Wilder's way of life had changed radically by the time he returned from Europe in mid-January 1929. He had resigned his job at Lawrenceville, and that decision freed him to relinquish the delicate balance he had maintained between his teaching and writing routines. Now he had to establish a new regimen.

Before he had left for Europe in the midst of his growing renown, he had signed a multiyear contract with the Lee Keedick Agency, a nationally known speakers' bureau, contracting for what turned out to be 144 lectures over several years' time. In mid-February 1929, he began his first series of lectures, traveling throughout the Midwest until May. On his return, he entered another writing residency at the MacDowell Colony, where he remained through June. While there, he began *The Woman of Andros,* a new novel and the third of the four books he had contracted to do for Albert & Charles Boni. Much of the rest of Wilder's summer was filled with social engagements and lectures, but he did manage to spend two weeks at his old tutoring camp on Lake Sunapee.

In September 1929, Wilder was off to Europe again, this time with his mother. They visited Bruges, Ghent, Antwerp, Munich, Paris, London, and Oxford, and returned to the United States in November. Wilder finished his new novel in October, and *The Woman of Andros* was published by Boni at the end of February 1930. In 1928, after the success of *The Bridge of San Luis Rey*, Wilder had acceded to his father's recommendation that he retain a local New Haven attorney, J. Dwight Dana, to represent him in his business affairs. Dana's representation gave Wilder control over the format and presentation of his new novel, a control he had not had previously.

The Woman of Andros was one of the top ten best-selling novels of 1930, although it was not the phenomenon that *The Bridge of San Luis Rey* had been. Reviewers admired his style and craftsmanship, but several of them had reservations about the relevance of this novel set in pagan times on an obscure Greek island because it was so removed from the practical experiences beginning to affect his reading public. The specter of Black Tuesday, the stock market crash on October 29, 1929, already haunted the American public, including the audience for literary novels.

Wilder's royalty income of approximately forty thousand dollars was not an insignificant sum in 1930. It was, however, an income subject to wide vacillations, a circumstance that had to be taken into account, because he had become the sole support of his parents and two younger sisters. His other siblings were self-supporting, with Amos teaching at Hamilton College in Clinton, New York, and Charlotte at Wheaton College in Norton, Massachusetts, and later at Smith College in Northampton, Massachusetts.

Wilder had invested a portion of his royalties from *The Bridge of San Luis Rey* in land in Hamden, Connecticut, just outside New Haven, and in 1929 he built a house there for his family. In the late spring of 1930, after he returned from a two-month lecture tour, Wilder, his parents, and his younger sisters moved into their newly built home, a residence referred to by the family as "The House *The Bridge* Built." The financial resources for running this household had to come from Wilder's earnings, because his father could no longer contribute to his family's economic needs; after several mild strokes, he was gently but firmly asked to retire from the associate editorship at the *Journal-Courier* in 1929. Wilder's sister Isabel, who remained at home, had begun to assist him with his voluminous mail, particularly when he was off lecturing or traveling abroad. His youngest sister, Janet, was a student at Mount Holyoke College, her tuition paid by Wilder.

Robert M. Hutchins, Wilder's friend from Oberlin and Yale, became president of the University of Chicago in 1929 and invited Wilder to teach there for two quarters a year, at a salary of four thousand dollars. Because he enjoyed teaching but also because he wanted the extra income, he agreed to begin his first quarter in April 1930. He taught a course in advanced English composition to a small class of students selected by him, as well as a larger lecture course on classic literature in translation. After classes ended in June, Wilder spent a month at the MacDowell Colony, working on six one-act plays. In September, he returned briefly to work in his new study in Hamden before going back to Chicago to teach in the fall quarter.

By 1931, Wilder seemed to have established a schedule that was flexible enough to accommodate his lecturing and teaching obligations without compromising his ability to travel and write. He began the year with a speaking tour that lasted through February, embarked for Europe in late March, returned in July, spent August and September socializing and writing, and then returned to Chicago in October to teach until the end of December.

The six one-act plays Wilder had completed at MacDowell were published in November 1931 by Yale University Press and Coward-McCann as *The Long Christmas Dinner and Other Plays in One Act.* The Boni firm was interested only in his novels, and Coward-McCann had published Wilder's first volume of his short plays, *The Angel That Troubled the Waters and Other Plays,* in 1928. It had sold well, coming, as it did, on the heels of the successful *The Bridge of San Luis Rey.* Two of the new plays in the 1931 volume, *The Long Christmas Dinner* and *The Happy Journey to Trenton and Camden,* had premieres at the Yale University Theater and the University of Chicago Dramatic Association in late November and early December 1931, respectively. Both of these, as well as another one-act in the collection, *Pullman Car Hiawatha,* anticipated ideas and stage techniques that would blossom in Wilder's full-length dramas at the end of the 1930s and the beginning of the 1940s.

In 1932, Wilder began the year teaching at the University of Chicago instead of lecturing on the road, and later in the spring he tried his hand at translating and adapting two plays. At the behest of Broadway producer Gilbert Miller, Wilder translated from the German and adapted Hungarian Otto Indig's *The Bride of Torozko.* But when the production opened, Wilder's translation was not used; the production closed quickly. The second was a translation from the French of André Obey's *Le Viol de Lucrèce* for Katharine Cornell, a leading actress of the day. The play, now entitled *Lucrece,* received a lukewarm reception in New York when it premiered in December 1932, and it closed shortly thereafter.

While Wilder was working on these adaptations and translations at MacDowell in June 1932, he also began serious work on his new novel, *Heaven's My Destination,* his first to be set in contemporary America. He hoped to finish it by April 1933, but it was not completed until the end of September 1934. Wilder's royalty income had dropped precipitously, from over $40,000 in 1930 to $13,300 in 1931, $9,200 in 1932, and $6,700 in 1933; as a consequence, he spent a good part of 1933 earning money to support his family. He was on the road giving lectures in January, February, and part of March. On April 1, he began teaching his spring-quarter classes at Chicago, and he stayed on through the summer term, earning four thousand dollars. After a short visit home in Hamden, Wilder departed by train for Los Angeles at the end of October, then sailed for Hawaii, where he was engaged to lecture at the university in Honolulu for two and a half weeks. Upon his return to Los Angeles, he lectured at UCLA for five days; made a short rest stop to visit with his friend Mabel Dodge Luhan at her ranch in Taos, New Mexico, in early December; gave more lectures in Kansas City, St. Louis, and Chicago on his way east; and arrived home in Hamden just before Christmas.

During the Depression, Hollywood was the one place where writers could earn large salaries. In Los Angeles during the fall of 1933, Wilder, who was genuinely interested in filmmaking as an art form, became acquainted with people in the movie industry. He spent approximately two weeks in Hollywood in March 1934, working on a screen treatment for a projected film about Joan of Arc. After Wilder taught in the spring at Chicago, he was invited back to Hollywood to work for Sam Goldwyn and RKO. When he returned to Chicago to teach for the fall quarter, he spent two weeks writing a film treatment for William Randolph Hearst's production company. For approximately ten weeks of film work, Wilder earned $11,500, twice his teaching salary and five times more than he had earned lecturing.

On his way home from Hollywood before the fall 1934 teaching quarter at the University of Chicago, Wilder again stopped at Mabel Dodge Luhan's ranch in Taos and finished *Heaven's My Destination*. The novel was published in England by Longmans, Green on December 3, 1934, and in the United States on January 2, 1935, by his new publisher Harper & Brothers, which bought the book from Boni and would henceforth be Wilder's American publisher. This fourth novel was successful and restored Wilder's bank account, earning approximately $27,000 during 1934–1935.

While he was teaching at the University of Chicago for the 1934–1935 academic year, Wilder met Gertrude Stein on November 25, 1934, when she spoke on campus. When Stein returned to Chicago for two weeks in March, Wilder lent her his apartment. Despite their difference in age (she was sixty-one and he thirty-seven at this time) and public renown (she was something of a literary curiosity, while he had been in the literary limelight for six years), they developed a friendship that became very important to both of them.

When Wilder finished his classes that spring, he spent some time in the Midwest, fulfilling speaking engagements, then returned east for much of May and June, visiting friends and joining family celebrations. That May, his sister Janet received an M.A. degree from Mount Holyoke, and in June, his brother married Catharine Kerlin, Thornton serving as best man. Shortly thereafter, he sailed for Europe for his first visit to the Continent in three years. He visited Gertrude Stein and Alice B. Toklas in France, went to Salzburg for the music festival (in the company of the political and literary hostess Sibyl Colefax, whom he had met in London in 1928 and who became a lifelong friend), walked in the Dolomites, and then spent time in Vienna, Innsbruck, and Paris. He returned to Connecticut for a somber family Thanksgiving: During October, Wilder's father had suffered a series of strokes, which left him paralyzed on one side; his condition worsened when he was hospitalized and operated on for an intestinal blockage. In spite of a grim prognosis, however, Amos Parker Wilder recovered enough to be tended to at home by family and nursing help.

In 1936, Wilder's grueling schedule of lecturing on both the East Coast and the West during the first three months of the year and teaching the spring and summer quarters at Chicago was interrupted by his father's death on July 2, 1936. He returned to teach after his father's funeral and concluded his classes. After six years of teaching, he resigned his position. He spent the summer of 1936 at home, and in early October, he left for new territory, sailing to the West Indies and stopping at several islands, where he searched for comfortable writing locales. Although he did not find an ideal place, he finished a writing project he had promised to do for Gertrude Stein—an introduction to her book *The Geographical History of America or the Relation of Human Nature to the Human Mind,* which was published in 1936. He had performed a similar service for her in March 1935, for *Narration,* a book of four lectures she had delivered at the University of Chicago.

The lecture commitments Wilder had made in 1929 were the only contractual obligations left that competed with his freedom to roam and write at will. He was free of that obligation by the end of March 1937, after spending the first three months of the year on the speaking circuit. During April and May, with the aid primarily of German translations, he wrote a new stage version of Henrik Ibsen's *A Doll's House* for a close friend, the actress Ruth Gordon. In June, after a five-year absence, he returned to the MacDowell Colony to concentrate on a new play, *Our Town.* During the summer, after serving as the first American delegate to the annual gathering in Paris of the Institute for Intellectual Cooperation, an enterprise that was part of the League of Nations, calling on Gertrude Stein, and attending the Salzburg Festival, Wilder completed most of his new play in a hotel in a small town near Zurich, Switzerland. He returned to New York in December for rehearsals of both *A Doll's House* and *Our Town;* the latter was to be directed by Jed Harris.

Wilder's adaptation of *A Doll's House* opened in New York on December 27, 1937. It was a great success and had a long run, closing in May 1938. When *Our Town* opened on February 4, 1938, and was similarly received, Wilder achieved the rare distinction of having two hits on Broadway simultaneously. In the spring of 1938, *Our Town* won Wilder his second Pulitzer Prize, this time in drama. At the end of March, Wilder left for Tucson, Arizona, to complete another play, a farce called *The Merchant of Yonkers.* It was to be directed by the Austrian theater director Max Reinhardt, whose career Wilder had followed for many years. Rehearsals began in November, and on December 28, 1938, *The Merchant of Yonkers* opened in New York. Wilder's Broadway winning streak came to an end when the production received lukewarm reviews and then closed on January 28, 1939, after just thirty-nine performances. Despite this temporary setback, he now not only was internationally recognized as a novelist but, with *Our Town,* had established himself as an innovative major talent in the literary area that had dazzled and attracted him since childhood, the theater.

110. TO SIBYL COLEFAX. ALS 4 pp. NYU

The MacDowell Colony
Peterborough New Hampshire
July 24 • 1929

Dear Lady Colefax:

If this is a long letter in small writing and crowded with matter, will I be forgiven for my frailty and broken promises? The time I thought I was writing you a letter and telegraphed the news was on my lecture tour. And lecturers ought to be forgiven the delusions that visit them in the nineteenth story of some strange hotel. The moment I sat down to write the bespoken letter, Heaven only knows what Reception Committee called up on the 'phone, or what reporter, or what new cousin, or what former pupil. Similarly any cables you receive from me next January and February must be regarded as fantasies and wish-fulfilment idyls. So great is the dislocation caused by a Lecture Tour that it is not until July that Friendship, Admiration, Gratitude and Obligation begin to collect themselves in the wreckage of my faculties.

This is the place for such a revival. The music of Edward MacDowell is not wearing well, but this Colony that his widow has built up in his name is a sufficient memorial. Edwin Arlington Robinson, our best poet, has been here about fifteen summers; Elinor Wylie wrote a great deal of her work here; Porgy and Death Comes for the Arch-Bishop and The Bridge of S.L.R. and Scarlet Sister Mary and Tristram were, all or partly, written here.[1] At nine each Colonist drifts off to a studio, a little house quarter of a mile from most of the other studios,

---

1 *Porgy* (1925), a novel by DuBose Heyward; *Death Comes for the Archbishop* (1927), a novel by Willa Cather; *Scarlet Sister Mary* (1928), a Pulitzer Prize–winning novel by Julia Peterkin; *Tristram* (1927), a Pulitzer Prize–winning narrative poem by Edwin Arlington Robinson.

set in deep pine woods, with views of hills and mountains, and doesn't see another human being until five o'clock. His lunch is brought by a cart and left on his doorstep without knocking. Naturally all that solitude is too austere a draught for me: I go walking or I play Patience or I go to the village to buy fountain-pen-ink. But finally one is caught by the contagion of concentration; a little routine is set up, and finally even I, the reluctant author, write a few pages daily.

It's still the Woman of Andros, my hetaira who is developing into a sort of Dr. Johnson.[2] Her sayings and parables and her custom of adopting human strays is weighing down the book. But die she must, and with unhellenic overtones, an anima naturaliter christiana.[3] I love to think that Terence's play on which, ever so inexcusably, I base the nouvelle was a favorite with Fénélon[4] and John Henry Newman. I'd love to introduce a strophe in salutation of those three lions with honey in their mouths. (As to Terence I don't know, but Strachey was a fool when he compared Newman to a dove and my Fenelon I take from the gallery of Saint-Simon, the true book for the shipwrecked, a sufficient compensation, Heavens, for a lost leg.)

The last bit of writing I finished was a preface for Sir Philip's book in its American edition.[5] I did my best with a subject matter I know nothing about; I tried a wandering personal essay; it may be stupid and childish. I hope not. Now that my "strength" is returning I hope to write him in a few days, a long overdue answer. If you see him, tell him that my silences are not the meter of my regard and that (you may guess from all this latinity what author I have been reading) my instability is passing, has passed.

There is a very fine novel by Ernest Hemingway (of "Fiesta") now

---

2 The heroine of *The Woman of Andros,* Chrysis, was a hetaera, one of a class of highly cultivated courtesans in ancient Greece.

3 Latin: a naturally Christian soul.

4 TNW noted before the opening lines of his novel: "The first part of this novel is based upon the Andria, a comedy of Terence who in turn based his work upon two Greek plays, now lost to us, by Menander." Fénelon (1651–1715) was a French prelate and writer.

5 TNW had written a preface for Philip Sassoon's nonfiction book *The Third Route,* published in the United States in 1929.

running serially in Scribner's Magazine.[6] It caused the magazine to be barred in Boston and I hear that 1500 indignant subscribers cancelled their subscriptions, but it is very fine work. ¶ Have you met Alfred Lunt and Lynne<Lynn> Fontanne and aren't they lovely? Give them my great love. ¶ Here's a very confidential secret. In the blessed engagement of Jean Forbes-Robertson and Jim Hamilton magna pars fui.[7] Jim and I once talked almost all night at the Savoy—I was packing to leave on a boat train and my back hurt too. But about 6 weeks ago I got a cable that read: Took your advice it worked congratulate us. Ach, doctor, heal thyself. ¶ I'm sailing somewhere in the first wks of Sept. I should love to go to England but I don't dare—I must also write on a play-notion that in the right hands could be lovely.[8] All I know is that probably I must see what the State Theatres and the Kammerspiele of Munich have been doing; and see my dear old Swiss lady that runs a 6-room pension at Juan-les-Pins. If you are here-or-there on the Continent I should love to cross your path for some meals and long walks and a merciless examination of life and letters in Our Times. ¶ I feel so ashamed at having failed you in a thing that I eagerly looked forward to. That is: seeing your son in New York. I live in New Haven and the few times I went to N.Y. were so involved in business and educational matters that I never found the spacious evening that the meeting required and promised. Is it still possible? Will it be possible the last wks of August and the first of Sept? ¶ I am to be a "special lecturer" in Comparative Literature at the University of Chicago during the Spring Term. Yes, Iliad and The Birds and Dante and Don Quixote and everything. And I can't even spell. ¶ I no longer admire Brahms. ¶ The Alfred Lunts already own a drawing by Augustu<s> John: if they want another tell them that Rosa Lewis in one of her apartments at the Cav-

---

6 Hemingway's second novel, *The Sun Also Rises,* was published as *Fiesta* in England. *A Farewell to Arms* (1929) was published in six issues of *Scribner's* magazine, from May through October 1929.

7 English publisher James Hamish Hamilton. The full Latin phrase is *quorum magna pars fui,* meaning "in which I played a great part."

8 TNW may be referring to "The Breaking of Exile," which survives as an incomplete manuscript and as a typescript carbon in the Beinecke Library at Yale University.

endish has that wonderful head of Euphemia Lamb[9] (you promised one day to tell me all about Euphemia Lamb) and everything in the Cavendish is for sale except rest and privacy.

So: forgive me, believe me and recognize one still ever

Sincerely yours
Thornton Wilder

<appeared perpendicularly in the left margin at the bottom of the last page>
As from: 75 Mansfield St., New Haven Conn.

111. TO NORMAN FITTS.[10] ALS 2 pp. (Stationery embossed Mitre Hotel / Oxford) Princeton

Oct 15 • 1929

Dear Norm:

Forgive my <u>haste</u> and everything.

It seems to me that my books are about: what is the worst thing that the world can do to you, and what are the last resources one has to oppose to it.

In other words: when a human being is made to bear more than <a> human being can bear—what then?

The Cabala was about these "extremities." Ones "nervous breakdowns."

The Bridge asked the question whether the intuition that lies behind love was sufficient to justify the desperation of living.

---

9 Lewis was a society caterer and the owner of the raffish and idiosyncratic Cavendish Hotel on Jermyn Street in London. TNW may be referring to a bronze bust (1908) by sculptor Jacob Epstein. The subject, Nina Forrest, was an artist's model and the wife of English painter Henry Lamb. Epstein called her Euphemia because she reminded him of the woman in Andrea Mantegna's painting of Saint Euphemia.

10 Fitts was in the class of 1919 at Yale and edited the monthly literary journal S_4N, which was founded in 1919 and to which TNW contributed frequently before it ceased publication in 1925.

The Woman of Andros asks whether Paganism had any solution for the hopeful enquiring sufferer and—by anticipation—whether the handful of maxims about how to live that entered the world with the message of Christ were sufficient to guide one through the maze of experience.

The Trumpet Shall Sound was given Dec. 1926 or 1927 at the American Laboratory Theatre in N.Y. About 35 performances in repertorie. Apart from the Lit never published<.> Now withheld for purposes of rewriting the close.

Yes a minor lit. editor.

No,—single,—no wife nor chillun.

The W. of A. (out late next Spring perhaps) is based on the action recounted that took place before the curtain rises on the first act of Terence's play.

Again forgive brevity etc
Ever yours
Thornt.

112. TO ISABELLA N. WILDER. TLS 2 pp. Yale

The Biltmore
<Los Angeles>
January 2nd, 1930

Dear Mom:

Sunlight, honey. Just terrible. Poinsettias and palms, everywhere. They haven't had any rain since July except a drop and a half in September. It's getting serious and everybody says they have a cough from the dust, but the dust isn't so bad as that and the sun is worth it. One day I went out to the beach at Santa Monica and just baked.

This city is getting near to two million people and has got to be seen to be believed. It's very American, only more so. I thought I had seen the limit of this kind of thing in Miami, but I spoke to<o> soon.

The first night I was here I went to see La Argentina dance.[11] Charlie Chaplin was in the front row, the present-day poverello;[12] and right behind me was Steve Benét and a young couple I knew in Juan-les-Pins. Argentina was wonderful, Oh!

I've been typing all afternoon and am wore out, so I can't think connectedly. The script will be done by tomorrow noon and sent to Isa by air mail and let's hope the English copy will reach Longman by the fifteenth.[13]

Mr. Keedick's Western agent is taking me to dinner at the Ambassador tomorrow night. He's a nice sort of Frank-Walls called Ainslie MacDougall. Apparently there are no new dates for me yet, so I can just lie on beaches and later sit in the Greek Theatre. At one of these lectures, he says, they are expecting two thousand people; count that off your abacus, yes, at a dollar and a half an admission. He says that last year at Toronto I pleased a number of people by my lecture and a number of others (on the committee) by making them four hundred dollars clear.

After this: No thousand, no speechy.

Never, mind, honig, next year I don't lecture nor teach nor travel. I just sit up on Dewberry Road,[14] or whatever it's called, and write play after play for Edith Evans.[15]

Just read a novel you'd better read if you want to know how terrible it is to run a boardinghouse in a small southern town. The novel is called Look Homward Angel[16] and is full of prose poetry and bursts

---

11 Argentine dancer Antonia Merce (1888–1936), whose stage name was La Argentina.

12 Italian: poor little person (this was an obvious reference to Chaplin's role as the Little Tramp).

13 TNW is referring to the manuscript of *The Woman of Andros.*

14 TNW is referring to his family's new home on Deepwood Drive in Hamden, Connecticut, then under construction.

15 TNW never wrote a play for English actress Edith Evans, and there is no record of her having appeared in any of his plays.

16 *Look Homeward, Angel,* by Thomas Wolfe.

of tears and every now and then it's even more sordid than the book about Andros.

It's true that this town is full of fungus religions and fungus medicine. Every apartment house window on the ground floor has a little card in the corner saying: "Mrs. Whoosiz: spiritual healing and advice." or "Naturotherapy Institute." There's a lot of Bible reading done in public by strollers with moving lips, or all a-dream on park benches; and you know I always felt that Bible reading in public or in the home was one of the less significant wrestlings with the angel.

Got Isabel's first batch of forwarded mail; and answered everything that had to be answered at once, at once.

I've lost my appetite for some reason. I walk twelve miles a day. My teeth are perfect; my appendix is out. Yet I don't approach any plate with a ghost of interest. (Well, there's a symphony tonight with Horowitz, that's something.) I guess I'm just homesick as usual. Or else I'm alone all the time, or else with some people that leave my pulse unhurried. Anyway I miss you-all a lot.

Aunt Grace[17] roasted an enormous bird and we had a nice four hours or more. I forgot to say a word about their Xmas present to me, and as I hadn't made any to them, they must have thought my conduct very strange. However am thanking them in a letter and trusting the rest of the oddity to kindly bewilderment.

I wish I had come Santa Fé. I looked out of the windows all day, especially all night and at dawn from my Lower, and liked it, but the Santa Fé would have repaid such gazing even more. And the fellow travellers were sad. Beside we all draw dividends from Santa Fé.[18]

There's no Ray or Pauline Hanna[19] in the telephone book.

There's going to be a very small crowd at the Pasadena lecture because there happens to be two big rival social events at the same moment. Ishkabibble.

I don't see how I can get to know Charlie Chaplin, though I was

17 Grace was the second wife of TNW's uncle Thornton MacNess Niven III.

18 TNW owned stock in the Atchison, Topeka, and Santa Fe Railway.

19 The Hannas were Wilder family friends in Berkeley.

so confident I could do it before. He looked awfully nice the other night; his hair is all gray, or rather white, at the edge of his ears.

Well, sufficient to the day is the Lawrence thereof.[20]

(A telegram was just brought me to the door and I tore it open and it was a New Year's greeting signed Contessa and then I saw it was addressed to a James Wilder. Yeah?)

Well, I love you more than Tunkantell. Mrs Johnson (Bill Hinckle's mother) sends you her best, and many pretty thanks. Tell Papa that Southern California is thataway; I still think that Florida, except for the dearth of concerts and <u>lectures</u>, is a better place to live.

love and pinings,
Thornt.

113. TO T. E. LAWRENCE. ALS (Stationery embossed Hotel Palliser / Calgary / Alberta) 4 pp. Private

As from: 75 Mansfield St.
New Haven, Conn
Jan. 20, 1930

Dear Mr. Shaw:

Your letter gave me great pleasure.[21] I too live so much in the great books and great music I admire that it becomes a sort of mortification to talk about my own books to people whom I value. The dejections of writing drive me to various Second Strings. I wildly sign contracts to teach or to go on lecture-tours (as now), and all to escape the self-assignments of my literary hope. At present I am cursed with the wish

20 TNW is probably referring to the letter he received from T. E. Lawrence (see letter number 113).

21 Lawrence wrote TNW a letter on December 12, 1929, praising his two novels but criticizing him for "aiming a little below your strength, to convey a sense of ease," in *The Bridge of San Luis Rey.*

to write a beautiful play for Edith Evans and her wonderful voice—before she is too old or too discouraged.

If I talk for a moment about your comments on my work, it is not that I am trying to justify my shortcomings. The inadequacies of one's book are the inadequacies of one's self and they have no surprises and no palliation from me. But I do not recognize the attitudes of mind you describe: the choosing of an easier subject in order to attain ease; and the determination, as though it were a matter of choice, to be in a given book, experimental or not experimental in language. I am too timid, without and within, ever to cast myself into the tradition of the stormy self-revealing books; all I can do is to mutter over and over to myself as I work: Mozartian form; Mozartian form.

But what book is it you refer to as your last in which you deliberately limited your intention? A paper I bought today says you have prepared a translation of Homer[22] which is wonderful news. I imagine the introduction you might do for it (though I have no doubt you refused to)—a long profound debate on the differences between living such actions and singing them. You are one of the few persons in the history of the world who has stood with a foot in each kingdom—Sophocles fought, and Dante a little.

It will be a long while before I arrive in England, but I hope to attempt what you have proposed, that I see whether it would be possible for you to leave the camp for a few hours. In the meantime know the pride I feel that you have written to me and my great admiration for the pages of the Seven Pillars of Wisdom & for yourself.

Sincerely yours,

Thornton Wilder

¶ From the window here I can see, though seventy miles away, the sudden barrier of the Canadian Rockies. The area of the greater peaks is fifty times the area of the Alps.

¶Five days ago it was 40 degrees below zero in Calgary.

¶Lecturing is an ignoble profession but it has these compensations.

---

22 Lawrence's prose translation of the *Odyssey* appeared in 1932.

114. TO SIBYL COLEFAX. ALS 4 pp. (Stationery embossed Hotel Palliser / Calgary / Alberta) NYU

Atlanta Georgia
Feb 20 • 1930

Dear Lady Colefax:

This letter pretends to be written you from Calgary. I have always hoped to write from some remote and colorful place that you have never visited. I did sit down to write you there (the thermometer fallen to thirty-five degrees below zero; and, seventy miles away, the frieze of the Canadian Rockies rising in a sudden barrier on the horizon), but the telephone kept ringing, the local lecture committee swept through the room and letters had to be postponed. It is always possible that you too have been to Calgary, have had lunch at the Ranchmen's Club and met the tremendous Mrs Winter.

I am still trying to make amends for teasing you about penmanships. The chief sacrifice I can make just now to solicit your forgiveness, the olive branch that costs most to pluck, is to write a letter myself—you remember how I disclaimed any possibility of correspondence while 'on tour'. Well, I am very much on tour, with ten close-packed engagements just ahead of me. So please <u>begin</u> to forgive me.

It is no news to you that America is stirring in its sleep. The other night, Monday, Hugh Walpole and I were announced to debate on whether Fiction or Non-fiction throws more light on experience. It was at Washington, D.C. and four thousand people attended. It looked like a football game. It was not a very good debate, Heaven knows, and you with your resources would have found your mind wandering to other things under the flood of truisms but the four thousand scarcely coughed—catarrhal February, too—while our humble little abstract ideas advanced and retreated in a very sedate combat. In all we furnish four great cities with that debate! I hope you are smiling more in amusement than scorn.

March tenth brings my trip to a close. It began January 6 at San Diego, California, and has covered a great deal of country. I begin to think I know why I am doing it. It is partly of course to assemble money to pay for the new house and its Steinway; partly to buy the thirty-five volumes of Saint-Simon in the edition grands écrivains de France. All that is true but only vaguely felt by me. I know now that the tours are Preparation. I don't know quite what they prepare for: I prepare and Circumstance fulfills. Sometimes I think I would like to be a College President: collect moneys and buildings and hospitals from millionaires, and once a week breath urgency into fatigued, limited and mostly jealous-hearted professors; and once a week (very successfully) excite my assembled students, wide-eyed, bewildered and so easily-excited students.

Another minute I think I want to be the head of a New York Burgtheater,[23]—bewitch money out of millionaires and build a repertory with Edith Evans, Haidée Wright,[24] Walter Huston and so on.

Do you like that?

At all events, I am burning out a host of awkward adolescent fears and maladjustments. I am actually serener. And the more people I meet the more I like people. I know America down to every absurd Keep Smiling Club, every gas station, every hot-dog stand.

April first I start teaching for two and a half months at the University of Chicago. Ten to twelve thousand students under President Hutchins, age 30 and an old friend of mine. "Tradition and Innovation—Aeschylus to Cervantes." 40 lectures (including Dante) with the students writing a 6-minute paper every morning to prove that they read the long assignment for homework. It's absurd, but its very American and is exactly what I want.

Do be patient with me and find a minute to comment on all this turmoil.

Ever sincerely
Thornton

---

23 The Burgtheater of Vienna, founded in 1776, is one of the earliest and most important theaters in Europe.

24 Haidee Wright (1868–1943) was an English stage and film actress.

50 Deepwood Drive, "The House The Bridge *Built."*

115. TO CHARLOTTE E. WILDER. ALS 4 pp. (Stationery embossed 50 Deepwood Drive / New Haven, Connecticut) Yale

<P.M. September 3, 1931>

Dear Sharlie:

I hear you are delighted about Yaddo, that you did a lot of fine work, and that you are looking very handsome.[25]

I hope from time <to time> you will come to Deepwood Drive, not only to cheer Mama, but to take advantage of the friendships you have arouséd in Mrs Canby,[26] Helen McAfee et alii et alliae (those should be in the Ablative.)

---

25 Charlotte had been selected as a resident at Yadoo, an artists' retreat in Saratoga Springs, New York, where she worked on her writing.

26 Mrs. Henry Seidel Canby, wife of the American critic and editor who was on the Yale faculty when TNW was an undergraduate.

If your New York life becomes expensive, do not hesitate to call on me. Do not crowd your soul by living on sandwiches and sausages

Amos has finished his thesis, and is far cheerfuller. Isabell has made much progress in her novel and is cheerfuller.[27] Mama is beginning to be aware of a home-economic-security and is cheerfuller. I am full of new wonderful thoughts and am cheerfuller, so your new well being should sustain ours—less wilder nail-biting, fears, and scruples and distrusts.

Ever thine
Thornton

Enclosed a small birthday present.

116. TO ISABELLA N. WILDER. ALS 4 pp. (Stationery embossed The Quadrangle Club) Yale

<Chicago>
Monday morning
<October 1931>

Dear Mom:

Forgive my being so long in telling you all about it.

I arrived none too early. I filled in the time with all kinds of things and assembled a lot more notes on the Iliad. Then on Tues and Wed I had to sit in the Gym which for those two days is turned into a Registration Hall. Representatives of each department and teachers with special classes sit under large placards bearings their names and the students approach them as though they were choosing dishes at a cafetaria. Its a great bazar of education: it is very interesting and very funny. All kinds of applicants came for my advanced comp.—some had been out in business for years; one had taught it at Mt. Holyoke; a man had been selling General Motors appliances at Kobe: a woman who had left a

27 TNW's brother would receive his Ph.D. from Yale in June 1933. TNW is referring to *Mother and Four,* Isabel Wilder's first novel, which was published in 1933.

husband at Grand Rapids to work three months with me on her deathless novel and who submitted as earnest of her genius an essay called Motherhood: A Vocation for Women. Well, you know me. Instead of saying with firmness that they are unsuitable I got all tangled up telling them they were too good for the course, that all they needed was to follow their own lights etc. Some cried; some argued; some phoned and returned and hung about and pleaded. But at last I picked a good eighteen. One negro who writes violent prose poems about Industry and the spilled blood of his people.

Classes met Thursday morning and I loved it. I was as nervous as though it were my first time. "Your assignment for tomorrow. . . ." I began in a loud voice.

Then Thursday a<t> noon a telegram came from Stanton Kennedy of Omaha (and Yale Law Sch.—I suppose you remember him)— "If I arrive Friday morning with manuscript will you receive me?" He arrived all right with his novel Proust-cum-Joyce. I'd read a few chapters while he mooned about by the lake. He was terribly nervous. ALL depends on the novel. Unless it is the greatest novel since War and Peace he will have to go into his uncle's law office or his father's construction work. He was somehow both nervous and lumpish, parasitic lumpish. And besides he was defeatest sneering fatigued. It comforted <him> to tell how awful Omaha's social life and its pretences to culture are. It comforted him to see in Chicago or in my beloved University little things that bespoke America's stupidities. It also comforted him to save money and to accept too many meals from me. Enfin—as Mme de Sévigné said—j'ai vu qu'il me préparait les délices d'un adieu.[28] So he went off Sunday afternoon with a letter to Cass Canfield.

Sunday afternoon

So I stole off to Prof Rafe Lillie[29] and played Four Hands and began to convalesce. When I got home at six I was told that the Pres. wished to speak to me on the phone. So I went to a little tray-on-your-

28 French: Finally I saw that he was preparing me for the delights of a farewell.

29 Ralph S. Lillie, a gifted pianist, was a professor of general physiology at the University of Chicago.

knees supper, just the three of us upstairs, and I told them about Jed and Ruth[30] and Isabel; and about Reinhardt and Du Schöne Helena[31] and he forgot his troubles and I forgot mine. And then I read them The Happy Journey and they were deeply moved[32]—And it was one of the nicest evenings we had ever had together. And no harm was done when I left them at nine because we were all dead tired.

The lake is more beautiful than you can imagine and the frieze of skyscrapers is as fine as ever. The Midway at my door is a perfect green lawn. My rooms are still pretty bare, though they have given me two rugs for the sitting room, two leather chairs etc. Do I dare ask you to send me the map of Scotland Lady Astor gave me—in the shelves at my right as I sit at the desk in my study. There is a big roll for mailing with it. I think. I could frame it and it wld solve the problem of the space over my fireplace mantel. Next time you are in N.Y. you must see The House of Connolly[33] and tell me about it.

Give my regards to Helen, to Phyllis, to Dr. Williams and to the Fultons. I haven't see<n> Percival Bailey yet but will today.[34]

Love to all
Thornton

---

30 Stage producer and director Jed Harris (1900–1979) was romantically involved for many years with American stage and film actress and writer Ruth Gordon (1896–1985).

31 German: The beautiful Helena. TNW is referring to Max Reinhardt's wife, German actress Helene Thimig (1889–1974).

32 TNW's one-act play *The Happy Journey to Trenton and Camden*, which was collected in his *The Long Christmas Dinner and Other Plays in One Act* (1931), is among the most performed of his shorter plays. In its use of such theatrical devices as the Stage Manager and the absence of realistic scenery, it anticipates his later full-length plays.

33 *The House of Connelly,* by Paul Green.

34 Helen McAfee, the managing editor of the *Yale Review;* Phyliss Trask and Dr. Williams were New Haven friends. The Fultons were TNW's next-door neighbors on Deepwood Drive. Bailey was professor of surgery at the University of Chicago.

117. TO ISABELLA N., ISABEL, AND AMOS P. WILDER. ALS 2 pp. Yale

<Chicago>
Feb 2 • 1932

Dear Mom, dear Isabel, dear Pop, dear Astrid,=[35]

Tomorrow morning at eight I give my annual rendition of Ugolino in the Tower.[36] Yes, that class now meets at eight. My alarm clock goes off at 6:30. When the doors open for breakfast at 7:00 there I am waiting with such impatience that I fall forward on my face like an eavesdropper. At ten o clock I give my other class the works with a psychoanalytical interpretation of La Rochefoucauld. Usually after two lectures I'm so tired, I go down town just to be away from people. I lunch in railway stations or somewhere, then gradually seep back to the Campus about 3:00 and begin to go into training for the two lectures on the morrow. I don't "go out" during the middle of the week; but when Friday comes around I get gay and "go out" in a big way. But all the time I'm worried about next week's lectures. I worry in my sleep and wake up wondering if I have enough notes to pull me through these eternal fifty-minutes. It's extra hard this term because both my classes are "preparation" engagements for me. Previously the ten o'clock class was Advanced Comp. and did not require anything but talent of me; now it requires diligence. Toward the middle of Feb begins a series I am giving in our "downtown college", that is 5 lectures on Tuesday evenings at the Art Institute (Chicago's Metropolitan Museum) on Sophocles for English Readers. It is billboarded all over town, and all the North Shore ermine dames are preparing to go, so there's some more lectures. SO you see I'm longing for March 19th. Am I!! And I think I'm taking a year's leave from the University. I haven't told Bob yet.

Bob was thirty-three the other day. Maude's birthday is Thursday.

---

35 Astrid may be a reference to a family pet or may just be TNW being whimsical.

36 As depicted by Dante in the *Inferno*, Ugolino della Gherardesca (ca. 1220–1289) was accused of being a traitor to the city of Pisa, arrested, imprisoned, and left to starve in a tower with his sons and grandsons.

Little dinners in the bosom of the family. The family consists of June Preston and me. Franja[37] finally had her tonsils out, but has had a long dragging temperature: so Franja simply lives in the children's hospital of our Clinics. Its just next door and so very convenient. She's not really ill; Franja likes it: it's merely more convenient so. The Doctor says she ought to be in another climate, but Maude won't leave Bob so what can you do about it but leave the baby in the hospital where the climate is practically Bermudan.

Cornelia Otis Skinner is performing for two weeks in town. I met her "out"; we talked of Helen Andrews etc; I dread going to see her show; her phlegm bores me.[38] And speaking of monologuists I sent a cable to Ruth Draper and received a friendly cable in reply.

The wife of the Governor of Wisconsin writes to ask me when I am coming up to stay with them. She says she is polishing up Ole Bull's bed[39] for me. I shall go up in two weeks I think for a Sunday night. Moral: home town boy makes good.

Girls, please do me a favor. See, if on my desk you can find my two volumes, Everyman's Library, of Don Quixote with my marginal jottings. Perhaps you can only find Volume One. If its there please send it to me with kisses.

Tomorrow, dearies, you are going to see Charles Laughton as Detective Poirot. Perhaps this very evening Isabel was to rehearsal for hours.[40] He's a fine actor and a delightful person. Has Mama got to know him. His accent alone will be enough to slay her and then comes his charm. Hoop-wow-zowie. I bet you he's wonderful in that part; I saw ten photographs of his facial expressions in it.

Its now 11:30 and I must get to bed out of respect for my alarm

---

37 Franja, the eldest daughter of Robert and Maude Hutchins, was born in 1926.

38 Skinner was performing at Chicago's Studebaker Theater at the time. Andrews may have been a Wilder family friend.

39 Mrs. Philip F. La Follette, the wife of Wisconsin's governor, was referring to the bed that popular Norwegian violinist Ole Bornemann Bull probably slept in when visiting the governor's house in the 1870s; it was henceforth called "the Ole Bull bed."

40 Laughton played Hercule Poirot in *The Fatal Alibi,* a play by Michael Morton, and also directed the production. *The Fatal Alibi* was apparently playing in New Haven before its New York opening on February 8, 1932. In 1928, Isabel Wilder had graduated from Yale's Department of Playwriting and Production, a forerunner of the Yale School of Drama.

clock. Isabel: Write the German agent that I would sell him The Woman of Andros cheaply enough, but only on condition that it is:

① for Elizabeth Bergner[41]

② for German speech alone

She is coming to America soon I hear to play for English-speaking audiences and films. If she wanted to use it in English it would require a different contract and with an American film company.

See you all before long.
Love me hard
Thorny.

118. TO KATHARINE CORNELL. ALS 3 pp. (Stationery embossed 50 Deepwood Drive / New Haven, Connecticut) SUNY-Buffalo

April 8 • 1932

Dear Miss Cornell:

I should be proud to translate Le Viol.[42] It is an eloquent play in itself and the freedom with which it overrides the conventions of the stage should make it very fruitful and additionally important. It is full of little difficulties of literary tact and I hope to come and see you during your Chicago engagement, about May first, to ask your help on some of those passages.

The University of Chicago allows me to teach two Quarters a year and then absent myself two Quarters. My vacation has just begun. I am sorry I cannot be there during the whole engagement in order to see The Barretts[43] many times, but I shall be able to make up some of my loss.

---

41 Austrian stage and film actress Elisabeth Bergner (1897–1986) was a favorite of Max Reinhardt.

42 TNW's translation of André Obey's *Le Viol de Lucrèce* was titled *Lucrece*.

43 Katharine Cornell's touring production of *The Barretts of Wimpole Street* (1931) by Rudolf Besier was apparently playing in Chicago at this time.

I hope you are well and the continued performance of so exacting a part is not too trying.

Very sincerely yours
Thornton Wilder

P.S. My agent is Mr. Harold Freedman of Brandt and Brandt. I have asked him to make a reasonable arrangement with Mr. Goodyear.[44]

T.N.W.

119. TO SIBYL COLEFAX. ALS 4 pp. (Stationery embossed 50 Deepwood Drive / New Haven, Connecticut) NYU

Nov 2 • 1932

Dear Lady Colefax:

Many thanks for the encouragement to go and see Francis Lederer.[45] I shall try to call on him at the end of this week. German theatrical records are my hobby and I know a great deal about him.

Rehearsals for "Lucrece" begin very soon. Being only a translator I feel very remote from it. My heart-beat hasn't registered the slightest acceleration except at the moment that I realized that success would mean one hundred and eighty dollars a week. I'm so seldom mercenary—and never as regards my own works—that I cite that curious experience to you in order that you may see how indifferent I am. I am a great admirer of Kath. Cornell, the woman, and happy that this will bring us often together, but I distrust some of the casting and the commission for some music from Deems Taylor. I have never met

44 Freedman of Brandt & Brandt was TNW's dramatic agent from 1932 until Freedman's death in 1966. A. Conger Goodyear frequently served as Cornell's business representative.

45 Lederer (1899–2000) was a Czech film and stage actor. He appeared in New York in 1932 in C. L. Anthony's *Autumn Crocus.*

Robert Edmond Jones.[46] People say we look alike, talk alike and think alike; which bores me in advance.

I translated a piece for Gilbert Miller—Die Braut u. Torozko by Otto Indig from the Josefstadt Theater in Vienna. Not literature, but a delightful play. I hear Mr. Miller is disappointed that I did not alter it more. So I must sit down and alter it.[47]

The middle point has arrived of my year's absence from the University of Chicago. In the six months I have done the two translations and a third of a novel. The novel is very funny and very heartrending—a picaresque novel about a young travelling salesman in textbooks, very "fundamentalist" pious, pure and his adventures among the shabby shady hotels, gas-stations and hot dog stands of Eastern Texas, Arkansas, Oklahoma etc. His education, or developement from a Dakota "Bible-belt" mind to a modern grossstadt[48] tolerance in three years; i.e. the very journey the American mind has made in fifty years. I don't know what to call it, but I am thinking of this:

Heaven's my Destination
by
x x x

George Mercer Brush is my name,
America's my nation;
Ludington's my dwelling-place.
And Heaven's my destination.

(Doggerel verses which children
in the Middle West used to
inscribe in the fly-leaves of
their schoolbooks.)

The book has given me a great deal of pleasure. If it turns out that I am not a humorist and that the whole project was a lapse of judgment I shall not greatly care.

---

46 Composer and music critic Deems Taylor wrote incidental music for the production of *Lucrèce*; American set designer Jones did the sets.

47 At the request of Gilbert Miller, TNW did a second version of Indig's play, but when *The Bride of Torozko* opened in New York in September 1934, the adaptation was credited to Ruth Langner and TNW's name was not associated with the production.

48 German: big-city.

Lately I have been going up to New York a little and seeing people. My best friends there (Chicago holds my real ones) are Jed Harris and Ruth Gordon. Lately Edward Sheldon.[49] I have a sort of urchin's hero-worship (urchin-watching brilliant lion-tamer in spangles) for Norman Bel-Geddes. I like Marc Connolly,[50] but as it were a little helplessly: he has so little cultural or emotional fond, for all his gifts.

Had lunch last Sunday with Ruth Draper and we talked of Lauro.[51] Tears and everything. She confesses that she invites and cherishes grief; has been so shaken that she has no new monologues and so must tour new territory—South Africa.

Alex. Woollcott is a real pleasure too. The gaiety of good digestion combined with a curiosity about crime and flambuoyant personality whether it be Mary Baker Eddy or the Empress Carlotta.

Myself have dwindled to the least fashionable of authors. Few book reviews come out without a passing disparagement of my work. But I don't mind. I have a rather low opinion of my books myself, but am fairly conceited about the next ones.

I want to thank you very much for calling my attention to Charles Du Bos.[52] I derived a great deal from the Journal and the Byron. Less from the Gide. If you should see him, reproach him for being so slow about the Nietzsche et la symphonie héröique de la pensée à contre-courant. This used to be announced among the works à paraitre[53] and has now disappeared from the promises. To my dismay; for I need it. Nietzsche has been my great discovery of this last year, my meat and drink. Nietzsche does not trouble my faith, for I see already enough what Egon Friedell[54] meant in calling him "the last great believer in Europe;" but I need a great believer's help in isolating the essential

---

49 American dramatist (1886–1946).

50 American dramatist (1890–1980).

51 Draper was the fiancée/lover of Lauro de Bosis (see letter number 67).

52 French literary critic (1882–1939). The book on Nietzsche that TNW mentions was never published.

53 French: to appear.

54 Friedell (1878–1938) was an Austrian philosopher, theater critic, and actor.

from the accidental Nietzsche. So do what you can to provoke such a book—tortured footnotes and all.

I haven't liked anything F L Lucas has done since the manual on Tragedy. Not the poems. And the papers in Life and Letters don't stand long enough on one spot to be helpful. There was a grievous lapse of taste in his paper on France.[55]

Phillip Sassoon and I have fallen away. He came to Chicago and I got him a lecture at the University. He must have thought his audience was imbecile. There was a great deal of manner and charm and no substance. And when last in London he introduced me for one disastrous evening to his clique—a dinner at a Mrs Fitzgeralds, where were Cole Porter and Lady Cunard and others; and such unsavory double-entendres were flying about—my naive remarks were twisted before my face to the merriment of all. Finally they were ashamed of themselves and went to the other extreme and were very sweet and gentle to me in words of one syllable as though I were a peau-rouge[56] at an orgy at Sceaux.

At present my day-dream enthusiams are

Reinhardt's plans	The poetry of Mörike[57]	Nietzsche
Croce on 17th & 18th Century Naples[58]	The plays of Nestroy and Raimund[59]	Walter Winchell
The music of Bruckner	The Barthian mov'mt[60]	The new pieces of the Compagnie des Quinze[61]

---

55 English literary critic and poet F. L. Lucas (1894–1967) was the author of *Tragedy* (1927).

56 French: a red Indian.

57 German lyric poet Eduard Friedrich Mörike (1804–1875).

58 Italian historian, and philosopher Benedetto Croce (1866–1952).

59 Austrian dramatists Johann Nestroy (1801–1862) and Ferdinand Raimund (1790–1836). Nestroy's play *Einen Jux will er sich machen* (1842) was adapted by TNW as *The Merchant of Yonkers* (1938), which, in turn, he revised as *The Matchmaker* (1954).

60 Swiss Protestant theologian Karl Barth (1886–1968).

61 Internationally renowned theatrical company established in Paris in 1930 by French actor and director Michel Saint-Denis, who produced a number of plays by André Obey.

It's a little late for me to apologize for not having written you for so long; and to tell how much I enjoyed your letter written from the villa in the Goldoni-Casanova country.[62] I still hope that I may be near you in some continental town where we can have long walks and talks. You too are among my day dream enthusiasms: most people live haphazard, but you have been able to apply the same sense of form and style to your life that artists apply to the most secret and dedicated work of their midnight vigils: you apply direction and continuity and preparation and immediately effaced labor; and now look at your rewards: learning and great connaisseurship and friendships and immense usefulness.

Most sincerely yours
Thornton

120. TO RUTH GORDON. ALS 3 pp. Private

The Faculty Exchange
University of Chicago
June 18 • 1933

<appeared in a circle above and next to the salutation>
Dear Ruth: Aleck arrived after this was written. He tells me you are back in this country. Wish that you were here or would at least pass through here en route to Calif. Weather to Aleck's intense surprise is temperate and even cool. ¶ Mary Pickford wants me to write a play with her! ¶ Saturday Aleck, Kit, Gert and I are going to Genesee to sleep on army cots.[63] Ever Thornton

---

62 Italian dramatist Carlo Goldoni and Giacomo Casanova were both born in Venice in the 1700s.

63 TNW is referring to Alexander Woollcott, Katharine Cornell, and Gertrude Macy (Cornell's general manager) and their upcoming trip to the home of Alfred Lunt and Lynn Fontanne in Genesee Depot, Wisconsin.

Dear Ruth:

A few weeks ago—one night—I telephoned to a whole series of addresses in New York trying to speak to you. I upset the Barbizon and the Barbizon-Plaza and the office downtown and finally all I could reach was your Banker's Address.

I hope the difficulty meant that you had slipped quietly abroad and that this will find you in some delightful French or Swiss hotel,—and with a contract for some big part lying in the desk drawer. <appeared in the left margin next to preceding paragraph> **Excuse formalism; not yet warmed up. T.W.**

There's nothing to tell about me. I became very discouraged about my university connection 2 week<s> ago. I decided to tell Bob H that I couldn't come back for my two quarters next year after all. I teach worse and worse, instead of better. I talk awful rubbish. My days are dissipated amid so many types of activity that I cease to be anybody. Nothing I do has been sufficiently prepared. I go through life postponing thinking.

However I have been able to make some changes in the details of my life—place of residence, meals, hours etc and shall try again next year April to September. [I need the money for the running of Deepwood Drive. I get $4,000 for a half-year, which is pretty good, considering that I can live here pretty cheaply myself. To be sure, if I settled down to write consistently I could make a good deal more than that, but I hate to feel any necessity-money aspect to my writing.] <appeared in left margin opposite bracketed passage> **Confidential.**

Kit is in town; two weeks run has been extended to four. Friday night she let me escort her to a big flashy party for George Gershwin that the Byfield's gave in the cottage on top of the Sherman. The papers will have the announcement of her plans next Monday. November to April first repertory tour of all the one night stands of the middle west—Candida, Barrett's, Romeo. Opens with Romeo in Buffalo. Imagine. Then New York City in April. Guthrie rehearses Sept. in New York. Owen Davis's Jezebel, probably with Bankhead.[64]

---

64 American director, producer, and actor Guthrie McClintic (1893–1961), who was married to Katharine Cornell from 1921 until his death, coproduced (with Cornell) and directed Davis's *Jezebel* in New York from December 1933 to January 1934, but Tallulah Bankhead was not in the cast.

Last Sunday afternoon Mrs Barnes[65] and I drove up to see Alfred and Lynn. Gardening and painting their house. They were lovely and cordial.

Alex is coming this week to see the Fair.[66] I am putting him up at our Quad Club Wed Thurs and Friday nights; then he goes to Genesee Depôt. All this New York air suddenly blows through my academic round.

The Fair is not serious; but its fun. Artistically its one big lapse of taste, but on such a big scale that it becomes somehow important. I love it; I trudge all over those bright awkward acres, staring at my fellow-citizens. I see the back side of it: the immense personnel a little frantically earning a living, because scores of my students are selling hotdogs and pushing jin-rickshas and holding Information booths.

Janet graduated Phi B K and magna cum laude. The only Wilder to make the big grades. Amos got an honorary degree. Isabel has a lecture contract with Lee Keedick.[67] Ma has been through a long protracted alarming cold (fatigue—monotony) but is better. Father is vague and may become a trained-nurse problem.

I go to fulfil the engagement at the University of Hawaii in the middle of November, so be sure and let me have your father's address.[68] All September I shall be in New Haven resuming work on Heaven's my Destination and I hope slipping in to New York to see Jed rehearsing. Katherine Hepburn passed thru town the other day and talked to Mrs Barnes enthusiastically about Jed and The Lake. Jed's happiness is one of the ingrediants of my happiness, and every hint of these plans

---

65 American dramatist, novelist, and short story writer Margaret Ayer "Peggy" Barnes (1886–1967).

66 The Chicago World's Fair of 1933–1934, known as "A Century of Progress," was located on 424 acres of lakefront, close to downtown Chicago.

67 TNW's youngest sister graduated from Mount Holyoke in June 1933. His brother received an honorary D.D. from Hamilton College, where he taught from 1930 to 1933. Isabel Wilder gave lectures during 1933–1934 on "Novel Reading and Novel Writing" and "The Modern Stage in America and Europe" under contract to the Lee Keedick Agency.

68 Ruth Gordon's father, former sea captain Clifton Jones, had retired in Hawaii.

gives me a good warming afternoon's meditation. It seems to me that The Green Bay Tree will come wonderfully out of his hands.[69]

I shall be here through August. If there are any errands I can do for you in this country, please let me. Give all my best to Jed and if the mood should strike him some midnight to write me a letter I should be knocked over with joy. Give my regards also (French or English) to notre ami.[70]

And as for yourself a ton of admiration and deep regard.

Ever

Thornton

121. TO EDWARD SHELDON. ALS 4 pp. Harvard

The University

Aug 7 • 1933

Dear Ned:

In asking to be forgiven for so long a silence, I can simply hurl myself on two things: your magnimminity and THIS LONG LETTER which is at once a request to be reinstated in your good books, and a mark of the joy that does lie in writing letters to you once one can get started.

Now I'm started. The joy has begun; and I make so bold as to feel the first steps of my forgiveness.

Yes, the Summer Quarter goes on and on. The students are now on an average of fifteen years older than my usual pupils. These Summer students take notes furiously; one ventures a harmless sally and a

---

69 Jed Harris produced and directed *The Lake*, by Dorothy Massingham and Murray MacDonald, in New York between December 1933 and February 1934. Katharine Hepburn appeared in a starring role. He also produced and directed *The Green Bay Tree*, by Mordaunt Shairp, between October 1933 and March 1934.

70 French: our friend.

hundred pairs of owl's eyes gaze, surprised and troubled, then bend over their notes and put it down.

That's the Eight O'Clock Class (The Inferno and the Don Quixote); in the Composition Class (ten o'clock) they are no less earnest, only very timid about speaking up in class. There I wish I were back among the twenty-year-olds who write better stories and discuss them more spiritedly.

Nevertheless I'm enjoying the Summer term. I expected to be vexed and woeful because of the weather; but I find it not so bad after all. I enjoy the Fair, great silly American thing that it is; and I enjoy the visitors. Scarcely a day goes by without a letter or phone call to the effect that some old friend of mine (or my father's<,> brother's<,> sisters') from China, California, Oberlin, Princeton, Lawrenceville, Yale, etc. . . is in town. I can't take 'em all to the Fair, but I take some. And I enjoy it all.

Even Ruthie showed up.

> (Gordon that is. 25 minutes between planes at the Air Field—two in the morning.
>
> The finest girl in the world—sic—and the drollest and most original.)

Kit was here four weeks and Guthrie a day or two. Kit was finer than ever, but I had to see the play again—fifth time. I have the sensation of looking into the soul of Sidney Howard: just what he thinks about things; what he thinks about Art, and Love, and Men.[71] That's what repetition shows to me.

And if that is a very uncharitable remark on my part, please forgive it and put it down to the fact that my nerves are exacerbated by teaching for four months without one week's intermission.

Aleck stayed for three days at our Quadrangle Club under my protection and was a great joy. After classes I would go over to his room and find him, immense and jocular, writing letters to his immense circle, reading in proofs all the books of his friends, doing this and doing that, perfectly happy and quite ready to tell some stories prodi-

71 American dramatist Sidney Howard's *Alien Corn*, directed by Guthrie McClintic and produced by and starring Katharine Cornell, was playing for a month in Chicago.

giously well. Soon we would start off to the Fair and there in a Ricksha, his genial stomach pointing to heaven, he would weave about the grounds. He began by not liking the Exposition, but pretty soon it began to creep about his bones and he ended up loving it squarely to the square inch.

He and I went up to spend the weekend with the Lunts, and found them rested and busy and absorbed in little domestic momentous activities. Lynn learning French off gramaphone records—for what part?—and Alfred, rising at six to water the garden and weed it and simply to examine it judiciously. We lived practically Nudist, eating wonderful things playing anagrams and falling on the floor in coils over Aleck's grave deliberations about Jed or Noel or Mrs Campbell or Dr Libmann or himself.[72]

I went up for another week-end at Janet Fairbank's.[73] Peggy Barnes was there and told me that you spent the Summers of your boyhood there, and I asked just where and took a walk toward it; and this, dear and incomparable Ned, is why I was so particularly moved:

The first weekend I spent at Lake Geneva I rose early Sunday morning and slipped out of the house for a long walk before breakfast. I took the path that ran along beside the lake at the bottom of the lawns. It was beautiful, of course, with early mist and horizontal sunlight and dew on the cobwebs, but I wondered why it was poignantly beautiful: and then suddenly I knew. It was more than that; it was the lake's smell, and the particular seaweed moss on the stones at the water's edge and the cray-fish holes beside the piers: that was my boyhood, too. Until the age of nine I lived in Madison Wisconsin and spent my Summers at Maple Bluffs on Lake Mendota, less than a hundred miles away. And though since then I have known lakes in England and China and Ohio—Carnegie Pond in Princeton and Lake Whitney and Lake Sunapee (very treasured, that one) and Lake Como and the Austrian lakes, none of them have that particular bundle of smells, nor those effects of light and air. My joy was an atavistic rediscovery.

---

72 TNW is referring to Noël Coward, Mrs. Patrick Campbell, and possibly prominent American physician Dr. Emanuel Libman.

73 American author and suffragette Janet Ayer Fairbank was Margaret Ayer Barnes's older sister.

And now to it has been added the news that you and I have the same standards for lakes; there we first heard waves lapping on shores with a sound that other lakes never quite repeat.

So call <us> cousins.

We're related through the Lakes.

A great many grotesque things happen in my life.

One day I was working quietly away in my tower room when the phone rang.

"Thornton, darling, this is Texas. Thornton, I want you to do me a favor. But you don't have to do it if you don't want to—it won't make any difference in our friendship; but if you feel you can, it would be a great favor to me."

"Why, Texas, I'd be proud...."

"Well, lissen, do you know Colonel Moulton?"

[A former professor at the University, professor of astronomy, who went into business and finally became Director of Concessions at the World's Fair—hot dog stands and Morrocan village etc.] I allowed I knew him slightly.

"Well, Thornton, I'm thinking of taking over the Dance Ship on the Midway, I and my Gang, and so, Thornton, he wants to know if I'm all right, if I keep an eye on my girls—and you know, Thornton, if they were my own daughters I couldn't take better care of them. And all he knows is the worst about me, the headlines and all that....Now if you could write him a letter...."

So I wrote him a letter, making an honest woman of Texas Guinan[74] and she got the job.

One day I found a telegram: "Have been trying to reach you by phone all day....could you come to the Blackstone...Mary Pickford."

There she was short, dumpy, speaking bad Kansas vowels, but still young and beautiful and inspiring tremendous confidence. Would I write a play with her; for Lillian Gish; a second part for her, if Miss Gish and I thought she could do it.

---

74 Mary Louise Cecilia "Texas" Guinan (1884–1933) was an American stage and film actress. During Prohibition, she had become a speakeasy hostess and was known for floor shows that consisted of scantily clad female dancers, whom she often took on the road.

Then she told me the plot. The one kind of plot I couldn't do anything with. She, whose sense of the theatre is sound as a bell in every department save one: now she must begin to be a heavy thinker and go in for theosophies and heavy-isms.

Contrast of the Orient and Ourselves. Two sisters in China. One goes to Paris and becomes "sophisticated." We Westerners live nervous artificial lives; we drink too many cocktails.

And so on.

I went away very sad, but devoted to her.

September's not far off. Save me an evening, Sir, about the 7th or 8th, because through all this diversity and spottiness and intermittence, I need to count more and more on the fixed and constant and unshakable friends of which rare community you are the Prince and high Example. And it is with that kind of dependence I sign myself

Your friend
Thornton

122. TO MABEL DODGE LUHAN. ALS 4 pp. Yale

Hollywood Aug 29 • 1933[75]
c/o Edington-Vincent, Inc.
Equitable Building
After Sept 10 • at
Taos, thank God.

Dear Mabel:

How kind and patient you are with my apparent vagueness. You know that it is not mere shilly-shallying. The central enthusiasm of my Spring this year was that I was to spend August and September at Taos, under your humorous and disciplinary eye. Then came a telegram from Hollywood offering a salary that sent all the Wilders into yells of deri-

---

75 TNW incorrectly dated this letter; it should be dated August 29, 1934, and follow letter number 128.

sive laughter. No one was worth that much, no one. A month of it would have been sufficient to save Keats and Mozart combined from malnutrition to a happy old age. The Wilders don't understand money, but they understand the fantastic. This money meant a trip to her ancestral Hebrides for mother; a relief from anxiety (imaginary, but real; imaginary, therefore real) during a protracted invalidism for father; summer in biological research stations for Janet; and for me, many warming little odds and ends to do during the six months at the University this Fall. For me also out here was always the invitation to look at and get into this gigantic hard-working "folk" industry.

Sam Goldwyn (Jupiter) called me out to add words to a former silent picture of Ronald Coleman's<Colman's> called "Dark Angel". The other day however he asked me to write a new climatic closing scene to Anna Sten's "We live again" (Tolstoi's Resurrection).[76] I did three scenes of it in all; the<y> have been "shot" and so I have had my baptism on the films.

Naturally I can hardly work because of the absorbing pressure of the contacts in town; imagine for instance my surprise and pleasure when Adrian[77] showed us his movies of Taos.

So much to tell you.

I came here for four weeks, but Jupiter took up an option on two more, and implied that he would beg me to stay beyond. I work furiously to get it done so as to leave by the 8th. In the meantime the publishers press me to send the last unwritten chapter of my novel; and that must wait until I get into the glorious air of New Mexico.

I guess I'm the craziest most unstable least sérieux of your friends, but I <am>

devotedly and affectionately yours
Thornton

---

76 Goldwyn produced *We Live Again* (1934), starring Russian-born film and stage actress Sten (1908–1993), whom Goldwyn had brought to the United States.

77 Film costume designer and couturier Gilbert Adrian (1903–1959), known simply as Adrian, designed costumes for many famous films; he also designed clothes for numerous wealthy women, including Mabel Dodge Luhan.

TNW and Mabel Dodge Luhan.

123. TO ALEXANDER WOOLLCOTT. ALS 2 pp. Harvard

Here
Today.
<Chicago>
<August(?) 1933>

Dear Aleck:

Enclosed Mr. Knickerbocker's letter. In the same mail I received Martha Dodd's thoughts about him. La belle Still-Waters-Run-Deep looked at him hard, I assure you.[78]

---

78 H. R. Knickerbocker, a well-known American journalist, was an international correspondent for Hearst's International News Service. Martha Eccles Dodd (1908–1990) met TNW at the University of Chicago, where she studied for three and a half years before becoming assistant literary editor of the *Chicago Tribune*.

What! Not one creditable letter from the whole ricksha fleet?

No, not one.

[Generalization deduced: There is one race that is not to the swift. We homely hunchbacks, phthisic and bespectacled, learn to write so that the invisible readers think that in life we must be "Pard-like spirits beautiful and swift."—Parenthesis ended.]

Please write and thank Joe Foster (Temple University, Philadelphia—now Daggett Roller Chair Co, C. of P.) for his letter. I told him I'd ask you to. Probably you've done it already, in which case forgive my bossy tone.

Friday came around and you weren't in the New Yorker. Five days' anticipation is really stunned by such a disappointment and the thought that your strength had gone into "The Snake in the Grass" was not consolation enough; nor was the appearance of the September Cosmopolitan with some pages that fatten without enhancing my Big Treasured portfolio of your work.[79] The Fridays are lately so surpassing one another that to miss one seems a loss that later regularity cannot repair.

Is your play going to be put on at the Music Box Theatre by Sam Harris with one of those smooth productions that smell of Valspar[80] or is a bit of it here and there to be left to the imagination of the audience? My students (yes, in the Dante-Cervantes class) stop at the end of the hour to tell me how they loved "Dinner at Eight" and asking me to comment on it in class, and all I can think of is an Italianate chauffe<u>r hissing his jealousy to a lady's maid up in the boudoir.[81]

I guess I'm cranky today.

Jed telegraphed me to meet him at the airport Saturday for a twenty-minute talk, but I was at Lake Geneva and missed him. I'm doubly sorry, because I've found the actor to play Mr. Dulcimer.[82]

---

79 Woollcott's "The Sage of Fountain Inn" appeared in the September 1933 issue of *Cosmopolitan*.

80 A brand of wood stain and paint.

81 *The Dark Tower,* written and directed by Woollcott and George S. Kaufman and produced by Sam H. Harris, ran in New York from November 1933 to January 1934. Harris also produced *Dinner at Eight,* by Kaufman and Edna Ferber, which ran in New York from October 1932 to May 1933.

82 A character in *The Green Bay Tree,* who was played by James Dale when Jed Harris's production opened in October 1933.

Aleck, did I ever tell you about that American sixteen years old who stopped to see some friends in Dublin; the friends were helping make scenery at the Gate Theatre, so he helped swab a flat or two; when the part of the Duke in Jew Süss[83] couldn't be filled they persuaded him to take it and he was so wonderful that the whole town was staggered; so they had him play Othello and it was wonderful beyond belief: the Abbey then broke all tradition and asked him to play Lord Porteous in The Circle[84] to continued consternation. He—still sixteen—was so confused and humiliated by all the praise and interest (It's not hard to act: all you do is have fun putting on a make-up, then you go on the stage and say the lines) that he resolved to leave town and never act again. So he said goodbye to the Gate, playing both Hamlet's father and stepfather and such power and authority and fascination had never been seen.

He left the stage to become a writer. He's now eighteen; has a long play about John Brown. I gave him one of those galvanizing talks (that are really directed at myself) and now he wants to act again. Armed with my letters he is soon going to New York. Apparently its something daemonic: he is a rather pudgy-faced youngster with a wing of brown hair falling into his eyes and a vague Oxford epigrammatic manner; the pose is from his misery and soon drops under a responsible pair of eyes like mine. The name is Orson Wells[85] and it's going far. Are you interested?

That's not the only wunderkind either. The just-graduated Senior John Pratt[86] who did the wall decoration in the Tap Room of Alpha Delta Phi (did I show you those) came in last night with two portfolios of wonderful witty macabre drawings that would throw you into an ecstacy. There's one of a Greek candy store with a soda-fountain in fake marble and a trellis full of paper roses and a stack of candy boxes with

---

83 Play (1929) by English dramatist Ashley Dukes.

84 Play (1921) by Somerset Maugham.

85 TNW is credited with being instrumental in introducing Orson Welles to the American stage.

86 John Thomas Pratt (1912–1986) became a costumer and set designer. He worked especially for African-American dancer and choreographer Katherine Dunham, whom he married in 1941.

red silk ribbons that would throw you into an (—I said that before). And an Ascension in which some very odd angels are heaving a soul up to Heaven with the greatest difficulty.

Harvard and Yale and Princeton stew in their sad defeatist juice. These boys matured from inside outward instead of vice versa. They come from Wisconsin and Indiana respectively. And in ten years the United States will be the most stirring, comic, gay and truthful country in the world. ¶ Have a happy time working, and every now and then look out of the window in a sudden abstraction and remember that I am devoted to you and my name is

Thornton

124. TO J. DWIGHT DANA.[87] ALS 2 pp. Private

50 Deepwood Drive
New Haven Conn
January 18 • 1933<1934>

Dear Dwight:

This is a belated report. I am back from Hawaii. They paid me on the spot, though it required some special transaction on their part to prevent my being paid in script or something.

Boni knows that I expect to put most or all of my MS in their hands by April first; but they also know me well enough not to go forging ahead with promotion until they're sure I've finished.

Cass Canfield of Harpers' moans about, hoping that something will happen that will bring the text to him. If Boni's can't pay a just advance etc.

You'll be horrified to know the money I have been turning down.

---

87 Dana became TNW's lawyer in early 1928; and he continued to represent him until 1951, the year Dana died.

The Chicago Herald Examiner wanted me to come out and do a daily report of the Wynkoop Murder Trial.[88] The Holliday Tours want me to go on a very de luxe yacht trip of the Greek Islands—seven weeks from New York to New York. The Spring Tour has Mrs Astor and Dowager Vanderbilt—that kind of tour—me to give half an hour talk every morning in the lounge on things Greek. Expenses and.

Now telegrams are passing to the effect that I go to Hollywood and write up Joan of Arc for Katherine Hepburn (Merion Cooper-George Cukor set-up—very choice, the group that did "Little Women".)[89] Rosalie Stewart agent, very superior, will get the money she thinks I deserve and a three months guarantee. Presumably Mid-June to Mid-Sept. I shall take that if it's offered to me.

Lee Keedick will send you in a few days the money from the St. Louis lecture. Enclosed (sep. cover) divers chicken-feed, forgive my delay. I have five hundred dollars in the Chicago Bank, if you need any of it to ciment the cracks in the New Haven Bank.

If the movie plan doesn't turn out, Mabel Dodge Luhan of Taos, New Mexico, has offered me a house for the summer near her, with the invitation to meals up at her ranch.

Isabel's novel will also and more certainly be done April first.[90]

Greetings etc.

Sincerely yours
Thornton

88 TNW is referring to the trial of Dr. Alice Wynekoop, who had been accused of murdering her daughter-in-law, Rheta, in 1933.

89 TNW's treatment of the Joan of Arc story for George Cukor and Merian C. Cooper was not used, but the script is in the George Cukor Collection at the Margaret Herrick Library of the Academy of Motion Picture Arts and Sciences in Beverly Hills, California, as well as in the Beinecke Library at Yale University. It was published in the October 2003 issue of the *Yale Review.*

90 Isabel Wilder's second novel, *Heart Be Still,* was published in 1934.

125. TO MABEL DODGE LUHAN. ALS 4 pp. (Stationery embossed 50 Deepwood Drive / New Haven, Connecticut) Private

Railroad: approaching Lamy <New Mexico>
May 15 • 1934
After April 2, Univ. of Chicago

Dear Mabel:

Here I am again, hanging out of the window, looking at the country I already claim as "well-known" to me. I wish I could stop, but I'm off on one of those loony unsoundly-motivated errands of mine. I've been called to Hollywood for two weeks of "conversations" about Joan of Arc (Jeannette D'ay, to her). We're to assemble a movie about her for the use of Katherine Hepburn. Then I take train again and rush from the station to take up my first classes. I'm craw-crammed with lore about the Maid; she certainly was wonderful beyond words, but I don't know whether I'm very excited about the projected movie. I accepted the call because it appealed to all that's worst in me, I suppose,—the love of <the> trip, the joy of accepting an interruption and evasion from duty (the completion of my novel), the curiosity of seeing new faces and new moeurs.[91] I agree with Muriel that the Lord has turned his face away from Southern California and laid upon it the punishment that Friedell said He laid upon the Renaissance: he <has> taken their souls away. But how interesting that makes it; worth going these thousand miles to see.

If the forty page outline of the movie which I am required to prepare after these conversations, inspires the Powers with any confidence that I have a knack for such things I am to be recalled in the early summer to write the picture and be present during its shooting. And that news came just as I was on the point of writing you that I was willing to override my feeling of obligation to the MacDowell Colony, and was asking you to let me come to Taos.

---

91 French: customs.

It still seems likely that I may. During these two weeks they can pick my brains and throw me away like a squeezed orange. I'm willing. Then some other hands can come in and show Jeanne falling in love with the Duc d'Alençon (Percy MacKaye) or Dunois (Schiller), doing what neither the British goddams nor Cauchon himself ventured to believe.[92]

This leaves my coming to Taos in doubt, but do not let it inconvenience you in the matter of the disposition of the guest-house. All I will ask of you, if it will be possible for me, will be your encouragement to come to the town.

Very little has happened since I saw you. For the most part I sat up in my study playing solitaire, keeping strict the statistics of the Viennese theatres and writing my novel. I took one "unsoundly-motivated" trip to an adventurous little college in North Carolina. (22 students and 14 faculty members, none of the latter receiving a cent of salary. The college broke away from Henry Holt's in Florida with a loud academic scandal.)[93] Every now and then I sallied into New York for a few days among the New York wits (Alex Woollcott, Dorothy Parker, Marc Connolly) or the theatre people (Jed Harris, Ruth Gordon).

Muriel[94] had lunch with me one day, but I had something contrary on my mind that day and I must have been a wretched companion. She seemed very well and full of life, though in suspense about the publisher's opinion of her book.

¶ When Jeanne was assembling her armor she told some of her company that they would find her sword behind the altar of the Church of St. Catherine of Fierbois at Tours. And sure enough there it was covered with dust. They asked her if she had ever seen it: she said no,

---

92 TNW is referring to two other fictional treatments of the Joan of Arc story: Friedrich Schiller's play *Die Jungfrau von Orleans* (1801) and Percy MacKaye's play *Jeanne d'Arc* (1906). The "British goddams" refers to English soldiers, and Cauchon was the bishop in charge of Joan of Arc's trial.

93 TNW is referring to Black Mountain College, which opened in 1933. Its founder, John A. Rice, had been fired by Hamilton Holt, who was president of Rollins College in Winter Park, Florida, at the time. Some of the faculty and students at Rollins followed Rice to Black Mountain.

94 American writer Muriel Draper.

but that her Voices had told her about <it>. She carried <it> in many engagements, and guess where it suddenly broke into pieces: while she was whacking with the flat blade of it, the poor prostitutes who hung about the camp. Even Tolstoi couldn't have thought up that detail.

As a person she was certainly a saint; as a historical phenomen<on>, she was certainly a case of supernatural intervention.

Well, I wish I could stop off here and talk to you all evening about her, you knitting beside the fire of piñon wood. Perhaps late Summer we can climb into the car and go down and see it.

Give my regard to Tony; and count me among your happiest and most devoted visitors.

Sincerely yours
Thornton

126. TO J. DWIGHT DANA. ALS 1 p. Private

University of Chicago
May 16 1934

Dear Dwight:

Thank you for the annual statement. Contents noted.

Enclosed find FIRST MOVIE contract. I submitted the treatment within the date indicated. Telegram rec'd from head of Agency Firm (Edington, Vincent, Inc. Equitable Bldg. Hollywood.) "Entire office enthusiastic about your magnificent treatment of Joan of Arc." They passed it on in twenty mimeographed copies to the firm of RKO which is now, under Clause 4, ¶ 2, required to notify me as to whether they liked it enough to call me back under the option. If they rec'd the treatment, say on May 5th, they must get word to me within two weeks—that is: by Sunday. Then I have ten days to decide whether I want to go back and work on it for a measely $13,500. And I guess I will. It will be a good picture.

Clause 4 troubles me a little. I must furnish completed work within sixty days of their notifying me. I meant: within sixty days of my being at liberty from University work. However if by the letter of the contract I could do it by July 18, although I would prefer doing it by 60 days from June 17. Anyway they're a very friendly and enlightened firm (Merion C. Cooper, Lawrenceville School, is King; and 1st Lieut. is Kenneth MacGowan,[95] long one of the best dramatic critics in N.Y.)

I sent Bonis and Longman's the first six chapters of my novel and am now polishing off the next six; after that two more to follow.

Many thanks as ever

Sincerely yours
Thornton.

P.S. Last week Ickes offered Bob H. the post of Commissioner for Education for the U.S.A. Bob refused, partly because the salary was insufficient even to pay his insurance. N.B. He ought to have a J. Dwight Dana in his life to give him the sensation of having private means. ¶ P.S. 2: my regards to your partner and my best wishes for the new firm.[96] P.S. 3: Last week I turned down Thousands. Sixty four of the greatest banks in the country have taken a nation-wide radio-hook-up hour. Music—Tibbett, Bori etc.[97] and talks to persuade a singed public that the banks are nice kind institutions that love their depositors. I was to deliver pocket sermons and tabloid success stories of farmers' boys who ROSE. I felt I had your permission to refuse that "opportunity for usefulness."

T.

---

95 After a successful career as a drama critic and as the director of New York's Provincetown Playhouse, Macgowan had gone to Hollywood as a story editor.

96 Harold Ickes, who offered Robert Maynard Hutchins the post, was secretary of the interior at the time. Dana's partner was Frederick H. "Fritz" Wiggin. The firm was henceforth called Wiggin and Dana.

97 American opera singer Lawrence Tibbett and Spanish opera singer Lucrezia Bori.

127. TO JOSEF ALBERS.[98] ALS 4 pp. Albers Foundation

50 Deepwood Drive
New Haven Conn.
July 1 • 1934

Dear Mr. Albers:

It was fine to hear from you and to know that your work goes on (and now in oil and in wood carving!) and that you have been finding continual audiences for the work here and abroad.

I am very ashamed of not having written you before. My delay was due to the fact that so far my efforts had been met with disappointment. The approaches I made to introduce your work in Chicago (The Arts Club and a dealer of modern art) were met always with the greatest interest, but with the word that one must wait: all the long difficult fight to persuade people to learn abstract painting has been done in the French school; and that they are not ready yet to adjust their eyes to that wholly new series of approaches which is the German abstract. Braque, Picasso and Gris and Léger have only recently become "classics" in Chicago, and the "Governors of the Public Taste" are going to consolid<at>e those victories first.

Similarly, I have talked with Daniel Rich of the Art Institute School of your distinguished teaching gifts. I shall have an opportunity to repeat and insist during the Summer for I hear that he will be in New Mexico when I am there.

However I am very happy to help you approach Mr. Harshe.[99] I don't remember ever having met him, but I probably must have at one time for a minute at some function or other.

It is only a matter of time and patience until you find the audiences and appreciation over here that your gifts have found in Europe. I shall continue to work on the matter in such ways as my contacts permit and hope someday to have a small share in the pride of having been useful to you.

---

98 German artist and former Bauhaus professor Albers (1888–1976) emigrated to the United States in 1933. He became a member of the faculty at Black Mountain College.

99 Robert B. Harshe was director of the Art Institute of Chicago at the time.

Please give my regard to Mrs Albers and receive my thanks again for the help your methods and your work gave me in understanding the modes of art that lie ahead of us in the next century.

Sincerely yours
Thornton

128. TO ISABELLA N. AND ISABEL WILDER. ALS 2 pp. Yale

<Hollywood, California>
Aug. 25 • 1934

Dear Gairls

Suddenly there was a flurry Wednesday afternoon. Mr. Goldwyn wanted Paul Green and me to see the just finished "We Live Again"[100] (Tolstoi's Resurrection). Something was wrong with it; and we were to tell him what it was. Well, we told him,—the ending was suddenly, cheaply unpreparedly happy. "Gentlemen, I throw myself on your mercy. I want you each" (including Praskins the original author of the script) "to write a big closing scene. We have only one day to shoot it—Friday, because Fredric March" (who plays Dmitri) "is going to Tahiti and can only give us one day's work."

Well, we all went off into different corners and wrote the scene. I appeared with mine at 3:00 on Thursday. The plan was to pool the best points of all three scenes, but the final scene was almost entirely mine. But it took from 3:00 to half past eleven to cut it and shape it in endless long conferences <and> at last it was done; we were all dog-tired but happy. Then one of the under-executives entered with the expression of greatest gloom: "Miss Sten has just telephoned that she has a pimple on her nose."

It wasn't funny; it was tragic.

The shooting took place the next day. The pimple was indubitably

100 When *We Live Again* was released in 1934, screenwriting credit was given to Leonard Praskins, Maxwell Anderson, and Preston Sturges.

there, right on the end of her nose. Her close-ups could be taken after March's absence, but the shots with them both in couldn't be taken closer than eight feet, which greatly damaged the intimacy and intensity of the scene.

As usual they took the scene twenty-thirty times. March had had to memorize my lines at 8:00 o'clock and play them at 10:00 and kept forgetting them.

Anyway, I am baptized in the movies. My first lines have gone over, directed by Reuben Mamoulian.

Mr. Goldwyn met me in the corridor and said he had seen the film; that it was a very beautiful scene; that it topped everything that preceded it; that he was very grateful to me.

Draw your conclusions.

Charles Laughton was rushed off to the hospital and operated on for an abcess in the rectum.

I am calling on him this afternoon.

Today is Sat and I am driving up to the Mt Wilson observatory to see the nebula in Andromeda. (Going with Dick Hemingway an ex-pupil at Lawrenceville: I gave him 28 on the final exam: he is now a contract player at Columbia.)

Ruthie-the-Pooh leaves for N.Y. next Tuesday and a wonderful part in the first Guild Play.[101] In the meantime she is being given very elaborate tests at Metro—four of them.

I think I leave for Taos Sept 10.

I just got your letter about Isabel's being up and about again. Never to swim? All yesterday I thought about her book's coming out and have orders in 3 stores here, but they are slow getting here.

A thousand salutes & best wishes.

Ever

Thornt.

---

101 Ruth Gordon played three roles in the Theatre Guild's production of James Bridie's *A Sleeping Clergyman* (1933), which ran in New York from October to November 1934.

129. TO CHARLES LAUGHTON. ALS 2 pp. UCLA

Chateau Elysee Hollywood
Sept 2 • 1934

Dear and splendid Charles,

No wonder they discourage visitors when the visitors are as excitable as I was on my last visit, one minute enthralled by medical stories and the next minute overcome by something plus forte que moi.[102] At any event I earn my living by my imagination and if every now and then it takes things into its own hands, it's not for me to complain.

I have been very eager to come and call on you to show you these two clippings from the Neues Wiener Journal (Sept. 12 and 19th).

You said you admired Raimu[103] and here is Raimu admiring you. He is being interviewed in Paris by an unnamed correspondent:

> <clipping pasted into the letter:>
> Und was sagt der Schauspieler? „Ich gehe gern ins Kino," erzählt Raimu, der unbestrittene Liebling der Pariser, „um mich zu sehen. Auch gestern sah ich mir den Korda-Film „Das Privatleben Heinrichs VIII." an."– „Wieso?" frage ich erstaunt, „Den Heinrich im Korda-Film spielen doch nicht Sie, sondern Charles Laughton!"– „Pas Possible!" entsetzt sich Raimu. „Ich sagte mir während der ganzen Dauer des Films: das kann nur ein einziger Schauspieler so blendend spielen und dieser Schauspieler bin ich..."

"And what does the actor say? 'I enjoy going to the movies,' says Raimu, the uncontested favorite of the Parisians, 'in order to see myself. Only yesterday I was looking at myself in the Korda film The Private Life of Henry VIII.' 'What!' I cried, amazed, 'it wasn't you who played Henry, but Charles Laughton!' 'Not possible!' replied Raimu, 'the whole time the film was going on I kept saying to myself: there's only one actor who can play as dazzlingly as that, and that one actor is myself.<'>"

The second clipping is from an interview with Stefan Zweig:

---

102 French: stronger than I.

103 Raimu was the stage name of French stage and film actor Jules-Auguste Muraire (1883–1946).

<clipping pasted into the letter>

„Das Privatleben Heinrichs VIII." etwa, in dem sich Charles Laughton zu einem der populärsten Schauspieler der Welt emporarbeitete. Laughton, der übrigens in der Verfilmung meines Buches über „Maria Antoinette" mit Norma Shearer die führende Rolle spielen wird, könnte heute selbst in der europäischen Hauptstädten Haftspiele bei vollen Häusern veranstalten, ein Wagnis, das sich vor ihm kein anderer englischer Schauspieler leisten konnte.

"The Private Life of Henry VIII, for example, in which Charles Laughton has elevated himself to being one of the most popular actors in the world. Laughton, who moreover will, with Norma Shearer play the leading rôle in the picturization of my book Marie Antoinette would be able today to fulfill guest performances to full houses in all the capitals of the Europe, a venture which before him no English actor could undertake."[104]

I'm not so sure of my words in this translation, but that's the general idea.

I hope you'll be out and well again before long. I'm as eager to see the Ruggles as I am the Barrett.[105] When I realized the other day that it was your Epikhodov I saw, the breath went out of me in my pleasure at adding a new item to my collection:

Cherry Orchard
Silver Tassie
Pickwick
Payment Deferred
Fatal Alibi

and the movies:
Payment Deferred
(in a submarine with Tallulah Bankhead and Cary Grant)[106]
Henry VIII

---

104 When the film *Marie Antoinette*, based on Zweig's 1932 biography, appeared in 1938, Norma Shearer played the title role, but Laughton was not in the cast. He had declined the role, which was played by Robert Morley.

105 Laughton was in the films *The Barretts of Wimpole Street* (1934) and *Ruggles of Red Gap* (1935).

106 The film TNW refers to in parentheses is *Devil and the Deep* (1932).

But then what a lot I've missed.

Bella Gordon got off, leaving Bella Hayes[107] terribly solitary. Bella Gordon's tests at MGM dazzled the powers over there and I think something big will come of them. Bello Wilder's life goes on much as usual. Tuesday he must turn in a WHOLE SCRIPT of an intermittently interesting movie to Jupiter Goldwyn. Tell Bella Lanchester[108] that Wednesday night I am going to Jupiter's dinner for Prospero Reinhardt and then I shall get the man's own ear to sow the 20th and last of my urgent persuasions that God and Shakespeare's own Puck is right in town. Also tell Bella Lanchester to call me at once if there is any book you want, any errand I can do, etc.

I hope earnestly that you are already well restored, that you are tranquil in mind, that in the long stretches when you are alone you turn over in your mind all the wonderful creations of the imaginations that you were sent into the world to perform, and that you realize that you are surrounded by the thoughts of so many that admire you as an artist and love you as a person,—among whom remember

Your devoted friend
Thornton

130. TO ISABELLA N. WILDER. Wire 1 p. Yale

1934 SEP 8 PM 6 48

HOLLYWOOD CALIF 8 31 8P
MRS AMOS WILDER =
50 DEEPWOOD DR NEWHAVEN CONN =
WAS OFFERED AND TURNED DOWN SOLO JOB ON NEXT GARBO PICTURE STOP ROLLER SKATED WITH WALT DISNEY TAOS NEXT TUESDAY LOVE = THORNTON.

107 Ruth Gordon and Helen Hayes.

108 Elsa Lanchester, Laughton's wife.

131. TO HARPER & BROTHERS. TL (Copy)[109] 1 p. Private

September 29, 1934

Harper & Brothers
49 West 33rd Street
New York, N.Y.

Dear Sirs:

I hereby consent to the assignment and transfer by Albert & Charles Boni, Inc., to you of the book rights in the United States and Canada, first serial rights and the manuscript so far as it has been completed, of my new novel entitled "Heaven's My Destination", it being understood that in consideration of such assignment and of my consent thereto you assume and agree to perform all of the undertakings of said Albert & Charles Boni, Inc., contained in the written agreement between said Albert & Charles Boni; Inc., and myself, dated July 18. 1934, in so far as they relate to the rights thus assigned to you.[110]

Very truly yours,
Thornton N. Wilder

132. TO MABEL DODGE LUHAN. ALS 4 pp. Yale

The best University
Oct 7 • 1934

Dear Mabel:

You will be astonished to hear that I am happy. Yes, ma'am,—partly the after-effect of the breadth and clarity of the days in your

---

109 This appears to be a secretarial transcription of TNW's letter; the original letter has not been located.

110 Harper & Brothers acquired the rights from A. & C. Boni for four thousand dollars on August 29, 1934, for TNW's new novel, *Heaven's My Destination,* the third and last novel he had contracted to write for the Boni firm, and he was now free to become a Harper & Brothers author.

valley, and the breadth and clarity of your nature, and partly the warming absurdity of two things that happened since I returned here. The first of these (confidentialissimo) was that President Roosevelt asked Bob Hutchins to leave the university for nine months and assume the directorship of the whole NRA.[111] The absurdity of that call does not lie in any inadequacy on Bob's part; nor in any difficulty of the job itself. It lies in the spectacle of how the world works; how merit finds its own level; how the threads of life—I first knew Bob as a gangling evangelist's son being elected to the presidency of my Freshman class at Oberlin, Ohio, and have known him ever since in hot water with a large company of bystanders continually predicting his downfall,—cross and recross. There is something beautiful and lyrical to the Comic Spirit about the emergence of certain threads from the shuffling and reshuffling of apparently aimless circumstances. And for that something I can only find the word Absurdity. Bob wrote the President a letter of acceptance asking however for a more distinct statement of his powers. We will know today or tomorrow whether it is settled. Then Bob and Maude, two rather lonely young souls, beautiful as pards, articulated like race-horses, will move to Washington,—Bob indifferent to the fact that the post is unlovely, doomed to checkmate at best, dangerous,—grateful aware only that it is difficult, unboring. C'est beau! C'est très beau![112]

Similarly I was called up from New York the other day. William Randolph Hearst and Marion Davies have just arrived in the country, filled with an impassioned idea: Marion Davies wants to do Twelfth Night in the movies.[113] Will I prepare the script? Will I assume the audacity of writing additional dialogue? Of course, I will. I'm an adventurer; that means: that all the values of life fluctuate. One minute honor and decorum seem to be a worthy price to pay; the next minute impulse seems superior to society's respect; One minute art's discipline; the next minute, observing and interfering. The fact that such a curious nexus as an ex-follies girl and a newspaper millionaire who

---

111 The National Recovery Administration, designed to help rebuild and strengthen the nation's economy. Hutchins did not take the job.

112 French: It's beautiful! It's very beautiful!

113 Hearst and Davies never made a film of *Twelfth Night*.

pathetically adores her and Wm. Shakespeare and myself should appear is more interesting than all the dignity and artistic honor in the world. Uncle Pio is the most loving portrait I ever made of myself—not Chrysis.[114] ¶ Since in the 20th Century the Sublime has departed the earth, let us at least cherish the beautiful image of the ridiculous.

The next night.

In a few minutes I shall call New York to ask Ruth Gordon how her great opening tonight went.[115]

A few weeks ago Maude Hutchins was in New York. Leonard Hanna[116] invited her out to lunch. He inquired whether she would like to meet anyone else. She, Marie-Antoinette-disdainful said: "No, no—I don't want to meet anyone else." Later Leonard told her he had thought of having her meet Ruth Gordon; and Maude was cut to the heart with regret and remorse: that was the one person in the world she wanted to look at. ¶ For years I have jokingly said goodnight to Maude with the words: "You're the second finest girl in the world", and she always knew that I meant she was only surpassed by Ruth.

I told all this to La Gordon adding: "Uneasy lies the head that wears a second best crown."

She telegraphed back: "I loved your letter."

No wonder!

After I left you in Santa Fé I went to the Santa Fé Art Gallery and then took a nap. I bought my ticket for the Chief that night, and went to dinner at Witter Bynner's.[117] There was a considerable company: The Knees, McCarthy, that writing woman, etc.[118] After dinner Witter read from his satirical sonnets. The reception was sycophantic and

---

114 Uncle Pio, a character in *The Bridge of San Luis Rey,* is the actor-manager of "La Périchole," a young girl he found singing in a tavern. Chrysis, a beautiful courtesan, is the major character in *The Woman of Andros.*

115 *A Sleeping Clergyman* opened on October 8, 1934.

116 Leonard C. Hanna, Jr., was an art patron and an important benefactor of the Cleveland Museum of Art.

117 American poet Witter Bynner (1881–1968) lived in Santa Fe for many years.

118 American photographer Ernest Knee (1907–1982); his wife, American painter Gina Knee (1898–1982); and, probably, American poet Daniel Clifford McCarthy, who in 1936 purchased Santa Fe's Villagra Book Shop.

tongue-tied. I grew more and more sombre. Finally my opinion was asked. You would have been proud of your little Thornton (né Caspar Milquetoast). For once in my life I spoke up. I said they were not only monotonous in form and cadence, but in attitude. The average reader—in spite of the brilliant verbal coinage—would finally push out his lip in repudiation. "You have invective without passion and yet analysis without objectivity." I tried not to be too harsh to Witter among his idolators but he got the idea that the portrait of the portraitist emerges from the portraits as even more unlovely than the sitters.

The Knees drove me to the train,—Mrs Knee is a gracious very-young presence.

The observation car of the Chief takes on the quality of the smoking-car of an ocean-liner. I played craps with John Boles, Francis X Shields and Jacques Catelier.[119] If you don't know who these world figures are, ask Spud.[120]

Tomorrow at nine I give a lecture on the Second Canto of the Inferno—Beatrice, the Virgin Mary and Virgil. Isn't <u>that</u> ridiculous? The earth is old; the mind of man is crammed with a strange hodge-podge; let us extract from it what intellectual delight we may from a sheer admiration of its strangeness.

Give my deep regard to Tony. I sincerely hope he can call on me when he comes to town. The telephone in my new apartment is Midway 7030. If I'm not in, telephone messages can be left for me at the office of the apartment house downstairs Dorchester 7080.

Today I mailed some Bach-Stokowski gramaphone records to Brett,[121] in your care. Do play them over before you pass them on: they represent my religious ideas: sentimental, personal anthropomorphic, intimate. My notion of God is much like that of a negro revivalist, and Bach's wasn't far from it. There are two pieces of music I would like to

---

119 Boles was an American stage and film actor. Shields was an internationally ranked amateur tennis player who appeared in small film roles.

120 American poet and journalist Walter Willard "Spud" Johnson (1897–1968), who founded the small-press magazine *Laughing Horse,* also worked for a time as a secretary to both Witter Bynner and Mabel Dodge Luhan.

121 English artist Dorothy Brett (1883–1977), along with D. H. Lawrence and his wife, Frieda, went to Taos, New Mexico, in 1924 and became an integral part of the art colony there.

be performed at my funeral (Westminster Abby) Weelkes' madrigal " 'Happy, oh happy he' who despising earth's rewards, lives far from<"> etc and Bach's last choral prelude "Schmucke dich, oh meine Seele"— 'adorn thyself, oh my soul'—

Well, it's two o'clock in New York and Ruth hasn't got home from her curtain calls yet.

I have been scouring the town for some very good chocolates to send you.

Ma'am, I am bound to you in great admiration and affection all my life and am

devotedly yours
Thornton

133. TO SARAH M. FRANTZ.[122] ALS 2 pp. Princeton

Faculty Exchange
University of Chicago
Oct 13 • 1934

Dear Mrs. Frantz:

What's become of all my hopes and plans to come into New Jersey, look at my old homes, take my accustomed walks and greet my friends again? Apparently this division of my life between Chicago and New Haven is cutting down my chances of free impulsive excursions. I no longer get to Peterborough in the summers, either; and now a new element has entered: I work in Hollywood a few months every year. I am very interested in the movies as a form; I am working very hard at its peculiar technique, and after a few years of apprenticeship I hope to be allowed a chance to write one that is all myself and all deeply felt. Besides it has fallen upon me to sustain several members of my family and the earnings out there are a great help.

---

122 A friend from TNW's days at Princeton in 1925–1926 (see letter number 89).

The Fall Quarter has been going for two weeks. I enjoy the teaching as much as ever; am very proud of the university and its wunderkind president.

I was so dilatory in handing in the closing pages of my novel that I am afraid the publishers will not be able to get it out by Xmas. Once a book is written I lose all interest in its further journey—its cover, its promotion, its appearance. The publishers go insane over my delays; at heart they enjoy that kind of worry and all the scheming that goes with salesmanship.

A good deal of the book is tough, full of bad words and life's unlovelier traps; but I hope you will see that none of the coarseness is there for cheap display. The subject of the book goes quietly on under the surface din: the earnest humorless undefeated hero trying to live an extravagantly idealistic life in the middle of a cynical defeatist world—a Gideon-Bible travelling salesman. On the title page I placed the motto from The Woman of Andros so that readers wouldn't think it was merely a rowdy comic book—"Of all forms of genius, goodness has the longest awkward age"—namely priggishness, preachiness, confusion etc. I hope it will be somehow useful to a lot of troubled young people.

Has your St. Bernard grown up to be enormous? Have you grown accustomed to the High Church ritualism at the First Church?

Give my best to Janet and Alison. When my Greek gets better I shall write a letter in it to Alison and she can return it with red-pencil corrections.

When Sunday evenings you sing the Blake hymn or the one about "The day thou gavest now is ended" with its long loping melodic line, remember me and my great pleasure in being at any time in your company.

Always devotedly and affectionately yours
Thornton

134. TO AMOS P. WILDER. ALS 4 pp. Yale

University of Chicago
Oct 25 • 1934

Dear Da:

Many thanks for your notes.

Please do not think I am sensitive about which secretaries share our correspondence. I am grateful also to anyone who is kind enough to help you.[123] I have never had any sense of secrecy about any of my affairs.

I am glad you say you are pretty well. I am feeling fine—but by Friday afternoon of every week I am ready for a rest. ¶ I wish I could get back to the geneological shelves of the Yale Library and polish up that Houghton ancestry. ¶ Rumors have begun to tell me that my new book will find friends. ¶ Am looking forward to Isabel's visit. Mrs Hobart Johnson asked us both up to Madison for Sunday night, but Isabel will arrive too late for it. Mrs Johnson spoke of you with great regard and affection and sends cordial greetings

Isabel will sleep in the bedroom of my nice little apartment and I shall snooze away in the sittingroom. I leave the house for WORK at seven and I hope she'll sleep until ten and get a big rest. ¶ I will talk to her on the subject you mention; and then she can talk to me on the subject you dictated to her. We are both over THIRTY years old, but we will talk to one another as tho' we were seventeen and we will come out very sensible, cautious, joyless and shrewd.

Bob Hutchins spends much time in earnest talk with Pres. Roosevelt. What's going to come of it, I don't know. ¶ Good Alex Woollcott is in town and I'm going down to dinner with him. ¶ I love my classes, and my classes like me. ¶ I've given up worrying
anxiety
nail-biting
and I hope you have too.

I hope my twelve sons will one day remember me as smiling and

123 Because TNW's father was ill, he was using private secretarial help.

serene. In my house no one will be permitted to mention MONEY. ¶ The view from my window is very beautiful,—mostly sky.

yr. loving son
Thornton

135. TO J. DWIGHT DANA. TL (Copy)[124] 1 p. Private

The University of Chicago
December 9, 1934, a Sunday.

Dear Dwight:

This is your crazy client speaking.

Sometime before Christmas you'll get a long distance phone call from New York; a certain John Ely will want to make an appointment with you.

He wants me to be the editor of a class woman's magazine. Like Good Housekeeping, only with the new unstuffy realistic smartness that is coming across the urban mind and that has been developed by the New Yorker and Time. There have been countless disasters in the effort to bring out a new magazine; only two have succeeded since 1900, the two named above. All the rest, especially in the woman's world, are old and are gradually slipping and getting out of touch with the new mentality. Mr Ely's will be forwarded for a selected superior clientele, beginning gradually.

Ely's own business is selling advertising and promoting schemes. He claims to be the last word in the engineering power of space-selling to advertisers. He claims complete ignorance about the editorial end; but how he can sell space. We'll make a million in no time; yes, sir.

He has all the figures to show you, with the plans for selling stock and so on. He claims I would have to put no money in it myself, beyond buying one of the four hundred shares. All profits he divides

---

124 This copy appears to be a secretarial transcription of TNW's letter; the original letter has not been located.

equally with me. He has a complete staff of women under me experienced in food products, fashion ad<v>ice etc. All I do is lend my name, build in ideas, select the fiction, and have an editorial talent in choice of illustrators, jokes, and so on.

There's no pressure on you or me to accept it. But I wish you'd listen to him and look over the diagrams.

Why should I even consider it? For the same reason that I go to Hollywood: adventure, color, the exhilaration of even pretending that I have a part to play in the immense bright stream of Twentieth Century activities. These things have no relation to my midnight secret life of literary composition. I'm Jekyll and Hyde. With the side of me which is not Poet, and there's lots of it, I like to do things, meet people, restlessly experiment in untouched tracts of my Self, be involved in things, make decisions, pretend that I'm a man of action.

We have made no commitments. Listen to his story; see if its sound as business; the only thing we risk is its being dull.[125]

(Thornton Wilder)[126]

136. TO C. LESLIE GLENN. ALS 3 pp. Yale

<Chicago>
<March 1935>

Dear and royal Les:

What a louse I am.

But the Bible commands you to forgive me 70 X 7 and I, the louse, greedily point to it and profit.

"I think," "as far as I know", "probably" "very likely" I shall be back April first 1936 to teach the Spring Quarter. The University has

125 Nothing came of this possible position for TNW.

126 This is handwritten, presumably by a secretary in Dana's office.

now given me one year off—April to April. Maybe with plays on Broadway or something or other I shall not return. But I don't know any reason now why I shouldn't, except that I teach worse and worse in the classroom itself—tho' if I do say it, I get better and better as a "campus character" in general circulation, accessible to all comers. Some mornings I rise up and swear that I shall never teach again, that I must go away and become a writer etc. Other days I rise up and love it, the everything, the classes, the tumult on the stairs of Cobb Hall.

What a silly pathless creature I am.

People are still writing to tell me of their contempt for my book "that I made fun of religion to earn money for myself."[127]

Amos had a kind of nervous breakdown. CONFIDENTIAL. Phobias and tics. Started off by intestinal flu. He feels much better now.

I didn't give Geo Brush enough of the intermittent moments of joy and reassurance. They are his due. The diagram of goodness was falsified by not exhibiting also its occasional inner reward. That was very bad of me; I was so intense about his troubles that I didn't <u>think</u> of it. SO my next book won't be harrowing: <u>it will</u> give pleasure. ADSIT DEUS.[128]

At present I am the secretary, errand boy-companion of Gertrude Stein who is teaching here for two weeks—a great, sensible, gallant gal and a great treat.[129]

Yes, yes, we've been narrowing religion. I've been reading Goethe.[130] For a time we can go out among the vaguer theists and pan-

---

127 TNW is referring to *Heaven's My Destination*, whose protagonist is George Brush.

128 Latin: God be with me.

129 TNW met American poet, novelist, and critic Gertrude Stein on November 25, 1934, when she spoke at the University of Chicago while on a lecture tour of the United States. President Hutchins invited her to return in March 1935 to teach a special course, with TNW to select her students.

130 Goethe was one of TNW's lifelong intellectual heroes.

theists and borrow for a while the Alpine airs of their cosmos-wide views; then come back to our personal aspects again without being harmed. It will be the right pendulum swing from the 19th century thing, that was so closely "God told me I should give up tobacco."

It's twelve-thirty. I must lecture on the Antigone at 8[00] tomorrow. I must send you back to your spiritual exercize of "forgiving". All my best to Georgie & the chillun.

Love me beyond my desserts or however it's spelled.

Ever

Thorny

137. TO J. DWIGHT DANA. ALS 2 pp. Private

University of Chicago
April 9 • 1935

Dear Dwight:

Don't be mad.

I gotta do this.

There's a very brilliant student here, in philosophy and metaphysics.

His father's a superintendant in Swift's, but he has a large family and can't do very much for the young man who must go abroad for a year's study rather than stew along in our Grad. School which is very poor in Philosophy.

I would like you as soon as possible to send $600[00] to

Fred. R. Davis
6827 Dante St
Chicago

with a word that you had been asked to do it by Wilder for the further education of his son Robert.

Mr. Davis, Sr, and Mrs Davis have already talked this over with me and know that it is coming.

I assure you this is a very brilliant investment in the future. Two of his profs have already told him that he has struck upon a developement in the theory of Time that seems extremely important and Gertrude Stein had a talk with him on it (metaphysics is one of her preoccupations, too) and she told me she thought he was remarkable.

So concede me this.

I'm sending you some other material on other matters, (royalties etc) tomorrow.

Ever sincerely
Thornton

138. TO LEWIS STILES GANNETT.[131] ALS 4 pp. Harvard

University of Chicago
April 16 • 1935

Dear Mr. Gannett:

I've had a minor nervous shake-down lately and dare not fling myself into a long letter about my enthusiasm for this university. I went to Yale and did graduate work at Princeton; through some friends I have seen a good deal of Harvard. The classical American education as viewed on the Eastern seaboard is really all wrong: it trains (in imitation of England) for a ruling class; America has no such thing. It trains for a 19th Century image of what is Important, True and Beautiful. Their very buildings as architecture <u>educate</u> badly. And the faint steam of money that rises from everything, (the Morgan Bros partners among the trustees—Yale spent 33,000<,>000 on buildings alone during the depression), the gentility tone, the dilettante radicalism, the unvital view of taste,—all 19th Century.

We live in the 2nd most beautiful city in the world; and the city most characteristic of what the next 50 years will be like. We are very contemporaneous. Hutchins has drawn a curriculum directed squarely

---

131 American journalist and writer (1891–1966). What prompted TNW's letter to Gannett could not be determined.

at his picture of a gifted, realist, excited student. North, West and South of us are great universities with over 10,000 students each—Wisconsin, Northwestern, and Illinois—we have 3,000 undergrads and 3,000 grads.—They are free, famous for their football and fraternity racketting and for their laxity in class-grades. We cost 100 dollars a quarter; have long had lamentable football and have a reputation for being difficult in studies: so by natural selection only those students who have heard about the intellectual life come to us. We have had 5 Nobel prizemen on the faculty and the atmosphere of no-nonsense austerity in the Grad schools has drifted down through the whole mass. Hence we are a slightly cold-hearted university; of a laboratory unsentimentality.

Think it over.

We are bad for certain kinds of students, I confess; but hundreds of them thrive on it.

Yours for the whistling high airs of the 20th Century.

Selah![132]

Sincerely yours
Thornton Wilder

139. TO WILLIAM FRAZIER. ALS 4 pp. (Stationery embossed On board the / Cunard / R.M.S. "Ascania" <heading crossed out by TNW>) Rice

July 5 • 1935
c/o American Express Co
Rue Scribe
Paris, France

Dear Mr. Frazier:

Please forgive my delay in answering your letter. My teaching schedule all Spring at the University of Chicago was so hard that I fi-

132 Hebrew: "Pause and reflect!" (This word recurs frequently in TNW's letters.)

nally got a little shaken in health because of it. I obtained a year's leave of absence and am now sufficiently recovered to take up my correspondence again.

Your letter interested me very much and on the whole I am sympathetic with your & George Brush's position. I hope that in a rereading of the book you have been able to see that I am not making fun of the hero. His instinctive goodness and his instinctive view of what is essential in living is far superior to the groups among which he moves. But I hold that he has been badly educated—badly educated even in religion. The fundamentalist tradition in American protestantism has made into fixed hard unimaginative laws the substance of the Gospel. All that is censorious, literal and joyless in the Calvinistic-Methodist-Baptist tradition is based upon a misreading of the New Testament and a failure to see that most of that tone in the Old Testament is expressly superceded in the New.

However I meant George Brush to be seen as learning in episode and episode better how to render his instinctive goodness and unworldliness effective. It's an Education Novel. I didn't write the close clearly enough, I see now: I meant to show George Brush disappearing into the distance still doing many things that are absurd in the eyes of the average hardboiled citizen, but nevertheless exhibiting the advance he had made over the position he held in the opening pages.

I intended that everyone should find something of his or her self in George Brush,—and of the best of themselves, too. I know that much of my father and my brother and myself is there, and many people recognize themselves in him. I was very glad to get your word to the same effect, and hope a second reading will remove your feeling that I wrote it to make fun of great and good qualities

Sincerely yours
Thornton Wilder

140. TO MABEL DODGE LUHAN. ALS 4 pp. Yale

Salzburg Austria. Sept. 13. <1935>
Next Tuesday (and then until Xmas)
c/o American Express Co.
Vienna.

Dear Mabel:

I'm not only a silly fellow; I am downright crazy.

How could I have written you the enclosed letter and then never mailed it.

Now you will have reams of letter and that is no favorable light for any letter writer.

Paris was no more lovable than I had expected; but the Italian Art Show[133] was very wonderful indeed.

I stayed eight days with Gertrude Stein at Bilignin. Automobile trips in the environs; an intense preoccupation with two dogs; Alice B Toklas's sublime housekeeping; and Gertrude Stein's difficult magnificent and occasionally too abstract and faintly disillusioned alpine wisdom about the Human Mind, identity, the sense of time and How we Know. I am devoted to both of them, but in the presence of Gertrude's gifts one must occasionally scramble pretty hard to realize one's <u>self</u>, collect it, encourage it, and trust it. (All that is of course, very confidential.)

The Salzburg Festival was an unprecedented success this year. The tiny streets rocked with Rolls-Royce's and English accents. The central point was the incredibly elegant tense and diamond-sharp figure of Toscanini calling out the horns. Time after Time Heaven was taken by violence and capitulated. Bruno Walter alternated on the Mozart evenings and wooed the ensemble, like a gentle and grieving father, begging the musicians to give him the next ten bars quite perfectly, please.

---

133 The 1935 Exposition of Italian Art from Cimabue to Tiepolo, held at the Petit Palais in Paris.

Reinhardt's production of Faust has ghosts of circus and Ziegfeld, but commits the mistakes that it requires genius to commit.[134] And at the heart of it there is a little simple wonderful Gretchen who grows from gentleness to terror and madness and builds the greatest performance I have ever seen.

My philosopher-friend and I have hiked through scores of vallies between Dolomites and peaks and passes and glaciers.[135] But at last I am very restless to settle down and work—horrified that so much of my vacation has gone by

"And my late Spring no bud nor blossom sheweth."[136]

Vienna is <a> very gossipy—intriguing—personality immersed capital and already from contacts made at the Festival its networks of hospitality-cum-self-interest have begun to stifle me.

I shall probably have to go to that hill forty-five minutes away to live. I dont pretend that the temptation to waste the weeks in going and seeing and grouping comes entirely from without; its within too, and I must manage it. At all events, it <is> very unlike the wonderful lucid hours in your valley, when the hours fall one after another, invitations to one's best expectations of one's self and enhanced not interrupted by your splendid self.

All my best to you both.

Ever

Thornton

---

134 Max Reinhardt's lavish production of Goethe's *Faust* was one of his most famous. TNW consulted with him on the script for this production.

135 TNW was traveling in Europe with Robert Frederick Davis, the young undergraduate student whose foreign study TNW supported (see letter number 137). TNW had arranged for Davis to study philosophy in Vienna.

136 TNW slightly misquoted John Milton's "On His Being Arrived at the Age of 23": "But my late spring no bud or blossom sheweth."

141. TO AMOS N. AND CATHARINE K. WILDER. ALS 4 pp. Yale

American Express Co.
14 Kärtnerring Vienna[I]
Sept 22 • 1935

My dear Brother and Sister:

A thousand greetings.

Selah!

Just a word to you before the war breaks out and before I have to slip across borders by night dressed as a Rumanien jewelry peddler.

I think of you as having everything I haven't got. You have a home, a continuity, a job. I've loved my European trip, yes'mam, the boat; the stay at Fontainbleau, the walks in those woods, the stay with the wise and kind G. Stein, and the hikes through the Tyrol, and The Festival at Salzburg with the giant activities of Toscanini and Reinhardt, and now Vienna with its bewildering hospitality—but I'm longing to settle down, as you have, and start a routine of working and reading and of quiet evenings at home. I think I can begin it about next week, but until then I remain a hotel-room boy surrounded by cracked and overflowing suitcases.

My German, anyway, is coming on apace, and the Hong Kong-Shanghai beginning apparently placed the vowels and consonants correctly in my mouth. My reading-German has likewise so far improved that I can tear up and down Goethe and Thomas Mann and Freud like they was English.

I guess there's going to be a War soon. Italy had 500,000 men in manoevres in their northernmost mountains when I was there and now your Geneva[137] is on pins and needles. How you two must be watching that: the immense gain in prestige that is possible; the ir-

137 Catharine Kerlin Wilder (1906–2006) lived in Geneva from 1929 until 1933. She worked summers for the American Committee for the League of Nations and taught at the International School there. She met TNW's brother in Geneva.

reperable loss that is possible. Amputated, strangled Austria hasn't money enough to buy a cannon even, so the Austrians sit in cafés all day over one mokka and wax witty about dictators and empires. Delightful people with something both oriental and mediterranean in their attitude to leisure.

So you see there is no real news to tell you, but I send you my cordialest fraternal affection.

Ever

Thorny

142. TO HILDA DOOLITTLE.[138] ALS 4 pp. Yale

American Express Co.
Kärntnerring<Kärtnerring> 14
Vienna[I]
Oct 2. 1935

Dear H. D.:

I am a contrary erratic urchin. Scarcely had I arrived in town, (after some splendid Tyrolian hiking and some great music at Salzburg) and been given the heaping schlagobers[139] of Viennese hospitality, when I suddenly became a surly hermit and retired up here at the Hotel Cobenzl to work. It's not really to work, yet, but it's a mood, long walks in the autumnal woods, desultory reading of the Austrian classics—Grillparzer, Nestroy, Stifter[140]—and a pleasant non-dejected brooding. So I have not presented yet the letters you so thoughtfully enclosed.

---

138 Full name of American poet Doolittle (1886–1961), who used the pen name H. D. and was known for her interest in the Greek classics.

139 Viennese dialect: whipped cream.

140 Austrian dramatists Franz Grillparzer (1791–1872) and Johann Nestroy (1807–1862) and Austrian novelist Adalbert Stifter (1805–1868).

When in this solitude my inner monologue gets too loud and wants group-life again I shall descend from the hill and knock at doors again.

You ask which Greek plays America has had a look at in the last few years:
Sophocles' Oedipus Rex—bad productions every few years.

Sophocles'	Electra (Mrs Pat Campbell as Clytemnestra. Also Eugene O'Neils Mourning Becomes Electra which was immensely successful rehashed the whole Agamemnon subject-matter.)
Euripides'	Medea, given by both Blanche Yurka and Margaret Anglin. It is about to be revived with a fine negro actress as the wild woman from Colchis.
Euripides'	Trojan Women was given a few matinées by a Peace Propaganda Society.
	The Yale University Dramatic Society with a woman guest-star gave Hyppolitus (G. Murray) so well that there is talk of reviving it in New York but perhaps not.

The public must by now have forgotten Granville Barker's immense stadium productions (New York, Yale and Harvard) of The Trojan Women and Iphigenia in Tauris.

The Bacchae was a great success in two of the girls' colleges, but has not been seen in New York. The Lysistrata of Aristophanes ran for two years all over the country.

So: how about the Alcestis? or the Iphigenia in Aulus? or perhaps a new Hyppolitus.

I have seen Dr. Modern from time to time and always with pleasure. And she has been very helpful in finding a room for my friend, Robert Davis.

If I return by London or Paris, I shall look forward to some good talks, and the pleasure of reading your MS.

Ever Sincerely
Thornton Wilder

143. TO GERTRUDE STEIN AND ALICE B. TOKLAS. ALS 4 pp. Yale

American Exp Co Kärmtnerring<Kärtnerring> 14
WIEN[1]
Oct 14, 1935, a beautiful autumn afternoon.

Dear Friends:

So I shall see the Rue de Fleurus[141] at last and my friends in it. And the pictures around them.

I still don't know when. I beg you not to change your plans one jot—because I can come to you in either place perfectly well. I still haven't the faintest notion when I'm leaving here. There's so much in town here that vexes me, the kind assiduities of authors, playwrights and stage directors—such phone-calls, such<.> When can I talk to you about New York, and Perhaps you can tell me which are the best literary agents. Such meetings in café-houses. The way strangers call up and ask for an appointment is the limit. And even if I were hard as nails about putting them off what can I do, if at social gatherings every body wants to make an engagement for a good long talk, freighted with self-interest.

Excuse all this self-pity.

There are compensations. Prof Freud was told that I had expressed (under pressure, but certainly true) a wish to see him, and he asked me to go yesterday at 4:15 to his villa in Grinzing. I was all alone with him for an hour and a half, and it was fine. He's seventy nine. He talked of many things: "I don't do anything any more.... loss of interest... satiety...impotence." "The poet we call Shakespeare was the Earl of Oxford...the sonnets are addressed to Wriothesley who was about to marry Oxford's daughter when Oxford fell in love with him himself." "I could not read your latest book...I threw it away. Why should you treat of an American fanatic; that cannot be treated poetically." "My sister-in law admires your Cabala the most; I do not think so." (One of the characters makes a slighting reference to Freud in it!) "I am no

141 The rue de Fleurus is where Stein and Toklas lived in Paris.

seeker after God. I come of an unbroken line of infidel Jews. My father was a Voltairean. My mother was pious, and until 8 I was pious; but one day my father took me out for a walk in the Prater—I can remember it perfectly and explained to me that there was no way that we could <k>no<w> there was a God; that it didn't do any good to trouble one's head about such; but to live and do one's duty among one's fellow-men." "But I like gods" and he pointed to handsome cases and cases full of images—Greek, Chinese, African, Egyyptian—hundreds of images! "No, my work did not require any particular intellectual gifts—many people could have done it—the quality I had was courage. I was alone, and every discovery I made required courage. Yes, the courage to publish it, but first the courage to think it, to think along that line." "Just these last weeks I have found a formulierung[142] for religion." He stated it and I said I had gathered it already from the close of Totem and Tabu.[143] "Yes," he said, "it is there, but it is not expressed. Hitherto I have said that religion is an illusion; now I say it has a truth—it has an historical truth. Religion is the recapitulation and the solution of the problems of one's first four years that have been covered over by an amnesia." "No, I am as unmusical as I am unphilosophic." "My daughter Anna will be so sorry to have missed you. You can come again? She is older than you—you do not have to be afraid. She is a sensible reasonable girl. You are not afraid of women? She is a sensible—no nonsense about her. Are you married, may I ask?" !!!

Really a beautiful old man.

What a lucky boy am I. My cup runneth over.

For my own help and for the pleasure of it I have begun a vast apparatus of pencilled glosses on the margin of your MS; but I shall erase it all before you can see it.[144] That's the way I close in on it and really digest. And the more I see, the more I see. 'Küss' die Hand.[145]

Robert's German goes on like wild fire. He has started at the University. He is reading the book, slowly, intensely and devotedly. I hope

---

142 German: formulation.

143 Freud's *Totem and Taboo* (1913).

144 The manuscript was Stein's *The Geographical History of America or the Relation of Human Nature to the Human Mind* (1936), for which TNW wrote the introduction.

145 German: I kiss your hand.

he'll write you about it; but his awe of you and his distrust in himself have awful battles.

I have the courage to write, anyway—even if its such shifty, disorganized letters as these last. The trouble with me is that I can't be soul-happy outside of my beloved U.S.A and that's a fact. So I think I'm sailing from Havre or Southhampton on Nov. 2. But first I'll have five days in Paris and every day I'm going to pay a call on two of my most loved Americans in the world. Oh, say can you see what I mean. So again Küss<e> die Hand, Küsse die Hande Thornton

144. TO ALEXANDER WOOLLCOTT. ALS 8 pp. (Stationery embossed The Graduates Club / New Haven, Connecticut <heading crossed out by TNW>) Harvard

50 Deepwood Drive
Dec 1. 1935
second snowfall of the season,
Connecticut very beautiful.

Dear Alick:

It was a great disappointment to find you gone, disappointment that practically ran to grievance.

Lot of things that happen to me take a sheen on them from the thought that they can someday be recounted to you.

Yes, my encounters with Picasso and my conversations with Freud and my idolatry of Daisy Fellowes and my account of Colette disciplining her cat, and certain confidentialissima about Gertrude Stein,—all these things have begun to fester within me for lack of your sardonic receptivity.[146]

Joe Hennessy[147] tells me you'll be back in January. I'm afraid that by that time they will <have> acquired that patina of fiction which

---

146 Singer sewing machine heiress Daisy Fellowes (1890–1962) was a well-known fashionable socialite, and TNW is referring to Colette's novel *La Chatte* (1933).

147 Joseph Hennessey was Woollcott's adviser, manager, and closest friend.

Max Beerbohm, Alexander Woollcott, TNW.

pleases the undiscriminating,—the dinner table retellings before the unexacting have falsified the images. Only the very truth is good enough for you.

Anyway I'm so devoted to you that I think the stuff will be shocked into its pristine state for you.

My father is in extremis, surrounded by nurses.

Amos and his bride spent Th - ks - ng Day with us. Very happy.

Thursday afternoon I have been asked to tea with Eleanora von Mendelssohn[148] who has a project to propose.

---

148 Eleanora von Mendelssohn (1899–1951) was a German-born American actress.

I am writing a work of humor, and am rereading Frank Stockton.[149] Is he an emerging American classic?

G. Stein has written a very good book. I don't know yet whether it's a very great book. She does. Bennett Cerf[150] says the rewards of her previous ones were so slender that he doesn't dare publish this one ("The Geographical History of America, or the Relations between Human Nature and the Human Mind".) Gertrude and Daisy Fellowes and P. Picasso (and Bennett Cerf) want it to be published with the text on one side and my explanatory marginalia on the other, reproduced in my own handwriting. I don't want to do that. It's true that I can clarify many an apparently willful inanity and (by the help of those wonderful conversations show it to be brilliant phrasing and thinking, but there are long stretches I cannot; and its those stretches where the pretentious explicator ought to be strong<)>.

Sybil says that a number of Noël's plays are very fine indeed.

I've been reading all your Reader, with great pleasure and your afterwords are happy as they can be, esp. the one about me.[151]

¶ Forgive me, but Lynne Fontaine is all wrong about Katharina.[152] Slight as Shakespeare's drawing may appear it has richer implications than that. (signed: Prof. Wilder.)

Give my best to Scrivener Brown;[153] and come back to a great big bear's hug from your unestrangeaballe

devoted

Thornton

---

149 Stockton (1834–1902) was an American novelist, short story writer, and editor.

150 Cerf (1898–1971) was the cofounder of Random House, Stein's U.S. publisher.

151 *The Woollcott Reader: Bypaths in the Realms of Gold* (1935), a literary anthology, included TNW's *The Happy Journey to Trenton and Camden.*

152 Lynn Fontanne played Katharina in a production of Shakespeare's *The Taming of the Shrew* that ran in New York between September 1935 and January 1936.

153 H. Leggett Brown was Woollcott's secretary.

145. TO SIBYL COLEFAX. ALS 2 pp. NYU

50 Deepwood Drive
New Haven Conn.
Jan 23rd 1936

Dear Sybil:

Your letter was so good and interesting that I want to answer it at once.

I saw Aleck yesterday. He went off the air because his sponsors objected to his discussing "controversiable subjects," meaning sundry polysyllabic slurs on Hitler and Mussolini.[154] Aleck refused to promise to restrain himself and his contract was not renewed. He devoted his last broadcast to a fiery discussion of Free Speech. He became increasingly conscious of his vast audience (he let fall casually the words "eight million") and was moving more and more into pathos, moral indignation and the righting of wrongs. He espoused the 'Seeing Eye' (training dogs for the blind); then a certain lady who collected cast off spectacles to distribute among the poor (his announcement of this good work practically crippled the postal service on Long Island); then poor Mr. Lampson, an administrator of Stanford University in California whose wife slipped and drowned herself in the bath, but who was sentenced to die for her murder.

His next book however will belie all this ethical responsibility. It will be called the Brotherhood of the French Poodle Owners, and will treat of Graham Robinson and his Mouton, Booth Tarkington and his Figaro, Gertrude Stein and her Basket, and himself and his Pip. He may be flying abroad in a few weeks to gather material for this work; if you see him, pretend that this is news to you.

The dejections of the Summer are all over, and he says that he never felt better in his life.

---

154 From 1929 to 1942, Alexander Woollcott hosted "Town Crier," a fifteen-minute weekly CBS radio show. When Cream of Wheat, Woollcott's sponsor, did not renew his contract because of his criticism of Hitler and Mussolini, CBS persuaded Woollcott to stay on until they found another sponsor.

Two weeks ago I went to Philadelphia to be by at the opening of "Ethan Frome." It was like a big three-day house party at the Hotel Ritz. Conversation until half past three every night. Pauline Lord, Ruth Gordon, Raymond Massey, Keith Winter, Helen Hayes' mother, Guthrie McClintic (who staged it) and K. Cornell, vacationing between Juliet and Joan.[155] The atmosphere was one of an assured success, since justified by the opening in New York two days ago. Ruth was sublime: every year sees the approach to final triumph of intelligence, will and character over a host of disadvantages. The disadvantages were voice, appearance, lack of a sense of "dress", undependable taste arising from her environment when a girl, and the heart-wrenching and career-blocking association to Jed. All New York giggled fifteen years ago when she forced a doctor to break her knees in order to straighten her legs; well, it's a sample, anyway, of the incredible determination. Fortunately, on top of it she has genius and intelligence. Within five years she'll be the first actress here. Its Mrs Fiske, over again. It's Rejane.[156]

I no longer get much pleasure from theatre-going but I never get tired of the atmosphere about theatres. The only other occasion that rivaled the Philadelphia visit was a hotel-house-party at Atlantic City surrounding the try-out of Mr. Gilhooly[157] of Liam O'Flaherty: Helen Hayes, Charlie McArthur, Aleck Woollcott and Jed. Jed was then worth two million, insolent and brilliant. Charlie the greatest raconteur of dreadful long macabre stories of Chicago gangster death cells (and of the vie amoureuse[158] of David Belasco); and all the while Aleck brilliant and waspish with envy of the only two better talkers than himself in America. Very funny.

In two weeks I say goodbye to the family for a long time: two

---

155 *Ethan Frome* had been in tryouts in Philadelphia before opening in New York on January 21. Lord, Gordon, and Massey were in the cast. Katharine Cornell had just appeared in *Romeo and Juliet* in New York and would star in George Bernard Shaw's *Saint Joan*, scheduled to open in March.

156 Minnie Maddern Fiske (1865–1932) was one of the leading American actresses of the late nineteenth and early twentieth century. Gabrielle Réjane (1857–1920) was an equally famous actress on the French stage in the same era.

157 *Mr. Gilhooley*, a play by Frank B. Elser, based on O'Flaherty's 1926 novel, had been in tryouts before opening in New York in October 1930.

158 French: love life.

months' lecture-tour and then teaching at Chicago the whole Spring and Summer Quarters. The tour is an ignoble affair: I no longer believe what I say, no longer "hear" what I say. The only thing to my credit is that I manage to get through the tour without saying Capital I. The travelling involved is wonderful to me; I take endless long walks in the suburbs of the cities. This trip carries me all the way to Los Angeles and brings me two new cities, Tulsa, Oklahoma, and Salt Lake City, Utah.

The Hutchins Christmas card: MPMH is Mrs Hutchin<s>, Maude Phelps McVeigh. She comes of the McVeighs of Virginia, a line of thrilling distinction she often tells us. The angel on the card was colored by her daughter Franja, aetat circa VIII.

> (Boston Jan. 28 • 1936. Up here a few days to see my brother and new sister; and to take long walks through old streets and to see the Museum which is incandescent with Van Der Weyden's St. Luke painting the Virgin)

Thanks for the suggestion of Miss Bowen's A House in Paris.[159] I shall get to it right off.

Broadway theatre is being described by its admirers as being "at its best" this year. I havent seen many of its successes. At Helen Hayes' Victoria the box office feels itself insulted if one asks for a ticket before April.[160] The wonder child of promise, Clifford Odett's looked long at Chekhov and confused the Russian diffuseness with Jewish nervous-system fever. He offers the tableau as a demonstration of the spiritual bankruptcy of the American Middle Class. Bankrupt we may be, but our symptoms aren't the same as those in the Gordon Family of "Paradise Lost."[161] At the final curtain there is his customary motto-speech to the effect that none of the exhibited anguishes would be possible under the communist state. Well, Leopardi[162] in his journals, after hearing some Utopians talk all night wrote: "I seemed to hear them claim

---

159 Elizabeth Bowen's *The House in Paris* (1935).

160 Hayes appeared in *Victoria Regina* (1934), by Laurence Housman, from December 1935 to June 1936.

161 Clifford Odets's *Paradise Lost* (1935) ran in New York from December 1935 to February 1936.

162 Italian poet Giacomo Leopardi (1798–1837), author of *Pensieri* (1845).

that out of a million contented citizens they could be sure of a million happy souls." (I thanked you before, I hope, for calling my attention to the Marchesa Origo's book[163] and the reading that flowed from it.)

Jed has sent me Elizabeth Femme sans Homme. I am to report with the speed of light whether I think he ought to produce it. Dull scenes up until 10:15 and then two very interesting scenes, too interesting, illegitimately interesting.[164]

Your description of Sacha Guitry's collection of letters[165] is enough to make one weep. And the abbé Mugnier, too.[166]

Forgive these loose jottings. I'll hope to do better on the tour.

Ever devotedly
Thornton

146. TO CHARLOTTE E. WILDER. Wire 1 p. Yale

CHICAGO ILL MAR 22 <1936>

MISS CHARLOTTE WILDER=
313 WEST 25 ST=
DEAR SHARLIE I THINK ITS SPLENDID POWERFUL AND GLORIOUSLY ORIGINAL HAVE NO QUALMS HOMAGE AND CONGRATULATIONS=[167]
THORNTON.

---

163 Iris Origo (1902–1988), author of *Leopardi: A Study in Solitude* (1935).

164 Harris did not produce *Elizabeth la Femme Sans Homme,* by André Josset.

165 TNW may be referring to Guitry's memoir *If Memory Serves* (1935).

166 TNW is undoubtedly referring to the diary of the French cleric Abbé Arthur Mugnier (1853–1944). Mugnier's diary covers the years 1879–1939 and offers portraits of such literary figures as Marcel Proust, Anatole France, and Jean Cocteau.

167 Charlotte Wilder's first book of poetry, *Phases of the Moon,* was published in 1936; it was the cowinner of the Poetry Society of America's Shelley Memorial Award.

147. TO ALEXANDER WOOLLCOTT. ALS 4 pp. Harvard

6020 Drexel
<Chicago>
Aug 15 • 1936
Lost my fountain-pen

Dear Alick:

I love you.

Troubling and preposterous fact.

But human nature being what it is, candor compels me to add that I love you for what you can do for me.

The soul of man is a sink-hole of greed, self-interest and malice.

But let us at least confess it and by robbing it of its deceptions, so rob it of half its terrors

As Edmund Burke said.

Today, I love you wolfishly because I have just rec'd my royalties from the Woollcott Reader and they're enormous.

Can I lend you some, by any chance? Can I put you under obligation—to me in anyway? Just write me—simply and without hesitation—if I can.

MGM says it won't invite me unless I promise to come for more than six weeks. So I said until Dec 5.

What do you suppose it is? Pride and Prejudice for Norma Shearer? There are rumors of a Benjamin Franklin for Charles Laughton.[168]

Oh, Aleck. I suddenly remembered your jacket. I've got the string—and I'll get the box and paper Monday. Don't be mad. All will end well.

I was sublime on the two Oedipuses the other day—sublime.

These last months I've been as happy; what do you suppose it is? Do you suppose the approach of forty is bringing me to my natural age? All my friends are nail-biting, full of alarms and most of them have cause; Spain and England are in a bad way; Germany and Italy are

---

168 TNW did not return to Hollywood at this time. Norma Shearer never made a screen version of *Pride and Prejudice*; nor did Charles Laughton ever play Benjamin Franklin in a film.

enjoying the brutish state of cattle—but nothing casts me down. I even enjoy my thoughts. Chicago—the only oceanic city in the world—is very beautiful these days.

It just occured to me: Perhaps its God!

If I count you not among my chiefest joys may my right hand lose it's cunning.

Yr. devoted and cunning
Thornton

148. TO JANET F. WILDER. ALS 4 pp. Yale

Port Castries
St. Lucia
British West Indies[169]
Nov. 16 • 1936

Dear Janet:

It's beautiful here. Tropics—mahogonany, banyan, iguanas, mangoes, volcanoes, beautiful seas, noble blacks.

So hot that I can't take very many of my long-walks.

Everywhere ants. Millions of 'em.

Sea-bathing is overrated; water so tepid. I yearn for the slap of a cold wave. Oh, to look at a snowflake.

How are you, sweetness?

At St Thomas in the Virgin Islands where I spent four weeks, there was a Miss Lilienfeld, official geneticist to the Emperor of Japan. She works on the exceptions to Mendel's Law. Do you find her name in your learnéd journals?[170]

Dearie, in the Virgin Islands the early Danish planters introduced the Mongoose to kill the snakes, which they did. They also tormented

---

169 TNW had sailed for the Caribbean on October 9.

170 TNW's sister was studying for her Ph.D. in zoology at the University of Chicago.

the rats which promptly took to the trees and have ever since made their homes up among the coconuts. The mongooses also killed off most of the birds. On Dominica the planters introduced the fer-de-lance so that their slaves would not run away into the bush. Now the fer-de-lance abound and the planters' children sitting in the public park with their governesses are bitten and die. MORAL: do not interfere in nature's ecological equilibrium rashly.

I arrive in NY Nov. 30; Dec 6–10 at Berea; then Chicago.[171] Save me a meal.

I miss Chicago and the campus, honey, and you in the middle of it. Whatjadooin? Are you well? Are you heart-whole? I feel a thousand miles away; I don't even know if you've received yet the inheritance of your pa. Lordy, if you get much richer you'll be wearing evening gowns by day. ¶ Give my best to Gladys;[172] keep some of the Fine Arts ventilating your scientific life; when you're hesitating as to whether to buy a new dress or hat, swallow hard and do it. ¶ My love to the Lillies.[173]

It won't do any good to answer this letter because I'll be there in no time and will wring more facts out of you than you would choose to put down on paper.

Be gentle as the serpent and wise as the dove. Like the Bible says.

Your
Thornton

171 TNW was going to Berea College in Kentucky, where he had spent the summer of 1917 working on the farm there, to visit Robert Maynard Hutchins's parents, William J. Hutchins, the president of Berea, and his wife. William J. Hutchins had been a professor of homiletics at Oberlin College when TNW and Robert Maynard Hutchins were students there, and TNW often visited the Hutchins's home during that time.

172 Gladys Campbell (1892–1992), a student of TNW's in Chicago, was an educator and a poet, taught at the University of Chicago and at the University of Chicago Laboratory School, and presided over a poetry club in Chicago that TNW attended.

173 Ralph S. and Helen M. Lillie (see letter number 116).

149. TO ISABELLA N. WILDER AND ISABEL WILDER. ALS 4 pp. Yale

Hotel Buckingham 43 rue
des Mathurins. <Paris>
July 20 • 1937

Dear Ones:

Imagine!

Meetings opened today. The morning was devoted to a very French Ouverture Solennelle. A ministre; Herriot; compliments and abstract nouns.[174]

After a great luncheon given by the secretary-Adjoint of the League at the Grand Hotel, we returned to begin the real work.

Scarcely had an hour gone by when a secretary whispered to me: "M. le Président (Paul Valéry) espère que vous prendrez la parole après M. de Madariaga."[175]

It was about language and the American enormities had been touched upon.

I spoke and though it was against the rules of the conference I was applauded!

It was a Defense of the American Language. The entirely different psychological character of the American has led to a long struggle to refashion a language that was built up over centuries to describe another type entirely. I gave some illustrations of these profound differences and when I struck off the formula: "an Englishman hopes that tomorrow will be like today, though a little better; an American even when he's happy hopes that tomorrow will be very different from

174 TNW replaced Frederick Paul Keppel, president of the Carnegie Corporation, as the American delegate to the Second General Conference of National Committees for Intellectual Cooperation of the League of Nations, which met in Paris in July 1937. Edouard Herriot (1872–1957) had served three terms as premier of France, the last of which was in 1932.

175 Spanish diplomat, historian, and writer Salvador de Madariaga y Rojo (1886–1978). French: "The President (Paul Valéry) hopes that you will speak after Mr. Madariaga."

today."—then, Mr. Gilbert Murray[176] and "Passage to India" Forster were delighted and M. Valéry turned with pleased surprised<surprise> to his right and his left.

Anyway, all the ideas were Gertrude's.

At six o'clock, reception and sit down buffet with champagne at the Hotel de Ville, and speech from the Mayor. We sign the livre d'or de Paris.[177]

Tomorrow lunch at the Ministère des Affaires Etrangères.[178] As for me, I'm a boy that likes champagne.

Delightful time at our end of the table at lunch today: M. Oprescu, Prof of history of art at Bukharest; Paul Hazard of the Collége de France (a charmer)<;> Dr. Yu Ying, of the Univ. of Peking, and a Signor Pavolini, president of the Fascist Confederation of Artists and Writers, who was given my book by his best friend on the very day that friend was to be killed in the Abyssinian War!!! We had a dandy time over that succession of wines and were very witty indeed.

I had a good long heart-to-heart tea with Sibyl at Armenonville in the Bois; then she took the train back to London and work, work, work.

This year the only fault with Paris is that I don't sleep very well.

Now I go out every night at twelve and get a tisane. Mother, Isabel—make yourself a tilleul[179] out of that box up in my study window.

¶ The only people who looked sour at my offering today were Mssrs Jules Romains and Georges Duhamel.[180] Je m'en fiche.[181]

I'll hope<hold> my tongue all tomorrow and then speak again on Thursday.

---

176 Gilbert Murray (1866–1957), British classical scholar.

177 French: the golden book of Paris (the official guest book in the City Hall).

178 French: Foreign Affairs Ministry.

179 French: lime-blossom tea.

180 Romains (1885–1972) was a French novelist, dramatist, and poet; Duhamel (1884–1966) was a French dramatist, novelist, critic, and poet.

181 French: I couldn't care less.

Ran across Malcolm Cowley in the American Express and took him to a meeting. Awfully nice fellow. Had been down to Madrid.

More soon.
Haven't I been good about writing?
Thine
Thornton

Mme Bousquet of the enclosure is the Lady Colefax of Paris. Great friend of Proust, Anatole France and Henri de Régnier.[182]

150. TO ISABEL WILDER. ALS 6 pp. Yale

Poste Restante Salzburg
Aug. 25 • 1937

Dear Isabello:

Got your letters an hour ago—you know, the Post Office by the Cathedral.

Telegraphed you both to come over.

Why not?

Some rooms in a little pension; by the Riviera. Cheap. Sunlight. Walks. Make Ma work hard at French. Make Ma loaf. Little train trips up and down the little coast. Would even help my work.

If Ma resists leaving the house you might come for two months to a Zurich pension.

Sure.

If I get a telegram from you favorable, I telegraph Fritz Wiggin to release you all due moneys and don't skimp. Be comfortable.

And don't think its chilly of me if I don't come to Paris to meet, that's all. I'll wait for you anywhere else, but I won't go to Paris.

---

182 Marie-Louise Bousquet, a journalist famous for her artistic salon, was the editor of the French edition of *Harper's Bazaar.* Régnier (1864–1936) was a French Symbolist poet.

Now rê Situation.[183]

Your shock will have 3 phases:

① To pride.

② To your View of your Future.

③ Real affection.

Only the third is worth suffering.

Separate the strands and stamp on the first two.

Suffer the third, purely and honestly until it gets done with.

The Second:

Again separate 2 strands.

Don't overdo that notion that a woman has nothing to say or be or give unless she's wife-mother-and-home-decorator.

We're all People, before we're anything else. People, even before we're artists. The rôle of being a Person is sufficient to have lived and died for.

Don't insult ten million women by saying a woman is null and void as a spinster.

You say you're old plain and poor.

A. You're not old. Rhetoric. Self-pity; Old is not a term of disparagement even if you were old. A woman of 36[184] is old only <on> the verandah of a country-club dance. And only there.

B. You've not only an attractive characteristic extraordinar<i>ly like-yourself face, but you have the mysterious gift of dressing to it, realizing it. When you enter a room the others are every time arrested, charmed & engaged afresh over your delightful presence and its delicate harmony with your personality.

If you want to see some women cursed with plainness I'll show you some.

So Ⓑ is theatrical. Rhetoric self-pity.

POOR? Think it over. Yes and no. And Yes because you allow it to gnaw you.

---

183 TNW is referring to the unhappy end of a romance in which Isabel had been involved.

184 When this letter was written, Isabel was thirty-seven, not thirty-six.

The Scotty business.

Lots of its Pathological.

Does pathological mean that anyone's to blame?

He's a big healthy male? Why isn't he married?

What's he do about sex and the owning-four-walls instinct?

Believe me: There's a psychic fear of going thru with a thing. He's ill.

And you, too. From some deep infantile Father-love-and-hate you brought up a lack-of-confidence in that realm that colored the air without you're knowing it.

Otherwise a Command would have shone through you.

What of it?

Out of these infantile conditionings we make our strengths as well as our weaknesses.

In the long run its not important.

The Self is more important then the Social or Amatory situation; more important than hereditary obstructions.

Digest the experience by reasoning; accept the suffering insofar as it is not crossed will and false pride—convalesce and start thinking of other things.

I'm writing a letter to Ma at the same time about Salzburg. It would look bloodless to put that into this same letter. Read her the first page of this.

As for Insomnia: don't try to fight. Relax. Read a little. Play solitaire. Keep your thoughts of<f> thatta.

Better take a trip to Europe. There's plenty of money.

love!!!

Thornton

Gertrude Stein and TNW.

151. TO GERTRUDE STEIN AND ALICE B. TOKLAS. ALS 4 pp. Yale

Poste Restante Salzburg
Aug 26 • 1937

Dear Endeared Dears:

So at last I decided to buy some stationery and resume correspondence.

I've changed unrecognizably.

For the worse.

I've decided to live entirely for pleasure.

Yes.

Never try to think again. Never try to write again. Just pleasure.

The other night after a performance of Falstaff, wonderful, too, I went, as one must, to the Mirabell Bar. Went into the Casino and gambled a little, così cosà,[185] then sat drinking and talking with friends until the Bar closed. No one wanted to go home; so we went, as all true Dedicated Drinkers must after curfew, to the IIIrd Class waiting-room at the Railway Station, and there we sat until eight in the morning. The party was slightly mixed. It consisted of Erich Maria Remarque, the author of "All Quiet on the Western Front," and Carl Zuckmayer, author of Der Hamptmann von Köpernick, an elegant play; and a wonderful German Archbishop—incognito and in civil—on obligatory vacation; and Frau Tal,[186] my German publisher; and a Swedish streetwalker. Just us. At 4:45 every morning Mass is read in the Station for the line workers, and the Host was solemnly carried among the outstretched legs of us dogs, no disrespect to Pépé.[187]

Pleasure comes in all shapes and sizes and its now what I live for. For instance: there are two polychrome baroque archangels on the altar of the Peterskirche in poses of flight and ecstacy that no human body could ever assume, and as far as I'm concerned they're my definition of ART. For instance: the meals in Austria are deplorable, deplorable, but the Sacher-torte and the cup of chocolate that goes with it at the Café Tomaselli (founded 1704—Mozart as <a> child, played with the little Tomaselli's and no doubt lingered about when the cakes came out of the oven)—pleasure, that's what they are, pleasure, and that's what I live for.

After the close of the Festival on the 31st I'm going to linger in town a week.

Do you think I will ever regain my Former Viewpoint?

Anyway New or Old I count you among my Pleasures, and that's what I live for.

Your
Thornton

185 TNW no doubt meant the Italian *così così*: so-so.

186 Lucy Tal was the wife of TNW's first German publisher.

187 Stein's and Toklas's Chihuahua.

152. TO ISABELLA N. AND ISABEL WILDER. ALS 4 pp. Yale

American Express Co. Zurich
Wed 11:20 A.M. Sept 15th or 16th 1937

Dear Ones:

In an hour or two I'm taking a train for Sils Maria or Sils-Berseglia (the sunny side). I get to St. Moritz at about half past 6: tonight. Lord, I was almost chilled off the whole excursion when I found I had to pass thru St Moritz and probably spend the night there. However, a good 3rd class pass. I'll go to the whatever-little-hotel by the Station, honey. You know me. Anyway this is the "Worst Season" of the year for St. Moritz, tho' the most beautiful.

Kinder,[188] I've finished the Second Act of Our Town and its just lovely, as is the opening of Act III. I'm just a dandy dramatist, looks like.

What do you think of this enclosure?[189] If the fella who had been collecting Reinhardt statistics five years ago had seen that he'd have fainted dead away.

Ma, there's simply nothing doing in my life, but I'm—there's only one word to describe it—happy. Now isn't that funny. I do an hour's work every morning, like silk off a spool and then I mosey the rest of the day. Walks toward all parts of the town and country; its a darlin restful place. To be sure it rains most of the time, but don't wet much. Swiss rain's different.

And I take it back that there are no mts here—they're at the other end of the lake and they're awfully big they shock you, they look so big, but they aren't in sight much of the time.

Seems like I'll finish Our Town by Friday and then I'll polish up Nestroy-Molière for Reinhardt. (If Jed hears about that, he'll be terrific.) Then I do the Prince of Baghdad which is the best of em all and

---

188 German: Children.

189 The enclosure has not survived.

the minute I finish that I'll get on a boat and come home to you, everything forgiven.[190]

Stay just as sweet as you are, because that's the way echoes of you are all thru the play and I don't want to find that its unhistorical. Sure, one remark esp. that you made to us years ago is in the Second Act and it radiates the whole play.

Your loving son
Thornton

153. TO ISABELLA N. AND ISABEL WILDER. APCS. Yale

In the Post office, Zürich.
Thursday night. Oct 28 • 1937

Dear Girls:

Saturday night I leave for four nights in Paris to confer with Jed. Jed telephoned from London for 20 minutes the other night. He wants to know if "Our Town" would be a good play for the Xmas season in New York. Would it?!! And guess who might act the lanky tooth picking Stage-manager? Sinclair Lewis! He's been plaguing Jed to let him act for a long time; and there's a part for his famous New England parlor-trick monologues.[191] Don't tell anybody anything about it, but Ma, would you like to file into a New York Theatre with me to see Our Town—think it over. ¶ Heavenly autumnal weather here.

love to all
Thorny.

---

190 "Nestroy-Molière" refers to TNW's reworking of Johann Nestroy's play *Einen Jux will er sich machen* into his play *The Merchant of Yonkers,* which also included TNW's reworking of a scene from French dramatist Molière's 1668 play *L'Avare (The Miser).* "The Prince of Baghdad" refers to a play TNW worked on throughout the rest of the 1930s; it has not survived.

191 At social gatherings, Lewis enjoyed impersonating people by performing mimicking monologues.

154. TO MAX REINHARDT. ALS 3 pp. (Stationery embossed Century Club / 7 West Forty-Third Street / New York) Theatermuseum

As from: 50 Deepwood Drive
New Haven, Conn.
Dec. 9 • 1937

Dear Prof. Reinhardt:

Just before Miss Adler called me up in Zürich I had been to Paris for a few days and there read to Jed Harris one of the two plays that I had been working on since the Summer. It goes into rehearsal next week and as it is still not yet quite finished, he has installed, or rather imprisoned me, in a house on Long Island and the work will be finished in a few days.

All this arose much earlier than I had intended and is now delaying further my opportunity to finish the play based on Nestroy's Einen Jux will er sich machen.

My plan is to go away—possibly to Tucson, Arizona,—and finish it, as soon as "Our Town" opens in New York, which will be around New Year. How long that will take I do not know but I should think about a month.

It is still the height of my ambition that it would interest you.

As I told you in Salzburg, it is in no sense a translation. My second most important character does not appear in Nestroy at all. Into the middle of the First Act I have inserted the wonderful scene from Molière's L'Avare where Frosine the marriage-broker tries to interest Harpagon in a young girl.[192]

I told Jed Harris firmly that you were to have the first "refusal" of the play, but I asked him to give me some help and advice on a certain difficulty I had met in the Third Act. To prepare him for it I read him the Second Act which he said was "a perfect piece of farce-comedy writing."

At all events, I have grown very fond of it and am very impatient to resume work. If you liked I could send you the first Two Acts by

---

192 As reflected in the play's title, TNW considered Horace Vandergelder the most important character in *The Merchant of Yonkers* and Mrs. Levi the second most important.

January first; but I presume that you would rather receive the whole at one time.

Naturally, I may be mistaken about my fitness to write that kind of play; but I will never lose my desire of being some day able to offer you a text which it will interest you enough to produce.

Kindly give my regards to Frau Reinhardt.

Very sincerely yours
Thornton Wilder

155. TO J. DWIGHT DANA. ALS 4 pp. Private

Two days in New Haven.
Monday Dec 20 1937

Dear Dwight:

Theatre business is funny.

Especially Jed's.

Went out to Chicago and saw 3 performances of Doll's House. Enormous Opera-House packed with people.

Yet Jed's losing money. 2 of the 4 stars are getting a thousand a week and percentages. Some performances (Mon & Tues. nights) sink to gross of 1100.

Jed says I get $150 a week, but it's still to come—retrospective, too, on 10 weeks of tour.[193]

As to the new play, he mentions the (Dramatist Guild's) contract; but still no contract.

I feel partly responsible for the delays because the play up until yesterday was still not all written.

---

193 TNW's translation of Henrik Ibsen's *A Doll's House,* drawn heavily from German sources and starring Ruth Gordon, had its premiere performance at the Central City (Colorado) Opera House on July 17, 1937, followed in the fall by a successful thirteen-week pre–New York tour that ended in Chicago. During its run, it was described not as a translation or adaptation but as a "new acting version." TNW was paid eventually.

He's undoubtedly in money-trouble but:

It doesn't prevent him from snatching me off the dock and imprisoning me in a cottage on Long Island—swankiest section, Roslyn and Cold Spring Valley—to finish the play.[194] Butler and Cook and everything.

Theatre business is funny.

Frank Craven, our "star" has a contract, but I haven't.[195]

However, I'll insist on it from the first day of rehearsals—presumably after two postponements—the middle of this week.

I now live in New York at the Columbia University Club—(circa 6) West 43rd St.

I realize that all this contract delay is highly irregular, but I'm in such of <a> mess of friendship-collaboration sentiment with Jed, and with the sense of guilt about the unfinished condition of the play that I can't pull myself together to insist.

One way would have been to have asked Harold Freedman of Brandt & Brandt to serve as agent, but that would have hurt Jed's feelings mighty bad.

There's a possibility that the play will be a smashing success—an old theatre-hand like Frank Craven seems to be thinking so.

Maybe not.

In the meantime Max Reinhardt in California telegraphs all the time to see play No #2—also still unfinished.

So I guess I'll be financially all right if I can tide over this interium—including the various cheques I'll have to draw for Xmas favors.

The Austrian Govt came through with that 56 dollars.

Enclosed the recipes for Mrs. Dana. Alice Toklas "prepared" one whole dinner. They look mighty elaborate to me; but good. And look at the extravagant materials they require. With the exception of the salad which is creole, they are old French family "secret cuisine." The

---

194 TNW completed the manuscript of *Our Town* on Long Island, but he continued rewrites during rehearsals in New York.

195 Craven played the lead role of the Stage Manager in the premiere production of *Our Town,* produced and directed by Jed Harris, which played in New York for 336 performances between February and November 1938. TNW signed the production contract on January 12, 1938, ten days before the play opened at the McCarter Theatre in Princeton, New Jersey.

typist unfortunately bound them up in the wrong order—straighten'm out and it's a dinner.

Until I can get the exact address for the Columbia U. Club I get my mail in NY at the ΑΔΦ Club 136 W. 44th St.

I got so many irons in the fire that here's hoping one of them pans out o.k.

Cordially ever
Thornton

P.S. Of course I won't sign the contract until I've sent it down to you.

156. TO GRACE CHRISTY FORESMAN. ACS 2 pp. (Card embossed A MERRY CHRISTMAS / AND / A HAPPY NEW YEAR) Yale

<P.M. December 20, 1937>

Dear Grace:

Just returned from the most rewarding trip I ever made abroad, to find myself in a turmoil of work: my own play goes into rehearsal next week—after divers rewritings I am doing every day—; and my adaptation of A Doll's House opens Dec. 27 with continuous conferences and alterations.[196]

So I can only steal a few minutes to send you again all my most cordial greetings. Another year has gone by without my being able to go to Oberlin. I'd love to see every inch of it again and especially with Emily pointing out her favorite places and naming the new ones.

We're all well. My niece, Amos's little Catherine, is her grandmother's joy as well as everybody's.[197] Charlotte stays in N.Y. working on some vast novel we're not allowed to see. Isabel'<s> found a good

196 TNW's version of *A Doll's House* opened in New York on December 27 and played for 144 performances, closing in May 1938.

197 Catharine Dix Wilder was born on January 31, 1937.

reception for her 3rd.[198] Janet is at the University of Chicago, all absorbed in Biology and moving on to a PhD. Mama doesn't look a day older to me; but she claims she's an old lady. She's active and diverted, and still serves as dog on whom her writing children (Charlotte excepted) try their stuff.

The summer abroad taught me regular work and solitude. I was 2½ months in a little hotel five <miles from?> Zürich.

And as soon as the present flurry is over I'm going to try and recreate the same hideaway somewhere in America: Quebec or Arizona, and write plays #3 and #4.[199] (No #2 is practically finished and Max Reinhardt is very interested in it.)

I hope you're all fine, and would love to hear from you on the details. I thought of you all with particuliar affection when I spent a day in Lawrenceville last Spring. It takes an hour or two to recover our Lawrenceville among the smart new buildings and plantings but it's there... and especially in the Chapel.

My new play is full of the sentiment of past time and old friends—though it's laid in a New Hampshire village—and I think you'll like it. I'm not having it published for the general public until I've done a lot more; but I shall probably have a number of copies printed off for my friends, and I specially hope it will give you pleasure.[200]

All my best to your household; my deepest interest and affection to Emily; and I hope you'll think of me always as

Your devoted friend
Thornton

---

198 Charlotte Wilder's novel was never published and it has not survived. Isabel Wilder's third novel, *Let Winter Go*, was published in September 1937.

199 TNW frequently changed the titles of his play projects as well as the numbering of them when he referred to them in his correspondence. Play "#3" may be the one variously referred to as "Haroun al-Raschid," "Arabian Nights," "The Diamond of Baghdad," "The Prince of Baghdad," and "The Hell of the Vizier Kabäar." The latter survives as an incomplete holograph manuscript, dated 1937. Play "#4" may refer to "Homage to P. G. Wodehouse," act 1 of which survives in two versions in holograph manuscript, dated 1952–1953; or it may refer to an early outline of what became *The Alcestiad, or A Life in the Sun* (1955). The evolution of this latter play can be traced from undated fragments in holograph notebooks to the corrected typescripts (dated 1955), all of which survive in the Beinecke Library at Yale University, as do all the other manuscript materials mentioned above.

200 This limited edition of *Our Town* was never published.

157. TO SIBYL COLEFAX. ALS 8 pp. (Stationery embossed Century Club / 7 West Forty-third Street / New York) NYU

January 2 • 1938
(the first time I've written the date of the new year.)

Dear Sibyl:

Day after day has gone by and I've kept putting off my report of these new developements.

The first thing to tell is that On the Whole everything has been pleasant, exciting and friendly.

There was one night when under an angry insomnia I planned a long letter, practically withdrawing my play from the producer's hands; but the thoughts of 3:00 a.m are very unreasonable things and in the morning I knew it had been nonsense.

Jed had made some admirable alterations in the order of the scenes, and some deletions that I would have arrived at anyway, and proposed the writing of a transitional episode that seems quite right. He has inserted a number of tasteless little jokes into the web, but they don't do much harm and they give him that sensation of having written the play which is so so important to him. The main tendency of his treatment is to make the play "smoother" and more civilized, and the edge of boldness is being worn down, that character of a "primitive" with its disdain of lesser verisimilitude; but I guess the play remains bold enough still.

Rehearsals began last Wednesday. (today is Sunday). When the actors (sitting about a table) first read the Third Act to one another they all wept so that pauses had to be made so that they could collect themselves. Frank Craven will be superb as the Stage-manager; and he loves the part. The chief danger is that the mothers are being played by experienced and well-known "character women" who seem unable to get the dry understatement of a New Hampshire housewife. They drip sweetness, and cannot understand anything between the extremes of nagging mean old rural women and ministring angels. Jed keeps saying: "No, darling, <u>dryer</u>, <u>dryer</u>."[201]

We're having trouble putting the Second Act ("Love and Mar-

---

201 Mrs. Gibbs was played by Evelyn Varden; Mrs. Webb was played by Helen Carew.

riage") into good shape. The difficulty doesn't seem to be where I expected it: in the wedding ceremony and the "hallucinatory" episodes, but in the scenes that lead up to it. Undoubtedly that Act is the least solid of the three; but it has some good moments. It now opens thus:

Stage manager Three years have gone by in Grover's Corners.

Yes, the sun's come up over a thousand times.

Winters and Summer<s> have cracked the mountain a little more and the rains have brought some of the dirt down into the valley.

Some children who weren't born before have begun to speak regular sentences; and a few people who thought they were mighty young and spry have found they can't bound up a flight of stairs like they use-ta, without their heart flutterin' a little.

Some older sons are settin' at the head of the table; and some people I know are now having their meat cut up for them.

All that can happen in a thousand days.

Nature's been pushing and contriving in other ways, too. Yes, the mountain's been reduced a few fractions of an inch; and millions of gallons of water have gone by the mill; and some young people have fallen in love, and got married, and here and there a new home has been set up under a roof.

Almost everybody in the world gets married,—you know what I mean? In our town there aren't hardly any exceptions. Almost everybody climbs into their grave married."[202]

etc. etc.

That's setting it in the frame of "cosmic reference", yes?

---

202 TNW made slight revisions in the text of *Our Town* before publishing it.

The opening night of Doll's House was very brilliant, Attention close; applause emphatic. Jed disappeared and I went home with Ruth (ushered from the theatre by two detectives, because of an autograph-crowd at the stage-door) in a taxi loaded with boxes of flowers.

All the signs of a smash.

So everybody was surprised to find a very mixed reception in the press. Some said Ibsen's stage technique creaked; some that Ruth had not been able to harmonize the frivolous Norah at the beginning with the raisonneuse[203] Norah at the close.

But Wednesday did $1800 in two performances, very good.

However there's some doubt. The expensive orchestra seats are sparse; and the balcony is always sold out. So the rear seats downstairs are sold out at balcony prices; but the $3:30's won't go. The Four-star cast doesn't permit Jed to lower the prices through-out and make it a frankly economical intellectual's play. We don't know what'll happen. The two performances yesterday—New Year's day, were damaged by an ice-blizzard.

I love the <u>money</u> side of the theatre; just disinterestedly love it.

Ruth's fine, gay and gallant and throws herself into every performance—and what an exacting part; on the stage almost every minute—only one short scene in the IIIrd Act when she isn't there—and that Tarantella![204]

Behind Jed's back I've been working on the play for Reinhardt. I promised him the First Two Acts by today.

It's going to be very good. And full of riotous acting opportunities.

And now I long to retire into some hinterland—Quebec or Arizona—and get down to Baghdad. My play opens 3 weeks from last night in Princeton, New Jersey; perhaps an advance performance in New Haven, too. Probably for New York in the Henry Miller's. (all wrong; that's a drawing-room theatre; my play should be in a high

---

203 TNW probably meant the French *raissonable*: reasonable.

204 The tarantella that Ruth Gordon, playing Nora, performed in act 3 of the 1937–1938 production of *A Doll's House* was choreographed by Martha Graham.

old-fashioned echoing barn of a place with an enormous yawning stage on which is built the diaphanous "Town".)

I've scarcely seen a soul. Aleck is entering the Sam Behrman play, to play the rôle based on the character of Rudolph Kommer—(ungraciously described in the advance publicity as a "Long Island parasite"). He was to have played it for the first time in Philadelphia a few night's ago, but Miriam Hopkins illness has postponed the opening. Rumors from the Chicago tryout say the play is so ill-constructed that rewriting has been very drastic; and maybe the whole venture is to be discarded.[205]

I'm a New Yorker now. Only three nights at Deepwood Drive since I came back. Mother's fine; but Isabel is shaken; surprises herself by bursting into tears too often. She's coming up to New York for a week next Sunday and maybe convalescence can be hastened with a complete change of place and tempo.

What you tell me about the repercussions of our Recession on the English retail trade makes me wince and cry out; but I'd rather be told bad news than not.

Jan 3 • 1938

An entire day up in my room at the Club. Polished off Act One of the Nestroy play (still no title) for the typist. It's just glänzend[206] now. I wasn't "needed" at rehearsal; they're still reading around a table. As soon as they get on their feet, I'm going to be present.

Now I'm going to walk almost down to the Battery to get some air and exercize. Oh, to be a long way off, but I did have a fine day of working even here.

I'm coming over to read to you late next Summer. If the Bagdad play is good, it's going to be dedicated to you,—so you'll want to be hearing your own play. Stay well; and count me as your devoted friend

Thornton

---

205 S. N. Behrman's *Wine of Choice,* starring Woollcott, ran in New York in February and March 1938, but Hopkins did not appear in the New York cast.

206 German: brilliant.

158. TO JED HARRIS. ALS 2 pp. (Stationery embossed The Copley-Plaza / Boston Massachusetts) Morgan

<January 1938>

Dear Jed:

Now it's time for me to retire for<from> the play for a while and get a "fresh eye."

My eye has become so jaundiced that I can no longer catch what's good or bad.

I'm going to New Haven tonight and sleep for a couple of days.

I've got a whole set of Nature's Warnings = twitches, and stutterings and head aches. I'll rejoin whenever you think best and when I'm pepped up again. Did you see me trying to hold on to consciousness during Marc's play?[207] You seemed as fit as a fiddle, and fresh as a daisy.

Ever

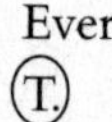

P.S. Friday afternoon—

I shall be at the hotel from 6–8 working on some closing lines. Shall bring them to the theatre at 8.20. I hope to take the 9:00 train. If you feel seriously that I can be useful here of course I shall stay—Leave word at hotel or theatre. If I go Ed. Goodnow[208] will notify me by telegram of where we are next week so I can rejoin.

T.

---

207 TNW may be referring to *Having Wonderful Time,* produced and directed by Marc Connelly, which was running in New York at the time.

208 Edward P. Goodnow was the production stage manager of *Our Town.*

Jed Harris, Frank Craven (the Stage Manager in the original Our Town *production), and TNW.*

159. TO ALEXANDER WOOLLCOTT. ALS 7 pp. Harvard

Boston, Copley-Plaza, Jan. 27 • 1938

Dear Aleck:

To me it's quite simple.

Success is accorded to a work of art when the central intention is felt in every part of it, and intention and execution are good.

Jed lost courage about my central intention and moved the production over to a different set of emphases. The result is that the vestiges of my central attention that remain stick out as timid and awkward excrescences.

Our reviews say that it is a nostalgic, unpretentious play with charm.

But what I wrote was damned pretentious.

The subject of the play now is: homely, humorous, touching aspects of a village life; of a wedding there; on to which is added a sad and all but harrowing last act. At the matinée yesterday there were storms of nose-blowings and sobs. A lady who called for a friend at five o'clock saw emerging a crowd of red eyes, swollen faces and mascara stains.

That can be attended to. And one of the reasons that it is so abrupt a change of tone is that all the strength of the earlier acts has been devitalized.

The subject of the play I wrote is: the trivial details of human life in reference to a vast perspective of time, of social history and of religious ideas.

It's too late to change it into a genre play. The succession of brief scenes can only be justified against the larger frame; if it had been written as a picture of rural manners it would have been written differently.

The First Act ("A day in our Town") has two interruptions—columns, pillars, set there throwing lights of "cosmic reference" on to the surrounding scenes.

"We want to know more about our town. I've asked Prof Walton of our State University—"

And we get the Geological position—Devonian Basalt—two to three hundred million years old.... The Anthropological report: Early Amerindian stock...tenth century of this era...Migration 17th Century English brachiocephalic blue-eyed stock...Some Slav and Mediterranean. Then from Editor Webb: the Sociological "Middletown.": 85% Republic. 10% Democratic etc. Not long, but trenchant. Then questions from the audience.

"All right now we'll go back to the life in Grover's Corners. It's two o'clock in the afternoon...<"> and so on.

Jed has done that without conviction. The Professor (adored by the audience and always clapped to the echo) is a caricature. Editor Webb, instead of a shrewd ironic Yankee...is a garrulous Irish mugger, Tommy Ross.[209]

---

209 Professor Willard was played by Arthur Allen; Mr. Webb was played by Thomas W. Ross.

The afternoon goes by. Boy and girl back from High School. Mother and Daughter. “Mama, am I good looking?”

Then the Second Interruption.

Now we want to look back on it from the future.

What became of some of these people. The Milkman. The Druggist.

What shall we put in the corner stone of the new bank for people to read a thousand years from now. “Y’know, Babylon once had 2,000,000 people and all we know is the names of the royal family. There the father came home from work. The smoke rose from the chimney, same as here. We’re putting a copy of this play in so people’ll know more about us than the Treaty of Versailles and the Lindbergh Flight..... This is the way we were in our living and our doctoring and our marrying and our dying.”

Jed says those things interrupt the affectionate interest in the family lives before us.

Frank Craven is embarrassed by them.

But that’s the central intention of the play. And it is picked up everywhere.

At the height of the Wedding Scene, the company freezes while the minister (Frank Craven) says over their heads:

“I’ve married 200 couples in my day.

Do I believe in it? I don’t know.

M marries N. Millions of them.

The cottage, the go-cart, the Sunday afternoon rides in the Ford, the first rheumatism, the grandchildren, the second rheumatism, the deathbed... <”> etc.

<“>Once in a thousand times it’s interesting. Let’s have Mendelssohn’s Wedding March.<”>

Yes, Alec it’s a great play. And all good people are deeply rejoiced by it. But from what’s there now they have to guess and grope for that side of it.

The first mistake was in the casting of Frank Craven, Tommy Ross, and the Professor.

The dangers of Irish blood.

Frank is lovable and we’re grateful for that. But oh, for that deep

New England stoic irony that's grasped the iron of life and shares it with the house.

The rest of the play is beautifully cast and superbly produced.

A great packed house in Princeton was deeply absorbed. Applause interrupted scene after scene. Laughter swept the house. Here, too, that is happening tho' to thin business. And always something is the matter at the heart of the play.

Jed didn't sleep or eat for days. Rosamond Pinchot's death[210] fell like a bomb into the middle of everything. She had loved the play and was at rehearsals. Jed has been kind and controlled to all the actors, except in overtiring them with interminable rehearsals, delays and all night work. The girl Martha Scott will be the next great actress in America.[211]

I'm all right.

I fight for the restoration of lines and for the removal of Jed's happy interpolations of New Jersey-New Hampshire.

Lord, I'm remote from it <in> many ways—wrapped up in Play #2, a beauty; reading, walking.

Until last night at 1:30 Jed wouldn't listen to a suggestion from me.

Ishkabibble.

But I continue fighting.

But I'd rather have it die on the road than come into New York as an aimless series of little jokes, with a painful last act.

At the opening night here a deputation of 41 small-town people from the skirts of Mount Monadnock—from Peterboro and Jaffrey and Keene—came down and presented me with a gavel of Cherry Wood and an eternal membership in the Mt. Monadnock Association. The faces. And they'd seen a play that was about something they knew.

Jed's thinking of closing here Saturday night; rehearsing again, and picking up the New Haven dates that you abandoned.[212]

It's fine that you feel that your play is now all right.

---

210 In the early morning of January 24, 1938, Pinchot, who was Jed Harris's personal assistant and lover and who had designed some of the costumes for *Our Town,* committed suicide.

211 Scott made her Broadway debut in the role of Emily Webb.

212 The production of *Wine of Choice,* in which Woollcott starred, opened in New York without playing in New Haven.

In Vermont we will look back on these unrests.

As soon as this is on or off I shall dash out to Tuscson, Arizona; recreate the solitude, long walks, and happy work which I knew in Zürich; plays no #3 and #4 are coming in sight.

How proud I was to be told by Ned[213] that I had the resources of a playwright well in hand. And I learn. I am an apprenti sorcier.[214] That's all the<that> matters.

love, dear Alec, as ever,
Thornton

160. TO J. DWIGHT DANA. ALS 3 pp. (Stationery embossed The Graduates Club / New Haven, Connecticut) Private

Jan 29 • 1938
Sat. morning.

Dear Dwight:

Enclosed the first cheque—$100.00 advance-money.

Boston reviews cautious but not unfavorable.

"Variety" has (I'm told) a ferocious review of the play, from the Princeton opening.[215]

Business in Boston very bad; but even so better than Julius Caesar[216] which had rave reviews.

Curious situation.

---

213 Edward Sheldon.

214 French: sorcerer's apprentice.

215 The *Variety* review of the January 22, 1938, performance of *Our Town* in Princeton, signed Rosen and titled "Plays Out of Town: Our Town," appeared on January 26 and called TNW's play "not only disappointing but hopelessly slow" and predicted that it "will probably go down as the season's most extravagant waste of fine talent."

216 The Mercury Theatre production of *Julius Caesar,* produced by Orson Welles, was playing in Boston at the time.

Many enthusiasts. My fan mail. Charles R. Codman[217] (whom I don't know): In thirty years of playgoing one of the most absorbing plays I ever saw. Edmund Wilson: last act the most terrific thing I ever saw in the theatre.

Marc Connolly came down and told Jed it was magnificent.

So with all those plus and minus marks Jed cancelled the second week in Boston (losing, he says, $2500 on the two weeks) and opens at the Henry Miller Theater in New York on Thursday.

I suffered plenty this week in Boston, over cuts and alterations.

But it was a lot of fun, too.

Came back to New Haven to rest.

In any event, my pulse is calm, and I'm learning plenty.

Ever

Thornton.

P.S.

Rê Doll's House

You see I thought I was making the translation as a present to Ruth Gordon.

Never mentioned it, however, as such to her or Jed.

Never mentioned money.

Similarly Ned Sheldon gave his translations of The Jest and Tolstoi's Redemption to John Barrymore; his adaptation of Camille to Ethel Barrymore.

If Doll's House really turns into a big hit now, maybe I'll be able to move toward some payments.

At present it's turn for the better has enabled Jed to make some daring expenditures on my play. Our Town looks cheap but is very expensive. 45 actors; and not two but five electric switchboards.

T

217 Codman was a Boston Brahmin, who later became well-known as an aide to General Patton in World War II.

161. TO J. DWIGHT DANA. ALS 3 pp. (Stationery embossed The Graduates Club / New Haven, Connecticut) Private

Sunday night.
<February 6, 1938>

Dear Dwight:

Funny thing's happened.

Ruth phoned down it's already broken a house record.

In spite of the mixed reviews when the box office opened Saturday morning there were 26 people in line; the line continued all day, and the police had to close it for ten minutes so that the audience could get into the matinée; and that $6,500 was taken in on that day—the two performances and the advance sale.

Imagine that!

Friday night both Sam Goldwyn and Bea Lillie were seen to be weeping. Honest!

It was very expensive being a dramatist.

Three opening-nights—telegrams to some of the actors, bouquets to leading ladies; a humidor to Frank Craven; gift of seats to a few friends; hotel expenses at Princeton & Boston (the contract says Jed should have paid.)

Now I'm going to be momentarily expensive—leaving for Arizona about the 17th, with a week in Chicago—and after that, very economical.

Isn't it astonishing, and fun, and exhausting?

Ever
Thornton

162. TO ERNEST HEMINGWAY. ALS 8 pp. (Stationery embossed Century Club / 7 West Forty-Third Street / New York) JFK

March 1 • 1938

Dear Earnest:

Should've written you long ago; but it would only have been repeating what I said over the phone.

However something new has come up.

Jed told me he was stipulating that if he does this play, he must ask you to accord him first option on your next three.[218]

Don't do that.

You've seen him now, and know that extraordinary bundle of lightning flash intuitions into the organization of a play; vivid psychological realism; and intelligence, devious intelligence.

But maybe you don't know the rest: tormented, jealous egotism; latent hatred of all engaged in creative work; and so on.

Use him for his great gifts—one play at a time only. But don't presuppose a long happy collaboration.

My distrust of him is bad enough, but others go far farther than I do and insist on a malignant daemonic force to destruction in him. Anyway, his professional career is one long series of repeated patterns: trampling on the friendship, gifts and love of anybody who's been associated with him.

I feel something like a piker to write such a letter as this. Because he has done, in many places, a fine job on my work. But the friendship's over all right. He's the best in N.Y, Ernest, but after this I'm ready to work with duller managers, if only I can get reliability, truthfulness, old-fashioned character, and coöperation at the same time.

So . . . one play at a time.

This afternoon I'm leaving for 2½ months in Tucson. Long walks,

---

218 At one point, Jed Harris had taken an option on Hemingway's play *The Fifth Column*, but eventually he bowed out of the project. The play was adapted and heavily altered by Benjamin Glazer for a Broadway production in the spring of 1940.

solitude and work. Perhaps some amateur Indian-remains archaeology on the side.

All my best to you. The play is stunning. Jed's suggestions sounded good—only arrive at the moment when you think the text is set and then stick to it. Be sure you get a Dramatist Guild contract; that gives you full power over the "words".

The best agent—and with Jed you must have an agent (I haven't rec'd a red cent yet! I will—its not dishonesty on his part; its just bad mental habits of deviousness) is Harold Freedman<,> Brandt & Brandt, 101. Park Ave.—agent for Sidney Howard, Phil Barry<,> Sam Behrman etc.

All my best to Mrs Hemingway; salute Capt. Dart[219] for me.

Regard & admiration
Thornton

163. TO CHRISTINA HOPKINSON BAKER.[220] ALS 7 pp. Yale

General Delivery.
Tucson Arizona
March 27 • 1938

Dear Mrs. Baker:

Many thanks for your kind and helpful letter.

I never foresaw for a minute that the Last Act would, for some people, approach the harrowing, nor that it would even seem to so many to be a fairly "new" point of view.

---

219 Captain Rollin Dart, a former Loyalist officer in Spain, was appointed by Hemingway to represent him in negotiating for stage productions of *The Fifth Column* while Hemingway was in Spain covering the Spanish Civil War.

220 Widow of George Pierce Baker, who, after teaching playwriting at Harvard, moved to Yale in 1925 and helped found the Yale School of Drama.

Lordy. I'd built my house with those ideas so long that they seemed to have the character of simple self evidence.

I suppose that I got it from Dante. I had to teach the Inferno and the first half of the Purgatorio at Chicago. I had in mind especially the Valley of the repentent Kings in about the 8th Canto of the Purgatorio. Same patience, waiting; same muted pain; same oblique side-glances back to earth. Dante has an angel descend nightly and after slaying a serpent who tries to enter the Valley every evening, stands guard the rest of the night. Most commentators agree that the allegory means: from now on the Dead must be guarded from memories of their earthly existence and from irruptions of the old human nature associations.

Catholic doctrine holds that, I think, though the custom of prayers for the dead has been built up to a shade of If-we-think-urgently-of them, they-will-think-gratefully-of-us.

At all events I do not mind from critics the charge of immaturity, confusion, and even pretentiousness. It's a first play; it's a first sally into deep waters. I hope to do many more—and better—and even more pretentious. I write as I choose; and I learn as I go; and I'm very happy when the public pays the bills.

At present in this wonderful desert air and penetrating sun light I am finishing a big long four-act low comedy. To me it seems just as hard to do and just as exciting. Max Reinhardt is very pleased with the first two acts I sent him and says that he wants to put it on.

I hope to be back in New Haven in the early weeks of May. There's another aspect of Our Town I'd like to ask you about,—some people find in it an embittered pessimism about human nature and its "being in the dark." Maybe that did slip into it without my noticing it; and then Jed Harris heightened it by certain cuts he made in the text.

I wish the great and good Professor were still alive—there are so many things I'd like to ask him, too.

In the meantime, my thanks again for your word.

Sincerely yours
Thornton Wilder

164. TO J. DWIGHT DANA. ALS 2 pp. (Stationery embossed Santa Rita Hotel / Tucson, Arizona) Private

General Delivery. Tucson, Arizona, April 4 • 1938

Dear Dwight:

I was about to mail you the enclosed card, when your second letter arrived with the contract.

Item (I) in my letter is now taken care of.

I think the contract is fine, an exemplary contract. I shall return it as soon as I can find someone to witness my signature.

Now I have a very interesting thing to lay before you:

A letter from Richard Aldrich, last Summer's director of the festival at Central City, Colorado, that presented "A Doll's House."

"Dear Thornton,

I've just heard from Denver that a check for $450 made out to you personally on July 25th was endorsed "Thornton Wilder, for deposit, Jed Harris," and deposited in the Irving Trust Company, New York. In other words, Harris or his manager must have forged your name and stolen this money which was due you for three weeks royalties on "A Doll's House" at Central City.

This is, of course, a prison offense and I suggest that you turn the matter over to your lawyer here in New York provided Harris does not pay you $450 immediately.

We have all stood a great deal from Jed Harris but I don't feel that any of us need stand for outright thievery as this appears to be.

If I can help in any way please feel free to call on me.

As yet I have not heard from Harold Freedman so I think I shall telephone him today. All good wishes.

Sincerely yours
Dick Aldrich
(The Cape Playhouse, Inc.
67 West 44th St. NYC)

I telegraphed at once:

Dear Dick, for former friendship's sake I don't want to challenge Jed on this yet & will approach indirectly through Sidney Hirsch.[221] Thanks and Regards.

And I have just written Sidney Hirsch:

"Dear Sidney, An unpleasant thing has come up which we can smooth over by acting as quickly and quietly as possible. ¶ For the sake of my long friendship with Jed, I want it to be cleared up as soon as it's possible and before the other people start to make any noise about it. ¶ The people in charge of a Doll's House Festival at Central City last Summer have found out that I never rec'd any royalties. ¶ They say that a cheque.....for $450 was made out in my name and that it was endorsed and deposited in the Irving Trust Co, N.Y. ¶ God knows I never endorsed it. ¶ They are very angry and might raise a serious charge. ¶ I just telegraphed them asking them not to do anything about it and saying that I would approach you on the matter. ¶ If it were merely a matter of my money I'd let the matter run until you and the office felt it was convenient, but now the only way to quiet it down would be to pay it to Dwight Dana of New Haven. Sorry, Sid, to have to write you a letter that sounds so ill-natured, but you can see how much worse things are at stake. ¶ Cordially ever, Thornton."

That's all pretty sweet and diplomatic, but I can imagine that Jed caught in the Lie Direct might be a very violent fellow, and the other uncontracted royalties of Doll's House may still be saved from the fire.

Now, I've got to apologize to you for writing long letters, but damme I wager this one isn't boring.

Ever

Thornton

221 Jed Harris's business manager. The money was apparently stolen by a member of Harris's staff; Harris made good on the loss.

165. TO RUTH GORDON. ALS 4 pp. (Stationery embossed The Beverly-Wilshire / Beverly Hills, California) Private

June 21 • 1938
Tues. at 5:15 p.m.
sitting upstairs waiting
for the telephone call to
say that Rosalie Stewart[222]
has come to tea with me.

Dear Ruth:

I keep wondering how are you, whether you're enjoying yourself. I see you at Wilton, at Qualigno's, at the Moat House in Kent, at St. Tropez with the René Clair's, at "Le Corsaire". Here's hoping that you've blown all the layers of fatigue from Doll's House.

I got here Sunday afternoon and saw that Helen Hayes was giving her only performance of The Merchant of Venice that night,—so I went.

Well, Ruthie, to begin with: the production and picture in it was that of a fatigued 1899 Baltimore stock company. Tasteless, empty-conventional. Doublets and hose picked out of the costumers just after they'd been returned from serving at a Masquerade at the Masonic Temple. Tasteless, tasteless. The moonlight slept upon the bank in the shape of a disk of green light down Stage Right. The supporting company—the Salanios, Gratianos<,> Jessicas and Nerissas were bad beyond belief.

Helen spoke distinctly, a fact which stood out so conspicuously that you knew at once that she had been on the stage before. But her charm, and her six graceful comedy gestures were so thin, so little-girl, and so far from breadth and womanliness and deep inner spontaneity, her love for Bassanio was so smiling-matter-of-course, her assumption of bossy authority in the Court room was so snippety, that all you could

222 TNW's Hollywood agent.

say was: she has no imagination, she has no music, she has no mature woman-nature.

Forgive me, Ruth, I just tell you what I think. Destroy this letter.

And Shylock.

He looked well, and spoke clearly.

But imagine a Shylock without hysteria, without understandable forgivable fury. A Shylock in his senses.

The pound of flesh exaction becomes a hateful ugly cold calculating bitchiness. And an audience 70% Jewish, with the headlines from Europe burned into their minds could only sit in horrified grief. A Shylock who is not frantic with his wrongs and eloquent, is an insult to a 1938 audience. Sofaer[223] was so afraid of ranting that he sold his race down the river.

And yet, Ruth, I was glad I went. Shakespeare is wonderful, wonderful. Next to Homer the greatest natural storyteller that ever lived. Under all those obstacles the scenes would each begin to collect its eternal vitality. Even there as each scene came to a close I'd sigh with intellectual pleasure.

You'll be surprised to hear that the best acting of the evening came from Pedro de Cordoba[224] who as the Prince of Morroco deliberated over the caskets, you could see him thinking, spoke richly, paused significantly, and took his departure with manly regret and Renaissance breadth and the audience burst into grateful applause.

Had dinner at the Reinhardts last night and read them the play.

Helene Thimig called for me here, driving her car. That dear wonderful face and exquisite voice.

They've lost everything, live frugally. Obstacles arrive every day. The Chamber of Commerce has just vetoed the Blue Bird[225] in Hollywood Bowl and may cancel the Faust. Only my play will be left.

---

223 Abraham Sofaer played Shylock.

224 De Cordoba was in the original cast of TNW's *Lucrèce* in 1932–1933.

225 *The Blue Bird* (1908), a play by Maurice Maeterlinck; TNW helped Reinhardt touch up his production of the play in California.

The Max Reinhard<t> Workshop opens next Monday (Faculty includes Paul Muni, Walter Huston, etc). Difficulties there every moment. Think of what their daily mail must bring them as news of Vienna every day. Think of what they once knew, the palace on the Tiergarten in Berlin. But they never wince or sigh or allude to all that. I simply love them. He made a few suggestions: the stolen supper party in Act III should come to a moment of hilarity and abandon; when the stage is divided by the screen with two plots going on simultaneously there should be one more moment at which both halves are related. In some trembling I read him the (new) monologue that Mrs Levi has in Act IV and asked him whether it was not too earnest for the play. When I was finished he looked at his wife and said in German: You see, he is a poet and turned to me and said: No, I have always said that in a comedy—and near the end—there should always be one moment of complete seriousness and by that the audience can see that also the comedy parts are not just pastime.

Well, I'll report to you, best of soldiers, from time to time. Don't trouble to answer; enjoy yourself.

Ever your old
Thornton

166. TO ALEXANDER WOOLLCOTT. ALS 4 pp. (Stationery embossed The Chief / Santa Fe) Harvard

Texas in a small way
<early July(?) 1938>

Dear Aleck:

You shall be the first to know.

I'm entering into a very tender union and both of us think that you should be the first to know.

I'm going on the stage.

I'm replacing Frank Craven for 2 weeks.[226]

That is to say: I'm memorizing the lines. I'm insisting on two days' rehearsal with the stage-manager before Jed sees me. (You can imagine how even the most shy and considerate suggestion from Jed would dry up my hypothetical art).

[Besides I have a far better and more experienced and congenial coach in Dr. Otto Ludwig Preminger of Vienna's Josefstadt[227] who is waiting at the Ambassador Hotel to encourage & guide me.—Confidential]

I'm going to make Jed pay me 300 a week which I shall give to the Actors Fund.

Of course, maybe I can't and won't do it. But there's a chance that I can transfer the best of the lecturing experience and the result might be a pleasure to me and to them.

The memory hazards are immense.

Anyway: what's life if it isn't risk, venture, taxes on the will-power, diversity, and fun?

My only real fear is that I may make the play spineless and boring and Dr. Preminger—honest as the day—will tell me, if I do.

=I leave The Merchant of Yonkers during its casting week. And I dote on you

Thornton

---

226 TNW played the Stage Manager in *Our Town* in New York for two weeks in September 1938.

227 Actor and film director Otto Preminger, who began his career working with Max Reinhardt in Vienna.

TNW as the Stage Manager in Our Town.

167. TO J. DWIGHT DANA. ALS 2 pp. (Stationery embossed 50 Deepwood Drive / New Haven, Connecticut) Private

5959 Franklin Ave
Hollywood, Calif.
Aug. 18 • 1938

Dear Dwight:

Many thanks for the good long letter and the enheartening statistics.

Yes, here I am still sitting around.

However the Faust opens on Tuesday, and then the Professor can give his attention to my play.

Delos Chappell (of Denver; Yale, about <'>17; producer of Father Malachy's Miracle) is flying to town to see me and Reinhardt; perhaps he will be the Manager of Reinhardt's production of the play. It will be a great help,—financially, and personally.

You will be interested to know that I have been turning down many offers to write for the movies. Harry Cohn of Columbia offered me $5000 a week (sic) to finish off the script of "Golden Boy" and De Mille today wanted me to do some work on "Union Pacific."[228]

It's good to know that those monies are still a possibility, but it's better to know that one doesn't have to call on them yet.

For I certainly have been spending,—life here, the summoning of Isabel, the trip to New Mexico, and just now (to Mother's violent protests) I sent Mother $500 for her trip to Scotland with Janet. I am especially glad to do that, because Mother has not budged from Deepwood Drive for many years and Janet, winter and summer, has leaned over microscopes in the fumes of a laboratory.

And now my clothes are falling to pieces and next week I am going to get a suit of clothes.

However I have faith that there will be considerable income next

228 *Golden Boy* and *Union Pacific* were both released in 1939; TNW did not appear in the screenwriting credits for either film.

year and nothing I do (except an occasional dinner at these dazzling restaurants) is really wasteful.

My friends tell me that all the expenses of this trip can be deducted from income-tax as necessary concomittents of a professional course. The other day a typist made six copies of my play and when I paid the bill ($25) he automatically leaned over, receipted it, and said: "For your income-tax report." And now others tell me that I should do the same for the apartment rental. As well as the $25 a week I paid Isabel as my secretary; and all our combined transportation.

I used to think it was painfully hot here, but it must have been far worse there; so may you and Anna[229] have a delightful vacation, and I shall see to it that Fritz will be dragged into an unbroken succession of unsavory Broadway-gutter litigations, breach of promise cases, embezzlements and mayhem.

To think that I might have been in New England all these months!

Ever

Thornton

168. TO ALBERT EINSTEIN. ALS 2 pp. (Stationery embossed The Graduates Club / One Hundred Fifty-five Elm Street / New Haven, Connecticut) CalTech

As from:
50 Deepwood Drive
New Haven, Conn.
Sept 19. 1938

Dear Prof. Einstein:

Your letter[230] made me very proud and happy,—for many reasons most of which you can divine. But one of them is that I know your love

229 Anna English Dana was J. Dwight Dana's wife.

230 Einstein had written TNW a letter, in which he praised *Our Town*.

of great music and I like to link your generous word with that. It is from a life-long devoted listening to Bach, Beethoven, Mozart and Palestrina that I draw, as best I can, certain aspirations towards form, breadth, and expressiveness.

Your letter reached me in California where I was working with Prof Max Reinhardt on the production of my next play, a broad farce with social implications, based on Nestroy's Einen Jux will er sich machen. It will be produced in New York in November. There too I dream of catching the "folk" vivacity of Figaro, Leporello and Papageno,[231] and the on-rushing high spirits and vitality of the close of a Brandenburg Concerto. I hope you will not feel it to be presumptuous that we beginners say that we work in the shadow of such glorious examples.

I hope that I shall retain your good opinion in my future work, and again accept my thanks for your kind word.

Sincerely yours
Thornton Wilder

169. TO HELENE THIMIG REINHARDT. ALS 4 pp. (Stationery embossed 50 Deepwood Drive, New Haven, Connecticut) Theatermuseum

Sunday midnight
Nov. 20 • 1938

Dear Mrs Reinhardt:

Last night I sent you a jubilant telegram; tonight I am still more jubilant. This afternoon the Professor, for the first time, ran through the Fourth Act. Even in a first reading like that what one saw was dazzling virtuosity in direction. Wonderful! As each character and situation developed all of us involved—including the Professor—would be

231 Figaro, Leporello, and Papageno are characters in Mozart operas.

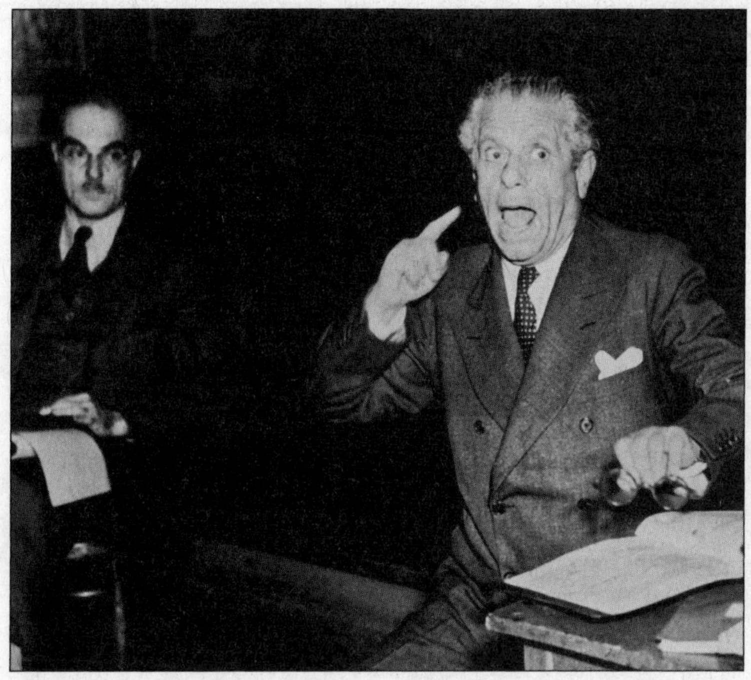

TNW and Max Reinhardt in rehearsals for The Merchant of Yonkers, *November 1938.*

shaken with laughter. Then this evening he returned to the First Act: the play opens like a scene from Charles Dickens.

As I said in the telegram there are still some hesitations in casting; but the Professor was so pleased with the good progress of two of the actors that I think he will decide to retain them. Because of certain contract reasons tomorrow—Monday—is the day he must decide. After the fifth day of rehearsal a rejected actor must be paid two weeks' salary.

The whole matter of Jane Cowl,[232] her fitness for the part, her willingness to receive direction, her relation to us all,—that is all a comedy in and around this comedy. Very funny and a little touching:

232 Cowl played Mrs. Levi in the premiere production of *The Merchant of Yonkers.*

ACT ONE: "I cannot play a part if I am directed; the part must grow up within me in my solitude."

ACT TWO. "He seems to know his business; and he's getting some very effective acting out of those others. But when my turn comes, I'll just read my lines quietly; *I* don't have to give a performance at rehearsals. I am who I am."

ACT III "I'm terrified. I *can't* possibly be as dull an actress as I've been these last three days. What'll I do? How can I play this part, with all those riotous scenes surrounding me? I'm terrified. Shall I ask *him* for help....?!!?"

ACT IV "Prof. Reinhardt, I want you to direct me, just as you do the others."

ACT V Joyous coöperation.

So far, we're only half-way through Act IV of the above Scenario, but I know the rest will come before long, and will be very good when it does come.

The Professor seems very well to me; but for myself I am surprised at the hours we must all keep for four weeks! The one hour for dinner between six at<and> seven would be all right, but the Professor never gets the full hour—there is a stage-designer, or costume designer, or music arranger, or an actor delaying him with questions! = However I didn't mean to cause you any concern: he looks well and works with ever new fresh energy.

But the important thing is to tell you again that he is doing glorious things with the play—among actors that are on fire to please him—and with the happiest author one could find.

Sincerely, devotedly
Thornton Wilder

Part Four

WAR AND AFTER: 1939–1949

AT THE END OF JANUARY 1939, JUST A FEW DAYS BEFORE THE short run of *The Merchant of Yonkers* ended, Wilder embarked for Veracruz, Mexico, on the S.S. *Siboney.* He traveled in Mexico and crossed the border into Texas, stayed in Corpus Christi for a while, and improved his Spanish significantly. By mid-March 1939, he was back in New Haven and New York, attending to business before sailing for Europe, where he spent time visiting friends in France and England during May and June. From early July through early September, he was back at work playing the Stage Manager in summer-stock productions of *Our Town* in Massachusetts and in Bucks County, Pennsylvania.

Between rehearsals and performances, Wilder became engrossed in James Joyce's recently published novel, *Finnegans Wake.* Already a great admirer of Joyce, Wilder was keenly involved from the first in an attempt to track down clues and word puzzles and to tease out meanings and intent in this complex and difficult book. His absorption in *Finnegans Wake* was to become a source of mental recreation for the rest of his life.

After spending a short time working in Atlantic City in October 1939, Wilder rented an apartment in New York City for four months. That fall, he wrote two nonfiction pieces, "Some Thoughts on Playwriting" (published in 1941) and an introduction to a new translation of Sophocles' *Oedipus Rex* (not published until 1955). At the request of producer Cheryl Crawford, he began an adaptation of *The Beaux' Stratagem*, an English Restoration comedy by George Farquhar, but he completed only half of it before putting it aside in the late fall. During this period, he took on another project, which unexpectedly required a great deal of energy and time: He became a consultant on the film version of *Our Town* after refusing to write the screenplay. Because Wilder declined to be paid for his services, the film's producer delivered a surprise Christmas present to Wilder's door: a Chrysler convertible with a rumble seat.

After Wilder gave up his New York apartment in mid-March, he returned to Hamden, Connecticut, for a short time. While there, he took lessons in order to brush up on his driving skills, and on April 1, 1940, he set out on an auto trip to Florida. During that trip, an idea for his next play began to take shape, in part because of world events. On April 9, 1940, Germany invaded Denmark and Norway. Before he drove north in May to attend the *Our Town* film premiere in Boston, Germany had invaded France, and the British army was now preparing the evacuation of Dunkirk. By the time he began a monthlong writing residency at the MacDowell Colony in June, Italy had declared war on Britain and France. On June 14, 1940, the German army occupied Paris, and on June 22, France surrendered. He had given his new play the working title *The Ends of the Worlds;* while he was at MacDowell, he drafted act 1 of the play, which he was now calling *The Skin of Our Teeth*.

After a short respite at home and on Neshobe Island in Vermont, the summer retreat of his good friend Alexander Woollcott, Wilder again performed in *Our Town* in summer theaters in Massachusetts, this time from mid-July through mid-August. After a second trip to Woollcott's island home, he paid a visit in October to Madison, Wisconsin, his birthplace, to speak on "Religion and Literature" at the centennial celebration of the Congregational church his family had attended there. He made a detour to Chicago to visit friends before settling in for a month and a half in Quebec and Montreal. During that time at the end of 1940, he began to refine acts 1 and 2 of his new play.

It was not until a year later that Wilder finished *The Skin of Our*

Teeth. Teaching and professional obligations occupied the hours that might otherwise have been devoted to his writing. In January 1941, he attended President Roosevelt's inaugural festivities, but he was also in Washington to study contemporary Latin American literature at the Library of Congress and to hone his Spanish-speaking skills. He had accepted a State Department Bureau of Educational and Cultural Affairs assignment for a three-month, three-country goodwill trip to meet with literary artists in Colombia, Ecuador, and Peru. Upon completing this mission, he delivered a twenty-one-page handwritten report to the State Department and then began teaching three classes at the University of Chicago in June. As soon as he gave his last examination on August 28, he was off again, this time to London as a delegate to a PEN (an international association of poets, essayists, and novelists) conference, which began on September 10. He visited his aunt Charlotte and Sibyl Colefax and experienced the London blackout. After the conference ended, he toured several bombed-out cities in Great Britain and gave talks and lectures as far north as Glasgow.

When he returned to America in mid-October 1941, he lingered in Hamden, then drove to Quebec, spent Thanksgiving with Woollcott in Vermont, and secluded himself in Newport, Rhode Island. Against the backdrop of the December 7 attack on Pearl Harbor and the U.S. declaration of war against the Axis powers, he worked on act 3 of *The Skin of Our Teeth,* which he finished at his home in Hamden on New Year's Day 1942.

With the United States at war, Wilder was asked to work on two military training films for the government, which he did. However, he wanted to do more than just write for his country. Despite his age (he was then forty-five), he wanted to be part of the military effort. At the same time, he was seeking a producer and director to mount his new play, which employed even more experimental theatrical techniques than had *Our Town.* By May, he had found a producer and had passed the interviews and physical examination for acceptance into the U.S. Army Air Force. About the same time, he received a telegram with an offer from Hollywood film director Alfred Hitchcock to work as a consultant and screenwriter on a projected film about a murderer's involvement with a small-town family. Although he was not initially enthusiastic, he accepted the job, because the promised salary of ten thousand dollars for five weeks' work would provide financial security for his family if his play turned out to be unsuccessful while he was away at war.

He was solely responsible for financially supporting his mother and two middle sisters, Isabel and Charlotte. The author of three novels published in the 1930s, Isabel lived with her mother in the family home. She had become increasingly involved in helping Wilder manage the details of his writing life; with his absence for military service, she became his personal representative during the premiere production of *The Skin of Our Teeth.* Charlotte had left her teaching position at Smith College in the mid-1930s, then worked as a journalist and published a second book of poetry, *Mortal Sequence,* in 1939. In February 1941, she suffered a severe mental collapse. After a year's hospitalization, during which she had not responded to treatment, nor had her condition improved in any way, Wilder undertook to provide the expensive long-term care that it was indicated she would require. His eldest and youngest siblings were married and financially independent. His brother, Amos, was beginning what would become a long and distinguished academic career as a New Testament scholar. His avocation as a poet would be confirmed in 1943, when his third volume of poetry appeared. Janet, the youngest sister, had completed her doctorate in zoology and was teaching at her alma mater, Mount Holyoke, when she married in the spring of 1941.

Wilder enjoyed his association with Hitchcock on *Shadow of a Doubt.* The screenplay had to be completed on a cross-country train ride from California in order to ensure Wilder's arrival on June 26, 1942, in Miami, Florida, where he was scheduled to report for basic military training on June 27. After completing his course in Miami, Captain Wilder was sent to Harrisburg, Pennsylvania, for six weeks of intelligence training. He was next ordered to Hamilton Field, north of San Francisco, where he joined the 328th Fighter Group. While he was there, *The Skin of Our Teeth* opened in New York on November 18, 1942, to favorable reviews; but shortly after the opening, a controversial article appeared in *The Saturday Review of Literature.* Written by two men who were engaged in writing a key to *Finnegans Wake,* it accused Wilder of borrowing ideas and details from Joyce's novel for *The Skin of Our Teeth*, and though they did not use the word, they made a thinly veiled accusation of plagiarism. Wilder chose not to reply publicly.

That December, and during the second half of Wilder's first year in the military, he was assigned to the Pentagon. He was sent to various bases around the country and was charged with writing an air force manual. During this time, he continually sought to be sent abroad. At the end of May 1943, just after he had received his second Pulitzer Prize in Drama, the newly promoted Major Wilder received orders to Constantine, North Africa, with the Twelfth Air Force at the headquarters of the Mediterranean Allied Air Force (MAAF). He was a staff officer working with the British, with duties that included interpreting the use of reconnaissance photos for the planned invasion of Sicily in July 1943. Shortly before the invasion, he was transferred to Algiers. He had served almost a year in North Africa by May 1944, when he was moved to Caserta, Italy, where, in August 1944, he was promoted to the rank of lieutenant colonel. For his military service, he was awarded the Bronze Star. In the spring of 1945, Wilder was ordered stateside to Miami to await his discharge, which came in September. The results of a health assessment by his family physician precluded his accepting the job he had been offered, U.S. cultural attaché in Paris.

Wilder exhibited some restlessness upon his return to civilian life, and by the end of October, he was off in his car to Florida. During the journey, he began writing an epistolary novel, *The Ides of March,* which dealt with Caesar, Clodia, Catullus, and Cicero. Despite interruptions both pleasurable (an acquaintanceship with Jean-Paul Sartre in New Haven and a continuing immersion in existential philosophy) and necessary (attendance at committee meetings in New York), he had written the first sections of his novel by May 1946. This productivity came to a halt at the end of June, when his mother, vacationing on Nantucket island with Isabel, became ill and died. She had cancer, had refused to see a doctor, and had concealed the gravity and extent of her condition from her sister and her children. After his mother's death, Wilder spent July on Nantucket with Isabel, then left to act in previously scheduled summer-stock productions. From the fall of 1946 through that Christmas season, Wilder remained, for the most part, in Hamden with Isabel. During those four months, he kept busy, writing an introduction to the translation of *Jacob's Dream* by the Austrian poet and dramatist Richard Beer-Hofmann, composing a short play for his fellow members to celebrate the centenary of New York's Century Club, and playing the Stage Manager in a recorded radio broadcast of *Our Town* for the Theatre Guild in New York.

In January 1947, Wilder drove down the Gulf Coast, boarded a tramp steamer for the Yucatán Peninsula, and resumed writing his novel. When he returned to the United States in mid-May 1947, he continued work on *The Ides of March* and began to write a promised introduction for *Four in America*, a book written by his recently deceased friend Gertrude Stein. Wilder finished the introduction in July and his own novel in October. *The Ides of March,* his first novel in thirteen years, was published in January 1948 and received generally positive reviews. At the time, Wilder was in Europe on a two-month visit, staying with old friends in London and then going to Paris to see his new friend Sartre, who had earlier asked him to translate his play *Mort sans sépulture* for an American audience, a task Wilder was now ready to undertake. During the spring, with no writing project of his own at hand, Wilder became engrossed in a scholarly endeavor that vied with his devotion to unraveling the puzzles in *Finnegans Wake*—dating the plays written by Lope de Vega, the eminent Spanish dramatist of the late sixteenth and early seventeenth centuries. This passion also preoccupied him for many years.

After two months playing the role of Mr. Antrobus in *The Skin of Our Teeth* in summer theaters in Massachusetts, Connecticut, and Pennsylvania, and intervals of Lope studies, Wilder embarked with his sister Isabel in September 1948 for a six-month stay in Europe. At Robert M. Hutchins's request, he had agreed to give a series of lectures in Germany. The first of these would be given in Frankfurt-am-Main in November. He and Isabel made stops in Dublin and Paris before he delivered his Frankfurt lecture, "The American Character as Mirrored in Literature." From Frankfurt, he went on to lecture at the universities of Heidelberg and Marburg. His final stop in Germany was Berlin, where he spoke with students for two days during the period of the Berlin Airlift. While his sister and he were in Switzerland on Christmas holiday, *The Victors,* Wilder's translation of Sartre's play, opened Off Broadway, to mixed reviews.

At the beginning of 1949, the two Wilder siblings, seeking a warmer climate, traveled down to Italy and then to Spain, where he pursued his Lope studies. In February, they sailed back to the United States. Beginning in 1948, and throughout 1949, Wilder worked on a play he called "The Emporium," but a third act continually eluded him. He put the script aside for a time in order to write an address to be given at the Goethe Bicentennial Festival, a celebration of music and talks to be held in Aspen, Colorado, from June 27 to July 16. Goethe was one of Wilder's intellectual heroes, and his old friend Robert M. Hutchins, as chairman of the celebration, had asked him to join the roster of distinguished speakers and had also placed him on the committee. Wilder delivered his lecture, "World Literature and the Modern Mind," and assisted two other speakers, one of them extemporaneously, by translating their addresses from German and Spanish into English as they delivered them. Wilder remained in Aspen through September, then returned to the East Coast for some solitary work time in Newport. After a more convivial stay in Saratoga Springs, New York, he joined his family for Thanksgiving. Following a few excursions to New York and Washington, D.C., he ended 1949 in Hamden. With both his parents deceased, he was now the head of his Connecticut household.

170. TO SIBYL COLEFAX. ALS 2 pp. NYU

Cuernavaca, Mexico. Feb 7 • 1939

Very dear Sibyl:

Your letter from Settignano reached me here and I loved it for itself and for the thought that you were receiving beautiful sights and sounds and company. When I came to the words: "Perhaps you'd say one must not have such oases in these times," I burst out laughing. Imagine ascribing such a sentiment to me. The more such restorative hours come to such gallant standard-bearing souls as Sibyl, the better for all concerned.

I, too, am in a beautiful place, but without any such wonder-talker as Bernard Berenson.

It's beautiful here. I can raise my eyes and see Popocatapetl,—lines second only to Fujiyama. And I have seen pyramids older than Egypt's; and gold-leaf baroque corruscating and festooning ad majorem gloriam Dei,[1] and a wonderfully touching Indian peasant life and art, and miles of this extraordinary renascence in contemporary fresco-painting.

Mexico's a great experience, but I can't work here and after four weeks of it I'm ignominiously crossing the border into my own country to walk, and bask and work at Corpus Christi, Texas, by the sea.

There are a number of reasons in many kinds:

I can't sleep nights because of the altitude.

I can't shake off a cold because of the alkali dust. The dry season began last October!

My eyes ache in the whitest sunlight I ever saw.

I can't digest the food, a highly specialized food.

And I can't rid myself of the anguish behind the landscape. Oh,

---

1 TNW misquotes the Latin phrase *ad majorem Dei gloriam:* to the greater glory of God.

Mexico's deep deep in blood and iniquity. The world is, but even China doesn't whisperingly remind you of it continually as this place does.

First, in these old civilizations,—there is one temple here where there were six thousand human sacrifices a year. Then the terrible era of the conquistadores, with their half-frivolous half-hysterical slaughter. Then the great land-owners and whip-bearing exploitation of the Indians; and now graft, graft, fine words and graft.

I take my walks through Indian villages, and through the streets of the towns, and there it all is: the patience, the hopelessness and the nobility of the Indian. And as for the Mexicans, their appearance, their taste, their women, their business practices, best not to go into that through the postal service.

So compare my walks (I'm always harping on my walks, but my walks are my work) compare them with those of the Salzkammergut, or the Zurichersee, or Tucson, or New Hampshire, or even the West Indies.

(At this minute it is sunset, and the sunlight lies red-gold over the foreground, with its bougainvilleas and oleanders and the mountains in the distance are in blue and purple veils and the tops of the volcanoes are rose snow.)

¶¶ The Merchant of Yonkers closed after a five-week run. I hope Alec. is right when he says that it will have a revival after a few years, in the American idiom, and declare and justify itself. In the meantime the text has gone to the printer's and you'll receive a copy before long.[2]

"Our Town" is in Chicago doing good business through a precedent-making blizzard.

I have been wrestling with the Alcestiad and have reached a temporary truce.[3] I will resume the struggle in Texas. It's all a matter of

---

2 *The Merchant of Yonkers* opened in New York on December 28, 1938, ran for thirty-nine performances, and then closed in January 1939. *The Merchant of Yonkers: A Farce in Four Acts* was published on April 13, 1939, by Harper & Brothers in an edition of fifteen hundred copies. Alexander Woollcott's prediction came true when the rewritten version of the play, now called *The Matchmaker,* ran in New York from December 1955 to February 2, 1957, a total of 486 performances. The musical comedy version of the latter—*Hello, Dolly!*—ran in New York from January 16, 1964, to December 27, 1970, a total of 2,844 performances.

3 TNW wrestled with *The Alcestiad* for many years. In the summer of 1938, he had written to his dramatic agent Harold Freedman of his "dream" of having the play finished the next summer for presentation at Max Reinhardt's festival in Hollywood, but that did not happen.

diction. The structure is clear; the idea-life is exciting; but how do they talk. I keep trying to find an utterly simple English prose, but it keeps coming out like a translation of a Greek classic, at one moment, and like a self-conscious assumption of homely colloquial speech at the next. I foresaw that it would be hard, but not as hard as this. It looks to me as though I ought to do it in blank-verse. I've long known that I'd have to come to verse some day, but to begin it now—with this play—would mean a year of studio, of constant exercises in verse, of disciplining myself; for to change one's medium is to change one's mind. Yes, some day I am to write verse, but I think I should approach it through the lyric. To enter it by way of blank-verse is to begin at the end, and a costing job. However, it is still possible that it can be done in prose and that Texas will show me how. Those heroic simplifications of the Greek myths must be met with some special strangeness in the approach: we've seen how Cocteau and Giraudoux did it, with iridescent concetti[4]; and Landor did it, with a mixture of dying-fall musicality and latinizing aphorisms. I want my way to be a plainness, a purity, an absence of rhetoric that will be a strangeness in itself, but it's hard.

If it turns out to defeat me—defeat me, I hope, only temporarily—because the subject is golden, there are a host of other subjects crowding in the notebooks, and most of them come with innovations (i.e. revivals of lost excellences) of form. I'm surer and surer that explicit scenery and the naturalistic method have run the theatre into the ground. There will be from me no repetitions of 'Our Town' but there will be the freest possible treatment of time and place. However, I hope to be writing to you about my work from Texas before long.

Guess who was on the boat from Havana to Vera Cruz? Beverley Nichols.[5] I liked him. Left a little sad by the emergence from the precocious twenties, but very nice.

I'm sorry that in my abrupt plunge from New York I was not able to meet Sir Ronald Storrs[6]; his letter has just been forwarded to me.

---

4 Italian: ideas (in this context, the word *style* would be a closer approximation of TNW's meaning).

5 Beverly Nichols (1898–1983) was an English novelist and dramatist; he is best known today for his books on gardening.

6 Storrs (1881–1955) was a British colonial official and a specialist in Middle Eastern affairs.

I've always heard that he is one of the most delightful people in the world and I would have loved to have known him.

Today's newspaper tells of Chamberlain's affirmation that England will associate itself with France if the latter is attacked. What a year last year was! Will next year be living just day by day under allowances of hope? Best not count our disasters before they're hatched.

At all events I catch myself daydreaming that you will be able to accept Mrs Crane's invitation to come to New York.[7] And then, too, if I get a good stint of work done I'm coming over. But always always I send you my devoted affection

Ever

Thornton.

171. TO ELIZABETH N. PAEPCKE.[8] ALS 4 pp. (Stationery embossed 50 Deepwood Drive / New Haven, Connecticut) Schlesinger

March 26 • 1939

Dear Pussy; dear Mrs Thompson:

Your telephone call put me in such a quandary that I couldn't make out whether the performance had been advanced from last Friday to Wed the 22nd or postponed until Wednesday the 29th and I'm afraid I've lost my chance to send a telegram.[9]

My quandary was this: the impossibility of explaining over the telephone the fact that I have never sat in the audience and seen one of

---

7 Josephine Porter Boardman Crane (1873–1972) was a well-known patron of the arts and a founder of the Museum of Modern Art in New York; she was the widow of former Massachusetts governor Winthrop M. Crane.

8 Chicago philanthropist Elizabeth Paepcke (1902–1994) was involved in many cultural activities both in Chicago and, later, Colorado. In 1950, she founded the Aspen Institute and the Aspen Music Festival with her husband, Walter.

9 TNW is probably responding to Paepcke's invitation to attend the performance on March 31 by the drama group at the Woman's University Club of Chicago of his one-act play *The Happy Journey to Trenton and Camden.*

my plays. Even hovering about the back rows I have never seen an entire performance. (except when taking part which is far from "seeing.")

Alec. Woollcott arranged a performance—and I hear and can believe that it was quite wonderful—up in Vermont—among real Grovers' Corners people; and yet I could not bring myself to go.

I use<d> to be bewildered and inclined to scoff at Eugene O'Niel <O'Neill> when I heard that he never attended his own plays, but now I understand.

The mixed emotions; the intensity of attention; the sensitiveness at variations in rendering; self consciousness, embarrassement, self-deprecations.

All I can do is to ask you to understand, or if not understand, forgive.

If there is still a chance of my being able to send a telegram let me know.

Cordially ever,
Thornton

172. TO HUNTINGTON T. DAY.[10] ALS 4 pp. (Stationery embossed The Graduates Club / One Hundred Fifty-five Elm Street / New Haven, Connecticut) Private

Friday morning
Sept. 8 • 1939

Dear Mr. Day:

As I told you my aim is to warn Mr. Lesser that I cannot take so large a share in the planning of the movie, since so large a share would inevitably lead to the general impression that I completely authorized and was responsible for the final picture.[11]

Mr. Lesser is in Clayton New York (Thousand Islands regions on the St. Lawrence, getting a long overdue rest); he planned to meet me

---

10 Day, a New Haven attorney, was a partner in Wiggin & Dana, the law firm that represented TNW.

11 Film producer Sol Lesser had proposed a movie version of *Our Town*.

in New York Tuesday the 12th for five days of continuous work on the movie-script

I suggest sending him the following telegram:

<“>Dear Mr. Lesser

much worried by your final indication that a five day collaboration between us on a first working script could be interpreted as my ultimate authorship and responsibility for the finished picture stop for me responsibility always means close conscientious detailled collaboration throughout and as I told you I cannot extend that at this time stop I suggest that I meet you in upper New York for one day more of congenial planning with financial compensation and then I withdraw. always extending to you and the picture my cordial best wishes but unable to serve as partial worker where the responsibility should rest on a screen writer continuously present stop hope that you see my point of view in all good will and friendship sincerely yours

Thornton Wilder”

Will you phone my house 7-3436 as to whether you approve of this and I will send the telegram off.

Cordially

T. Wilder

173. TO SOL LESSER. ALS 2 pp. UCLA

Monday Oct 9 • 1939
50 Deepwood Drive
New Haven, Conn.

Hope you don’t mind my writing you on my “work paper”, it’s a sign of congeniality.

Dear Sol:

Returning to New Haven I found the yellow pages of corrections and now have everything before me.[12]

---

12 On October 5, Lesser sent TNW a “First Rough Draft” for an *Our Town* film; the draft was prepared by Frank Craven (the actor who originated the role of the Stage Manager) and screenwriter Harry Chandlee. A typescript carbon is in the Beinecke Library at Yale University.

The cuts in Mrs. Gibbs-Mrs. Webb shelling beans are all right with me; also the transferred speeches from the Stage-Manager to Mrs Gibbs in the Last Act. Also the omission of the Birthday Scene from the opening sequence. And I have always realized that 88–92 would require cuts.

Of the new lines the only one that sounds out of character is shot 142 page 84 "Promise me I'll always be your girl."

Now that you've restored the opening breakfast-and-going-to-school-scene are there still some lines you want from me, or is this material from the book sufficient?

Now for some comments on the whole:

My only worry is that—realistically done—your Wedding Scene won't be interesting enough, and that it will reduce many of the surrounding scenes to ordinary-ness.

Did you ever see a Wedding Scene on Stage or Screen that followed through normally?

Either it was interrupted ("Smiling Through", and "Jane Eyre" and "It Happened One Night") or it showed the Bride hating the groom ("The Bride the Sun Shined On"), or some other irregularity.[13]

On the stage with "Our Town" the novelty was supplied by

① economy of effect in the scenery.

② The minister was played by the Stage Manager.

③ The thinking-aloud passages

④ The oddity of hearing Mrs Soames' gabble during the ceremony.

⑤ The young people's moments of alarm.

You have none of these. By a close-up of Mrs. Soames even her gabble will lose its oddity and shock. Here is a village wedding and the inevitable let-down when it all runs through <u>as</u> <u>expected</u>.

Now, Sol, it's just you I'm thinking about; will you have as <u>interesting</u> a picture as you hoped?

This treatment seems to me to be in danger of dwindling to the Conventional. And for a story that is so generalized that's a great danger.

The play interested because every few minutes there was a new bold effect in presentation-methods.

---

13 The first of the three films mentioned is titled *Smilin' Through;* the play TNW refers to is titled *The Bride the Sun Shines On.*

For the movie it may be an audience-risk to be bold (thinking of the 40 millions) but I think with this story it's a still greater risk to be Conventional. This movie is bold enough in the last sequence, but apart from the three characters who talk straight into the audience's face, there's less and less of that novelty and freedom and diversion during the first forty minutes.

I know you'll realize that I don't mean boldness or oddity for their own sakes, but merely as the almost indispensible reinforcement and refreshment of a play that was never intended to be interesting for its story alone, or even for its background.

I shall probably have some notions to send you soon,—I've asked my sister to read the script, too ,—and shall be writing you again soon.

All my best to all, as ever.

y'r' old
Thornton

174. TO WILSON LEHR.[14] ALS 2 pp. (Stationery embossed 50 Deepwood Drive / New Haven, Connecticut) Yale

Nov. 26 • 1939

Dear Wilson:

Please forgive me being so long in thanking you for the beautiful pot of aster-chrysanthemums (that's all I know about'm; but I enjoy'm none the less). I water them faithfully and they stand in the window getting a lot of sunlight and making chlorophyl like mad per since Creation. The delay was due to the fact that Sol Lesser is in town again and worried about his script and requiring a big upset in my daily working routine. He's now thinking of employing Lillian Hellman as the scriptwriter and Sam Wood ("Mr. Chips") as the director.[15]

Suppose Lillian let go and showed us a script revealing how every-

14 Lehr graduated from the Yale Drama School in 1939; he later taught theater at Brooklyn College.

15 Hellman did not work on the script of *Our Town*, but Wood did direct the film.

body in Grover's Corner loathed one another, with some pretty dubious goings-on rê Rebecca Gibbs' tattling.

The old Beaux Stratagem progresses but I don't really think there's any practical entertainment there.[16]

I'm getting fond of my N.Y. apartment and the long quiet hours that pass. Finnegan's Wake still makes great inroads into my time and I've untangled some more of its knots, but there remain a million.

Stop in for a drink some time when you're free, and again many thanks for the happy thought

Ever
T.N.

175. TO GERTRUDE STEIN AND ALICE B. TOKLAS. ALS 4 pp. (Stationery embossed The Graduates Club / One Hundred Fifty-five Elm Street / New Haven, Connecticut) Yale

50 Deepwood Drive
New Haven, Conn.
Jan. 28 • 1940

Dear Ones:

Last year I lost my little black engagement-diary-address book.

Is your address 5 or 15 or something else rue Christine? Would the postman correct such a mistake? All my notions of France go into my doubt; so I shall send this to the post ladies of Belley; they too have a very low opinion of all letters not addressed to themselves.[17] But I think (some day) they will forward this to you, just to get it out of their way.

16 TNW had begun work on *The Beaux' Stratagem* in September, but he stopped in December, having completed only about half the adaptation. Holograph and typed versions are in the Beinecke Library at Yale University. TNW's adaptation was completed in 2005 by American dramatist Ken Ludwig and was directed by Michael Kahn for the Shakespeare Theatre Company in Washington, D.C., in 2006.

17 Belley was the town where Stein and Toklas received their mail when they were at their house in Bilignin in the Rhône Valley.

I have no news.

Health, inertia, and a shocking busyness over trifles

I have a New York apartment until March 15, and I am all adazzle about my new acquaintance, New York. Walks, walks, subway rides, then more walks. To all proposals—dinners, committees, lectures,—I say no—not as formerly a defensive anxious apologetic no, but the easy no of the indifferent and absent-minded. I don't go to the theatre,—this is the year that the movies have finally risen and surpassed the stage.

I like it.

Just as that summer at Peterborough I laid everything aside and read The Making of Americans,[18] read, and reread, and made cross-references and went about in a waking dream of complete immersion in it; so I have been for months engaged with Finnegans Wake, decoding that unbroken chain of complicated erudite puzzles. I've only skimmed the surface, but I know more about it than any article on it yet published. Finally I stopped, and put it away from me as one would liquor or gambling; I ceased tearing off to the public library to verify Persian moon goddesses, and the astronomical conditions over the British Isles in January, and the Danish word for goat.

But it was wonderfully absorbing while it lasted.

Mabel Luhan is in New York and has opened a salon. The first Friday night it was on Civil Liberties; the second: T.W. will elucidate eight pages of Finnegans Wake; the third Psychoanalysis and Medecine; the fourth on Censorship. I had much hope that it would be a Something, but it wasn't. It takes a will of iron, and Mabel hasn't that, so it's petering out.

The movie magnate for "Our Town" confused because I would accept no money for the interminable conferences over the script, gave me an automobile for Xmas. I don't like 'em, but there it is. So when my apartment-lease is up I shall take it and drive far away.

I had some hours with Robert Haas and he has sent me his thesis which I like very much; now I am eager to go back and reread The Geophophical<Geographical> History. I hope he goes on to do a very very good book about you. I wish I could hear Bob Davis's discussion

---

18 Stein's *The Making of Americans: Being a History of a Family's Progress* was published in Paris in 1925 and was reprinted in an abridged edition in the United States in 1934.

of the Haas thesis. His aperçus would leap farther and brighter than Haas's, but his soul has gone murky like his English style. Clouds of smoke.[19]

A letter from Sir Francis[20] asking if I could see any kind of call or engagement for him in America. The galleries and dealers; the glazed paper women's magazines;—he must have closer approaches to them than I have. I'm still deep in Austrian exiles and in trying to establish Max Reinhardt in a dramatic school in New York or in a college near here, and I've had some success in finding teaching posts and pension grants etc, etc. for teachers and writers, but I wouldn't know where to turn for Sir Francis.

The Hutchins were in New York for a few days during the holidays.

It would take the whole of a drive to Vienne and back to lay that situation before you.

I summarize it by saying that Maude's going crazy and in such a way that one is torn between pitying her for a desperately sick mind and hating her for a vulgar pretencious tiresome goose. Such dances as she leads Bob, with tantrums, caprices, changes of mind and talk, talk, talk.

And the effect of it on the two daughters!

The Wilders are fine. Isabel at last starts in this week on a job. She is to be assistant to the supervisor of the Connecticut branch of Federal Writers Project. Charlotte will have after many years a volume of prose ready this spring—Proust-like evocations of her childhood in Berkeley and China. Janet rec'd her PHD from the University of Chicago and is teaching at Mt. Holyoke. Amos's Katharine is about to give us another baby.[21] Mother is fine.

Is it still possible you will be over this Spring. When I get back to

---

19 Haas was a graduate student at the University of California in Berkeley. After he heard Stein lecture there, he began corresponding with her about her work and wrote his master's thesis, which was titled "An Analysis of the Present as an Aesthetic Process in the Critical Writings of Gertrude Stein." Davis was the University of Chicago graduate to whom TNW introduced Stein and Toklas when TNW and Davis traveled to Europe together in the summer of 1935.

20 Sir Francis Rose was a twentieth-century English painter.

21 Charlotte Wilder's second book of poetry had been published the previous year. TNW's nephew, Amos Tappan Wilder, was born on February 6, 1940, in Boston.

New York I shall verify through Lee Keedick and Mr. McCullough how things are progressing.

(Tuesday—back in New York)

A letter came from you this morning. I deserve your reproaches, but shall mend my ways.

I called up Lee Keedick today. He is out of town but his secretary (an old friend of mine—that demon of personalizing everything always sets me to wooing secretaries—yes. yes, it's to take the curse off business transactions and to apologize for the exchange of moneys) tells me that some important decision on the matter of your tour is to be reached this week.

Now I'm reading another splendid book: The letters of Madame du Deffand to H. Walpole.[22] The absurdity, the agony, the dazzling crystalline French—"les grandes passions sont celles de quatre-vingt ans" said Disraeli.

How I wish, dear sister-stars, that I could rush into your dear sitting room (amid barking) and kiss you on both cheeks and read the MS of Paris, France.[23]

Ever thine
Thornton

176. TO SOL LESSER. ALS 4 pp. (Stationery embossed 50 Deepwood Drive / New Haven, Connecticut) UCLA

Easter night <March 24, 1940>

Dear Sol:

Sure, I see what you mean.

In the first place, I think Emily should live. I've always thought so. In a movie you see the people so close to that a different relation is established. In the theatre they are halfway abstractions in an allegory;

22 *Horace Walpole's Correspondence with Madame du Deffand and Wiart,* edited by W. S. Lewis and Warren Hunting Smith, had been published the previous year.

23 Both the English and American editions of Stein's *Paris France* were published in 1940.

in the movie they are very concrete. So in so far as the play is a Generalized Allegory she dies—we die—they die; inso far as it's a Concrete Happening it's not important that she die; it's even disproportionately cruel that she die. Let her live—the idea will have been imparted anyway.

But if she lives, I agree with you that after all that grave-yard material the survival may seem too arbitrary and abrupt and out of relation to the Stage-Manager presiding over the experience.

Hence:

Your first suggestion is fine.

sick-in-bed we hear her say, faintly: I want to live! I want to live.

Then the whole graveyard sequence and the return to the birthday and back to the sick bed; and a louder "I want to live."

This may give the impression that all the intervening material was a dream or hallucination that took place in a second of time—that is: between her second and third cries of "I want to live"—which is the right idea.[24]

Now as to the stage-manager's relation:

I don't think we have to ask whether Emily has told him her "dream". I like to think that the audience even in this version, can accept that he knows everything.

I suggest that in the place you mention, Frank says:

"Out at Emily's and George's farm, though, they're still up—talking over the new baby" then a moment's pause, and a look straight into the audience: "—the new baby that Emily's been able to live for." Then the view of the room through the window, . . . and perhaps adding during it, a sort of grunt and: Its like one of those European fellas said: <">Every child born into the world etc. etc." That might send the audience home with a better taste in their mouth (if the implications of the return-to-the-birthday scene have given a repudiation-of-life sensation, as it did to so many during the stage-representations.)

I've just laid this before the family and they like it; but if you still think we should look farther, drop my<me> a card and I'll fire back with some more.

---

24 In the film version of *Our Town,* Emily Webb lived.

You know how delighted I am at the fine testimonies that have come in to you about the picture.

Cordially ever
Thornton

177. TO SIBYL COLEFAX. ALS 4 pp. NYU

The MacDowell Colony
Peterborough, N.H.
June 14 • 1940

Dear, dear Sibyl:

What times, what things to live through! The mind cannot grasp a small part of the agony undergone, and of the further disasters possible.

Your word months ago that you were sure it would be a long war terrified me, but now I draw comfort from it. Long enough to sustain the best we know, and long enough for America to help.

A few days ago I received a letter from Lynn and Alfred asking me to telegraph the President and my Senator in answer to President Conant's (of Harvard) appeal to expedite the means whereby material could be sent abroad; I had already sent off the telegrams. All too slowly the formalities in Washington are unrolling to some effectiveness.

The Middle West remains obstinately "isolationist", but even that is thawing with a swiftness unprecedented among us—but can it be swift enough to match the acceleration of historical action as we see it taking place abroad.

Each day seems more in crisis than the last—in a few minutes I go back to the "main house" to see what has happened today—and so, each night and each morning.

June 17.

Waiting. Waiting.

And now the news of France's capitulation.

All I can do is send to you my love and a thousand thoughts you can divine, and over here to exert myself in every way I know to make people realize that our aid and participation is essential—to some I can put it (for it is no less true) as pure self-interest; to others and to myself I put it Humitarianism = Civilization. A civilization without instinctive brother-participation with the Thing-France and the Thing-England is no civilization.

Let the thought of me enter as a whisper into your dejected moments and as a voice into your moments of courage, fortitude and hope.

Ever affectionately
Thornton

178. TO RICHARD BEER-HOFMANN. ALS 4 pp. Harvard

Returning Friday to
50 Deepwood Drive
New Haven, Conn
August 6. 1940
(Cohasset, Mass.)

Dear Dr. Beer-Hofmann:

How often during these months of vast and terrible events have I longed to sit with you and hear and feel your contemplation of them.

I continue to receive letters—veiled by the exigencies of the censorship, but nevertheless very significant—from a friend in London, and from Miss Gertrude Stein who remained through a deluge of refugees and German soldiers in her house a few miles below Lyons.

I don't know whether Dr. Steiner[25] has told you the story I told him: how that I drove a long distance across the state of Vermont, full of happy expectation of seeing you—to Woodstock, Vermont,—inquired for you at the Post Office, telephone office and telegraph office—only

25 Austrian writer, poet, and editor Herbert Steiner.

to realize finally that you were in the other Woodstock,—a kind of mistake that I make, alas, too often.

During the six weeks in the deep green shade and solitude at the MacDowell Colony I at last found my subject for the new play and finished the first act, and on Friday I shall be back in New Haven again, for some months of uninterrupted work upon it. In this one it seems I call upon still free-er uses of the stage, as to scenery, time, abstraction and audience collaboration. This one is sub signo Aristophanis[26]—the subject is the ordeals that man has had to pass through, including the Ice Age (sic), and the method is buffoonery and lazzi.[27] Difficult, difficult, but I hope I can "get it right." It has all colors in it—violence, anguish, detailed realism of the contemporary American scene, and low comedy—but the color I have most difficulty in encompassing is that Aristophanic intermêde[28] of pure dream-like lyric poetry.

There has not been much application in my reading. I have read Lord Rosebery's Napoleon: the Last Phase (not very good); Keyserling's book on South America—a mixture of exalté theorizing and sharp observation; very curious and often rewarding;[29] rereading the little selection of Mozart's Letters,—glorious stuff; and Kleist's stories—the despair of narrators.

Do tell me, dear and noble Doctor, if there is any book I can procure for you; any errand or service I can render. We are suffering many hot days, but I hope that your evenings are cool, and that you find much beauty in the place where you are. Are there some music-makers there? I have been starved of great music this last month and hope to replunge in it, even if only by gramaphone records. Give my devoted regards to Frau Czuczka-Beer-Hofmann, and accept the affectionate greetings and friendship of one

Sincerely yours
Thornton Wilder

---

26 Latin: under the sign of Aristophanes (that is, comedy). The new play became *The Skin of Our Teeth.*

27 Italian: jokes.

28 French: interlude (French is *intermède*).

29 Alexander Keyserling's *South American Meditations.* French: exalted.

179. TO VAN WYCK BROOKS.[30] ALS 3 pp. (Stationery embossed The Century Association / 7 West Forty-Third Street / New York) Pennsylvania

As from: 50 Deepwood Drive
New Haven, Conn.
Sept 18 • 1940

Dear Mr. Brooks

James Joyce is in very straightened circumstances in the South of France. He has begun a new novel. Padraic Colum[31] is collecting a few names to append to a letter to the Nobel Award Committee in Sweden. It will be brief and not make large claims for its nominee.

The following have consented to sign it:

Archie Mac Leish<MacLeish>
President Hutchins
Mr. & Mrs Colum
Eugene Jolas[32]
Sinclair Lewis
Dorothy Thompson.

I have written Aldous Huxley and Edmund Wilson. If you would also consent to sign it I think I shall venture to approach President Conant. With these names the list would be closed.

The letter is a purely private one to the chairman in Stockholm and every effort shall be made to prevent its getting into the press.

Could you drop me a card with your yes or no. Should you feel it inadvisable, we will respect your decision and the matter will remain confidential.[33]

Sincerely yours,
Thornton Wilder

---

30 American critic and biographer (1886–1963).

31 Irish poet and dramatist Padraic Colum (1881–1972). His wife, Mary (1884–1957), mentioned below, was a literary critic.

32 Jolas (1894–1952) was a poet, journalist, and founder of the literary magazine *transition*.

33 James Joyce never received the Nobel Prize.

180. TO SIBYL COLEFAX. ALS 2 pp. (Stationery embossed 50 Deepwood Drive / New Haven, Connecticut) NYU

Sept. 26. 1940

Dear Sibyl:

Such thoughts go out to you day by day, and especially night by night, when the ordeal is most drastic. Each days report, the advance and the set-back, I read in the light of Lord North Street and its unquenchable spirit.[34]

We have all the feeling that great new resources of confidence are permitted to us. Terrible though the ordeal may still be, you now know some of the things they haven't been able to do.

Our country is being rent by the coming election. There is something exhilarating about the very violence of the partisanship. I am fanatically for Roosevelt and of course a large part of my feeling is that more than any man in the country he sees all that we can and must do for the Allies and can put the measures into effect, skillfully driving through the oppositions.

Last Sunday noon with a group of pro-Roosevelt writers I went to lunch with the President at Hyde Park,—and Sibyl, I looked about—your friends, so many of your friends! (I received an invitation to join the Pro-Willkie Writers Committee; and looking at all the names there was no one I admired except the agéd Booth Tarkington, and no one I knew, or that you know, unless it be John Marquand.)

But there on the lawn at Hyde Park were Alice Duer Miller, Marc Connolly, Beatrice Kaufman<,> Edna Ferber,—a letter from Bob Sherwood was read,—and a dozen others. We are all going on a nationwide broadcast tomorrow night, and may the rightness of our cause give us persuasion and conviction.[35]

---

34 Lady Colefax's house on Lord North Street in London, where she was living during the German air raids.

35 On September 27, 1940, TNW participated in a radio program on the NBC Blue Network, moderated by Eleanor Roosevelt and presented under the auspices of the Women's Division of the Democratic National Committee. He was one of eleven prominent writers and stage performers who discussed their support for Roosevelt in the upcoming election.

Woollcott would of course have been there, had he been able.

Roosevelt will probably win. The relapse of the New York Times from his support and the coolness of Lipman[36] and Dorothy Thompson are incomprehensible to me. The opponents' charges that he is usurping autocratic powers, that he is "conceited", that he is buying the peoples' votes with public works, that he is inciting to class-warfare, that he is corrupting the American character by creating a dole population—each of these can be answered so easily. It looks to me like merely the irruption which all political thinkers ascribe to so much political activity—from Plato to Montesquieu—the "sourde"[37] deep visceral resentment envy-grudge against the Superior Man. Roosevelt is not a great man, but he's disinterested, tireless, and so instinctively active and creative that his bravery about it does not look like bravery; free from fanaticism; without spite or retaliation (some anecdotes Bob Hutchins told me: FDR laughs at the discomfiture of his opponents, like a boy who has played a practical joke—not like the snarl of an injured brooder). The great thing is that he's always doing things and most of them are good.

There in the shadow of your great war and linked to it is our little one.

God give you strength, dear Sibyl, and an occasional serenity. My imagination falls short of conceiving a small part of the strain you are under and the thousands of concerns that must pass through your mind every day. From time to time I allow myself to dream of the day when these struggles will be over and we can sit on some beautiful hill-top and turn it all over in silence. May it be in our time that Satan hears again, emerging from his bas-fonds,[38] Heaven's recurrent NO.

With such love,
Thornton

36 American journalist and political columnist Walter Lippmann.

37 French: muffled (French is *sourd*).

38 French: underworld.

181. TO ZOË AKINS RUMBOLD.[39] ALS 3 pp. (Stationery embossed Chateau Frontenac / Quebec) Huntington

As from: 50 Deepwood Drive
New Haven, Conn.
Nov. 18 • 1940

Dear Mrs Rumbold:

Your kind letter made me walk on air and fills me with pleasure every time I think of it.

I wish I could come into that beautiful house I remember so well and have a talk with you about The Merchant and its troubles in New York and the modest second wind it's acquiring in the Little Theatres around the country.

Since you are a friend of the play I <would> like to tell you about two thefts in it, from very high quarters: in the First Act, the scene where Mrs Levi tries to interest the Merchant in an imaginary young girl Enestina Simple, is stolen—five pages almost verbatim—from the scene between the Marriage Broker Frosine and Harpagon in Molière's The Miser (no one's ever noticed it); and Mrs Levi's epigram about money: "Pardon my expression, but money's like manure,—it's not worth a thing unless it's spread about encouraging young things to grow," is from Bacon's Essays ("for money is like unto compost which is of little worth save that......").

I'm like a woman I heard about who was arrested in Los Angeles for shoplifting. Her defense was "I only steal from the best department stores, and they don't miss it."

I wonder if you guessed that your writing to me would give me particular pleasure,—could you see that your opening in The Furies[40] made me say to myself: yes, that's right, the monologue is one of the theatre's most telling devices.

For that, and for so many vital things in your plays, and for this kind and thoughtful letter,—many thanks.

Sincerely yours,
Thornton Wilder

---

39 Zoë Akins (1886–1958) was an American dramatist and screenwriter.

40 Akins's play *The Furies* (1928).

182. TO ISABELLA N. WILDER. ALS 2 pp. (Stationery embossed 50 Deepwood Drive / New Haven, Connecticut) Yale

<Washington, D.C.>[41]
Tues. night. Jan 21 <1941>

Dear Mom:

Telegraphed you two hours ago.

Drove in from Baltimore this a.m; worked in my cubby hole (where I am now; 8:30 p.m), then at 4 or 5 drove to Alexandria and was accepted by the hotel that had to turn me down last Friday, the George Mason.

You saw it—it's on the main street (the Country's main street, U.S. I<)>—so that's settled.

I found a garage 3 blocks away.

Most days I shall bus or train into town.

x

Tomorrow I must come to N.Y. four hours each way, for that old Committee on Relations between Xians and Jews. But I can study Spanish going and coming so that's all right.

My train leaves here at 8.

x

Yesterday was fine and fun & as far as my participation went as rapid and superficial and inconsequential as a tea at the Lohmans.[42]

I picked up a taxi about 1:20 and thought that with my special card "to be placed on the windshield of the automobile" could get anywhere. But the crowds were so thick that one couldn't even get to a policeman to ask the permission to drive through. So I walked and finally after trampling on piccaninnies and grinding down grandmothers, I got to <a> cop & was admitted onto the Ave that was cleared for the parade due 2½ hours later. Long semi circular awning on the East front. Gave up hat and coat, and joined a long slowly moving line pass-

41 TNW was in Washington, D.C., for the inauguration of Franklin D. Roosevelt and was invited to the White House reception.

42 Carl A. Lohman and his wife were New Haven friends.

ing thru "basement" corridors hung with portraits of former presidents and their ladies. I looked about among my fellow guests and decided I was among campaign-debts. A voice said: "Dontcha know: we used to see him in Little Rock." The long line mounted some stairs and suddenly was at the front door of the W. H. Band playing. And Mrs R, alone, shaking every hand. She did not recognize, but smiled nicely. There were no presentations. So I strolled into the East Room crowded with people eating cold meats in vegetable salad. Yes, I said: tycoons, ward heelers. Then I suddenly recognized from her fotos the former Mrs Vincent Astor; then I saw Thurman Arnold;[43] then the Les Glenns. (The President had done the traditional visit to Les's church that morning at 10:30).[44] With them we strolled into the Dining Room. At the left old Mrs R[45] was rec'ing in the Red Room. Cordell Hull passed. I shook hands with Raymond & Doro Massey and Madeleine Sherwood (Bob with influenza at his hotel). Happy greeting with D. Thompson. Then Elmer Rice! Then in the Dining Room, I can't remember them all: Bishop Atwood,[46] Doug Fairbanks Jr.<;> the Frankfurters; Georgiana[47] for some reason knew both Wallace and Chaplin, and we talked quite a while with each (Wallace—nicest face in the world): Chaplin lectured us on the Brotherhood of Man. I was both very impressed with him, and yet dying of boredom at what he said.

No sign of the Pres. Then Nelson Eddy! and Helen Gahagan and Melvyn Douglas! Georgiana seemed to know a great many of the women—her father having been head of the U.S. Chamber of Commerce here. I lost the Glenns when I stepped in to see Madame R. again, and presently circa 2:45 came out and went back to the Lib. of Congress not having had tickets for the grandstands for the Parade.

Here, I've written that all very lifelessly but it'll have to do.

---

43 Head of the Antitrust Division of the Justice Department at that time.

44 Glenn was the minister of St. John's Episcopal Church on Lafayette Square, opposite the White House.

45 Sara Delano Roosevelt, the president's mother.

46 Julius W. Atwood was the former Episcopal bishop of Arizona.

47 Georgiana was the wife of C. Leslie Glenn.

¶ Wish I hadn't double-promised old M^c^Cracken I'd come to N.Y.

¶ Guess who I saw lunching with a man at the Roger Smith today—and who saw me!—Guess.

Yes—Virg. Withington.[48] Her mother'll be here Thursday. I asked them to lunch Sat (I only "see" people at weekends) if her mother's in town still. ¶ I've found a very good book by an Ecuadorian—so I won't have to be insincere in Quito

more soon

love Thornton

183. TO ALEXANDER WOOLLCOTT. ALS 2 pp. (Stationery embossed 50 Deepwood Drive / New Haven, Connecticut) Harvard

Popayán
<Colombia>
Palm Sunday
<April 6> 1941

Dear Alec.

Will this reach you?

In these countries you put the air mail letters into the hands of young ladies behind a grill and they put the stamps on. Rumor says that when your back is turned, they soak the stamps off, re-sell them to another foolish client, and destroy your letter and his.

That would make you angry? Dishonesty?

Not at all.

That is charming. Inconvenient, but charming.

It is an inconvenient by-product of their individualism

48 Withington was a Wilder family friend from New Haven.

What are other people's letters and other people's postage stamps compared to one's own fascinating and voracious life. With those resold and resold postage stamps one can buy for oneself such delicious things as a pair of shoes, for one's lover such delicious things as a half-dozen Gilet<te> razor-blades, and for one's grandmother such a delicious thing as 50-years respite from Purgatory.

It is impossible to be angry at a Colombian.

Besides I am more than half-Colombian.

I envy them that drop of Indian blood that would efface the passage of time and that would confer on me a patience as wide as the ocean, even if at times it would let me fall into a vacancy that's like despair, and a paralysis of the will that's like petrifaction.

And I envy them that drop of negro blood that would inure me against discomfort under the heat, and would set my blood circulating with a godlike well-being, even if it did bring with it a preoccupation with sex so obsessive that any other activity in life would seem like a boring automatism.

No, but I'm very Colombian. If anyone shows any sign of liking me I lay my heart in their hand without asking <for> a receipt. I confide the story of my life to the first person who alludes to a lesser known incident in his own; I am subject to a melancholy that—it's the only kind—does not proceed from any occasion in external life: meaningless melancholy. I have a passion for poetry and tears come into my eyes at the mention of a great poet's name.

When I left Bogotá night before last my thirty friends-til-death arranged an event: a copy of the movie of "Our Town" was discovered in far-off Cartagena; it was air-posted to the capitol. We all saw it at 11:30 p.m. I spoke. They spoke. We separated at 1:30 with embraces and tears and promises of return. Cordell Hull has other things on his mind, but in one corner of his domain, his will had an unpredictable extension.

It's a pity that this letter won't reach you,—but its impossible to be angry at a Colombian.

Next week I embrace Ecuador.

your friend sea-changed
Thorny

184. TO RUTH GORDON. ALS 1 p. (Stationery embossed Gran Hotel Bolivar / Lima / Peru) Private

LIMA <Peru> May 26. 1941.
leaving Sat. by Plane—Miami, Sunday
night

Dearest Ruthie:

Everytime I was on the point of wishing you were here to share some of these persons and things I suppressed the wish: No, Ruthie doesn't like mountains. You can't enjoy these countries on any other terms. Everywhere mighty peaks.... eternal snow.... Cotopaxi.... Chinborazo.... El Misti.... Only at that price can you see the glittering baroque churches of Quito, dear, covered with gold leaf so thick that it could balance beggared Ecuador's budget; or the melancholy dreamy Colombians, every one a poet, and everyone bursting into tears when you mention poetry; but living in a country divided by three great ranges so that you visit the other cities either in an hour by plane, or in a month by donkey back; or Peru, a handful of Spaniards or almost Spaniards driving Rolls Royces through a myriad Indians.

I've liked it. I've done pretty well what I was sent to do. I've made good friends with scores of writers and educators. They've all planned to come up and stay with me when the monetary exchange permits and Mama will be Señora for years to come to a procession of darker-skinned intellectuals.

I'm glad I made it clear to my committee that I wouldn't write about this trip. Writing's only fun when you can tell your truth, and my truth about these countries is winning, appealing, complex, aching, frustrated, hopeful and dejected.

I have been completely cut off. I do not know what you have been playing. I saw your name in electric lights on a movie theatre in Bogotá (I have no camera); but I hope to see you soon. I shall be teaching in Chicago all Summer—but with my car—so every Friday noon to Tuesday morning I shall be in some obscure hotel on the Michigan shore writing plays. Give Jed my love. Only Chinborazo can give an idea of how I admire and value and love you,

Ever

Thornton.

185. TO NOËL COWARD. ALS 3pp. Private

<London>
The Savoy 2:00 a.m
waiting for a 4:00 a.m.
broadcast. Oct 9–10, <1941>

Dear Noel:

First of all the title is genius: with spirit and blithe you already lay the ghost and shroud the death's head.[49]

and then the whole treatment of Madame Arcati. What is genius but combining the unexpected and the self-evident,—so that at the same moment you are saying both: "How surprising!" and "How true that is!"

And what a performance from Miss Rutherford—

and then. turning it all on Edith. By quarter of four I was saying: How the Hell can Noel get us out of this satisfactorily? And then you did—like that.

Elvira—perfect. That voice.

I wish you'd been Charles.

I thought Fay Compton was hitting pretty hard.

Tell the director how brilliant his work was. For instance, that moment when Elvira knows she has caused Ruth's death. Oooo!

Only thing I didn't like was the last three minutes. Hard, I call it. And a little longueur[50] in the early part of Act II.

This play—and London Pride—and the Destroyer picture—falling from one sleeve within two years, and such years.[51] That's telling 'em. That's England talking.

God bless you
Thornton

---

49 Coward's play *Blithe Spirit* had opened in London in June 1941, with Margaret Rutherford as Madame Arcati, Kay Hammond as Elvira, Fay Compton as Ruth, Cecil Parker as Charles, and Ruth Reeves as Edith.

50 French: length (TNW no doubt meant it was a bit lengthy).

51 "London Pride" is a song Coward wrote in 1941. The "Destroyer picture" refers to *In Which We Serve*, which Coward wrote, codirected, and acted in. It was not released until 1942, but the British press had begun discussing the film in late August 1941.

186. TO J. DWIGHT DANA. ALS 2 pp. (Stationery embossed 50 Deepwood Drive / New Haven, Connecticut) Private

Jan 29. 1942.

Dear Dwight:

Memo: rê Michael Myerberg.[52]

Have known him about five years, first in Hollwood, where he had an office.

Principally, he is Leopold Stokowski's manager. He put through Stokowski's Tour of South America with the American Youth Orchestra, and the tours in this country; managed his relations with Walt Disney for "Fantasia"; and his business with the gramaphone companies.

Altho' he's only about 38 he has been in the entertainment business a long while, as promoter, sometimes manager. He began many years ago by being the first to place college-boy bands on ocean-liners; then he placed ballet-units in musical comedies; managed the Humph<r>ey-Weidner<Weidman> ballet,[53] and the Catherine Littlefield Philadelphia Ballet.

For years he has maintained an experiment studio for making movies with marionettes, which he claims will be the next new sensation in the movies to supercede cartoons. The only thing I know that he actually managed on Broadway was a Ballet-Drama on Voltaire's <u>Candide</u> with Humph<r>ey and Weidman about five years ago, but he claims 30 productions on Broadway, by which I suppose he means various revues to which he furnished specialty numbers, etc.

He is married to the daughter of Margaret Matzenauer.[54] His wife under the name Adrienne is a star in night club singing and has been appearing in the Rainbow Room and Féfé's Monte Carlo, which are tops in the profession.

---

52 TNW had met Myerberg at Mabel Dodge Luhan's Taos home in 1938. When Jed Harris declined to produce TNW's new play, he turned to Myerberg.

53 In 1928, dancers Doris Humphrey and Charles Weidman had established a school as a dance company, which toured the United States in 1938. In 1933, the company performed *Candide,* choreographed by Weidman.

54 Matzenauer was an opera singer.

So you see it's that part of the entertainment business that Anglo-Saxons don't know about, vague but omnipresent, and that the French call cuisine, dickering, middleman, promotion. The thing that separates him from the fly-by-night adventurers in the profession is his matter of fact reticence, his absence of loud-mouth boasting, and his earnest desire these last years to get into things of high standard.

I feel sure he is honest, and that he is very effective and capable. He has a cordial letter of commendation from Cordell Hull on his conduct of the Symphony's tour through Brazil, Argentina, etc, which was a very difficult thing to manage.

He is very enthusiastic about the play.

He has in mind engaging the young manager director, Shepard Traube, who has just struck a great success with Angel Street.[55]

My feeling is that though he may not be the best overseer on the production of so difficult a play (after Jed that would be Orson Welles, who is deeply engaged in a new movie) that nevertheless he is a person to whom I could best turn over all that overhead aspect of a production in perfect confidence, thus leaving one free to work out the artistic aspects. Given the troubled times, and the need for haste, if it is to go on this Spring, I think his enthusiasm, energy and command of resources are just what it needs. He feels the cast should have Big Names—which, given the peculiar state of the theatre business at this time, is right—and immediately began thinking of George M. Cohan and Fanny Brice. The first is wrong casting and the second is fine. He knows these stars' managers (and themselves) and again relishes that kind of persuasion and dickering.

He is not a member of the Manager's League, but I assume that that part will be conducted by Shepard Traube, who is. What is he then? He is the agent in the sense that Brandt and Brandt ought to be, but isn't,—the live-wired activator, taking care of all those things that the layman can't do.

I'll be seeing him again this evening and will report further.

Cordially ever,
Thornton

---

55 American producer, director, and writer Shepard Traube produced and directed *Angel Street,* which ran in New York from December 1941 to December 1944.

187. TO LYNN FONTANNE AND ALFRED LUNT. ALS 4 pp. (Stationery embossed The Century Association / 7 West Forty-Third Street / New York) WisHist

Week-ends: 50 Deepwood Drive, New Haven
Otherwise: Columbia University Club, 4 West 43 St. NY

Feb. 5, 1942

Dear Friends:

I didn't answer Lynn's lovely letter, because I knew that I soon would have another matter to write you on. Jed with the manuscript was being silent week after week and I foresaw I would have the text back and be released of the promise to give it into his hands first.

Then I didn't write you with the sending of the script because such letters—half deprecation—are so unnecessary.[56]

But now with Alfred's telegram, of which—whatever happens—I shall always be proud, I shall write a letter about the play even before receiving Alfred's letter.

x

Lately, my eyes have been opened with a shock to one aspect of it.

It's struck some people as "defeatist." I have only read it to a few friends, mostly in our academic group in New Haven. One distinguished doctor said that it haunted him for days but that "the government ought to prevent it's being shown"; others variously said it was "anti-war" or "pacifistic." And I suddenly remember that Sibyl, who heard the first two acts in London, said that the Second Act was "so cruel."

And three or four days ago my eyes were opened, and I could see with amazement how I had given so wrong an impression of what I had meant.

It's that old thing again: that New England shame-facedness and

---

56 TNW had sent Lunt and Fontanne a completed script of *The Skin of Our Teeth* in January, hoping to convince them to play Mr. and Mrs. Antrobus and perhaps to convince Lunt to direct it. Lunt, who at first reserved judgment, ultimately found the play "very obscure" and declined the opportunity for both of them.

shyness of the didactic, the dread of moralizing, the assumption that the aspirational side of life can be taken for granted.

I had omitted (through thinking it self-evident!) any scene of conjugal love and trust between Mr. and Mrs Antrobus; and any speech that would give open voice to her and to his confidence, through discouragement, in the unshakable sense that work and home and society move on towards great good things.

Now with a sort of eagerness I have set to rendering more explicit all things which for me were always there and which I now feel to be urgent for expression. With what mortification I now see that the Second Act—vindication of the unit of the family—exhibits only the exasperating side of children and the "nagging" side of Mrs Antrobus; and how especially I shirked Mr. Antrobus's broadcast to the Natural World; and how the positive affirmative elements of Act Three are muted and evaded to the point of spiritual thinness.

x

Jed's objections which he says apply only to the second and third Acts have to do with theatrical contrivances and "tricks." He doesn't specify which ones he objects to; but the ones I have resolved to modify are in the last act.

I have tried writing the Third Act straight through, without the interruption of the Rehearsal of the Hours-as-Philosophers, and am preparing some less obstrusive way of giving the impression of the overarching world of time, weather and natural history that surrounds the Antrobus family.—But the chief thing is to inform all that with the tone of warmth and courage and confidence about the human adventure which I had too much "taken for granted."

x

I don't have to tell you what hopes I keep in relation to you both.

But it's enough for the present that Alfred's telegram tells me of his warm interest in the text itself. And any suggestions from that comprehensive God-given understanding of what the theatre is in heights and depths are reward enough for me.

With devoted affection
Thornton

Post-script:

This Michael Myerberg whose association with the play was published as manager, is an old friend who is really serving in the capacity of what Brandt and Brandt never really has done. He is not a member of the Manager's Association; there is no contract between us; and his enthusiasm led him to "do something about it" as inspirator and friend.

T.

188. TO HAROLD FREEDMAN. ALS 2 pp. (Stationery embossed 50 Deepwood Drive / New Haven, Connecticut) Private

Feb 20. 1942

Dear Harold:

Your letter is so kind and helpful that I am going to reply to it in very confidential terms—just for you and Janet,[57] and Mrs. Freedman, if she is interested.

First: the history

Back of that is the Unsatisfactoriness of Jed, the Ideal Director and the Atrocious Manager.

My life-long feeling that plays should represent a series, and a developement, not each an isolated New York package-ing.

Hence, the resort to Reinhardt.

Since we have no Manager-plus-director units in this country (the formula that has been behind every great theatre manifestation in Russia, Germany, Austria and France) I still continue gropeing to help set one up.

I am still believing in M. Myerberg, even though he is making

57 Janet Cohn, Harold Freedman's assistant.

some brash flighty mistakes according to the promotion ideas that he brings with him from the aspects of the entertainment business that he has been associated with hitherto. Apparently my successive scripts are floating in and out of all sorts of unlikely offices, etc, etc. But he is very alive. A fresh air blows through all the plans. The only thing I don't like is that it's still indistinct as to whether he is promoter or manager. When we approached the Lunts and discussed approaching Orson Welles, he seemed perfectly ready to retire from manager-activities and give it over.

Today, I'm going to insist that he enroll among the managers or return the scripts to me (since it looks as though we cannot produce until next Fall) wait and begin all over again from the beginning later. In which case he can be Manager, if he wants, but a real Manager with contracts and everything.

x

Most confidential:

I think Kazan is the director I've been hunting for. Fine comedy; superb stage movement; and dry economy in emotion.

He is very enthusiastic about the play. But is committed to the Paul V. Carroll for the next two months.[58]

Frederic March is eager to play it. And I'd settle for Mrs March, but only as the Mother, and with the proviso that she and ourselves might find her unsuited as rehearsals advance. (F. March shows signs of being willing to seek his career alone!)

Kazan's and March's commitments would only permit us a hurried late Spring try-out; and this is not an out-of-town tryout play.[59]

x

Since then it resumes in the Fall, maybe we'd better begin from scratch and try for Orson who is an old friend of mine and never forgets that I "discovered" him.

x

---

58 Elia Kazan did direct *The Skin of Our Teeth*, but at the time TNW wrote this letter, Kazan was scheduled to direct Paul Vincent Carroll's *The Strings, My Lord, Are False* in May 1942.

59 Fredric March and his wife, actress Florence Eldridge, who frequently acted together, did originate the roles of Mr. and Mrs. Antrobus; but at this time, March was committed to star in the film *I Married a Witch* (1942).

Anyway, I'm not downcast. Except for one thing: I'm always forgetting that I'm the head of a household and am presumed to be earning my living by my pen. Jed used to foster that notion that I'm a gentleman of vast private means; I'm damned if I'll fall in with that rôle forever.

All cordial regards, Harold, and now I return to the government movie I'm working on, also—practically gratis![60]

your old friend
Thornton

189. TO ISABEL WILDER. ALS 2 pp. Yale

<Hollywood, California>
Tuesday night, May 26 <1942>

Dear Isabel:

Many thanks for your letter and clippings. Latter better than I expected.

Got a really sensible letter from Michael about. Very harsh on Kazan's work, but still confident of his powers au fond.[61] "For Sabina I think we need a big theatre personality, and I don't think she's a big theatre personality." But he sent her the script last week.[62]

Work, work, work.

But it's really good. For hours Hitchcock and I with glowing eyes and excited laughter plot out how the information—the dreadful information—is gradually revealed to the audience and the characters. And I will say I've written some scenes. And that old Wilder poignance about family life going on behind it.[63]

---

60 During the first few months of 1942, TNW wrote the scripts for two army training films, *Manuelito Becomes an Air Cadet* and *Your Community and the War Effort*, an assignment arranged by Archibald MacLeish, who was assistant director of the Office of War Information.

61 French: fundamentally.

62 TNW is probably referring to Tallulah Bankhead, who did play Sabina in the original production.

63 At this time, TNW was working with Hitchcock on the screenplay for *Shadow of a Doubt*.

There's no satisfaction like giving satisfaction to your employer. I hope I give it to the Army too. Satisfaction to yourself is fleeting, spite of what the moralists say. And satisfaction to the public does not interest me.

Last night and tonight I've worked, too. But this climate drives you early to bed.

Tomorrow night Bob drives Helen to the station. She's going to Ardmore, Oklahoma, for a while to stay with her mother. The day after he goes to New York to do a government movie. Then they come back here in July to continue work on the play.[64]

I was at their house during the the ¾ hour blackout Sunday night. As they don't have rehearsals here, it always means something. Usually a mistake by the Interceptor Command. No ack-ack fire, I'm sorry to say.

An air-raid warden was run down by a unlighted car and killed.

Rosalie fine.[65]

Hermann Weissman immature as ever.[66] But rich. He says C. Chaplin wants to see me. I've offered next Mon. or Wed. evenings.

Friday morning, maybe, Mr. Skerball,[67] Mr. Hitchcock and I fly up to San Francisco to visit the town of Santa Rosa, 50 m. N. of the Bay, scene of our movie. They return the same night. I stay on and moon about the place another day. Sic.

Tonight who should be going in the door of Villa Carlotta at the same moment as I but the MacMillans. I had a cigarette with them in their luxurious apartment. "What a coincidence! Who could believe it."

He has a number of pupils. Yes, pupils. I'm in the best of health, thank you.

I drive better.

---

64 American dramatist and screenwriter Robert Ardrey had been TNW's student at the University of Chicago, and TNW was his mentor thereafter. Ardrey's wife was Helen. The play mentioned may be *Jeb* (1946).

65 Rosalie Stewart.

66 Herman Weissman was one of two people credited with the adaptation for the 1944 film of *The Bridge of San Luis Rey.*

67 Jack H. Skirball was the producer of *Shadow of a Doubt.*

TNW and Alfred Hitchcock at work on Shadow of a Doubt.

Will I ever get—during the five weeks—so that I won't feel as though I ought to be home writing the script? I've done about 30 pages out of a hundred and thirty. Each step is complicated plotting and of course that gets denser and more complex as it goes on. But I like it.

And tomorrow we "pick up" the first cheque. Never did I love money more purely.

It's 10:45<.> I can't keep my eyes open.

Listen. My contract says I must be here until the 26th. Rosalie says if the script is done, etc, I can ask for three days off earlier—pleading preparations for the Army. As there will be no more transcontinental civilian air passage, the most I can hope for is plane-passage to Kansas City. Then train to Chicago—Albany—Rutland. One night with Woollcott; pullman to Boston and home. Speriamo.[68]

Love

Thorn.

---

68 Italian: Let's hope.

190. TO RUTH GORDON. ALS 2 pp. Yale

5959 Franklin Ave. Hollywood
June 11 <1942>

Dearest Ruthie:

Repeating my telegram:

Your letter blew like a high wind through the insipid airs of this town.

x

Enclosed a signed affidavit of homage. I'm delighted to send it to you and delighted to be able to send it to you.

x

I can never retreat from positions that have been ratified by reciprocal friendship. Gadgett's to do the play.[69]

I'm now going to tell you an awful thing, but don't tell anybody:

It's very hard for me to take the slightest interest in any of my things once I've written them. There they are, and they can go their separate journeys amid success or failure, amid good or bad production—I'm already a thousand miles away. My première, my applause and my hisses (and my 300th performance) have already taken place at my writing desk.

Isn't that awful?

So about Sabina. You were Sabina in Quebec; just as you were Mrs Levi in Tucson. I roared at you. I knelt before you. I carried home your flowers after the first performance. Never have I been so happy in the theatre.

I feel quite calm in the fact that you will some day be Mrs. Levi and Sabina in the future. You created the rôles and you can resume the creation whenever you choose. Last year or this year doesn't matter. Besides, it looks as though you were going to insinuate yourself into my future plays, too.

I have very little temporal sense. I'm not impatient.

---

69 Elia Kazan's nickname was "Gadge."

So if the Natasha thing holds you, do that; and if that developes any difficulties, do come to us and let us know at once.[70]

x x

Captain Wilder reports for "special duty" at Miami on the 27th. So as to get every last minute out of me, Mr Skerball, Mr Hitchcock and I will probably fly to N.Y. about the 21st and continue work in a New York hotel room. Besides, Mr Hitchcock will be photographing the wastes of the Jersey marshes and the working-men's roominghouses of Passaic for the prologue of our picture.

Honest, Ruth, the picture is good. At the end we descend to a little fee-fo-fi-fum, but for the most part its honest suspense and poignancy and terror. Today Hitch told me that he had had Little Foxes shown to him yesterday and that he'd picked Patricia Collinge for our mother. I told him you were en route and to hold his horses. I've asked him to look at the Magic Bullet.[71]

x x

Oh, Ruthie, I was never in better health. Never looking forward to anything more than the Next Chapter.

The only thing I lack is company.

I went to dinner at George Cukors. (with Barbara Hutton Reventlow and Cole Porter and some glamor-food). He's very nice and we got on fine. But that's not the company I want. And René Clair came to a cocktail party Sol Lesser gave for me. He's fine; but he looked tired and harrassed, and slipped away back to his cutting-room.

Jed was asked to the same party. I expect its too much to expect that he'd have come.

Anyway, soon or late, near or far,

somebody loves you:
Thornton

---

70 There was some discussion of Gordon playing Sabina, and she may well have been the actress TNW had in mind for the part when he wrote the play; but she was not offered the role. In December 1942, she opened in New York in a production of Chekhov's *The Three Sisters*, playing Natalya Ivanovna.

71 Patricia Collinge played Birdie Hubbard in the film *The Little Foxes* (1941), as well as the role of Emma Newton in *Shadow of a Doubt*. Ruth Gordon played Hedwig Ehrlich in the 1940 film *Dr. Ehrlich's Magic Bullet*.

191. TO ROBERT MAYNARD HUTCHINS. ALS 2 pp. (Stationery embossed Universal Pictures Company, Inc. / Universal City, California) Chicago

June 16. 1942

Dear Bob:

It's been a long time since I owed you an account of the fits and starts of my life. The trip to England was a great experience, but I was unequal to digesting and realizing very much of it.[72] I am easily rendered insensible by too much to see, too many people to talk to. The days were crowded with inspections of ruins, of defense activities, airplane factories, bomber commands, luncheons, interviews with workers, journalists, Ministers, dinners, writers, and so on. A more scrupulous conscience than mine would be shadowed by the fact that British taxpayers paid out about a thousand dollars to transport me there and back; but it <is> sufficient for me that I enjoyed it. Probably my socio-politico-welt geschichtliche[73] reflexions on it are unworthy of a child of ten.

I came back and finished my play. I am not ready to ask myself if its a very good play. It's design is that of a very good play and maybe the design is actually present in the text.

Then I began moving toward the Army and the movement culminated this morning at 9:30 when I took the oath of office. I am Captain T.N.W, 0908587. I arrive the 27 at Miami for six weeks training in basic soldierly and then I go to Harrisburg for six weeks training in the Army Air Intelligence Officers Training School.

To put it briefly:

> Only men between 19–24 can pilot the new bombers. At twenty-five the psychosomatic reflexes no longer respond.

---

72 From September 10 to 13, 1941, TNW and John Dos Passos attended a conference in London of the International Committee of PEN, the writers' organization. TNW stayed past the end of the conference and was able to witness the war firsthand, not only in London but also as he traveled around the country visiting friends, military bases, bombed cities, and addressing meetings as far north as Glasgow. He returned to the United States on October 18.

73 German: world history (German is *Welgeschichtliche*).

> But the young pilots are emotionally immature. Returning from raids where they have killed, or where their friends behind them, gunners etc have been killed, they approach the Interrogators Table in an inner turmoil. They do not wish to speak to a human being for 24 hours. The<y> fantasize or worst of all develope mutism.
>
> The Army has sent out word that there must be a new kind of officer at the interrogators' table. It's not enough to know maps, read photographs and compute ballistics. There must be a psychologist, etc. He must know with which pilots he must be hard as nails, with which he must be patient and indirect. Yes, all War is ugly, not less so when it tries to be humane.
>
> So it was laid before me.

Entering the Army in wartime is like getting married: only the insecure feel called upon to give the reasons for their decision.

So I won't go into them. But it's a pleasure to describe the relieved rush with which I turn my back on civilian life. The level to which 'society' has fallen, the fine arts, the 'public speech', the talk one has to exchange. The Army, imagine, is a place where one no longer hears the War 'intelligently discussed'.

In der Anfang war die TAT.[74]

And to think that Archie MacLeish first approached me with a view to entering his bureaus. I told him I didn't want to write for my country and I didn't want to sit in an office for my country—and instead of being antagonized, he helped me to this.

Well, this was being set in motion, and suddenly the invitation came from Hollywood to write a murder-script with Alfred Hitchcock, from whom murder and suspense have no secrets. With barely five weeks of liberty I decided to come out here. I wanted to make some more money for my dependents in the event of a long war. I came cynically, and what happened?

I'm fascinated. Our work is very good. It's not literature. But the wrestling with sheer craft, the calculations in a mosaic of exposition is bracing.

---

74 German: In the beginning was the deed. (TNW misquotes Goethe's line from *Faust*: ("Im Anfang war die Tat!")

It's almost over.

x x

The Closing of the Door—that to Civilian Life—is almost pure joy and the anticipation of what's ahead: being pure instrument, however modestly, in a movement-wave that's so important to me is all joy; but looking backward I have one big regret: That in the last years of intermittent writing and intermittent ill-organized experiencing I have not made myself to rejoice myself enough in two friendships: you and Amos. It's only secondary to say, though true, that you are one of the persons I admire the most in my whole life. For what I mean, it is more essential to say that you are you, and to the I that is I that is a great good real right Fact and Thing.

When Armistice Day comes among the many things it will mean, my God (to Greece and the Ghettos of Poland, and the paddy planters of China, Oh my God) I shall walk among the bonfires of celebration; I shall permit myself a luxury of cynicism about mankind and civilization, but I shall be thinking of you and Amos and Gertrude, and saying that The World may wag its way hither and yon but as for me I shall love my friends and do it much more wisely than "before the War."

x x

I seem to have fallen into the mood of a Heroickal last farewell, so tell Maude to snip a piece of a ribbon from her hair or sash and I'll wear it like a paladin on the field in her dear name. I ask that your three daughters stand on the battlements shading their eyes toward the West for me.

Anfang
und
Ende
Alt
und
neu[75]

affectionately
Thornton

75 German: Beginning and end, old and new.

192. TO ISABELLA N. AND ISABEL WILDER. APCS 1 p. Yale

Hotel Woffard<Wofford> Room 323 Miami Beach
Monday Noon
<June 29, 1942>[76]

Dear Ones

The more I suffer the more I like it. We're on the drill field at 7:00 a.m and already dripping wet; and I love it. And scarcely a moment to think until six. In quarters absolutely at 8:00; lights out at 10:00. Packs of work and a sense of no time to do it, but I love it. ¶ Tomorrow (confidential) I am ordered to meet the Press for the first & last time with Capt Clark Gable and Capt Don Ameche. ¶ So far being in the Army is expensive—always new books, equipment etc to buy. Our first pay cheque contains an additional $150.00 for uniforms. ¶ Last night I hunted for Toby.[77] He is not in the Hotel Royal. Janet is misinformed. But there is a hotel Royal Palm and a hotel Royalton. Tell Janet. Verify. Do not worry about my "sufferings"—I was never happier and seldom in better health. I live to make myself rewarded for diligence and alertness. No time for letters ¶ 600 of us. A nice roommate Lt. Powers of Fargo S.D. Love,

Thornton

193. TO ISABELLA N. WILDER. ALS 2 pp. Yale

Hq. 328th Fighter Group
Hamilton Field
Calif.
Oct 7 • 1942

Dear Mom: Here I am under another duty. Last Friday, never to be forgotten, I was Officer of the Day for the whole Post. I told you about

---

76 The postcard was postmarked June 30, 1942, which was a Tuesday.

77 Winthrop Saltonstall Dakin (1906–1982), who had married TNW's sister Janet on March 22, 1941, before entering the U.S. Army Air Force.

that. Tonight, I'm merely Officer of the Day in the 328th Group. That means I sit in the great echoing barracks of an Office between 12 and 1 at noon and from 5–10 in the evening. I've fortified myself with peanuts and milk chocolate and at ten o'clock I shall go to one of the most fascinating all-night lunch stands in the world—the one maintained in Hangar 9 for all night aircraft repair workers and for whatever flyers may descend on us from A—ia and A—ka, and God knows where else.

I've got to point out to you again that these extra duties (I've also just finished my 3rd Investigator's report on a Court-Martial case) are not imposed on me because of my splendid soldierly capacity; all new officers are saddled with them; they're supposed to be the corvées[78] of the service.

Do you want to know a secret,—a non-military secret?

Well, I always knew that a large part of my reluctance to write was due to my cramming myself with reading. The impulse to write arose from a spring very near the appetite to read and the latter could easily quench or substitute itself for the former. Well, I haven't read a book since I've been to Miami, except one detective story and Giraudoux's Bella[79] which I picked up at home during my delicious long week-end. There was no thought of reading nights at Miami or Harrisburg; but here—altho' there is no end to study I could do on enemy planes, artillery etc—on the whole my evenings are free. I get up at 6:15 by bugle call and go to bed at 9:45, but that time after dinner is free. I feel the need of literature; but (a) I'm in no position to get it and (b) I wouldn't even like to read if I had it. (I was surprised at how less-good "Bella" seemed)<.> SO—as simply as falling off a log I found—a solution: I started making my own. I began the Alcestiad. I write only about 10 speeches an evening. If I find that it moves into the center of my interest, or keeps me awake at night, I'll have to give it up. But so far it contributes its fragment tranquilly every night. And on Sundays I can do a larger portion.—As I see it now its very Helen Hayes. Anyway, so far its still a secret.

78 French: drudgeries.

79 Novel (1926).

Isabel writes me that you're about to be thrown into the throes of a great decision. I shan't push.

Another letter from Aunt Grace; they're going up to San Francisco to see an eye specialist for Uncle Thornton. But I don't get to San Francisco alternate weekends as I hoped. My chief's wife is there, so my days off will come in the middle of the week, if at all. Fortunately the Army believes in leaves, tho several day furloughs are only extended in war-time for convincingly stated reasons. It is impossible that I could come East for the opening of the plays.

Lots of love, honey, early and lately.
Thorny

194. TO SIBYL COLEFAX. ALS 2 pp. NYU

Captain Thornton Wilder, A.C.
To Lady Colefax, 19 Lord North St.
Westminster, London.

Hq. 328th Fighter Group. Hamilton Field, Calif
Oct 9. 1942

Dearest Sibyl:

After those months of training I am at my first job, and what I'd like to talk about are all those stirring and moving things about me.

It's no secret, however, to say every corner of the place is directed to the great end and that some of the corners are very near the crucial places. I'm still healthier than I've ever been and as happy.

For change I can go every two weeks and spend some thirty hours in San Francisco. I kept wondering last Saturday whether you had ever seen it. I spent a part of my childhood on the Bay; its as beautiful as ever, especially toward late afternoon.

On the way here I stopped and had a Sunday breakfast with the Hutchins. Maude has again shifted her medium and has done some brilliant watercolors. She has also printed some verses in "Poetry".[80] If I transcribed some, it would only give you an access of anger, for they canalize perfectly that aspect of her which irritates, that cool narcissistic impudence. Bob "missed the train" of public leadership, once <and> for all, and is on a siding, for life, I'm afraid. Maybe not.

Others are wrestling with the rehearsals of my play. I can scarcely believe it myself, but it opens in New Haven next Thursday, a week from last night. We have a brilliant cast: Fredric March; Florence Eldridge, his wife; Tallulah Bankhead and Florence Reed (as the Fortune-Teller.) A cast of 40 and an investment (not mine!) of $40,000. It will tour outside of New York for six weeks, being licked into shape. Isabel is serving as my proxy and says that rehearsals have gone swimmingly as far as the text is concerned, though there have been many clashes of personalities. Tallulah has tried to show all the other actresses how to do their job and when they have not taken her advice she has flounced off to her hotel and resigned. So far she has returned almost penitently each time. She loves her rôle (Sabina) as well she might, and is very acute about the whole play when the demon is not possessing her. The text is almost established. My last week at Harrisburg I wrote them a new close to Act II and some crowning motto lines for Mr. Antrobus in Act III. Last Sunday from San Francisco I sent them a new treatment of a middle portion in Act I (eliminating the Ancestors scene which had turned out to be unclear in rehearsals) and heightening the atmosphere of impending cold and danger.

But now I'll tell you a secret, a non-military one. During the four months I've been in the Army I've not read a book nor felt that I wanted to; nor is what one would call reading possible. But literature I must have about me, and <I> have been driven to make my own. I've been going to bed at quarter of ten, but for a week now I've gone to bed at ten: every night I write from eight to ten speeches in a new play, the several-times attempted and discarded one, The Alcestiad. The second Act (i.e. "play") covers the same material as Euripides', but from a different point of view; the First on the marriage of Alcestis turns on the wonderful legend of how Apollo came to live, disguised, as a shep-

---

80 Maude Hutchins published four poems—"I Asked Her," "Absent-Minded Poet in Washington," "Suitor," and "Gold"—in the September 1942 issue of *Poetry*.

pherd working for King Admetus for a year; the last act is the old age and "mysterium" of Alcestis. The whole is how Alcestis learned to hear Apollo speaking to her through circumstance,—Deus Reconditus.[81] I have always wanted to dedicate The Skin of Our Teeth to you, and especially to you "in London", because it represents my thoughts about endurance and fortitude in War; but maybe the elements of horseplay (i.e. my avoidance of pathos; and indirect approach to 'elevation') and perhaps the semi-chaotic jumblings of historic allusions render it unsympathetic to you. Perhaps, on principle, you don't like dedications at all. Perhaps you would prefer "our" Arabian nights play,[82] if I could ever see it as a whole, or The Alcestiad. The text goes to the printers in about five weeks. Unless I hear from you accepting the dedication. I shall send it to them undedicated. If you are willing I suggest the form "To Sibyl Colefax, in London." Don't let this be a moment's worried bother to you: Your word is my law.[83] ¶ Alec seems very high-spirited. Ruthie is finishing a movie before joining Kit Cornell for the Three Sisters.[84] ¶ Apart from that I know nothing but my absorbing task and the engrossing communiqués in every morning's paper.

Much love and constant thoughts
Thornton

195. TO ISABEL WILDER. ALS 2 pp. Yale

<Hamilton Field, California>
<October 21, 1942>

Isabel: Here's the letter I wrote Michael: show it to Tallulah and Freddie and the two Florences and Gadget if you think fit.

---

81 Latin: God is concealed.

82 TNW is probably referring to "The Hell of the Vizier Kabäar" (see letter number 156).

83 When *The Skin of Our Teeth* was published in 1943, it appeared with no dedication.

84 Ruth Gordon appeared in two movies that were released in 1943, *Edge of Darkness* and *Action in the North Atlantic.*

Dear Michael:

Certainly something must be the matter.[85]

And I don't want to hear the story from other people but from you.

What lines have been removed from the play that I or others would regard as integral?

What actors have been removed that would seem to so many people as essential?

And why couldn't these things have been done without so much sincere alarm and regret?

Remember that no actor or co-worker ever worked with Reinhardt who didn't long to work with him again.

Remember the same of Charles Frohman.[86]

Remember that no actor or co-worker ever worked with Sam Harris who wasn't crazy to work with him again.

And remember that no one (except Ruth) ever worked with Jed without loathing the thought of ever working with him again.

The great manager is also the peak of consideration and tact, even when business considerations or decisions as to entertainment values require his doing difficult things.

And they deeply value actors and actors' peace of mind and find ways to secure their undistracted concentration on the play.

Do, Michael, drop me a letter about all this and do everything to establish so fine a company into the harmonious working unit they have a right to be.

I want them to admire you and long to work for you in many future great productions.

Ever your old
Thornton

---

85 Shortly after *The Skin of Our Teeth* began its pre-Broadway run in New Haven on September 15, TNW received telegrams from both Reed and Bankhead telling him that Myerberg had fired three actors and was sabotaging the play.

86 Frohman was a well-known Broadway producer.

196. TO MICHAEL MYERBERG. ALS 3 pp. WisHist

New address:
329th Fighter Squadron
Hamilton Field, Calif.
Oct 27. 1942

Dear Michael:

Just returned to find your letter. Its what I've waited for—your acc't, and I assure you that I haven't let myself be pushed around by others accounts.

I won't try to answer it fully, being punch-drunk with fatigue tonight, as so often.

Naturally I am astonished at the degree of Tallulah's difficulty; but I am convinced by your description. So, conceding that the lion-tamer's technique is necessary, I still hope for the day when such provocation of her hatred can be gradually transferred to something more paternalistic; that would be the real triumph. And such a triumph over the managers who've had to deal with her formerly.

A telegram from Isabel arrived at the same time as your letter saying the reviews in Philadelphia were uniformly favorable. My first thought was of your investment. I should hate to think that the results of the final performance would be that you had been clipped. I was flabbergasted to hear that you had raised only 10,000 dollars. O my God! Does that mean that no one, under any conditions you could accept, came forward with any more money than that!!

I'm sorry that Isabel has seemed to be drawn into the magnetic field of our stars agitations. They have almost a right to such agitations—being artists going through the throes of bringing to birth. I think she likes to frequent them. I know I do; but her letters to me don't seem to be excitable. She loves to discuss the play in itself, and does it very well, giving me a clear and enthusiastic picture of long passages of the performance.

The Marchs have each written good "manly" letters and I have more and more admiration for them as persons. I hope you can find occasions to express your admiration for their work and to do them some kind of "favors" of regard. Actors and public speakers (I know!) and performers need such things, as dry soil needs rain.

As to the close of Act I: once they have established audience-relationship and effectiveness in the comic spirit, I hope they can gradually bring it around to the human-exciting, letting the comic merely enter by flashes. Sabina's cry at the close should be one of the big signifigances of the play—whether the audience laughs or not, the idea should be planted at 9:30—"Save the human race" and the rest of the play can practically rest on it,—but its highest effectiveness comes from a background not of comic but of suspense-hope-effort-excitement in the scene that it springs from.

I reproach myself for not having written Gadgett more frequently. The letters that began to come in from discriminating friends (with world theatre backgrounds) in New Haven and Baltimore[87] agree that he has done a masterly job with such difficult material. I hope this brings him the recognition he deserves and that he is the director the American scene has been waiting for and that, God willing, I can call on him down the years for all kinds of plays.

x x

It's late and I must turn in.

But one more word:

To felicitate you and Adrienne on the good news:

I hope it's a girl this time—with her mothers voice and beauty, and with her father's power of grasping situations.

I can keep both military and non-military secrets; I'm proud to know this one.

More soon
your old
Thornton

87 *The Skin of Our Teeth* had one-week runs in Baltimore, Philadelphia, and Washington, D.C., after New Haven and before its New York opening.

197. TO ROBERT FROST. ALS 2 pp. Virginia

As from: 50 Deepwood Drive
New Haven. Conn.
Thanksgiving Day
<November 26> 1942
Los Angeles.

Dear Robert Frost:

Had it been possible you would indeed have received some tickets for the opening of the play.[88] The reasons why it was impossible would make a long and complicated story, briefly: on the 15th I was in California; on the 16th I was on Long Island (on a military order that had no connection with the play); your telegram of the 17th was forwarded to the wrong address, and was received on the 18th when all the tickets had been disposed of. I did not go to the opening and left the next day for Spokane, Washington. As the Bible says: When they say unto a Centurion, go; he goeth.

But far more interesting to me than your seeing the play, would have been the chance of me seeing you. My days are spent in, on and about khaki. I'm starved for wider views.

But the work is fascinating. Until that order of the 15th I have been (after months of training) Intelligence Officer of the 328th Fighter Group, Hamilton Field, California; being knit into three squadrons of pursuit pilots being "activated" for combat duty. That Order pulled me out of that and put me on a committee that is preparing a certain Air Force document that requires our visiting many of the Fields in the country. Whether I go back to my Group after this 60 days of Detached Service, I don't know. I hope so.

I look forward to our next walk and talk, cher maître

Most sincerely
Thornton.

---

88 Apparently, Frost had wanted to attend the New York opening of *The Skin of Our Teeth* on November 18.

P.S. Half a year ago I gave Alex. Woollcott that ardent Vermonter, a collected edition of your poems.

Aleck has always said that he has a closed mind to poetry. "There's nothing in poetry that couldn't be said as well in prose."

I begged him to read you "as though you were prose" and the poetry would arrive later.

He now asks me which of yours I would recommend for inclusion in an anthology he has been asked to prepare for men in the services.

I made my suggestions. I think he is consulting many persons.

Not long ago a Marine quoted to me "West-Running Brook,"[89] but it was a more than usually literate Marine. The only reading I've seen in the hands of soldiers is pulp magazines.

And as for officers, myself included, they don't read at all.

T.

198. TO ISABEL WILDER. ALS 2 pp. Private

Washington, D.C.
December 17. 1942[90]

Isabel: Send this to the Saturday Review.[91]

First go upstairs and verify the fact that Finnegans Wake is 600 pages long. I think it is.

Then erase this note.

Love and giggles,
Thornton

---

89 A 1928 poem by Frost.

90 The date and the place of origin appear at the end of the original letter.

91 In its issues dated December 19 and February 13, 1943, *The Saturday Review of Literature* published a two-part article by Joseph Campbell and Henry Morton Robinson, "The Skin of Whose Teeth?" The authors called TNW's play "not an entirely original creation, but an Americanized re-creation, thinly disguised, of James Joyce's 'Finnegans Wake.'" Not wanting to dignify the accusations by answering them and further inflaming passions, his attorney and family advised against replying; TNW's letter in response to the December 19 article was never mailed. Either TNW saw an advance copy of the article or the issue appeared before December 19.

To the Editor of the Saturday Review of Literature.
Dear Sir:

Many thanks for your telephone call and your request that I comment upon the article in the Review pointing out some real and some imagined resemblances between my play, "The Skin of Our Teeth", and James Joyce's novel, "Finnegans Wake".

At the time that I was absorbed in deciphering Joyce's novel the idea came to me that one aspect of it might be expressed in drama<:> the method of representing mankind's long history through superimposing different epochs of time simultaneously. I even made sketches employing Joyce's characters and locale, but soon abandoned the project. The slight element of plot in the novel is so dimly glimpsed amid the distortions of nightmare and the polyglot of distortions of language that any possibility of dramatization is out of the question. The notion of a play about mankind and the family viewed through several simultaneous layers of time, however, persisted and began to surround itself with many inventions of my own. If one's subject is man and the family considered historically, the element of myth inevitably presents itself. It is not necessary to go to Joyce's novel to find the motive of Adam, Eve, Cain, Abel, Lilith, and Noah.

From Joyce, however, I received the idea of presenting ancient man as an ever-present double to modern man. The four fundamental aspects of "Finnegans Wake" were not to my purpose and are not present in my play. Joyce's novel is primarily a study of Original Sin and the role it plays in the life of the conscience. Its recurrent motto is St. Augustine's "O felix culpa!" Nor could I use its secondary subject, the illustration of Vico's theory of the cyclic seasonal repetitions of human culture.[92] Nor could I find any place for its primary literary intention, the extraordinary means Joyce found for representing the thoughts of the mind while asleep, the famous "night-language". Nor could I employ his secondary literary intention, the technical tours-de-force whereby through puns and slips of the tongue he was able to represent several layers of mental activity going on at the same time and often contradictory to one another. If I had been able to transfer to the stage

92 Italian philosopher Giambattista Vico (1668–1744).

several or any one of these four basic aspects of the book, wherein its greatness lies, I would have done it and would have gladly published the obligation at every step of the way.

The germ of my play, once started, began to collect about it many aspects which had nothing to do with Joyce. It fixed its thoughts on the War and the situation of the eternal family under successive catastrophes. It groped to find a way to express dramatically the thought that the great "unread" classics furnish daily support and stimulation even to people who do not read them. But principally the play moved into its own independent existence through its insistence on being theatre, and theatre to such an extent that content was continually in danger of being overwhelmed by sheer theatric contrivances. I can think of no novel in all literature that is farther removed from theatre than "Finnegans Wake".

The writers of the article in the Review list a long series of resemblances. Only those who have pored over the novel can realize how patiently the authors must have searched through that amorphous dream-texture to assemble them and how surprising it is to find them confronting the concrete theatrical material they are supposed to parallel. Maggie Earwicker's letter buried in the rubbish heap behind her house becomes the letter of proud and indignant self-justification that Maggie Antrobus throws into the sea over the heads of the audience? Well, all the Margarets in the world can be presumed to have written letters that were important to them. In the most wonderful chapter in the novel, Anna Livia Plurabelle, river and woman, looks for a match to search for some peat to warm her husband's supper. The authors of the article quote this passage and tell your readers it resembles Mrs Antrobus and Sabina asking for fuel to warm the household against the approaching glacier. By such devices your authors could derive "Junior Miss" from "Lady Chatterly's Lover". The ant-like industry of pedants, collecting isolated fragments, has mistaken the nature of literary influence since the first critics arose to regard books as a branch of merchandise instead of as expressions of energy.

Should a group of men of letters represent to me that the dependance of my play on Joyce's novel is so close as to justify adding a note of acknowledgement to the theatre program, I would willingly accede to their opinion. I have placed such a note twice before; once in The

Women of Andros, though Terence's riotous farce had been changed into a reflective tragedy, and once in "The Merchant of Yonkers", though its principal personage did not appear in the Austrian prototype at all. The first of the credentials of my advisers in this matter, however, would be that they had decoded all six hundred pages of Joyce's crowded and mighty novel and realized how great were its differences from my three act comedy.

Sincerely yours,
Thornton Wilder

199. TO MONTGOMERY CLIFT. TL (Copy)[93] 1 p. Billy Rose

March 23, 1943

Dear Montgomery Clift:

My sister has only just told me of your ill health. As grateful author I have the best of reasons for regretting your withdrawal from the play,[94] but the important thing is that you restore your health before you have overtaxed it and that you restore it for a long and triumphant career in the theatre.

I hope you are going somewhere for a long rest under wise care. Do not trouble to answer this letter now, but when the convalescence is well on its way, I should be very interested to know what you are thinking about, what you are reading, and what you are seeing; (this last shows that I hope you are considering our Western desert country where most of the invalids I've known have got ringingly well—"seeing" means the profile of mountains around Tucson.)

Be patient in your resting. Give in to resting. Put the present agon of the world out of your mind—with the invalid's legitimate permitted

93 This is a transcription of TNW's letter; the original has not been located.

94 Clift played the role of Henry Antrobus in the premiere production of *The Skin of Our Teeth.*

selfishness.—Read and think over only the works from which the stress has been removed by the author's art—about suffering but not of it—Sophocles not Euripides; Mozart not Beethoven; late Shakespeare not middle.

Think of yourself as surrounded by the grateful thoughts of your friends—among whom I hope you count

Sincerely yours
Thornton Wilder

200. TO MICHAEL MYERBERG. TL (Copy)[95] 2 pp. Private

Last hours at the Billetting office, Air Base,
Presque Isle, Maine.
Hereafter: APO # 4002, c/o The Postmaster, N.Y.
May 21, 1943.

Dear Michael:

Try and remember at what moment you arrived at the point when you were <u>unable to discuss the production with anybody.</u>

It would teach you a lot about yourself, your past and your future.

What was the moment when you locked up your mind in a steel brace.—and transferred the operations of the reason over to sheer blocked unlistening will?

From that moment you talked like a hysterical madman,—building up exaggerations; contradicting yourself hit or miss; substituting wish-fantasies for arguments.

Notice our last conversation:

I said in a spirit of sheer discussion, and with your interest in mind, that the decisions you were making were all gambling (i.e. taking a chance on Tallulah's returning to the part; taking a chance on the

95 This is a transcription of TNW's letter; the letter has not been located.

public's finding any interest in the play with Hopkins and Nagel in it) and you answered that you'd never made a wrong move yet.[96]

What kind of answer is that?

In the first place, it's untrue; a manager whose 3 stars abandon a successful play the minute their contracts run out has bungled his managerial function in a way that would make Charles Frohman, Belasco, Sam Harris and Max Gordon[97] laugh with contempt.

In the second place, it's a wishful fantasy. It's a little venture at prophecy. Business isn't conducted by boasts and predictions; neither is war.

In the third place, it shows how completely emotional your whole relation to the production has become. Your answer shows that for you the whole production is staked on your self-consciousness.

The moment that happened your ears became closed to discussion; you dried up any approach of friendship that I could make toward you; and you became a tiresome bore.

Through emotional self-justification you began raving about how Conrad Nagel and Miriam Hopkins would give better performances than Freddie and Tallulah; and how Tallulah's record in THE LITTLE FOXES[98] proved that there'd be no audiences for her in this play,—you knew in your gizzard that that was all eye-wash, but you were deaf and dumb and thought that Harold[99] and I were infants.

You broke the approach of friendship; you made discussion impossible; and you became a hysterical bore.

That's what the practice of hate does. By design and by your own confession, you employed hatred as an administrative method from the beginning. It took; and the blood has rushed to your head ever since.

---

96 In June 1943, Tallulah Bankhead, Fredric March, and Florence Eldridge took advantage of clauses in their contracts and left the play. They were replaced by, respectively, Miriam Hopkins, Conrad Nagel, and Margalo Gillmore. The play ran through the summer, to decreasing audiences, and closed on September 25. The next week, it opened in Boston, prior to a planned national tour; but after one week of a two-week run, now with Lizabeth Scott as Sabina, it closed and there was no tour.

97 Gordon was a theatrical producer.

98 Tallulah Bankhead starred in the premiere production of Lillian Hellman's play *The Little Foxes* (1939).

99 Harold Freedman.

Now you imagine that everyone hates you and you plunge from one distorted position to another.

For God's sake, clear your head.

You have a large theatrical property.

Manage it judiciously, and from a distance.

It's a play basically requiring high standards; maintain them.

Don't listen to Shubert Alley wise-guy advice; they don't know anything about this kind of property.

See that it satisfies the highest type of audience in every town,—then the hoi-polloi will follow. But if you direct it to the hoi-polloi, they won't like it and you'll have lost any solid following.

You have my friendship waiting for you when you've emerged from your illness, and show yourself again an able business man; a cool clear administrator; and a worker in the arts who is unshakeably set on only being connected with the highest standards procurable.

When you can assure me of that, I'm

Your old friend,
Thornton

201. TO ISABELLA N. WILDER. ALS 2 pp. Yale

Censored
T.N. Wilder

HQ NAAF A-5
APO 650
c/o Postmaster NY NY
Sept 15 • 1943

Dear Mom:

Lovely long letter from you.

I am delighted to learn from you that I am the one of your children who is now most a subject for your concern; for I am not likely to cause you any beyond what your imagination can invent. The city I was in for a month and a half had many mosquitoes, but the citizens were proud to say that none of them had been carriers for ten years. This is hard to understand, because the city was very dirty, as they all are here. At present I am about 10 miles from another famous city; here the mosquitos are carriers and we sleep under nets. A number of my colleagues have had short fits of malaria, dysintery, etc. I suffered with the latter for one day. I confess I do not take the atropin table<t>s urged on us by the Medical Corps and placed in every mess. I don't like drugs of any kind, unless you call whisky a drug and I get none of that here. Africa is the continent of insects. I think using Lifebuoy soap has kept me fairly unmolested.

A-5 has moved into a wealthy Mohammedan's villa. Seven rooms about a large central court. Hideous "European" murals. A Squadron Leader; (i.e Major) a Flight Lieutenant (Captain) and I share a room, and are a congenial and gratifying example of "combined staff" harmony. The Mediterranean is a heavenly blue. The place-names of the region are famous in warfare, ancient and modern.

It's true that I was in one raid which I shall remember as the most magnificent display of pyrotechnics that a small boy could imagine. 40 planes of the enemy did little damage and were driven off with losses. It was at 4:00 a.m. and you know how I like early rising.

I loved your going to Hartford to shop with Mrs Burton, and would like to see what you both bought. And I loved Isabel's account of your gira[100] to Boston, the Pioneer, the visit backstage, etc. And I liked best your determined resolve to live well past 90. Take care of yourself, especially on those back stairs. Try not to be a concern to me and I'll take care not to be one to you.

Lots of Love,
Thornt.

---

100 TNW means hegira.

202. TO ISABELLA N. AND ISABEL WILDER. ALS 2 pp. Yale

Mediterranean Air Command
APO 512
c/o Postmaster, NY, NY.
Dec. 20(?) <1943>

Dear Ones:

A new address

I don't dare think how long it may have been since I last wrote.

We moved because we have a big piece of new work to do, and we had to begin the work before and during the work<move?>. We're back in the second city in which I was stationed before. I love it when the work is concrete.

This afternoon when we asked our boss, the Group Captain, whether there was to be a "office conference on progress" he stopped and thought a minute and said, "No,—my advice to all of you is to go out and take a long walk." Oh, boy,—I walked home and took a nap which was mighty welcome.

Now, dears, I gotta tell you an awful thing,—I am now established in a billet of delicious comfort!! It weighs on me. Two other officers and I have a 5 room apartment on the main street of the city (elevator and everything); we have a bonne à tout faire,[101]—une "perle",[102] who adores us. We draw comestibles from the quartermaster and she cooks our breakfasts and dinners. The minute we take off a piece of clothes she whisks it away and washes and irons it, and refuses to think of keeping a record and being paid for it. What's more, her soups are delicious, her coquilles (from G.I. salmon with bechamel sauce), everything.

She is slightly touched with what G. Stein calls "cook-stove crazi-

---

101 French: a housekeeper.

102 French: a pearl.

ness"; but I like her fine and she's recounted the story of her 56 years to me with details which would have startled the late Delia Porter.[103]

I get up at quarter to seven from between real sheets. I bathe cold, but I could bathe hot, if I dared manage the alarming looking geyser which has a pilot-light on, like a perpetual votive flame. I take bus, tram or hitchhike a considerable distance to the hut ("Nissen hut") in which my desk is. Lunch at "Senior Officers' Mess". Start home about 7. Loud welcomes from Françoise. Dinner and early to bed to read a little Balzac before turning out the light. Such are the rigours of war.

Another thing has arrested us all from writing. No one can settle for us what our address is. We have risen one echelon higher, yes, ma'am. I am now the head of Mediterranean Air Command Air Plans III. All MAC is one APO number. Should we or not, include our section? Is it a breach of security? Yet if we omit it, would correspondence ever reach us?

Darlings, your packages are piled up in one corner of my armoire. Christmas day will be like any other day probably; but one of my housemates has ordered a turkey from a farmer (an American!) 15 miles from this city, and that we'll have on the Eve and I'll open my packages by myself in my luxurious bed after dinner.

Dec. 21

Again interrupted.

Work increases. I love it, and enjoy the approval of my bosses. Someday I shall a tale unfold.

This letter'll never get off, if I don't give it up to the Sgt. now.

Look at the date.

We don't even think Xmas yet.

But

tons of love

Thornton

---

103 Delia Lyman Porter's inspirational gift books, published in the early 1900s, offered quotations for every week of the year.

203. TO EVELYN SCOTT METCALFE.[104] ALS 2 pp. Tennessee

T.N. Wilder, Major AC
HQ MAAF
APO 650
U.S. Army
July 28. 1944

Dear Mrs Metcalfe:

Indeed I understand very well the assumption behind your letter that Charlotte judging by her letters may be soon permitted to return to normal living.[105] We have it often, too, after a visit to her when her conversation for the most part gives every indication of being restored to herself. I have not seen her since I came overseas, more than a year ago. For a time she had seemed to benefit greatly from the shock treatments and several of the nurses said that they had never seen such improvement in her type of illness.

Unfortunately, however, the lucid interval and the balanced letter are only a part of the story. For us the distressing part is the sudden bottom falling out of a conversation and the disappointment to our hopes: the sudden insistance that she has only been ill a year; the announcement that there are many people going around in the world saying that they are Evelyn Scott or Thornton Wilder, but that they aren't and that we must protect ourselves against them. From the doctors' point of view a still more conclusive reason that she is not well enough for removal is the fact <that> she towards the doctors—all of whom have

104 Evelyn Scott (1893–1963), a Southern novelist, poet, and essayist, met Charlotte Wilder at Yaddo in 1933, corresponded with her thereafter, and was one of the two women to whom Charlotte dedicated her first book of poetry, *Phases of the Moon*.

105 In late February 1941, Charlotte Wilder had had a mental breakdown in New York City. She was hospitalized in private hospitals in New York City and White Plains, New York, for several months, where she received the accepted treatment of the day—electric-shock and insulin-shock therapy. When she did not show any improvement, it was decided that she had a deep-seated condition that would require continued hospitalization. She was transferred to the Harlem Valley State Hospital in Wingdale, New York, where she received drug therapy. After an initial positive response to the drug she was being given, Charlotte became depressed and distant. In January 1945, the family would move her to a smaller, private facility in Amityville, New York.

been unfailingly tactful and discreet—she maintains an implacable silence & pretends not to see nor hear them.

Fortunately for my own reassurance that no injustice is being done Charlotte's opportunity for the best surroundings conducive to her recovery is the fact that Dr Tom Rennie, the head of the Psychiatric Section of the NY Hospital and one of the most distinguished doctors for mental illness in the country is a friend of mine; has interested himself in Charlotte's case and is able to read the reports which we are not allowed to see. He assures me that there is still a measure of hope that she may rejoin the outside world and that he will continue to follow her case and let us know when he thinks that she has sufficiently recovered to justify a change of background.

Sincerely yours
Thornton Wilder

204. TO ISABELLA N. AND ISABEL WILDER. ALS 2 pp. Yale

HQ MAAF APO 650 Oct 17, 1944

Dearest Twain: Suddenly I'm aware again that quite a time must have elapsed since I last not only vowed each morning to get a letter off before the day was over, but did it. My days are more and more cluttered with other duties than my military. The American service personnel who are interested in putting on plays have urged me to let them do Our Town, and I can't offer any very good reasons not to, so a group of soldiers with little theatre and professional experience and some WACs are already rehearsing. In addition, I was pushed into being Acting Chairman—I at least insisted it was only "acting"—of the committee supervising all productions at the Hq., and now there's a perfect fever of theatre going on.—there were highly successful runs of "Outward Bound" "Rope" "French without Tears" and <">Pirates of Penzance" and now four companies are rehearsing Arsenic and Old Lace, Blithe Spirit, Tons of Money and Our Town. All this requires a

TNW as a lieutenant colonel in the Army Air Force.

lot of coordination and committee and club meetings, and is accompanied I'm sorry to say with a lot of underground politics and some very bitter feuds. I'm getting out of the chairmanship as soon as I can, and will restrict myself solely to overseeing the Our Town. ¶ The Wing Commander is back from his wedding journey[106] and the eternal teasing of him by the entire staff will soon die down, speriamo.

The capitols of enemy held Europe, are falling<.> Riga and Athens these last few days; two more any day now.

We gave a goodbye party to another of our staff who got an appointment at the Pentagon. I was told the same could be had for me for the asking but I replied that I didn't want to go there or home, until this mighty action had seen its ending.

---

106 TNW's British intelligence counterpart, Roland Le Grand, was married in Rome in October 1944; TNW served as the best man.

It's getting colder, dearies. I don't wish to harrow my mama, but it certainly is idiotic the way that during the day I forget to call up the billetting officer and ask for another blanket. I only think of it nights when it's too late!! So I put rolls of Sunday NY newspapers under my lower blankets—newspapers are very good insulation—and my heavy raincoat over my feet and over the two other blankets—can you bear it, mother?—and make out very well. Today, and no later, I shall call up and arrange for everything. My colleagues who were here last winter say that seven blankets is par.

Rê Xmas presents. Well, dears, edibles are highly welcome. Due to my not going to mess at noon and merely nibbling sweets. From the PX we can draw unlimited fruit juice so that prevents my picnic lunches from being downright deleterious. What is most deleterious, however, is sitting down to a full dinner at noon. As for the rest, any practical clothing from underwear to sox are also welcome. Heigh-ho—what I want most is to give you some big hugs and lie on the hearth rug and listen to the radio describing the reconstruction activity after the war.

lots of love and you'll hear from me oftener.

Thine Thorny

P.S. I'm still in top health, girls, explain it.

205. TO ISABELLA N. AND ISABEL WILDER. ALS 2 pp. Yale

HQ MAAF APO 650 c/o P/M NY NY Nov. 10, 1944

Dear Ones.

Such fascinating packages arriving from you every day. The smaller ones I shall dip into as comestible in order to augment my picnic lunches,—ie that retirement to my tent, disdaining the plethora of the mess, and opening a can of fruit juice, etc, etc, reading a few pages of

Freeman on Lees Lieutenants or Croce on old Naples,[107] occasionally catching a cat's nap, etc.

Our Town rehearsals go on pretty well. I've rec'd very high approval for the transfer from an air combat unit of a sergeant who was asst stage manager at the Los Angeles production—so I won't have to give so much time to it. The "Stage Manager" does pretty well, but he's atrocious in the clergyman's speech at the wedding. How that must have been misread in the many small-town productions. It's not a small-town comment on the ceremony!

I loved your letter on the garden. I love all your letters and don't deserve them. Its downright abysmal how few I write: between rehearsals on alternate nights; Hq. Theatre Club committees (very stormy) on other nights; a new military committee I'm on and which requires writing up reports on other nights, I get very little time. Since with old fashioned scrupulousness I refuse to using<use> the working day for such things. This minute it is 0825 and my colleagues have not yet appeared.

Nice letters from Eliza and Rebeckah Higginson.[108] Helen Hawey<?>[109] sends me impetuous greetings from time to time and even got a book to me without my having requested it (Little Coquette—tepid Tilleul)[110]

Day follows days with an featureless uniformity, a sort of winter quarters monotony. Some pleasant new officers have joined our section to replace those who sweated to get themselves into the Pentagon. An order suddenly closes all civilian restaurants in Italy to service personnel, so the little Italian grape arbor trattoria to which I took many an acquaintance is now out of bounds. I paid a last visit to

---

107 Douglas Southall Freeman's *Lee's Lieutenants,* a three-volume work, was published in the 1940s. Italian historian and philosopher Benedetto Croce (1866–1952) was born in Naples and lived there for most of his life.

108 Rebekah Higginson met TNW when he was in Arizona in 1936–1937. She had three children, none of whom was named Eliza. TNW may have meant her daughter Sally, with whom he became a close friend and correspondent.

109 TNW may be referring to film actress Helen Hawley.

110 TNW is probably referring to *Little Coquette: The Story of a French Girlhood* (1944), by Renée de Fontarce McCormick. In referring to tepid linden tea (*tilleul*), TNW means uninspiring reading material.

Signora Napolitano (the family name) and to little Catarina (aged 10—but what a capable little manageress since she speaks Inglis) with many protestations of undying affection.

The wedding which I practically staged is a great success in many ways. Already Mrs L. (Flight-Officer WAAF) knows she is to become a mother, so by regulations she is hustled back to England by the first boat, discharged from the service (tho' honorably) and generally encouraged to increase the population of the United Kingdom. I have been a very close party to all this, even my rich store of learning in gynecology being put to service, so there'll be lots of tears to shed when Eileen leaves her husband and "loco parentis".

Oh angel-mama, the letter I wrote to make you happy, succeeded only in distressing you. I cannot repeat too often that I love my tent and my fixtures and my getting up and my lying down. It's not only comfortable in itself, but I have a temper which finds things comfortable about me, what a fortunate young man, and how devoted to his mother and sister to whom he sends his love

Thorny

206. TO EILEEN LE GRAND. ALS 2 pp. Private

HQ MAAF APO 650 U.S. Army.

Feb 15 • 1945

Dear Eileen:.

You can imagine with what absorbed interest I read your letter (and reading correctly, I hope, still further between the lines) and with what interest I listen to Roland as he thinks aloud about you, which he loves to do with such moving affection.

I try to imagine what the life is like there. I'm angry angry angry at the weather. There's nothing harmful about outdoor cold as long as one is warmly dressed and if there is, at least occasionally, sunlight. Its long been noticed that very young children thrive on outdoor cold, if they're warmly dressed. Their faces seem not only <to> bear the cold better than ours, but even rejoice in it. But, oh. I wish you had more sunlight.

I've been thinking over, as you asked me to, some occupation for your time and attention that can remove you at least for a few hours every day from the routine-domestic and the self-occupied reverie. (There's nothing wrong in itself with long meditative hours about yourself and Roland and the child; its only that there comes the moment in such thoughts daily when they start repeating themselves and going around in circles; that is the moment when they turn into dejection, or worry, or self-pity, or conscious loneliness: and that moment one must rise firmly above and occupy oneself at something else.) <appeared perpendicularly in left margin> **Rê all this I remember my dear Gertrude Stein once saying that 'the business of life is to create a solitude that is not a loneliness'. And that's where the fine arts and the intellect and each person's creativity comes in. My regards to MM.**[111]

What I am going to suggest is this that you set aside a number of hours every week to go to the University or municipal libraries (if you find yourself getting interested this may turn into several hours a day) to read and study systematically: the Psychology of Children. I have known a number of young mothers whose friends or doctors placed such volumes in their hands, but they read them only desultorily. They were too absorbed in maternity itself; they told themselves that the "maternal instinct will enable them to supervise the early years of their children, etc." But it is a science, and one which has made extraordinary advances in modern years. Moreover, it is a profession requiring training and skill. I hope (and there is every reason to believe) that you and Roland will live a long long happy life together; but maturity teaches us to look in the face all the accidents which <u>might</u> arrive in the future. It is only one advantage of the project I suggest that if under certain contingencies you could demonstrate that you were well-read in the psychology of children you would find yourself eagerly sought after. One thing we're sure of in the world of the future is that the Governments are going to interest themselves in the physical and mental well-being of children.

The one drawback against the above suggestion is that the latest

---

111 Probably Margaret MacDonald, a friend of the Le Grands.

studies about it are full of material which laymen would call: "unwholesome." The world's authority is Dr Anna Freud, whom I know, the daughter of the great Doctor. Don't begin, then, with the psychoanalytic books on the subject; save them until the later stages. The really important thing now is that your mind is principally filled with confidence, gratitude, and proud tenderness. Whatever vexations the daily life and the weather and separation and the stringencies of wartime living may bring, do, do combat as far as possible any mental inroads on your sovereign mind: there we can all be rich, serene, and (blessèd word) independent. Perhaps one way to combat just such vexations is to tell Roland about them (and me, if you had time; or me through Roland). He won't misunderstand as long as you can assure him that you're also proud and happy to be Mrs Le Grand and mother.[112]
God bless you,

Thornton

207. TO LAURENCE OLIVIER. TL (Copy)[113] 2 pp. Yale

HEADQUARTERS MEDITERRANEAN ALLIED AIR FORCES
APO 650, U.S. Army

February 18, 1945

Laurence Olivier, Esq.
New Theatre,
London, England.

Dear Mr. Olivier:

It has been a great satisfaction to me to know that you and Miss Leigh are interested in putting on "The Skin of Our Teeth". Through my sister Isabel's letters I have followed the various negotiations including the preposterous deal Michael Myerberg got into with Miss Mannering. I hope that has been straightened out and that your title to it is

112 Julian Le Grand was born on May 29, 1945; TNW was his godfather.

113 This is a transcription of TNW's letter; the original has not been located.

completely clear.[114] Isabel writes that your return to the service is due and that you will have time to direct but not to appear in the play. My admiration for your work is such that I am equally satisfied with this arrangement and hope that it can be put into effect.

I was delighted to hear that your idea was to caste the play with "unknowns" and to so direct them that the result would be a sort of half-way approach to an American manner. Such a procedure might improve on the one drawback I felt behind the New York presentation: the performances of the principals were excellent throughout, but they projected them with the studied precision one would look for in "The Wild Duck". My idea is that the play could give practically the sense of improvisation, a free cartoon, "The History of the Human Race in Comic Strip". At one time I hoped there would be a performance by negroes whose spirit of play, spontaneous emotions, musical voices and uncomplicated idealism (Rodin's Adam!) would have captured this quality so well.

All negotiations about my plays have been handled from New York and New Haven to such an extent that I do not even know who is acting as my agent in London. Could I ask you therefore to see that the following appointment is offered to Lady Colefax, in the earnest hope that she will feel able to accept it, and that the appointment is understood and negotiated through that agent?

It is my hope that Lady Colefax will serve as the Author's Representative and working very closely with the producer, will have full authority to answer for the author and represent him in the following ways:

1. The advisability of cutting certain lines and business or adding others necessary to the better understanding and effectiveness of the play.
2. Consultant on scenery and costumes. It is recommended that in deliberations on casting her opinion should carry considerable weight.

---

114 In 1943, Michael Myerberg made a secret deal for the British stage rights to *The Skin of Our Teeth* with a little-known English actress and producer without informing TNW's agent. This option expired in July 1944, and Myerberg resold the British rights, this time with TNW's knowledge and enthusiastic approval, to Vivien Leigh, Olivier's wife.

3. It is hoped that from time to time during rehearsals and performances she will circulate among the company and be accessible to the performers. It has been my experience that the author or his representative can adjust slight inconveniences and personal frictions in such a way as to aid the morale of the production out of all proportion to the apparent importance of such service.

For these services the Author's Representative will receive 10% of the author's royalities computed prior to the deduction of taxes.[115]

I hope the production will give you pleasure during its preparation and gratification with the results.[116] Kindly convey my regard to Miss Leigh also.

Sincerely yours

208. TO HARRY J. TRAUGOTT.[117] ALS 2 pp. Private

50 Deepwood Drive
Hamden 14
Connecticut
(Only lookit:
AAF Redistribution Station No #2
1020 at<?> AAFBU
Squadron H, Flight 455-C
Hotel Caribbean, Miami Beach, Fla)
May 20. 1945

Dear Harry:

Now hold your horses. This is what happens when you return for reassignment.

---

115 For various contractual reasons and because rehearsals were too far advanced, this arrangement did not take place.

116 The English production of *The Skin of Our Teeth,* directed by Olivier and starring Leigh as Sabina, ran at the King's Theatre in Edinburgh in March 1945 and opened in London at the Phoenix Theatre in May 1945, receiving favorable reviews.

117 Traugott had met TNW in North Africa in 1943, when he, as an enlisted man in the air force, was assigned to be TNW's clerk. He went to Italy with TNW in 1944 as his chief clerk. At the time of this letter, Traugott was in Italy, awaiting reassignment and hoping to be promoted to the rank of staff sergeant.

Within three or four hours of arriving at the post of debarkation (hold your hats, now) you're en route to your home on a 21-day visit. (I waived that in order to expedite matters and God what a fool I was.) Then you report to a Redistribution Station.

You bring your wife, if you choose. You live in a luxury hotel at the seashore—Santa Monica, Calif., or Atlantic City, or here. For nine days you have about two appointments a day. Physical exam, or Classification test, or orientation lecture. (Are you following me?) This applies to Enlisted Men or Officers, because they're all in this very hotel, wives, too; the only protection against reciprocal contagion being that we're on different floors.

Then you have to wait, some a few days, some months for their orders.

I'm in such a mess of red tape as has never been seen. Some Authorities say it'll be two months before I even get to the Separation Centre. Archie Macleish phoned down yesterday, saying he'd effected my separation from the War Dept, but the separation within the Air Force is a thing that'll pretty much have to take its own course. Anyway, tomorrow noon I start being on Inactive Status, which is Step One. With that I can go home and do my waiting, but I travel at my own expense. Query: crazy to learn tomorrow whether Inactive Status gives me gas and shoe ration coupons. All the shoes I got are those I stand in, and my family is certainly going to look for gas coupons after the first hug has abated.

May 22. 1945—Continued over.

Okay. I go North tomorrow on thirty days' leave while the Headquarters meditate on my forward application for separation from the service, with the State Dept's appointment submitted as Inclosure #1.

Well, well, well, won't it be funny to see the family again and the New Haven Green? I've been here over two weeks, but I don't feel I've appraised the United States yet. This town is as bad as Los Angeles and I hope no one ever takes it as an index of what the country has to offer. It's a honkytonk de luxe and always has been.

I still have that feeling of being a piker through my running off and leaving you and Bernie and Morrill[118] on that..... ship. I hope all

118 Other clerks with whom TNW and Traugott worked in Italy.

goes well with you, that you get interesting jobs until its all over, and that you get the advancement that lies just ahead of you. When I spoke of that to Col. Burwell, he acted surprised to hear that there was a Tech. sergeantship on the T.O. I hope he's keeping it in mind.

When I phoned my family they told me that a cable from Laurence Oliver and Vivien Leigh had just arrived congratulating me on a big success in London with the play. I hope it's true, as much for their sake as mine, because that play will always have brickbats and indignant customers, whatever the critical reception is.

I've already written the Wing Commander; give my regard to Col. Alston and tell him I'll write him soon. And do me one favor: I was prevented on that last day from running around to find Wilcox. Do look him up and tell him he has my lasting esteem and that I shall always be glad to hear from him. The opportunity to do him a favor of any kind would always tickle me. The same applies to you ten-fold, Harry and don't forget it, Indianapolis.

Yours in war and peace
Thornton Wilder

209. TO SIBYL COLEFAX. ALS 4 pp. NYU

Back in a week or two at: 50 Deepwood Drive
Hamden 14, Connecticut
(AAFRS No. 2, Miami Beach, Florida)
August 20 • 1945

Dearest Sibyl:

Two letters from you, though written on the 2nd and the 11th, arrived this afternoon. 'Ate 'em up.

I'll take up some of the agenda seriatim and then I'll see what I've stored up to report.

RETREAT: We've just been released unlimited gasoline (but tires are hard to get). I'm thinking now of going, not to Colorado, but to Acapulco, Mexico. Driving there viâ Chicago (i.e. the Hutchi, Amos and my wunderkind nephew); down the Mississippi to New Orleans (Sibyl, what meals—): then to Texas, and down the great "new" road to Mexico City. Down SW past Cuernavaca (where I once went to work, but the work wouldn't come), past Taxco with its famous little cathedral to Acapulco on the sea. It's become very swank, unfortunately: Hollywood flies down there week-ends to marry and millionaires to fish for black marlins (having caught one, you sometimes have to "play it" for five hours). But there are many hotels strung along the black cliffs, a Mexican Town of 20,000, and I hope little subsidiary plages up and down the coast.

THE NEW PLAYS: (Thanks for asking.) For Alcestis I want Elizabeth Bergner. Who else? In the first act, an exaltée faintly "goose"-like young girl; in the second, the greatest golden young matron of all tradition; and in the last the agéd slave, water-bearer in her own palace, with scenes of tragic power and mystical elevation. Who else? And all to be played against that crazy atmosphere of the numenous that is possibly hoax and the charlatanism that may be the divine. And the preposterous-comic continually married to the shudder of Terror. When Heracles goes down to wrestle with the Guardian of the Dead for Alcestis, it's no joke and yet the great generous demigod is terrified and very drunk. I sit here writing one big scene a day (awaiting orders in this luxury hotel, my window over the surf and the greenest ocean,—with next to nothing on, for its very hot and humid); the play is a chain of big scènes à faire.[119] But oh, Sibyl, it's very hard and every-other day it seems clear to me that it can't be done. The whole play must be subtended by one idea, which is not an idea but a question (and the same question as the Bridge of San Luis Rey!); and each of these scenes must be balanced just so and not give a wrong impression about that idea. And no two minutes of it must be too romantic, and none too pedestrian, and none too comic, and none too grandiose. And the great temptation is "to just write it any old way" and trust that "no one will notice" anything but its dazzling theatrics. Oh, dear.

"The Hell of Vizier Kâbaar", that will be more difficult still, but in a different way. That will require the good old-fashioned plot-

119 French: obligatory scenes.

carpentry that I've never done; the joiner's art that must be then rendered invisible, as though it were perfectly easy (like the last movement of the Jupiter, God save the mark.) The danger of the Alcestiad is that the effectiveness may be greater than the content (to which Jed replied, quoting an old Jewish exclamation: "May you have greater troubles!" but what greater trouble could an artist have?) The Hell of..... can't run into that danger. It's content is not a hesitant though despairing question.[120]

THE OLIVIERS: Oh, dear. I'm afraid that I may have said something in one of my letters that hurt their feelings. I've never met them; but even to strangers in whom I have such confidence as I have in them, I run on so, I babble, as though I'd known them twenty years. I assume that they know me, that idiotic bundle of conceit and modesty, of dogmatic assertion and exasperating non-commital; of excessive intimacy and intermittent withdrawal. At a pinch I can write a formal letter. But I can't write an almost-formal letter, and so I'm always getting the tone wrong. Anyway, I honor and admire them boundlessly. I hope they will dismiss me as crazy, rather than think me rude.

CHURCHILL: Do you still have the feeling that the election could be described as showing ingratitude to the Prime Minister? Or that, the first week past, he would interpret it so? Never did he have a better press than the valedictory one, over here. But I'm like to get beyond my depths in your politics or ours.[121]

KIERKEGAARD: Strange things happen when I start raving about S.K. I blew a blast of him, over some cocktails, at Cheryl Crawford. She couldn't wait until Brentano's opened next morning and marched off with Either/Or (a vast mixed dish) and The Theory of Dread (the first half of it, uncharacteristic metaphysics). I recommend starting with two little volumes Fear and Trembling and Philosophical Scraps[122] (or Remnants as sometimes translated.) Anyone<Anyhow>, if you are indeed tempted, and thus have given me permission, I shall send you copies, perhaps my copies with their vociferous marginalia, if

120 For earlier references to this unfinished play, see letters numbers 156 and 194.

121 Wartime prime minister Winston Churchill and his Conservative party had been defeated in the national election in July 1945 by the Labour party and its leader, Clement Attlee.

122 The title was *Philosophical Fragments.*

I can get them back from the latest borrowers. The best sign that I like a book is that it has left my house. Yes, beauty, art, and memory are enough. As bargainers say: I'll settle for them. But the point of S.K. is that he begs us not to settle for them too soon; the prizes beyond those things he makes more enviable exactly by making them more difficult and more painful (just where protestantism has been saying they are easy and consoling.)

I must go or I'll miss mess. All my colleagues are ex-PW from Germany. Stories!

Sibyl dear, (as brides say: "I want you to be among the first to know") I have been awarded the Order of the British Empire. That with my Legion of Merit brings my three years of the war to a happy close. There are few satisfactions greater than knowing you have the approval of your superiors in a job which involved their responsibility as well as your own. When I heard of this, I thought of my favorite Britisher in the world: "Sibyl will be pleased,<"> I said; <">Sibyl, who's done so much for me, who's worked over me.<"> There's a part of my heart that is forever England and over it is a little band of pink and grey ribbon.

(Mess call.)
Lots of love
Thornton

210. TO BYRON FARWELL.[123] ALS 2 pp. (Stationery embossed 50 Deepwood Drive / Hamden 14, Connecticut) Private

Jan 2. 1946

Dear Byron:

Fine.
Fine.

123 Farwell met TNW in Capri during the war. In 1946, he was beginning his studies for an M.A. in English at the University of Chicago.

x

Delighted that you both met the Chief.[124] Though I'm concerned about his being x-ray'd.

x

Emmet Rogers.[125]

A nice enough fellow—but, believe me, acting is not a profession for adults. It is mostly entered into by the kind of person who has no intention of being an adult, and once in it the very exercise of the profession breaks down most of the traits that make for being-the-master-of-one self.

Think of how extra bad it is for a man:

ⓐ You must say words which are not your own.

ⓑ You must assume emotions—which are not spontaneously prompted.

ⓒ You must be aware, down to the finest shade, of what you look like.

ⓓ You live to please, impress, or gratify strangers.

I've known many actors and Larry Olivier is the only one who has not been trivialized and soften<ed> by those requirements.

x

Your paragraph on the U.S. and your idea of a livelihood is written as though you expected me to disagree with it word by word.

x

No, no. Since these things are real to you it's important you do them ⓐ live outside the U.S. ⓑ teach English to support yourself. ⓒ deliberately set your marks for a very limited income.

All I say is do not concretely or mentally pour your thought into that as a life-long picture. Because:

ⓐ one falls into the danger of confusing one's impatience with one's fellow-countrymen and one's impatience with human beings. The trouble with America is that its full of Americans, that's certainly true, but it's not a more pleasing thought when one reflects that (in the mass) England's full of the English; and so on. I have known many

124 Robert Maynard Hutchins.

125 TNW is probably referring to American stage actor Emmett Rogers.

expatriots (this does not include refugees) and I swear to you that I've only known one who was not devitalized by it, and that was Gertrude Stein. Aldous Huxley is palpably thinned out by it; the American "artists" in Rome; the worldlings and the couples with jobs in Paris ("Oh, we adore Paris; we wouldn't think of going back to Baltimore!!<">) whom I knew; such people at Capri; at Taxco; at Oxford. Without realizing it one has been made American by living here the first 15 years of one's life; to slip away from coping with it is to injure oneself.

ⓑ All right—one teaches a subject 5 or 8 hours a day in order to make the livelihood by which one exists. But isn't that a second prize? Isn't the first prize to make one's livelihood with joy, as well as one's leisure? Five hours to drudgery in order to have 8 in which one "lives"—but the happiest lives are those in which there is no division between "working" and "enjoying".

ⓒ Money. Through the Grace of God you happen to have the finest wife in the world.[126] Never forget, however, that straightened means bear down on the wife twenty times harder than on the husband. However, clever she is in running up meals "by magic", in cleaning and dusting as tho' it were "fun"—they pay. They pay not only by work, but by preoccupation; it literally and inevitably takes their mind. Women live and love to serve us; it's part of our business to prevent them doing it beyond a certain point. ¶ Money has three dignified uses (and they do not include owning beautiful things or providing recreation)

1. Saving time
2. Reducing drudgery
3. Furthering the health and education of children.

Well—never did I feel so like an uncle, nor so devoted to my nepotes

Ever

Thornt.

---

126 Byron Farwell's wife was Ruth Saxby Farwell.

211. TO EILEEN AND ROLAND LE GRAND. ALS 2 pp. (Stationery embossed 50 Deepwood Drive / Hamden 14, Connecticut) Private

March 9. 1946

Dear Friends:

It is not only work which has kept me silent and interrupted my correspondence with even my best friends. It is a sort of post-war malaise which I won't go into further lest I give the impression of self-pity or misanthropy or melancholia. It's none of those things. Call it out-of-jointness, and forgive me. I think I've recovered now. Whatever it was it didn't overcloud the fact that I love the Le Grands, old and new, and always shall.

As I think I told you, red tape delayed my demobilization from May to September. The papers must have been lost in some officers in/out baskets. I didn't greatly mind; some of the time I was allowed to wait at home; the rest I spent in the hotels of Miami Beach which had been turned into "redistribution" quarters; but waiting-time is not conducive to work, and perhaps what I wanted was a good excuse not to settle down to work. Finally out I took a trip to Florida and Georgia and did begin work, but its been slow, reacquiring habits of concentration and perserverance.

In the meantime I have been "inhabited" by two compelling enthusiasms. An accident turned my attention to the problems connected with the chronology of the (circa) 500 extant plays of Lope de Vega. I hurled myself into scholarship, spending 10 hours a day in the University Library and making trips to libraries 100 miles away in search of further sources, and I discovered new data. I think that this passion was a useful therapy: pure research has nothing to do with human beings; it has little even to do with taste or aesthetic judgments. Finally I saw that the ground I was working in was a Life-work; wider and wider vistas opened. It was Escape, and finally I willed myself to quit it. Roland, if you want to prepare a thesis in the Spanish golden age, I'll send you all my notes. There's a beautiful thesis there, in a territory where all the Spanish and international scholars were in error. Ready for the asking.

Lately, I have been absorbed by Existential philosophy and its literary diffusion, especially in France. Jean-Paul Sartre has been here, and I have seen him many times. Your London reviews are full of it. It is fascinating, not as nihilistic as it appears to be on the surface, and it is magnificent evidence that France remains a great power, whatever its political and economic situation.

The Alcestiad is almost finished. It waits on one last clarification which I must clear up in my own head, philosophically, before I can project it into the web and woof of the lives of my characters. I have also begun that novel-in-letters about Julius Caesar and the scandal of the profanation of the mysteries of the Bona Dea.[127] I should say that the two works are racing in competition except that such slow work could scarcely be called a race.

Now that I am out of my acedia[128] sufficiently to write letters, I shall write Pank, and Vera and Mike Morgan and the Trolleys, but I've begun with you, dear Kinder. The silver mug is all engraved with Julian's name, but we were told that it can't be sent. My sister Isabel is going to London with the newly-formed "Our Town" co., and if she goes by boat she can bring it.[129] That may be very soon. I may follow in the Autumn,—oh, what good talks. Oh, what dandling of babies. Oh, what insidious instruction in an American accent to say "Uncle Thornton!" Heartfelt blessings on you all—

devotedly
Thornton

---

127 TNW is referring to what became his novel *The Ides of March*, published in 1948.

128 Latin: ennui.

129 Pank refers to Leonard Thomas Pankhurst, TNW's commanding officer at the MAAF headquarters. Mike Morgan and Leonard Trolley were RAF servicemen with whom TNW had worked in Italy. Isabel Wilder went to England as her brother's representative when *Our Town* opened at London's New Theatre on April 30, 1946, with Marc Connelly as the Stage Manager. The London production received mixed reviews.

212. TO RUTH GORDON AND GARSON KANIN.[130] ALS 2pp. (Stationery embossed The Viking / Newport, R.I.) Private

<P.M. March 30, 1946>

Kinder, Kinder, dear Kinder:

Excuse me if I sound smug, but I'm in a beautiful place under a beautiful sun and I haven't a trouble in the world except that I'm penniloius, tubercular, and I'm not sure whether what I'm writing is worth a bean. Apart from that I haven't a trouble in the world and am inanely happy.

Now let's hear about you.

Kinder, do you read plays? Jean-Paul Sartre has given me the American disposition of a play he's written that would freeze your gullets.[131] Will any American manager produce it? Five French Maquis are variously tortured and raped by some Petain militiamen. But it's not about the Resistance movement; it's about the dignity of man and the freedom of the will. There's not a cliché in it; its as bare as a bone in New Mexico; five characters wear handcuffs through the entire play; every agony in it must have been experienced in Europe a thousand time<s> and yet no American manager would venture to present it and we're not grown-up enough for it and we're not worthy of the U.N.O.[132] and so let's think of other things.

When are you two going to get a rest? Now, really; life's short enough as it is. I'll bet you Garson hasn't had a 15-hour sleep for four years,—at least not without anxieties marching through his dreams like Hessians. I'll begin to think that you two are bitten by the hornets of Ambition or the wasps of Competition. Swear to me on the Prayer-

---

130 Gordon had married Kanin in 1942.

131 Sartre asked TNW to translate his play *Morts sans sépulture* (1946), which opened in Paris in November 1946, to great controversy. After meeting with Sartre in February 1948, TNW did the translation. The play, now titled *The Victors,* opened in New York on December 26, 1948, and ran until January 22, 1949, Off Broadway at the New Stages Theatre.

132 United Nations Organization.

book and Talmud that you aren't; that you're sane, that your love for one another and the love that we extend to you is/are calmatives enough. You are successes, you are, because you're loveable intelligent wonderchildren, but I'm beginning to think that there's a slight admixture of Mexican jumping bean in you too. I wish to address the one nonchalant philosopher in the family and send my love to Jones.[133]

I wouldn't scold the Kanins, if I didn't feel lots of love

Thornton

213. TO AMOS N. WILDER. ALS 2 pp. (Stationery embossed 50 Deepwood Drive / Hamden 14, Connecticut) Yale

May 31 <1946>

Dear Amy:

Can't believe it. Isabel's was over twice that. Glad to see that it's deference to the Cloth.[134]

No, never heard of E. Rosenstock-Huessy.[135] Glad to read anything you recommend and will return scrupulously.

Had some hours with A Camus. Lord be praised, I didn't like him as much as Sartre or I'd have committed my time away in translations, services, etc. But I respect him and Le Mythe de Sisyphe is fine romantic writing, though he'd hate to hear it called that.

Isabel heard Dylan Thomas read some of his poems in London (she sat two yards from the Queen!), fine self-forgetting projection she says. He dresses "non-gentleman". The distrust and unkindness of

---

133 Jones Kelly Harris, who was born in 1929, was Ruth Gordon's son by Jed Harris.

134 TNW may be referring to a discounted travel ticket for his brother, who was an ordained minister.

135 German philosopher Eugen Rosenstock-Huessy (1888–1973) emigrated to the United States in 1933 and taught at Harvard and then Dartmouth. Amos Wilder may have recommended Rosenstock-Huessy's *The Christian Future or the Modern Mind Outrun* (1946).

Englishman to Englishman along those hair-fine social categories has to be seen within the military framework to be believed; in what century did this profound evil enter English life? The infiltrations of vulgarians into the Serenissimi[136] circles during the Industrial Revolution? That is just what Proust describes in his world, but there it didn't result in the fear, nay panic, in an Englishman's heart lest he be addressed cordially by some one! So of course Dylan Thomas wears colored wool shirts. How wonderful that the Scots lack any shade of it and move in and out. English life, not imitated and not catalytic, but unaffected.

The Achilles' heel of the French is property and avarice (not luxuria[137]); of the British "Racha, thou fool";[138] of the Americans, self-righteousness—and here I am displaying it.

Our girls here are fine.

Our house is honored this week-end by two Golden Guests, Laurence Olivier and Vivien Leigh. Larry, the greatest English actor in 200 years, says he is using the drive down here to study Lear which he brings to London in the Fall![139]

Love to you and your Loved-ones
Thorny.

214. TO RUTH GORDON AND GARSON KANIN. ALS 2 pp. Private

Last days at Nantucket.
As from: 50 Deepwood Drive Hamden 14 Conn.

July 23. 1946

Dear Ones:

At the end all her dear traits became clear to us again but in a new light: her self-effacement in loving and serving; her Scots inde-

---

136 Italian: the most serene.

137 Latin: lust.

138 TNW is referring to the passage in Matthew 5:22, thereby meaning contempt of others.

139 Although only thirty-nine, Olivier played Lear in a production he directed. *King Lear* opened at London's New Theatre on September 24, 1946.

pendence and desire to endure whatever she had to endure, alone; her distress at "putting people out"; and finally one we had never seen before,—the call for help.[140]

Isabel has been wonderful throughout.

I dread writing Vivien, Binkie,[141] Sibyl, etc. that I am not going abroad, after all. I shall be at Deepwood Drive until Christmas, finishing the novel and sort-of re-establishing a home. Important for Isabel is the feeling that she is needed and useful somewhere; otherwise—you can see—she seems to hang in mid-air.......

My hard work begins next Monday. I'm looking forward to those five weeks. Summer theatre's so damned occupying. Carol Stone is to be our Sabina at Cohasset; the other productions will be full of old friends. Doro Merande, Coolidge, Tom Coley, etc.[142]

The novel's full of glitter now that Cleopatra has arrived in Rome, but its also getting deeper, wider, and more preposterous,—yes, that's the word for the burden of vast implications I've assigned myself.

We've been reading about the March's possibly taking part in Miss Jones.[143] I'm sure that under Garson's hand they'd be fine; but I'll have to hover about in the last row disguised. Florence was very incensed by a moderate letter I wrote her and I doubt that she'll ever consent to speak to me.

Monty Clift writes me that Garson was a wonderful help to him in the tangles of Hollywood negotiation. I'm afraid that fellow's going

---

140 Isabella Niven Wilder died on June 29, 1946, on Nantucket.

141 British theater manager Hugh "Binkie" Beaumont.

142 TNW played the Stage Manager in *Our Town* at Westport, Connecticut, August 5–10; he played Mr. Antrobus in *The Skin of Our Teeth* in Cohasset, Massachusetts, August 19–24; and he played the Stage Manager in East Hampton, New York, August 26–31. Among those with whom he performed, several had been involved in the original stage production of *Our Town*. Doro Merande had played Mrs. Soames, a role she also played in the film version. Philip Coolidge had played Simon Stimson. Thomas Coley had played a baseball player and had also served as one of the assistant stage managers of the original production.

143 TNW is referring to Gordon's autobiographical play, *Years Ago,* in which Fredric March and Florence Eldridge played Gordon's parents, Clifton and Annie Jones. The play, directed by Kanin, ran in New York from December 1946 to May 1947.

TNW as George Antrobus in The Skin of Our Teeth.

to get caught in delays, re-tests, refusals of scripts, and a whole season will go by without his having played anything or ending up as the Young Man rejected by Barbara Stanwyck's daughter.

Garson, William Layton writes me that there is talk of his being asked to read for the part of the New Republic Editor in one of your companies.[144] At his request and in dutiful memory of Woollcott who's secretary he was, I hereby put in a word for him. He's just come back from the London "Our Town"; was the Radio Operator in a year of "The Man who came to Dinner"; a Marine in the Pacific for years; a trained actor, with a steady unvarying authority that was a benefit to the whole London venture, and a fine fellow. To be reached through Joe Magee of the Wm Morris office.

Try and remain modest and unspoiled, dears, in spite of the fact that you're the best, brightest, sturdiest, most gifted and most lovable urchins in the world.

your old
Thornton

215. TO ALICE B. TOKLAS. ALS 4 pp. (Stationery embossed 50 Deepwood Drive / Hamden 14, Connecticut) Yale

October 8 • 1946

Dear Alice:

These last weeks, in whatever company I've been in, I've silenced the aimless talk that goes on in order to tell them about Gertrude, about the several Gertrudes, the Gertrude who with zest and vitality could make so much out of every moment of the daily life, the Gertrude who listened to each new person with such attention and could make out of her listening such rich reinforcing friendship, the Gertrude of intellectual combat who couldn't let any nonsense or sentimentality or easy generalization go by unpunished, and finally the greatest Ger-

144 Several companies performing Kanin's highly successful stage comedy *Born Yesterday* (1946) were going to tour the country. Alexander Woollcott had died in 1943. Layton went on to have a successful career as an actor, a director, a teacher, and a writer. He moved to Spain in the 1960s and became important in the theater world there.

trude of all, the inspired giant-Gertrude who knew, and who discovered and who broke the milestones behind her.[145]

Oh, miserable me, I lost my mother this summer. I havent a right sense of time. I've lived as though I assumed that we'd have these infinitely treasurable people always with us. I never foresee their not being there. It may be that this makes my losses twice as cutting, but I think it has one consolation: while they were alive I had them really as a possession, I didn't feel them as temporary. My Gertrude is always there, as she was there before I knew her, which is to say: always here.

My poignant self-reproach at not having written her is acute. It doesn't help that I remember that she taught me how all those audience-activities—"articles", letter-writing, and conversation itself are impure at the source,—but oh! that I had at least sent her signs and signals of my ever-deeper love and endebtedness.

At the time of her death, so soon after my mother's, I was booked up with engagements acting in my plays in the summer theatres. I was unable in that stupifying work to write an adequate, a half-adequate article for one of the weekly reviews,—revolted though I was at the incomprehension of their papers about her. Again, this unmarked sense of time came into play—that someday when I had realized fully her loss and had penetrated still further into the greatness of her achievement I should write what I remembered and what I had come to grasp.

During the War I was not exposed to any particular danger or even tension; I have no right, compared to my friends in combat, to claim any long slow and difficult readjustment; but nevertheless that's what I've been undergoing. I seem only now to be emerging from a long torpor and misanthropy and paralysis of the will. My outward health soon recovered—the disabilities that prevented my fulfilling the appointment to the Embassy in Paris—but the psychological effects have dragged on for a long time.[146]

145 During an operation for cancer, Gertrude Stein lapsed into a coma and died on July 27, 1946.

146 In some of his correspondence from early March through early June 1945, TNW had indicated that he looked forward to an expected assignment as cultural attaché at the U.S. embassy in Paris; however, upon his return from Europe, he was advised by the Wilders' family physician to rest for a period of six months to a year.

I do not know whether this silence and "absence" led Gertrude to believe that the literary executorship of her work would better be transferred to another person.[147] If she felt so, I would very well understand it. If, however, she wished me to assume it I am as eager as ever and I hope as efficient. I mention it because I have interested the editors of the Yale University Press in a possible publication of Four in America which seems to me one of her most significant as well as her most charming works. It is the one I dreamed of publishing myself "the next time I made some money." My money-making capabilities have slowed down, along with the rest of me, and if this turns out to be a real offer of publication I think it should be accepted. In whose hands would you like to place the negotiations?[148]

I have not said anything, dearest Alice, about the loneliness you must be feeling. All I can say is: WASN'T IT WONDERFUL TO HAVE KNOWN AND LOVED HER? What glory! What fun! What goodness! What loveableness!

Everything one can say falls short of it. Someday before long I shall try to put all that down in words as carefully chosen as I can choose them—in the meantime she grows in my mind and heart and realization. Her greatness in the larger world has scarcely begun yet; long after you and I are dead she will be becoming clearer and clearer as the great thinker and the great soul of our time.

With much love, dear Alice,
much love

Thornton

---

147 Two days before she died, Stein made a will, in which she directed her executors to provide Carl Van Vechten with the funds that he deemed necessary for the publication of any of her unpublished works.

148 *Four in America* was published by Yale University Press in 1947, with an introduction by TNW, which was a contractual precondition to its publication.

216. TO SIBYL COLEFAX. ALS 4 pp. (Stationery embossed 50 Deepwood Drive / Hamden 14, Connecticut) NYU

January 7.
<19>47
Monday

Dear Sibyl:

That's the chief thing I have to say so I write that big.[149]

So, dear, I put this Fall into *living* in Deepwood Drive, and refocusing the ménage after it's loss. We coped with the community; we went to people's houses and we had people in. All this became positively mountainous over the holidays, what with eggnogs and everybody's relatives visiting from out of town. Such greetings over cocktails; such "now we have to hurry on to the Tuttles or the Donaldson's, or the . . . . .".

So that's done. The house is repainted. Isabel is installed in a great wheel of social give-and-take that will occupy her for years. During my absence a friend of long standing is coming to live in the house.

My sense that any particular value of heart or head is transmitted in "conversation" has never been very strong. It was much sapped during the War. So I went through all this with mounting fretfulness. I even developed a technique of coping with it. Dreading the conversations of others . . . . on politics or literature or on our neighbors . . . . I resolutely set about talking myself on what interested me. During those obligatory two hours after rising from table at a dinner party or even in the meleé of a cocktail party, I too often threw my partenaires[150] into consternation by insisting on telling them about Lope de Vega, Freud's theory of the physiological basis for avarice, Kierkegaard and the "leap". This practice cannot be acquitted of egotism; but it was not at least complacent egotism, for I did not enjoy it. It was a *modus vivendi*.

---

149 TNW wrote the salutation in large letters.

150 French: partners.

At last I can go. On the 15th of January I start driving to Mexico. And oh the exhalation of Relief and the joys of holding my tongue.

The work on the novel stumbled. But just last week I rolled up my sleeves to do a page or two to keep it in hand, and it came fine. [A sample from the Notebooks that Cornelius Nepos kept for potential biographies he might write some day. He had had Cicero to dinner and lured him into talking about Caesar. Cicero's fear, envy, and incomprehension comes out as wit. Very funny. This book ought to have every color, and I knew that it had developed without much being funny—now it's got some very funny places and will have more, juxtaposed with much that is painful and much that is, I hope, beautiful.]

So, dear, I shall miss Henry Uxbridge[151] and John Gielgud. In the light of Lady Anderson[152] all your recommendees are so joyfully rewarding that I regret this much. But I shall be at San Miguel or at Manzaniko.

Look at this wildly self-centered letter. Well, I am spiritually ill from lack of solitude. I shall return healed and a Franciscan brother of the human community. Now that the Dioscuri (Larry and Vivien,—I like to think of happy married couples as twins) are resting I shall venture to write them a letter. Yours are of such fascination and vitality that we forget that you are surmounting pain

You will hear from me oftener when finally I am not in the situation of a bear <u>frustrated</u> <u>of</u> <u>his</u> <u>hibernation</u>.

Lots of love
Thornton

151 Probably Charles Henry Alexander Paget, earl of Uxbridge (1885–1947).

152 London hostess Ava Bodley, Lady Anderson (1896–1974), wife of British politician Sir John Anderson.

217. TO JUNE AND LEONARD TROLLEY.[153] ALS 2 pp. Yale

As from: 50 Deepwood Drive. Hamden 14. Connecticut
New Orleans, La. Feb. 23. 1947

Dear June; dear Leonard:

I throw myself on your forgiveness. I had a sheltered life during the War and have no right to talk of post-war maladjustment, but that uprooting in my middle age did have bad after effects on me. One of them was a relapse into melancholia, lethargy and unsociableness. The death of my mother and the consequent necessity of settling in New Haven (i.e. Hamden) all Fall in order to rebuild the home for my sister after it had lost its center, all added to this. What I needed was to work, and in order to work, solitude, so soon after the New Year I left home and came down here. Tomorrow I take a tramp ship to Yucatán, and that will be sufficiently "cut off" and solitary. So I ask your forgiveness; and plunge at once into answering your questions.

a. Common Sense says that you shouldn't cross the water now,—and yet...... On the one hand, you know our Actors Equity rule that a non-American citizen engaged for a rôle here must wait six months at the termination of that rôle before assuming another. [Occasional exceptions are made when a manager goes before Equity's council and asserts that such-an-such a non-American actor is the <u>only</u> one he can find to fill a given part.] Moreover, jobs are hard to find. Your theatre structures were reduced by bombing; our<s> by the fact that movies buy up the houses and convert them into cinema halls. There's an awful dearth of theatres and plays wander around the provinces waiting to enter New York when a theatre tenancy is vacated.

And yet! There's always the chance that a manager about to put on a British play would snap you up. For instance, John Golden plans to

---

153 Leonard "Tom" Trolley served as a clerk to TNW and Roland Le Grand at the MAAF headquarters in Caserta, Italy. He met his future wife, June, while both were acting in the RAF Players group there; and his nickname was taken from the name of a character he played. Since she was an officer and he was not, there were great difficulties regarding their marriage; TNW helped them surmount military red tape, gave away the bride, and arranged the wedding reception.

TNW with June and Leonard Trolley following their wedding in Rome on February 12, 1945.

put on J. B. Priestley's The Inspector Calls.[154] I imagine there must be several roles in it that you could do; but Golden would have been interviewing hosts of young actors, British or pseudo-British

b. Movie work and radio would I think be out of the question until you had a number of engagements to point to as "experience". Entrance to those fields is dark and mysterious. I know some awfully bad actors who flourish in them, and some excellent ones who can't get a look in.

c. However, if the English stage is as blocked as our<s> is, and you may temporarily have to go into some other kind of job anyway, like the hotel business, or "gentleman front man" in a firm selling motor boats or motor cars, etc; maybe it would be right for you to cross over anyway—and do both your "earning a living" and your theatre career over here. The world's going through an awful time; everywhere it's hard; great migrations are taking place everywhere; one's "nationality" is no longer as sacred a matter as it used to be. If you bright young children have to struggle and suffer somewhere, maybe you could do it here, where opportunity is perhaps a very few degrees less cruel. I don't dare call what I'm saying advice. Perhaps June's mother may have some thoughts in the same direction. We're such old friends that I can say at once that I'd practically adopt you and would lend you the money to sustain yourself until you got on your feet. Such a transplantation should only be contemplated, however, if you sadly and inevitably accept the fact that you would at least for a time have to make a livelihood outside the theatre, and probably with an ultimate view of taking out citizenship papers here.

I'm including two letters, one to Larry and one to Hugh Beaumont. [That crossing out is because at first I thought I'd not include covering envelopes; but I've decided to send them also, for maximum efficacy.]

As part of my malaise, dear children, I gave up working on the Alcestiad, though it was well into the 3rd Act and was very beautiful. But my ideas about life had changed and I felt it to be sentimental. Instead I'm working on my novel about Julius Caesar, told in letters ex-

---

154 A production of Priestley's play *An Inspector Calls* did have a New York run from October 1947 to January 1948, but it was not produced by John Golden.

changed between the characters.—and such characters!! Caesar, Cicero, Catullus and Cleopatra!! And that's what I shall be doing in Yucatán next week. Letters will be forwarded to me promptly from Hamden and I promise to reply promptly and faithfully. Forgive an old bungling misfit of a foster-father; I'm better already and know that I shall be all my better self by Spring.

Write me your thoughts on these things.

Ever devotedly though undeservedly

your old pal

Thornton

P.S. My regards to Wilkinson.[155] I rec'd a cable from him and am delighted that he used my name and hope good came of it.

218. TO LILLIAN GISH. ALS 2 pp. Billy Rose

New Orleans, La.

April 1. 1947

Dear Lillian:

It's a joy to get a letter from you and to think about you.

Now as to this proposal, I don't say yes or no, but I call your attention to the following points:[156]

(a) The plot-lines have no real tension. The novel combines two famous well-tried plot motives<:> the Magdalene-Thaïs story (or Fallen woman with heart of gold) and Camille (Fallen woman barred by social opinion from achieving a happy union). But my novel has robbed both of these stories of their popular pull. Chrysis is helpless silent and dies having won a success only in her mind. And Glycerium-Pamphilus story is a matter of waiting helplessly and then coming to very little.

---

155 Arthur "Wilkie" Wilkinson, an RAF flight lieutenant who was instrumental in opening Caserta's Royal Palace Opera House for repertory plays open to all service branches during the war. He was a professional actor in civilian life.

156 Gish contacted TNW about doing a film version of his 1930 novel, *The Woman of Andros.*

All the characters are externally passive and engaged in waiting.
ⓑ Have you ever noticed that the one costume that always looks phoney and corny on the screen is the Graeco-Roman? Modern man cannot wear that dress and appear real. Think of the "Passion Plays" and the De Mille Quo Vadis, Ben Hur and The Sign of the Cross. The only way to get away with it is by extreme "character" types, like Charles Laughton as Nero or Claude Rains as Caesar.[157] Otherwise, everybody looks like dead chromo illustrations of ancient history.
ⓒ Readers of Andros write me all the time. The thing<s> they like about the book are the descriptions of nature, and the "thoughts" of the characters. Now there's certainly room for thoughts on the screen, sure,—but they only live on the screen when they are carried by strong situations and strong emotions. Now the Woman of Andros from the point of view of action is pale, muted, and passive. In a novel characters can suffer and meditate, but on the screen wouldn't it all look dreary and spineless?
ⓓ Suppose you hopped up the plot for the screen. Contrived real clashes between the characters. Then I think you'd run into another danger,—in those unconvincing costumes, no one would believe it. Lots of action and crisis but all looking like wax-works charades or a Sunday School pageant. To bring any vitality to Ben Hur they have to work up a vast spectacle and was there any real vitality? And to make Quo Vadis come alive don't they crown the picture with a mighty orgy? (In Hollywood I used to have lunch with the script writer who was trying to think up a sensational item to "top" the orgy. I think he ended up with naked women bound to the backs of bulls. All concerned knew that the "story" wasn't holding the audience, so that they had to inject sensation and spectacle).

But, dear Lillian, I don't say yes or no. I've always believed that you have a magnificent sense of all aspects of movie and theatre. At various times Pauline Lord and Blanche Yurka approached me about a play

157 Cecil B. DeMille was not involved in either *Quo Vadis* (1924) or *Ben-Hur* (1926), but he did direct *The Sign of the Cross* (1932), in which Laughton portrayed Nero. Claude Rains played Julius Caesar in the film *Caesar and Cleopatra* (1945).

from it; an opera for Helen Traubel[158] was written from it (she sang arias from it at concerts, but the opera was never put on). I feel that it is just about material for a short novel, some word-landscapes, and some semi-philosophic reflections: to expand it would break its back; to transfer it to the stage would reveal the fact that none of the characters really pull themselves together to do anything until it's too late; and to picturize it would reveal that it falls into a series of melancholy tableaux.

All this is merely subject to your judgment and intuition. And it comes with

devotedly
Thornton

219. TO EVELYN MACHT.[159] ALS 2 pp. Yale

en route to Mayfair Inn
Sanford Fla.

April 7. 1947

Dear Evelyne:

I've known unpublished writers who thought their work was very great indeed and I've known unpublished writers who've feared they were very bad,—but you seem to be both.

When you ask me for the name of a Columbia University teacher who would read them over—what am I to think? That idea would never occur to a reader<writer> with any self-confidence at all. What made you ask for that? If you are a writer of high originality and power what on Heaven could a Columbia University academic do for you?

I repeat what I told you before—if you are a writer of assured powers the first thing to do is to try and sell it through the usual channels,—that is agent or publisher. It may be that your work is so

158 Traubel was an American opera singer.

159 American writer and sometime actress; there is no record that Macht's work was ever published.

highly original that they won't be able to appreciate its merits, but at least you <u>try them first</u>.

I wasn't condescending to you. I was paying you the compliment of assuming that you would at least begin by sounding out the professional ways of doing things. Readings by Columbia Univ. professors are not professional.

x

Your letter is very angry with me.

I don't think I deserve it.

But not only is your letter angry at me, but for the second time, you get in some sideways sneers at me. Don't do that.

If you have a friend whose singing, or painting, or writing you don't like you either ⓐ drop the friend entirely ⓑ tell him roundly you don't like the work, and discuss it as far as he wishes to discuss it ⓒ adopt the plan of never mentioning the work at all—(that's what I do in hundreds of cases). But the one thing you don't do is to let fall passing sneers, like side-swipes, and then go on as though you hadn't said anything at all. It gives you the appearance of thinking that you are wonderfully superior and smug—and I hope that's not what you intended.

Thornton

220. TO HELEN HAYES. ALS 4 pp. (Stationery embossed The Century Association / 7 West Forty-Third Street / New York 18, N.Y.) Billy Rose

As from: 50 Deepwood Drive
Hamden 14, Conn.

Feb 28. 1948

Dear Helen:

I would be ashamed to take up your time with any request of my own, but I am doing it on behalf of a great actress and a gracious delightful woman.

I have just returned from Paris where I saw much of Jean-Louis Barrault and his wife Madeleine Renaud.[160] They are at the Marigny—on the Champs-Elysées—having a great success in a repertory which includes "Hamlet"; Marivaux's <">Les Fausses Confidences"; Molière's "Amphytrion"—with glorious scenery by Christian Bérard[161]; and the Gide-Kafka "The Trial".

I met them first at a friend's home and then I used to sit and eat and drink with them after the performances. And I noticed that Madame Renaud had a most unfortunate hand at make-off <make-up>. Off the stage without being classically beautiful, she has a fascinating and endearing face; on the stage (in plays that go into paroxysms about her beauty) her make-up did her every injustice.

Finally, I felt that I knew her well enough to mention it. She received my remarks with gratitude and anxiety. I then told her that I was once present when one of our first actresses gave to another of our first actresses—you to Ruth—your "formula", worked out from a long experience on both stage and screen. I said that naturally such a thing required great readjustment from person to person, etc, etc. All that she understood. I told her I would see whether such a formula could be obtained. At our leave taking her last words were an imploring repeated "You won't forget."

It seems surprising that a Frenchwoman would be so unskilled. I think the explanation is that she rose from the Conservatoire, to the Odéon, to the first place in the Comédie Française and that the French (innovators in so many things; conservative in others) were still passing on a maquillage[162] suitable for gaslight.

Mme Renaud is not tall; has light brown hair, and a complexion neither strikingly white nor pink. I think she could adapt any suggestions given to her.

Could your secretary type out that "plan", together with the names of the ingredients which I would forward to her?

---

160 Barrault and his wife founded their own acting company in 1946 at the Théâtre Marigny in Paris.

161 Bérard was a well-known costume and set designer, as well as a painter.

162 French: make-up.

Maybe this is all impractical, but I know you will not mind my having tried to further a good service in the sisterhood of great actresses.

with devoted admiration
ever
Thornton

Hamden, Conn.

221. TO GLENWAY WESCOTT. ALS 2 pp. Yale

As from: 50 Deepwood Drive, Hamden, Conn.
Princeton Inn, Princeton, N.J. en route
April 7. 1948

Dear Glenway:

To be so generously commended by you sets off such a hurlyburly of self-examination and self-reproach, mixed with the delight, as you can hardly imagine.[163] I am suddenly reminded of all the negligences and shortcuts, of the fact that I go through life postponing the book I shall really "work at", as you so dedicatedly do. You are the only writer of our time who sovreignly means every word and weighs every word's relation to every other. The thought of you reading mine aloud to your friends is very exciting to me because I can imagine you—as good actors do for our plays—subtly repairing balances and tactfully filling hiatuses. To all but the most attentive the book looks like a sedulous array of erudition and painstaking assembled mosaic,—Lordy, it's what the architects call an <u>esquisse</u>-<u>esquisse</u>,[164] an impenitent cartoon. It was, in fact, my post-war adjustment exercise, my therapy. Part

---

163 TNW is responding to Wescott's praise of *The Ides of March,* published on January 16, 1948.

164 TNW misuses the French term *exquise esquisse,* or exquisite sketch.

almost febrile high spirits and part uncompleted speculations on the First Things.

All this is why it was so warming to know that falling into your heart and mind, you could see all that and understand all that, and yet, as you say, love it. Because with all its incompleteness it urgently asks to be loved. And that so many have denied it. It's been called frigid,—when its all fun and about the passions; it's been called calculated,—when its recklessly spontaneous; it's been called hard,—when it's almost pathologically tremulous.

This fact that (and about the plays!) everybody "gets me wrong" has made me accept the fact that I'm a very funny fellow. And it extends to my personal self and is reflected in your letter. The notion that a parti-pris[165] could have prevented my seeing you in New York is unthinkable. Were you in New Haven, I should be importuning you continually to talk the night out over beer. Why, no month goes by but what I remember and profit by things you let fall at Villefranche,—on Beethoven's style compared with Mozart's, an extraordinarily enlightening remark on James's The Golden Bowl,—those are extraordinary resources and if I were not inertia in person I would long since have travelled far to tap them. But here I am this very funny fellow, glad to drop in at cocktails anywhere in New Haven, speaking at any Veterans Wives sewing circle, if it's in New Haven; going to New York "on business", then getting a fit of shyness rather than call up friends, and eating alone at little boites in the West Forties and dropping in alone at whatever trembling pianist may be coping with a début at Town Hall.

Look, for instance, at what I am doing now, and what has delayed my reply to your letter. Idiotic!—I've been working all day and far into the night on the chronology of the plays of Lope de Vega (but out of the 500, only those between 1595 and 1610). Passion, fury and great delight. Yes, a compulsion complex. Sherlock Holmes as scholar. I am certainly the world's authority and can correct all the scholars before me, but cui bono? only 20 people in the world would be interested. It is perhaps my harbor from the atomic bomb. In the meantime, letters mount up; duties neglected;—this is the funny fellow.

---

165 French: preconception (French is *parti pris*).

Next day—New Hope, Pennsylvania.

There are lots of ways in which I've watched you these years,—for instance, in those sideshows (sometimes called duties) of an author's life, prefaces, translations, recommendations, political statements. Next to you, I do it least of our colleagues; and I think you are right that we shouldn't do it at all. (Ernest Hemingway used to do <it>; he has abandoned it, not however on grounds of principle, I think.) I'm getting a firmer No as I grow older and I often mutter to myself: Glenway Westcott's right.

This is only one of a score of matters that I would like to submit to you some day. I'm about to be fifty-two years of age, but I still have an enormous appetite for advice; I seek it out and I act upon it; and you have always held for me the character of a sage.

So that's one of the reasons why your letter was so much more than gratifying, and I thank you a thousand time<s>

Ever most cordially
Thornton

222. TO MAXWELL ANDERSON. ALS 4 pp. (Stationery embossed 50 Deepwood Drive / Hamden 14, Connecticut) Texas

July 5 • 1948

Dear Max—

Don't have to tell you how happy your letter made me.

Yes, I by-passed large quantities of the material that, given the title, should have been there,—the political life behind the conspiracy. For that I took refuge in—and overexploited the most exciting element of a letter-novel: the "jumps", the hiatuses. Similarly, the Girls are harrying me about what they feel to be an omission,—what <u>did</u> Caesar feel about Cleopatra after he surprised her with Marc Antony? To that question I feel, smugly, that I gave the indications sufficiently. But the full picture of why Brutus did what he did I skimped.

x

Max, for over two years I've been working on Lope de Vega,—often 10 hours a day in happy contentment. It'll be a short book "The Early Plays of L. de V." for scholars only, all footnotes, no "literary" appraisal.[166] I've been able to date play after play through observing his theatre practice, rôles tailor-made for the performers, etc. But some day I'd love to tell you about himself. At certain periods of his life he was finishing a play about every eleven days. Fascinating to see that the stupifying fecundity proceeded from the fact that he wrote from every motive for writing, good or bad: for money, for prestige, from vindictive competetive spirit (sideswiping savagely his great contemporary Ruiz de Alarcón and cool to Tirso de Molina[167]), from autobiographical overflow and confession, and of course from intoxication at the multiplicity of character and circumstance.

My labors have been sheer PhD work and I should have done it in my twenties, but I'm still living as though we were to live until a hundred and fifty.

That we all wish for you.

Thanks again and cordial regard

Thornton

223. TO ALICE B. TOKLAS. ALS 4 pp. (Stationery embossed Century Club / 7 West Forty-Third Street / New York) Yale

March 19 • 1949

Dearest Alice:

Passing through New York after three days in Washington. Am discontented with myself because of (the customary) dispersal of in-

---

166 TNW never published a book about Lope de Vega but he did publish two essays based on his research: "New Aids Toward Dating the Early Plays of Lope de Vega," which appeared in the book *Varia Variorum: Festgabe für Karl Reinhardt* (1952), and "Lope, Pinedo, Some Child Actors, and a Lion," which was published in the journal *Romance Philology* (1953). Both essays were reprinted in TNW's *American Characteristics and Other Essays,* ed. Donald Gallup (New York: Harper & Row, 1979).

167 Juan Ruiz de Alarcón (ca. 1581–1639) and Tirso de Molina (1584–1648) were Spanish dramatists.

terests. Went down there ⓐ to be photographed in the "T. W. Suite" at the Hotel Raleigh, at the request of the manager of the Hotel Raleigh,—only it turned out that Life Magazine had changed its mind and was not proposing to publish the series of photographs of the titular suite incumbants in their respective suites, and ⓑ to address a (for Washington, pathbreaking) writers' club made up of white and Negro members,—that turned out to be very pleasant, but more sociable than earnest.

However I improved the visit by going to call on Ezra Pound in what he energetically call<s> the "loony bin"—i.e. St. Elizabeth's Hospital for Mental Disorders under the Army.[168] After long experience with Charlotte I am accustomed to the atmosphere. Ezra Pound alternately talks very interestingly and very tiresomely. Even in a visit of two hours I learned to guide the conversation off the reefs of anti-semitic frenzy and off his messianic omnisciense on politico-economico-financial reform. I had not remembered ever meeting him before, but he reminded me that we had met at the Adolfo De Bosis home, 1921 in Rome![169]

Alicia, the modus vivendi at Deepwood Drive is not better but worse. I don't want Isabel to cook meals for me, so I often go down town to eat and often naturally take her with me. So that's not only a meal but an automobile ride and generally a shopping tour to furnish forth future meals, and thus given over two hours so that I myself then succumb and propose further additions to it, calls, etc. Moreover, since eating has become such a drama we both accept with alacrity all invitations to eat at the homes of others,—and of an evening that's seven to eleven. It is sinking very low when one dines with friends in order to eat conveniently. On the train home I am going to mull this over and I think you can divine the announcement I must make.

Funny thing happened: the Modern Language Association held its vast annual Congress in N.Y. between Xmas and New Year, thousands of professors and instructors, listening to papers, from Beowulf to

---

168 Pound was confined from 1946 to 1958 in St. Elizabeth's Hospital in Washington, D.C., after having been found psychologically unfit to stand trial for treason.

169 See letter number 67, which describes this time in 1921, although Pound is not mentioned in that letter.

Guillaume Appollinaire, hour after hour. Well, on renaissance Spain day the head of the Spanish dept at Harvard[170] read a paper on "The Investigations of Mr. Thornton Wilder." I'd never met him; he was reta<i>ling material from my practically delirious letters. My academic friends claim it was a shocking breach of faith and etiquette. I on the other hand am proud and pleased. There is no flattery like piracy. Besides I have enough bullion in my cargoes to stock a dozen piratical papers.

In spite of the "bothers" I have described on the opposite page I am boundingly well and unjustifiably happy. Like a fatuous old uncle I continue to scold my callers for dejected and disheartened behavior and I broadcast trumpery advice like some columnist dispensing counsel to the love-lorn. But I can see also that I'm storing up "courage"—i.e. unrepentant assurance to say "No"—to evade a lot of claims and appeal<s> (such excellent ones, such duty-heavy ones). Yesterday I seized a piece of paper and resigned from the P.E.N. Club a friendship whose highly artificial flowers had long since faded.

Isabel assures me that she's very well. She wasn't pleased with her interview with her doctor; he disagreed with her as to why she was so greatly improved. Like her mother and like a great many women she feels that she has an instinct for medical matters that is superior to eight years' exclusive study of them. (I put that into the Ides of March, and I remember rocking with laughter in my chair while I wrote the lines.) So you see that she's not only well in body but confident, nay even majestic, in mind.

So I'm withdrawing from circulation until the Goethe Festival in July. Thereafter I'm acting in the summer theatres a bit. Thereafter I think I may do that movie—a movie all movie ur-movie—with the great Italian Vittorio de Sica and that brings me to Europe.[171]

Isn't this stationery beautiful? Isn't this handwriting beautiful (I've lost my fountainpen)? And beautiful is the bubbling sensation

---

170 Professor Courtney Bruerton.

171 De Sica had expressed interest in collaborating with TNW. In 1952, TNW prepared for him a treatment of a film about Chicago, based on a Ben Hecht story, but the project was abandoned. TNW later salvaged some of the script for his one-act play *Bernice* (1957).

that arises in me while I am writing to you and seeing and hearing you before me,—the only good thing that that wicked element AUDIENCE can give.

Devoted love
Thornton

224. TO SIBYL COLEFAX. ALS 2 pp. (Stationery embossed The Hotel Raleigh / On Famous Pennsylvania Avenue at 12th St. / Washington 4, D.C.) NYU

May 15 • 1949

Dearest Sibyl:

Cross my heart, I was good as gold all last week at Atlantic City. Walks and work. The play talked to me and informed me of several structural changes that have set it off into growing again. Here too I am working. My only distractions being visits to great poets—Ezra Pound, Alexis Léger,[172] and Czeslaw Milosz. (No, I don't even pretend to read Polish, but many that do assure me he is a classic in his lifetime and he is a rare person.) A week here and then I don't know where I go. Announcing I was to be in the South enabled me to refuse a battery of chores (honorary degrees which you are no more allowed to refuse than the invitations to be Best Man.... etc, etc.)

No, I am not acting this summer.

At the Goethe festival I loathe my share: the brief opening address of welcome (assigned me by Jove) and another address; but I rejoice to hear Schweitzer, Ortega y Gasset, Curtius and the others and to sit by them at table. This time last year I had to give the baccala<u>reate sermon (the screaming irony that I can't now spell it) and accept a degree at Kenyon—the whole thing enchanting by the campus of the

172 French poet and diplomat Alexis Léger used the pen name Saint-John Perse.

dear old Ohio college and the President's family but raised to golden privilege by 3 days relaxed companionship of Jaeger, the greatest Grecian of our time. (Bob wept went<when> Harvard stole him from Chicago.)[173]

By now you will have heard that Bob married his "secretary" a beauteous sloe-eyed divorcée with a six year old daughter.[174] That's probably why he's not dining with you.

The comments of peripatetic American prof's on Bob H. as an enemy of humanism make my hair stand on end. It's true that he doesn't think that an "art school" is an important part of a University, just as he doesn't think a school to make electrical engineers and sanitation experts, journalists, etc is the work of a university. But no one has done more to put the right value on the study of the "humanities", to confront the students with the great books themselves, and not with books about them. It is even he who has revived the word "humanities", divorced it from its impure relationship with the "social sciences" <and> carefully distinguished it from its ancillary philology, etc. Why, now even Harvard and Princeton have imitated him and set up the Divisions of the Humanities, so that the professors of Greek and Romance etc will sometimes have occasions to meet one another.

I wish you to grieve with me that Basket, Gertrude's and Alice<'s> white French poodle has been very ill. This is Basket III—the first (forever famed in song and story) was given her by Picasso, II by Picabia. You have not forgotten that it was the sound of Basket I lapping water that made clear to Gertrude the distinction between poetry and prose,—a distinction hitherto never never clarified.

---

173 Robert M. Hutchins, who was now chancellor of the University of Chicago, was the chairman of the 1949 Goethe Bicentennial Festival in Aspen, Colorado, one of several worldwide commemorations of the writer's birth. TNW, who was a member of the Goethe Bicentennial Foundation, gave the brief opening address and delivered a formal lecture, "World Literature and the Modern Mind" (reprinted in *American Characteristics and Other Essays* [1979] as "Goethe and World Literature"). Ernest R. Curtius was a German literary scholar and critic; Werner Jäeger was a German philologist and classicist.

174 Hutchins, who was now divorced from Maude, married Vesta Sutton and adopted her daughter, Barbara.

I think I'm sending someone to see you. Someone so gifted and so nice. So rare these days to find someone as deeply gifted who is without fever and without assertion, who has his field of what he knows so deeply and soundly within him that it never occurs to him that his self is socially negotiable. This is Robert Shaw, the wunderkind of choral directing, Toscanini's valued "preparer" of his IX Symphony and Verdi's Requiem, and director of his own Collegiate Chorale. From him Bach and Palestrina and Purcell and the Madrigalists have no secrets. He will, I hope, prepare our great Handel Festival at Newport in the summer of 1950,[175] revealing the great sunbursts which are the mighty fugal choruses of Judas Maccabeus, etc. I could wish that he simply had tea with you, but he will probably shrink from presenting his letter. I often think that the people we would most wish to see walk three times around the block and then decide not to call on us, fearing that they have nothing which could interest.

How I am hoping that the Tuscan and Ligurian sun has been of great benefit to you. Or whether you will embrace the Great Potential and come to Arizona this fall. If you don't come here I shall cross to see you. That—as tart people say—is all there is to it. And don't forget that other alternative: I have 100,000 irremoveable marks in Germany.[176] We could go to Bad Homburg or Bad Nauheim or Baden-Baden and you could lie in the mud-filled copper baths where your sovreign, Edward VII, renewed his youth like the eagle.

Lots of love
Thornton

175 TNW attempted, with the support of Rudolf Bing, to establish such a festival in Newport, Rhode Island, but he did not succeed.

176 Under postwar occupation currency regulations, TNW's German money earned from royalties could only be spent there.

225. TO AMOS N. WILDER. ALS 2 pp. (Stationery embossed Goethe Bicentennial Foundation / 135 South La Salle Street / Chicago 3, Illinois) Yale

<Aspen, Colorado>
July 7. 1949

Dear Yamus the Bamus:

Selah!

Yes, it's just wonderful being 52 because you can then be excited over things without being so excited that you're incapable of absorbing 'em.

Batteries of concerts and lectures assault you—often three a day.

Eminent scholars call on you to come out of the large audience to make a comment on a lecture just delivered by an eminent scholar. It's wonderful to have outgrown visceral panics about public speaking.

But I've become the pack mule of the convocation.

Dr. Schweitzer gave his lecture in French last night. Translation made in NY by some journalist hack or by one of those swooning ancillae that smother Mahatmas. Terrible. This English text was read antiphonally with Dr. S. from the platform.

Today I was sent for. Would I touch up the English text for its German presentation tomorrow and would I read it antiphonally for him?

Ditto: Don José Ortega y Gasset. Only for him I am to be first and sole translator of his Second Lecture and I am to read it with him from the Podium.

In addition, Bob H. who only arrived yesterday begs me (i.e commands me) to redeliver my own lecture to the Second Series Guest-Subscribers who are arriving by every bus, plain<plane> and train today.

God forgive me, but I was pretty good, and I know now where I can improve it.

And the music we're hearing, and the endowed hands I've been shaking: Rubinstein in Beethoven's IV, Milstein and Piatagorski in Brahms' Double; Erika Morini in the Mendelssohn; and that dear brown angel Dorothy Maynor[177] in songs.

---

177 Maynor was an African-American opera singer.

TNW and Albert Schweitzer at the Goethe Bicentennial Celebration in Aspen, Colorado, July 1949.

I had two hours rehearsal with the Old Man this afternoon. He can't get into his head who I am, so when I begin Mon frère, Amos, le reverend Amos Wilder, that's more than he can cope with, but I'll get there yet.[178]

I love the Convocation, and the colleagues, esp. Fairley of Toronto and Simon of Israeli.[179] I love the mountains

I love the schoolteachers who stop me on the street, and the students who've hitchhiked across the country to sample this. But most of all I love Goethe. Nobody ever loved anybody like I love Goethe. And

178 TNW is referring to Albert Schweitzer. TNW's brother was a graduate student in theology at Mansfield College, Oxford, when Schweitzer went there in February 1922 to deliver the Dale Memorial Lectures. Because Amos Wilder knew French and Schweitzer's English was not strong, Amos helped him with his correspondence.

179 Scholar, critic, and painter Barker Fairley and educator and philosopher Ernst Simon.

this is the poem I analize & translate at the close of the lecture, finally reading it in German.

Jawohl! Das ewig Wirkende bewegt
Uns unbegreiflich, dieses oder jenes,
Als wie von ungefähr zu unserm Wohl,
Zum Rate, zur Entscheidung, zum Vollbringen.
Und wie getragen werden wir ans Ziel.
Dies zu empfinden, ist das höchste Glück,
Es nicht zu fordern ist bescheidne Pflicht,
Es zu erwarten, schöner Trost im Leben<Leiden>.[180]

Not a dry eye in the house. And I slay 'em by pointing out the implications of the penultimate line. We are not permitted to ask Nature to be unnatural.

There are a number of flies in my ointment but I shall not stoop to recall them.

When our festivals are over, I shall stay on here and finish my play.

Bob's mother and daughter leave tomorrow. I've scarcely seen him.

Dinner this evening with Paepke's, Nitze's et alii.[181] A great pleasure seeing the N's again. Isn't it awful not having got back to Chicago for so many years which I love so and which has so many people I value (including Abou Ben Adhem[182] and family).

I realize this letter sounds like <u>euphoria</u> and you are putting it down to the altitude or to drink,—no, no, mostly it is Goethe. Perhaps too it is the elation of plain brute fatigue. Pack-mule fatigue.

Lots of love to Kay,[183] and to the children.

---

180 TNW's translation of this passage appears in "Goethe and World Literature" in *American Characteristics* (1979).

181 Chicago businessman and philanthropist Walter Paepcke (1896–1960), chairman of the Container Corporation of America, made Aspen, Colorado, the site of the Goethe Festival. In 1950, Paepcke and his wife, Elizabeth "Pussy" Paepcke, created the Aspen Institute; Elizabeth was the sister of Paul Nitze, who held major positions in several presidential administrations and was instrumental in establishing Cold War policy. His wife was Phyllis Pratt Nitze.

182 TNW is referring to the poem "Abou Ben Adhem" (1838) by James Leigh Hunt. TNW obviously means his brother and the latter's family in this regard.

183 Amos's wife, Catharine.

The Spaniards (imagine what the French would be without vanity and combine it with what the Italians would be without excitability) have a thousand expressions of spiritual cortesïa<.>[184] One of them

"You owe me love"
Thornton

226. TO HERBERTH HERLITSCHKA.[185] ALS 2 pp. (Stationery embossed Goethe Bicentennial Foundation / 135 South La Salle Street / Chicago 3, Illinois <address crossed out by TNW>) Yale

Until Sept 2.
Hotel Jerome,
Aspen, Colorado.
<P.M. August 15, 1949>

Dear Herberth:

Your recommendations for the contract with Burmann-Fischer[186] have been thought good by the Wiggin and Dana firm and will have been forwarded to those concerned. As usual I can't follow them. Play-contracts, radio, acting, movie-work contracts are hard enough for me to read, but they're crystal-clear compared to these. And those are read by others for me.

I'm sorry about the misunderstanding rê William Faulkner. I've never met him and never corresponded with him. I've always heard that like Eugene O'Neil he's even worse than I am: he never answers

---

184 Spanish: courtesy (Spanish is *cortesia*).

185 Austrian-born translator Herberth Herlitschka (1893–1970) was the German-language translator of TNW's early plays, *The Bridge of San Luis Rey,* and all his subsequent novels except for *Theophilus North,* which was published after Herlitschka's death. TNW shared his German-language royalties equally with Herlitschka, an unusually generous arrangement.

186 TNW's contract was with the German publisher Bermann-Fischer.

letters at all. For twenty years Ernest Hemingway also tore up all letters except those from his girls and from his hunting, bullfighting and skiing pals. Max Perkins handled all his publishing business.

Yes. I recognize with regret that its perfectly possible that—without meaning to—I've been bloodily heartless in relation to you and your rights. But why? I'm not bloodily heartless to others. Just yesterday I signed a responsibility for hotel debts up to 250 dollars and gave another 100 dollars to a granddaughter of a Furstin Hohenloe[187] and the daughter of a knight who'd got stranded in town and a sort of high class vagrant and who had to get out of town or she'd be jailed. Two weeks ago another case. Why am I a lynx for human trouble wherever I see it and apparently blind as a bat in regard to you? Because your statement of your interests always comes wrapped up in such a network of contractual negotiation. I try to support justice and I try to recognize human need, but negotiation-details tend to represent for me neither necessarily justice nor need. They represent bartering and the marketplace and that's something I know nothing about. For a long time I had to earn my living by jobs and I taught-taught-taught, but I never came anywhere near the problems of commerce and that will always remain a great big blind-spot with me.

I hope you do not mean the same thing by sneers that I do, for I'm sure that in letters to you I never employed them.

I enclose another letter about that plagued Warship Story. It's a miracle that they dug it up out of an old edition of the "Yale Literary Magazine". [188]

I've written 'em:

ⓐ It may circulate until Dec. 1950 without charge, that it then reverts entirely to me.

ⓑ That you are my sole translator, and

ⓒ that Burmann-Fischer is now in possession of German rights to my works.

If indeed you will be going to Vienna there is a much greater

187 The Hohenlohes were a German noble family.

188 TNW's story "The Warship" had appeared in the *Yale Literary Magazine*'s Centennial Number in February 1936.

chance of my seeing you than in London—a great great city but uncongenial to me—to the same degree that Vienna even in distress remains and always will be my favorite capital in Europe.

All my very best wishes to you both
your old friend
Thornton

P.S. My English protégés the Leonard Trolleys have returned to 37 Ladbroke Square after a year and a half's trial of NY. and the hope of establishing themselves in the New York theatre and taking out citizenship. The NY stage is going through an awful crisis, the rising demands of the combined unions making <it>—as it also does in publishing—increasingly difficult to bring a product to market.

TW

227. TO CARY GRANT. ALS 2 pp. Academy of Motion Picture Arts and Sciences

Hotel Jerome
Aspen, Colorado
August 23 • 1949

Dear Mr. Grant:

Excuse this working paper.[189] In fact, it is a sign that I am taking a thing seriously.

x

There is no possibility that I should undertake work on a movie-script of the first two book<s> of Gulliver's Travels, but I enjoy discussing and offering my suggestions for whatever value they may have. If ever I work on a movie again it will be an 'original'; Vittorio

---

189 TNW wrote this letter on lined paper.

de Sica has approached me on the matter and when my present play is finished, I'm going to try and find a subject and a treatment that would suit him.

x

But the Gulliver's Travels is a fine idea and—certain difficulties mastered—should make a film that you and Mr. Hawks would be very proud of and which would delight millions.[190]

x

The first thing that occurs to me is this:

Don't treat it as a fantasy. Treat it as dead-pan sober-serious travel-experience.

Such it was for Swift's first readers (Gulliver's journeys 1701–; book published 1726). It was for them, as we say, in modern dress). It belongs to the catalogue of great farces and great philosophical works that say: grant me one big preposterous premise and I will develope the consequences in cold logic, and without any further strain on credulity (Don Quixote; Robinson Crusoe, and the best farces of Avery Hopwood[191]). From such a treatment comes the real explosive force of the humor and the social criticism. In this way, your picture would have a real superiority over the Russian puppet-treatment[192] which was constantly adding conscious drollery to the basic text.

x

The ideas in the book—over the telephone you mentioned the high and the low-heeled and the Big-Endians and the Little-Endians—would not be as effective as on the page. Discussed from the screen or photographed they would appear labored,—simply because the continual spectacle of Little Men and Enormous Gulliver would be so overwhelming that it would dry up every interest except itself. There is quite sufficient and terrifying social significance in the view of civilization by pygmies or giants to take care of itself.

---

190 Grant and Howard Hawks had contacted TNW about writing a film adaptation of Jonathan Swift's satiric masterpiece. This project was never realized.

191 American dramatist Avery Hopwood (1882–1928).

192 *The New Gulliver*, a 1935 Russian animated film using the stop-motion technique, directed by Aleksandr Ptushko, in which puppets were used extensively.

x

Your real difficulty lies in the question:

Do you need to add some plot? Love-interest (given the difference of size!) is out of the question; but what is lacking is any person-to-person relation between anybody and anybody.

Can you hold the interest of audiences for two hours on the situation GIANT-PYGMY?

Gulliver's Travels is not a work of narration; it is not even a travel-book; it is a work of exposition. It is almost entirely without movement.

x

You have a choice: to take the risk of photographing the exact text, trusting that the visual excitement of great-and-small men will hold up to the end.

Or: taking constant liberties: having Gulliver really intervene in a war between the people of Lilliput and Blefusco; having Gulliver really have an absurd but touching tendresse (and farewell) with the Queen of Brobdingnag,—things like that.

I suggest that you attempt the latter.

x

Your deference over the phone to my being occupied and having no time, etc, embarrassed me. Wherever I am, I am always a lazy loafer, a very intermittent worker.

If you and Mr. Hawks would wish in addition to seeing this increasingly famous valley and also talk over this very exciting project, I should certainly be delighted. On the afternoons of the 27th and 28th the Budapest String Quartet is giving two concerts (the 28th is both the birthday of Goethe and of Mrs Walter Paepcke). If that sounds too much like a distraction, any other day would be all right up to my departure for the East on September 3.

Sincerely yours,
Thornton Wilder.

Hotel Jerome Annex, Room 321

228. TO HEINRICH WALTER.[193] ALS 4 pp. (Stationery embossed 50 Deepwood Drive / Hamden 14, Connecticut) Private

Oct 28 • 1949

Dear Dr. Walter:

Unfortunately the request you convey comes at a time when I cannot do anything about it. I must absorb myself completely in the completion of this work.

You may wish, however, to recast some of the following items into a sort of interview:

① a large portion of Our Town was written at the Hotel Belvoir<,> Ruschlikon.[194] It was a stimulation to know that in immediately adjacent houses Brahms was reported to have written the Liebeswaltzer and Conrad F Meyer the Balladen.[195]

ⓑ For several months I walked into the city every evening and walked back to my hotel—in addition to long walks in the surrounding country. Often in the City I attended the performances at the Stadttheater and the other theatres for drama and opera.

ⓒ The absence of representative scenery has never been felt by me to be an innovation, but a "restoration" of dramatic conditions as established in Elizabethen England and the Siglo de oro of Spain.[196]

ⓓ The aim of the last act is not to present a statement about the life after death but merely a point of view of how life should appear to

---

193 German journalist and editor Heinrich Walter, who had emigrated to the United States after World War II, had met TNW in Stockbridge, Massachusetts, in the summer of 1948. At TNW's invitation, Walter interviewed him thereafter in New Haven and subsequently submitted further questions to him by mail.

194 This hotel in Rüschlikon is five miles from the center of Zurich.

195 Brahms's *Neue Liebeslieder* was composed in Rüschlikon in 1874. Swiss novelist and poet Conrad Ferdinand Meyer lived in the nearby town of Kuchberg. His *Balladen* was published in 1867.

196 The golden age of Spanish literature extended from the early sixteenth century to the late seventeenth.

us while we are alive,—the "after death" situation is only a metaphor and is borrowed from the picture given in Dante's Purgatorio
ⓔ "Our Town" is an attempt to present our daily life against the perspective of vast stretches of time; "The Skin of our Teeth" is similarly civilization as viewed against vast stretches of time; the play I am working on now is, perhaps, the subjective life of the individual so viewed.[197]
ⓕ Like all my plays, "Our Town" is filled with borrowings from Our Masters. Emily's farewell to the world is from Achilles' praise of the things he had valued in life: his "fresh raiment" becomes "new-ironed dresses"; his wine—naturally—becomes coffee.

As I was writing this your second letter arrived.

I think it surprising that "Welt am Sonntag" cut the first paragraph which must have explained to the readers that the interview took place at the Goethe Feier in Colorado.

Yes you may certainly borrow from Mr. Jungk and I'm sorry that I cannot now send a more extended "interview".

Sincerely yours
Thornton Wilder

---

197 TNW is referring to *The Alcestiad,* or *A Life in the Sun,* as it was titled in its premiere production at the Edinburgh Festival in August 1955.

Part Five

HONORS: 1950–1960

DURING THE 1950s, THORNTON WILDER WAS ENGAGED IN INtermittent travels, writing projects, and civic events, which often included receiving honors from governments, universities, and professional societies. After a three-month trip to Europe in the spring of 1950, which included Lope de Vega research in Spain, Wilder flew back to the United States in May to participate in a college production of *Our Town,* give an address, and receive an honorary degree. He took the position of Charles Eliot Norton Professor of Poetry at Harvard for the academic year 1950–1951. The terms of this prestigious appointment required that he live on campus, give six public lectures, which would then be published by Harvard University Press, and generally make himself available to the Harvard community. Wilder made himself so available that in March 1951, he collapsed from exhaustion and a sacroiliac condition and spent a month in the hospital. He gave five of the six Norton Lectures and stayed in Cambridge after his appointment ended to prepare them for publication, a task that proved to be extremely difficult. In an effort to make progress on the essays, he changed his location, spending two months in France, then three months back in the United States, where he traveled from Pennsylvania to Florida.

In May 1952, Wilder received the Gold Medal for Fiction from his peers in the American Academy of Arts and Letters. At the same time, writing projects new and old invited his attention: a possible screenplay set in Chicago for Italian director Vittorio de Sica, the rewriting of some plays he had put aside earlier, and the completion of the Norton Lectures for Harvard University Press. He revised three of the lectures at this time and they were published in *The Atlantic Monthly* in July, August, and November 1952. The film did not materialize and his playwriting projects were temporarily put aside.

The State Department asked Wilder to represent the United States as head of the American delegation to an arts conference sponsored by UNESCO, which would be held in Venice in September 1952. He was assigned to write the general report of the conference, and as soon as he completed this, Ruth Gordon asked him to revise *The Merchant of Yonkers* for her. Wilder spent the next eight months in Europe, where he worked on the play, as well as socialized with friends and pursued Lope de Vega research. When he returned home in May 1953, he had completed most of the revisions and a scholarly article on de Vega. The article was published in August 1953, just as he was putting the finishing touches on the script for Gordon at the MacDowell Colony. The revised play was titled *The Matchmaker.*

During the fall of 1953, Wilder was in Newport, Rhode Island, one of his favorite writing hideaways, trying to complete a third act for "The Emporium." Although he had begun the play in 1948 and worked on it over the years, a final version continued to elude him. He drove south for the winter and turned northward again with the coming of spring, his car filled with his journals, notes for the rest of the Norton Lectures, his *Finnegans Wake* material, his manuscripts, including the still-unfinished "Emporium," and the usual quantities of mail to be answered. He spent the spring and early summer of 1954 in various locations on the East Coast, then sailed to England in mid-July to attend rehearsals of *The Matchmaker,* which was to have its premiere at the Edinburgh Festival in August. The production received wonderful notices, and after touring England in October, it opened in London in November, to rave reviews.

After the Edinburgh success, Wilder left for the Continent in early September 1954 for a round of lectures in Germany and socializing in Paris. By mid-October, he was settled in Aix-en-Provence, ready for solitude and work. Following some Christmas travel to Switzerland, he returned to Aix and resumed writing. During this time in Aix, he took short breaks in Italy and Spain, then returned to the United States in April 1955. While in Aix, Wilder had worked on *The Alcestiad,* a play he had begun in the late 1930s and then turned to again in 1942, when he was stationed at Hamilton Field. Although it had been no more than half finished when he resumed work on it in 1954, his writing had advanced far enough by mid-January 1955 that he'd entered into negotiations to have it performed at the Edinburgh Festival in August 1955. The festival managers believed that Wilder's title might be off-putting for their audience, so *The Alcestiad* was retitled *A Life in the Sun.* Wilder continued to work on the play throughout the spring, and in mid-July 1955, he sailed to England for another round of rehearsals and another Edinburgh Festival opening in August. This time, however, his play was not well received.

Wilder spent the early fall of 1955 on the Continent, enjoying the company of his friends. In mid-October, he returned to the United States for rehearsals and out-of-town tryouts of *The Matchmaker,* which was scheduled to open in New York on December 5. He went back to Europe before that opening because he had arranged to meet with Louise Talma, a composer whose music he admired and with whom he planned to collaborate on an opera. They had first encountered each other at the MacDowell Colony in 1953, and throughout 1954 both of them had searched for a libretto idea. Wilder suggested they consider *The Alcestiad,* and when Talma agreed, they began work. For Wilder, this meant the attractive idea of immersion in a new writing form. He remained in Europe, traveled, began work on the libretto, and met once more with Talma before returning to the United States, arriving on February 29, 1956.

Wilder also began a new drama project in May 1956, a series of "Four Minute Plays for Four Persons." Soon they exceeded his imposed limitations and he began to envision them on an arena stage. Between social engagements and travel, he continued to work on these plays, as well as on the *Alcestiad* libretto. He spent some time at home, but he was also on the move, looking for places to work. For the next year, he traveled around the East Coast, went to the Southwest, and then on to Mexico. In April 1957, a few days before his sixtieth birthday, he and his sister Isabel sailed for Europe. They visited friends in Paris, traveled to Brussels to see *The Matchmaker* performed in French, and went to Switzerland and then to Bonn, where Wilder was given a signal honor for intellectual achievement: He was inducted into the Orden Pour le Mérite für Wissenschaften und Künste. After this, he returned to Switzerland for rehearsals of the German-language production of *The Alcestiad* in Zurich. It was well received, foreshadowing the play's popularity on the German and Austrian stages. Wilder returned to the United States in July 1957 to spend the summer in New England, having completed a one-act satyr play to accompany *The Alcestiad;* titled *The Drunken Sisters,* it was published in *The Atlantic Monthly* in November 1957.

Acceding to another request by the State Department, Wilder flew to Germany in September 1957 to participate in the dedication of the new Congress Hall in West Berlin. Two of the new one-act plays he had written in 1956, as well as a play he had written much earlier, were among the seven plays presented by American dramatists on that occasion. Wilder performed in two of his plays and was master of ceremonies for the entire program. After the festival, he visited Bad Homburg before going on to Frankfurt in October to receive the German booksellers' Peace Prize, the first American to be so honored, and to give his address, "Culture in a Democracy," in German to an audience of two thousand people. That same fall, he received an honorary degree from Frankfurt's Goethe University and was awarded Austria's Medal of Honor for Science and Fine Arts.

After he returned to the United States in December 1957, Wilder spent most of his time at home in Hamden. Then in February 1958, he journeyed to Washington, where he received a medal from the government of Peru. Soon thereafter, he resumed his peripatetic writing life. This time, he drove to California to confer for a week with Louise Talma. He drove around Southern California before heading home to Deepwood Drive in a leisurely fashion. During this period, he continued to work on his one-act plays for an arena stage, which he now conceived of as part of a series based on the seven deadly sins.

When Wilder returned home in June 1958, he embarked upon what had by now become a summer routine, driving around New England, where he visited friends or enjoyed quiet times alone. Once autumn set in, he packed up his manuscripts and notebooks and sailed for Europe, where he spent the winter and early spring of 1959 in several favorite locales in Austria, Switzerland, and Italy, places that suited both his desire for company and his need for solitude in order to work. At the end of March 1959, he returned to Hamden and attended to his mail and business matters before setting off yet again. This time, he drove to hideaways in Saratoga Springs and Newport. Between May and October 1959, Wilder devoted himself to a number of projects: He agreed to have his one-acts produced in the arena-style Circle in the Square Theatre in New York once they were completed; cleared his latest libretto draft with Louise Talma; performed in a summer theater as the Stage Manager in *Our Town* (his last appearance as an actor); and helped with an adaptation of *The Ides of March* for the stage. He also resolved to abstain from his time-consuming Lope de Vega and *Finnegans Wake* studies.

In the fall of 1959, Wilder sailed for Europe. He traveled in Germany and Switzerland, spent a couple of weeks in Paris, and then visited Italy. After leaving Italy at Christmastime, he took a long sea voyage, finding, as always, that a shipboard routine was beneficial for writing. He was back in Hamden by the end of March 1960 and remained at home much of that spring. In the summer and fall of 1960, his writing materials at hand, he roamed around New England, then drove south for the winter. He put aside some projects dating from the beginning of the decade, such as "The Emporium" and the overdue Norton Lectures; others he continued working on, such as the libretto for *The Alcestiad* opera and the unfinished one-act series concerning the seven deadly sins. There were new projects, as well. He agreed to write another libretto, an adaptation of his one-act play *The Long Christmas Dinner,* for use as a short opera by composer Paul Hindemith. He also began a new series of one-act plays based on the seven ages of man, one of which—*Childhood*—was published in *The Atlantic Monthly* in November 1960.

Wilder ushered out the year 1960 in New Orleans. More than ever before, as he reached his mid-sixties, he was feeling that the demands of his public life were impinging on and interfering with his writing, and he yearned to find a way to escape these obligations for a sustained period of time.

229. TO MARGARITA DE MAYO.[1] ALS 2 pp. (Stationery embossed 50 Deepwood Drive / Hamden 14, Connecticut) Vassar

Midnight and a half
Jan 12–13. 1940?<1950>

Dear Margarita:

I strongly suspect
I strongly suspect
I strongly suspect
that the enclosed envelope contains an honorarium
I've long made a rule
I've long made a rule
I've long made a rule
never to accept an honorarium from any educational institution.
I'm very well fed
I'm very well housed
I'm very well clothed (only I don't take care of my clothes)
by the Entertainment business and movies and readers.
So I delight
So I love
So I rejoice
to give my services when I can to young people in schools and colleges.

And never have I been happier doing it than under your charming and gracious auspices

Your friend
Thornton

---

1 A professor of Spanish at Vassar College in Poughkeepsie, New York, de Mayo met TNW in Aspen at the Goethe Bicentennial in July 1949. She arranged for him to give a lecture, "The Spanish Theatre of the Seventeenth Century," at Vassar on January 12, 1950.

230. TO AVA BODLEY, LADY ANDERSON. ALS 4 pp. Rice

American Express Co.
11 rue Scribe <Paris>
March 19 • 1950

Dear Lady Anderson:

My last hour in London I stopped by the Authors Club in Whitehall Court (for once it had not been able to lodge me; long booked-up, they said, by visitors to the Ideal Homes Exhibition) and there found your kind messages. I'm sorry I had not received earlier the change of hour for Thursday's lunch,—every moment being so delightful.

Mr. Sitwell presented me with a copy of his book on the Netherlands[2] which I promptly read—at Dover—with continuous pleasure and a mounting desire to go right back to Holland. Mr. Sitwell is a determined individualist; we must take him on his terms. He resolutely refuses to discuss the Big Things in order to call our attention to overlooked beauties and half-hidden oddities. He says that there is nothing new to be said about the grandes machines[3]—the great churches and canvases; but it is precisely from such richly-furnished minds as his that we could obtain fresh lights on the great masterpieces. Wouldn't it be fun to get him in a corner some day and make him talk about "The Night Watch" or the "View of Delft"?

I leave Friday for the few weeks in Spain—long walks, musing, and work. I am so conscious of having been "bad"—of neglecting work in order to pursue a variety of interests—and of having been impeded by my sister's illness,[4] that I have determined to make this really a solitary Trappist work-siege. Hence my feeling that I must deny myself the splendor and violence of Holy Week at Seville. The moment has come when I must make and not receive. Hence, too, my confused

---

2 *The Netherlands* (1948).

3 The term *grandes machines* is usually used to refer to large French history paintings, although TNW uses the term in a more general context.

4 Isabel Wilder had fallen in her home and suffered a concussion.

and absurd remarks at lunch—which certainly laid me open to the charge of fatuity—about being annoyed by reporters. The happiest occasions in my life were those days when as dreamy student-vagabond—boundlessly un-noticed—I visited foreign countries: to recover that is all my aim.

If I finish my play this spring, then I can give my summer—or part of it—to work on Lope de Vega in the archives of Spain, and then I may ask you for the introduction to the Duke of Alba.[5]

The reason why I have been able to make so great an advance in Lope studies is that I selected a limited moment in his career. Other Lopistas treat of his entire life and work—the most immense output in all literary history; they can do no more than scratch that vast surface. I fixed first on 1599–1600, and began making explorations in depth, widening gradually. Under this microscopic treatment passages and documents began to reveal more and more material; and now I know my way about his life and works from 1590–1606. (The poet did not die until 1635, writing voluminously the whole time).

We know that Lope withdrew from the service of the Duke of Alba during the early months of 1595; but scholars have been in much doubt as to when he entered it. We have a play dated in Lope's autograph Carlos El Perseguido November 2 1590. Only a microscopic Lopista would notice that in it a wicked duquesa is the daughter of a duque Albano. Throughout the next ten years Lope was to use the name Albano with deference and even affection, because of the syllables <u>Alba</u> that it contains—including writing plays, poems, and a novel referring to the marriage and sentimental history of the Duke who had been sent "into Coventry" by Philip II for shifting from one bride to another on the eve of his wedding. Hence Lope was not yet secretary by the end of 1590. Soon after Lope had a daughter whom he christened Antonia probably after the Duke Don Antonio. In May 1593 the Duke's brother Don Diego de Toledo was killed by a bull in a fiesta. Lope wrote a most beautiful threnody for the occasion, but in the comedias I have found two allusions to this death which have

5 TNW probably is referring to the seventeenth duke of Alba, Jacobo Stuart-Fitz-James y Falcó (1878–1953).

never been remarked before—in modern times—and which help me to date the plays.

And so it goes in a vast and fascinating puzzle.

The stay in Dover was not a success. The Lord Warden Hotel is no longer in operation. Friday it rained hourly and I did not make any trips beyond climbing to the Castle and to all the nearby cliffs—and write letters—and read Mr. Sitwell's book.

But this long 'rambling' letter is merely to thank you for the delightful occasion last Thursday and to send my regard to yourself and to Sir John.

Sincerely yours,
Thornton Wilder

231. TO AARON COPLAND.[6] ALS 1 p. LofC

St Jean de Luz <France> Easter morning <April 9> 1950

Dear Aaron:

You've got a short memory. We've been over all that before.

I'm convinced I write a-musical plays; that my texts "swear at" music; that they're after totally different effects; that they delight in the homeliest aspects of our daily life; that in them even the life of the emotions is expressed contra musicam.[7]

Music and particularly opera is for the unlocked throat, the outgoing expressive "idea and essence" behind our daily life. I hope my play<s> don't lack that idea and essence but they singularly shrink from any explicit use of it. They are homely and not one bit lyrical.

But I'm delighted that you are applying yourself to opera and the musical play and very proud that that born impresario, Dr. Bing has

6 Copland wrote TNW on March 23, asking him about doing the libretto for an opera version of *Our Town*, with the music to be composed by Copland. Copland had been asked to do so by Rudolf Bing of the Metropolitan Opera.

7 Latin: against music.

expressed this good opinion of me. Give him my regard. And you—find a suitable text—and all good courage and best wishes to you.

Cordially ever
Thornton

P.S. Just got here from attending the Holy Week procesiones at Valladolid[8]—great theatre in the best sense—and all surrounded by the great motets of Victoria[9] whose wonderfully plangent type of musical phrase just suits that week's events

232. TO VIVIEN LEIGH AND LAURENCE OLIVIER. ALS 4 pp. (Stationery Embossed 50 Deepwood Drive / Hamden 14, Connecticut) British Library

July 19, 1950

Dear Friends:

You're just about packing to come over.[10]

I'm very glad of it.

I'm of the same mind still: Come over and make a lot of dough; come over and get a lot of that Western sunshine; come out of England for a while—all so that you can go back and give England the renewed refreshed height of your gifts.

To each of those clauses I could give further detailed developements (and how I'd enjoy it) but I'd soon sound even older than I am.

You'll find the U.S. in a State of Tension, but its a different kind of tension. You may even find it bracing.

Last week I went to New York and saw two dress-rehearsals of

8 Valladolid, a city in central Spain, is famous for its Holy Week *procesiónes,* or processions.

9 Spanish Renaissance composer Tomás Luis de Victoria.

10 Olivier and Leigh were going to Hollywood, where Leigh was going to play Blanche DuBois in the 1951 film version of Tennessee Williams's play *A Streetcar Named Desire* (1947); Olivier was going to play George Hurstwood in *Carrie* (1952), a film version of Theodore Dreiser's novel *Sister Carrie* (1900).

Gar's The Live Wire. It opened in Ogunquit, Maine, on Monday night and the NY Times reports that it was well received. It's better than The Rat Race, but as I told Gar: Why is it that you who love your friends and are so generous-minded about praising them,—why is it that you don't introduce likeable characters into your plays? This play exhibits two carefully elaborated portraits of the type heel—one male, one female. Curtain.[11]

Ruthie is desolate that she must be away from Faraway Meadows[12] just at the time that Vivien will be there. [This may all be changed, tho': the paper announces the<that> Michael Todd is bringing The Live Wire into New York on August first.] I suppose you know Ruth's schedule for the summer, two big rôles. And that they just sold two originals to the movies.[13]

I, too, am desolate, for I must be away. I'm kinda ashamed to tell you where I shall be. I "open" on August first in "Our Town" at the Wellesley Summer Theatre—the twelfth company I've played it with. Every time I report one of these engagements to Sibyl she boils over with indignation,—all I can say is that I advise every playwright to get somehow somewhere that side of the footlights.

x

Nothing in New York to recommend to you except Shirley Booth's performance in Come Home, Little Sheba.[14] Wonderful.

x

---

11 Garson Kanin's play *The Live Wire,* directed by Kanin and produced by Michael Todd, ran in New York in August and September 1950. Kanin's play *The Rat Race* ran in New York from December 1949 to March 1950.

12 Faraway Meadows was the Kanins' country house in Sandy Hook, Connecticut.

13 Gordon was scheduled to appear in the pre–New York tryout of Jane Bowles's *In the Summer House* at the Westport (Connecticut) Country Playhouse during the week of August 21, 1950, but the engagement was canceled; she did appear at Westport during the week of September 11 in Garson Kanin's adaptation of the French play *The Amazing Adele,* by Pierre Barillet and Jean-Pierre Gredy. The two original movie scripts Gordon and Kanin sold to the movies may refer to *The Marrying Kind* and *Pat and Mike,* both of which were released in 1952.

14 William Inge's *Come Back, Little Sheba,* starring Booth, ran in New York from February to July 1950.

I've decided to give my new play to Jed Harris. (But it's still not finished!)

Judith Anderson begs me to adapt Cocteau's La Machine Infernale for her.[15] She wants to play Jocasta and the idea is that I should so rewrite the last act that Jocasta and not Oedipus learns first the horrifying facts of the case. I reread the play and found it chic, pert, and anything but tragic.

¶ Letters from Sibyl from Rottingdean and Sissinghurst—so she can move about again. Praises be.

¶ At last I saw The Cocktail Party.[16] Here it closes at 11:15. I (and a large audience) was grateful and absorbed until 11:00; and when the answers began to come through I was angry as a boil. No, sir, life is not restricted to two choices only—dreary inconsequentiality or absolute sainthood. No, sir. T. S. Eliot does not like people; he is in some stung quivering revulsion against our human nature and he retreats into that extreme position of Aut Christus aut nullus.[17] Any fifty pages of War and Peace (also about "polite society" and about suffering struggling human beings) would sear his little play into the bloodless bowel-less thing it is.

¶ There! I went and got angry and now there is little room to tell you how I love you, how I rejoice that you're going to have a change; that you're going both to have lots of fun and do lots of brilliant work. Oh, oh, oh, I wish I could be in Hollywood and we could all have supper at Ciro's and eat enormously and drink lots and talk, talk, talk. About the Abbey[18] (I love every inch of it); about you; and about

your devoted old
Thorny

15 TNW did not adapt this 1934 play by Jean Cocteau.

16 Eliot's play ran in New York from January 1950 to January 1951.

17 Latin: Either Christ or no one.

18 Notley Abbey was the couple's home in Buckinghamshire.

233. TO ROBERT W. STALLMAN.[19] ALS 4 pp. (Stationery embossed J-31 Dunster House – Harvard University – Cambridge 38, Massachusetts) Virginia

<appeared above the stationery heading>
last days at

August 17. <1951>

Dear Bob:

There are a number of questions involved in your letter—some of them mutually exclusive:

1. Steve was a wonderful fellow. Did he express himself saliently in letters? I don't know. I must have some from him in my files, but I suspect that—like my letters from Hemingway, etc.—they are always about plans to meet, or about some piece of business. "Our generation" seldom wrote letters of analysis or theory to one another. Our key was the jocose. The justification for publishing letters are (1) historical—data relating to social implications of a period or (2) a natural gift for letter-writing—a mysterious endowment not necessarily a concommitent of literary genius or even of intelligence. For instance, E. A. Robinson and Willa Cather seemed to have lacked it. It is very possible that Steve had it, too,—but before you launch out on this venture, get hold of several hundred and weigh the matter.

2. One of the finest things about Steve and Bill[20] was their generosity to younger writers. Whether from such letters of guidence you could assemble an art poétique is a possibility. There your problem would be: have you enough material and does the material—like Rilke's—build itself up into rich generalized lessons. Or does it spread itself into repetitions of injunctions, and into hundreds of specific suggestions about individual poems (which would require the printing of the younger poets' poems).

3. Letters of the Benét-Brothers' Circle.

---

19 TNW first met Stallman during the Depression when the latter was an able but poor undergraduate at the University of Chicago. TNW anonymously assisted him financially. Stallman got a Ph.D. in English at the University of Wisconsin and was, at this time, teaching at the University of Connecticut in Storrs. He approached TNW to write him a letter of recommendation to the Guggenheim Foundation for a volume of Stephen Vincent Benét's letters. This project was never realized.

20 William Rose Benét, Stephen Vincent Benét's brother and fellow poet.

Would they be interesting enough?

As I say, it seems to me that that generation was self-conscious about letter writing and much given to the casual wise-crack. Consider it thoroughly.

Down the years I have written scores of recommendations for Henry Moe.[21] Every year at least half a dozen applicants ask me to speak for them. I have resolved to limit my calls on his attention to two a year. If in your application you can affirm that the Benét Letters are of constant high interest and/or offer a wealth of suggestions on the practice of poetry, I should be delighted to further your application.

Thanks for the invitation to Storrs. After this over-loquacious year I am taking a long vacation from speaking.

Isabel and I sail for Europe on Sept 14. I may have to return almost at once to continue my work in the vicinity of one of our great libraries; but its going to be a Trappist year.

All cordial best wishes
to you both
Thornton

234. TO HOWARD LOWRY.[22] ALS 4 pp. (Stationery embossed 50 Deepwood Drive / Hamden 14, Connecticut) Wooster

S.S. Saturnia—in Halifax, NS harbour—arriving NY Monday
Nov. 4 • 1951

Dear Howard:

You wrote me a good richly packed long letter over a year ago. Vous me pardonnerez; c'est votre métier.[23]

---

21 Secretary of the Guggenheim Foundation.

22 Lowry was president of the College of Wooster (Ohio) at this time.

23 French: You will forgive me; that's your profession (TNW is playing on "Le bon Dieu me pardonnera: c'est son métier," a quote attributed to Catherine the Great and, in a slightly different form, to Heinrich Heine).

The year at Cambridge was the hardest I ever spent; but that was entirely my fault. I broke down with a sacroiliac dislocation (real but psychogenic) and spent 4 weeks in Mass. Gen.—the best hospital in the world, I guess. I enjoyed my illness, very much, but emerged from it to resume the hard work. The Chas Eliot Norton professor gets a lot of dough for merely giving 6 lectures and being in residence with a faint implication of being accessible to a select portion of the student body. Well, with that old Maine-inherited conscience of mine I'm always in servitude <u>when I'm paid for something</u>. So every time the phone rang I said 'yes'—not to 'social' events (I made the rule never to cross the River Charles) but to speak; and the forums and discussions group and hospital benefit committees and Harvard Dames clubs and so on are legion.

I suppose the ground cause is this: I am an observer and an onlooker; so I fear and dread lest I <u>look like</u> an observer and an onlooker. I make every possible motion to appear to <u>belong</u>, to be in and off <of> a community. Well, by the time I left I knew every third person I passed on the street—I sure was a citizen of Cambridge—but it was the most difficult year of my life.

The Norton lectures have to be published. I think I'd have refused the invitation, if I had realized to the full extent what that meant. I'm not an essayist; I'm not a critic; I'm not a "non-fiction" man. I don't mind casting forth generalizations and sententious dicta from a platform—but those are not dogmatic but merely tentative discardings from one's "personality." And of course my discourses cant be printed as spoken. The Germans have a proverb: Schön gesprochen, schlect gedrückt."[24] So now I'm rewriting the lectures for the eye. Much of it is an expansion of the remarks I made at the Convocation when you did me so much honor.[25] But now I derive my observations on the American temper from my findings in Thoreau, Melville, Whitman,

24 German: Beautifully spoken, badly printed.

25 TNW received an honorary Doctor of Humane Letters degree from the College of Wooster in May 1950; the idea in the address he made on that occasion, "The American," about the essential loneliness inherent in being an American, was one he expanded upon in his Norton Lectures at Harvard.

Emily Dickinson and Poe.[26] (Many of the ideas I got from Gertrude Stein.) So all Summer I worked worked worked and every day since. This brief trip to Europe—thirty days was partly to call on my agéd friends Alice Toklas and Max Beerbohm and partly for the never failing restoratives which are for me slow-crossings. Much restored I am. I leave my sister Isabel in Rome where she will spend the winter; our Deepwood Drive home is rented to friends (but serves as my address); I go to live in a few rooms over a drugstore in New Hope, Pa.—easy driving distance to the Princeton Univ. library (but not to live in Princeton—for we know what that would lead to.)

I resolve for a year to be a bear; an unsociable boor; a recluse. Each sunrise I shall feel free to devote the day to the Nortons; or to the Lope studies; or to the Palestrina work; or to Finnegan's Wake; or to my new comedy.[27] To be sure, I am not cutting myself off from humankind; but my acquaintances are of the sort that one makes in bars—illiterates, analphabetics, who don't know anything about Culture and who don't wanta.

I should have thanked you long ago for The Matthew Arnold—from which I have derived many hours of lofty, serene though slightly tristful pleasure. Your apparatus is exemplary: just what we need and never too much and never im-pertinent. The book in higher education and the rôle of religion is in a field where I flag.[28] I'm only happy close to the specific and the individual. This is a reflection on me, not on your handling of the subject: I never could read far in Bob Hutchins'

---

26 TNW titled his Norton Lectures series "The American Characteristics of Classical American Literature" and delivered five of the required six before he became ill. He revised three of the lectures and they were published in *The Atlantic Monthly* as "Towards An American Language" (July 1952), "The American Loneliness" (August 1952), and "Emily Dickinson" (November 1952). All three were reprinted in TNW's *American Characteristics and Other Essays* (1979).

27 Besides being involved with his ongoing study of Lope de Vega and of *Finnegans Wake,* TNW was studying the music of the Renaissance composer Giovanni Pierluigi da Palestrina. The new comedy he was working on was probably "The Emporium," which remained unfinished at his death; incomplete holograph sketches, acts 1 and 2, and a story summary are in the Beinecke Library at Yale University.

28 Lowry had edited several books on Arnold, so it is difficult to determine for which one TNW was thanking him; but the second book he mentions is Lowry's *The Mind's Adventure: Religion and Higher Education* (1950).

pages on higher education, either. Question of temperament and what the French call "formation".

In a few minutes I go ashore and stroll about the dreariest town in the hemisphere.

This slow crossing has been brightened by a most interesting new friendship: Alma Mahler Werfel. Wife of four remarkable men each in a different art—Gustav Mahler, Oskar Kokoshka, Gropius and Franz Werfel, and mistress of as many more.[29] The Egeria[30] of high format. Vestiges of her great beauty and more than vestiges of extraordinary galvanic femininity.

Yes, Howard, after I've finished by<my> bearish year, I dream of descending on your community again. Wooster has coalesced with Oberlin in my associational field and emerged on top. Give my regards to your mother, and to that woman whose name I have forgotten but of whom I remember such grace of mind and person, and to all the friends, especially Bill Craig and Myron Peyton.[31]

Flag not in your splendid work; but don't overdo.

Lots of regard
Thornton

P.S. Tinker's better than he's been for years.[32]
PS II The El Greco book is a continuing joy.[33]
P.S. III Want to hear about your findings rê South American colleges.
P.S. IV Delighted that Bob Shaw went to you again. Do you see how many daemonic elements pull him in many directions?

---

29 Alma was married to Mahler, Gropius, and finally to Werfel. She never married Kokoshka, although she had a three-year affair with him prior to her marriage to Gropius.

30 TNW is referring to Egeria, the water nymph in Roman mythology, who was King Numa's consort and provided him with advice. Her name became identified with any woman who was an adviser to or a supporter of a famous artist or political figure.

31 At this time, William C. Craig was a professor of speech at the College of Wooster and Peyton was a professor of Spanish there.

32 Yale English professor Chauncey B. Tinker was now seventy-five years old. He and Lowry had collaborated on *The Poetry of Matthew Arnold: A Commentary* (1940).

33 This book may have been presented to TNW during his stay at the College of Wooster.

235. TO ISABEL WILDER. ALS 2 pp. (Stationery embossed Holland-America Line) Yale

The Col. Club
Wed. noon—train to New Haven at 3
<Fall 1951>

Dear Isa—

So I had lunch with Sharlie.[34] She's most definitely better in every way. Hat and dress downright smart. She's now forbidden liquor and smokes only some expensive de-nicotined cigarettes. Her diet seems to have been much relaxed or enlarged or whatever you call it. Her color's good.

But the fact that she's almost completely well merely means that there's less and less to be interested in while she's talking.

I thought that at one point the conversation was going to reveal an alarming angle, but no, it turned out to be merely tiresome; here it is.

"The other day I did an awful thing. Perhaps, I oughtn't to tell you.....But there's a movie house nearby where they show good pictures and there's a man who takes your tickets and tears them in half....and maybe I oughtn't to tell you this..he has a friend who he says has written a great play and he doesnt know what to do with it next. And he asked me if I knew anybody who was in the theatre and wrote plays. And I told him about you but I said that you were away in Europe...And that maybe when you come back...."

I sat silent.

I wouldn't mind reading a 2,000th play, but the picture of getting her and me in fine chatty relationship with the ticket-taker.

So she only sighed and said.."Well, I guess I can't go back to that theatre for a while yet."

---

34 After her serious mental breakdown in 1941, TNW's sister Charlotte had not responded to treatments. In 1947, she had undergone a prefrontal lobotomy at the Neurological Institute of Presbyterian Hospital in New York City. Two and a half years later, she had appeared so much improved that, with financial assistance from TNW, she began to live independently in September 1950 in an apartment in Greenwich Village, her former neighborhood in New York City.

Her conversation is full of these people she falls into conversation with.

And that's bound to be. That's Greenwich Village anyway, and one can only hope that something doesn't flare up.

Dinner last night with Monty, Mira[35] and Elizabeth Taylor. He and Eliz did a lot of tender cheek to cheek, but that's all. He says she's been given a fright about men and about her own emotions as a result of her brief marriage to Billionaire Hilton.[36] She's a very lovely 19-year old and I can't know whether she'll develope strongminded or gentle, or knowing or negative or what. And she doesnt know either.

You can imagine the craning necks wherever we went, ending up at the St Regis bar at two in the morning.

My cold has almost entirely disappeared now.

In a few minutes I gotta transport my luggage to the Grand Central: oh what a chore!

Well, now I'm crazy to read your first letter from Rome. So much hangs on the weather.

Happened to pick up a book at the Century—a bereaved family had privately printed the verses and letters of a Mrs Laurence Peck [aunt incidentally of the Pierson Underwoods].[37] They had a villa in Rapallo about 1927 and some letters from there are about how in March the weather was alternately divine and dreadful—rain and cold.

Well, you can think of me most of this week deep in the Yale Library. I'll deliver the trinkets to Rose; call on Catherine Coffin and Helen; learn the latest about the Withingtons,[38] but I'm not going to "eat" in homes, if I can help it. Just pass through 'em. I'm going to begin my life as a bear.

---

35 Mira Rostova, Clift's close friend and acting coach.

36 Elizabeth Taylor had married Conrad "Nicky" Hilton, Jr., heir to the Hilton hotel business, in 1950, but the marriage lasted only nine months.

37 These, privately printed, were later published as *Letters and Verses of Clara Boardman Peck* (1951).

38 Rose Jackson, Catherine Coffin, Helen McAfee, and the Withingtons were New Haven friends.

Note for Gallup: "Gabrielle was scheduled to take her departure on 1 November, and I devoutly hope that she has done so."[39]

Love (to both!)
Thorny

236. TO THEW WRIGHT, JR.[40] ALS 2 pp. Private

1440 North Atlantic Avenue. Daytona Beach Fla
Sunday night <ca. December 23, 1951>

Dear Thew:

Was that suspense terrible?

I mean: did you expect an SOS every minute?

Well, I have yet to see a house in that 7-mile built up area along the beach which is called Daytona Beach that hasn't a sign on it saying Vacancy. Like a chatty waitress said: I think it's overbuilt itself.

Well, I got a little bungalow and the window I sit at sees the surf between two houses<.> Another man has an apartment in the same bungalow, but by a separate entrance and I haven't seen him yet.

Weather just wonderful. Girls were standing in the breakers today surf-fishing.

And I'm doing just what I came for: being silent; and working.

I haven't a single appointment in the world until that Oberlin one in June.[41]

I've only taken this for a month.

If by then I've done a good hunk of work I may drive down to Key West; work there a bit, then leave my car and go over to Habana.

---

39 Donald Gallup was curator of the Yale Collection of American Literature. Because of his friendship with Gertrude Stein and Alice B. Toklas, he was instrumental in obtaining their papers and artworks for Yale. Gabrielle was Toklas's maid.

40 Upon Dwight Dana's death in 1951, Wright became TNW's attorney.

41 TNW and his brother, Amos, both received honorary degrees from Oberlin College in June 1952.

I eat around. Everybody says the season's not begun and there's nobody here; but there are thousands—either old folks from the farm or honeymoon couples; and they too eat around. The food isn't good, of course, but I never was choosey that way.

One of my ears has cleared up. I can't hear my watch ticking with the other.

My landlady's name is Mrs Joseph Ginsburg. Like all landladies she has a beautiful daughter (in her opinion); and like all girls who fancy they are beautiful she had to come over and slay the new lodger.

Very funny about my name. Mrs Ginsburg like all the motel and hotel clerks where I stopped and wrote my name did a take on it. Where had they heard it before? In sports? in crime? am I under investigation? a playboy millionaire? since none of them ever crack a book it never occurs to them that it would be literature. But they think they've heard it before and it leaves 'em confused and puzzled. The younger ones ask. The older ones—foxy—probably go and phone Cousin Beulah who once taught school and who reads the papers. At Williamsburg the hotel manager called up and asked if I was comfortable. I guess he thought I was writing a piece for Saturday Evening Post on how phoney the Williamsburg Reconstruction is.[42]

Well, you can see the results already of having to hold my tongue. It makes me loquacious on paper. You'll have to put up with a lot of this. Or else fly down with something for me to sign.

There's no phone here, but Mrs Ginsburg next door is Daytona Beach # 5320

I always forget to ask you: can you read my handwriting? I think it's fine, but that's what I think of my singing, too.

Well, the sound of those waves breaking makes me sleepy.

All my best to you and yours

x

Think it over
Thornt

42 In 1926, John D. Rockefeller had begun restoring the town of Williamsburg, Virginia, to preserve its eighteenth-century past.

237. TO MALCOLM COWLEY. ALS 4 pp. (Stationery embossed The Princeton Inn / Princeton, New Jersey <heading crossed out by TNW>) Newberry

50 Deepwood Drive Hamden
March <1952>

Dear Malcolm:

Wish I could be there—not for the performance, but for the dress rehearsal. That would give me a chance to urge them not to make the last act lugubrious. (But I got to be in NY April 1—those tickets bought long in advance for Caesar and Cleopatra.[43])

There's one word in Our Town that causes me endless distress. At the close of Act II the clergyman thinks aloud and ends up with "one marriage in a thousand times is interesting." How did I happen to give such a chilling and cynical impression? because I had incorporated into myself G. Stein's use of the word—and I had failed to realize that the rest of the world didn't use it in the same sense.

She'd say: human nature is occupying but it's not interesting; it's the human mind that's interesting.

Or: Science is not interesting; once you know that there can be an answer to a question it is not interesting... etc.

What she meant was: basically important... or of significance for all.

What I meant was: "a Mozart is born....<">

It's awful the way one's "associations" can play one false; but I suppose its worse not to have a lively network of just such associations.

[One of the reasons I like to play that rôle is that I can attempt to "save" that moment; I do the first half of the speech dreamy and grave and then suddenly break out into <a> smile on that word!]

I'll soon have the first two (rewritten) Nortons to send you. As

---

43 Laurence Olivier and Vivien Leigh played on alternate nights in George Bernard Shaw's *Caesar and Cleopatra* and Shakespeare's *Antony and Cleopatra* in New York from December 1951 to April 1952.

non-fiction you may wish to see a short paper I did for "Poetry" on the death of Joyce and which has been widely reprinted esp. abroad.[44]

x

I've decided to insert a short passage about Emerson into the Norton book.

Isn't he awful? Yet how that colossus bestrode the world for so long! his ideas basely, soothingly, flattering all that is facile and evasive in the young republic. Wonderful field for the Marxian kind of literary criticism. The very syntax breathes 3 meals a day with hardworking maids in the kitchen preparing them while the Seer entertains these messages and promptings from the Over-Soul. Melville's copies of the Essays are in the Harvard Library and its a joy to see how Melville dug his pencil into the page in scornful annotation.

x

What do you read for sheer recreation after the day's work?

Anything I can lend you?

Have you ever done a Kierkegaard course?

Have you got a strong stomach and can you read Jean Genet—and Sartre on Jean Genet?[45]

Have you read Cécile, the recently discovered sequel to Constant's Adolphe?[46]

x

'Thought I was going up to the Institute meeting on the first, but was reminded that I had that Caesar date.

Still ashamed of myself for speaking at that other Institute meeting against the candidacy of Oscar Hammerstein. Hell, what did it matter? Why should I have gone on the warpath as to whether he were a lyric poet or not?—Especially, as it was interpreted by many as a movement of rabid antisemitism. Ever since June I've held my tongue on every subject—and that's why I feel so well.

---

44 The Joyce essay, "James Joyce, 1882–1941," had originally appeared in the March 1941 issue of *Poetry*. It was reprinted as a chapbook by the Wells College Press in Aurora, New York, in 1944. It was later reprinted in *American Characteristics and Other Essays* (1979).

45 Jean-Paul Sartre wrote *Saint Genet: Actor and Martyr* (1952).

46 Benjamin Constant's novel *Cécile* was probably finished in 1811, but it was not published until 1951; Constant's best-known work was his novel *Adolphe* (1816).

When you've got a clear spell from whatever other work you're doing I'll drive up and bring a packet of material.

Ever
Thornton

238. TO ELIZABETH SHEPLEY SERGEANT.[47] ALS 1 p. Virginia

As from American Express Co. 11 rue Scribe Paris
Venice Oct 11. <1952>

Dear Elizabeth:

At last the racket has abated. I am alone, wearisomly writing the 3 reports for the State Dept.

I've got loyal friends. Of such a thing as the Conference, they cry: Oh, you're just the person. How glad we are you are representing us. Etc. Horsefeathers. That kind of oratory and marshalling of material and public argumentation, I am a perfect dub at. You know the pressure that made me go. The Conference I think was useful but not at the overt level. I wont take time here to weigh its successes and insuccesses.

This is my first visit to Venice. More fascinating than anything had prepared me for. I find nothing in it of Thomas Mann's discovery of morbidezza.[48] Beautiful as the fabric is, my chief joy is in the painting—in the Veronese<,> the Tintoretto<,> Titian and Bellini Venice. Oh glory oh art. I went to Florence for 3 days. Those edifices of ivory green and rose, dear, are still there; Michelangelo's figure still lost in deep thought or under the ban of sleep. Venus is still blown toward us on a shell. I shall never be sufficiently grateful to Gertrude Stein for having directed me from being an ear-man to an eye-man; it

47 TNW had met American journalist and biographer Elizabeth Shepley Sergeant (1881–1965) in the late 1920s.

48 Italian: softness (TNW is referring to Mann's *Death in Venice* [1912]).

was late in life but now that education of the eye is bringing me profit. When I was last in Florence I thought Santa Maria Novella was "that uninteresting church by the railway station". Heigh-ho.

Where do I go next? I don't know. I'm having a tug of wills with Ruth Gordon who wants me to come to Paris to confer with Tyrone Guthrie over that potential London revival of The Merchant of Yonkers.[49] But I don't want to go to Paris. I want to go to a little hotel in St. Moritz (already under snow) and work at what only pleases me. What is there to confer about? Let them come to me. I think that Monday or Tuesday I will entrain for Milan and there at 1:25 take the autobus arriving at 6:10 in St. Moritz..... think of that drive, past Como, up up the dramatic Italian alps and then in evening light in the square of that Swiss village.

Oh, how badly I run my life. How I postpone from year to year the establishment of those conditions under which I can work. And I don't mean work in the sense of producing volumes, I mean work in the sense of working on and in and with myself. I am a slow digester and a slow ruminator, altho' I carry some of the external signs of a "bright" and a fast one. No, no,—I am a monastic and an umbraticle <umbratical> type who long since went astray among the volatile and the worldly. This has been my complaint for many years and yet I do nothing about it: you may well say that there must be something about it that I like.

It has been raining all day. The gondoliers under my window have been quarreling with one another, loud, loud, all the time. A barnyard of angry raised voices. There is a beautiful passage in the Wings of the Dove where James describes Venice in bad weather; he does not mention this effect.

This letter shows my incoherence and ill-humor. I shall not be myself until I am settled in Switzerland. And now my ink has given out. I shall go to the Piazza San Marco to buy some ink! On the 15th you will be done with your book—you will celebrate the fact by your

---

49 Guthrie was not involved in the production of *The Merchant of Yonkers* that opened at London's Embassy Theatre on December 27, 1951, but he did direct the revised version of the play, *The Matchmaker,* which opened in Edinburgh on August 23, 1954, and in London on November 4, 1954.

party to<for> the Colonists.[50] Give them all my affection—Yes, I shall be all but there: the last of the flowers but always the Lordly Hudson.

Tout dévoué[51]
Thornton

239. TO AMOS N. AND CATHARINE K. WILDER. ALS. 2 pp. Yale

c/o American Exp. Co. 11 rue Scribe Paris
last day at St. Moritz Switzerland
Nov. 20. 1952

Dear Ones:

First: the translation of Hölderlin's poem[52] is splendid, noble and moving.

Second: just sent off some goodies to the children.

I hope to hear that Catharine in her cell at Clères found Tappy to be gradually adjusting. I've tried to remember back to my childhood. Father sent me to the craziest places. I seem to see a difference between saying of such experiences: "I suffered there" and "I hated it". I hated my summer working on the farm at San Luis Obispo Calif. I hated it but endured it and continued in my (free) evenings all the eager reading and writing that was boiling in my head. Did I ever "suffer" at such transplantations? That is another thing: that is to feel oneself aban-

---

50 TNW is referring to Sergeant's book *Willa Cather: A Memoir,* which she had worked on at the MacDowell Colony. It was published in 1953.

51 French: completely devoted.

52 Amos Wilder's poem "Autumn Fires" was later published in his poetry collection *Grace Confounding* (1972). It was the custom of Amos and his family to send one of his poems as a Christmas greeting, but on this occasion they sent the poem at Thanksgiving because they were in Frankfurt for the year, where Amos was at the University of Frankfurt-am-Main as an exchange professor. The two children were at boarding schools—Catharine ("Dixie") at the coed International School in Geneva, Switzerland, and Tappan ("Tappy") at the all-male Ecole des Roches in Cléres, France.

doned in a totally unrelatable world. It may be, dear ones, that the French over the centuries have made so schematic an all-French-motivated school that an American boy can only feel "abandoned in an unrelatable world." You know that I do not like the French nature—while admiring many aspects of their mind. And least of all in this century when they are aware that they have fallen out of phase with the stream of spiritual advance. France is in malaise. They have not the British fortitude and they have not the Italian "resources in nature." Their celebrated vanity (vide Stendhal passim) has been offended. The result is that they have even less human warmth than they had in their good ages. Sécheresse de coeur. Sécheresse de Coeur.[53] Tappy is the most winning outward going fellow in the world. If he cant make a friendly situation for himself, no one can.

I leave next Tuesday to live in Baden-Baden—on my frozen marks. Rumor says I have thousands. I'll report to you when I have explored the matter.

Give me a little time. I may join you in Gstaad. I'll find some hotel or pension nearby. However, I may bring a company—Sally Higginson,[54] Montgomery Clift, the Kanins even. People who can't make up their mind attach themselves to me. And I can't always make up my mind. My projects of work must come first—I've evaded work so long. So—à bientôt.

Loads of love
Thornton

53 French: hard-heartedness.

54 Higginson met TNW in Tucson, Arizona, in 1938, when she was nine or ten. TNW had a letter of introduction from a mutual friend to Higginson's recently widowed mother, who had taken her three young children from Boston, Massachusetts, to spend several months in a dryer, milder climate.

240. TO ESTHER W. BATES.[55] ALS 2 pp. BU

Will be home by the end of April

As from Hotel zum Hirsch, Baden-Baden

Stuttgart March 16. 1953

Dear Esther:

Isabel has at last sent me the Virginia Quarterly.

I write to you instead of to Mr. Scott.[56]

If I wrote to him something artificial would inevitably creep into the expression of thanks and appreciation; and perhaps an element of constraint into his feeling that he should reply.

What better intermediary than the deep pool of understanding which is Esther Bates?

Mr. Scott is the first person to have put on paper a recognition of the fact that the play is in counterpoint between the particular and the universal and he has found many striking ways of calling attention to it.

Is the play cruel?

I don't know.

Some have said so.

Mr. Scott seems to think not.

Committed Christians are severe with me that I indicated without pressing their eschatology—I "dilletante'd" with the Great Affirmations. "The triumphant doctrine of the immortality of the soul one does not whisper tentatively." That is right. All I did was to borrow the muted hope of Dante's Purgatory; but his purgatory is a stage in a longer journey whose destination is—Dio mio!—not left in doubt.

---

55 American dramatist Bates (1884–1977) met TNW at the MacDowell Colony in 1924, where she was known for being able to transcribe Edwin Arlington Robinson's minuscule handwriting into readable manuscript form.

56 Bates was a close friend of American poet and critic Winfield Townley Scott (1910–1968), whose essay "*Our Town* and the Golden Veil" appeared in the Winter 1953 issue of the *Virginia Quarterly Review.*

Deep at the genesis of the play was the fact that I, as a young student in Rome, went on archaeological expeditions; saw an axe bring to light a once-busy streetcorner. There is a Pompeii aspect of Grovers Corners. (Ever since New York and Chicago are potential Pompeiis; and under my window much-bombed Stuttgart is an industrious ant-hill in a Pompeii—but that is "The Skin of our Teeth".) The theme-words of Our Town are: hundred, thousand, million. I have no other subject; but now it is the one soul in the billion souls.

There is another literary borrowing in the play that may interest Mr. Scott: the catalogue of Emily's goodbyes is after that of Achilles in the underworld. As a shoplifter said to a judge in Los Angeles: I only steal from the best department stores and they don't miss it.

One more point: when Emily "returns" there is not even the table and two chairs: all, all is in our minds.

Give my deep thanks to Mr. Scott. I feel as though he had made the play respectable. Does he realize the extent to which it embarrasses "professionals"—professors and critics? "We're all very fond of it in a way, but it's not really a play about anything like those of x and y.<"> Just as Skin of Our Teeth was never listed among the war plays—everybody knows a war play when he sees one and obviously that's not one. (It was in Germany that it became the war play and families denied themselves meals to see it for the third and fourth times in icy auditoriums. Funny!)

I'm going to be in Peterboro August and Sept. I'm speaking at the Jaffrey Forum Aug. 28.[57] You want a ride?

Devotedly
Thornton

---

57 TNW's talk at the Amos Fortune Forum in Jaffrey, New Hampshire, was titled "Modern Literature and the Inner Life."

241. TO SALLY HIGGINSON. ALS 2 pp. (Stationery embossed Columbia University Club / 4 West 43rd Street / New York 18, N.Y.) Wisconsin

<appeared with arrow pointing to heading>
Someday get into the Vassar Club, dear—you can't imagine how tranquil you'll be.

As from 50 Deepwood Drive
Hamden Conn.
May 13. 1953

Dear Sally, ma belle et ma bonne:[58]

Just a word to tell you what a pleasure it was—Ware Street et obiter.[59]

And what interest I take in your trip and the work you'll do there.[60]

Let your old uncle urge you:

(a) women's writing has to be truer than men's. Yes, it does. To be really good. Men can construct literary works—not because they are inherently more capable than women—but because society for so many thousand years has put them in a situation where they have more self-confidence. The strength of women's writing must come from their fierce truth-telling—see Katherine Mansfield's Journals and letters.[61]

Your business as you face the task of being a writer is to be cruel to yourself—always more fiercely honest to tell your truth. She kept

---

58 French: My beautiful and good one.

59 Latin: and so forth. Higginson lived on Ware Street in Cambridge, Massachusetts, and invited TNW to tea or drinks. He suggested she invite some friends as well, which she did, and there was a group of about ten people.

60 After having graduated from Radcliffe College, Higginson wanted to be a writer and go to Paris.

61 Mansfield's journals and letters were edited after her death by her husband, John Middleton Murry: *The Journal of Katherine Mansfield* (1927) and *The Letters of Katherine Mansfield* (2 vols., 1929).

calling it being purer. You can't afford to copy other writers—because that would be making it easier for yourself. She copied Chekhov; in her case it did no harm, precisely because he was the humblest and purest author she had seen.

Your truth—that's what you must uncover—first in a Journal to yourself. Then in your stories.

This doesn't mean that the material must be (what they call) "awful". The simplest things admit of a hundred ways of telling: yours must be the one real right way for you.

ⓑ Don't be in a hurry. To be published; to be praised; to be "justified" in the eyes of others. Set yourself a five-years-plan. Mature your art without haste and without any desire to impress the neighbors. Rejoice that you are you. Your writing is you, and you have no need to rush out and assert yourself.

ⓒ Don't read many current books, the talked-about smart literature of the day. Have by your bedside always some of the great Unattainables. Let them be your companions, your weather.

In the meantime, rejoice in people, in the diversity of life—affectionately, watchfully.

Love and you will be loveable.

Don't be impatient, and people will find in you a haven. ¶ You are dear to your devoted uncle

Thornton

242. TO CHARLOTTE E. WILDER. ALS 4 pp. (Stationery embossed 50 Deepwood Drive / Hamden 14, Connecticut) Yale

<P.M. June 6, 1953>

Dear Sharlie

Lord's sakes . . . it's been an age since I wrote you . . . . and yet I write from 8 to a dozen letters a day, most of them as dull as the letters they answer.

Many thanks for the suggestion about Cobb's Mill Inn[62]...it is in a beautiful location; but too expensive. I took Maude Hutchins and 2 of her daughters there once.....ouch, got away with barely my shirt on.

Today we drive up to Janet's at Amherst,[63] so as to be nearer to [Confidential: The Univ of New Hampshire] where I get a degree on Sunday. I'll be eight times a Doctor! Wouldn't that amaze your father? [All those conversations of his with Dean Jones, pleading that poor grades be forgiven.[64]] I tole 'em frankly I could not make a speech. Most of these "Honors" are accompanied by a request for a Commencement address...—but no more. A hood in exchange for a speech is not an equal swap.

I've got over my indisposition, honey, and I beg and pray you have made much progress.

Remember: you don't <u>only</u> eat to support your body; you eat to support your soul.

Do you eat slowly?

Do not read while you eat—do as the Mohammedans do: eat in silent admiration: eating is thanking,—thanking for being. Why don't you put a little half-solemn, half-playful ritual into eating?[65]

x

Honey, why will you collect old papers?

I'm the quickest tearer-upper in the world. Isabel's always afraid that I'm about to throw away some "treasure". Well, I aint got any

---

62 Cobb's Mill Inn is on the Saugatuck River in Weston, Connecticut.

63 Their youngest sister and her husband lived in Amherst, Massachusetts.

64 TNW's father had lobbied his Yale classmate Frederick Scheetz Jones, dean of Yale, to get TNW admitted there in September 1917.

65 TNW's concern about his sister's eating habits stemmed from Charlotte's bout with a hemorrhaging gastric ulcer, brought on by irregular eating and a general disregard for her health and physical surroundings. That illness resulted in a six-month hospitalization in 1952 in a halfway house at the institution in Amityville, Long Island, New York, where she had lived from January 1945 until September 1950, when she had begun to live independently. She returned to her Greenwich Village apartment after her convalescence and after assuring her doctors and her siblings that she could take care of herself. But she was unable to do so; the ulcers recurred and she required an operation that involved removing most of her stomach. On July 18, 1953, she was readmitted to the house in Amityville and her apartment was vacated. She spent the remainder of her life in institutional settings.

treasures and I don't want any treasures. I like rooms as near to monastic cells as possible. The Thew Wrights come to dinner not long ago and I filled up their arms with books to take home—Isabel making anguished signs. Bare walls bare floors—that's my ideal. Again: to support the soul. As Thoreau cried: "simplify, simplify, simplify!"

Old papers collect dust: asthmatic, choking, wearying, unclean, unorderly dust.

I'm coming to New York soon!!!!

Lotsa love
Thorny

243. TO AMOS TAPPAN WILDER. ALS 2 pp. (Stationery embossed 50 Deepwood Drive / Hamden 14, Connecticut) Private

Please give the accompanying leaf to your Angel-Mother:

<p.m. July 3, 1953>

Dear Tappie
Greetings!
Greetings!

You sure wrote me the nicest nephew's letter ever received in the History of Uncles.

You bet I'll be at your house lots of the time.

I'm going to the Mountain Ash Inn[66] for a lot of reasons:

(1) So as not to crowd you in your cabin.

(2) So as not to be in your mother's way <u>all the time</u>.

(3) Because writers <u>love</u> inns—there are so many <u>strangers</u> there to learn things from.

---

66 A summer inn in Brooklin, Maine, approximately six miles from TNW's brother's family home.

④ Because I know my bad character—when I work mornings I'm uuuugly—I bite and bark and snarl.

⑤ So as to have a place to invite YOU to come to.

Think this all over.

Aren't I too heavy to go in a boat-race?[67]

WAVES OF LOVE
Uncle Thorny

244. TO AMOS N. AND CATHARINE K. WILDER. ALS 2 pp. (Stationery embossed 50 Deepwood Drive / Hamden 14, Connecticut) Yale

Veltin Studio Thurs. am
<MacDowell Colony>
<September 10, 1953>[68]

Dear Ones:

Lovely letter from Kay. Yes, the summer of 53 is over; right cold this morning—38° and lots of tomato plants spoiled, as I heard from local gossip when I was downtown getting early breakfast today. Yet only six days ago we were on the last day of 11 of woeful heat and humidity.

Yes, I went to see Charlotte. Amazing. Best she's been since her first illness. Climbs up and downstairs like you or I; her conversation has lost those passages of irritation and suspicion. ("Why don't those Italians and Jews go back to their own country", "I used to like X on the radio very much, but the other day she said something so shocking.

---

67 TNW's nephew was racing a Brutal Beast class sailboat in Blue Hill, Maine.

68 "(Sept. 10, 1953 from McDowell Colony)" supplied here in another hand, probably that of TNW's brother.

I wrote her that saying things like that could lose her her audience and her position").

I saw Dr. Roller (head—I think—of the Medical part of Long Island Home... but maybe he's co-head of the whole thing with Dr. Squires... on second thoughts I think he is a psychiatrist too... well, I don't know). He said that there had been a radical change in Charlotte's attitude: she now acknowledges she did have a nervous breakdown and she is willing to concede that her family was acting for her own good and not merely maliciously restraining her liberty... etc. etc.

She talks of getting back as soon as possible to her New York apartment. No one ventures to tell her yet that it has been cleaned up and disposed of. If she went back would the disastrous cycle repeat itself? Cigarettes and coffee instead of food; mental instability because of malnutrition; new ulcers; constant vomiting; break down? Maybe not. At present she is not smoking. She can eat anything and retain it. But, of course, she is filled with the determination to get back to her apartment and her "work."

Amos shouldn't feel that he has to go: the secret of her cure is this all-inclusive bland self-centered self-sufficiency. There are two kinds of self-conten<te>dness: one is the anxiety-ridden, the other is the bland idyllic. At present she is in No 2. If he feels he wants to go, the drill is phone the Long Island Home, Amityville, to ask when it is convenient to come. (Officially callers may only come afternoons; as she is in Garden Cottage; for private medical patients convalescing, exceptions may be made for us. I went 11:00 a.m.) Ask on the phone whether it will be possible to see Dr. Roller. (We Wilders are too self-effacing; doctors expect the "family" to visit them, and it is part of the doctors' self-esteem.<)> Make a fuss over Charlotte's nurse Mrs Best. I didn't know whether I should slip her a ten-dollar bill in an envelope. I didn't. At the discharge of a patient, that is customary. Perhaps I'll try it next time. Passing through Amityville village get Charlotte a half-pint of vanilla ice-cream. She can always share it with Mrs Best or the "nice patient next door." I took a little book bought secondhand at the Gotham bookshop[69] (I doubt whether Charlotte has sufficient

69 The Gotham Book Mart in New York City, a popular gathering place for writers.

consecutiveness of mind to read adult literature; but the assumption is maintained; I saw War and Peace on her bureau; she hadn't begun it yet. She follows the more horrifying crime news in the Hearst papers.)

I know you don't like my tone about Charlotte, but you know me: my admiration for (x), who fought her way up and out of some appalling "conditioning" can only be maintained by dint of being indulgent toward (y) who gave up the struggle. We don't know all the facts about either x or y; but we must cling to the principle of freedom and responsibility. Poe—whom I have been re-studying for the Harvard book—destroyed himself—just as a part of Charlotte in her subconscious is out to destroy her—but Poe's infantile conditioning was horrible and his fight for life was tremendous. When he was not drunk, Poe was unfailingly attentive to others. That is the criterion. Beatrice Kendall[70] has broken down in much the same way as Charlotte, but Beatrice has always expended herself for others to the point of irritating officiousness.

I haven't yet made up my mind where I shall live through the Fall. Nor even where I shall go October first. I'm tempted to try Washington D.C. I'm a Consultant or something like that at the Library of Congress and they'll give me a cubicle in the stacks; and I've always liked the city. Shall I do that? Anyway, my uprootedness is a subject not of anxiety but of pleased reverie.

Lots of love to you all—I'd love to "follow" the steps of Dixie's first weeks at the new school.[71] (Don't take too seriously my animadiversion on coëducation; I'm not a dogmatic man). It'll be a very exciting year for Tappy, too,—any minute the "life-bent" may emerge.

Ever
Thorny

---

70 Daughter of William Sergeant Kendall, dean of the Yale School of Fine Arts from 1913 to 1922.

71 Catharine Dix Wilder entered Dana Hall School, an all-girls boarding school in Wellesley, Massachusetts, in September 1953.

245. TO EDWARD ALBEE.[72] ALS 2 pp. Private

As from: 50 Deepwood Drive Hamden Conn

Key West, Fla Nov. 22 <1953>

Dear Edward:

Greetings.

Delighted to receive your letter.

Yes, indeed, send me the play in couplets. I still have no fixed address down here so send it viâ Hamden.

You say that the answer to your finding acceptance by editors is: "Time and work".

Yes, but....

That's not enough.

Cultivate also a deeper concentration of all yourself on the poetic act. One preparation for it is this: let me beg you not to read too much contemporary prose and poetry. Expand your imagination's picture of what poetry does by withdrawing into yourself for a short time daily to read some of the great writing of the past. It's often valuable to do this in some foreign language. It wouldn't hurt if you made a sort of ceremony of it: quietly shut the door, sit down, relax, open the book, make your mind a serene blank cup for a minute: then slowly read Beaudelaire<Baudelaire> or Mallarmé or Rimbaud—for instance.

Something like that.

And remember: don't only write poetry; be a poet.

I like the poem you have sent me. The mood is admirably conveyed. But wasn't the poem on its way to a greater intensity? Before you used the title: Letter from Florence. This too has something of the

72 TNW met Albee at the MacDowell Colony in the summer of 1953, when Albee was there to visit his partner, American composer William Flanagan (1923–1969), who had a fellowship there. When Albee showed him the poems he'd been writing, TNW reportedly advised him to try writing plays. As a result, Albee began writing a verse play, "The Making of a Saint," and wrote TNW asking if he would look at it and enclosing a poem he had written.

"letter" quality—that is, talking. The talking cries out to pass to the next stage of singing, of praying, of bursting....

Something like that.

Give my best to Bill

Cordially ever
(T.N.)

246. TO MARCIA NARDI.[73] ALS 4 pp. (Stationery embossed 50 Deepwood Drive / Hamden 14, Connecticut) Yale

Feb 25 • <1954>

Dear Marcia—

Found your special delivery when I returned last night.

x

Enclosed find...etc. Do not think of repaying it.

x

Deeply interested by all you say about women in work and love.

The only thing I wish to say about it now is that the financial-security anxiety under which you live is greatly coloring your thoughts on the matter. Any secondary or additional anxiety in a woman's life (her conviction that she is ugly; or her fear of imminent illness; or the vicinity of someone who she thinks hates her;)—all such anxieties translate themselves promptly into a basic vague monstrous thing that one can only call "the humiliation of being a woman". [Centuries-old; Christianity-fostered, alas; in large part men (i.e. male) constructed and emphasized.]

In my opinion there is no such thing as the humiliation in being a

73 American poet Marcia Nardi (1901–1990) most likely had met TNW in the summer of 1953 at the MacDowell Colony.

woman, but billions have felt there is and feel so still. I hope that someday your work will be one more step toward removing that old-old prisonhouse. In the meantime, fight its shadows and its threats when they tend to "frighten" your mind. Femelle de l'homme[74] is a splendid blow against it. Keep up that proud, courageous, attitude,—that striking back at those who wish to remake woman into their condescending, minifying image of woman.

x

Through all this difficult time, please take good sensible care of your health. Let me be a stuffy old uncle: every day, preferably morning, take a half-hour walk—standing very straight, (from the frieze of the Parthenon), not looking at the passersby), breathing deeply but effortlessly, and thinking of the high and excellent and of your true proud relationship to it. Eat the simplest things and eat them slowly.

I hope to come to N.Y. before long. I will give you warning and hope that I shall find you free for dinner.

Eugene Davidson head of the Yale Univ. Press wants you to submit your poems for the "Yale Series of Younger Poets" whose editor is Auden. Does that seem too parochial-cliquey for you? Would you be ready? I recited some of yours to him (and to Sir Herbert Read[75]) and they were greatly struck.

Affectionate regards ever
Thornton

P.S. Neither Virginia Wolf<Woolf> nor Simone de Beavoir <Beauvoir> are true advocates for woman. Their very intensity arises from a lack of candor. More of this when I see you. . . .

74 A poem by Nardi that she sent to TNW; it was published in the October 1964 issue of *The Atlantic Monthly.*

75 Read (1893–1968) was an English poet and literary and art critic.

247. TO MICHAELA O'HARRA.[76] TL (Copy) 2 pp. New Dramatists

April 2, 1954

Dear Miss O'Harra:

In a way I ought to be ashamed of having asked that you give up so much time to write me a letter—but the letter's such an admirable piece of exposition that I'm going to hold it—or lend it back to you—in order to enlighten others also.

I have no skill nor practice in the form of exposition that you do so well. Let me just try a few jottings.

*

Older I grow I see that playwrights (in the early stages) discover and nourish themselves in only one way: being in the theatre, hanging around theatres. Fifty hours backstage are worth a thousand in audience-seats.

So I think very little of playwriting classes. (Prof. Baker was a magnet only; potential dramatists went to him; but his two most gifted, O'Neill and Wolfe, left after a short time—In his nine years at Yale, he "made" no playwrights, except Paul Osborne and Paul didn't even finish his one year).[77] Discussion groups—workshops in which they read to one another—are a little better—but only for courage, not for content.

Think of all our masters who worked backstage <u>first</u>. They don't even have to have been associated with good plays, (Ibsen at Bergen,[78]

---

76 American dramatist Michaela O'Harra (1911–2007) founded New Dramatists in 1949 as a monthly craft seminar for young playwrights. She apparently asked TNW for suggestions to be given to fledgling playwrights and she then printed his reply in the bulletin or newsletter that New Dramatists sent to its members. TNW's original letter has not been located; this appears to be a secretarial transcription.

77 Among the students George Pierce Baker taught in his '47 Workshop at Harvard University between 1905 and 1924 were Eugene O'Neill and Thomas Wolfe. After moving to Yale University in 1925, he taught American dramatist Paul Osborn (1901–1988).

78 Henrik Ibsen served as a stage manager with the National Stage in Bergen, Norway, before beginning his career as a dramatist.

wasn't); it's enough they smell the paint and the audience and the working from that side of the curtain. (Composers don't go to concerts!)

Next best is attendance at rehearsals. (You note I put very little faith in attendance at performance—as a member of the public.) You kindly refer to me: let me state my youthful formation. In the grammar school and high school of Berkeley, California, it would seem that I'd have little chance to know backstage theatre; but no: Margaret Anglin, and Maude Adams, and Edith Wynne Matheson<Matthison>,[79] and the University's English Club were always putting on plays in the Greek theatre; and I climbed walls and was thrown out by guards and I hid behind back rows, but I saw hundreds of hours of rehearsals.

When painters and composers get together they don't talk about content (in content, no one can help you and you don't want anyone to help you), they talk about fabric, about medium, and all those things that go under the head of technical resources.

So much for the formation.

Now the plays are being written.

Is silence and solitude and isolation and leisure necessary for playwriting? It certainly is for poetry and musical composition. It is probably desirable for all artistic work. But most dramatists we read about seemed to have lived in a city turmoil—Goldoni and Congreve and Shaw and Beaumarchais and Sheridan, to name some in the second rank.

Which is related to my third proposition:

They all coped with the theatre, the commercial theatre of their day. To be sure, Shaw had that quasi-suburban venture the Vedremo <Vedrenne>-Barker Theatre, but notice how almost at once he began to aim for the West End—for Ellen Terry and Sir John<George> Alexander and Arnold Daly,[80] etc.

At present our off-Broadway theatres are our most hopeful market for gifted young playwrights—but there's a kind of danger in it, too. In

---

79 Anglin, Adams, and Matthison were among the most popular stage performers of the first quarter of the twentieth century.

80 Shaw's earliest plays were produced by Harley Granville-Barker at London's Court Theatre, which was managed by J. E. Vedrenne. English actress Ellen Terry, English actor-manager Sir George Alexander, and American actor Arnold Daly all appeared in plays by Shaw.

the theatre one writes for PEOPLE,—not for people-of-a-certain-taste. Off-Broadway theatre tends to please other interests before basic theatre storytelling: sociological tendency; a poetic-literary spinning. (Wasn't CAMINO REAL a perfect off-Broadway field-day in this sense?[81])

So I suggest:

(1) Divert playwrights to be stage managers. Use funds, if necessary to buy them jobs as assistant stage managers in summer theatres.

(2) See if Broadway shows won't let them sit backstage on the electrician's bench.

(3) For their "time to write", arrange to select your most promising playwrights and apply for their admission to MacDowell Colony, Yaddo, Huntington, Hartford; or buy a shack at Cape Hatteras.[82] (The poet St. Jean-Perse<Saint-John Perse> got one there for $12 dollars a month.)

Do not be too tender-hearted about their careers. What poets we admire have earned their living by their pen? Marianne Moore, a librarian; William Carlos Williams, a Pediatrician; Wallace Stevens, an insurance executive. Dozens of us have been teachers. It's too bad. It's probably hurt us, but it's only killed a few of us. But the one thing "we" didn't do was to write rubbish in order to earn the money to write literature.

A dramatist will be helped by doing a man's task of earning a living, but he will only be harmed by using his faculties as a dramatist in writing what he cannot respect. I have seen it over and over again in my pupils and young friends who have done routine Hollywood or routine radio and advertising writing.

Well, now, I haven't been much use to you. I'm sorry. We are all impatient for the next crop of playwrights who will bring some quality into the Broadway scene. But that is a matter of authentic endowment and no means has ever been found to produce that. Thousands of plays are being written by young people (and the postman certainly brings

---

81 Tennessee Williams's *Camino Real* had opened on Broadway. Its run at the National Theatre from March to May 1953, a total of sixty performances, was a significant failure.

82 MacDowell, Yaddo, and the Huntington Hartford Foundation's colony in Pacific Palisades, California, afforded artists short-term residences.

me a lot of them.) Their principal shortcoming—(that they aren't superior writing)—we can do nothing about. Their next shortcoming—that they lack basic stage-movement—can only be improved by extended frequentation of theatre-in-production. Not advice; not guidance; not round-table discussion; not theatre-attendance; not (and here you'll be angry with me) not primarily a production of their own plays, (in productions of one's own plays, so much anxiety and ego-susceptibility, and hopes 'n fears, and impulsive advice from Tom, Dick and Harry are involved; that there's little clear mind left to learn anything).

Lots of best wishes—

Sincerely yours,

SIGNED: Thornton Wilder

248. TO RUTH GORDON AND GARSON KANIN. ALS 2 pp. Private

Poste restante   Aix en Provence

or Hotel Thermes Sextius

All Souls Day <November 2, 1954>

Très-bons et très chers—[83]

All the time I've been sort of on my knees praying that Ruthie'll be able to say: why, <u>that</u> opening wasn't any strain at all!—that the deep rewards of all that wonderful selfless devotion to her task of these ten weeks will have that happy issue—an effortless, oh, a buoyant opening.[84]

On that phonecall from Birmingham the other night all I wanted to ask, and did ask, was: was Ruthie well and did she feel well in the rôle; and then I could have used £5 of phonebill asking was the <u>finale</u>

83 French: Very good and very dear ones.

84 After ten weeks on the road, *The Matchmaker* opened at London's Haymarket Theatre on November 4, 1954.

TNW, Garson Kanin, and Ruth Gordon in Berlin for the pre-London tryout of The Matchmaker, *September 1954.*

of Act III back in place and a thousand other questions. Now I'm crazy to know if the dressingroom at the Haymarket is magical for both comfort and tradition. (I called on John Gielgud for a moment there, in September; it looked like a drawingroom to me.)

I'm longing to be there for the Second Night; but—you know me—I haven't the faintest desire to be there at the First.

I am, however, represented in the First Night audience, and by one of the finest fellows I ever knew—Air Vice Marshal Pankhurst. He was my boss during the year in N. Africa and the year in Italy. No one, they say, ever liked an employer since business began; but that's not true. Pank was so tensely unsmilingly a conscientious leader that the other officers didn't like him very much; but I loved him and he knew it and he was very fond of me in that emotion-bound English way (the finest dogs, too, would give anything to be able to talk). He was so conscientious (outwitting those Germans) that he could almost never laugh. But I was able to make him laugh, and often. Those conversations in front of the Mess Bar after midnight.... under straye stars.... "Well... uh... Wilder, how do you think things are going?" "How do you mean, sir?" Mrs Pankhurst will be there, too; I never met her, but as a result of the appalling candors of exile and homesickness, I learned more about her than I shall ever know of Anna Karenina or Isabel Wilder. I used to be able to make him laugh and I now pass on that worthwhile task to dear Ruthie.

Now while writing this letter I've almost come around to wishing I could be at the Opening Night. There's a right kind of nervousness and a wrong kind of nervousness. The right kind arises from our anxiety that everything should go right for us; the wrong kind from our anxiety that everything should go right for them. I love the right kind of nervousness; I had it at Newcastle and it was very heady and exciting. But big capitals engender the second kind,—now, well—there must be something wrong in my argument somewhere, because we're certainly in this business to please: Garson sometime will point out my lost stitch to me.

Oh, dear, its one-ten in the morning; and I want to go down and get tight; but in little compact adorable Aix they take in the sidewalks at ten-thirty (no street-walkers, either; tutt-tutt, provincial University town). Of course, there are the brilliant and raffish salles de jeu;[85] but I don't want to get tight under a thousand chandeliers, I want to sit on a terrace on the most beautiful street in the world, the Cours Mirabeau, hearing those plashing fountains and staring with slowly glazing eyes into the falling beech leaves, and brood about how I love the Kanins and about all I owe to the Kanins, and then start weeping weeping about how wicked and unjust I am to the Kanins, and ungrateful and unworthy, happy happy tears, until the garçon wakes me up. In vino veritas. True, true, all true.

Thy

Thornt.

85 French: gaming rooms.

249. TO MARCIA NARDI. ALS 2 pp. Yale

Poste restante Aix-en-Provence Jan 10 1955

Dear Marcia—

Sorry about this delay in answering. I only found your two letters here when I returned from a holiday visit to my sister in Switzerland. I'd told them here only to forward telegrams and registered mail.

The chief thing that distresses and surprises me in your letters is the account you give of all those rejections of your poems by the very magazines which I feel should accept them gladly. Poems enter circulation through having aroused the active enthusiasm of a few readers—through such a reader I am happy to see that your book is to find a publisher.[86] I hope—especially as I am to remain out of the country for a while—that you will find more such readers who will do battle for you.

But it's hard to see how you can make personal relations with such championing admirers while your life goes on as it is,—and not only because you are cooped up in New York.

Now grab your hat because I'm going to talk to you in the tone of an old uncle:

You describe three "shattering emotional experiences that you have been through" that leave you "ill in both body and soul." Now look, Marcia. I've known such experiences, and no week goes by but that some distraught friend writes me about such experiences—but I'm afraid you're the kind of person that no one can help; you're the person who likes 'em, who rushes toward 'em; who (worst of all) <u>returns</u> to 'em. I think you've got some foolish romantico-erotic notions mixed up in your head. Why should you be "shattered" that J.E. should return to his wife? You should have forseen it from the first day. One glance is enough to show you that he's a very prudent middle-of-the road man. And you <u>returned</u> to this "monster" as you describe him, your former husband? I think you're a sort of emotional goose; you read too

86 Nardi's *Poems* was published in 1956 by Alan Swallow, which was based in Denver, Colorado.

many bad novels when you were a girl. You justify it by invoking the claims of the senses. Well, we all know about them; but in adults the claim of the senses is always linked with other claims—enrichment, tranquility, children, etc. But I'm afraid that with you its linked with a very appetite for suffering, and perhaps with an image of yourself as a grande amoureuse,[87] as a noble wronged loving woman. THREE, Marcia? And one of them a Repetition?

Now, you sit down and have a good talk with yourself. You don't sound like a woman out of the 20th Century—you sound like a "willing victim" out of bad French novels, 1901. And I should think it'd all have a bad effect on your poetry. These abused, spurned and abandoned women are out of date. Yes, I know they exist and I've just seen a lot of one of them—but they accept their sufferings differently. They have more resilience, more pride and dignity and resilience.

Formerly when I recommended that you get a job I grieved about it—because I regretted the time so diverted from the writing of poetry. But now I don't grieve at all: I don't think you'll write any more superior poetry until you change your attitude. You're not enough like Shakespeare's heroines; you havent a strong enough spine; you have out-dated cobwebs in your head. You're Greenwich-village-y, 1912.

Now, I always feel ashamed when I indulge in this kind of preaching. And my shame takes the form of sending a cheque. I can't afford it, but here it goes.

I think you know that I write you this way because I believe that you will outgrow all these stages and write beautiful things,—searching beautiful truth things. You know that, don't you?

Your old friend
Thornton

87 French: a great lover.

250. TO IRENE WORTH.[88] ALS 2 pp. Yale

Paris Sunday — Jan 23. 1955
en route to
Hotel Sextius
Aix-en-Provence, (B. du R.)

Dear Miss Worth:

Never have I seen so many Parisians going to church. Even the most tepid are bounding along to fling themselves on their knees. Why? There's only one subject of conversation in Paris—the alarming behavior of the Seine.[89] All day (and at 4:00 in the morning when I was coming home) crowds stare, silenced and appalled, at that coiling flood. The French lose very little sleep over disorder in other countries; but the fact that disorder can take place in France leaves them speechless. (Dieu, est-il français?[90]) I wish some power the giftie'd gie' 'em to see that they are introducing a similar disorder into international affairs.

I skipped out of London leaving a number of matters unresolved. There's going to be a clash between an irresistable force and an immovable object. Tony will urge powerfully that the play's cast be recruited in Canada; and Binkie[91] will ask how that can be subsidized. And Wilder, the most difficult and irrational of beings, will have left his deposition that he doesn't want the Canadian forces to present the play in Edinburgh, unless Canadian audiences have had their just right to see it in their home base; and Mr. Hunter[92] will insist that the play should not be seen prior to his unveiling in his own Festival. And Tony

---

88 Actress Irene Worth played Alcestis in the world premiere of TNW's *The Alcestiad* (retitled *A Life in the Sun*), which opened at the Edinburgh Festival on August 22, 1955, directed by Tyrone "Tony" Guthrie.

89 In mid-January, the Seine rose to flood level, necessitating removal of artworks on the ground floor of the Louvre and causing the evacuation of thousands in the suburbs of Paris.

90 French: Isn't God French?

91 Hugh "Binkie" Beaumont, whose company, H. M. Tennant, coproduced *A Life in the Sun* with the Edinburgh Festival Society.

92 Sir Ian Bruce Hope Hunter was the artistic director of the Edinburgh Festival.

will say "I cannot adequately caste this play in Shaftsbury Avenue, and I wouldn't have time to do it, if I could." And Binkie and Hunter will say, "We have your commitment that you would put this play on in Edinburgh and—wind or high weather—you shall and will." Whereupon I go blithely off to Paris which—as *The Importance of Being Ernest*<*Earnest*> says—"hardly shows a very serious disposition at the end."[93]

I hope, gracious lady, that you are not caught between the millstones of those differences.

I'm accustomed to a dim view of the success of my works on the part of those who must "promote" them. When I took *The Bridge of San Luis Rey* to my publishers, they shook their heads; they "liked" it, but they saw that it was for a restricted circle of readers and hoped that I would bear in mind a larger audience. They found so little of interest in *Heaven's My Destination* that they resigned it to another publisher. *Our Town* went so badly in a Boston try-out that the manager cancelled a second week and almost did not bring it into New York. (He engaged the Henry Miller Theatre that was only available for a week and a half.) *The Skin of Our Teeth* received such crashingly bad notices that the manager was cancelling the New York opening, when he heard that Freddie March was asking his agent whether *he* had enough money to buy it.

So I'm almost *braced* by the fact that (reported to me in a letter by Mr. Hunter) Binkie does not feel that this play could ensure a Edinburgh-to-London removal (to say nothing of a trip around the provinces *en route*). So after all this writing of mine and after all these hopes (and all these 'conferences') there is to be a two-week or hopefully a three-week presentation of the play and *finis*! I think that's awfully funny. Is the play so off-beat as all that? so intimidatingly highbrow? If there had been no question of the Edinburgh Festival, couldn't I have found a West End manager to believe in it? Anyway, I've arranged that after the Edinburgh run, all the rights to the play return to me, so that I shall seek to place it with a New York manager.

---

93 The quotation is from act 2, when Jack indicates that his brother Ernest had "expressed a desire to be buried in Paris" and Chausuble observes, "I fear that hardly points to any very serious state of mind at the last."

Apparently you and I are the only persons who believe that the Suburbanite could become absorbed in this play and recommend it to his or her neighbors. When Binkie has given you a text, do select one or two friends whose judgment is sound also on "entertainment values" and see if they too think it is commercially hopeless. I love men and women so much—and the ordinary man and woman (to whom the play is a sort of hymn)—that I should be very confused, if I woke up at 57 to discover that I was writing works in which they were unable to see themselves reflected. Oh, Lord! have I become library-dusty and out-of-reach-cultured!!

I'm finishing this letter at Aix—and I wish I could wrap up some of this Provençal sunlight and send it to you... I'm now going to sign my first name and I want you to pull yourself together to meet the affront in my next letter, of my addressing you by your first—to which will be added the indignity of my (for a while) thinking it in two syllables. But since it means PEACE you cant be indignant for long.[94] Its use will be, madam, just one of my ways of expressing my admiration, gratitude and

regard,
Thornton

251. TO THEW WRIGHT, JR. ALS 2 pp. Private

<Aix-en-Provence>
Feb 19 <1955>

Dear Thew—

Well now, what was I saying?

Oh, yes.

So I got back from Marseille, where I picked up my dough,[95] and after a while I went to a dive where I often go. This is a University

94 Irene was the Greek goddess of peace and the name derives from the Greek word.

95 Wright had wired money to TNW.

town and very controlled. I went to the only place that stays open almost all night. Certain people have warned me against it—its the gangster (that's a French word) and sporting place, but I'm an old acquaintance. The dame that runs it, half Martinique negress, and her husband and boy—why, they're old friends. She made me an aioli—a Provençale dish almost solid garlic, and was my guest when we all ate it together. I'm the American with horn-rimmed spectacles who speaks bad French, but they speak worse. I was a year in French North Africa, reportedly a hotbed of pickpockets, but I never lost a thing and here I havent lost a thing yet; but we're a real worldly-wise crowd down there. Every now and then I meet there<?> my friend Régus Toussaint (translated: of the King-all Saints); he's a pimp and hangs around all the bars getting customers for Madame Francia's. I<'ve> been to Madame Francia's. She's only got three girls, and for years in Marseille (30 kilometres away) she had 25. But all France—even Paris—has closed down, institutionally, on such stuff. They allow her to operate here for an extraordinary reason. She showed me her medals. God damn it, France, England, and America had given her impressive citations and medals for her work in the French Resistance. She'd hidden aviators and transmitted messages and organized railway bombings, and she was an old whore and madame. Life's bigger, wider, fuller than the deacons ever dreamed it was.

So I went tonight to this joint and had my oysters and my omelette and my bottle of wine and it was all less than a dollar; and everywhere else France is killingly expensive—so my advice to you is to stick to the half-world, and semi-criminal because its more interesting and more human and lots cheaper.

I got back from that week in Italy where I'd paid the bills for Isabel and the German translator and everywhere I'd asked people to come to dinner and you know how it is and when I got back it was more expensive than I'd thought....... Hence my S.O.S. to you. I think they must have mislaid your remittance a while—but efficiency is not to be expected in this charming country—especially not of French employees working for an American firm.

It's time we invented a Cable code name for you, and I've a good mind to register THEWIGDAN.

But I know I won't have any occasion to S.O.S. you again.

I'm just bent double with the kind of jobs I hate most—"preparing" the definit<iv>e Matchmakers for the translators (and for later publication). Writing a piece on What the Alcestiad is about for the Edinburgh publicity.[96] And oh! the letters. I must write about 600 a year, but then I get bawled out for not writing twice that many.

I'm afraid that I've hurt Isabel's feelings: I gently suggested that I didn't see why she had to spend all that money to return to Europe again to see the new play at the Edinburgh Festival. I didn't tell her (but she might have seen it long ago) that—during those harrassed times—it not only adds to "the things I have to think about", to be "nice" about, but it also reduces the occasions when I can have a little deserved recreation. A sister is not a wife; and although some brothers in literature or the arts, have had sisters who were as omnipresent and "necessary" as wives, I'm not one of them; in fact, I'm one of the most extreme goers-alone I ever came across. Even from Isabel's point of view—in my eyes—I am constantly aware of the fact that she does not sufficiently see that it is <from> oneself and the developement of one's own qualities that one makes a satisfactory life—not in being present passively at places where "things are going on". Her talents are writing, housekeeping, hostessing, and being a resource to her friends....But her writer-brother is having a new play come out in Scotland,—is it mean of me to suggest that its not necessary she should be there? I suppose it is. (With the other productions she was actively useful—that depended on the temperament of the director. This director Guthrie doesn't call on any outside help—even I could be absent.)

If I get my present chores in hand, I hope to set down an itemized bill of some of these business trips...for income tax.

Yet all the time a new play is trying to move into my consciousness. Hell, it's hard to organize my life...but at least I'm doing it a little better in France than in the U.S.

But oh I'm getting ready to come home

Ever

96 TNW's "Notes on *The Alcestiad*" was published in the program for the Edinburgh Festival production; it was reprinted in volume 2 of *The Collected Short Plays of Thornton Wilder* (1998).

252. TO ALAN SCHNEIDER.[97] ALS 2 pp. Yale

Gibraltar—sailing tomorrow for U.S
April fool's Day 1955

Dear Schneider—

Fine!

Great!

Scores told me how good your Catholic U. production was.

Yes, the unframed stage is getting to be self-evident,—what promise for a new Theatre age.

Don't come to Washington to hear the damn lecture. Anyway, I repeat it at the YWHA on May 2.[98]

Maybe you hate hearing authors read their plays: I'd understand it. But I think I'm reading the new one[99] to a few friends in my sitting room at the Algonquin on Sat. night April 9—verify by phone. Bring wife and baby unless author's readings revolt them, too. <appeared in the left margin, with an arrow pointing to it from the last sentence of the paragraph> **confidential**

In Europe don't go to theatre much—saw nothing arresting.

There are 20 ways of doing Skin. I have no idea how it should be done. When I began it I saw it as <a> comic strip—Fanny Brice and Ed Wynn[100]—giant Punch and Judy with balloon-speeches coming out of their mouths—and Sabina tearing around serving breakfast on

---

97 Alan Schneider (1917–1984), who, while teaching at Catholic University of America in Washington, D.C., had directed a production of TNW's *The Skin of Our Teeth* in 1952. In 1955, he directed a major revival of the play, starring Helen Hayes as Mrs. Antrobus, George Abbott as Mr. Antrobus, and Mary Martin as Sabina. The production, produced by Robert Whitehead (1916–2002), ran in New York for twenty-two performances in August and September 1955 before going to Paris as part of the American National Theatre and Academy's Salute to France program.

98 On April 18, 1955, TNW read the first two acts of *The Alcestiad* at the Library of Congress; on May 2, he gave a lecture/reading, "Culture and Confusion," at the YM-YWHA in New York City.

99 *The Alcestiad.*

100 Wynn was known for his "Perfect Fool" character.

roller-skates—sort of Ubu Roi.[101] Then as I wrote on that old Wilder pathos-about-family-life began to get into the act. The characters lost a lot of their out-size.

I used to think the climax and core-kernel was "We're all as wicked as we can be and that's the God's Truth"—a line Tallulah[102] hated and used to mumble ("But it doesn't mean anything")

L. Olivier never played Antrobus in London but he did on the Australian tour—I saw a rough dress rehearsal in London before they sailed. He was wonderful in each act—but in the last what a picture of brutilised war-fatigue gradually assembling a few things to cling to. I've never seen a Mrs A that I'd buy. I've seen school-marms and injured tragedy-queens, and agitated hens (peacock-hen; in Milan).

I always cry when Sabina declares that from time to time she's got to go to the movies.

See you soon.

All best to all three of you.

Cordially

Thornton Wilder

And lots of regards to Robert Whitehead; tell him I'm ashamed I wrote a play with so big a cast and so many technical problems. (But the new one's worse.) Am writing Mary and Helen.

---

101 This play (1896) by French dramatist and novelist Alfred Jarry is a stylized burlesque and had a great influence on Dada and surrealism.

102 Bankhead played Sabina in the original 1942 production of *The Skin of Our Teeth*.

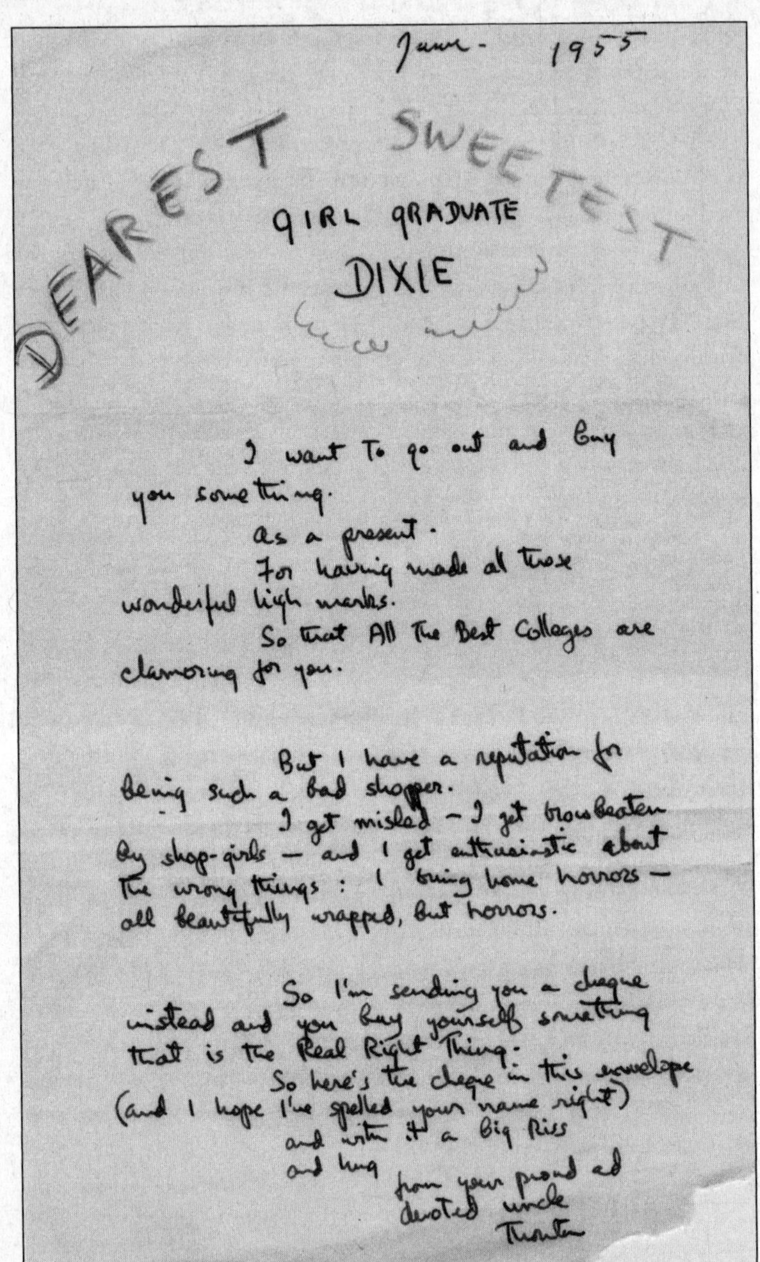

June - 1955

DEAREST SWEETEST

GIRL GRADUATE

DIXIE

I want To go out and buy you something.

As a present.

For having made all those wonderful high marks.

So that All The Best Colleges are clamoring for you.

But I have a reputation for being such a bad shopper.

I get misled — I get browbeaten by shop-girls — and I get enthusiastic about The wrong things: I bring home horrors — all beautifully wrapped, but horrors.

So I'm sending you a cheque instead and you buy yourself something that is The Real Right Thing.

So here's the cheque in this envelope (and I hope I've spelled your name right) and with it a Big Kiss and hug

from your proud and devoted uncle

Thornton

An example of TNW's multicolored decorative letters. The word "DEAREST" is written in blue pencil, "SWEETEST" in red pencil, and the design under "DIXIE" in blue pencil.

253. TO CATHARINE DIX WILDER. ALS 1 p. Yale

<June 1955>

DEAREST SWEETEST
GIRL GRADUATE[103]
DIXIE

I want to go out and buy you something.

As a present.

For having made all those wonderful high marks.

So that All The Best Colleges are clamoring for you.

But I have a reputation for being such a bad shopper.

I get misled—I get browbeaten by shop-girls—and I get enthusiastic about the wrong things: I bring home horrors—all beautifully wrapped, but horrors.

So I'm sending you a cheque instead and you buy yourself something that is the Real Right Thing.

So here's the cheque in this envelope (and I hope I've spelled your name right)

and with it a big kiss

and hug

from your proud and
devoted uncle
Thornton

---

103 TNW's niece graduated from the Dana Hall School in June 1955 and entered Radcliffe College that fall. The date was supplied in another hand, presumably that of Catharine Dix Wilder.

254. TO FRANZ LINK.[104] ALS 2 pp. Private

50 Deepwood Drive Hamden, Connecticut USA
Nov. 7. 1955

Dear Herr Link:

Many thanks for your letter and for your very perceptive comments on The Bridge of San Luis Rey. I read them with great interest, and intellectual pleasure, and gratitude for your generosity; but I hesitate to comment in return. I distrust bringing upward to the conscious analytical level, in myself (in relation to my own works) the various processes, and influences which enter my novels and plays. I have always assumed that every artist is a tireless critic—a selector, a rejector, a discriminator—but that those operations take place—as it were—"in the dark." The practice of writing seems to me to be the gradual acquisition of ever increased experience, in the organization of such thought and material,—an experience which frees him from the consciousness of "fabrication" and opens his mind more and more to the appearance of spontaneous and "lyric" expression.

Hence, I do not look back at my works; do not re-read them. I even become ill at ease when I recall them. "Forward!" "Let's make another."

These last months I have been called to duties, from place to place, so swiftly that much of my mail has not yet caught up <to> me. Your paper on Goethe will probably arrive here soon—though I must sail for Rome on the 18th to have long conferences with the composer who is setting my new opera-libretto to music.[105] I shall look forward to reading it, however, when I return.

One comment I will make—since you have asked for it!—on the "style" of the Bridge—on a relatively superficial aspect of the style. During the years preceding the writing of my first two novels I had been reading intensively in the literature of the French grand siècle.

104 Link (1924–2001) was a leading German scholar of American literature during the postwar period.

105 TNW was working with Louise Talma on an opera version of *The Alcestiad*.

The Marquesa de Montemayor is "after" the Marquise de Sévigné—the colors heightened in the Spanish colonial atmosphere. Those formal portraits with which I introduce the principal characters are in the manner of Saint Simon and the memoirs of the Cardinal de Retz, La Rochefoucauld, and even the portrait-making in the sermons of Bossuet and Bourdaloue. Hence the "removed" tone, the classical, the faintly ironic distance from the impassioned actions is an expression,—even a borrowing—from the latin thought-world. Thence comes also the occasional resort to aphorism.

I have read and reread your Herbstnacht in der Grosstadt with grateful pleasure. As to the story, I feel that dreams,—real or supposed—are a perilous art-form. They "invite" a certain irresponsibility.

All best wishes to you and many regards,

Sincerely yours
Thornton Wilder

255. TO THEW WRIGHT, JR. ALS 2 pp. Private

Hotel Vesuvio Naples, Nov. 28 <1955>

Dear Thug—

Just about the only ocean crossing I failed completely to enjoy. Don't quite know why. First my digestion and my sleep failed to function. I thought it was too much drinking maybe—i.e. a little at 5; a little at dinner; a little after dinner; a little at midnight. So I substituted coca cola in the later hours (horrible); no improvement. The ship's company was less than galvanic, but that never puts me off; I can be attentive to anybody. (Had to sit at the Captain's Table with various State Dept and Amexco V.I.P.s and their ladies.[106]) Myerberg put Alan Schneider on the boat to pick my brains about their forthcoming pro-

106 TNW went to Europe for the Paris production of *The Skin of Our Teeth*, which was partially funded by the State Department and by American Express.

duction of Waiting for Godot (Bert Lahr and Tom Ewell!) and sure—free gratis for nothing I retranslated by dictation the whole play . . . rather enjoyed it but it took time and mind and energy from other things.[107] No, the root of the whole trouble was the damned air-conditioning. Hermetically sealed in a room with that

LATER: Feel better already. Oh, Naples . . . . nothing like it. Sun today . . . Reporters; refused to do radio and TV . . . pleading.

I want to stay on here a few days—besides, I'm not ready to present Louise with her finished text

Mon. I was sort of crazy to think that I could ever have done all that: returned from Switzerland for the Matchmaker,[108] returned to Rome for Louise, returned to America for Mexico. (I should begin to know now after a hundred experiences that my judgment of what is possible in future time is always ALWAYS wide wide of the mark. Especially in writing I should never set any kind of dateline.—I'm inclined to think that I can only write "fast" when there is no pressure.)

LATER: Happened to see a Hamburg paper with a review of The Matchmaker—so beautiful a review that for the first time in <my> life I wrote the critic, on a Xmas card. The same play opened in Zurich yesterday. That play sure is giving pleasure in central Europe. I tell myself that some day it'll get a production in USA of which I would approve every bit of it.[109] Its of no importance that I may not be there to see it. To hear these Germans talk about it, you'd scarcely guess that it was the same play. ¶ A sixteen page letter from that young woman who (with her mother) ran the bar Mimosa at Baden Baden and who was undergoing psychoanalysis. An extraordinary letter: women can be at the same time both boundlessly happy and boundlessly unhappy at the same time and get it all understandably down on paper.

---

107 Schneider directed Beckett's 1952 play. Produced by Michael Myerberg and starring Lahr and Ewell, it opened at the Cocoanut Grove Playhouse in Miami, Florida, in January 1956, to negative reviews. Wilder's dictated translation was not used in the production and has not been located.

108 *The Matchmaker* was scheduled to open in New York on December 5, 1955.

109 Although TNW was always loyal to Ruth Gordon and pleased at the success she made with *The Matchmaker,* he appears to have favored an ensemble interpretation of the play, closer to the European farce tradition than to the more rambunctious, star-driven American version.

Well, I'll never get this letter off if I go on adding desultory items like this.

Give my love to Danda and to the other bright and beautiful girls in your home[110] and a world of Xmas greetings and new year greetings to you all—

your old
Thornt

256. TO ERIC BENTLEY.[111] ALS 4 pp. (Stationery embossed 50 Deepwood Drive / Hamden 14, Connecticut) Penn State

Jan 5. 1956

Dear Bently—

Greetings.

Yes, I've spent all those countless infatuated hours over Lope. My attention was mostly absorbed in finding the clues that would help to date them, an extra-literary preoccupation; but I was constantly aware of the genius, too. There are several hundreds of plays which I have read many times. Even in the most mechanical of them, there is somewhere the mark of the lion. And always a wonderful relation to theatre and to the ways his contemporary audience "followed" a story. And by 1610 every play is a masterpiece or near it—and that's a great many.

I've long despaired of any ability on my part to make a translation. The problem is despairful enough in the case of Molière and Schiller and Racine, but rendered far more difficult still in that of

110 Danda was Wright's second wife, but whether TNW is referring to Wright's children by his first wife or to daughters his second wife had from a previous marriage cannot be determined.

111 Bentley had asked TNW to provide a translation of or an introduction to a Spanish play for the third volume, *Six Spanish Plays* (1959), of his four-volume *The Classic Theatre* (1958–1961).

Lope. (As it is more difficult still in that of Calderon[112] who was a really great poet and a great spiritual myth-maker, in addition—which Lope was not.)

If Shakespeare were suddenly discovered in 1956, in an old Warwickshire chest,—would the modern world be willing to accept that Viola-Cesario Rosalind-Ganymede business—Portia's caskets, the first act of Lear and the last of Measure for Measure? I feel certain that it's only the fact that they have been played continuously, generation after generation, that makes the conventions work. Lope employs all those (and those with an added fantastication from the Spanish temper) and heaps on them a great many more.

Take the sonnet directed, at crisis, to the audience. They loved it, and Lope uses it most beautifully. As: In the openings of his two finest play<s> Fuenteovejuna and Peribánez the lovers play a sort of renaissance game: I love you with an A.. with a B... with a C... It must be cut (do you realize that probably Fuenteovejuna is probably the most frequently played play in this decade? since the USSR commanded that it be played in every theatre in Russia) and when it is cut the balance on which the play rests is shattered: the agony is turned into mere melodrama.

But I believe that English-readers should have the opportunity to divine what the lion's work was like.

I cannot write a preface. (I go through life writing as little "non-fiction" as possible—since I do it badly and with excruciating effort<.>) But I send all my best wishes to the venture.

I suggest that the following plays would be the most accessible:

Fuenteovejuna
Peribánez
Los Commendadores de
Córdoba (but not the three together, because of certain resemblances in the plots.)

and for comedy

La discreta enamorada (the only play I ever saw on the stage—at Stuttgart, where they had robbed it of almost all of its enormous charm.)

---

112 Spanish dramatist Pedro Calderón de la Barca (1600–1681).

La dama boba
Los melindres de Belisa

one or the other; there is a resemblance in plan. The former much played—by Maragunta Xirgú<,> Garcia Lorca's actress.[113]

The Barraults have been doing El perro del hortelano which I admire boundlessly but I dont think that in translation it puts Lope's best foot forward. It is very delicate chamber-music,—until the closing scene.

For pictures of customs and manners there is Santiago el verde or La vallana de Getafe<.> His power in making vast heroic "epics" from Spanish history—each one that I can recall has some elements that would seem infantile to present day readers.

Lopistas are generally agreed that La Estrella de Sevilla—which passed in Germany for a century as his masterpiece—is not by Lope. "Finely designed and poorly versified." Perhaps a thief's reworking of a lost original (stolen to sell to another manager.)

Again—all best wishes—and my sister joins me in sending many regards

Sincerely yours
Thornton Wilder

257. TO HENRY R. LUCE. ALS 1 p. (Stationery embossed 50 Deepwood Drive / Hamden 14, Connecticut) LofC

Moving gradually north
Mexico City
August 14 • 1956

Dear Harry:

Been in thc wilds of Mexico—where often mail is brought by donkey—slow and not always certain.

---

113 Spanish stage actress Margarita Xirgu (1888–1969) was a friend of and a frequent performer in the plays of Spanish dramatist and poet Federico García Lorca.

Yes, I've been working on that bundle of notions about America (The Charles Eliot Norton lectures at Harvard, 1950–1951; Panoffsky was only seven years late in delivering the printable text to the Harvard Press.[114])

I shall keep my promise of letting your staff see them; but its doubtful whether you can find them serviceable. I'm casting them into unconventional forms—following certain ideas of Gertrude Stein—in an effort to renew "exposition." There'll be dialogue and catechism and inner monologue and interruption and oddities of pagination: anything to give to the didactic pretended-omniscient essay some of the character of thought itself: process not stasis; journey not rest.

Anyway, even if it doesn't lend itself to excerpt-publication I hope old HRL gets some lively agreement and disagreement out of it and some laffs.

You can imagine how distressed I was to read about Clare's illness. To think that she—who is fortitude and courage and total commitment to so exacting an office should have had that burden added to it—all the worse for being puzzling and inexplicable. Do convey my sympathy to her, my wishes for full restoration, and my ever-admiring affection.[115]

All cordial best to you ever
Old Thornton

Isn't it a pleasure to see in Hersey the "tone" of us Old China hands.[116]

---

114 German art historian and essayist Erwin Panofsky's Norton Lectures were published as *Early Netherlandish Painting* (1953).

115 Luce's wife, editor, journalist, dramatist, and politician Clare Boothe Luce (1903–1987), had been appointed U.S. ambassador to Italy in March 1953. In 1956 she was forced to resign because she contracted an illness diagnosed as arsenic poisoning, attributed to paint chips that had fallen from the decorative ceiling in the bedroom of her official residence.

116 American novelist and journalist John Hersey was born in China to missionary parents and spent several years there. Hersey's 1956 novel, *A Single Pebble,* deals with an American engineer who is sent to China in the 1920s and falls under the spell of Chinese culture.

258. TO MAXWELL ANDERSON. ALS 4 pp. (Stationery embossed Gideon Putnam Hotel / Saratoga Springs / New York) Texas

Returning to.
50 Deepwood Drive
Hamden, Conn.

Nov. 13
1956

Dear Max—

All right, if you say so.

But I'd have been mighty proud to find and send you a copy of the book from me.

Of all the works I've done that book comes nearest to what one could call fun.[117] Fun to shift from voice to voice; to build up the complicated time-scheme (there are several howling boners in it); fun to parody the apparatus of a work of scholarship; fun to force the reader to assume that people have been much the same in all times and ages (that society dowagers, for instance, babbled, then, much as they do at their committee meetings now; and the figures now known to every schoolboy regarded one another as anything but lasting historical giants).

I turn purple whenever I think of my translations of Catullus. It's not the first nor the last time that I go into a sort of tunnel of deluded bad judgment. Had I read those in a book by someone else (even at the time I was doing them!) I'd have burst out into howls of derision. I seemed to have combined the worst effects of plaster-cast classicism with those of what England calls Wardour-Street.[118] Ouch! The tricks that subjectivity overstrained with good intentions can play on oneself.

I'll give you $2\frac{1}{2}$ guesses as to what lady well known to the U.S. public—daughter granddaughter descendant of senators, governors etc

117 TNW is referring to his epistolary novel *The Ides of March* (1948).

118 TNW's reference to Wardour Street relates to archaic language used for effect. The expression derives from the London street where a large number of antique shops were once located.

etc gave me some "lights" on how a Clodia ticked (the revolt against being duped by society's genteel facade).[119] For a Caesar I was richly fed by a great admiration for the thousands of pages of Simón Bolívar's correspondence: a lofty smiling half-sad unshakenness in the face of the betrayal of friends and beneficiaries.....

One of these days I want to recapture that mood of having sheer fun in writing a thing—which is no where near the same thing as writing a funny work.

All devoted best to you both

Ever
Thornton

259. TO LOUISE TALMA. ALS 2 pp. (Stationery embossed 50 Deepwood Drive / Hamden 14, Connecticut) Yale

Thursday
<November 29, 1956>[120]

Dear Louisa—

Well, an unforgettable time. The French have a phrase for it: toujours égale à elle-même.[121] You may have each morning's panic for yourself, but I won't be a party to it. Do remember—you who are so often victimized by self-doubts—that the achievements of any given moment are not that moment's sudden taking hold of strength, but are the results of a lifetime's choices and rejections, a lifetime's discipline, a lifetime's adherence to what one admires and what one relegates. You are still haunted by some notion that each good idea is a haphazard descent from the skies—yes, it is also that—but in addition to gratitude

---

119 TNW is referring to Tallulah Bankhead, whose father, William Brockman Bankhead, was Speaker of the U.S. House of Representatives and whose paternal grandfather, John H. Bankhead, was a U.S. senator.

120 The date for this letter was supplied in another hand, presumably that of Louise Talma.

121 French: always equal to herself (by which TNW means she is always up to the task at hand).

to the skies one has the legitimate expectation that all the dedicated work of one's previous years are also there as support and incitement. This is the popular misunderstanding of the word "inspiration": all work is breath from without, but it is also the reward of being ready—for years—for hundreds of previous inbreathings. You are a wonderful composer because you were an unobstructed listener to just such promptings in the past.

In a hurry
Just ate.
Now I gotta take Isabel downtown
to the movies.
More tomorrow.

That play about the criminals has grown and grown. It's called Bernice now. It's bigger and more terrible.... it's sort of darkly grand.[122]

Be a goooood girl and a lassen Sie sich nicht quälen bein Arbeiten gnädigte und Himmel-begapte<begapt> Frau.[123]

Dein[124]
Thornt

260. TO EILEEN, ROLAND, AND JULIAN LE GRAND. ALS 2 pp. (Stationery embossed 50 Deepwood Drive / Hamden 14, Connecticut) Private

December 19. 1956

Dear dear Friends—

This is the Grasshopper speaking.

---

122 TNW salvaged *Bernice* from the scenario he sent to Vittorio de Sica in 1952. That scenario was based on Ben Hecht's 1943 novel *Miracle in the Rain,* and TNW retained "the returned convict" and "the Negress as advisor" from the scenario in writing *Bernice.*

123 German: Please do not let yourself be tortured by work, gracious and heavenly-gifted lady.

124 German: Your.

That foolish fellow who never settles down, who fiddles away, neglects his debts of affection, procrastinates, and assumes that every tomorrow will be sunny. And that every tomorrow will be a splendid letter-writing day.

His only excuse is that from time to time he can borrow some qualities from his antagonist the Ant, and burrow down and do a little work. I've just finished five new one-act plays and am deep in two more. My hope was to send a privately printed copy of these as a Christmas momento to a few friends. But with them I fell into another old failing—the inability to draw finis: three of them still await one last touch, one last real right brushstroke.[125]

Anyway, you shall have them in time. (Of several of them the subject-matter is heart-rending and far from suitable for the season.)

Enclosed please find an item to decorate your tree.....I wish I knew Julian's tastes now and could participate in the conspiracy to surprise and delight him.

There is little news of me except work. "A Life in the Sun"—hateful title imposed upon him<it>—is going on journeys. A wonderful composer is making an opera of it—in the "12-tone series" style—now difficult listening for many, but to be the normal musical speech of the next generation; and as Die Alkestiade is to be played at the Zürich Festival in June, from whence it will probably travel the German language countries.

I am coming abroad late spring. I do not know yet whether I can come to England. If I do, we shall have a joyous reunion.

---

125 In his *Journal* entries for December 2 and December 13, 1956 (*The Journals of Thornton Wilder: 1939–1961,* ed. Donald Gallup [New Haven: Yale University Press, 1985] 257–259), TNW noted the dates of six one-act plays he had begun. On November 9, he began a play "reflecting my reading in Zen and Mahayana Buddhism" (this play may have turned up in another form); on November 12, what became *The Drunken Sisters*, the satyr play for *The Alcestiad*; on November 17, *The Wreck on the Five-Twenty-Five;* on November 23, *Bernice;* on December 2, "The Attic Play," which he noted lacked an "all-shaping idea" and which was probably discarded; and on December 9, "Shakespeare and the Bible," which was never completed to TNW's satisfaction. *Bernice* and *The Wreck on the Five-Twenty-Five* premiered as part of a program of short American plays presented to dedicate the new Congress Hall in West Berlin in September 1957. The casts included TNW, Ethel Waters, Lillian Gish, James Daly, Hiram Sherman, Cynthia Baxter, and John Becher; the director was Lamont Johnson. In 1958, TNW began working on a series of short plays based on the seven deadly sins, with *Bernice* representing the sin of pride. He did not complete the series, and *Bernice* was not staged again in his lifetime.

TNW with godson Julian Le Grand, Edinburgh, 1955 or 1956.

Give my deep regard to Dr. Francis[126] and all the family there.

And lots of love to you all
and a Merry Christmas
and
A happy New Year
To
Dear Julian—and Dear Eileen and Dear Roland

Thy
Thorny

---

126 Dr. Graham Francis was in charge of Edinburgh's Royal Infirmary and was married to Roland Le Grand's sister Noelle.

261. TO RUTH GORDON. ALS 4 pp. (Stationery embossed 50 Deepwood Drive / Hamden 14, Connecticut) Private

AM DEAF AGAIN
WITH MY WINTER
COLD—MUST'N'T see anybody

Wed. Jan 23 <1957>

Dear Ruthie—

The French translation:[127]

Rueful regret: that that's what it is: an unusually faithful translation.

I had hoped for a fascinating gallic transmogrification.

x

I changed myself—I fancied—into a French theatregoer; and I say with confidence that—unless you are playing in it—would be a prompt, lamentable failure.

x

It has, in itself, no qualities that arrest the attention of the French.

Each country has its own cherished tensions: The Germans like to hear behind the play Destiny-and-Fate—and vague philosophical allusions to Last Questions (my Alcestiad is going on at the Zürich Festival in June and will go like wildfire all over the German municipal theatres.)

The French love florid language (Giraudoux) and sharp eyes about our deplorable human failings (Anouilh) and above all the cat-and-mouse game of sex-impulse versus sexual legal and religious conventions. (The French Theatre would collapse if the Church and State ceased to presuppose monogamy. The Russians don't think that adultery is even interesting.)

The French have also some of that Latin emotionalism about the family. They can be caught by excruciating sentimentality about pater-

127 TNW is referring to the French translation of *The Matchmaker.*

nity and maternity (1000 performances of Le Rosaire, and La Bonheur de Jour and Mon Curé chez les Riches.)[128]

But our play has no "knowing" consciousness of sex; it has no family relationships whatever.

Without you in it,—it would utterly bore them. It is fade; it is plat. Worst of all, all the characters, except Dolly, are niais.[129] Ducreux[130] cannot cope with Cornelius. You can see him trying to make Cornelius somehow interesting.

The one little tentacle our play contains that might arrest our French theatregoer is that there's a certain amount of talk about money; and there is the Dolly-role as a femme forte.[131] (You know my theories about the French admiration-hatred and capitulation before a femme forte)

But, Hell, from the point of view of the French infatuation about money, it's downright incomprehensible about money. It's full of a Protestant-Puritan condition of being "unimpressed" by money; and Dolly is a femme forte who is not at all proud of her qualities as a femme forte; she is neither vainglorious nor cruel (aren't they fascinantes when they're cruelles<crueles>!)[132]: Hell, she wants to be friends with everybody; that is not in the formula at all.

What remains?

Ruth Gordon's performance.

Ruth's being able to see whether she can connect with an audience is unerring. Ruth knows Paris theatre-life. Does Ruth divine that she can express her powers in this rôle, in this play, among those factors?

I feel fairly certain that the play would expire every time she left the stage. Would Ruth wish to bear the burden of solely animating a play before which the audience was remote?

There is my main comment.

x x x x

---

128 *Le Rosaire* (1926), a play by André Bisson; *La Bonheur de Jour* (1926), a play by Edmond Guiraud; *Mon Curé Chez les Riches* (1925), a novel by Clément Vautel.

129 French: *fade,* bland; *plat,* dull; *niais,* vacuous.

130 Louis Ducreux was the French translator of *The Matchmaker.*

131 French: strong woman.

132 French: *fascinantes,* fascinating; *crueles,* cruel.

SOME INCIDENTAL OBSERVATIONS–

Cornelius completely defeats M. Ducreux.

Cornelius doesn't want to fly the millinery shop because Mrs Molloy would think him a *mufle*. No, no, no. *Mufle* means stupid pretentious bore,—naïve perhaps, but assertive bullheaded. Cornelius in the cupboard scents *l'éternel féminin*.[133] Imagine. Cornelius asserts that Mrs Molloy *est la plus jolie femme du monde*.[134]

Very clever the way Ducreux removed all reminiscences of the Molière borrowings.

VANDERGELDER: Vous avez un amant que vous cachez dans les armoires.[135]

Exactly. That's the way the play should sound in Paris. But unfortunately, the whole course of the play doesn't sustain and support it. That's the play that I sort of hoped Ducreux would furnish. Out of Feydeaux instead of out of Nestroy. Hélas.

Love to you and Gar—

Looking forward to seeing you when I'm well.

Thy

Thorny

Tell Gar I now own a Thunderbird.

262. TO LOUISE TALMA. ALS 2 pp. (Stationery embossed 50 Deepwood Drive / Hamden 14, Connecticut) Yale

Marineland, Fla

Feb 8 <1957>[136]

Dear Louisa—

Things happen to me. Lord be praised. Often they might seem little to others, but they can be big to me. I arrived yesterday at the

133 French: the eternal feminine.

134 French: is the most beautiful woman in the world.

135 French: You have a lover whom you hide in the closets.

136 The year was supplied in another hand, presumably that of Louise Talma.

motel connected with this unused "aquarium". Its restaurant is run by an old friend of mine Norton Baskin, widower of Marjorie Rawlings.[137] I went to see again (through underwater peepholes) that world of sharks and great turtles and baleful moray eels and countless fishes; and then the trained porpoises. Any animal doing a quasi-human "trick" is at once moving and disturbing to me, but porpoises leaping high out of the water to ring bells and to catch and return footballs and to cast basketballs into high baskets fill me with a sort of troubled anguish. The tricks are so undignified; the effort is so sublime. All created things aspire to mind. Dinner that evening—yesterday—at Norton's restaurant coincided with an alumni reunion—program enclosed—of an adjacent College for the Deaf.[138] I was invited to dine with them; I was introduced to the guests by the toastmaster (in sign-language): thereafter I autographed scores of their programs, handed to me by them with such shining friendly faces. There were well over 90 there. Most remarkable of all was the "reading" of the college's "hymn". The deaf can spell out any word, letter by letter, but why spell out when you can find a gesture that can convey the word? When you can touch your forehead for "think" and your heart for "feel"? Notice in the hymn the words: <“>from sea to sea<.>” This became F – ~·~·~·~ – T – ~·~·~·~ : See those little waves for the sea? What this woman did with a sort of hieratic solemnity was a dance with her hands, but the dance was far nearer language than the dance generally chooses to go. Isadora Duncan would have been shaken: Delsarte would have felt himself, mistakenly, justified.[139] For me, it was an evening in secret correspondence with the afternoon,—with the dolphins.

I picked up from the window of a tourist's giftshop in Myrtle

137 Novelist Marjorie Kinnan Rawlings.

138 TNW enclosed with this letter the program for the Edward M. Gallaudet Memorial Dinner of the St. Augustine Chapter of the Gallaudet College Alumni Association, held at the Dolphin Restaurant in Marineland, Florida, on February 7. Gallaudet (which is now a university) in Washington, D.C., is the only institution of higher learning in the United States devoted exclusively to the education of hearing-impaired students. The "adjacent College for the Deaf" to which TNW refers is the Florida School for the Deaf and the Blind in St. Augustine, but it was not their alumni who were meeting.

139 François Delsarte (1811–1871), a French acting and voice instructor, emphasized the importance of gestures and poses to the act of expressing oneself.

Beach (among "remainders" marked down) a not very good book about Mallarmé by Wallace Fowlie[140]—the man who lost his whole Guggenheim check in a Chicago bank, you remember the story. And at one place in it I was poignantly recalled to you, dear Louise—for I read that often when Mallarmé was writing he was visited by such palpitations of the heart that he could not continue. After a time he tried to dictate to his wife, but found no alleviation there. And then I was recalled to myself, with reproach, for I know I am not sufficiently sérieux to earn, to deserve such palpitations and such throbbing in my ears.—I'll send you the Mallarmé book; it is enough that it is filled with citations of the full poems.

Tomorrow I push on. Monday night I am having dinner with my aunt in Winter Park.[141] I can hear most that is said but there is too much humidity here for me to recover completely. Soon I'll be turning around and starting north again.

Love
Thorny

263. TO CASS CANFIELD. ALS 1 p. (Stationery embossed Hotel Ambassador / (Krantz) / Wein I) Yale

October 28. 1957 [Play[142] opens at the Burg here a week from tomorrow; then in Munich two days later.]

Dear Cass:

I've got a problem
And an idea.
Is the idea practical, feasible, profitable, and in good taste?

For two years now Louise Talma has been composing music for an opera, the book by me, based on the Alcestiad.

---

140 Fowlie's *Mallarmé* was published in 1953.

141 Charlotte Tappan Niven had retired in Winter Park, Florida.

142 *The Alcestiad*.

She had a Fulbright to the American Academy in Rome; summers she's at the MacDowell Colony; now she's at "Yaddo", Saratoga Springs, in January she goes to the Huntington Hartford Colony, in S. California. She's writing wonderful music. She's widely admired and esteemed. And all this time is taken away from her teaching post as Professor at Hunter College.

In other words, she's getting no salary.

Every year I put a thousand dollars to her account—to pay the mechanics of copyists when the time comes—music paper etc. But she wont accept any money for herself, not could I afford to give her money comparable to her Hunter College salary.

Rumors reach me that she is living on very narrow means.

How, how, how—to get money to her—across the barrier of her pride and independence?

Now—naturally an enormous correspondence has taken place between Louise and me about OPERA, about our Opera; about other people's operas. About all these stage performance<s> of the Alcestiad in Edinburgh, Zurich, Frankfurt, and now in Vienna. But also there are letters to and from Ruth Gordon about the Matchmaker (Edinburgh, London, U.S.)<.> Letters to and from Sibyl Colefax about London and New York theatre. Max Reinhardt about the Merchant of Yonkers. Jed Harris etc about Our Town. Olivier about Skin of our Teeth. Even Gertrude Stein.

Could you see a book:

LETTERS ABOUT THE THEATER: By and to THORNTON WILDER

Word has reached me that I'm supposed to be a very droll fellow, especially about the theatre. (Some of the vivacity would have to be toned down in fact) and Lord knows, Ruth Gordon writes hum-dingers. The letters wouldn't have to be solely about the theatre, either. At least we wouldn't cut out a description of Acapulco or from Sibyl's letters an account of England in wartime..... or from Alec Woollcott's an account of a visit to Booth Tarkington, etc. I think it would be a practically uproarious book.

Query: Would it be bad taste to publish one's own letters in one's lifetime?

SUGGESTION: my sister Isabel to edit it.

PURPOSE: Dough. Solely Dough. I think that Louise—many of whose letters would be included—would accept the royalties from this work seeing that they go to subsidize our common project, the opera.

Think it over. Take it to the Lord in prayer.

If there's any difficulty about "permissions" we could limit it to Woollcott; Colefax; Ned Sheldon; Ruth Gordon; and Louise Talma. Ruth and Garson Kanin arrive here tomorrow for a week. I feel sure that they'd love it—there's 20 copies sold already.[143]

Cordially ever
Harper's Problem Child
Thornton

I liked your son enormously. If I live long, and if you hand over the reins to him—have you sufficiently prepared him for the fact that Wilder is the House-Trial,—that he combines the worst features of a grasshopper, a gnat, a sloth, and a jay-bird? Start induring him now.

TNW.

264. TO EDWARD ALBEE. ALS 2 pp. (Stationery embossed 50 Deepwood Drive / Hamden 17, Connecticut) Private

August 17 <1958>

Dear Albee:

[Forgive pencil. Late at night. Hellishly hot. Don't want to go around the place hunting for ink, if any.]

Much impressed by The Zoo Story.[144] Many far-plunging insights. Much focusing on the speaking and the carrying image.

---

143 This project was never realized.

144 Because no U.S. company would produce it, Albee's play premiered at the Schiller Theatre in Berlin in September 1959 on a double bill with Beckett's *Krapp's Last Tape.* It was produced in New York, again with *Krapp's Last Tape,* in January 1960, at the Off-Broadway Provincetown Playhouse.

Congratulations.

I don't think it would play half as well as it reads. The men—the concrete men there—would get in the way. Not a matter of acting talent: a matter of how.

The trouble is that your content is real, inner, and your own, and your form is tired old grandpa's.

[I couldn't stand this. I did go and get some ink. Connecticut,—very hot.]

The number of plays I've had to read (Obliging Wilder, judging contests) about chance encounters—Central Park benches. Whimsy or stark or dear Romance. "Do you mind if I talk to you?"

It may well be that someday a Kafka or a Becket<t> will come along and show that it can be done, but oh! what difficulties you made for yourself before you'd really started.

Why does your sense of form, your vision of the how lag so far behind your vision of the what? It's as tho you were frozen very young into the American "little theatre" movement. Because this gulf between the stage-mode and the inner gift means that finally you have no style. You don't even have a slightly ironic play on the kind of theatre you are employing—as I think I remember you having had before. [Just as Kafka's style is a constant play on very matter of fact bureaucratic documents.]

Anyway, I wish you well. I think you have much to say. And I have one recommendation which I urgently bring before you: write much, write many things. Only that way will your imagine<imagination> teach you to make your mode as original as expressive as your thought.

Give my regard to Mr. Flanagan and he can illustrate my point, I'm sure, for the principles of musical composition.

And many thanks
Sincerely yours
Thornton Wilder

265. TO KAY BOYLE.[145] ALS 2 pp. (Stationery embossed 50 Deepwood Drive / Hamden 17, Connecticut) Yale

August 29 1958

Dear Kay—

Your letter was forwarded to me at the end of March when I was driving to the Pacific Coast, reached me in New Mexico, and in that life of successive motels, fell into the wrong hamper of papers—certain notes and projects which I have only now reopened.

I humbly humbly beg your pardon.

Yes, indeed, I would wish to join all those who express appreciation for Samuel Beckett (I saw Godot twice in Paris; once in London: once in New York). And I read and reread the other plays and novels, and eagerly wait for more.

If the wretched mistake of misplacing your letter has not put me out of the running, except as enthusiastic supporter, I should be happy to join you in sponsoring him.

I doubt that we would have success at the first try; it will take persistance. "Honorary membership" is as strongly contested as membership. Many years ago several of us tried to get Faulkner into the Academy. I called in my neighbors Dean Wilbur Cross and Prof C. B. Tinker—both declared that they would never vote for such a coarse writer (their expressions were variously stronger.) And Cross was the biographer of Sterne and Fielding, and Tinker's early work had been largely devoted to Boswell.[146] For them, only two-hundred year-old

---

145 American writer Kay Boyle (1902–1992) had written TNW to enlist his support in getting Samuel Beckett elected to honorary membership in the American Academy of Arts and Letters.

146 Cross was the author of *The Life and Times of Laurence Sterne* (1909) and *The History of Henry Fielding* (1918). Tinker was the author of *Young Boswell* (1922) and the editor of the two-volume *Letters of James Boswell* (1924). TNW's point is that Sterne, Fielding, and Boswell were all recognized for the earthiness of their writing.

"candor" can be condoned and even admired as "humanity." Can't professional intellectuals be ti - i - i -resome?

Command me, dear Kay. (and forgive me.)

With a world of
regard to you both
Thornton

266. TO AMOS TAPPAN WILDER. ALS 2 pp. (Stationery embossed m/n "Vulcania,, / "ITALIA" / Societa di Navigazione / Genova) Yale

CONFIDENTIAL.

Stopping 16 hours at Lisbon tomorrow
Nov. 20. <1958>

Dear Tappers:

When you were raking the leaves that afternoon and asked me how you should understand your Aunt Isabel's varying reactions in regard to the visiting young lady, I "ran away" from the explanation. It is difficult to make because it seems to reflect disparagingly on someone we love and to whom we are indebted. But Uncles must answer their Nephews questions. That's what uncles are for, God help them.

x

When Saints do a kind act for their fellowmen we can be sure that they never mention it, complainingly or with self-gratulation, and they don't want to hear a word of thanks. But there are very very few saints. Now women and especially spinsters live to serve, and they find a large measure of self-justification from serving. And all except the saints are often given to dramatising their kind services—sometimes as martyrdoms, or as heroic achievements and nothing makes them feel so good as to <be> lavishly thanked. So, Nephew, never hesitate to lay it on thick.

Now you're both a Kerlin and a Wilder. That will make a very unhappy life for you unless you keep reminding yourself of it, and so understanding it and above all laughing at it. For instance, the Wilders scarcely know what a home-life is. A home-life is a house in which there are, as a matter of course, three meals a day; where there's a guestroom in which it's a pleasure to house a guest. There's no home-life at Deepwood Drive. There are no meals at Deepwood Drive unless there are guests (then the meals are rather elaborate and very very good). Wilders aren't interested in meals, are not interested in the mechanics of life, it's time-worn customs and routines. To have a guest in the house rather frightens us: we've lost the habit of a well-run house; it's not lack of money or lack of good-will; it's sheer loss of know-how. You've noticed that Aunt Isabel doesn't get up until 9:30.

I've just been reading a novel "Le Fils", probably the 411th by my friend George<s> Simenon.[147] I read: "Chaque couple, quoi qu'on fasse, n'est pas seulement formé de deux individus, mais de deux familles, de deux clans. Son espirit, son mode de vie, n'est jamais qu'un compromis entre deux esprits, deux modes de vie differents, et il est fatal que l'un ou l'autre l'emporte. C'est une bataille, avec un vainquer et un vaincu, et il est naturel que cela provoque des ressentiments." That goes also for individuals, and for you. The Kerlins are sure of themselves and are quick to establish an order in the daily life they lead. The Wilders are turned in on themselves; they are self-sufficient but not through strength but through insecurity; they do not like others to make inroads upon their personality; they have no basically congenial or willing relation to the community around them. This shut-in-ness infuriates those who as<are> fond of us. Your father is most himself when he's shut in with his books in his study and I never cease to admire your dear mother's patience. Aren't you surprised that Isabel, during my long absences, stays alone in that big house? There are many

---

147 Georges Simenon's novel *Le Fils* was published in 1957. The passage quoted from his book deals with the fact that any couple comprises two distinct individuals, both of whom bring to the relationship their own history and way of life, and thus the nature of the relationship is always one of compromise.

single women—widows, divorcées, spinsters, living oh so reluctantly alone, who would be delighted to make a double home with her; but she's a Wilder and that's the Wilder pattern.

All this is going to come out in you. Here in your letter to me you reproach yourself for being "absent-minded, forgetful, and undiplomatic." That's the Wilder in you. The Kerlins don't waste time reproaching themselves. They're very fine folk and know as everyone must that they occasionally fall short of what they would expect of themselves; but they don't torment themselves.

A third element in Aunt Isabel's attitude to the week-end guest was her sense that the girl had "put it over on you" by inviting herself for two nights. Isabel's very quick to judge women severely. It was from her fondness for you that she took up arms against this demoiselle. On the way to New York I heard a good deal also about the fact that the young lady had not yet written her a note. That was not so much because Wilders are "formal" and cling to old-fashioned conventions as that my sister wanted credit for the inconvenience of returning from New York to receive her. Et cetera. Et cetera.

The chief thing I want you to learn to do is to laugh—to understand these things with laughter. Otherwise the Wilders can barely survive. The over-independent gypsy-self-sufficient side of them is so out of step with the majority of men and the self-reproachful self-condemning side is so constant that only laughter and constant work of some kind can keep them healthy.

Many thanks (but we decided that thanks can be taken for granted) for your letter. Write me some more, especially when you're very happy <u>or</u> very depressed.

lots of love

Uncle Thornton

267. TO FRANK SULLIVAN.[148] ALS 4 pp. (Stationery embossed 50 Deepwood Drive / Hamden 17, Connecticut) Cornell

a Thursday
<May 21?, 1959>

Dear Frank =

Was on the road by 6:30 a.m.

Got into the Algonquin well before 11:00, followed by a cloud of State Troopers, like Keystone Cops<Kops>. Put 'em off the scent, though,—first by unfurling some bunting that said JUST MARRIED and slowing down. They dashed by me like a school of minnows. Then I started off and accumulated some more cops. Eluded them by raising my superstructure YONKERS DIAPER SERVICE. I didn't have to employ my third camouflage.

Saw Dotty at the Academy session (where she and Capote and Arthur Miller were honored). Never did I more wish for a mind-reading radar than when she stood up and bowed to the assembly. Mrs Arthur Miller was in the eighth row applauding.[149]

So who did they place me between at lunch? Lucky Wilder! Between Carson McCullers and Djuna Barnes. "You're not eating that good roast-beef, Carson," I said. "I can't cut it up," she said. So I—synchronizing with the television cameras—cut her meat very nicely. "I just saw that exhibit of your work in the Paris show about American-Expatriates-in-the-Twenties, Miss Barnes." "Must've been horrible!" "No—very attractive. I went with Miss Toklas." "Never liked her!" "Really—and Miss Stein?" "Loathed her." "I was especially interested also in the Joyce exhibit." "Detestable man."

---

148 American journalist, humorist, and author Sullivan (1910–1972) lived in Saratoga Springs, New York. He wrote humorous articles for *The New Yorker* for many years and was a member of the Algonquin Round Table in the 1920s.

149 At the annual ceremony of the American Academy and Institute of Arts and Letters on May 20, 1959, Dorothy "Dottie" Parker was inducted as an academician; Truman Capote received a Grant in Literature; and Arthur Miller received the Gold Medal in Drama. Miller's then wife was actress Marilyn Monroe.

And they could have placed me between Dottie and Marylin <Marilyn>.

x

Well, that's the penitence I had to pay for the good hours with you.

x

I owe you a dollar.

x

But who's going to reimburse me for the beverages I had at the Colonial[150] waiting on the chance that you'd turn up?

x

Tonight in Hamden it is as hot as (fooled you that time) gulyás.[151]

Ever

Thornton

268. TO LOUISE TALMA. ALS 5 pp. (Stationery embossed Hotel / Algonquin / 59 West 44th St., New York 36, N.Y.) Yale

Oct 3 <1959>[152]

Dear Louise:

I arrived here yesterday afternoon and found your letter waiting for me.

The first thing I wish to say about it is that I see that you are suffering. This calls out all my sympathy. I am distressed that you are unhappy.

The second thing is that you are suffering for no reason at all. Your suffering is real, the grounds for it are made up out of your own head.

---

150 The Colonial Tavern in Saratoga Springs, which Sullivan wrote about in his collection *Through the Looking Glass* (1970).

151 Hungarian: goulash.

152 The year was supplied in another hand, presumably that of Louise Talma.

The third is that you are unjust to me.

How do you suppose big productions are negotiated?

If I sent an elaborate play to the Theatre Guild, and they wrote back that they accepted; and if they said they could produce it in the 1959–1960 season but would produce it in the Fall of 1961, I'd call at the office and shake hands. I'd smile. They'd smile. They<'d> say: we'll be thinking over casting and choice of director. And I'd say I'll be thinking over casting and choice of director. They'd say we'll send you a contract. And I'd say thank you, I'll be away, but my lawyer or agent will read it and send it to me and I'll sign it. And then we'd smile and shake hands. And I'd go.

If the play were to be performed, however, within the next few months, I'd cancel my sailing, and we'd go to work at once on various details of production.

If the opera The ALCESTIAD were to be produced within the next eight months, I would certainly stay long enough to be of moral support to you in the details of production. THE COMPOSER is THE "AUTHOR" of an OPERA—the 90% predominant 'true author' of an opera. When the time comes that this opera goes into production I shall be present at whatever conferences you wish me to attend.

You have known for a long while that as soon as Isabel's health permitted, I must get away. I must escape from Connecticut and from Greater New York which extends as far as Hartford. I am leaving October 15; anybody who saw the life I lead would have wished me to leave Sept 1.

I think its very melodramatic of you to write "I have worked uninterruptedly four years with utmost devotion and under great pressure to make a fine work.....for you....and now you go away at the crucial moment.<">

Wem sagen Sie das?![153] The heroic years of work I love and honor.

---

153 German: To whom are you saying that?!

The finished product I love and honor. The rhetorical pointing out of it to me seems unworthy of you.

The phrase "for you" means I hope for my words—which you have gloriously transcended—; and for my pleasure which you have overwhelmed; "for me" in its dedication which honor I bear proudly. But great works of art should not be considered as for any single person or group of persons

---

Presumably in the next 90 days a committee of musicians will recommend to Mr. Bing that this opera be accepted or rejected. The decision will be made through a study of the score. Every person associated with such procedures assures me that it is unthinkable that the DECISION be reached by PIANO performance of the score. Any piano performance would come much later—when the work has been accepted—and will certainly be reduced to the Maestro's ernest and deferential inquiries about many CRUCES. They hate the piano as a substitution for orchestra. PIANO Partchers<?> are for artists rehearsing with their coaches.

I leave in a few minutes for Hotel Claridge, Atlantic City, where I shall be finishing two plays for the typist.

Please show this letter to Dr Elizabeth.[154]

None of us escape suffering, but let us be sure we suffer about essential things. You have made me suffer at the spectacle of you in great distress over an emotional imagined situation of your own making.

Lots of love
Thornton

154 Talma indicated in a handwritten footnote appended to the letter that this referred to Elizabeth Goodman Freiman.

269. TO GILBERT AND JANET TROXELL. ALS 2 pp. (Stationery embossed: Hotel / Curaçao / Intercontinental / Waterfort, Willemstad, Curaçao, Netherlands Antilles) Yale

Jan. 11. 1960

Dear Troxells:

It's the duty of every tourist in far places to represent the rewards of foreign travel as enviable. It is unsporting to share with the stay-at-homes the slightest intimation that there are many hours in the day when one does not know what to do with oneself, that there is a limit to the numbers of times when one can pinch oneself and say ‘oh what a privilege to be actually here’.

But.

There were three cruise shiploads in our port today.

As I sat on the terrace before lunch sipping my coca cola this is what I heard:

‘Oh, isn't that too cute for words! I didn't see that in any of the places I was at.’ ‘My niece is starting her second bracelet; see, I got her this charm—it's the Dutch coat of arms, I guess’.—<“>I got this for my maid; she'll love it.—The lanjree<lingerie> I saw—you can get it at half the price in Milwaukee.—There's a girl in our office just crazy about stamps.—Lend me one of your cards, will ya; I got to write my mother or she'll kill me. Look! I wrote Trinidad; isn't that awful?”

Like I always said: There's nothing so narrowing as foreign travel. By the time I've been five months away I'm right back to my Wisconsin boyhood; I start yearning for peanut butter sandwiches and a tricycle.

By sunset Wednesday I'll be in Miami, Florida, and can start feeling international again.

I've got some new material to submit to Lincoln Street,[155] but I'll

155 The Troxells lived on Lincoln Street in New Haven and were part of a group to which TNW often read his plays in progress.

linger in the south a bit in the hope that Isabel will feel like coming down.

You will charitably ascribe the dullness of this letter to the heat.

Thy devoted
Thornton

I enclose the latest card from my mysterious correspondent. I assume the message is in Arabic. Who can it be?

270. TO LOUISE TALMA. ALS 8 pp. (Stationery embossed 50 Deepwood Drive / Hamden 17, Connecticut) Yale

Sunday
<March 20, 1960>[156]

Dear Louise:

What makes me thoughtful is that Mr. Bing didn't ask you to lunch.[157]

If he—or his consultants—approved the work, he would
ⓐ have asked you to lunch; and
ⓑ given us some glimmer of his appreciation.

xx xx xx xx

You know me by now: that I don't give a damn about the disfavor of this group or that. I glory in the opera and have the serenest confidence that it'll be heard innumerable times. Nor am I crazy about the Met with its aroma of opera-grind and star-adulation. Nor about City Center[158] whose public is being crammed with subsidized patriotism-inspired mediocrity. Where is both joy and dedication? Where is hushed listening?

---

156 The date was supplied in another hand, presumably that of Louise Talma.

157 In a note appended to this letter, Louise Talma indicated that Rudolf Bing had asked TNW to lunch to discuss *The Alcestiad*.

158 The New York City Center of Music and Drama on West Fifty-fifth Street between Sixth and Seventh avenues opened in 1943. From 1944 until 1964, it was the home of the New York City Opera.

TNW and Louise Talma.

xx xx

If Mr. Bing is very Viennese suave and kind. "We particularly wish that you had chosen a contemporary subject—" (that's Mrs Belmont's note[159])—"the work is one of extreme difficulty" (any respectable crowd could sight-read Vanessa[160]). Delicate Refusal.

xx xx

As I say, I shall hold my tongue until my silence has drawn all the position<s> out of him. Then I shall ever so lightly adumbrate the overtures from elsewhere and my overtures to elsewhere.

---

159 Eleanor Robson Belmont (1878–1979) was a major patroness of the Metropolitan Opera and the founder of the Metropolitan Opera Guild. TNW attempted to get her to intercede with Rudolf Bing on behalf of *The Alcestiad* opera.

160 *Vanessa*, an opera by Samuel Barber, with a libretto by Gian-Carlo Menotti, was first performed at the Metropolitan Opera in January 1958.

xx xx

If I'm now mistaken, and if Mr. Bing (who has learned to make it a practice never to show enthusiasm about anything) does take the other line: . . . . "very much like to considerate it . . . . don't see how I can fit it into the next two seasons . . . . would you and Miss Talma be very distressed if we asked you to wait . . . of course, we would wish to have the première . . . ." etc. Then I shall find the need of putting on a little pressure—not so much for advancing the date, but for nailing him down to a real committment.

xx xx xx xx

Now, Louise dear, I love to dine with you at any time; I love to be with you at any time—but I get as nervous as a witch when I'm in a conversation that goes round in circles and that's what we do on this subject. And I get as nervous as a witch when any artist of stature starts talking about what THEY say—critics, neighbors, friends, wringers of hands, tearful loved-ones. Think of the works of art that the world loves and honors that have been repudiated, kicked around, had to wait for their éclosion (I hope that's French).[161] Why, it's an honor to be rejected. And every now and then when you say something in that realm of status-nervousness or prestige-fearful I'm struck dumb. I cant find an answer. I'm embarrassed to look at you. You are so unjust to yourself. The composer of The Alcestiad should walk the streets and the corridors of Hunter College with the presence of the Nike of Samothrace.

This "self-consciousness" on your part I put down to residence at places like the MacDowell Colony—and that's why I look back on it with discomfort. Art in a world of kaffee-klatsch and "Rowena is having a one-man show in Wilmington, Delaware."

xx xx xx

I'm certain that it's best for all that's best between us that we don't have dinner Thursday night and dont talk around in circles and dont get me nervous as a witch. But, if certain positions to take—relative to Mr. Bing—have become clearer to you, do write me about them. I shall obey you implicitely and I know I shall grasp them much better in

---

161 French: birth.

the written form. ¶You remember that I have to return to that promised engagement in New Haven on Friday night with Mrs. Coffin. I wont know where to telephone (about Bing's lunch) during the afternoon; and I can't get out of my dinner party before 11:30 or so. Probably I shall best send you a night-letter.

xx xx

I was contracted to A and C. Boni for a second novel: They almost turned it down because they felt it was written "for a small overcultivated circle of readers," i.e. *The Bridge of San Luis Rey*

On tryout the manager cancelled the second week in Boston because the reviews were so bad. *Our Town*

The Lunts "liked" *Skin of our Teeth* but would not consider playing it because it was so defeatist. It reached New York and never was there a play "where so many people walked out at the end of the first act"

Merchant of Yonkers failed in Ncw York—with not morc than 100 words altered in<it> ran three years as *The Matchmaker*. Edinburgh—London—New York—to Los Angeles.

Bonis so disliked *Heavens My Destination* ("the American scene is not natural to you . . . and the comic spirit is not either<">) that they gave up their contracted right to it and let me carry it to Harpers.

xx xx

There's nothing that leads to more wasteful expenditure of the creative energy than to depend on the verdicts of others.

xx xx

Whenever I hammer this doctrine I feel fine and I hope you're laughing, too

Lots of love

Thornt.

271. TO GERTRUDE HINDEMITH.[162] ALS 2 pp. (Stationery embossed 50 Deepwood Drive / Hamden 17, Connecticut) Yale

April 11. 1960

Dear Mrs Hindemith:

Many thanks for your letter.

I must now explain to you this great delay in replying to it.

Your letter was received here while I was about to take the slowest boat on the seas from Naples to Central America; it was forwarded to Venezuela, but I did not get off the boat at Caracas because there were riots in the streets. The agency in Caracas did not forward mail for weeks while I wandered from Curaçao to Florida. By that time it was to late to reach you in Switzerland as you said you were leaving for Paris and America. In Florida my sister joined me—convalescent after an operation. My concern over her improvement made me postpone all other interests. Finally, arriving home, I asked Grace Donovan[163] where you could now be reached.

Please forgive this long delay.

x

I am indeed proud that your great husband has taken this interest in setting my play to music. I am most happy to leave in his hands any work of adaptation he would find advisable; his skill in the literary aspects of musical forms is well known and admired.

Of all my plays it is the one that has found the widest variety of receptions. At some performances it has been played to constant laughter; some listeners are deeply moved and shaken by it; some find it cruel and cynical ("What? The dead are forgotten so soon?") I once

162 Gertrude Hindemith, the wife of composer Paul Hindemith (1895–1963), had written to TNW to express her husband's interest in composing an opera version of TNW's one act play *The Long Christmas Dinner.* The opera, with score and German libretto by Hindemith (translated from TNW's English version of the libretto), had its world premiere in Mannheim, Germany, in December 1961.

163 The wife of Richard Donovan, who was on the faculty of the Yale School of Music at the time.

saw a production at the Stadttheater in Baden-Baden, infinitely slow and lugubrious—it took forty-five minutes.

When I wrote it, I directed that the characters as they age draw gray wigs from under the table and adjust them on their heads. I have seen it "work" quite effectively; but at most performances it has not been necessary; the actors have been able to indicate the advancing years by pantomime alone.

x

Whether Professor Hindemith approached such a work in English or German, the question of a German text would ultimately arise. The present German text is by Herberth Herlitschka who lives near Ascona. I assume that Professor Hindemith has also had much experience with translators and knows that they are the most sensitive, the most easily "wounded" of human beings. Considering all the problems of translation that does justice to the musical line, your husband would, of course, be the ideal translator. If for any reason he were too occupied to do this, I trust the work would be assigned to Herr Herlitschka, who is a splendid translator, who has a rich musical background, and who particularly prides himself on just such adaptation toward musical requirements.

x

I hope that the unfortunate delay in replying to your letter has not caused yourself and your husband to change your mind about this project. It is with deep pride and happiness that I would know that any work of mine was to be expressed in music by so great a composer.

With many regards to you both,
Very sincerely yours,
Thornton Wilder

272. TO AMOS TAPPAN WILDER. ALS 2 pp. (Stationery embossed Hotel / Algonquin / 59 West 44th St., New York 36, N.Y.) Yale

Aug. 2. 1960

Dear Taps:

Uncles should write sententious letters to their nephews. Polonius-style.

But today I scratch my head and I haven't got a glimmer.

You say you are about to turn to history and plunge into the "glorious past." Watch your semantics.

"Glorious" is a concept which external-minded people apply to external things. Everybody thinks that Vth Century Greece was a glorious age—but Sophocles "the happiest man in antiquity" decided that next to dying quickly the best thing was never to have been born at all, and in the next generation Plato spins constructions that will keep him from falling into despair about man and society—The Republic is an opium dream. The Age of Louis XIV—"glorious"? La Bruyère wrote: "What are those blackened animals I see leaning over in the fields—can they be men?" A century later they straightened up and there were rivers of blood.

FOUND THIS AMONG MANY OTHER UNFINISHED LETTERS IN MY DESK.

Others say we study history in order not to repeat the mistakes we see there.

That was the hope of 19th Century "meliorism"; much was made of the phrase that "History repeats itself". That is held by very few now. The circumstances we confront <u>while</u> <u>we</u> <u>live</u> <u>them</u> are different from any others that ever befell. As Prof. Whitehead[164] was never tired of saying "every occasion in the existence of a conscious being is unique.... happens but once." The resemblances to previous occasions are there for the non-engaged to see and be impressed by (all historians, except the very greatest, are the quintessence of "outsiders"); but they

164 English philosopher and mathematician Alfred North Whitehead (1861–1947).

are not <the> heart of the matter. For instance, China and Greece and Rome and Crete fell to invading forces from the North; and we will probably "fall" before invading forces from the Russian north. Descriptions of a recurrent phenomenon (that men age and die, for instance; that tyrannies provoke revolts) do not alter behavior.

There is a kind of history that I find absorbing but I do not know its name. It is the bringing-to-light of the successive images and myths and prompting that move the masses of men, for good and ill. It is therefore "psychological"—the very word was first coined a hundred years ago. It is the meteorology, the ever-shifting weather of man's and Man's minds. This study lies partly in religion, in ethnology, in psychoanalysis, in comparative mythology. It's focus is on mind—of which mere events have to <be> cautiously read. That's why the Bible and Herodotus are such great histories and why most history books are unreadable after ten years (how fast they supercede one another, always claiming to be nearer the "truth" than their shallow predecessors.)

The whole category "history" and "historians" in our time has become <a> mere academic stagnant pool. Occasionally the universities through<throw> off an historian who goes in for vast syntheses—Spengler and Toynbee—but though that's better than the Diener Arbeit[165] of most historians, they get entangled in their own systematizations. Their master and mine is Burckhardt.[166]

Well, I'll never mail this letter if I don't stop at the bottom of this page. I send you the enclosed Christmas present well before Christmas, so you can be thinking over what you want. ¶This minute Aunt Isabel tells me you'll be away for ages—so I must send this to Cambridge. I wish I'd got it off earlier.

Love
Uncle Thornt.

<appeared perpendicularly in left margin>
Not reread: punctuate and re-spell to taste

165 German: grunt work.

166 Jacob Burckhardt (1818–1897), Swiss historian of art and culture.

273. TO JANET AND WINTHROP DAKIN. ALS 2 pp. (Stationery embossed 50 Deepwood Drive / Hamden 17, Connecticut) Yale

Friday
<late November 1960>

Dear Janet Dear Toby
Selah!
Lobet den Hern![167]

x

x

x

First, I want to say that again I had a lovely day at your house on Thanksgiving and then another following.

x

x

x

There were only two flies in the ointment:
One: that I there discovered how completely I had lost whatever little practice I had had with the piano; and
Two: that there were no new drawings of Toby<'s> on the wall, and that he is in danger of losing whatever considerable practice he had.[168]
It's too late for me to regain mine, but it's not too late for him to recover and to advance. He must have a very real aptitude for one of the first he did—the shoe—is still one of his best, and is a very good drawing indeed.

x

x

x

I have been in Newport most of two days and have scarcely said a word, except indispensible greetings to the staff etc. and going without speaking is—like going with<out> eating—always most beneficial to me. It has been very cold here, but we did not have the flurries of snow that

167 German: Praise the Lord!

168 TNW is referring to his brother-in-law's hobby of sketching in pencil and ink.

Boston and New Haven has had and surely you have had. I hope I walk in and on snow, before I leave for the South. There will probably be plenty of it when I return in mid-February.

x

x

x

Now I have something to ask Janet.

Frankfurt am Main has asked me to write a play to open their new theatre in September 1963.

I can't do it, of course, unless I get a good IDEA.

And maybe I could write a play, good or bad, and they might not like it.

So many things may rise to prevent it. But.

I have an idea or two ideas that might set me planning and plotting. One is how down through families and cultures and centuries the destructive elements in one generation can produce good elements in the next; and how the good elements in one generation could produce bad effects in the next—a sort of birds' eye view of a hundred years; the audience recognizing the strands of certain qualities from parents to children, saint to rogue; hero to fop; rascal to patriot, and so on. With the general tenor that something more than moral judgment is at work—that what struggles to be free (in criminal or in hero) is what is ultimately valuable for society.[169]

And the other: that it takes many hundreds years of this mixed-mixed-social-anti-social living to produce a community helpful to the individual.

And for that I'd like to meditate <on> that illustration you gave me of the succession of trees on an Illinois sand dune.

Will you be thinking that over?

I don't want it now—I won't want it until well after Christmas. And even then it need only be six lines (of the length of the lines I'm writing now) like: grasses to low bushes (1000 years); low bushes to willows; willows to soft oaks (300 years) soft oaks to hard oaks (500 years). Something like that.

---

169 This was the germ of TNW's novel *The Eighth Day* (1967).

Again lots of love to BOTH
TO BONNIE and JINGLE
and to BRAVA and GREY-Y[170]

Thy
Thornts

274. TO LAURENCE OLIVIER. ALS 2 pp. (Stationery embossed 50 Deepwood Drive / Hamden 17, Connecticut) British Library

(Newport, R.I.
Dec 10 <1960>...returning home
today.)

Dear Larry:

Rê: Far From the Madding Crowd.[171]

Had never read it. A thousand thanks for calling my attention to it. Read the first two thirds of it in a whirl of admiration. Delight in the chorus of yokels; the sureness of Hardy's hand which comes from his observation of nature and of farming.

Above all his power to make us believe that the characters are really in love—that makes most novelists seem immature.

But it has two big weaknesses:

It runs down badly in the third part. Very few of those novelists escaped that resort to crowded Victorian melodrama, wild coincidences taking place under thunderstorms, etc. Hardy made it worse by claiming to identify these goings-on with a philosophical and even theological meaning. He pulls the artificial strings of his puppet-show and

170 Bonnie and Jingle were his sister's Morgan horses; Brava and Grey-y were the Dakins' cats.

171 Olivier had apparently asked TNW whether a stage version of Thomas Hardy's 1874 novel would be feasible. The project was never realized.

then declares that God is a sardonic showman piling up tragic and ironic catastrophes upon poor human beings.

Hardy even says so in Far From the Madding Crowd: near the end of Chapter LIII: "Even then Boldwood did not recognize that the impersonator of HEAVEN'S PERSISTENT IRONY towards him......" That's the views that makes Jude the Obscure and The Dynasts nearly unreadable and which almost ruins The Mayor of Casterbridge.

Bound up with this, because it increases so in the third part is the behavior of Bathsheba.

As Alec Woollcott once said of Eleanora von Mendelssohn: "There comes a time when you can no longer do anything for a girl who persists in making every mistake." And Bathsheba sure does plunge from one blunder to another.

x x

But.

Just the same.

It's a stunning novel.

Any dramatization of a novel that succeeds amazes me. My friend Paul Osborne has done half a dozen of them. I should be so distressed by what one would have to omit that I'd lose confidence in saving what one could save.

But I wish you every success, if you do go to work with it.

xx xx

I saw the Kanins in Boston. They're working at an awful pitch of tension, shaping and reshaping that vast project.[172] I believe it will be a success, but at what a cost. I get downright mad at the extent to which it has removed Ruth and Gar from all other interests, from all other exersize of their gifts, from their friends.....It's as though they had gone to Tierro del Fuego for eight months and aged themselves in building an attractive gazebo there.

xx xx

On the 16th I start driving South. Gas stations, roadside restaurants, villages, motels. Shenandoah Valley. The Mississippi. I'm going

172 *Do Re Mi,* a musical for which Garson Kanin wrote the book and which he directed, ran in New York from December 1960 to January 1962.

to spend Christmas in New Orleans. I only know about 3 people there and I'm not going to call them up until after the holidays.

People say: "But won't you be lonely, Mr. Wilder?"

And I say: "I HOPE SO!"

(N.B. I shall have a corner table every noon at Galatoire's.[173])

x

Confidential: Paul Hindemith has made a chamber-opera of my old one-act play The Long Christmas Dinner. It's a jewel. It's a treasure. Vienna wants to put it on in its June Festival. Especially if Paul and I run up another one to fill out the bill.[174] I hope to do that in New Orleans, though I'm a slow worker. The Maestro can fill his sheets of music paper as fast as the hand can travel.

x

Please give my affectionate admiration to the radiant, strong, sincere, gifted, beautiful young lady I met in the elevator.[175]

your old

Thornts

P.S. That was a mighty silly conversation we had with Mr. M. in your dressing room about doctorates.[176] But you were unkind to forget yours from Tufts! And I lied because I now remember that I have not ten but nine, and my best three (Harvard, Yale, and Frankfurt am Main) dont equal your best. My brother's got one that beats us all: The University of Basel on its 600th anniversary.[177]

TNW

---

173 Famous New Orleans restaurant.

174 In 1959, TNW had started, but then put aside, a libretto for a second short opera, titled "July August September." It was never completed; holograph manuscript fragments survive in the Beinecke Library at Yale Library.

175 Probably English stage and film actress Joan Plowright, whom Olivier would marry in 1961; he and Vivien Leigh were divorced in 1960.

176 TNW went to see Olivier in the New York production of Jean Anouilh's *Becket* (1959), which ran from October 1960 to March 1961. It was produced by David Merrick, who may be the "Mr. M." referred to in the letter.

177 The University of Basel was founded in 1459, and thus was celebrating its five- hundredth anniversary.

275. TO LOUISE TALMA. ALS 2 pp. (Stationery embossed 50 Deepwood Drive / Hamden 17, Connecticut) Yale

<New Orleans>
Dec. 31. 1960
7:30 p.m. waiting to go to a
reveillon party

<appeared above salutation at a slant in left margin>
I can't drag myself to reread this—punctuate to taste Ⓣ

Dear Louise:

Well, the holidays are almost over.

Here, they won't be over until Tuesday the 3rd (Monday is another holiday—banks closed and all—because of the Sugar Bowl Game; this year the Rice (Texas) Owls are playing the U. of Mississippi Rebels (sic), and I can tell you the passions run high. Since Friday night the racket in these hotel corridors until late at night....<)>

x

New Orleans has a great deal of charm but along with the charm you're constantly aware of that fact that for decades the South got no real education. Some fellows went to Princeton; some got as far as Harvard ("The Sound and the Fury"—do you remember the closing words? "I don't hate the South; I <u>don't</u> hate it!")[178] I was going to save for you a manifesto in this morning's paper by a group bent on keeping the public school system undefiled. Well, the syntax and the coherent thinking of its ringing paragraphs threw an odd lite on the education they were so impassioned about.

Anyway, it's all very interesting. This is the third large community of French-outside France that I've seen a good deal of: the Québecois; the Colons of Algeria; and these Créoles. These are easily the most

---

178 The last words of William Faulkner's novel *Absalom, Absalom!* (1936), spoken by Quentin Compson (who is also a character in Faulkner's 1929 novel, *The Sound and the Fury*) in response to the question "Why do you hate the South?": "*I don't. I don't! I don't hate it! I don't hate it!*"

engaging. Besides they're the only group that brought their refinement in cuisine with them.

x

So I promised to write something about the Emily Dickinson volumes.[179]

Before I forwarded them, I cheated: I read them myself. And somewhere in volume II I remembered that you said you like to read volumes that I had marked. (I always mark up a volume—often making an additional index of my own.) So I began. And then I noticed that I was underlining to correlate certain things between the lines that I can only call the gossip aspect. And I became ashamed of myself and stopped. Leyda (I gave him some letters of introduction when first he went to Amherst, many years ago—having much admired the similar "log" he did on Melville) has done a very curious job as editor. Apart from a few circumspect remarks in the introduction he hasn't said boo! I suppose that's because he promised all those people who ransacked their attics and also because he must efface himself before the Big ED works being given out of the Houghton Library by Johnson[180] (without which his volumes would have been impossible.) But what he does is leave us this semé[181] of items; we can weigh, speculate, and probe if we wish.

I profoundly admire her poetry. But as with Joyce I feel no admiration for her character. I don't believe in all that fulsome language of endearment. I detest the constant seeing her loved ones snatched away, gone to Heaven, especially the newborn babies whom she consigns to the ground at once. There is a terribiltà[182] all over the place, muffled, muted. And I wish Leyda had shared with us all that additional matter he must know. What an awful place Amherst was! All that religiosity,

179 *The Years and Hours of Emily Dickinson* (2 vols., 1960), edited by Jay Leyda, who also edited *The Melville Log: A Documentary Life of Herman Melville, 1819–1891* (1951).

180 Lawrenceville School English teacher Thomas H. Johnson edited the three-volume *The Poems of Emily Dickinson* (1955); wrote *Emily Dickinson: An Interpretive Biography* (1955); and edited *The Letters of Emily Dickinson* (1958).

181 French: semantic portion.

182 Italian: fearfulness.

and how atrociously they treated their "ministers." It's all a putrescent protestantism. What a woman, Sue![183] All the hatreds in those two houses. Leyda should have told us (since there is so much about them) that Austin loathed his father yet when his father died, he dyed his hair red to resemble him. The father was a tormented s.o.b. but one evening he had the church bells rung to call the town's attention to a particularly fine sunset.

And out of that the poems came!

x

I thank you, dear Louise, and shall thank you daily while I live for those two volumes that will be arriving for my Christmas.[184]

Love

Thornt

Jan 2. 1961

Going to the "symphony" tomorrow night. Arrau is playing the Schumann and a Chopin.

<appeared on back of envelope>
Word has come that I've got to go to the Skin of Our Teeth European tour company—try out in Palm Beach...So I'll leave here about next Satdy.

183 Susan Gilbert (1830–1913), Emily Dickinson's closest friend, married Emily's brother, William Austin Dickinson (1829–1895), in 1856. Susan and Austin lived next door to Emily for the rest of the poet's life.

184 In a note appended to this letter, Louise Talma indicated that this referred to the full score of acts 2 and 3 of *The Alcestiad*.

Part Six

JOURNEYS: 1961–1975

AS 1961 BEGAN, THORNTON WILDER VOWED TO WORK ONLY on novels and plays; he stopped writing essays and introductions, and he discontinued giving lectures and speeches. He had several current writing projects in his portfolio as he drove north after spending February 1961 in Florida. The libretto for *The Alcestiad* opera was completed, and the libretto for the Hindemith opera of *The Long Christmas Dinner* was almost finished and would be ready in time for its December 26 premiere in Mannheim, Germany. Wilder was also at work on the two series of one-act plays, "The Seven Deadly Sins" and "The Seven Ages of Man," for the arena stage at New York's Circle in the Square Theatre, and these manuscript materials were packed in his luggage when he left in March for a two-month trip to Italy, Switzerland, and Germany.

After his return from Europe, Wilder worked on several of the plays at New England summer retreats and continued this writing throughout the fall. There were to be fourteen one-acts in all, but only three were ready to be staged. His "Plays for Bleecker Street," so called because the Circle in the Square was on Bleecker Street, opened on January 11, 1962. *Someone from Assisi* was from the "Sin" series and *Infancy* and *Childhood* were from the "Ages" series. Wilder kept working on both series, and, as was his habit, he did not attend the premiere. Instead, he was in Atlantic City, helping Jerome Kilty, a young actor/playwright friend, adapt Wilder's 1948 novel, *The Ides of March,* into a play. Shortly thereafter, Thornton and Isabel left for Frankfurt, Germany, for the rehearsals and premiere of *The Alcestiad* opera, which was scheduled to open on March 2, 1962. "An Evening with Thornton Wilder" was held in Washington, D.C., in April. At this event, Wilder read from his work in front of an audience that included President Kennedy's cabinet and invited guests. Less than a month later, he drove to Arizona to become a self-styled "hermit in the desert," planning to live anonymously and write for two years. He set off in his car on May 20, 1962, and arrived in Douglas, Arizona, on May 26.

Wilder stayed in Douglas, with occasional visits to Tucson, for a year and a half. While he was working on the one-act plays around Christmastime in 1962, he decided to change course. He began a new novel, which he would work on during his entire stay in Douglas. Since he was unsure at the outset whether this project would continue to flourish, he did not mention it to his sister Isabel until March 1963. He intended to be in Arizona for two years, and he planned to leave only for a brief trip, scheduled for September 1963, when he was to receive the Medal of Freedom from President Kennedy in Washington. The ceremony was postponed twice, once because of the death of the president's newborn son in August 1963 and then because of the president's assassination. A new date for the ceremony was set, and Wilder left Douglas in late November in order to reach Washington for the presentation of the award by President Lyndon Johnson on December 6.

Having decided not to return to Arizona, Wilder traveled to Hamden and then went to Cambridge, Massachusetts, to attend his brother's retirement dinner at the Harvard Divinity School and spend the Christmas holidays with his family before setting off in early January 1964 for a four-month stay in Europe. That month, after he had left for Europe, a musical based on his play *The Matchmaker* opened in New York; the great success of *Hello, Dolly!* gave the Wilder finances a tremendous boost. His goal during his time abroad was to complete his novel, but he began to realize in April that it would be significantly longer than his previous ones. In May 1964, he booked passage on an Italian ship traveling from Genoa to Curaçao, a three-week voyage that would allow him to continue writing in comfort and without interruption.

He remained in Curaçao for a week before flying to Florida, where his concentration was hampered by the necessity of driving himself around and visiting his aunt Charlotte Niven, who was now living in St. Petersburg. When he reached Hamden at the end of June, Wilder had a routine eye examination and a cancerous mole was discovered near his left eye. He subsequently underwent surgery to have the tumor removed, then spent most of July undergoing radiation treatments. By August, he was pronounced fit enough to resume his travels around New England. By mid-September, he was off to Quebec, and by December, he was able to make the long car journey to Florida.

In January 1965, Wilder was ready to return to Europe to continue work on his ever-expanding novel. Reversing the route he had taken from Europe the previous spring, he flew from Florida to Curaçao and embarked on a leisurely three-week Atlantic crossing, this time to the French Riviera. He spent six weeks writing in Europe, then embarked on another three-week ocean voyage, returning to Curaçao. He was back in Florida by mid-April. May 4, 1965, was the only inflexible date on his calendar that year. That was the day Wilder was due at the White House to receive the first Medal for Literature award from the National Book Committee, which was presented to him by Lady Bird Johnson. After that, he was off to New York to see, for the first and only time, the long-running *Hello, Dolly!* and, as promised, pose for publicity photos for the show. Early June found him in New Haven to attend his forty-fifth Yale reunion; he remained in Connecticut for most of the summer, working on his novel, and then spent several weeks in August with Isabel on Martha's Vineyard. With the manuscript of his unfinished novel in tow, Wilder sailed for Europe with Isabel in October. They stayed three months; in early February 1966, Wilder embarked on his now-preferred leisurely ocean voyage from Genoa to Curaçao, then flew to Florida, where he spent three months writing.

Upon his return from Florida, he spent a short time at home in Hamden, then set off to writing retreats in Stockbridge, Massachusetts, and Quebec. He spent August 1965 in solitude at New Haven's Hotel Taft before joining his sister on Martha's Vineyard for September.

When Wilder traveled, he could set the parameters of his writing and social life. This solved the difficulty of declining invitations and offending friends and family. As a solitary vagabond, he could also make the abrupt changes of locale that sometimes helped to stimulate his thought processes when he felt stymied in the midst of his work. Wilder had been working on his novel full-time since January 1963, and now it was almost completed. At the end of October, he returned to Europe, visiting Paris and Munich. Then on November 26, 1966, in Innsbruck, Austria, he signed off on the proofs of the new novel, *The Eighth Day.* He spent Christmas in Switzerland, traveled in Italy, then sailed back home and arrived in Hamden a few days before the March 29, 1967, publication of the novel, three weeks short of his seventieth birthday.

After the publication of *The Eighth Day,* Wilder retired to Martha's Vineyard for two months. He wrote for several hours each day, trying to find the ideas and imagine the form that would shape his next creative venture. He changed his locale at the end of June, traveling to Stockbridge, New York, and New Haven, then returning to Martha's Vineyard in September, where he and his sister bought a house. Wilder stayed on the island for the month of October, still with no definite writing project in mind. In November, as was his custom, he returned to Europe for the winter months, and, unusual for him, spent more than a month in Paris. Isabel joined him there for Christmas and then they left for their regular haunts in Switzerland, Austria, and Italy. While he was abroad, Wilder learned that *The Eighth Day* had won the 1968 National Book Award for Fiction. It had been on the *New York Times* best-seller list for twenty-six weeks.

He did not return to the United States for the ceremony; his thoughts were focused on the future and on his next "real right" writing project. He continued to write, as well as reading, rereading, and annotating the books in his collection, whether an old copy of Goethe's poetry, a volume on Kierkegaard's philosophy, or a new paperback treatise on linguistics, archaeology, or social science. Wilder was particularly interested in the authors whose fiction and nonfiction works informed or influenced the thinking of young people coming of age in the 1960s. When that generation challenged established social institutions and practices, he observed with interest the civil rights protests, dissent over university governance, and demonstrations against the

Vietnam War, attempting to interpret these events in a more inclusive, universal context. This was especially true during the summer of 1968, when he was recuperating on Martha's Vineyard from a long-delayed hernia operation. Wilder recovered in full and, like clockwork, was off to Europe in November to remove himself from interruptions to his writing life.

These periods abroad were as important to Wilder as the slow ocean voyages to get there and the hotel rooms he lived in; he considered the ships and rooms his "places of business," his essential workplaces, his "offices." This way of living was modified in the next few years, however. Soon after Wilder's fiftieth Yale reunion in June 1970, he began to experience serious vision problems. In late June, he learned that this was a circulatory, rather than an ocular, problem. He was suffering from hypertension, and because his sight was reduced to some degree, he was advised to limit the time he spent using his eyes. During the almost three months he was in residence on Martha's Vineyard, an additional ailment—severe back pain—also limited his activities. In the late fall of 1970, accompanied by his sister, Wilder took his last trip to Europe. Since he was no longer allowed to live at high altitudes, they spent the two months of their stay mostly in Venice and Cortina, Italy. They also went to Innsbruck and Zurich for a short time before returning to Italy, where they stayed in Naples. Wilder worked four hours a day, despite the problems caused by high blood pressure, poor eyesight, and intermittent deafness. He was on the brink of an idea for a new novel.

More than two years before, in February 1968, in Europe, he had begun a semiautobiographical, semifictional series of sketches drawn from different stages of his life. He continued to develop the separate pieces during his international and domestic travels thereafter. Now that Wilder's journeys were limited to low altitudes, he spent the winter months each year in New Mexico, Texas, and Florida. When he returned to Hamden in the spring of 1972, the "real right" idea coalesced. He envisioned the protagonist for a projected chapter of his memoir as the hero of an entire novel, one devoted to his adventures in Newport, Rhode Island. Wilder began and finished this novel, *Theophilus North,* in his seventy-fifth year, writing it from April 1972 to April 1973. His final book, it was published in October 1973.

He began work on a sequel, which he was calling "Theophilus North—Zen Detective," even as he was plagued with increasing health problems: a slipped disk, increasing blindness, continued high blood pressure, breathlessness while walking even at an unaccustomed slow pace, and, in September 1975, an operation for prostate cancer. Despite his poor physical condition, Wilder remained the same energetic and cheerful conversationalist as always, particularly at Thanksgiving dinner in 1975 in New York with his old friends Ruth Gordon and Garson Kanin. That holiday week in the city proved tiring, however. He returned from New York on December 6 to his home in Hamden, "The House *The Bridge* Built." On December 7, still feeling tired, he took an afternoon nap and died in his sleep of an apparent heart attack.

276. TO NED ROREM. ALS 2 pp. (Stationery embossed 50 Deepwood Drive / Hamden 17, Connecticut) Private

June 25 • 1960<1961>

Dear Mr. Rorem:

Many thanks for your letter and interest.[1]

Sure, I'd be proud to have you find something there that you could set to music.

But I'll have to ask you to wait a year.

There are three operas now being written to words of mine—and probably a fourth which has been pending a long time. This constitutes a sort of glut. I wouldn't mind it, but the first two composers take the view that it diminishes their chances at getting a hearing, or some reservation like that.

If, after a year's wait, you should still be interested, I would be inclined to ask you to consider the question as to whether it is worth your while to set to music such brief pieces. Those three-minute plays were more planned as dramatic exercises or sketches—than as practical theatre-pieces. I'm inclined to think that drama (and musical drama) doesn't really begin to work under half-an-hour. But I'm not certain about this and we can discuss it later.

I wish I could suggest something for you to work on, in the meantime. I've never heard of anyone setting Edna Millay's Aria da Capo[2] to music. More and more I hear of productions, here and in Europe,

---

1 American composer and diarist Rorem wrote TNW to ask permission to set to music some of TNW's three-minute plays; this project was never realized. In March 2006, Rorem's opera version of *Our Town,* with a libretto by American poet and librettist J. D. McClatchy, premiered at Indiana University in Bloomington.

2 Verse play (1919) by Edna St.Vincent Millay.

of those fragments (imitation of an American revue) grouped around T. S. Eliot's Sweeney Agonistes[3]j

I'm sorry this letter may be a disappointment; I hope it's only a delay.

All cordial best wishes.

Sincerely yours
Thornton Wilder

277. TO MARTHA NIEMOELLER.[4] ALS 2 pp. (Stationery embossed 50 Deepwood Drive / Hamden 17, Connecticut) Wisconsin

July 25. 1961

Dear Miss Niemoeller:

Late in life I have taken a great interest in the Noh plays—first through Fenollosa and Pound.[5] A Japanese translator (of my work) sent me as a present a most satisfying selection with a rich annotation. It's a very great manifestation of theatre.

And I wish I had known it earlier in my life. My plays may seem to reflect some elements of Chinese and Japanese theatre but—in spite of the years I spent in the Orient as a boy—I have not been aware of any influence prior to the '40s that could derive from the East. My

3 *Sweeney Agonistes: Fragments of an Aristophanic Melodrama* (1932) was an uncompleted experimental verse play.

4 At this time, Niemoeller was a graduate student in English at the University of Wisconsin in Madison, writing an M.A. thesis on the influence of Noh plays on some modern authors.

5 After the death of American art historian, author, educator, and Orientalist Ernest Francisco Fenollosa (1853–1908), his wife gave his notes and papers to Ezra Pound, asking him to be her late husband's literary executor. Pound published two books of Noh plays based on Fenollosa's manuscripts: *Certain Noble Plays of Japan* (1916) and a study of Japanese classical drama, *Noh, Or Accomplishment* (1917).

use of a "free" stage has other sources. (To this day I have never seen a Noh or Kabuki performance—and no Chinese theatre except that program of "selections" which Mei Lan Fang[6] gave in New York in the 30s.)

My admiration for Noh was first caught by Claudel's account in L'Oiseau du Soleil Levant (have I remembered that title correctly?)[7] but by that time I had already written the plays you name.

No, I never met Copeau[8] or Claudel.

So all I can say is that I deeply regret that I had not known Noh earlier. The six devices you list can also be found in other forms of drama. What I would have borrowed would be

Ⓐ the two-part drama—real, then supernatural.
Ⓑ the device of the journey
Ⓒ the relation of protagonist and chorus-observer.
Ⓓ the ideal spectator seated in the audience
Ⓔ the entrance of the Spirit across a "bridge".
Ⓕ perhaps the use of quotations from classic poetry

All cordial best to you in your work

Sincerely yours,
Thornton Wilder

P.S. Both the addresses you give are very near my birthplace—heigh-ho 64 years ago

TNW

6 Mei Lan-Fang (1894–1961), the best-known singer, actor, and dancer of the Beijing Opera, toured the United States in 1930.

7 Paul Claudel's *L'Oiseau noir dans le Soleil Levant* (1927) was a collection of essays and prose poems written during his tenure as ambassador to Japan (1921–1927).

8 French director, producer, and theater critic Jacques Copeau (1879–1949) was a founder in 1913 of the Théâtre du Vieux-Colombier in Paris, which introduced such innovative techniques as the use of minimal, suggestive set designs.

278. TO RUTH GORDON AND GARSON KANIN. ALS 2 pp. (Stationery embossed Hotel Taft / New Haven, Conn.) Private

Sunday eve
August 27 <1961>

Dear Labor-Day-Week-End Merrymakers:

Look at where I am!

In a temple of sheer romance.

Time stands still here. Down the corridor Miss Ruth Gordon is studying the new act-ending for Saturday's Children. Down another Garson Kanin is worrying about whether Judy Holliday can replace Jean Arthur.... Tallulah is screaming at Michael Myerberg. (A few years later she is (in The Eagle has Two Heads) throwing "that Marlo Brandy" out of the cast) and a few years later I'm sitting on the floor in Gadget's suite after the first performance of Streetcar and Brando looks in the door for a minute with supreme contempt at all us effete intellectuals.[9]

Sheer romance.

x

I'm going to evoke delighted pictures of you all in the penthouse of The Sands at Las Vegas; but I'm going to congratulate you that I'm not there.

There's an old almanac saw that "the friends of friends are friends." Nothing is less certain.

Alec tried to endear me to Neysa (a frost), to Cornelia Otis Skin-

---

9 TNW was reminiscing about earlier times spent at the Hotel Taft in New Haven, where the Schubert Theater was a major venue for pre–New York tryouts. Among the productions he remembered were *Saturday's Children* (1927), a play by Maxwell Anderson that starred Gordon; *Born Yesterday* (1946), a play written and directed by Kanin that featured Holliday in a role that had been intended for Jean Arthur, who had to leave the out-of-town tryouts due to illness; *The Skin of Our Teeth* (1942), TNW's play starring Tallulah Bankhead and produced by Myerberg; *The Eagle Has Two Heads* (1947) by Jean Cocteau, starring Bankhead, who insisted that Marlon Brando be fired from the production before it went to New York; and *A Streetcar Named Desire* (1947) by Tennessee Williams, directed by Elia Kazan and starring Brando.

ner (a freeze); but to Alice Duer Miller (soul-mates)* Sibyl tried to kindle a congeniality with Vita Sackville-West and Miss Mitford (arctic); with David Cecil and Cecil Beaton and Morgan Forster (not a vibration); but with Max Beerbohm (the flowers of friendship). Gertrude took this kind of lamp-lighting very seriously and suffered at her failures: who could like Bernard Fäy or Sir Francis Rose?[10]

The reason I don't mix well is because I'm a "confiding nature." Hence I fall silent when there are more than five people in a room. One can't confide one's tentative notions to a roundtable, to a circle; nor—save very exceptionally—to <a> new acquaintance.

Enuff.

x

I hope I thanked you ringingly for the delicious dinner at Côte Basque and for the joy of seeing you—and Ruth so adorable in that dress (at the time I groped to describe it—the word came to me later: isn't it "eyelet" embroidery, or something like that?)

x

Folks, after your quoting—on the phone—that wish of George Brush,[11] I went downstairs to see if I had a copy. Yes, there it was. I certainly haven't looked into it for 25 years. I read it. Long passages I seemed never to have read before. I must say I think it "holds". Second, I was reminded of my feeling soon after writing: it could have been a longer book and each episode could have been longer. My passion for compression sure had me in its grip. It actually cries out for expansion—legitimate expansion to make its points. Thirdly, what a sad book it is! Fourthly, how the Depression hangs over it like a stifling cloud.

After Gertrude Stein continued her journey—having stayed 2 weeks in my apartment at the University of Chicago—she wrote from some place like Cornell:

---

*And we're all indebted to Alex for Gus Eckstein who met him through Kit?[12]

---

10 "Alec" refers to Woollcott; American illustrator Neysa McMein; English novelist and biographer Nancy Mitford; English literary scholar and biographer David Cecil; English novelist E. M. Forster; and French academic Bernard Fäy, who was head of the Bibliothèque Nationale during the Pétain era and was imprisoned after the war for his role as a collaborationist.

11 The main character in TNW's novel *Heaven's My Destination* (1935).

12 Gustav Eckstein was a professor of physiology and psychiatry at the University of Cincinnati; "Kit" refers to Katherine Cornell.

"People tell us you have published a new book. Why did you not tell us you had written a new book. [No question mark.]"

So I sent the book—that book.

"We have read your book. Yes, in the middle it has balance. It is such a pleasure when a book has balance. Yes, I can say that in the middle it has balance."

And, rereading it, I became aware of the moment when the book swung into balance. And the whole damn thing would have been in balance if I'd let it ride more easily and not tried to be so sec[13] and compressed and drastic. I should'a reread Don Quixote—of the relaxed free rein.

Lots of love
Thornt

279. TO URS HELMENSDORFER.[14] ALS 2 pp. (Stationery embossed 50 Deepwood Drive / Hamden 17, Connecticut) Yale

Oct 14. 1961

Dear Herr Helmensdorfer:

Yes—long before I met M. Obey I had been deeply impressed by those first two plays he wrote for the Compagnie des Quinze,—Noé and Le Viol.[15] But I never saw either of them in French and for several years I was not even able to find a copy to read. The Professors don't always realize that literary influence can be propagated by the slightest of intimations: I had merely read brief accounts of the plays and of their productions. (Similarly I was deeply influenced by Paul Claudel's ac-

---

13 French: dry.

14 This letter was printed in facsimile in the program of the Würtemburgische Landesbühne 1961/62; the program was for a production of André Obey's play *Vom Jenseits Zunuck*. TNW's letter was in answer to a letter from Helmensdorfer, who was a director at that theater and had written TNW to tell of the production and to request a statement from him about Obey and the latter's influence on his work.

15 In addition to Obey's *Noé*, the Compagnie des Quinzes staged his play *Le Viol de Lucrèce* (which TNW translated in 1932).

count of a Noh play long before I was able to read one—if it can be said that any Westerner can really read a Noh play.)

Michel St. Denis' method of staging—as I read about it—was also a large part of this influence: the treatment of Noah's Ark—the fact that Tarquin prowling through the house walked merely between posts set up on the stage; the figures of the two commentators—all that was very exciting to me and led to my writing The Happy Journey to Trenton and Camden, The Long Christmas Dinner—and later the longer plays.[16]

It was years later when I had dinner with M. Obey one night in Paris, the recollection of which is of his great distinction of mind and spirit.

I send all my cordial wishes for the success of your production.

With many regards,
Sincerely yours
Thornton Wilder

280. TO LOUISE TALMA. ALS 2 pp. (Stationery embossed 50 Deepwood Drive / Hamden 17, Connecticut) Yale

In festo sancti
Valentini 1962
<February 14, 1962>[17]

Dear Louise:

Where there's a will there's a way.

---

16 In his "Notes for the Producer" in the 1934 acting edition of *The Happy Journey to Trenton and Camden,* TNW wrote, "Although the speech, manner and business of the actors is colloquial and realistic, the production should stimulate the imagination and be implied and suggestive." These short plays, written in 1930–1931, eschewed conventional scenery, used pantomime to simulate activities without the use of props, and, in *The Happy Journey,* introduced a Stage Manager, TNW's version of "the two commentators," about which he had read.

17 TNW was on the S.S. *Ryndam,* on his way to Europe to meet Louise Talma for the Frankfurt production of *The Alcestiad* opera.

I went to the Captain and said:

"Captain, the Atlantic Ocean's awfully wide. There's a letter that I'd like to get to a certain party in Europe. And I can't afford radio-telegraphy. Can't you think of some other way?"

"Well, let me see.—They're training porpoises and sea-gulls; but they haven't quite taught them yet to read addresses."

"Oh!—Aren't there some inhabited islands we could stop at? The Canaries or Ascention?"

"Look here, Mr. Wilson, since you're so serious about this, I'll tell you what I'll do. I'll make a left turn and stop at Halifax in Canada. Would that suit you? I won't mention it in the Log—see what I mean?"

"Put it there, Captain. You wait and see if I don't *always* cross on the Dutch Line."

"Are you and Miss Watson comfortable?"

"Oh, yes. My sister has her bed-board and I have my . . . a-hem . . . basins . . . I have only one very small criticism to make . . . I'll keep my voice down to a whisper: the orchestra doesn't quite play in tune."

"You don't say!! I thought they did the Potpourri from *Madame Butterfly* very nicely"

"Oh, that.—Yes, all those quarter-tones and super-imposed keys added a certain interest that isn't always there. But in that place where the Geisha says that some day Lieutenant Pilsbury[18] will come,—you know, there's real pathos there: because I doubt *if he could find her*."

"How do you mean?"

"Well, Captain, it's like your charts. He'd be looking for her in E-Flat and she wouldn't be there."

"Why, Mr. Wesley—where'd she be?"

"Well, today I got the impression she was out shopping, at a considerable distance, too."

"Well," replied my Captain, drying his eyes, "there's nothing like those old Japanese myths to move the human hear<t>: *Madame Butterfly* and *The Mikado* . . . and *Japanese Sandman*.[19] Now, Mr. Williams, I'll stop in at Halifax, if you'll do something for me."

---

18 In Puccini's opera, the principal male character is Lieutenant Pinkerton.

19 "The Japanese Sandman" was a 1920 song.

"Yes, indeed, I will. What is it?"

"I want you to sit at my table so we can have some more meaty conversations like this. You can't imagine the amount of drivel I have to listen to. And: in that letter of yours that we're making this little détour for—be sure you put some more of this good sense into it—and this inspiration . . . How . . . how did you plan to end your letter?"

"I thought I'd simply say

'with love,
Theodore.' "

281. TO CASS CANFIELD. ALS 2 pp. (Stationery embossed Ritters Park Hotel / Bad Homburg v.d.H.) Yale

Last days in Frankfurt
March 13. 1962

Dear Cass:

At everything I do these days I whisper happily to myself "for the last time."

Last lecture, last class, last "dinner coat", last première, ... its a great feeling. By mid-May I shall be in the desert of Arizona, . . . loafing, cultivating my hobbies (Lope de Vega, Finnegans Wake, Shakespeare)<,> learning Russian, refurbishing ancient Greek . . . And after a while, doing some writing. I should have retired long ago.

An odd thing happened at our opera-première here . . . . unprecedented ovation . . . curtain calls for 19 minutes. The composer Louise Talma naturally elated . . . then in the next few days the critics' reviews: none denied her mastery of means, but all but two have been severe. These things don't affect me (an old battered ship) but it is especially hard for Louise with her first large work and coming after that undoubted appreciation by the audience.

Rê Goldstone. A friendship picked up in officers' messes in the army. Well, I tried to be obliging. I submitted to the Paris Review thing groaning; but most of it was from tape and many answers I submitted in longhand.[20] But I told him that that was to be all. Imagine my horror when I heard that he was writing to old friends (Bob Hutchins and Harry Luce etc) for character sketches etc. Hell's Blazes!! What could be more mortifying. And for them to think that I was behind it—gloatingly waiting for any pretty things they might say about me.

I've told Goldstone over and over again that I won't have it. But he has the skin of a rhinoceros. All his fellow-profs at N.Y.U<.> are publishing—have gotta publish. And he's got his teeth set.

I won't help him one inch.

And I've written several friends to slap him down.

If there's ever to be a book about me (and what an uneventful putter-putter book that will be) let Isabel do it. It's not any harsh truths that I mind, its the unfocus'd admiration of a Goldstone—which also contains almost unknown to himself a good measure of animus,—especially now when I've had to treat him so badly.

Anyway books about living persons are inevitably porous—I helped Eliz Sergeant chapter by chapter through that book on Frost[21] and a woeful task it was.

I'm going to Berlin next Saturday (I've always admired the Berliners) and shall give a reading (my LAST) at the Amerika Haus. Thereafter "I have one more river to cross Oh Lord", I've go<t> to go to Washington for a "Wilder Evening" (confidential) before Certain Listeners.[22]

THEN . . . Oh, Glory. . . . The cactus and the rattlesnakes. I'll be away about $2\frac{1}{2}$ years and then return 20 years younger and with a portfolio of stuff for Master Harpers.

All cordial best to the House.

Ihr alter Freund[23]
Sagebrush Thorni

---

20 In 1942, TNW met Richard Goldstone during officers' training in Miami. Goldstone became an academic; in December 1956, to help him with his career, TNW arranged for Goldstone to interview him for *The Paris Review.* The interview appeared in the Winter 1956 issue.

21 Elizabeth Shepley Sergeant's *Robert Frost: The Trial by Existence* (1960).

22 TNW is referring to the Kennedy administration–sponsored program "An Evening with Thornton Wilder," which would take place the following month in Washington.

23 German: Your old Friend.

282. TO IRENE WORTH. ALS 2 pp. (Stationery embossed Hotel Steinplatz / Berlin-Charlottenburg 2) Yale

March 18 • 1962

Dear Irene:

Oh, it's awful; oh, it's shameful, I've owed dear Irene a letter for so long. FIRST, to thank her for the Empson book.[24] I revel in it; I read it over and over. I don't agree with every word; time after time he's the outrageous enfant terrible. He gets Milton's God mixed up with the God he revolted against in some Church of England he was forced to attend when he was 12. But he's so full of ideas—of splendid digressions—of gallant crusades (for Dalilah, for example). It's about time he settled down from all this flambouyant Don Quixotism and did another really focus'd book, but until then I'll joyously follow him across heath and jungle slaying beasts real and imaginary.

Now—you're to do Lady Macbeth "most of the year" in Stratford[25]—and what else? You shouldn't pine to do his Cleopatra. It's not grateful; it only looks grateful. The play should be called Antony and Octavius. Shakespeare was much more interested in that scene of the drunken triumvirates on the boat than in the amours in Egypt. With "Cleopatra" in the title no wonder directors have to scissor scissor the last act. Won't they let you do A Woman Killed with Kindness? Or a restoration or Lady Teazle?[26]

I hope you got some pleasure out of the Elizabeth in Rome[27] and that there are some passages in it where I can cry out "Theres Irene actin' great." And tho' it's incidental, I hope you had many a feast in Rome—of art and of knives-and-forks—and of good talk.

---

24 William Empson's *Milton's God* (1961).

25 Worth played in a Royal Shakespeare Company production of *Macbeth* during the 1962 season at Stratford-on-Avon.

26 *A Woman Killed with Kindness* (1603), a play by Thomas Heywood; Lady Teazle is the leading female character in Richard Brinsley Sheridan's play *The School for Scandal* (1777).

27 Worth played Queen Elizabeth I of England in the Italian film *Il Dominatore dei sette mari* (1962), which was released the same year in the United States under the title *Seven Seas to Calais.*

Maybe you're in London now and Isabel has been seeing you. In which case you'll know our news but I'll sketch it lightly.

With our opera we had the damnedest experience. The House gave us all we could ask for: five singers (led by Inge Borkle)—a noble conductor—countless rehearsal hours (the score is devilishly difficult) and the première was followed by an unprecedented ovation—19 minutes—over 40 curtain calls. Naturally, Louise thought this was IT. Then in the next few day<s> the region's critics: cool to worse. To be expected we were told by the Director: an opera by an American!... by a woman!...by a composer of French background i.e. understatement of big situations instead of the Wagnerian-Straussian soaring-racket. Now the reviews have begun to come in from farther off—Zurich etc...much more favorable especially to the stature of the music. And the public is filling the house (I heard the first three) and the silence during the big scenes and the applause is very real.

But, damn'it, those reviews have so far prevented other opera houses from picking it up and a Publishing House from adopting it. Damn, damn, double damn. Anyway it is beautiful music and in time it will be rediscovered.

I shall soon be far away. Farewell, O world. Arizona desert—$2\frac{1}{2}$ years. A bum. Loaf, read, learn Russian, polish up my Greek, do Lope de Vega and Finnegans Wake...and finally start some writing of my own. Go for weeks without saying a word (oh blessing) except buying avocado pears and helping to close bars at 2:00 a.m.

But before I plunge into this long-delayed obscurity I've been splashing like a seal in its reverse. The Russians wouldnt dare encroach on Berlin while this publicity-mad hostage is here. I'm dining with General Clay[28] tonight and reading from my works Tuesday to autograph-frantic maenads. I'll bet you're raising and lowering your chin and muttering "Old Thorny thinks he likes solitude and cactus, but just wait....he's the biggest popinjay in the puppet-cabinet; he'll be back from his sandpile from<in> two months calling attention to himself like a blasted Rubirosa."[29]

---

28 Lucius D. Clay, who was serving as the representative of President Kennedy to the citizens of West Berlin during the construction of the Berlin Wall.

29 Dominican diplomat, polo player, race car driver, and international playboy Porfirio Rubirosa.

Any bets?

Berlin is fascinating in itself but oh the art treasures in the Kaiser Friederich-Museum, beginning with the Nefertite.

Lots of love
Thy
Sagebrush Thornt'

283. TO GLENWAY WESCOTT. ALS 2 pp. Yale

S.S. "Bremen" approaching New York, March 30. 1962

Dear Glenway:

I hope you felt sort of more free knowing that T.N. would postpone reading your words until they were freed from time and place—like those rooms which we once lived in and loved but into which other people have moved; they are ours in the truer if not in the literal sense.

Anyway, I knew you understood.

Isabel thinks very highly of them and says there are some pages about the very nature of the novel that I am greedy to read.[30]

x

The older I get the more things I find funny. I really ought to grow a pot-belly and resemble those ribald drunken old poets that are pictured sitting under cliffs and waterfalls on Chinese wall-hangings.

x

For instance: I ask a woman to write an opera with me. This seems, after Dame Ethel Smythe,[31] to be the second time in all history that a woman has set out to write a real "grand" opera. The sound sturdy musicians in the orchestra pit at Frankfurt took a sardonic view of all this. And they engaged in a furtive conspiracy—not to sabotage

30 Wescott's *Images of Truth: Remembrances and Criticism* (1962) included a chapter titled "Talks with Thornton Wilder."

31 Smythe (1858–1944) was an English composer and suffragette.

the work; that's not German, that's French and frequent there—but to test her out. But Louise Talma is métier to her fingertips (acquired under that terrible whiplasher Mlle Boulanger[32]). Louise stops the piccolo-player in the corridor: "You did that high trill on C splendidly but what was the matter with the G-sharp iterations?" "Gnädige Frau, it's not playable." And she showed him a fingering. Things like that get around. The conductor asked her to show Percussion a certain riffle on the snare-drum. And finally they were playing like angels. Why is it that I find such things funny?

x

And. So it gets around that I plan to go to Arizona to be a hermit—without shoe-laces necktie or telephone.[33]

Well, the realtors swamp me with offers of 20 room houses in 40 acres with swimming-pools. (The letters are full of facetious remarks to show that they know, too, the Bohemian side of life.) A woman offers me a ghost-town which she had won in a contest from the Saturday Evening Post.... This is absolutely true... It had been called Stanton but the Post changed the name to Ulcer Gulch and so it is called now on the map.... A woman offers me a house where she had been happy with the husband who designed it: it is in the form of a star for aspiration and a spider web, because the spiders are the greatest of all architects. There is no square room in the house, but there are four bathrooms.

It's not hard to see why I find those returns funny.

x

Less amusing is that they stage a play of mine about St Francis... I wanted one almost blind, toothless, but a flame of happiness; and they give me a man who could be a full-back on the Indiana football team tomorrow and who has just risen from mountains of corned beef and cabbage.[34]

x

So you're working on the Odyssey—that's one of the things I'm to

---

32 French composer, conductor, and teacher Nadia Boulanger (1887–1979), whose students included Louise Talma.

33 By the end of May, TNW would settle in Douglas, Arizona, a small town on the Mexican border.

34 TNW's one-act play *Someone from Assisi*, with Lee Richardson as Father Francis, had opened in New York at the Circle in the Square on January 10, 1962.

do in the desert: renew my Greek. The widow of Karl Reinhardt has just given me his posthumous book Die Ilias und ihr Dichter[35] . . . The conjectures of scholars about the layers . . . the growth of its structure . . . The lost epics which it reflects . . . This book all the richer because it is made up of notes written over many years which he did not live to re-shape into a stately volume.—the immediate insights of a great scholar. Not funny, but fun.

x

Please share this letter with Beulah[36] . . . . under her grave glance is concealed a boundless capacity to find things funny—especially young chaps from Wisconsin

like

your devoted old friend
Thornton

284. TO LOUISE TALMA. ALS 2 pp. (Stationery embossed 50 Deepwood Drive / Hamden 17, Connecticut) Yale

May 17. 1962

Dear Louise:

Delighted, delighted about the Colony. Tho' it would have been "fun" to think of you here in August, both Isabel and I were concerned about some of those crushing days that can descend on us here.[37] (Yet, too, there can be halcyon days for a week on end, even in August.)

L. Bernstein,[38] whom I recently met "in society" will be at the Colony. What do you think of that? Are you going to tell him right to his face that he'd better re-contemplate Beethoven?

---

35 Reinhardt's book, which concerns Homer and the *Iliad,* was published in 1961.

36 Beulah Hagen, Wescott's sister, was an assistant to Cass Canfield at Harper.

37 Talma indicated in a footnote to this letter that if she had been rejected by the MacDowell Colony, TNW and Isabel would have offered her their house in Hamden.

38 Leonard Bernstein.

Oh, I'll betya he'll be charmed by you—transported—and things will come of it that'll almost persuade me to buy an air-ticket and fly east.

Remember my prophecy.

x

So you want to know what the Washington "do" was like?[39]

What did I talk about with M. Malraux.

I talked about "good evening" and that was all—and not even in French.

Gracious sakes, there were 162 guests.

The high points for me were ⓐ meeting Scott Fitzgerald's beautiful "Shakespearean" daughter who remembered a walk we took in a rose-garden when she was eleven[40] ⓑ meeting Balanchine and telling him, plump, in his face all that I owed to him and ⓒ the President in the handshake line saying: "I want to thank you, Mr. Wilder, for what you said about last week" (at my "reading" in the State Department.★)

The greeting line was alphabetical and we were a nice little contingent in "W"s: Penn Warrens,[41] Wilder, Tennessee Williams.

I sat at the Vice President's table with Alexis Léger, Mrs Lindbergh, Mrs Bohlen, Robert Lowell.[42]

The first Lady was glorious in a white and pale raspberry Dior.

The food (Vendredi, maigre[43]) was perfect.

★ When Mr. Ribicoff introduced me to the audience I said: "I am delighted to be here, but even if I were not here and another was here in my place I would be delighted to read about it......Washington has become like a lighthouse on a hill by the interest it takes in those things for which we spend our lives....restoring a surprised self-respect....<"> (something like that.)

---

39 TNW was a guest at the White House dinner on May 11, 1962, honoring French author and critic André Malraux, who was France's minister of cultural affairs at this time.

40 Frances Scott ("Scottie") Fitzgerald Lanahan, whom TNW had met in February 1928, when he spent the weekend at the Fitzgeralds' house in Delaware (see letter number 107); she was six at the time of TNW's visit.

41 Robert Penn Warren and his wife, the writer Eleanor Clark.

42 Anne Morrow Lindbergh; Avis Thayer Bohlen, the wife of Charles "Chip" Bohlen, the American ambassador to France at this time.

43 French: (Friday, light). TNW is referring to the fact that since the dinner was held on a Friday, meat was not served.

TNW with Secretary of Health, Education and Welfare Abraham Ribicoff on April 30, 1962, at the State Department, where TNW read excerpts from his work to an invited audience.

Stern-Rose-Istomin[44] played the Schubert E-flat superbly but the audience, excited by all that glamor and a little tight, did not behave as it should. (I sat by Mrs Sam Behrman[45]—and a lovely person she is—who is Jascha Heifetz's sister.<)> We listened. Lenny was the only musician there—they having been at the Casals night. I finished the evening at the Francis Biddles[46] with the Edmund Wilsons, the Saul Bellows, Balanchine, and Lowell.

Fun?

A little contretemps took place involving our hosts which I will only tell you in confidence in 1965 (not involving me, deo gratiâ.)[47]

---

44 Violinist Isaac Stern, cellist Leonard Rose, pianist Eugene Istomin.

45 Elza Heifetz Behrman, wife of playwright S. N. Behrman.

46 Francis Biddle, a lawyer and former U.S. attorney general, and his wife, the poet Katherine Garrison Chapin Biddle.

47 TNW means *Deo gratias* (Latin: Thanks be to God).

I start driving west Saturday. Don Quixote following his mission. Friday I go to Long Island to see Charlotte.

I love the Rumpelmeyer passacaglia.[48] What a girl! I suppose that the surpassing difficulty is in allusion to my rusty old steps on the parquet. Oh, how often I shall think of those Frankfurt days in my new home and it'll all get more and more lyrical. And all on the tide of the rich right flowing music.

love
Thornt'

285. TO ISABEL WILDER. ALS 2 pp. (Stationery embossed 50 Deepwood Drive / Hamden, Connecticut) Yale

<Douglas, Arizona>
August 26. 1962

Dear Isa—

This letter's for Aunt Charlotte,[49] too, but prepare her for the insubstantial bulletins I'm reduced to.

Tonight, having eaten without break six of my own meals I drove over to the Copper Queen Hotel in Bisbee for dinner. I went all that way to get the sirloin steak and the salad. I don't like steak or lettuce (who can?) but a little voice kept saying I ought to, I should.

Now that I'm housekeeping I'm getting to be really like that small-town eccentric that I envisaged, and described to you in Patagonia. To get the paper—the mail—a little food-shopping is the only thing that takes me out of my room. That's not right.—oh, I go out to drive—and glorious drives they are; I meant: to walk.

x

---

48 In a footnote appended to this letter, Talma explained that she mentioned to TNW that during certain "somewhat frivolous" parts of the fugue she was working on she was reminded of the night the two of them danced at Rumpelmeyer's in Frankfurt.

49 TNW's aunt was visiting Isabel in Connecticut.

Girls<,> enough has not been said about the dangers of the kitchen. Several times I've almost lost an eye from far-spitting fat; and that lifting hot water from one place to another. I think a campaign should be made to warn us beginners. When I eat out, Sammy's or The Embers at Buena Vista and see all these brides (nicely nurtured girls who've married engineers in the hush hush Establishment—three children by the age of 25 but still brides) were they warned about this. Don't I remember our own mother—in Man<s>field Street days, and maybe in Mo<u>nt Carmel—always having accidents and cicatrices? Aren't I right about that? Please reply.

x

What do I like most about cooking? The various ways of doing eggs.

What do I hate most? Washing and drying drinking glasses. (That's because I inherited from both the Wilder and Niven side a compulsive perfectionism. I can never believe that the glass is clean and dry.)

What do I hate most about my kitchen as a work-place? Damn it, the four pilot lights. They're not, as in Deepwood Drive, unobtrusive little beacons; they're actual flames. At night they're four big eyes. And—in this weather—they're enough to heat the kitchen in themselves. You could fry an egg on them in 10 minutes—pfui!

What do I like most about my kitchen as a work-place? Why, the frigidaire. I moon about it. I dream about it. I think of all the workers for 10,000 years to whom it would have been a miracle. You remember my feeling about the obtuseness of Delia Bacon[50] (noble Christian woman) letting her Noras and Hilda's deform their bodies by stooping over those damnable washing troughs—so I think of the labor saved now... let's not talk about it. Let's just be grateful. And the money saved—when every dime meant so much in the mid-west and in these states.

x

Dear Aunt Charlotte I wonder what it'll be like when this letter reaches Hamden. The social interchange won't have begun (thank you, I don't miss it yet); I hope the weather won't be oppressive still; (it's ac-

50 American writer (1811–1859), whose only fictional works were a collection of short stories, *Tales of the Puritans* (1831), and a play, *The Bride of Fort Edward* (1839).

cablant,[51] here). I wish I could show you the acres of houses for retired people, like you and me, under the shade of these great mountains—acres, yet they in no sense crowd the landscape—the Biblical desert remains as on the day when Jacob worked for Leban and his two beautiful daughters.

x

I'm saving this letter to mail it when it will arrive when you do. Lots of love to both of you, from your vagrant

Thornt

286. TO CHARLOTTE TAPPAN NIVEN. ALS 2 pp. Yale

General Delivery, Douglas, Arizona

Sat'dy Sept. 8 1962

Dear Aunt Charlotte=

Sunday's my day for writing to Isabel, so I don't have to work until tomorrow.

One of the first things to know about a hermit is that he hasn't much to say. I'm perfectly content in my thébiade<thébaïde>.[52] Every now and then I get a faint twinge of nostalgia—for Martha's Vineyard and for the New England road; but then I take a sunset drive on my glorious desert and the uneasiness abates.

This is a very nice town of a little over 5000. Wide streets; one and a half with shops. We're right on the Mexican border and we're at least 50% Mexican descent ourselves. The Junior High School is catty-corner from where I live and the several hundred children who collect at 8:30 under my window are at least that per-cent of Mexican descent. There is no hoodlumism here among the working class; that's only at the top. The head of one of our chief banks has just had to go to prison for peculation.

The signs of frontier are all around us. Ready courtesy and much reserve. A real deference for women, immediately recognizable as dif-

51 French: overwhelming.

52 French: solitary retreat.

ferent from big city politeness. As frontier, very church-going. A leaflet was giving<given> showing me 36 churches in Douglas and immediate vicinity,—includes Spanish Baptist and Methodist and all sorts of cult churches and, of course, Mormons. You would go to St. Stephen's Episcopal Church.

We've just lived through July and August which I'll try not to do again. It's the rainy season—very little rain but mighty thunder and lightning every day—and humidity with the great heat.

But on the whole, I chose better than I knew. As far as I know only 4 people in town know "who I am" and they don't spread it. About once a month I go to Tucson (250,000) for a few days, partly to visit the University library.

Im "getting well" so fast that maybe my retirement from civilization may not be as long as I first thought it would be.

I am very eager to look over your retreat.[53] It's certainly much prettier than mine which just escapes looking like a barracks or even a tenement. But we have two tall Lombardy pines at our door like sentinals. I'm just getting to brief-chat relations with some of my neighbors,—an arthritic lady on the first floor who's reading W. Wilkie's One World[54] and a retired engineer who can only walk from the porch to his room. We have young couples too, teachers in the schools here. But I've made a resolution not to "get friends" with anybody for a year; so to my own surprise, I'm curbing my natural tendancy to expand. Have a good time in New England, dear Aunt Charlotte,—and when you rejoin your car—drive carefully.

I wish you could see the Y here—its the busiest place in town and the YWCA in nearby Bisbee is the second most imposing building in town. The town used to be much bigger than it is now—the fortunes of mining have made and unmade regular cities out here.

Lots of love
always
Thornt

---

53 TNW's aunt had moved from Winter Park, Florida, to a retirement home in Saint Petersburg, Florida.

54 Willkie's 1943 book, an entreaty for international peacekeeping after World War II.

287. TO ELIZABETH SHEPLEY SERGEANT. ALS 2 pp. Yale

General Delivery Douglas, Arizona—

Sept. 12. 1962

Dear Elizabeth:

Delighted to receive your letter. You dont mention when you are going home so I assume that you will stay on in Peterborough through September.

Yes, it must be "costing" to recall in writing (which is a higher concentration than reverie or conversation) the days of early childhood.[55] Gertrude Stein said: "Communists are people who fancy they had an unhappy childhood" i.e. the same people who can imagine themselves in a social order where nothing is ever ever wrong are the same people who can rewrite their past and declare that they went through years when nothing was ever ever right. It seems to me that the early years can be interpreted both ways: since neither memory nor prevision has begun to operate<,> the heavens and hells alternate without relation to one another.

I recently read the two volumes of Lawrence letters[56] (sent me by their editor Harry Thornton Moore—a pupil of mine at the University of Chicago.) I read the second volume first, partly because it contained reference to many people I have known, and because I assumed that the maturer letters would be of greater interest. But later I was to find that the first volume was far superior. How I envied that youthful bull-in-a china shop way of talking straight truth. (Oh, how often I should have done that—even though my view might have been wrong: the honesty in intention would have saved the venture; and from time to time I would have been, valuably, both honest and right.)

D.H.L was in those early novels a great novelist; but there was one serious dead-weight they had to carry. English women—through their situation—have not been "interesting" for a century and a half. They

---

55 Sergeant was working on her autobiography, which she failed to complete before her death in January 1965.

56 *The Collected Letters of D. H. Lawrence*, 2 vols. (1962).

can't be; their bringing up has been so stifling. I've always said that English actresses always behave like vicar's daughters at a garden-party where the Duchess is expected. The only actresses that count over there from Mrs Patrick Campbell, Meggie Albanesi;[57] to Edith Evans have had the redeeming drops of Jewish Italian or Celtic-Welsh blood. Women in Love is a fine novel—, but those two girls (Miriam?) are constantly reflecting Nanny-training. And I bet they were physically cumbrous. Any way all you have to do is to think of Anna K—or Emma B—or Natasha R—or to go back <to> Jane Austen's. (Dorothy in Middlemarch shows the transition.)

There's little to say about me except that I should have done this long ago. From time to time I get a pang for friends and conversation and music, but all I have to do is to take a late afternoon drive into this glorious desert and the velléité[58] abates. It's taken several months for the cobwebs to dissipate, but they're going—and little steady excited work-hours are beginning.

Since you don't mention your health I hope I can gladly assume that you're much better.

Will portions of the work you're on appear in periodicals? I'm to have something in The Hudson[59]—way off next January; but it's the University of Texas Review that pays—well, Texanly—and for sheer disinterested belles-lettres,—with a special interest however in that South West.

¶Now that I'm housekeeping a whole new field of curiosities has swung into view. The fact that I don't know a thing about cooking is a positive advantage: I improvise; I make advantage of ignorance. My deep regards to the Kendalls. Blessings to you and to your working hours

love ever

Thornton

57 Talented English stage and film actress (1899–1923), who, at the time of her premature death, had already showed great promise.

58 French: indecisiveness.

59 TNW's essay "Giordano Bruno's Last Meal in *Finnegans Wake*" was published in the Spring 1963 issue of the *Hudson Review.*

288. TO EILEEN AND ROLAND LE GRAND. ALS 2 pp. (Stationery embossed 50 Deepwood Drive / Hamden 17 Connecticut) Private

As from: 757 12th St. Douglas, Arizona.

[Tucson, Arizona]
Dec. 10. 1962

<appeared perpendicularly in left margin>
¶I told you, didn't I, that I found an allusion to Peperharow in the new edition of Boswell's Journal etc of Dr. Johnson in the Hebrides?[60]

Dear Les Grands:

Selah!

Lobet den Herrn!

I'm up in the big city for a few days to buy Christmas presents and—gee whillikers!—for a practicing hermit the ado of a city of 200,000 is abrutissant.[61] I return to my cactus stretches tomorrow. And, Eileen, to my own housekeeping, because my cooking though still modest, is improving.

There's not much I miss in The East ("civilization") but I do have other hankerings. I found myself with a longing for the sea and I drove for a day to reach Guaymas, in Mexico on the Gulf of Lower California, known to the Mexicans as El Mar de Cortéz. I was there almost two weeks and never grew tired of watching the waves come in as they did "before there were any of us around." And now (you'll think I'm frivolously restless) I pine to stand amid falling snowflakes.

x

Roland! You're going to stage The Matchmaker! (I wrote most of it in this very Tucson under the name of The Merchant of Yonkers some 24 years ago.<)>

Well, here are some reflections.

---

60 Peperharow is a small hamlet near Godalming, Surrey. Roland Le Grand was head of the Department of Modern Languages at the Charterhouse School, located in Godalming. A reprint of *Boswell's Journal of a Tour to the Hebrides with Samuel Johnson* was published in 1961.

61 French: exhausting.

You may find it too long. I wouldn't know where to cut it, but don't cut it by racing the three main dialogues between Dolly and the Miser (Heavens! I've forgotten his name!) Especially, not the dinner scene: it may give the effect of being rapid but an actress would lose her grip on it without calculated pauses followed by fresh attacks and changes of tone.

The longest laugh in the play has to be artfully watched. It's where Cornelius creeps on hands and knees into the "armoire". Have Dolly Levi perfectly motionless as she watches him; that builds up the "comedy" of I'm-going-so-self-effacingly-that-I'm-invisible. Don't get worried if the audience doesn't laugh at first and don't hurry it. The laugh should build and last until he's completely hidden in the cupboard.

The other big laugh requires a most expert actor: it precedes Melchior's monologue. He starts to return the newly found purse to Cornelius... Then half-way across the stage, turns and says to the audience "You're surprised?" The audience falls apart—partly, I think, surprise at being addressed directly—so that actor must do it very real, sincere... Implication: "you thought I was a low bum who'd certainly keep any money I found in public places."

I hope you remember Ruth Gordon's wonderful reading <in> Act IV to Vandergelder (now I remember his name)... "Horace... I never thought I'd hear you say a thing like that!!" Surprise—laughter—warmth. It lets the audience believe that they can be happy with one another. LOUD impulsive and very sincere.

I don't know what sweet old-fashioned melody you'll use for "Tenting Tonight" in the Cafe scene, but be sure that it's a real little pool of simplicity and aural beauty not without a touch of pathos.

Cast your Cornelius for true naïve idealistic. A touch of worldly-wise "knowingness" and the rôle is ruined. He is wide-eyed and bedazzled by woman and love....

And even more so his young companion: I hope you have an engaging young irrepressible.

Tell Dolly to advance on her monologue in Act IV with a meditative pause... The room empties; she alone on the sopha... change of mood... lost in thought, her eyes on the ground... collects the audience's attention for her first words.

Please give my THANKS to all the players and to the Technical Staff (who so seldom get thanked) and my cordial best wishes for a happy preparation and a happy issue. Tell them the way to combat nervousness before entering on the scene is to stand at the entrance and breathe evenly and serenely—not too deep—but smilingly. Acting's fun when the body is completely relaxed.

NOW I have almost no space left to wish you all a happy holiday. I sent on a little momento through the postal authorities today; I hope it gets through all right—it has to go through some kind of red tape in New York. . . . SPERIAMO as they say in Caserta. ¶A world of affection to you Eileen; this letter has been taken up disproportionately with the strains and stresses of Show Biz. ¶I wish I could SEE Julian. Is he in his last year at Eton? (All Americans believe firmly that there is a great deal of cruelty at Eton—I hope that's no longer true!) ¶And to you Roland

lots of old old friendship Ever Thornton

289. TO CATHERINE COFFIN. ALS 2 pp. (Stationery embossed 50 Deepwood Drive / Hamden 17, Connecticut) Yale

757 12th St. Douglas, Arizona

On or about Dec 11. 1962

Dear Catherine:

The Indians here used to communicate with one another over a distance by puffs of smoke; and that's what my letters are reduced to. As the months go by I have less and less to recount, but more and more in the way of affection and regard to express. I don't miss the centers of civilization, but I do miss the occasion to express affection and regard. Lord knows, one of the principal reasons I fled civilization was that I had to pretend such occasions so wearisomely often (all Americans play-act a social ecstacy—I more than others); now "society" is taking its revenge on me. Please accept the smoke and the bonfire under it; it says in papago language: bonjour chère Catherine.

It will require all your charity to understand me when I say that though I would be entranced to call on you this evening, and though it was always a happiness to come to dinner in East Rock Road,—an invitation to dinner with you tonight with the same friends would frighten me. I learned this on Thanksgiving Night at the seaport of Guaymas in Mexico. A friend had asked me to her house for the "rest of the turkey"; there were present two American couples, a Mexican couple and various children between 10 and 15. How quickly one becomes dishabituated. A dozen "personalities" in the room; two and three conversations going on; a distraction of lighting cigarettes and moving chairs and passing dishes and remembering names and being asked questions in non-sequitur.

And it can't be denied that people wear a different face when there are more than three in a room.

When you live in isolation, as I do, you read more attentively. I pick up paperback novels in bus-stations. Ordeal of Richard Feverel[62]—doesn't hold up. Return of the Native—doesn't hold up. Jane Austen: incomparable. How seldom readers seem to remark on all that contempt for the whole human scene that lies just under the surface,—oh, more than that: a desespoir contenu, une rage déguisée[63] . . . . . but by her art her spirit has been saved from mere spinster's waspishness and from cholor. In Moliere the same contempt became aggressive. A man of religious mind believes the human race is correctable. There is not a hope of that in these two. Jane Austen's only resource and consolation is the pleasure of the mind in observing absurdities.

¶Word from Italy has given me great pleasure. In Milan the director staging the Assisi play found that actor after actor turned down the rôle of St. Francis—as blasphemous? non-canonical?—finally he engaged one of the finest of all Italian actors, Renzo Ricci (and his dis-

---

62 *The Ordeal of Richard Feverel* (1859), a novel by George Meredith.

63 French: a contained despair, a disguised rage.

tinguished wife Anna Magni)[64] and report is that all three plays are a great success. I did not express aloud my disappointment at the playing in New York or my chagrin at the spiritless reception.... all a dramatist can do is to murmur: "Some day....."

¶The other day in Tucson I looked up an old Yale friend Jack Speiden, Yale '22, in the hope he was still running his dude ranch where I might go for a few days around Christmas and imbibe martinis in front of a great log fire. Well, he's retired; his wife is a grievous invalid with three nurses around the clock—a fall from a horse. Jack tried to persuade me to stay and dine with them Wednesday with the Paul Chavadjadzies <Chavchavadzes>—you know the spelling—I presume the parents of Bill's friend. But I returned to Douglas.

Instead I am driving I think to Taos. Mabel and Tony are no more.[65] Mabel rests and others are given a measure of rest. But I shall take Dorothy Brett out to dinner and ask her again of those old days— young D. H. Lawrence, Bertie Russell, Lady Ottoline, Katherine Mansfield...and about Mabel. It will be cold—it's about 8,000 feet high—I hope I have cold's compensation,—the beauty of snow.

Today (the 15th) I bought myself a Christmas present: a record player. I have three records, The Bach Magnificat; the Lotte Lehmann Lieder Recital; and the Mozart Sinfonia Concertante (Heifetz and Primrose).

From Tucson I sent a little <">something for your breakfast tray," just a pensee,[66] a puff of smoke but laden. To all, all the Coffins and the-in-laws much affection

devotedly
Thornton

---

64 Actor Renzo Ricci (1898–1978) was married to actress Eva Magni (1906–2005).

65 Mabel Dodge Luhan died on August 13, 1962; Tony Luhan died in January 1963.

66 French: thought.

290. TO AMOS TAPPAN WILDER. ALS 2 pp. (Stationery embossed 50 Deepwood Drive / Hamden 17, Connecticut) Private

757 12th St. Douglas Arizona

Dec 19 • 1962

Dear Tappie:

So you're a New Yorker.[67]

A New Yorker is like nothing else in the world.

I was once one, for about three months.[68] I took an apartment in Irving Place. Morning after morning I'd get up at dawn, or before, and walk to the Battery, each day by a different route—through Chinatown, Polish Town, Italian Greenwich Village, the Jewish acres around Grand Street. At the Battery I'd feel myself nearer Europe toward which I suppose I strained.

The sense of the multitude of human souls affects every man in a different way. It renders some cynical; it frightens many; it made Wordsworth sad; me it exhilarates. I must go back and submerge myself in it from time to time or I go spiritually sluggish. What I have fled to the desert from is not the multitude but the coterie.

The sense of the multitude of souls is not the same thing as that of the diversity of souls—Shakespeare is the writer of their diversity: an island-dweller could not apprehend the millions of millions. The Old Testament is the work most freighted with realization of generations and generations.

As a New Yorker open your imagination to it.

I was delighted to hear from your mother on the telephone that you're finding your classes absorbing: getting a good professor is a matter of sheer luck. In Oberlin I had one; in Yale I had none (but I had Tinker, though I was not registered in his course.) To be sure, I was not an assiduous student but any born teacher could have caught me—as

---

67 TNW's nephew was in New York to study at Union Theological Seminary.

68 TNW had rented an apartment in New York City from November 12, 1939, to March 12, 1940.

Baitsell almost did in Biology and Lull in Geology—mighty remote from my daily preoccupations. (But they have left their mark in a tireless curiosity about science.)[69]

A little Christmas present has fallen to me in my literary life. That short play about St. Francis had a cool reception in New York. Divers friends and unshakeable judges let me know that I had not really finished it, or thought it through, that it was not thoroughly cooked. And I—o so deferentially—agreed with them. But something inside of me said: "Wait, just wait." The three plays have just gone on in Milan. At first I was told that the director could find no actor who would consent to play Il Poverello. Did the rôle seem blasphemous or tasteless? or merely a colorless acting part? Finally the manager offered the play to a couple who are among the foremost in Italy, and the whole program is now a sensational success. MORAL: Pay no attention to the weather.

Now, Tappie, if you have to do an extended paper for one of your professors, and if you have to type it with carbon copies—please lend me one copy for one week. I not only want to read it because it's yours, but because I want to see the kind of material and approach that the school expects, and because, as your father knows, I have a wide-ranging appetite to read anything in the field of humanities (except Old Goodenough on Josephus and T.S. Eliot on the theory of college education[70]).

I hope you take some exercise. Do you go to a gym? I hope you take some girls out dancing. And I hope that 1963 is your best year yet.

Lots of love
Uncle Thornton

---

69 TNW is referring to Charles H. A. Wager with regard to Oberlin; at Yale, he studied with Chauncey B. Tinker, George A. Baitsell, and Richard S. Lull.

70 Erwin R. Goodenough was professor of the history of religion at Yale University; TNW may be referring to Eliot's 1932 essay "Modern Education and the Classics."

291. TO THEW WRIGHT, JR. ALS 4 pp. (Stationery embossed 50 Deepwood Drive / Hamden 17, Connecticut) Private

P.O. Box 144 Douglas Arizona

Jan 11. 1963

Dear Thew:

Oh, I'm a skunk.

I meant to write you at once when I heard you were in the hospital.

I guess—from my proximity to Mexico—I'm catching the mañanas; I know I am.

Have you been a difficult patient? Throwing dishes at the wall, and turning up the TV full blast?

It must have been interesting having that other veteran of the Pacific Islands there; because you never talk about your war experiences. Does he, Kit?[71] (And I go around ranting and raving about how I saved Europe—)

It turns out here that I'm not a 100% hermit. Once a month I have to go away. Usually to three or four days in TUCSON. But just as I went to Guaymas in Mexico over Thanksgiving to see the SEA, so I went to Santa Fe and Taos over Christmas to see the SNOW—and how I got it. My toes and ears darn near fell off. After 8 months here I'm a softie.

But I like it here completely.

I now have a considerable acquaintance but they are <the> type of persons that closes the bars. They say that Douglas and our sister-city Bisbee have the highest no. of churches per. cap. in the whole country. (It sure looks it.) But those exemplary citizens are safe in bed before I start going into society.

Tallulah is playing in Phoenix this week and I was half tempted to go up and sit up til four in the morning hearing four-letter words; but

71 Wright's third wife.

no! I've put all that kind of interest-curiosity behind. I've 'ad actors, I've really 'ad em.

I've been very pleased that the one-acters are getting a good reception in Milan—especially the Assisi one that left people cold in N.Y. They go on in Munich this month.

La Gordon writes that Gower Champion says that the plans for the musical Matchmaker are coming along great. Ruthie has been taking singing lessons (she told her teacher that she didn't want to sing half-talk half-sing like most actors do; no, she wanted to learn to sing LOUD, and she says she is singing LOUD.) Didn't I read that the rôle was being designed for Ethel Merman? (There's LOUD, for you.) Anyway Ruthie feels she has a lien on that rôle for life.[72]

When your knee's better I suppose you'll be going down with Kit (choose the baby-sitter wisely) to see Who's Afraid of Virginia Woolf? Ed. Albee has been telling interviewers that a conversation with me long ago made him turn playwright. If so I'm very proud. He sent me a copy of the text. Gee whillikers. Steel yourself. Its a blockbuster; but I admire it enormously.[73] And isn't it fine to have a new dramatist who speaks in his own voice?

Tell Kit that a score of expectant mothers have taken my advice: gaze at drawings by Raphael; listen to music by Mozart; float through the Parthenon and stroll about the Taj Mahal. Honest,—they've written me about it afterwards.

Get well serenely, you too<two?>.

To you both all best
from your old
friend Thornt

---

72 TNW is referring here to *Hello, Dolly!,* the musical based on *The Matchmaker.* It opened the following year, directed by Gower Champion and starring Carol Channing.

73 Albee's play ran in New York from October 1962 to May 1964.

292. TO RUTH GORDON AND GARSON KANIN. ALS 4 pp. (Stationery embossed 50 Deepwood Drive / Hamden 17, Connecticut) Private

P.O. Box 144 Douglas Arizona

Jan 14. 1963

Dear Kays:

I've been here 7 months.

x

It AGREES with me.

x

But le petit train-train[74] of my life makes me a poor letter-writer.

x

Tallulah and Estelle W. are playing Tucson at the end of the week in HERE TODAY.[75]

x

I'm half tempted to go up and sit with them until four in the morning. But I'd better not. That's a different world. I'm not ready to reopen that door yet.

x

Judith comes soon. Macbeth-scenes and Medea.[76]

x

And Celeste Holm. Road shows are reviving. Some agent sends them out, starting in L.A.

x

I enclose a glimpse of my activities. Note: I don't see a soul until long after sunset.

x

---

74 French: the little humdrum routine.

75 English actress Estelle Winwood was Bankhead's best friend from the 1920s until Bankhead's death; they frequently costarred on the stage. *Here Today* is a 1932 play by George Oppenheimer.

76 Judith Anderson, one of whose most famous performances was as the heroine in American poet Robinson Jeffers's 1947 adaptation of Euripides' *Medea,* which Jeffers wrote for her.

I found the last surviving honest garage mechanic and now my car goes like a dream.

x

I love hearing from you, but gee I have nothing to recount in return.

Love and kisses
Thornt'

SOCIETY NOTES

by our Douglas correspondent

A shower was given for RUSTY (barman at the Tophat) and his bride, at MIKE's on Route 80 in Silver Springs. Beer, dancing, and clandestine gambling were enjoyed by over 90 guests..... Among the presents were..... a can of Crosse and Blackwell's kippered herrings and a can of coffee for percolating, from the Professor.

x

On Saturday night Louie (engineer) and Pete (highway patrol) and the Professor crossed into Mexico and had dinner and danced and smooched at the Copa. They then went on to visit a house of ill-fame, where the Professor's Spanish was much in demand. All of the gentlemen returned to their homes at four in the morning, their virtue intact, but leaving most tender regrets with the beautiful young ladies.

x

Vera R., waitress at the Palm Grove, has gone to the Douglas Hospital for an operation. Among her callers was the Professor, who was not admitted to see the patient, but whose flowers were much appreciated.

x

The usual Stein Night (second Fridays) was observed at the Crystal Palace Saloon in Tombstone. Beer and tacos were much enjoyed by 85 guests. The beautiful "Duffie" (Miss Duffield) behind the bar was pleased to welcome her shy admirer, the Professor.

x

Mr. J. L. whose travels for electronic gadgets bring him frequently to Douglas received the help of the Professor in writing a letter to council and judge requesting that his alimony be reduced. Mr. J. L.

hasn't a bean; he lives in a trailer while his wife and two sons enjoy his six-room house. The Professor believes Mr. J. L. to the effect that he had never offended his wife in any way. She and another woman concocted a story about how he had struck her cruelly on six different occasions. Tie that!

x

Mrs A . . . B . . . a winter guest at the Hotel Gadsden again closed the bar ("one o'clock, ladies and gentlemen, thank you") in deep conversation with her friend the Professor. There are now not many chapters in Mrs B's life which have not been imparted to her attentive friend.

x

Dawson's on the Lordsburg road is becoming more and more a place of entertainment for our Young Married set. Miss Winnie Shaw—former waitress at the Gadsden<,> now cook at her brother's <u>Hamburgateria</u>—laughingly persuaded the Professor to dance with her. The crowded floor was soon cleared as the other dancers stood against the wall and watched the charming couple with admiration. Miss Shaw was told by her parents that she was related to the English dramatist George Bernard Shaw, which in view of her lively <u>ripostes</u> is not hard to believe.

x

293. TO CATHERINE COFFIN. ALS 2 pp. (Stationery embossed: 50 Deepwood Drive / Hamden 17, Connecticut) Yale

P.O. Box 144   Douglas Arizona

Feb 7. 1963

Dear Catherine:

Many thanks for the records. I'm perfectly delighted with them both—the Mozart Quartets and the Landowska. My collection is still so small that each of them has its own particular invitation; I have the feeling that I'd lose that pleasure in them if I had, as some of my friends have, a whole wall of them.

I suppose Isabel may have told you that the New York representative of Ricordi—music publisher of Verdi, Puccini etc—has entered into a 5-year agreement with Louise Talma to promote The Alcestiad. Schirmers has just published her Etudes. She's playing her new Passacaglia and Fugue next week at a concert in honor of Aaron Copeland at the Gardner Museum in Boston and the new Violin Sonata somewhere else and other performances are cracking on radio and in concert halls. I'm a good picker.

The Hindemiths were thrown into a consternation that I didn't fly to Europe to hear the first of The Long Christmas Dinner in Mannheim or the second in Rome and now that I'm not flying to New York.[77] Well, I've never attended the premières of my own plays. Shucks, it's the public that's on trial, not the authors. Hindemith's opera is a jewel; it will appear everywhere; I shall be catching its 500th performance somewhere.

"How vainly men themselves amaze
To win the Palm, or Oke, or Bayes;
And their uncessant Labours see..."[78]

That's the hermit's beads. "Shouts in the distance." I've just got a letter from Jerry Kilty. The Moscow Ministry of Culture has approved the dramatized Ides of March. It has been accepted for production in Warsaw; Turino-Milano-Roma October to December; London (with John Gielgud) in June. Paris in October.[79] I presume it's the same text that had a bad reception in Berlin. I wrote some new scenes for it; then my will-power broke down. It's tedious work to rewarm yesterday's porridge; and one can put no heart into putting patch-patch-patch on to a framework that was never designed as theatre. Had I intended to write a play on that lofty subject I would have gone about it differently in every detail.

x

I hope the worst of your winter is over—the famous winter of 1962–1963. Here, again erratic, we have plunged into full spring. We are in the 80's by noon. Oh, how wonderful the sun is—and the moon no less

---

77 The Juilliard School was going to produce the Hindemith opera of TNW's *The Long Christmas Dinner* in March 1963.

78 From "The Garden," by Andrew Marvell.

79 Although Kilty's adaptation of TNW's 1948 novel was somewhat successful in Berlin in 1962, it failed in London in 1963.

so these nights. I now have quite an acquaintance in town, through I still havent been in a single home. There's a Judge Hanson, 75—still on the city bench, who was born in Denmark. An omniverous reader and in small small way (he was director of the YMCA here and in Texas for years) a collector of pictures. Years ago in a second hand store he picked up a portrait of Walt Whitman (it was in Philadelphia) which he thinks is by Thomas Eakins. He's consulted some experts and has a pile of documents but as yet no full assurance. If it *is* an Eakins of Whitman, think of what value it would have in the national interest. I'm to see it this week for my *expertise*! Often when the bars close at one we rakes cross over into Mexico where they don't close if there's still one customer sitting up straight,—Louie, the town engineer, Eddie, the Federal A.A representative at the airport; Rosie the elevator girl at the Gadsden; Gladys (*great* company) the cook at the Palm Grove and her sister Mrs Hẹrt, an attorney. Well, well,—I'm the oldest by 30 years but nothing tells me so. The ladies drink *margaritas*, a tequila daiqueri that<'s> sipped from a champagne glass the rim of which has been dipped in salt. My best friend is Harry Ames who's been going through a terrible time—the chicanery and general bitchiness of his father's partner's widow has ousted him from his Round-UP bar and liquor store,—a long Balzacian story. Harry's wife Nanette has been crying for weeks. Harry will land on his feet, though. Harry and Nanette are college graduates—all of the above-named are except Rosie and Gladys,—but that doesn't mean, ahem, that the conversation turns on T. S. Eliot and Boulez.

Well, I'm going to play myself KÖCHEL 465[80] which I shall henceforward identify with you,—except that I don't want to associate you with any of those passages of "glimpsed unfathomable dejection," wonderful though they are. Give my love to all in Bill's house and to Massachusetts and Long Island.[81]

your devoted *cavaliere servante*
Thornt'

80 Mozart's Quartet in C Major, which apparently was one of the recordings Coffin had sent TNW.

81 Catherine Coffin's children, William Sloane Coffin, Jr., of New Haven, Edmund Coffin of Long Island, and Margot Coffin Lindsay of Massachusetts.

294. TO ISABEL WILDER. ALS 2 pp. (Stationery embossed 50 Deepwood Drive / Hamden 17, Connecticut) Yale

P.O. Box 144 Douglas Arizona

March 17. 1963

Dear Isa:

Well, the opera thing is over.[82] I know I would have found it very hard to live through. The easy thing about the Frankfurt occasion[83] was that it was a beautiful professional performance. It's as hard to be complimented as to be blamed for a performance when you know that some one or more elements in it (the recent Mr Antrobuses, or the actor playing St. Francis) absolutely deform the work. I'm tranquil about blame or praise if the work was adequately represented. Otherwise your lips are sealed; you're not allowed <to> utter a judgment on your team-mates.

Heigh-ho.

I wrote those people who wanted me to find an agent for the Nebraska play, and the inquiry about the long poem translated from the German—I got out of them both prettily. I signed the book for publisher of the Penguins. N.B. The last line of <u>The Matchmaker</u> is six words short there, too.

I had a dinner party last night. Harry Ames who has lost his bar the ROUND-UP, has no job; and his wife and mother. His father was what in Brooklyn would be a saloon-keeper but here in the West was a sort of city father, the most admired man in town, a hand in politics, friend of all the governors and senators—even of Isabella Greenway.[84] And his widow has the carriage and taste in dress of the best <of> St Ronan Street.[85] Harry's wife Nannette, very pretty, though she has

---

82 TNW's sister, as his representative, had attended the Juilliard School opera production of *The Long Christmas Dinner* and reported her disappointment in the opening-night performance. She said the orchestra was too loud, the tenor could not be heard in the sextet, and there was a general non-professional air to the whole production. She found the second night better, however.

83 The opera version of *The Alcestiad* had had its world premiere in Frankfurt on March 1, 1962.

84 Arizona Democrat Isabella Greenway served in the House of Representatives from 1933 to 1937. She also built the Arizona Inn, a well-known hotel in Tucson.

85 A fashionable address in New Haven, noted for its large and beautiful old houses.

been crying for weeks, Scandinavian, physical culture teacher until her baby came a year ago,—all very nice people and it never occurs to them to read a book. Cocktails, first in Apartment 6: I put Karkana cheddar and white fish roe on little crackers; and New York State champagne cocktails. After the first bewilderment they accept the fact that the Professor doesn't go into homes.

Well. I won't stew about any longer but come right out with it that I've written what must be 90 pages or more of a novel.[86] I can't describe it except by suggesting that it's as though Little Women were being mulled over by Dostoievsky<.> It takes place in a mining town in southern Illinois ("Anthracite") around 1902. And there's Hoboken...and Tia Bates of Araquipa, Peru, transferred to Chile[87].....and theres the opera-singer Clare Dux (Swift)[88]...and Holy Rollers....and how a Great Love causes havoc (the motto of the book could be "nothing too much") and how gifts descend in family lines, making for good, making for ill, and demanding victims. You'll be astonished at how much I know about how a family, reduced and ostracized, runs a boarding house. But mostly its about familial ties, and oh, you'll need a handkerchief as big as a patchwork quilt. The action jumps about in time, though not as schematically as in The Ides. The form is just original enough to seem fresh; its not really like usual novels.

This morning I was doing a passage (Sophia's nightmare) and was so shaken that I couldn't go. I've had a headache ever since.—It's terrible, the book!

All this since Christmas. I didn't venture to mention it earlier because project after project has wilted away. But I'm darn well certain now that this is here to stay. I think it was the record-player that set things in motion, some Mozart and some organ works of Bach. Nothing I've written has advanced so fast, but it doesn't worry me. Between the lines there's lots of "Wilders".

---

86 *The Eighth Day* (1967).

87 Mrs. Ana "Tia" Bates was the American proprietor of Quinta Bates in Araquipa, Peru, an inn that became famous throughout South America and attracted famous visitors from all over the world. TNW had visited there during his South American trip for the State Department in 1941.

88 Claire Dux Swift was married to Charles H. Swift, of the Chicago meatpacking family. TNW knew the couple from his days at the University of Chicago in the 1930s.

To think that that stroll that you and I took about Hoboken should have made such an impression on me! I must find out what kind of trees those were—lindens?

There's melodrama in it, too, and a trial for murder.

So that's the secret.

And you can imagine how my mode of life here now suits me.

I'm distraught on the two days of the week when I have to get out because the cleaning woman comes; I could eat glass with rage because I've mislaid my reading glasses; I postpone the boring necessity of taking my drivers test. I'm only ready for interruptions after sunset. I don't work at night—twice it led to two sleepless nights—I, who never have any trouble sleeping. (You should read the account of Mrs. Ashly's insomnia!)

Every new day is so exciting because I have no idea beforehand what will come out of the fountain-pen.

I hope Alice lives to read it; she has gently implored me to do a novel for a long time.[89]

love

Thornt

295. TO HAROLD FREEDMAN. ALS 2 pp. (Stationery embossed P. O. Box 144 / Douglas, Arizona) Private

<appeared above the letterhead>
Last days at

Nov 18 1963

Dear Harold:

It puts me in a very funny position to have to repeat to kind well-wishers that I think The Alcestiad is not a workable play. It makes me look like someone fishing for more and more compliments.

89 Alice B. Toklas died on March 7, 1967, three weeks before *The Eighth Day* was published.

I don't mind having a failure but I hate to involve others in a failure.

Mr. Strasberg[90] wrote me about the play, but (confidentially) his interpretation of the first two acts was miles from what I meant and his recommendation for the rewriting of the last act was unbelievable. That's not his fault, but mine. As I wrote Cheryl[91]: it's a pan of rolls that didn't get cooked through in the oven.

It's too bad.

The only way I can pull myself out of this awkward position is to do another so that these well-wishers can forget poor Alcestis

I've written Isabel that I'm not yet ready to return to urban civilization. I need one more year in some village, probably abroad. My new novel (not announced yet) is approaching its final draft. Then I'll "go theatre" again.

I'm sorry to be leaving the desert. It's done a lot for me.

But so will a change. Including (oh Lord!) a change of food. Can you imagine living a year and a half with almost never an attractive bit in<on> your plate?

But I'm well and cheerful and grateful to Arizona (the State where WATER is GOLD. You should hear the political thinking in the bars that I frequent! I was told the other night—in a fist-beating roar—that the late Mrs Roosevelt did more harm in the world than TEN Hitlers.) A woman working in the Douglas Telephone office asked an acquaintance "Who is that Mr. Wilder? Is he a communist?<"> Her thinking goes like this:

① He makes $8 long-distance calls (once a week to Isabel, yet <).>

② He doesn't own a phone.

③ He makes them through the central office so that they can't be traced.

④ He has a funny accent and even in August he wears a necktie

Q.E.D.

---

90 Lee Strasberg, the artistic director of the Actors Studio, had expressed interest in producing *The Alcestiad*.

91 Cheryl Crawford, who had cofounded the Group Theatre with Strasberg and Harold Clurman in 1931, also cofounded the Actors Studio in 1947.

Please give my affectionate best to Sam and Elza.[92]
and love to Sam<,> May and Bobbie[93]

from
Thornt'

TNW receiving the Presidential Medal of Freedom from President Lyndon Johnson in the White House, December 6, 1963.

296. TO AMOS TAPPAN WILDER. ALS 2 pp. (Stationery embossed 50 Deepwood Drive / Hamden 17, Connecticut) Private

Dec 29 • 1963

Dear Tappie:

D'une elégance! D'une beauté[94]

And particularly welcome now—can you guess why?

---

92 Sam and Elza Behrman.

93 May was Freedman's wife, and Bobbie was his son. Sam cannot be identified.

94 French: How elegant! How beautiful.

Not only are they warm and comfortable, but they are of this elegance.

For the next few months, perhaps the whole year, I must live (as so often before) on boats and in hotels.

Nothing impresses the stewards on boats and the chambermaids in hotels like a luxurious pair of pyjamas to spread on the bed every night.

I'm sorry to say it, but there's no snob like a servant. And I'm sorry to say it, but there's no ill-clad down-at-heel bum like your uncle. So now you've given me a chance to hold up my head and get a little more considerate service. Thanks, many thanks.

x

As you are beginning to think about writing a novel, here are some suggestions that would be of use to some young writers—but every writer is different and they might not apply to you at all:

(1) Don't begin at the beginning. Begin at some situation near the middle of the work that is livest to your imagination.

(2) In fact, don't begin a novel; begin a note-book toward a novel.

(3) This notebook contains not only scenes and bits of conversation that may find their place in the novel; but make it a sort of journal wherein you talk to yourself about the novel (objectify your thoughts about it, by writing them down.)

(4) Lots of novelists waste time and "poetic" energy and courage (the most important ingredient of all) by not deciding early what kind of novel it is. In some novels the reader simply hears and sees what happens; in others he hears the author's voice explaining and analyzing what's going on. The two methods may be combined but must be evenly distributed. You can't indicate for 30 pages that you know all about Jim and Nelly and then withdraw and merely exhibit Jim and Nelly for the next 30.

(5) You're a Wilder. Fight against the didactic,—the didactic-direct.

(6) When you are about one-third through your work, you will pass through a phase in which you despair of it, you loathe it, you loathe yourself, etc. Any work—a sonnet, a short story, or an epic poem. Always happens. Expect it. Be ready for it.

⑦ The theme of a work should express some inner latent question in yourself. It is best when this is so deeply present that no one else would recognize it. Without this you will become bored with writing.

⑧ It's a subtle help not to give your characters run-of-the-mill names. Unless you deliberately wish to render the run-of-the-mill nature of their lives. Not "Jim" and "Nelly"—but an occasional "Ludovic" or "Thomasina."

Happy hunting.
Again thanks—and love
Uncle Thornton

297. TO AMOS N. AND CATHARINE K. WILDER. ALS 1 p. Yale

Last weeks at Americ. Exp. Co NICE

April 21. 1964

Dear Kith'n Kin:

Many thanks for your greetings. Am enjoying my late sixties plus my existence en marge.[95] Things that would have vexed me once I shrug off: have had a head cold virus since January—with intermittent deafness. Ishkabbible. The dream of finding a Douglas-in-Italy couldn't work. Allez donc.[96] Had a hotel reservation in Cannes to embark on the 9th. Hotel phones...regrets...mistake....there was an earlier booking....The Film Festival....i.e. some film tycoon has given them a big bonus to swipe the room. All right, go fly a kite. I'll embark at Genoa.

---

95 French: life on the edge.

96 French: Let's get on with it, then.

Nothing makes much difference to me except the hours at my desk. The number<novel> is getting on well. Will be longer than I had foreseen. I should be getting down to Southern Illinois to get a look at the locale and read their 1902–1905 newspapers. But I've had great fun inventing how a coal mine is run, how a murder trial is staged. I'm no slouch either at describing copper mining at 13,000 feet in Chile. As we heard in The Importance of Being Ernest<Earnest> at the Thacher School in 1912: "Ignorance is like a beautiful exotic flower; touch it, and the bloom is gone."[97]

So I sail from Genoa on the 7th—BARCELONA—TENARIFE—the port of CARACAS—CURAÇAO. (I've done this all before—Curaçao is a perfect 18th century Dutch town—better than Delft or Haärlem—only peopled by beautiful octoroon maidens with burdens on their head. It'll be hot as blazes, but it'll heal my cold.) Fly to Miami. Get a drive-yourself. Fool around Florida. Call on Aunt Charlotte. But always the daily working hours.

¶Just read London Sunday literary reviews of Leslie Hotson's "Mr. W.H."[98] I've been very scared for him ever since he read me fragments of the book. Insufficient respect for the laws of evidence.

¶Olivier opens tonight in Othello at "his" British National Theatre.[99] He once told me he would never play Othello because it demanded a voice a full octave lower than his. The greatest living actor. I can believe that he's superb. ¶Have been reading (in French) HÉRODOTE: Histoires (love it): GOETHE: Les Affinités électives (I hoped for so much from this "old man's" novel; I can only believe that I've missed the point, or the points.) STENDHAL: Oeuvres intimes, all 1500 pages of 'em....droll,....pathetic...often bracing.[100]

---

97 The line is spoken by Lady Bracknell in act 1. The correct quotation is "Ignorance is like a delicate exotic fruit; touch it and the bloom is gone."

98 Shakespearean scholar Hotson's *Mr. WH* (1964) identified the individual to whom Shakespeare's sonnets were addressed as William Hatcliffe.

99 Laurence Olivier was one of the founders of the National Theatre Company, which was established in 1963.

100 *Elective affinities* was the 1854 translation of Goethe's 1809 novel, *Die Wahlverwandtschaften*. Stendhal's *Oeuvres Intimes*, edited by Henri Martineau, was issued by the French publisher Gallimard in 1955.

Lots of Balzac. I hope it can <be> said of me that I had at least a drop of his zest.

Now I've got to go to lunch. I don't really like French cooking—until suddenly some dish hits you in the eye. Day in, day out, the Italian is more my style.

I'll be terribly eager to know what Tappy's plans are.

I just wrote Dixie.

Loads of love to everybody and thanks.
Thy
Thorny.

298. TO JOHN O'HARA. ALS 2 pp. (Stationery embossed Rossini / "ITALIA" / Societá di Navigazione / Genova <Rossini crossed out by TNW>) Penn State

American Express Co. NICE (A–M)

February 18 • 1965

Dear John:

It was very generous and helpful and bracing of you to write that letter to me about rereading The Cabala. It's followed me around through several forwardings and has finally caught up with me here. It arrived when I was miserable, unable to shake off a cold (caught in the air-conditioning, a month before, in a Curaçao hotel—the big colds are caught in the tropics) and I was deaf and I was none too enthusiastic about the writing I was doing every day. Your letter galvanized me.

Most of that book was written at Lawrenceville by the Assistant House Master of the "Davis House." It was written after "lights out"—with interruptions ("Please, Mr. Wilder, I don't feel very good; I think I'm sick." "Please, Mr. Wilder, can I study downstairs for just half an hour, because I'm so worried about that exam tomorrow I can't sleep?") I had no problems about self-confidence and "enthusiasm" then. It didn't seem possible that anyone would want to publish it. I just wrote on about all those rich highly colored people, like a boy trying his hand at science-fiction. (In Rome, I had had no entree into such coteries as that!) I haven't looked at the book for years, but now—puffed up by your good opinion—I shall return to it.

So you'll soon be sixty! I hope you'll enjoy each succeeding decade as much as I have. Thank God I was never tormented by that panic over the passing of youth that beset Scott Fitzgerald and Hemingway. I think if you welcome each new decade you're allowed to keep all the past one's green inside you. Nothing ages a man or woman like clinging to an image of themselves that's gone by. It snowed in Nice last evening—unheard of!—and golly, how chipper I felt,—simply bucketed along.

I was delighted to hear of your Gold Medal.[101] Late, but all the solider for that.

Well, back to my drawing-board—and feeling fine as a result of a mighty kind salute from you.

Ever cordially,
Thornton

299. TO PHYLLIS McGINLEY.[102] ALS 1 p. (Stationery embossed Verdi / "ITALIA" / Societá di Navigazione / Genova) Syracuse

As from 50 Deepwood Drive, Hamden 17, Conn

April 2. 1965

Dear Miss McGinley:

I got a beautiful, generous letter from you.

I set it aside, as children do the biggest chocolate cream in the box.

Moving from hotel to hotel with my four pieces of hand-luggage—packed like rats' nests, I lost it. At intervals I'd search for it among the

---

101 O'Hara received the Award of Merit Medal for the Novel from the American Academy of Arts and Letters (not the Academy's Gold Medal) on May 20, 1964.

102 Canadian-born American poet (1905–1978).

letters, bills (membership in the Tombstone, Arizona, Preservation Society), summonses (to my 45th Class Reunion), old ship's passenger lists (an "x" denotes a friendship sealed for life), vaccination certificate (two weeks to run), clippings ("Canadian doctor declares babies suffer acutely from boredom", "Robert Graves modernizes 300 words and phrases for London production of Much Ado About Nothing"), snapshots, menus....

Twice I wrote my sister Isabel: urgent, send Miss McGinley's address. Finally, I'm on a slow slow ship—two weeks from Genoa to Curaçao—I really unpack. And there's your letter, plain as day.

It not only gave me the pleasure of its kindness, it arrived as a talisman and a sign. I'm at work on another; it looks as though it wanted to be long, I'm sorry to say. So I'm going through hopes and fears, and feverish spurts and arid spells. Hence, your message came at a real right helpful moment.

You mention "War and Peace". I bought it in French, for a change, to read on this slow-crossing. (French not a good idea; but it shows that Mrs Garnett[103] didn't even try to cope <with> the slang of the soldiers and the working people.) So I was on two oceans. Funny thing: in Anna Karenina I can see the architecture, the recurrent themes, designs (and even symbols—that abused word). But in War and Peace I can't isolate them; I know they're there because of the wonderful assurance—the freedom from anything approaching diffuseness or the merely episodic. But I can't yet see how it's done,—not that it matters. ¶I hope you know that fragment that Tolstoi wrote—the beginning of a sequel to War and Peace—opens with a picture of Natasha as a staid matron—I think a grandmother. I can see why he didn't carry it further.

Also I've travelled with another vast novel—said to be twice as long as War and Peace and Brothers Karamazov and Don Quixote. The only longer novel is Proust's. Have you guessed it? Written by a woman, about 1000 A.D.? (A whole long chapter has been dropped out in our version of it.) Well, I'm not a Japanese scholar, but I read much in the oriental religions; and I have the impudence to say that Arthur Waley—judging by his preface—hasn't a glimmer of what the true theme of the

---

103 English translator Constance Garnett (1861–1946), whose translation of *War and Peace* was first published in 1900 and was, for many years, the only English version of Tolstoy's novel.

The Tale of Genji <is>.[104] An Englishman wouldn't. We love our English cousins—oh, yes,—and we're in eternal debt to their literature—but no Englishman after the 17th Century could have any "windows open" to the oriental view of THE WAY. It's not a very large island. The islander can develop no apprehension of multitude—of the billions who have lived and died...billions and billions, which is warp and weft of the oriental consciousness. Genji dies about half way through the book (the novel gets better and better as it goes on) but the subject is the persistance and continuity of souls—in good and evil—not as biological heredity, but as the accumulation of good and bad karma—Lady Rokiyo's tormented jealousy in operation 50 years after her death is the clearest illustration.... but Genji—anything but a heedless Don Juan, he's a sort of saint manqué...who will arrive at felicity after a couple of thousand lifetimes,—a completely un-British notion. ¶You mention Pride and Prejudice. I love Miss Austen but I have one little skunner against her: women exasperate her. The only women she can like (as in Colette) are those avatars of herself in the middle of the book. Lady Murasaki has none of this exasperation and none of this self-regarding. She's rather neutral about women—but, then, she's mad about the fellas, and what a fella! ¶You've got to go to Shakespeare and Tolstoi for a clear statement: women are just as good as men (and even a little better.) ¶Genji was handsome as all get out—wasn't it great of Tolstoi to make that other suffering moral hero Pierre—uncouth, fat, and bespectacled? Everybody loves Levine, too.[105] I must go back and find out what he looked like—I forget.

Well, I'm wasting your time. And it's like a conversation in which I don't let you get a word in.

But, anyway, it's my frustrated way of telling you how indebted to you I am and how I shall always be

devotedly yours, Thornton Wilder

---

104 Classic Japanese work believed to have been written by noblewoman Murasaki Shikibu (978–1014), which is considered to be the world's first novel. TNW was reading the translation (1960) by English sinologist Arthur Waley.

105 Pierre Bezukhov and Konstantin Levin, principal male characters in Tolstoy's *War and Peace* and *Anna Karenina*, respectively.

300. TO CATHARINE DIX WILDER. ALS 4 pp. (Stationery embossed 50 Deepwood Drive / Hamden, Connecticut 06517) Yale

June 3. 1965

Dear Dixiana:

Many thanks, querida sobrina,[106] for your birthday greetings. On that day—Easter Eve—I had just arrived in West Palm Beach, Florida, had paid a months rent for a small apartment, had gone to a supermarket and laid in bread, butter, milk, eggs and CANNED SOUPS. It wasn't until noon that I remembered "what day it was" and I burst out laughing. Weeks later I happened to read that the days of the week in 1965 happen to fall on the same days in the calendar as they did in 1897,—so I learned for the first time that I (and my twin brother) was born on the day that the old English church used to call The Raking of Hell—when Christ, just before the resurrection descended into hell and redeemed the noble pagans who died before the Advent. There are old pictures of Him pulling up large throngs of them in a net. I've been trying to see if there's any symbolism, for me, in all this.

So now you're going to learn the great Spanish language—el lenguaje de los Reyes.[107] It's resemblance to Italian and French is merely historical; its "inner feeling" is very different from theirs. As I had occasion to write your father a few years ago, it has no elisions. Every syllable stands alone, like the Spanish character. One of the first words you'll meet shows its firm concreteness: I HAVE = YO TENgO. Get that T and that hard G. Italian: io ho French: j'ai. How weak, how unsubstantial. (The Spaniards ruled Naples for centuries, and in the Neapolitan dialect they rightly retained this Tengo and have long since forgotten that it's from the Spanish.)

I know what you mean about bogging down in La Vida es Sueño.[108] When you will have read a number of Spanish plays you'll have got used to their theatrical conventions—just as you're now used to Shake-

---

106 Spanish: dear niece.

107 Spanish: the language of kings. TNW's niece was going to take a course in Spanish at Harvard Summer School in order to meet further requirements for teaching credentials.

108 A philosophical drama (1635) by Spanish playwright Pedro Calderón de la Barca.

speare's girls going around disguised as boys—and you wont "notice" them. The way Calderón works out the magnificent image of Sigismundo brought up in a tower with no contact with the world except one old guardian is very fine. I hope you'll teach it some day!

It's hard to realize that your school goes on until June 25th.[109] As I remember it the last mile's the hardest,—grading the students. Heigh-ho!

In an hour Tappie will be here for lunch—its Archie Hobson's birthday and he and his mother will be here, too.[110] Then at 2:30 I have to go to a doctor's appointment, made 8 months ago—a check-up "look see" at the scar on my face.[111] As far as I can see it's all right. Then tomorrow I go to the Red Lion Inn at Stockbridge to work in seclusion until I come back here for a day or two at my 45th Class reunion. How we senior-citizens will scan one another for signs of general delapidation! I entertained the notion of going to the Beau Brummel Beauty Parlor and taking the "budget treatment"

Pour réparer des ans l'irréparable outrage,[112]

(do you spot where that verse comes from?) but no! I've resigned myself. I'll be the same old laughing bottle-hugging Silenus.[113]

If you're in Cambridge most of the summer, I may drop by—is dinner as good as ever at the Vendôme (or Lockobers?) and of course I love cocktails on the revolving carousel bar in Copley Square. If there is any fellow around that you're weighing in the balance you'd better bring him along. I'll try not to scare the daylights out of him. Am I formidable? I don't mean to be, but I've been told that I am.

Con mucho amor, mi niña
Tu tio[114]
Torntón.

---

109 TNW's niece was teaching French at Wellesley Junior High School in Wellesley, Massachusetts.

110 Archibald Hobson, the son of TNW's first cousin Wilder Hobson; Archie's mother was Verna Harrison Hobson.

111 TNW had had a cancerous growth removed from his cheek.

112 French: to repair the years' irreparable damage (from act 2, scene 5, of Jean Racine's *Athalie* [1691]).

113 The teacher and companion of Dionysus, the god of wine.

114 Spanish: (on first line) With much love, my child; (on second line) Your uncle.

301. TO AMY WERTHEIMER. ALS 2 pp. (Stationery embossed 50 Deepwood Drive / Hamden, Connecticut 06517) Yale

<appeared above the letterhead>
A few days in St Augustine soon at Triton Motel Sarasota Fla

April 7 • 1966

Dear Amy:

Thank you.

Thank you in advance of the day.

x

You're quite right, you haven't found my death in the papers nor any signs of my life.

There's a good reason for that: I'm not "news."

x

I never read Albee's The Sand Box<.> I hope the rôle of the Grandmother is not like that in his The American Dream

You're quite right,—Our Town is given less and less, but are you sure that it's been outpaced by No Exit? Anyway, they bear a partial resemblance to one another: the last act of my play suggests that life—viewed directly—is damned near Hell; his play says that the proximity of other people renders life a Hell—"L'enfer—c'est les autres."[115] Sartre told me that at the time of the first production he received scores of protests—They found that line too cruel "You are your life"—(i.e. there are no alibis.) It's a savage play. I hope you've got three remarkable actors for it.

x

I have to stay away from New England most of the year. When I catch a cold it fastens on me for months and makes me deaf.

x

Your letter sounds doleful: twice you refer to your imminent death, and once to mine; your hands are too weak to work, you say, on

115 TNW is quoting from Sartre's 1944 play.

those heavy Bibles and geneologies.[116] One of the greatest charms of the Amy of Blodgett's Landing was her beautiful laughter (in addition to her beautiful speaking voice). Don't lose that.

In the long novel that I've almost finished I assert roundly that life is <u>not</u> an image of hell. You will receive a copy from your

devoted
old
friend
Thornton

302. TO CHERYL CRAWFORD. ALS 2 pp. (Stationery embossed 50 Deepwood Drive / Hamden, Connecticut 06517) Houston

<appeared above the letterhead>
Returning soon to Triton Motel, Lido Beach, Sarasota.

Wrote this weeks ago— then lost it—now add the clipping from England. Sorry T.N.W.

St. Augustine Fla
Maundy Thursday <April 7> 1966

Dear Cheryl:

I love to get a letter from you.

I love to think of you.

x

116 Wertheimer was a bookbinder.

I've had to stay away from the North because when I catch a cold it lodges in my ear. Blindness is an affliction; deafness is a humiliation.

x

The theme of your play makes me nervous.[117] Milieu, however exotic, cannot pull us into a theatre by itself. Jews in China, Mormons in Uruguay, Yankees at King Arthur's Court. In fact milieu is dangerous. We don't "believe in" the theatrical presentation of background unless it's subtended by things nearer to us: love (preferably young love); courage to survive, etc THE PASSIONS. Watch that script.

x

We are in a phase of the culture-climate of the Jews. A great jet-fuel of the human race. Thank God I have some drops of Jewish blood. But after centuries of contempt they are emerging into estimation and not only estimation but the goyim's expectation of greatness. First there was the condescending tolerance (Abie's Irish Rose), the admiring relish in the foreigness (Awake and Sing.) But they're bewildered and self-conscious (there's nothing worse in the world than being self-conscious—a teen-age agony.) and flustered (Herzog.)[118] Chagal<Chagall> (and Buber) have made it with charm, but only one has made it with the true note of the Jew—nobility, nobility athirst for the absolute: KAFKA. There, too, is the greatness of your Actor's Studio and its power to capture the gifted young. "Only those who are humble enough to strive for a difficult truth can enter this house." Do find some passage in your play to sound that note.

x

You know that you and I have never seen eye to eye about Bert Brecht.

Well, I've been getting some low reprehensible pleasures out of the reports of Günther Glass's play in Berlin.[119] (I've just come from Miami

---

117 TNW is referring to the musical *Chu-Chem*, which Crawford was coproducing at the time. The play concerns Jews who migrated to China in the tenth century.

118 The two plays and the novel TNW mentions also deal with Jewish characters.

119 Günter Grass's *Die Plebejer proben den Aufstand* (*The Plebians Rehearse the Uprising*) opened in West Berlin in January 1966. The character of the Boss in this play represents Bertolt Brecht.

where I could buy German newspapers and read lengthy accounts.) I'm ready to go along with a true Marxist. I love the literary criticism of Georg Lukács.[120] The world is furthered by passionate conviction, right or wrong, not primarily by judicious appraisal. Least of all by political dilletanti. Brecht wobbled, finally posed, finally played the opportunist.

x

Have you been reading the Shaw letters?[121] There's the preparation for the British elections last month. How astounding and right to find that his future wife's money founded The London School of Economics and the magazine The Economist.[122] You've read about the English musical comedy The Matchgirls—how instructive it is to learn that those dauntless girls were aided by a penniless Irish music critic and by Mrs Besant, the "muddle-headed" but fiery proponent of the Occult.[123] Civilization is furthered by <the> lunatic fringe.

x

LATER: April 17. Today's my birthday. I'm 69. I've put my foot into my 70th year and intend to enjoy it. Isabel's here to see me and our agéd Aunt Charlotte who's not well, in St Petersburg.

Thanks again—and all best wishes. Love to Cheryl and Ruth.[124]

your devoted
Thornton

---

120 Lukács (1885–1971) was a Hungarian Marxist philosopher and literary critic.

121 Volume 1 of *Bernard Shaw: Collected Letters*, edited by Dan H. Laurence, was published in 1965.

122 Charlotte Payne-Townshend Shaw was an active member of the Fabian Society and a patron of the London School of Economics.

123 In 1888, English social reformer and Theosophist Annie Besant was one of the organizers of a strike of women workers against the Bryant and May match factory in London's East End. *The Match Girls*, a 1966 English musical, tells the story of that strike.

124 Ruth Norman was Crawford's companion.

303. TO RICHARD GOLDSTONE. ALS 4 pp. (Stationery embossed 50 Deepwood Drive / Hamden, Connecticut 06517) NYU

Oct 6 or 7 1966

Dear Richard:

Every few days I get a letter from some old friend or acquaintance asking me if he or she should show him<you> letters of mine; or telling me that you have approached them for information about me.

Some of them are from persons who knew me long before I met you.

That implies that you are writing a biography of me. But I'm still alive. I have not yet appointed a definitive biographer.

There were a number of books written about Robert Frost before he died—one was by my friend Elizabeth S. Sergeant and she drew me into the composition of it to the extent of at least 20 letters (which she bequeathed to the Yale Library.) Now Robert Frost made it very clear to her that she was not writing a biography. (He had already selected his biographer.[125]) He pulled her short many times. She was writing—he kept reminding her—a memoir of a friendship, together with a commentary on his work. She would not have dreamed of "circularizing" his friends.

What kind of book are you writing?

Please make it quite clear to yourself what you are doing.

It certainly appears to my friends (and even casual acquaintances merely that are now writing me!) that you are collecting materials toward a biography.

If I get many more letters from friends and acquaintances I shall explode. I regard it as "undignified" to disturb friends for a "character reference," on the one hand, or "picturesque anecdotes" on the other.

Dr. Jones wrote me asking for recollections of Freud (for his Biography) and Lord David Cecil of Beerbohm (for his Biography<)>—when the subjects were dead. (Ditto Elizabeth Sprigge on Gertrude Stein)

---

125 Princeton University English professor Lawrance Thompson.

If I get any more of these I shall reply that you are a well-meaning young scholar—but that you have more zeal than judgment.

I suggest that you give your attention primarily to the work. As is my custom, I have not read the short books that deal with me, but I presume there is ample room for ideas—favorable or unfavorable—I don't care—as long as they are thoughtful—are <u>good</u> <u>criticism</u>.

Ever
Thornton

304. TO GRACE CHRISTY FORESMAN. ALS 2 pp. (Stationery embossed 50 Deepwood Drive / Hamden, Connecticut 06517) Yale

<appeared above the letterhead>
For a few months' hideaway (before the "summer people" come<)>, at P.O. Box 862, Edgartown. Martha's Vineyard, Mass

April 21. 1967

Dear Grace:

What a joy to hear from you

And to learn that you were not disappointed in the book.[126]

You probably saw that you were in mind in a portion of the book—there was a great hurlyburly of names and addresses when I sent out copies... I could not find your address in my "papers"—I still think of you as near Pittsburgh... or you would have been among the first to receive a copy.

You were married to one of the most honest and clearest-souled of men. As illness began to descend upon him I was filled with deep affectionate concern for you both. The experience made a deep impression on me—who had had at that time little experience of physical and spiritual suffering.

---

126 *The Eighth Day*, which had been published on March 29, 1967.

With no sense of intrusion, dear Grace, my imagination tried to understand the great ordeal you both underwent.

And many years later it reappeared in that book. But under what different aspects!

How different are Clyde Foresman and Breckenridge Lansing.

A greater part of Clyde's suffering was the attempt to alleviate your pain. Poor Breckenridge is all egotism gradually "thawed" through Eustacia's religious view of "love for the creature."

In an odd way "St Kitts" is for a time Davis House and Breckenridge Lansing is—in reverse—a tribute to the brave and noble man you married and you are Eustacia bearing a no less—an even greater burden—because you knew and you knew that Clyde knew that an end was approaching that only love could transcend.

A number of correspondents have already told me that those scenes are lacerating—almost too painful to bear—only endurable because of Eustacia's clairvoyance and largeness of soul. That is my tribute to you.

Give my love to Emily—and to Jack.[127] My book has already told you that I see these storm-tossed lives as stages in a vast unfoldment.

Indeed, I know well that LIFE-TIME is a loveless juggernaught that grinds lives in an atmosphere of fear, competition, and seldom-rewarded ambition. It had its part in breaking up the first marriage of my cousin Wilder Hobson—who later went to "Newsweek"! We must take a long view or we must despair.

If you have time, will you write me a word about "those matters"—because your life-story was one of the turning-points in my life.

I have begun "another"—and always at the back of my mind is the hope that (this time) I shall succeed in amusing you. The only amusement that's worth anything is that which is based upon a deep acceptance of the tragic background of life

With a world of affection

Ever

Thornton

---

127 The Foresmans' daughter, Emily, had been married to John K. Tibby, Jr., who worked at Time-Life. See letter number 305, which mentions the divorce. The couple, who had three children, later remarried each other.

305. TO JOHN K. TIBBY, JR. ALS 2 pp. (Stationery embossed 50 Deepwood Drive / Hamden, Connecticut 06517) Yale

<appeared above the letterhead>
P.O. 862 Edgartown, Mass. 02539

May 5 • 1967

Dear Jack:

Before I received your letter one arrived from Grace Foresman telling me of the divorce, of Emily's and Bill's interests. I'm glad to hear from you.

I hope for both of you that the new situation—since it had to be—is "working", that you're making a good thing of it.

I burst out laughing at your mention of p. 327 of my book. Old writing-hand though I am, it still comes as a surprise (even a shock) to me that readers find anything "usable" in my ruminations. I am so little of a dogmatic type that my first impulse is to exclaim "Oh, I didn't mean to be taken as seriously at that,—I was just kicking the subject around."

My sister Isabel will forward the Life-Time Tributes to Harry Luce soon. I just received a reply from Mrs Luce (Tempe, Arizona). She thought I was still living the "hermit" in Arizona and wished I would come up and spend a day with her: she wanted to learn about those early years of Harry that she had never understood. (Incidentally, she described herself to my sister as very lonesome.)[128]

Harry Luce, Bob Hutchins, my brother Amos and I (all near classmates in New Haven) are a very special breed of cats. Our fathers were very religious, very dogmatic Patriarchs. They preached and talked cant from morning til night—not because they were hypocritical but because they knew no other language. They were forceful men. They thought they were "spiritual"—damn it, they should have been in industry. They had no insight into the lives of others—least of all their families. They had an Old Testament view (sentimentalized around the

128 Henry R. Luce had died in February 1967.

edges) of what a WIFE, DAUGHTER, SON, CITIZEN should be. We're the product of those (finally bewildered and unhappy) Worthies. In Harry it took the shape of a shy joyless power-drive. And like so many he intermittently longed to be loved, enjoyed, laughed with. But he didn't understand give-and-take. Bob and Amos and I—bottom of p. 148!

I wish you'd known Brit Hadden.[129]

I wonder what school you'll select for Bill. Largely approve of your avoiding the big ones—but such decisions are closely related to the nature of the student.

Martha's Vineyard is my hideaway now—until the "summer people" come. Bad weather, seagulls and I.

If you feel like it some rainy Sunday afternoon open a beer and write me. (God, you typewrite elegantly.) Oh, I forgot, on Sunday afternoon you're on your boat,—well, Sunday night. Where were you born? Where did you school?—Are you making most of your own meals, like me? Since the divorce are you more of a convivial or less? Do you do a lot of reading? What are you reading?

Your loyal

Uncle Thornton

P.S. I gathered, between the lines, that Grace admires you very much. TNW.

306. TO WILLIAM I. NICHOLS. ALS 4 pp. (Stationery embossed 50 Deepwood Drive / Hamden, Connecticut 06517) LofC

<appeared above the letterhead>

Passing through N.Y. to see my sister Charlotte in the sanatorium on Long Island

---

129 Briton Hadden, TNW's and Luce's classmate at Yale and one of the most admired men in their class, cofounded *Time* magazine with Luce in 1923. They served in alternate years as the company's president until Hadden's untimely death in 1929.

Friday
<August 1967>

Dear Bill:

Many thanks for sending me your "talk."

The larger part of it is finely organized and phrased.

I think it's a very important movement (for good or ill) and not likely to be drowned out by civil rights riots.

I think you can very much count on its CONTINUING to change it<s> form:

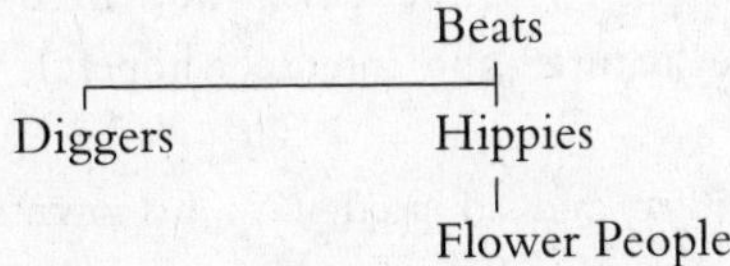

The Beats were vagrant (few women; you can't wander about with women); picked up occasional jobs (no begging) and little said about "smoking", etc. Lots of poetry-readings; quasi-religious viâ the Orient.

x

Hippies—sedentary community. Totally drug-oriented. Hence—as you point out—the atrophy of the "will". Debasement into panhandling and begging (very un-American.) Debasement of the ideological rationales—don't <u>know</u> anything about their Hindu chants or Zen disciplines. Omnipresence of women, but "pot" is very much a sex-substitute: "you pursue your beatitude; I'll pursue mine."

x

The Diggers: I wish I knew more about them (including the history of their name and their hats—a sect in England—deported as convicts to Australia—the altruistic mission of the sect survives all those vicissitudes and reappears in the Hippie movement.)

The Diggers show us all the admiral<admirable?> aspects of this Revolt of Youth; what it could have been, if it had not become devitalized and "fuzzied out" by pot.

x

The sad thing about youth is that it doesn't know anything.

The admirable thing about youth is that it truly desires to live correctly and to use sincerity—not convention—as the criticism of the "correct."

After the First World War German youth broke away from the German home,—and what a "home" it was: "if Paul-Jurgen and Grete do their homework every night of the week they can go for a walk in the hills with Papa and Mama on Sunday!"

To the consternation of all decent-minded people, the youth left the house and wandered over the world. Literary influences, also: they sang mediaeval latin songs to the zither; a certain amount of shocking free-love also, but a strong askesis: they repudiated beer as identified with the "fat" generation that had lost the war. They were emancipated—free, vocal, happy in "nature" and intensely hopeful. The Wandervogel movement.

And Hitler seized all that promise and adopted it to his own purposes—just as "drugs" have betrayed this movement. Because the young don't know anything.

Everybody blames the American home, but that's only part of the injustice to the young.

There's the school. The American School (and the German before it) have failed to render knowledge and the exercise of the mind attractive.

There's a terrible line in an old play by Thomas Corneille—brother of the great Corneille: Combien de virtus vous me faîtes haïr[130]

The American home can't help the young becomes<because> the parents, too, went to the American school.

Children love to learn. But they're fed "canned facts". The schools, outside the cities, look more and more like country clubs—which is all right—but English and History and Math still resemble punishments.

A revolt (and an understandable revolt) has been led into the wilderness by drugs.

But—as you say—it's discovering its own dead-end and bankruptcy.

But the movement goes on. And new young people are reaching 17 every day and will repudiate this generation.

130 The line, which reads, "O ciel, que de vertus vous me faites haïr," is from *La Mort de Pompée* (1644) by Pierre Corneille, not his less-famous brother.

I'm eager to see what's coming.

Damn it, I didn't mean to run on like this.
But, Lord!—I've battered your poor ear off before.
Again thanks for your fine address.
My regards to Gnädige Frau.

Your old friend
Thornt.

307. TO JAMES LEO HERLIHY.[131] ALS 2 pp. (Stationery embossed Norddeutscher Lloyd Bremen an Bord <TNW added "BREMEN" to the printed letterhead>) Academy of Motion Picture Arts and Sciences

<appeared above the letterhead>
until after Christmas at, or near, American Express Co. 11 rue Scribe, Paris.

Middle of the Atlantic
November 10 <1967>

Dear Mr. Herlihy:

Your letter gave me much pleasure

Forgive my being so long in answering. I was living all alone on Martha's Vineyard. SUMMER people gone, most of the eating places and bars closed—just us natives and the seagulls.

I was enjoying a breakdown—not a nervous breakdown, or a mental one—just a breakdown of the will. Nothing tragic, nothing even pathetic—merely dreary and unmanly—very Russian,—but deeper than mere laziness and sloth.

---

131 American novelist and dramatist (1927–1993) Herlihy was the author of the novels *All Fall Down* (1960) and *Midnight Cowboy* (1965), both of which were adapted into films, and the play *Blue Denim* (1958), which was also made into a film.

So much for apology. I've shaken off the condition on shipboard.

I knew your name—and with lively esteem—but I couldn't recall where I knew it. When suddenly I found in the local stationery shop a copy of ALL FALL DOWN. I'd never read it, but I remembered the movie well—not only for three striking performances[132] but for an overall searching honesty in all that suffering and a rich illustration of the world in which those persons lived. I'd made a mental note to get hold of the book, but other things intervened.

Well, I read it and the pleasure I got from it multiplied the pleasure your letter gave me.

Yes, you and I are Middle Westerners.[133] (I left my birthplace Madison Wisc. at the age of nine, but returned for two years at Oberlin—and then for six years teaching in Chicago.) But more than that we have a feeling about the Middle West's non-prosperous middle class that is not often found. We don't hate or mock it or sentimentalize it (Booth Tarkington) or condescend to it (Sinclair Lewis). It is, as it were, <">romantic" for us: we rejoice in the whole gamut from farce to tragedy. (For my part, I'm including not only The Eighth Day but the "road" and the Kansas City of Heavens My Destination.) Gertrude Stein has a very fine passage about how every writer should have the country he lives in and knows and the country he—in no trivial sense—romant<ic>izes. For the Elizabethans she said it was Italy; she lived in Paris but she "dreamed" about America. This is true about strata of society, too. My first book The Cabala was about a very rich milieu in Rome that I knew nothing about. My New Hampshire village in Our Town is pure imagination: I tutored in summer camps and I was a guest at the MacDowell Colony. I seldom entered "homes." I took late strolls and looked through windows. I lingered in stores and post offices. I looked and listened. I don't know whether your Cleveland comes from a saturation of actual experience: for me it has the solidity and fascination of a partially imaginative reconstruction. Have

---

132 Among the stars of the 1962 film of *All Fall Down* were Eva Marie Saint, Angela Lansbury, Warren Beatty, Karl Malden, and Brandon de Wilde.

133 Herlihy was born in Detroit.

you ever noticed that Farrell's Chicago[134]—for all its millions of words (and his undoubted gifts)—has no real "psychic color" of the place?

But oh! that Seminary Street, and that Florida!

And Clinton's suicide letter![135] And lots and lots of pages.

Belatedly
but with
plenty of
sincere thanks and regards
Thornton Wilder

I wish you could see your way to the theatre again,[136] but the trouble with the theatre (now days) is that you've got not only to tell your story, but you've got to devise some novel element in the manner of telling it,—to innovate in form, damn it.

308. TO SCHUYLER CHAPIN.[137] ALS 2 pp. (Stationery embossed Hotel Continental / 3, Rue de Castiglione / Paris) Yale

American Express Co. 11 rue Scribe Paris
Nov 29 • 1967

Dear Mr. Chapin:

Many thanks for your letter. I follow closely the work at the Vivian Beaumont Theater and am delighted that it has gained its stride and is doing fine things. All continued success to it.

---

134 James T. Farrell (1904–1979) was best-known for his three books about Studs Lonigan, a native, like Farrell, of Chicago.

135 TNW is referring to locations and a character in *All Fall Down*.

136 Herlihy wrote several plays prior to and after *Blue Denim*.

137 At this time, Chapin was in charge of programs at New York's Lincoln Center for the Performing Arts, which includes the Vivian Beaumont Theater. He had expressed an interest in producing *Our Town* there.

The thing that prevents my wishing to see my play in the Lincoln Center might seem to many a small idiosyncratic difficulty, but to me it's important.

That 30-year-old play has been done over and over again in school auditoriums, Sunday School halls, gymnasiums and theaters-in-the-round. I have seldom heard of its being performed in the theater for which it was intended: the conventional box-set stage with the brick wall at the back, the heating-system pipes, etc. I have always felt certain that a large part of the effectiveness of the original production came from the emergence of Grovers Corners—not from an abstract "non-place", but from that homely even ugly "rehearsal stage". (The same is true of "Seven<Six> Characters in Search of an Author.")[138] The audience's imagination has to fight doubly hard to overcome and transcend those concrete facts.

I was confirmed in this conviction when I read the reviews (and received letters from friends and strangers) of William Ball's revival last year in San Francisco.[139] They were surprised that the play had such meat in it; they had seen it often (usually with relatives in the cast) and remembered it as pretty and pathetic and easily forgetable.

So when I—at the age of 70—was approached on the matter of a "serious" anniversary revival, I was filled with the hope that we could have either of the two theaters of the first run: the Henry Miller or the Morosco,—or certainly one like them. There's poetry in Our Town—those crickets, the toot of the train's whistle approaching Contookuk; but its not the same kind of poetry as in the dramas of the Elizabethan age and the Spanish Golden Age—which rejoices in an abstract scenery-less setting. My "poetry" rises from little homely objects; it must win its poetry from steampipes and back stage ladders.

[This is odd coming from me, who later went all out for the arena stage.]

---

138 TNW is referring to Luigi Pirandello's 1921 play.

139 American stage director Ball (1931–1991) had founded the American Conservatory Theatre in Pittsburgh in 1965, then moved it to San Francisco in 1967.

Bill Schuman[140] has also written me a friendly letter. I've told him that I've written you. Would you kindly let him see these paragraphs?

And all best wishes to the work you are doing.

Sincerely yours
Thornton Wilder

P.S. And Morton Gottlieb[141] who, I think, didn't get the point when I tried to explain it earlier.

TNW.

309. TO CASS CANFIELD. ALS 2 pp. (Stationery embossed Hotel / Colombia Excelsior / 16126 – Genova Italia) Yale

Friday March 1. 1968

Dear Cass:

Isabel's phone call yesterday at dawn and her cable received this morning leave me in some doubt as to whether ("addressed to your home before Saturday noon") you wish a mere statement of my acceptance of the prize or an extended portion of a 500-word speech of acceptance. I have sent you the cable of acceptance and I now send you a few notes to add to a short acknowledgement of my gratification—to be delivered, I believe, on March 5.[142]

Isabel said that you already had some fragments of a letter that I wrote you which you intended to draw upon.

x

Here are some additional jottings which you may or may not wish to incorporate.

x

---

140 Composer William Schuman (1910–1992) was president of Lincoln Center at this time.

141 Producer Morton Gottlieb (1921–) was involved with many plays at Lincoln Center.

142 TNW was awarded the National Book Award in Fiction for *The Eighth Day,* but he did not attend the ceremony.

The principal idea that is expressed in the novel (and in its title) has been present in Western thought for some time—that Man is not a final and arrested creation, but is evolving toward higher mental and spiritual faculties. The latest and boldest affirmation of this idea is to be found in the work of Père Teilhard de Chardin—to whom I am much indebted.

x

It has given me pleasure to be both commended and reproved for writing an "old-fashioned novel." There is the convention of the omniscient narrator, reading his character's thoughts and overhearing their most intimate conversations. I have been more reprehended than commended for introducing many short reflections or even "essays" into the story. That is old fashioned also, stemming from Henry Fielding. I did this even in my plays: there are little disquisitions on love and death and money in "Our Town" and "The Matchmaker." I seem to be becoming worse with the years: the works of very young writers and very old writers tend to abound in these moralizing digressions.

It has somewhat surprised me that few readers have found enjoyment—or even noticed—the allusions, "symbols," musical them<e>s that are a part of the structural organization. These cross-references are not there to tease or puzzle; they are not far-fetched or over-subtle. It is hoped that they reward and furnish both amusement and insight in a second reading of the book. It is a device particularly resorted to by writers in their later decades.

x

So, Cass—if there's anything here that can save you time and trouble—use it—or just throw it away.

x

Again my thanks to the committee...deep appreciation, etc....

The hermit of Arizona will be home soon—but even more hermit-like than before.

A world of regard to you, dear Cass—and to Beulah who may have to decypher these words

Ever

Thornton

310. TO TIMOTHY FINDLEY.[143] ALS 2 pp. (Stationery embossed 50 Deepwood Drive / Hamden, Connecticut 06517) National Archives of Canada

April 20 • 1968

Dear Timothy:

Many congratulations. Thanks for your letter with the good news. Yes, indeed, Viking is <a> very fine publishing house.[144]

I'm glad you're turning to write for the stage. I'm sure you're endowed for it as well as experienced in it. Beware, however, of regarding yourself theatrically. You and your sense of guilt about Dr. King's assassination! In a very general sense everyone is daily responsible for some measure of injustice and ill will in the world—but you taking that crime on your shoulders—it's like putting on a penitent's garb in amateur theatricals and admiring oneself as a "Great Sinner." You rightly describe yourself as seeking "quiet"—well, don't endanger your own quiet by introducing imagined troubles like that.

For this play:

Select your subject carefully. One very real and close to you—not autobiographically but inwardly. Take long walks—view it from all sides—test its strength—its suitability for the stage. Then start blocking out the main crises or stresses. I suggest (though all writers are different) that you don't begin at the beginning but at some scene within the play that has already begun to "express itself in dialogue." Don't hurry. Don't do too much a day. In my experience I've found that when I do a faithful unforced job of writing every day that the material for the next day's writing moves into shape while I'm sleeping. Never hesitate

---

143 TNW met Canadian novelist, dramatist, and actor Timothy Findley (1930–2002) in 1954, when the latter played Rudolph in the Edinburgh Festival production of *The Matchmaker.* Through TNW, Findley also met Ruth Gordon, who, with TNW, encouraged Findley to consider a career as a writer. Findley enjoyed great success, eventually publishing eleven novels, three collections of short stories, six plays, and three books of memoirs.

144 Findley's second novel, *The Butterfly Plague,* was published in 1969 by Viking.

to throw away a whole week's good hard-won writing, if a better idea presents itself.

All cordial best wishes to you

your old friend
"T. N."

311. TO CATHERINE COFFIN. ALS 2 pp. (Stationery embossed 50 Deepwood Drive / Hamden, Connecticut 06517) Yale

April 22, <1968> some say

Dear Catherine:

This is one of the most heart-felt thank-you letters I ever wrote. I'm thanking you for pure intention. What could be more courtly?

Like some great lady of the Renaissance—a Borgia, a Medici, pupils of il grande Macchiavelli you extracted from me that I already owned the magistral recording by Fischer-Diskau<Dieskau> of Der Lied von der Erde.

A gift, an intention, à la hauteur[145] of yourself and—I hope—of me. So:

I thank you with the weight and expansiveness of my 72nd year.

x

Now I have a confession to make to you. When we saw you Thursday night I was all steamed up to tell you about my newly-acquired interest and concern about Professor Herbert Marcuse. It may be that you know more about him than I do. Besides, Thursday night I hadn't my ideas fully organized and I was afraid that I'd make a foolish exposition of them.

My hotel in Genoa was on the same street as the main building of the University. Constant protest agitation. I passed it the day that the

145 French: at the height.

students sat—hundreds strong—in the mighty portals and on the vast staircases to prevent the Rector and his council from entering his office. I assume they were at the "back doors,<"> too.) Among their banners and placards were

MARX MAO MARCUSE

and so the names were linked in Rome and Berlin. And Prof Marcuse was calmly giving Socratic interviews to pilgrims from all over the world in his office as Professor at the University of California in San Diego.

The first wide-spread revolt that has not been able to engage the cooperation or even sympathy of the laboring classes and the proletariat. He explains that.

In all ages a ruling hierarchy has exploited the slaves, the enfieffés<?>,[146] the industrial worker...and revolts have been about economic justice—ie money.

But now Capitalism has reached a new type of reducing men to servitude. The Technological Establishment makes sheep of men by making them "one-dimentional men": by publicity means it tells them what they want and gives them what they have been taught to want. The industrial workers and the bourgeosie like their new condition. They're seduced. <appeared perpendicularly in left margin beside previous three paragraphs> N.B. Marcuse is a Marxian but believes that Kremlin-Communism is doing exactly what Capitalism is.

The press (hence the students' hatred in Germany of the magazine-lord Springer[147]) feed them irrelevant pap; the universities form technological robots and irrelevant "culture"; the governments "absorb" and trim the claws of socialist parties—

All is soothing de-individualizing—

Marcuse showed the young what to revolt against; and how to go about it—

Massive resistance—with or without violence.

What he proposes (now their aim) is a dictatorship (yes) of the

---

146 TNW probably meant *en fieffé,* French, describing those who wandered and had no home.

147 German journalist and publisher Axel Springer (1912–1985), whose German tabloid *Bild* was attacked for its conservative viewpoint.

intellectuals who see through the technological strategy: a dictatorship which once having produced the New Man will be superceded, will disappear into thin air.

So utopian dream fantasies—again.

In the meantime we have this really "massive resistance" against the technological stupifying of man.

Love—every day of the year
Thorntie

312. TO WILLIAM A. SWANBERG.[148] ALS 2 pp. (Stationery embossed 50 Deepwood Drive / Hamden, Connecticut 06517) Columbia

July 25. 1968

Dear Mr. Swanberg:

Please forgive this delay of my reply to your letter of July 10. I have recently returned from the hospital after a serious operation.[149] I shall be out of circulation for some time.

Yes, I knew Harry Luce over many years. He was, for the most part, a shy and guarded man. I think it was the fact of our long association that made him particularly so with me. After college days I saw him seldom—always in large groups—once when he came to speak at the University of Chicago;—at the reunions of the Class of '20—I dined with the Luces twice in the Waldorf Towers. About 10 years ago Harry invited me to a meeting at the Chinese Inst<it>ute (if I remember the name of the institute correctly) to honor the recently dead Dr. Hu Shih.[150] He gave me no intimation that I was to be called on to speak. I went to this meeting in New York merely to express my regard for Harry. (I have never been sympathetic to the non-recognition of

148 American biographer Swanberg (1907–1992) was researching his biography of Henry R. Luce at this time (*Luce and His Empire* [1972]).

149 TNW had a hernia operation on July 2.

150 Chinese diplomat and scholar (1891–1962).

the People's Republic of China.) To my surprise I discovered that I had been assigned the rôle of concluding speaker on the program. I heard Harry introduce me as an old friend of Dr. Huh Shih. I spoke—to the best of my knowledge—of Dr. Huh Shih's work as a scholar and reformer of the Chinese language. I did not tell the audience (nor Harry until the close of the meeting) that I had never met Dr. Huh Shih.

I liked and admired much in Harry. I believe (with Charles Lamb) that "one should keep one's friendships in repair"; but that takes two.

I shall be here a number of weeks under house arrest. If you wish to mail me the photo from the China Inland Boys' School I shall endeavor to identify Harry; but I am still too tired to receive any callers except relatives and old friends.

All best wishes toward your task.

Sincerely yours
Thornton Wilder

313. TO E. MARTIN BROWNE.[151] ALS 2 pp. (Stationery embossed 50 Deepwood Drive / Hamden, Connecticut 06517) Harvard

July 30 • 1968

Dear Friends:

Absolutely delighted. Couldn't be in better hands.

Oh, how I hope it finds friends among you all.

There's usually an air of suppressed excitement about rehearsals—because its a large cast with so many "distinct" parts in it; and because the actor begins to feel an additional responsibility on him <u>because there is no scenery</u>.

If I'm not mistaken Martin—the kindest of men—will discover

151 English stage director and producer Browne (1900–1980) was putting on a production of *Our Town* at this time.

that he has to be as "mean" and tyrannical as a lion-tamer or as a Toscanini. Actors—by selection and training—are highly suggestible; they will try to impose the mood (not the content) of the last act on the first two. They will "grave-yard" the whole play. (Oh, the productions I've seen; this applies to The Long Christmas Dinner, too.) For two acts nobody has the faintest notion that they will die or even that time is passing (except the Stage Manager and he only indicates that he is aware of it by an increasing dryness of tone); and even in the third act the mood is not elegiac: it mounts to a praise of life that is not impassioned regret but insight—and affirmative insight. The poignance is not on the stage but in the hearts of the onlookers.

I love those moments when the actors are real loud—milkman with his horse; Emily and her school friends. We found that the biggest laughs in the play (and legitimate laughs) are when George decends to breakfast.

"Four more hours to live"—noise, real loud, of cutting his throat.

Breakfast with Mr. Webb. Long embarrassed pauses and glances while stirring their coffee, then MR WEBB—real loud!—"Well, George, how are you?" George almost loses his mouthful.

God grant you can find an actress who can say Emily's farewell to the world not as "wild regret" but as love and discovery.

[Did you recognize that that speech is stolen from the Odyssey—Achilles in the underworld remembers "sleeping<?> and wine and fresh raiment"!!]

N.B. It was GBS who said "Every child born into the world...etc"

I'll be interested to know if an English audience finds Emily's self-satisfactions (about being "wonderful" in her class studies) unappealing.

NB One Mrs Webb in ten is able to remain apparently unresponsive to Emily's appeal to her in Act III

I love dear Henzie[152] as Mrs Soames—real loud, her voice cutting across the wedding—the village gossip, etc. Fun.

152 Actress Henzie Raeburn (1896–1973), Browne's wife.

I'll send a cable

lots of love to you both

Thorny—

P.S. Had an operation July 2—hernia—am still under house-arrest—progressing fine—Isabel taking wonderful care of me. She sends her love, too.

TNW.

314. TO RICHARD GOLDSTONE. ALS 3 pp. (Stationery embossed 50 Deepwood Drive / Hamden, Connecticut 06517) NYU

Nov. 19, 1968

Dear Richard:

This is going to be an unpleasing letter for you to read
So sit down and reach for a cigarette.

x

I've been telling you for years that I'm not the kind of author that you understand—that you should treat. I'm not tearful, I'm not self-pitying, I don't view myself tragically, I don't spend any time complaining or even looking backward. I'm energetic, full of projects for the future, engrossed in other people's writing (Lope de Vega, Joyce), engrossed in what happens about me.

x

In July a week after my operation you wrote me a letter that contained some phrases that were so absurd, so obtuse, so lacrimose wrong-headed that I burst out laughing and then got mad. Damn it, you wrote:

"and each year I understand you better. I understand that your life has been difficult, filled with profound disappointments, with strivings and struggles, that the rewards have not been many."

Where the hell do you get that?

You get that out of your own damp self-dramatizing nature.

God damn it, I've lived a long life with very little ill health or pain [in the same letter you talk of the "great pain and discomfort.... all the agony" of my operation. Go fly a kite—it was amazingly free of discomfort; it was bracing; I wouldn't have missed it... you derive some dreary relish in draping other people with fake misery]. Struggles? Disappointments? Just out of college I got a good job at Lawrenceville and enjoyed it. I made a resounding success with my second book. The years at Chicago were among the happiest in my life. I got a Pulitzer Prize with my first play.[153] What friendships—Bob Hutchins, Sibyl Colefax (400 letters) Gertrude Stein, Ruth Gordon (hundreds of joyous letters, right up to this week).

What's the matter with you?

x

Of course my work is foreign to you.

You can't see or feel the play of irony.

You have no faculty for digesting serious matters when treated with that wide range that humor confers.

For you the woeful is "mature"—you chose the Pariah as a thesis-subject[154]—the solemn-humorless alone is "grand."

Go pick on Dreiser or Faulkner. Leave me alone. Write about Arthur Miller.

x

Also you've never understood—though I've warned you—that I am not interested in my past work. I refused to coöperate with those authors who put out books about it—poor Isabel had to bear the burden.

I can't help feeling that you so far misunderstand me that you think I'm flattered when you run up palliatory extenuating phrases about The Trumpet Shall Sound or The Marriage of Zabett (I can't

153 *Our Town* (1938).

154 Goldstone's 1960 Ph.D. dissertation at Columbia University was titled "The Pariah in Modern American and British Literature: An Illustration of a Method for Teachers of Literature."

remember a word of it—not even "the yellow lakes").[155] I suspect that every self-respecting author loathes hearing his juvenilia mentioned. Stop it.

x

In Gertrude Stein's Portrait of me she says:

"He has no fears.

At most he has no tears.

For them most likely he is made of them."[156]

"For them" means for a large part of the reading public—and for you—The Bridge of San Luis Rey and Our Town are tender, tear-drenched, and consoling. But they aren't, they're hard and even grimly challenging, for "he has no fears." Stop wringing your hands over me and find your own congenial subject.

x

I'm leaving a copy of your letter of July 10th and this letter with my literary executor

x

I'm sorry I've had to write this letter, but at 71-plus I must speak to you with absolute firmness (you have a way of not grasping what I've said a number of times) and I must clear my decks.

Sincerely yours
Thornton

155 The phrase "the yellow lakes" occurs in the first sentence of TNW's short story "The Marriage of Zabett," which appeared in the June 1917 issue of the *Oberlin Literary Magazine.* TNW's play "The Trumpet Shall Sound" was published in the October 1919, November 1919, December 1919, and January 1920 issues of the *Yale Literary Magazine,* and was produced in a slightly revised version in 1926 by the American Laboratory Theatre.

156 From chapter 6, "The Portrait of Thornton Wilder," of Stein's *The Geographical History of America* (1936).

315. TO CATHARINE DIX WILDER. ALS 2 pp. (Stationery embossed 50 Deepwood Drive / Hamden, Connecticut 06517) Yale

Nov 19. 1968

Dear Dixie:

Loved your letter.

Rê Mexico.[157]

I never got much relish out of Mexico City. Maybe the altitude leaves you with a faint malaise (don't move fast, or touch alcohol the first 24 hours.) Mostly because the young ambitious republic tried to build its capital in imitation of Paris of the Exposition style.

But the Mexico of the villages and smaller towns is a warm glowing mysterious proud and gracious thing—largely derived from the survival of Indian blood in the people (they are descendants of great civilizations, too.) The Spanish civilization was a great one, but its descendants in the new world exhibit too much and in adulterated form the old world characteristics—vanity, pompousness, insecure and easily injured pride, obstinacy, "closed minds."

Try to see something of the villages, especially on their market days. Note the eyes of Indians—obsidian black, but so watchful (not primarily distrustfully, but humanly) and so quick to catch a courteous or friendly overture. You have a tendency to be "little princess" shy and stand-offish—oh, don't be so with the Mexicans or you'll come to hate Mexico—catch the eye of every waiter and waitress, of every sales-girl, and watch the result; abound in muchas gracias and buenos dias, buenos tardes.

Even American tourists—they're crazy to talk to other Americans. Give them the outgoing warmth, too. You may find some tedious sides of the hosiery manufacturers from St. Louis—but you're a beautiful young woman. Get to know them: you can brighten their voyage.

x

157 TNW's niece was planning a vacation trip to Mexico.

Mural painting is one of the greatest of all art-forms. It's dead in Europe and in Boston (Sargent and Abbey and Puvis de Chavannes—in the Library—dead.). But it came to life in Mexico (from the Indian blood—how to cover a wall—)<.> We now know the once-fashionable Rivera was merely a gaudy illustrator; but Siqueiros and especially Orozco are magnificent.

x

The great betrayal, the Tragedy of Montezuma—

x

The charm and felicity of the folk-arts,—taste. Taste always resumes centuries of high culture—that the Mexican Indians have.

x

Maybe you'll have time to read D. H. Lawrence's The Plumed Serpent—a lot of it is downright silly, Lawrence's Messianic complex—but the description of Mexico City at the beginning and of the village life on the lake later—is masterful.

x

There are hundreds of travel books, mostly ephemeral. A good travel book doesnt date: Flandreau's Viva Mexico[158] is still as telling as though it were written this morning.

x

A trip to a foreign country can also be a renewal of oneself. Go to Mexico as a new Dixie. Be audacious, daring, fun-loving, vulgar, "Mexican"—I send you my CHRISTMAS PRESENT in advance—have (create) the hell of a time. I sail for Europe next Monday (Isabel follows me soon to Paris and Switzerland) but wherever you are you are my treasured niece

sez with love

Old Uncle Thornton

---

158 *Viva Mexico! A Traveller's Account of Life in Mexico,* by American writer Charles Macomb Flandreau, was first published in 1908.

316. TO JAMES LEO HERLIHY. ALS 2 pp. (Stationery embossed Post Office Box 862 / Edgartown, Massachusetts 02539) Academy of Motion Picture Arts and Sciences

<appeared above the letterhead>
Last day at

(Martha's Vineyard.)
until after Labor Day.
But my sister will be here and
will be forwarding mail.
July 25 <1969>

Dear Herlihy
Selah!

Here's the dope you asked about:

I got fed up with academic and cultured society. (As I put it: "if one more person asks me what I think of T.S. Eliot, I'll shoot<">). May 1962.

I decided to go to the desert and be a hermit. From the map I picked out Patagonia, Arizona. (As children we didn't say "Go to Hell!" but "Go to Patagonia!"<)> I drove across the country for the sixth time—love the Road, the gas stations, the motels—the fried egg sandwich joints.

My car began to stagger and poop out as I came to a hill and a sign saying WELCOME TO ARIZONA. I just managed to get to the bottom of the hill: DOUGLAS, ARIZONA. 1 1/2 miles from the Mexican border. I stayed there 20 months. No phone. Made my own breakfast and lunch. Closed* the local bar (midnight in that State.). 5,000 people—3/4 of them Mexicans come over the border to put their children in our schools. A once pretentious hotel for T.B's and asthmatics and arthritics—on its last legs, breaking up. A few small ranchers. Local airport staff. Bar "help", restaurant "help." (There was a bit of "society" there; engineers at a smelting works, with a country club, etc. but I never went into their homes and was never asked.) There was a vague notion that I "wrote", but whether it was phony Westerns or

---

* I mean: I was there until closing—had to be cajoled out.

books for children no one gave a damn. Once a week I drove 60 miles to Tombstone for dinner or Nogales; once a month to Tucson or Phoenix. Some casual and agreeable friends—no attachments, no claims or demands either way. JUST WHAT I NEEDED. Took me three months to blow the cobwebs of self-conscious genteeldom out of my head. Then I started the novel (I thought it would be a short novella.) A record player—I worked under the clouds of Bach motets and Mozarts last string quintets—just about the tops of all music.

So after 20 months I left, reluctantly, but I knew that inevitably the blessing of change that it offered would in time cease to be change.

Ever since I keep hunting for another "Douglas." Nearest to it are SPAS out-of-season. (I've never stayed here so late before but the give-and-take of hospitality is beginning to overwhelm any idea of work: all pleasant people: Lillian Hellman, the Feiffers, Mia Farrow,—like that.<)> I return in Sept, Oct—nobody here but the chowder-makers, the sea gulls and me.... St. Moritz out-of-season—Saratoga Springs out of season.

No, I didn't say the couch was the writer's enemy but I quoted George Moore: the writer must resist the writer's temptation—the desire to go out and find someone to talk with. Desultory conversation—gassing—is the enemy.

We have a hippy population on this island. But ours are "well-to-do" ones. It costs $5.50 to get on and off the island by ferry. The Police cracked down on them last week and jailed a dozen or more (there had been an FBI informer among them for months); they put their finger on the pushers. We have also a stratum of drop-outs—girls "waiting" in the bars and restaurants—very nice some of them. And men who talk your ears off about how they're learning from LIFE,—"the school of hard knocks" (laughter.) The girls are fine—the men are awful. Insecurely boastful; great intellectual pretension and bone-ignorant. Here's "Wilder's Law"—a man between 18 and 25 who for several years has done nothing becomes a misery to himself and a bore to others. It is written into the human constitution that MALENESS means work: homo faber.[159] The British aristocracy is no ball of fire, but it

159 Latin: the working man.

would long ago have struck out but for the law of primogeniture—only the oldest son got any dough: his brothers had to go into Army, Navy, Church, Diplomacy, or "running the Estate."

Look about you.

Went to Boston for 3 days.

Saw Midnight Cowboy. Much to admire. Some splendid performances. Something's missing. I shall read the book to find out. (There were Long Lines at the Box-office)

Mia was delighted to receive that book from you and with its inscription.

She's a very interesting girl. In my opinion her career is in great danger if she plays any more of those hex'd girls.[160] Her directors don't seem to distinguish between girls conditioned to neurosis and mentally arrested. She's strong healthy and intelligent and she's being forced into the straight jacket of an "image" which the public will soon weary of.

At present she is overwhelmedly in love. In a few weeks she will marry Maestro Previn.[161]

I returned Monday from Boston to find this community like a cow that's been hit on the head with a mallet.

They'd had to go through their exaltation about the moonwalk and their learning of the squalid Edward Kennedy behavior on their own doorstep.

Tough.

JLH,—you're as crazy as a coot, if you think I could enjoy conversation with the knowledge that someone was "taking notes."

So start reshuffling what you take to be your image of me.

I suspect you of being deficient in a sense of humor.

We'd better not meet—I'd constantly distress you.

As it say<s> in you-know-what book when other people are bellyaching about the incommunicability* of human-to-human, about their

---

* Wilder's Law No 401: "You can always communicate with someone else, if you don't talk about yourself."

160 TNW is referring to Farrow's role in the 1968 movie *Rosemary's Baby.*

161 Farrow did not marry André Previn until October 1970.

"loneliness", about the bondage to a technological civilization I get more and more elated, euphoric, happy, frivolous, trivial; and when others are in ecstasy about their halucygenic visions and their love-of-all-mankind and their kinship with the universe I get more and more sombre and metaphysically depressed. I'm terrible.

Arrange the flowers, sure; pet the cat, sure; but also do a number of hours daily of relaxed but single-minded work.

Glad to hear from you.
Old
TNW.

317. TO MIA FARROW. ALS 2 pp. Yale

Last five days at Neues Posthotel, St Moritz,
Feb 2. 1970

Dear Mia:

Ruth has given me your address and suggested that I write you—and I always do what Ruthie suggests, especially if it's something that I want to do, too.

I hesitated a bit, but then I said to myself: January and February are the two most cheerless months in the year—especially in England and New England—sunless, heart-in-your-boots months—and a letter from a friend that loves you is a cheerful thing on your breakfast tray.

My thoughts often return to the radiant gifted FRIEND you're waiting for (gifted by Papa and gifted by Mama).[162] My niece is to have a baby in April. You know the Spanish idiom for having a baby—dar luz a: to give light.[163] So Spanish! I've seen you with your own niece and an unforgettable sight it was.

I try to imagine what your life's like while you're waiting. I follow

---

162 Farrow and Previn's twins, Matthew and Sascha, were born twenty-four days later.

163 TNW means the Spanish idiom *dar a luz*.

the London papers and saw Andre's concert there and read the news of his forthcoming American tour. I wish Ruthie had told me what your plans are. Well, mine are fairly set: go to Milan Friday—two weeks—then to Genoa (stay in nearby Rapallo a few weeks)—take ship to Curaçao (Central America)—go slowly up the Carribean (I spelled that wrong, I think)—visit my mother's sister, 88—in Florida—then to Martha's Vineyard, end of April, with only a few days in New York and at home. I've been working hard—some stuff that'll make you laugh, I hope. With the years I'm getting less gloomy.

My thoughts keep returning to the time when the Chichester Festival approached you about doing a play. Romeo and Juliet would be best, but London and New York have been—for the time—surfeited with that in both film and ballet. I still dream of The Wild Duck for you, but your idea of A Doll's House is fine. I've never seen a very young Nora—who has? It's about maturing: it's about deepening spiritual insights. She's made some frightening mistakes—but through ignorance, through love of her husband and children. Now she resolves to live correctly, truthfully,—but the person who is nearest and dearest to her doesn't understand this "new Nora", this moral urgency.

You're a born actress. I dream of you constantly returning to the theater. And that's best in London with all those companies with that continual variety of good parts and plays. Look at Irene Worth—two years ago a great success in Heartbreak House (Chichester and London); then with the National Theatre with Gielgud in Seneca's Oedipus; now there<?> with the Royal Shakespeare Company in Tiny Alice.[164] Well, she writes me that she's to play Hedda in Stratford-on-Avon, Canada (where years ago she did All's Well that ends Well and As You like it with Alec Guinness.) She's just written me asking for my "ideas" about Hedda. All my life I've had ever-changing ideas about Hedda, but I haven't any more. I don't like plays about clinical cases, especially destroyer-women. But I love Irene's clear pursuit of "good plays in good companies."

But that's not the important thing just now. Now I see you sitting before an open grate in Eaton Square, gazing into the live coals and

164 Worth had played Miss Alice when Albee's play premiered in New York in 1964.

dreaming. From time to time you put on the record of Albinoni's Adagio—but that's too sad. A Mozart—have you Klemperer's recording of Mozart's Serenade for Thirteen Wind Instruments? Maybe André has recorded it, in which case forgive me recommending another. At intervals you turn the pages of one of these "art books" that have reached such a perfection in our time. Your eyes fall on Giotto's The Virgin's meeting with St. Anne. Both are very pregnant and there is such a hushed solemn gravity in their faces, in their embrace, as takes your breath away. Don't take time to answer these rambling thoughts, dear Mia. I put an address on the back of the envelope that will reach me for the next four weeks, on the chance that there is some way in which I could be useful to me<you>.

LOVE to all three of you
your devoted
Uncle Thornton

318. TO JAMES LEO HERLIHY. ALS 2 pp. Academy of Motion Picture Arts and Sciences

Milan Feb 12 1970

Dear James-the-Lion:

I don't know whether you're still a Roman Catholic in good standing, but I'll tell you a story that will reawaken old pieties. Yesterday was Ash-Wednesday. The carnival season came to an end,—carne = meat; the season before Lent when you could eat meat.

But we in Milan can eat meat for three more days—the only place in the WHOLE DEVOUT WORLD where one can eat meat without sin. Because we are enjoying the Carnivale de Sant' Ambrogio. Centuries ago this city had been smitten by the plague; we died like flies. Finally as Lent approached the pestilence abated. And our good Archbishop—later our Patron Saint—St Ambrose passed a miracle. The survivors of that terrible time needed to eat meat to keep up their strength. So our wise and tender father and leader announced that fasting would be postponed for three days. So ever since the City goes wild with feasting and rioting and civic pride while the rest of the world goes into sackcloth and ashes.

I hope the tears are rolling down your cheeks like marbles.

Pass the wine and have a little more of this steak; it'll keep up your strength.

x

I'd go crazy, if I weren't pursuing some hobby—absorbing, totally occupying train of inquiry. At present it's Greek Vase-painting. I've lived 72 and $\frac{10}{12}$ years without giving it a thought. For something I'm writing I needed just a small bit of knowledge about it.[165] (Not what they call <u>research</u>: I don't do research—that's why I make so many bloomers<bloopers?>.) Just enough to make a bit of literary magic about it. Couldn't get any books up at St Moritz, so I came down here and picked up a few. Fun? yes and more than that—exaltation. Also, for what I'm reading I felt I should know something about the Tibetan <u>mandala</u>. Before that it was Levi-Straus and structuralism. I think I told you about that. Now for these hobbies I hook on to a subject and read what the authorities have to say and then I start and construct my own theories. Every hobby is also an exploration, a constructive question-answering journey of my own,—"creative", as they say in college classes. Within no time I'm saying that those authorities, those professors are blind, stupid, academic-obtuse. These glorious objects were painted at a time when Athens was at its pinnacle—the great architecture, and sculpture, the tragedies were being written, the lung-expanding comedies. And yet: Athens was in mortal danger—the Persians were advancing; the war with Sparta was ultimately inevitable.

It seems never to have occurred to the scholars to ask what is the relation between the scene pictured on one side of the pot and the scene picture<d> on the other, why Bacchus and his frantic women-followers on one side and Hector taking leave of Andromache on the other. God damn it... in times of mortal danger (which is also <u>any</u> time in life, if you're really alive) you must encompass both poles—life and death (Bacchus's vine-plants which renew themselves annually—the

165 TNW is probably referring to one of the semiautobiographical sketches he was writing during this period.

life-enhancing force—and the death of Hector, the great and good. That's where the mandala comes in, too. James-the-Lion, see to it than <that> in every novel you write (NOVEL: a window on Life—and on all life] you touch all bases: death and despair and also the ever-renewing life-force, sex, courage, food, the family. I think you've always done that anyway, but know that you're doing it. Touch all bases to make a home run.

x

I'm shy of writing you because you want to make me into a guru of some kind. More and more I see the havoc that's made in life by overvaluation. After overvaluation there's always a bitter disillusioned morning-after. Marriages are wrecked by it; father-and-son relationships are wrecked by it. It's popular name is idealization. It would be terrible if we didn't have it—it's present everywhere around us, but oh, if we could only guard ourselves against OVER-valuation, we save ourselves a lot of shipwreck.

x

This is the Beethoven anniversary year.[166] He's not my topmost music-maker but he sure was a wonderful man. Now that you're as rich as Croesus, give yourself a journey from the early Septet through the quartets and violin sonatas to those last quartets. (I've never been able to hook on very much to the piano sonatas.)

x

I'm soon starting home by the slowest ship on the sea.

I've been writing some stuff that'll maybe make you laugh. You don't hate laughing, do you? Remember true laughing requires a wide departure from the self and its self-preoccupation. But, after all, I don't know you and maybe you're a buoyant roaring boy.

If Tennessee's[167] still there, give him my deep deep regard. Forgive this long-delayed answer to your letter and be sure that I'm always glad to receive one from you—now it must be viâ Hamden. I just got a buoyant letter from Mia—she reports that she and André are sitting in London happily awaiting the baby that's kicking boisterously within

166 The bicentennial of Beethoven's birth.

167 Tennessee Williams.

her. She just rec'd the British Academy Award nomination for best actress.[168] ¶I hope all's going great with you and the work.

Your old friend
(T.N.)

319. TO AMOS TAPPAN AND ROBIN G. WILDER.[169] ALS 2 pp. Private

Last day in Miami Fla.

April 18 • 1970

Dear Robin and Tapper

The great-uncle is as impatient as you are for the entrance on the scene.

I know you're looking about for a baby-sitter. Well, as you know, I'm a stay-at-home. I don't mind yelling and screeching as long as I'm certain that baby hasn't swallowed a string of beads or something<.> I'll assume the child is merely practicing to be an opera singer.

So when you're invited out to dinner just bring the bassinet up to my study (with the bottle and a page of instructions—your phone-number and the phone-numbers of the half-dozen best pediatricians in town (headed by my old friend, Dr. Betsy Harrison<?> who can always soothe me, too)

My terms are very high but I offer these services gratis to great-nephews and double-gratis to great-nieces.

So lots of love to dear little Gloriana or sturdy little Augustus.

And thanks for the birthday greeting.

love
Uncle T.

---

168 Farrow was nominated for a British Academy of Film and Television Arts Award as Best Actress for her role in *John and Mary* (1969); she did not win.

169 TNW's nephew married Robin Gibbs on June 15, 1968; their first child, Amos Todd Wilder, was born on April 22, 1970.

Wilder family, Thanksgiving 1970, in Amherst, Massachusetts. Left to right: *Amos N. Wilder, Isabel Wilder, Robin Wilder (holding Amos T. Wilder), Amos Tappan Wilder, Catharine Dix Wilder, TNW, Arthur Hazard Dakin, Winthrop S. Dakin.*

320. TO GENE TUNNEY. TL (Copy)[170] 3 pp. (Heading 50 Deepwood Drive / Hamden, Connecticut 06517) Private

December 4, 1970

Dear Gene:

There are certain long-time deeply valued friends whom I find it strangely difficult to write letters to. One of them is Bob Hutchins (President of "my" freshman class in Oberlin, 1915; my boss when he

170 TNW met heavyweight boxing champion Tunney in Florida in December 1927 and spent time hiking with him in Europe in the summer of 1928, an excursion covered extensively by the press. This is a secretarial transcription of TNW's letter; the original has not been located.

was President of the University of Chicago). Another, Bob Shaw, now director of the Atlanta Symphony. Another is your so-much-admired self. I think the difficulty is that I have to write so many letters on the relatively superficial discursive level—, that I shrink from the danger of falling into mere chatter with these friends. I notice that those two "Bobs" seem to understand this "bloc" (and perhaps suffer from it, too), because when we do meet—so seldom—we behave as though no lapse of time had taken place at all.

Just the same, it is not right; I think of you and dear Polly often.[171] I think of you often with the most affectionate laughter—the fun we had at the training camp in The Adirondacks; or with delighted surprise, as when I was trotting beside you and you turned to me (after stepping on a caterpillar) and quoted solemnly:

> "The humblest beetle that we tread upon in corporal sufferance feels a pang as great as when a giant dies."[172]

(Scientists tell me that Shakespeare wasn't quite right about that.)

Or I think of you with quiet joy, as in that beautiful wedding in the Hotel de Russie at Rome; or with apprehension, as when you felt indisposed in Aix-les-Bains.

Recently I have heard that you have been suffering considerable pain. Day before yesterday I met Mary Jackson[173] in the train going to New York; she was on her way to see Polly. I sent my love and we talked of you both with much admiration and love.

No one lives to my time of life without experience of pain—of body and of spirit. My trials of body have not been as extensive or as racking as yours, but I have known them. Each person meets these demands in a different way. I am not a religious man in the conventional sense and cannot claim that consolation that is conveyed in the word "trial" ("God has sent me this ordeal as a test of my confidence in Him

---

171 Polly Lauder Tunney, Gene Tunney's wife.

172 The quotation is from act 3, scene 1, of Shakespeare's *Measure for Measure:* "And the poor beetle, that we tread upon, in corporal sufferance finds a pang as great / As when a giant dies."

173 Polly Tunney's goddaughter.

and in His ordering of the world"); nor am I willing to endure pain in that spirit that so many noble men and women have done—merely stoically. My strategy—if I may call it so—is to attempt to associate myself to persons I love and honor in the past or to multitudes unknown to fame and barely alluded to in history. At three in the morning carried through the streets with a bursting appendix I murmured "This is nothing to what Dr. Johnson endured when he was "cut for the stone" (gall stones); ever after he took to dating his life from that experience. In 1951 while teaching at Harvard I was "struck down," as they say, by a sacroiliac dislocation. I was barbarously tended at the Harvard Infirmary (where they thought it was some kind of laughable charley horse). I was finally transferred to Massachusetts General. From time to time I could "lose myself" in an attempt to join those who had suffered ten times what I was undergoing—political <illegible>, heretics, the victims of Nazis, the great and the good. Physical pain is the summit of aloneness, of solitude. I tried to catch glimpses of a companionship in Endurance.

Very certainly I shall have to face such hours again—I shall think of you; I shall "telegraph" you.

The doctors have just "sprung" me after months of treatment—deterioration of eyesight and hypertension—and next week Isabel and I are taking a slow, slow ship, the Christoforo Colombo, to Europe: New York, Dec. 10—Venice, Dec. 23. Soon after Isabel returns here to look after the house; I stay on somewhere over there to resume work after this long interruption.

In the meantime I send you affectionate wishes for improved well being, memories of many happy hours in your company and in Polly's and my hope that you can understand and forgive my foolish immature difficulty about writing letters.

Love to Polly.

Ever,
(Signed) THORNTON

Mailed Dec. 11

321. TO EILEEN AND ROLAND LE GRAND ALS 2 pp. (Stationery embossed 50 Deepwood Drive / Hamden, Connecticut 06517) Private

April 25 1971

Dear Roland; dear Eileen:

Many thanks for your letter.

Yes, we know Julian's news.

We have met Damaris and found her most attractive and likeable.

No doubt you were much surprised at their decision to be married in Philadelphia when they were also planning to go to England so soon after to see you there ("To see the relatives" he wrote us.)

It would be hard to make clear to you what a thorough revolution has taken place in the mentality of young people during these last years. You are certainly aware of it—it is world-wide—without however grasping the extent.

They wish to do things their own way. No fussing, no interference, not even counsel. There are very few families that have not been confronted by this "independence," often to a heart-breaking extent. The root of it seems to be a shrinking from any claims that may be made upon them—emotional claims, approval or disapproval. This isolation often makes them unhappy but they will it.

I have watched this increasing for more than ten years and have seen it in my own near-kin.

You may have noticed that in all the years that Julian has been here I have never called on him in his rooms in Philadelphia.[174] Nor—though a very concerned godfather—have I intruded with a word of advice (unless asked, and I was never asked on any matter of importance) until about two months ago, on the delayed appearance of a thesis.

What kind of wedding do they want? Do they really want us to be present? Julian has never mentioned any church affiliation. I think it very likely that they want what in England you know as a visit to the Registry Office.

---

174 TNW's godson was working on a Ph.D. in economics at the University of Pennsylvania.

I love Julian and am ready to love Damaris,—may they long be happy—AND I am prepared to let them make all the conditions in this matter. Are Damaris's parents planning to cross the sea? In Our Town the congregaters and especially the mothers weep copiously. Those days are completely over.

I have been "poorly" as they say in the American language—eye-doctors, ear-doctors—respiration-doctors. Now at 74 I don't bustle about easily. I would like to propose that I give the young people a dinner in New York on the eve of their flight to England and let them go to the Registry Office with their co-evals.

In the meantime I await clearer instructions as to what the young people want. Do share with us how you feel about all this.

love
Thornton

322. TO ENID BAGNOLD.[175] ALS 4 pp. (Stationery embossed Post Office Box 862 / Edgartown, Massachusetts 02539) Yale

It's June 29th, they say;
anyway its 1972
and I'm 75 years
old, so I'm just
in condition for a little
epistolary flirtation.

Dear Enid:

So you're posting memory tests!

Well, you flunked right off: I've never worn a bowler hat or "growler"[176] in my life.

175 English novelist and dramatist (1889–1981).

176 English word for a porkpie hat, derived from the Yorkshire term for pie made with pork.

What did you wear? You wore a sort of land-girls uniform, just short of farmer's trouser overalls, because you took me around and showed me the cows you'd milked, the cabbages you'd hoed, and you were adorable; and two weeks later, you were just as adorable, very ladified, when you had dinner with me at Boulestins (where Paula[177] used to meet her gentlemen friends before she married into the Tanquerays.)

But I have forgotten the third way to open a play.

In the intervening 30 years, I've changed my mind often.

For a time I loved opening in silence. Feed the audience's eye with the stage-setting, if you have one to offer. Then a bit of pantomime in silence, to capture their curiosity. (Hamlet: nothing.—then a sentry—go—Gruff exchanges. Then a bull's eye: "Tis bitter cold and I am sick at heart"). The greatest living dramatist-actor-regisseur, whom you've just been seeing in London<,> Eduardo di Filippo[178] has wonderful silent openings. But I've totally forgotten my third recommendation of 30 years ago. Did you notice that after calling my first the "Figaro" opening, you gave as my second "Sir, you have raped my daughter!"—which is precisely the opening of Don Giovanni. I have never doubted that Mozart had a large share in the libretti of his operas—pace Da Ponte who is now resting in the cemetery of Trinity Church in Wall Street, New York.[179]

You are quite right that Ruth Gordon played in a play of mine—just over a thousand showings and she never missed a performance![180]—but far from having quarrelled she is my dearest friend and she and Garson are have<having> dinner with me tonight,—I having dined with them four times in the last two weeks and having put down my foot about the ignominy of such one-way hospitality. I must take them

---

177 TNW is referring to the heroine of Arthur Wing Pinero's play *The Second Mrs. Tanqueray* (1893).

178 Italian actor, dramatist, screenwriter, and poet (1900–1984).

179 Italian librettist and poet Lorenzo Da Ponte (1749–1838), who wrote the librettos for *The Marriage of Figaro, Don Giovanni,* and *Così fan tutte,* is buried in Calvary Cemetery in Woodside, New York.

180 Gordon played Dolly Levi in *The Matchmaker* for ten weeks on the road, then for eight months in London, and then in New York from December 1955 to February 1957.

out to a public place—because Isabel has left me alone on this island to work and I am wallowing in bachelor squalor—sheer Heaven!—and writing like a fiend possessed.

Oh, I wish you were dining with us tonight: I cannot yet give you the menu, but here are some items on the conversational agenda:

① Simone de Beauvoir's *La Vieillesse*. (As Mrs Fiske[181] said of a rival actress's performance "She played all evening with her hand firmly on the wrong note."<)> She seems to have no organ for the perception of innerness...but then that's very French...apart from Pascal (who is apart from everyone) the only great French authors who had that gift were Montaigne and Proust—and both their mothers were Jewesses...Gertrude Stein told me that Picasso's mother said (another Jewess!): "The only time that I realize that I am the mother of a grown-up son is when I look in the mirror."

② Your dear self—an account of your first play produced I believe in Santa Barbara—with that redheaded girl (Fitzgerald?) about an understudy who did away with the star. I wasn't there but I read about it avidly.[182]

③ A stern injunction not to neglect HANDEL—the manly nobility of his pathos, the buoyancy of his fugues (the twelve *concerti grossi*: he had suffered a stroke a year and a half before composing them), the sunburst splendor of his choruses in praise of God (*Israel in Egypt*, *Theodora*, and passim.<)> Be not ungrateful of the gifts of Heaven.

④ Dear Katharine Cornell with whom I am invited to lunch next Saturday, fragile but with an increasing etherial beauty and spiritual radiance.

⑤ The weather. ⑥ The locust-crowds of tourists; etc, etc.

As this letter is not without its flirtatious aggression I must add (to make you jealous, I hope) that although I am 75 years old I received this week two letters, not without notes of *tendresse*, from two actresses: one very old, Miss Mia Farrow and one, very young, from Miss Irene Worth a-tiptoe for Corsica. Do you know Goethe's poem to himself at eighty:

---

181 Minnie Maddern Fiske.

182 Bagnold's first play was *Lottie Dundass* (1941). The production in Santa Barbara starred Geraldine Fitzgerald.

Du......

Munter Geist....

....

Du auch sollst lieben"[183]

There is no age limit to creativity, but there are two required conditions: EROS at your right hand, Praise of life at your left.

Much love to the lady of Rottingdean[184]
devotedly
Thornton

323. TO MIA FARROW. ALS 4 pp. (Stationery embossed Post Office Box 862 / Edgartown, Massachusetts 02539) Yale

Oct 4. 1972

Mia Mia Carissima:

Loved your letter.

Loved your photos.

Loved your postscript (from André).

There is no news here except heavenly weather <last two words circled, with an arrow to text in left margin> **Three days later: still one perfect day has been following another.** and hard work. The Kanins were twice off the island for some time; they returned last night and we shall see them tomorrow here—when Isabel will cook some good things for them.

Your brother John and his co-worker Alden and a very nice girl came to dinner with us at the BLACK Dog. We had a very pleasant time and I think they did; but I must confess with chagrin that although I taught (and had conferences) for twelve years with boys and young men and young women between the ages of 15 and 25 (Law-

---

183 TNW is referring to the last stanza of Goethe's "Phänomen" (1814), written when the poet was in his mid-sixties. However, TNW has misspelled certain words and misquoted the final line.

184 Bagnold lived in Rottingdean, near Brighton, Sussex.

renceville School, University of Chicago, and Harvard) I find it very hard to reach the center of young persons of this generation,—the center of their interest. The center of their curiosités—the word has a richer and more dignified sense in French than in English. Whatever those centers are they keep them locked up from us older persons. But I like them and wish them enormously well.

I'm delighted that you are "reading" passages from the Midsummer's Night's Dream with MENDELSSOHN'S music under Erich Leinsdorff<Leinsdorf>. I can well understand that you're nervous because it's an aspect of the actress's art that's gone out of fashion for half a century. It's that kind of "extending" yourself that's going to be very useful to you as your career developes. That kind of presentation used to be called the mélodrame. Some Sunday evening ask some friends in to hear you read Richard Strauss's setting of Tennyson's Enoch Arden for speaker and piano. André will enjoy it, for the piano part is positively luscious. Your problem will be to keep the audience from laughing (I suppose it's really for a male speaker) but it does have a real eloquence, however dated, like turning over the pages of old family albums.

Do you know the Quaker use of the word "concern"? "I have a real concern for thee," they say. It means a sympathetic participation at a deep level,—not pathos, not anxiety, not mere wish "for every happiness" but a sharing in friendship of the recognition that basic existence is hard for everyone and can be sustained in Quaker quiet and reverence and innerness. My concern for thee comes from my knowledge that you carry so many concerns for others, and so well and so bravely.

Please have a concern for me. As my book[185]—I have been working very hard—approaches it's end more and more earnest notes about suffering in life insist on coming to the surface—and I want to "get them right" and then the book will end in a blaze of fun and glamor and happy marriages (at the annual "Servants' Ball" at Newport!); and you know what author I am trying to emulate.

What a lovely coronet of flowers you wear in the "wedding pic-

185 TNW was completing his novel *Theophilus North* (1973) at this time.

ture"—with a dress of a lighter color that's just what you should wear while reading A Midsummer Night's Dream—a mixture of Titania, without a royal crown, and of the dancers on the green when England was "Merrie England"—Perdita in A Winter's Tale. Lovely.

What a sad thing for us that we can't stay here into November and have some more happy hours at "your place" and at "our place." But Isabel's been under some strict regimen and has to see her doctor, and I have to interrupt my surprisingly happy "working vein" and attend to postponed matters in New Haven and New York.

We have changed our plans. We are not going abroad until early January. We have "escaped" too often the "family reunions" of Thanksgiving and Christmas—I far oftener than Isabel. My brother has just turned 77 (and is in buoyant health) and my great-nephew is two months younger than your boys—so we have a wide range at those celebrations! We sail on "our old friend" the "Cristoforo Columbo" and disembark at Genoa—maybe a few weeks at Rapallo and then back to our favorite hotel in Zürich—moderately good opera and often very good theater—rooms over the lake—an unexciting but congenial city. Isabel will return to Hamden (having missed the worst of the New Haven-Hamden man-high snowdrifts, breakdown of public services and facilities: because of the "miracles" of technology, winter in a medium-size city is getting to be worse than winter on a remote North Dakota farm.<)>

I wish I could sit beside you at André's concerts. (When Larry came over for the first time I used to sit beside Vivien at each "first performance"—Oedipus, The Critic, Henry IV Parts I and II—on his second trip she was playing with him, the two Cleopatras and The School for Scandal)<.>[186] And—there's no law against dreaming—I'd order the programs: Bach's seconde suite; Bruckner's V, VI or VII, Berlioz Romeo (again), Mozart G-minor, any Rossini Overture, Vaughn-Williams Pastorale, and Haydn, Sinfonia Concertante; Oh, yes, and I'd order André to direct a Mozart concerto from the piano and improvise

186 In May and June 1946, Laurence Olivier performed in New York with the Old Vic Company in the plays mentioned above. From December 1951 to April 1952, Olivier and Leigh appeared in repertory in Shaw's *Caesar and Cleopatra* and Shakespeare's *Antony and Cleopatra* but not in *The School for Scandal*.

the cadenzas on the spot. Did you ever imagine I could be so presumptuous?

My love to Matthew and Sascha. My love to Alicia. My love to Tina.[187] My love to the Maestro.

My love to the dear Lady who joins us all like the diamond on a necklace of the choicest emeralds.

In which Isabel also cries AMEN.

Thornt'

324. TO RUTH GORDON AND GARSON KANIN. ALS 2 pp. (Stationery embossed 50 Deepwood Drive / Hamden, Connecticut 06517) Private

April 20 1973

Dear Kind Kanins:

I've held this enclosure for weeks. Où est ma tête..?[188]

x

So I finished the plaguéd book. I'm accustomed to turn my back on a piece of work once it's finished—but it's something new for me to feel empty-handed and deflated,—to wake up each morning without that sense of the task waiting for me on my desk. Daily writing is a habit—and a crutch and a support; and for the first time I feel cast adrift and roofless without it. I hate this and am going to get back into a harness as soon as I can.

x

Received a composite letter from Mia/Irene Worth written from Mia's dressing room at the Three Sisters<.>[189] Irene's full <of> appre-

---

187 Alicia is André Previn's daughter by his first wife. Tina may refer either to Farrow's sister Tisa or to Frank Sinatra's daughter Christina "Tina," who was Farrow's former stepdaughter.

188 French: Where is my head?

189 Farrow had been appearing as Irina in Chekhov's play at London's Greenwich Theatre.

ciation of the simplicity and skill of Mia's playing of Irina—Irene is now in rehearsal at Chichester in<as> Madame Arkadina.

The papers announce that Mia is to film The Great Gatsby at Newport.[190] I wonder which place they have selected for setting.

x

I'm jolly well, thanks to Garson's tirelessly acquired wisdom and his firmness with me. I take all my medecines.

April 29.

Another time-lapse.

This house is in constant muddle. The book was finished but portions come and go to agents, typists, proofreader (la Talma) all in a muddle of missing pages, crossed letters, incorrect pagination, etc.

But I don't let this bother me much.

I was suddenly stung with an idea for a play and can't wait to get to the island and get back in harness. I must find a chauffeur—either a divinity school student who's glad of the job or O'Neil,[191] if he can get away from the Royalton Hotel (he could only do that on a weekend when maybe it would be impossible—I hear—to get a ferry boat reservation.)

Went to NY for 3 days (lunch at the Players[192] with Cass Canfield, Beulah Hagen and Isabel—in that private dining room—perfect); dinner at Laurent's with Carol Brandt and her husband[193]—delightful time, but ouch!). Forgive me but I saw A Little Night Music[194] without Hermione Gingold; I constantly forget that I am no audience for musicals. Was very depressed by the air-pollution; but have now recovered. Forgive the delay of this letter and accept

a load of love
Thorny

---

190 Farrow starred as Daisy Buchanan in the 1974 film *The Great Gatsby.*

191 American actor and director F. J. O'Neil, whom TNW met in 1950–1951 at Harvard University while O'Neil was an undergraduate there and TNW was giving the Norton Lectures.

192 The Players Club, on Gramercy Park in New York City.

193 In 1962, TNW had chosen Brandt & Brandt as the agency that would represent his nondramatic works. Carol Brandt's husband was Edmund "Pavvy" Pavenstedt.

194 The musical *A Little Night Music* ran in New York from February 1973 to August 1974.

325. TO C. LESLIE GLENN. ALS 2 pp. (Stationery embossed 50 Deepwood Drive / Hamden, Connecticut 06517) Yale

June 24. 1973

Dear and Reverend Doctor:

So you became a Dr. at Stevens Poly[195]: Did you remember that I spent a week there as your guest—in your absence—taking walks and taking notes on the Hoboken that I would fantasticate in The Eighth Day almost half a century later?

x

I'm mortified and distressed and confused that there's a sort of conspiracy going on around here to collect old letters that I wrote.... I think that gives the impression that I'm behind it and am pretentious and self-infatuated... I wasn't supposed to know about it... Hell! It's enough to make a fellow incapable of ever writing a spontaneous word again.[196]

x

Dear Les,—I shall never speak, read, preach, orate, act, or sing from any podium, platform, or even hearth-rug again. It's at least 15 years since I've done it.

My revulsion from it was so sudden and so intense that it was like a prompting of The Inner Light, (or like Socrates's daemon which never told him what to do, but what not to do.) Please convey graciously—as only you can—to your committee at the Corcoran[197] my appreciation of the invitation and my regret that my disabilities—hypertension and deteriorating eyesight—prevent my accepting it.

x

---

195 Glenn was a graduate of Stevens Institute of Technology in Hoboken, New Jersey; TNW first met him when they both taught at Lawrenceville.

196 TNW is undoubtedly referring to Richard Goldstone, who, despite TNW's requests that he not do so, continued to approach TNW's friends, collecting personal materials for his unauthorized critical biography.

197 Glenn had conveyed to TNW an invitation to speak at the Corcoran Gallery of Art in Washington, D.C.

Here's a joke I heard. I told it to Isabel and she's still laughing: Suppose that Wanda Landowska married Howard Hughes, divorced him and then married Kissinger—wouldn't her name be

Wonder Who's Kissinger, now?

Love to you and to dear Neville[198] with felicitations on her birthday

And to you

Theophilus

P.S. I'm sending copies of this letter to the Archives of the International Geriatrics Society; the Lapaloosa Wilder Fan Club, Lapeloosa, Arkansas; and to the FB.I, who intercept all my sinister mail anyway.

TNW.

326. TO PEGGY AND ROY ANDERSON.[199] ALS 4 pp. (Stationery embossed 50 Deepwood Drive / Hamden, Connecticut 06517) Redwood

Oct 11. 1973

Dear Peggy—Dear Roy

Dear Roy   Dear Peggy

The postman is bringing you my new book.[200]

It will certainly seem a strange book to you,—all about Newport! A Newport in large part spun out of my own head. You will be surprised—and probably intrigued at my presumption. But it all takes place in 1926—almost half-a-century ago. It should be read as one of those historical novels—highly romantic and extravagant.

I hope you find some amusement in it, but I hope you find also an affectionate picture of the beauty of the place and then I hope you

---

198 Glenn's second wife.

199 American artist Peggy Anderson and her husband, Roy, a musician, became friends with TNW during one of his stays in Newport, Rhode Island.

200 *Theophilus North* was published in October 1973.

find—what the first reviewers, even the more favorable ones, seem to miss—a deep emotion behind most of the stories (its really a dozen novellas which finally "come together" and justify it's being called one novel<)>. Please do find yourselves sincerely moved from time to time.

You'll be relieved to know that there's not a single portrait drawn from life in the whole book—least of all the hero, who is part "saint" and part rascal, a combination that is fairly rare in fiction.

x

I haven't been well these last months—had a lumbago (slipped disc) from sheer fatigue after finishing the book and had two separate 9-day hospitalizations. Am better now, but limp about cautiously.

Had to cancel my trip abroad. I was slow convalescing because I'm so old.

x

I should have written you this letter before you received the book but my energy ran low.

I hope all is well with you and that you are rejoicing under the "glorious trees of Newport"

Ever affectionately
Thornton

and love to Kitty-Pooh

327. TO HELEN AND JACOB BLEIBTREU.[201] ALS 3 pp. (Stationery embossed 50 Deepwood Drive / Hamden, Connecticut 06517) Columbia

Nov 3 1973

Dear Jack; dear Helen:

Delighted to receive your letter, though very sorry to hear of the trouble you have both been having with your health. I too have just

201 TNW may have first met Helen and Jacob Bleibtreu during the summer of 1942, when he was stationed in Harrisburg, Pennsylvania, to receive military intelligence training.

graduated from the use of a "walker" (or "aluminum petticoat") having been in the hospital 21 days for a slipped disc—my convalescence has been slow because I'm 76—but I've been cheerful inside and I see you are, with your lively recall of the Harrisburg days.

Naturally I'm proud to inscribe the book to you. The reviews have been generally favorable—a few LEMONS to keep me humble, but the big city reviewers don't seem to get the point of the book (reviewers don't read for pleasure but for pay and that dulls the perception.) They think it a topical book, picturesque social history, etc.

The hero as a child dreamed of becoming a saint—well, he fell far short of it but the dream remained and could not die. The book is about the humane impulse to be useful, about compassion, and about non-demanding love.

I hope you find it occasionally funny, too, but a very serious intention lies under the surface and becomes more evident as the story developes.

I'm sure Helen will see that it contains a great deal of homage to women (to all except "Rip's wife<">!).[202]

May you both be restored to excellent well being soon.

Even in our all-too-short meetings, I felt I was privileged to know you

with much affection
Thornton

P.S. The book returns under separate cover.

TNW

---

202 A chapter in *Theophilus North* titled "Rip" features a character named Nicholas Vanwinkle ("Rip") and his wife.

328. TO MICHAEL KAHN.[203] ALS 4 pp. (Stationery embossed 50 Deepwood Drive / Hamden, Connecticut 06517) Yale

Nov. 8 • 1973

Dear Michael Kahn:

Greetings.

I do indeed remember your fine work on those plays and remain forever grateful to you.

I'm sorry about my delay in answering you, but it was necessary.

Several years ago I gave the rights to make a movie of The Skin of Our Teeth to Miss Mary Ellen Bute (Mrs. Nemeth) who made that delightful film fragment of Finnegans Wake.[204] In the agreement between us I promised to veto any showing of the play within 50 or 60 miles of N.Y. She has been held up by financing but is eagerly planning the film.

I had to send out tactful feelers as to whether I remember the "mileage" correctly etc. At last she has replied that she would look favorably on a production of the play at Stratford.

Many have told me that they thought Miss Shelley[205] to be the next authentic comedienne of this country: Ada Rehan → to Mrs Fiske—to Ina Claire—to Ruth Gordon. (Talullah was a wonderful being, but she never gave the same performance twice.) I'd only seen Miss Shelley in The Odd Couple but I spotted the real biz.

So all's clear and I pass you over to Bill Koppelman at Brandt and Brandt.

---

203 Kahn had directed an evening of three of TNW's one-act plays—*The Long Christmas Dinner, Queens of France,* and *The Happy Journey to Trenton and Camden*—at the Off-Broadway Cherry Lane Theatre in 1966. At the time this letter was written, Kahn was artistic director of the American Shakespeare Theatre in Stratford, Connecticut. Kahn had contacted TNW about mounting a production of *The Skin of Our Teeth,* but the play was never staged at Stratford.

204 American film animator Bute's live-action film *Passages from Finnegans Wake,* which she directed and cowrote, appeared in 1965. Her film of *The Skin of Our Teeth* was never completed.

205 Actress Carole Shelley made her New York stage debut as Gwendolyn Pigeon in Neil Simon's *The Odd Couple* (1965).

I haven't seen many SKIN<s> but the ones I've seen where it worked best were in Germany. They knew what is was about: survival, terror and hope. They played it for the story line. They didn't stop to fool with gimmicks—there are gimmicks enough in the play itself—They played them for real. Georgio Strehler in Milan, being an ardent communist, directed the Antrobus family as members of the hated bourgeoisie—idiotic, vapid poseurs. Others—over here—are so busy horsing around that the curtain-scenes are a mere shambles of noise and confusion and miss any dynamic force. (One ended the play with newsboys rushing down the aisles crying "Extra—the atom bomb has fallen"—catastrophe number four.<)>

It is my impression that the structure of the Stratford stage dissipates tension—everything becomes "spectacle." The end of Act One is all focus'd about one fireplace; the end of Act Two is all focus'd about one narrow pier leading out into the sea.

x

Menace hangs over the people in every act.

Sabina is only aware of it at intervals. She refuses to face facts—she thinks one should live for pleasure alone (for a short time she seduces Mr. Antrobus to her position.) Her pathos is when she sees that events are too big for her to grasp. Mrs Antrobus—absurd though she sometimes seems to be—is the pivot of the play. I've never seen an adequate Mrs A.—dear Helen Hayes didn't have the voice or the stance[206] . . . it's hard to make humorless women sympathetic, but she must be sympathetic because of her single-minded will to survive.

Play it for melodramatic passion, and let the jokes take care of themselves,—the flare-up between father-and-son in the last act will be felt as organic in the play.

I'll hope to see you during the spring and have a good talk.

In the meantime enjoy the project.

Ever cordially

Thornton Wilder

---

206 Hayes played Mrs. Antrobus in the 1955 revival of *The Skin of Our Teeth*.

329. TO CATHARINE DIX WILDER. ALS 2 pp. Yale

Box 826 Edgartown Mass 02539

Sunday June 30 1974

Dear Dixie:

The weather's been miserable down here and I keep hoping that its better up north by you.[207] I don't mind honest rain but we've been having two kinds of weather I don't like: dull shilly-shally drizzle and hot weighty humidity—oppressive to man and beast. Whenever Isabel's not around I tend to relapse into "bachelor squalor." (I'm not really as untidy as that, but comparatively.) Since, like you I'm still convalescent (*still*, from that slipped disk) <(>I tend to let certain niceties lapse.) As not a soul has been in this house since she left except the master a measure of laxity can be presumed. Isabel arranged for a "girl" to clean up from time <to time> but "occasional help" in an overcrowded pleasure resort is proverbially unreliable. I make most of my own meals (*huevos rancheros* and Irish stews—from cans<)>—but I go out to dinner every other night and invite guests. The actor Robert Shaw is here, star of JAWS which is being intermittently shot all over the island. Bob dedicated a play to me—"Cato Street" which was played in England with Vanessa Redgrave in the lead, but had a short run.[208] The other night I took his wife actress Mary Ure and the governess of her children came out to dinner with me and I plied them with Champagne and we were joined by the eminent and elderly cellist Otto von Copenhagen and I made up for a week's silence and solitude. The Garson Kanins have been in New York and I'm going out to dinner with them tonight, but on the whole silence and solitude agrees with me very well.

Your father sent me a picture postcard of "Wilder Hall" in Oberlin. It didn't exist when I was there and wasn't named after our family; but I have happy memories of Oberlin and feel very loyal to it. Your father's letters are a big lift to me. I'm happy he's so full of *élan*; I'm not;

---

207 TNW's niece was at her family's summer house in Blue Hill, Maine, recuperating from an operation.

208 Cato Street premiered at the Young Vic Theatre in November 1971.

in spite of the account above I'm more and more of a stick-in-the-mud. I take a nap after breakfast and a nap after lunch and three naps between sundown and dawn. But I'm cheerful inside. Like you I'm convalescent. I think my vitality will return to me if I coöperate with it. Please you do too; let Nature take its own time in healing.

Give my love to everybody at Blue Hill. Be my advocate and urge them to forgive me for being such a bad letterwriter. Please be your own best friend and take it easy, very easy. Give my very best regards to Jerry.[209] Read three pages of Montaigne every day; play a quartet by Haydn every day; gaze at some pictures of Raphael every day,—they are the equible masters.

Lots of love, dear Dixie . . . don't trouble to answer this unless there's some useful thing I can do for you. Toujours ton vieux oncle qui t'aime tant[210]

330. TO ADALINE GLASHEEN.[211] ALS 2 pp. (Stationery embossed 50 Deepwood Drive / Hamden, Connecticut 06517) Hobart/William Smith

Oct 22, 1974

Dear Adaline:

Many thanks for sending me CALYPSO.[212]

---

209 A friend of TNW's niece.

210 French: Always your old uncle who loves you so much.

211 American scholar Glasheen (1920–1993) was an authority on Joyce and *Finnegans Wake.* She compiled three censuses of *Finnegans Wake* (1956, 1963, 1977). She and TNW corresponded about *Finnegans Wake* from 1950 until his death; their correspondence has been published in *A Tour of the Darkling Plain,* edited by Edward M. Burns and Joshua A. Gaylord (2001).

212 Glasheen sent TNW a copy of her essay "Calypso," which was published in *James Joyce's* Ulysses*: Critical Essays,* edited by Clive Hart and David Hayman (1977).

It seems to me an admirable exposition—brings together all those strands of reference.

But you know me and Joyce. William James used to warn his students from lingering long in the realm of the "abject truth." Joyce was certainly in relation with truth and all honor to him, but he also exhibited a delectation in the abject. We know many greater writers than he of whom that could not be said. How "unengaging" is the man we see in the letters and the biography. He was never "at home with himself," dans sa peau,[213] and had little warmth to extend to others,—neither were Eliot and Thomas Mann (cold fishes) nor Po<u>nd (in his later years—when young he was wonderfully generous-minded) nor, I suspect, Yeats. Yet how one would like to have been in familiar relations with Chek<h>ov or Turgenev or H. James or Freud (I was)

I assume you know Empson's paper[214] on what happened after the close of Ulysses. I can give you it—Kenyon Review, Winter 1956. Just drop me a card (or phone); otherwise I'll keep it in my Empson-collection.

Next time I'm in Zürich I'll go to the Kronenhof<Kronenhalle> Restaurant where they have Joyce's table marked as a shrine. I know a number of waitresses there who are proud to have served him often (on Mrs Edith Rockefeller McCormick's money,[215] I assume). I'm going to ask them if he took Norah[216] there often. I'll bet I know the answer. I'd like to have known Norah.

sez

your old friend

Thornton

---

213 French: in his skin.

214 Empson's "The Theme of *Ulysses*."

215 Mrs. McCormick, who lived in Zurich, was one of Joyce's benefactors.

216 Joyce's wife.

Last photograph of TNW and his brother, spring 1975, Copley Plaza Hotel, Boston.

331. TO MARY M. HAIGHT.[217] ALS 2 pp. (Stationery embossed 50 Deepwood Drive / Hamden, Connecticut 06517) Yale

Some are saying that it's April 12 1975

Dear Mary.

Before leaving for Europe (hope you had a lovely time) you sent me a beautiful American Wildlife Calendar. I was enjoying the pictures—

---

217 Mary Haight and her husband, Gordon, an English professor at Yale, were New Haven friends of the Wilder family.

the timber wolf, the woodchuck, the bison—and the mottos, Job, Walt Whitman. Dostoievsky, Dante—when I was thunderstruck to see my name—my birthday month, April…subscribed to a howling idiocy: "The best thing about animals is that they don't say much." I never wrote that! I never thought that! I yelled for Isabel and pointed it out to her, the tears rolling down my face. "Isabel! Somebody's played a cruel joke on me<.> WHEN DID I SAY SUCH A THING? Let's move to Arkansas until the laughter dies down."

"Don't you remember that Mr. Antrobus says it in The Skin of Our Teeth when the Dinosaur is whining about the Ice Age."

But I, I didn't say it."

Then I thought of all the damaging things that could be brought up against me from that same play:

The Child Welfare Calendar: "A child is a thing that only a parent can love" Thornton Wilder.

The Anti-War Calendar: "God forgive me but I enjoyed the war; everybody's at their best in wartime." Thornton Wilder.

x

No more playwriting for me.

x

[The next day.]

I've calmed down. I read my calendar to the end—and loved the pictures and the legends. Isabel assures me that intelligent people like Mary and Gordon Haight don't believe that I mean all those outrageous things that characters say in a book. I'm going to try and write something that doesn't misrepresent me in a farmer's almanac.

Affectionate greetings to you both and thanks for the beautiful picture-book

Old Thornt'

332. TO LEONARD BERNSTEIN. ALS 2 pp. LofC

Edgartown, Mass 02539

July 20 1975

Dear Leonard Bernstein:

As I told you on the phone:

I did not want an opera to be made of The Skin of Our Teeth.

But I admired and trusted you, and was persuaded. I trusted you and the fellow-workers you would select.

x

When your fellow-workers fell apart—who was left to write the book?[218]—I felt relieved of my commitment to you

x

Hereafter, while I'm alive no one will write or compose an opera based on that play.

x

Torn from its context, Sabina's opening aria "Oh! Oh! Oh!" sounds awful, unmotivated, synthetic vivacity.

The nearest thing to it would be Zerbinetta's aria (or rondo).[219] Who cares what her words are, except an implied comment on Ariadne's abandonment? These words bear the weight of a crowded historical story of many facets.

x

I'm sorry to disappoint you, but my mistake was to have said 'yes' in the first place; yours, to have not followed through with the original plan offered me.

Always with much regard
Ever
Thornton

---

218 In 1964, Bernstein and Jerome Robbins had worked with Betty Comden and Adolph Green for six months on a musical version of *The Skin of Our Teeth,* but the project was abandoned because of artistic differences.

219 TNW is referring to "Grossmächtige Prinzessin," an aria addressed to Ariadne in Richard Strauss's opera *Ariadne auf Naxos.*

TNW and Isabel leaving Martha's Vineyard for the last time, October 2, 1975.

333. TO DALMA H. BRUNAUER.[220] ALS 3 pp. Private

50 Deepwood Drive
HAMDEN Conn
06517

November 11 1975

Dear Mrs Brunauer:

Many thanks for your thoughtful and sympathetic paper about my novel.

I have often been reproached for not having made a more explicit declaration of commitment to the Christian faith. If I had had a strict upbringing in the Catholic Church—like Mauriac or Graham Greene—I would certainly have done so. But I was a Protestant and I was thoroughly formed in the Protestant beliefs—my father's, my school's in China; Oberlin!—and the very thoroughness of my exposure to dogmatic Protestant positions made me aware that they were insufficient to encompass the vast picture of history and the burden of suffering in the world. I think that in The Bridge I took flight into the R.C. thought-world in order to avoid asking the same questions—the novel is a novel of questions, remember. And show that even the R.C. background broke down before those questions,—Brother Juniper was burned because he questioned.

I took refuge in Chekhov's statement: it is not the business of writers [of fiction, like himself] to answer the great questions [let the theologians and philosophers do that if they feel they must] but <“>to state the questions correctly.”

Which brings us back to Gertrude Stein's dying words: “What is the answer?... What is the Question?” [Namely, what is Man on earth for?]

---

220 Brunauer, a professor of English at Clarkson College of Technology in Potsdam, New York, was studying TNW's work and had published an essay, “Creative Faith in Wilder's *The Eighth Day,*” in the Autumn 1972 issue of the academic journal *Renascence.*

At present I am convalescent from a serious operation[221] and cannot write you the long commentary that your paper deserves.

But I can express my appreciation of your admirable meditation. and my thanks and my regard

Sincerely yours
Thornton Wilder

Please convey my devoted regard to our dear friend Helen Hosmer.[222]
P.S. It may interest you to know—since you mention Franz Werfel that his widow (and Gustav Mahler's) Alma Mahler-Werfel asked my permission to entitle her (second) book of memoirs: "Du Brücke is die Liebe"!![223]

334. TO MALCOLM COWLEY. ALS 2 pp. Newberry

50 Deepwood Drive, Hamden, Conn 06517

Nov. 18. 1975

Dear Malcolm:

I shall always be grateful to you.[224]

It appears that you have sounded the note and indicated the direction to others.

---

221 In September 1975, TNW had undergone surgery at Massachusetts General Hospital in Boston for prostate cancer.

222 American educator Helen Hosmer was the director of the Crane School of Music in Potsdam, New York, from 1930 until 1966.

223 German: "The Bridge Is Love" (the last words of TNW's novel *The Bridge of San Luis Rey*). Alma Mahler Werfel's memoir, *And the Bridge Is Love: Memories of a Lifetime,* was published in the United States in 1958.

224 In the November 9, 1975, issue of the *New York Times Book Review*, Cowley reviewed Richard Goldstone's *Thornton Wilder: An Intimate Portrait* (1975), harshly criticizing Goldstone and praising TNW. In the December 21, 1975, issue of the *Book Review,* after TNW's death, there appeared an exchange of letters between Goldstone and Cowley. In these letters, which were even harsher than Cowley's review, Goldstone responded to the review and Cowley described Goldstone's book as "intrusive, condescending, shallow, [and] badly written" and called TNW "the most neglected author of a brilliant generation."

Reviewers of good will write me in sheer bewilderment at that book: apparently Goldstone conveys that all my papers etc were thrown open to him. I am also getting letters from friends and strangers, mostly mentioning your review—from, for example, William G. Rogers (G. Stein's The Kiddie)[225]

I still haven't read the book but am told that the charge of anti-semitism is laid at my father's door—(in the first draft it was charged to me, but Mrs Carol Brandt begged him to alter that]

This is how that arose: my first publishers A. and C. Boni contracted the "Lawrenceville schoolmaster" to four novels on the strength of The Cabala. I submitted The Bridge as contracted. The Bonis wrote that they wished it were more like The Cabala; that it was obviously intended for a small fastidious circle of readers but they graciously consented to publish it; I then submitted The Woman of Andros,—they deplored that it wasn't more like The Bridge, but they published it (at the depth of the Depression); I then submitted Heaven's My Destination and was told that I was out of touch with the American scene, especially the depressed areas, and assured me that "humor" was not my province and they waived their option on it—I took it to Harpers and stayed with them ever since. Forty years later Goldstone interviews Charles Boni—old and embittered—in New York and was told that I had abandoned the Boni firm because I was anti-Semitic. The truth was that I was faithful to them (though they were displeased with my work) until they refused my fourth book. Anti-Semitic? Oh, Gertrude! Oh, Freud! Oh, mothers of Picasso and Montaigne!

Montaigne is grand reading for us old men. He lived through woeful times and retained that equilibrium. His mainstay was neither religion nor the (later) reliance on reason and the Enlightenment's belief in progress, but on the wisdom of antiquity—especially Plutarch!

I'm guardedly convalescing and cheerful
and much indebted to you

Ever
Thornton

---

225 American journalist and author William G. Rogers met Stein when he was a young soldier in World War I, and she continued to refer to him as "the Kiddie" thereafter.

335. TO CAROL BRANDT. ALS 3 pp. Yale

50 Deepwood Drive
Hamden Conn 06517

Nov. 18. 1975

Dear Carol:

Many thanks for the splendid terms for Theophilus North among the German bookclubs. I'm delighted by the goodwill of my German readers; I wish that my love for things French found the same reciprocation. (We know that dear Madame Lemy<?> does her best.[226])

I've begun getting letters of indignation and consolation about my biographer's book. I will not read it; and Isabel returned to the publisher the copy "sent by the author" (but not inscribed to me within!)

I wish dear Isabel wouldn't get so energized by these annoyances. I try to rise to the level of resentment but (as with Dr. Johnson's friend) "cheerfulness is always breaking in." Judging by my correspondence Goldstone is probably receiving letters of outrage, too

I'm convalescing very well. Am waiting for permission from my doctor (appointment the 21st) to go to New York and take Isabel to see two movies which I can believe are very beautiful: S. Ray's Distant Thunder and I<n>gmar Bergman's Magic Flute. If I go I shall accept a friend's offer of a guest card to the Harvard Club where I shall be presumably cut dead (though I do have a Harvard degree.) I'm not very strong or confident on my legs yet, so I shall not venture out much—except to those movies—but I've been house-bound and hospital-cocooned so long that I can get a grand feeling of adventurous freedom from just strolling from 44th St to the New York Public Library. Herzliche Grüsse an den lieben Pavvy und an seine reizende Frau[227]

love
Thornton

---

226 TNW is probably referring to the French agent for his book.

227 German: Best wishes to dear Pavvy and his lovely wife.

336. TO EILEEN AND ROLAND LE GRAND. ALS 2 pp. (Stationery embossed Harvard Club / 27 West 44th Street) Private

Dec 3. 1975

Dear Eileen—and Roland in Bhutan—

Lovely to get your letter with all the news.—the house near Dartmoor the Quantock Hills—all that poetry of the west country too bad it's so far from Sussex.

All my commiseration to you on your operation. So many of our letters these days are exchanging news of illness. I too had a serious operation in a Boston hospital this summer but am convalescing well... though with depleted vitality. You'll be surprised to see the above address..The rivalry of Yale and Harvard is of long standing—but I wanted to get a change to hide away for 14 days in New York. So a friend gave me a guest-card to this club—12 doors from the Algonquin—Isabel joined me for three days at Thanksgiving Time.
Oh, Roland, I hope your work is deeply interesting and rewarding...I have no clue of Bhutan[228]..but I saw S. Ray's film laid in Darjeeling ("Anapara"<?>?) in the now fading splendour of the old hill resort hotels. (And Isabel and I just saw Ray's latest picture Distant Drum laid in the Punjab—very beautiful but sad.)[229] Eileen says you are in a valley of the High Himalayas and not coping with severe cold.

We were not happy in our 3 successive attempts to go South and escape the cold in Connecticut—Mexico (beautiful but no chance of meeting anybody but elderly Americans). Puerto Rice (as in most of the Caribbean, one is aware of the sullen resentment of the emerging self-determination.). Southern Florida (more elderly Americans.) Maybe at the end of the winter we shall try Martinique—still a département of France.

So far our Fall has been surprisingly sunny and temperate. Isabel

---

228 Roland was in Bhutan on one of the UNESCO assignments he accepted as an expert in secondary education.

229 Ray's film set in Darjeeling is *Kanchenjungha* (1962); the 1973 Ray film TNW is referring to is *Ashani Sanket* (*Distant Thunder*).

is well—that is bravely coping with her handicaps,—respiratory mostly. In New Haven we see our nephew and niece and our nephew's children.[230]

I am now old, really old, and these recent set-backs have taken a lot of energy out of me. I think I'm pulling myself together for another piece of work.

Thank you for your beautiful long letter. I hope you've found some congenial friends in the neighborhood; I'm getting more and more unsociable but I notice that most people (including Isabel) are kept lively by a diversity of friends. Give our love to the "Young 'Uns" and a world of affectionate greetings to you both

Thornton

---

230 Amos Tappan and Robin Wilder's daughter, Jenney Gibbs Wilder, was born on June 7, 1973. TNW died on December 7, four days after writing this letter.

INDEX

Note: Page numbers in *italics* refer to illustrations.